D1357010

5 127 496 5

Handbook of
Research Methods in
Human Operant Behavior

APPLIED CLINICAL PSYCHOLOGY

Series Editors:
Alan S. Bellack
University of Maryland at Baltimore, Baltimore, Maryland
Michel Hersen
Pacific University, Forest Grove, Oregon

Current volumes in this Series

A Continuation Order Plan is available for this series. A continuation order will bring delivery of each new volume immediately upon publication. Volumes are billed only upon actual shipment. For further information please contact the publisher.

Handbook of
Research Methods in
Human Operant Behavior

Edited by

Kennon A. Lattal and
Michael Perone

West Virginia University
Morgantown, West Virginia

Plenum Press • New York and London

Library of Congress Cataloging-in-Publication Data

Handbook of research methods in human operant behavior / edited by
Kennon A. Lattal and Michael Perone.
        p.   cm. -- (Applied clinical psychology)
    Includes bibliographical references and index.
    ISBN 0-306-45668-0
    1. Operant behavior.   2. Operant conditioning.   I. Lattal, Kennon
A. II. Perone, Michael. III. Series.
    [DNLM: 1. Behavior. 2. Conditioning, Operant. 3. Psychology,
Experimental--methods.   BF 319.5.06 H2363 1998]
BF319.5.06H37 1998
153.1'526--dc21
DNLM/DLC
for Library of Congress   98-28963
                                                              CIP

ISBN 0-306-45668-0

©1998 Plenum Press, New York
A Division of Plenum Publishing Corporation
233 Spring Street, New York, N.Y. 10013

http://www.plenum.com

10 9 8 7 6 5 4 3 2 1

Printed in the United States of America

Contributors

Alan Baron • Department of Psychology, University of Wisconsin–Milwaukee, Milwaukee, Wisconsin 53201

Daniel J. Bernstein • Department of Psychology, University of Nebraska–Lincoln, Lincoln, Nebraska 68588-0308

A. Charles Catania • Department of Psychology, University of Maryland Baltimore County, Baltimore, Maryland 21250

Thomas S. Critchfield • Department of Psychology, Auburn University, Auburn, Alabama 36849

John Crosbie • Department of Psychology, West Virginia University, Morgantown, West Virginia 26506-6040

Gina Green • New England Center for Children, E. K. Shriver Center for Mental Retardation, and Northeastern University, Southborough, Massachusetts 01772

Timothy D. Hackenberg • Department of Psychology, University of Florida, Gainesville, Florida 32611-2250

Stephen T. Higgins • Human Behavioral Pharmacology Laboratory and Departments of Psychiatry and Psychology, University of Vermont, Burlington, Vermont 05401

John R. Hughes • Human Behavioral Pharmacology Laboratory and Departments of Psychiatry, Psychology, and Family Practice, University of Vermont, Burlington, Vermont 05401

R. John Irwin • Department of Psychology, University of Auckland, Auckland, New Zealand

Kennon A. Lattal • Department of Psychology, West Virginia University, Morgantown, West Virginia 26506-6040

P. Scott Lawrence • Department of Psychology, University of North Carolina at Greensboro, Greensboro, North Carolina 27402-6164

James E. Mazur • Psychology Department, Southern Connecticut State University, New Haven, Connecticut 06515

Dianne McCarthy • Department of Physiology, University of Auckland, Auckland, New Zealand

Allen Neuringer • Department of Psychology, Reed College, Portland, Oregon 97202

Michael Perone • Department of Psychology, West Virginia University, Morgantown, West Virginia 26506-6040

Carol Pilgrim • Department of Psychology, University of North Carolina at Wilmington, Wilmington, North Carolina 28403

Seth Roberts • Department of Psychology, University of California, Berkeley, California 94720-1650

Carolyn Rovee-Collier • Department of Psychology, Rutgers University, New Brunswick, New Jersey 08903

Kathryn J. Saunders • Parsons Research Center, University of Kansas, Parsons, Kansas 67357

Richard R. Saunders • Parsons Research Center, University of Kansas, Parsons, Kansas 67357

David R. Schmitt • Department of Sociology, University of Washington, Seattle, Washington 98195

Eliot Shimoff • Department of Psychology, University of Maryland Baltimore County, Baltimore, Maryland 21250

Richard L. Shull • Department of Psychology, University of North Carolina at Greensboro, Greensboro, North Carolina 27402-6164

Jalie A. Tucker • Department of Psychology, Auburn University, Auburn, Alabama 36849

Rudy E. Vuchinich • Department of Psychology, Auburn University, Auburn, Alabama 36849

Paul Weisberg • Department of Psychology, University of Alabama, Tuscaloosa, Alabama 35487-0348

Dean C. Williams • Parsons Research Center, University of Kansas, Parsons, Kansas 67357

John T. Wixted • Department of Psychology, University of California at San Diego, La Jolla, California 92093-0109

Preface

The experimental analysis of behavior began with a white rat. In the hands of B. F. Skinner, it was the subject of pioneering experiments in the 1930s that gave rise to an increasingly sophisticated appreciation of the environment's role in the acquisition, maintenance, and modulation of behavior. Although rigorous experimental control of environment–behavior relations was achieved first with rats and later with pigeons and other nonhuman animals (hereafter in this volume, simply "animals"), it was assumed from the beginning that the principles that emerged would apply to humans. The assumption of relevance led some researchers to interpret interesting cases of human behavior in terms of the principles from the animal laboratory. Others sought ways to extend and adapt the methods of animal research to the direct study of human behavior. We briefly review the history of the experimental analysis of human operant behavior in the first chapter of this volume and will not duplicate it here. At this point, suffice it to say that the extension of the methods of analysis of animal behavior to that of humans posed substantial methodological and conceptual challenges. The impressive array of methods represented in this volume attests to the skills of dedicated investigators in (1) extending and modifying extant methods used in the study of animal behavior to that of humans and (2) creating entirely new methods that address research issues not previously studied with animals, for example, human verbal behavior, other social interactions, and self-management.

Operant behavior of humans is studied in both laboratory and applied settings. Such investigations yield data relevant to basic processes and effective treatment of behavior disorders. At the edge, distinctions between basic and applied research are, like Skinner's rats, fuzzy, so that such distinctions are often more a matter of judgment than fact. Except that they require tinkering with procedural details of experimental arrangements, the settings in which basic research is conducted are less important than the problem under study and the goals of the research. The present volume is focused on the methods used when the goal is to study basic behavioral processes. This focus seems invited: Despite remarkable growth in the experimental analysis of human operant behavior over the past 20 years, there is no compendium of the methods used in the analysis. Applied topics are not considered, although, of course, the research derived from the methods described herein may have implications for applied behavior analysis. Furthermore, it is unlikely that any volume could cover every conceivable topic in its bailiwick and the present volume is no exception. We do hope, however, that the range of topics we have selected is sufficient to provide both detailed information on a range of specific research problems and areas as well as more general information about the experimental analysis of human behavior that could be used in many content areas and research settings.

An edited volume can be no better than its contributions. We thank the authors of the chapters of this volume, laboratory scientists all, for their willingness to share their considerable expertise with others who might be interested in the experimental analysis of human operant behavior. We thank Professor Iver Iversen of the University of North Florida for his help in planning the volume and in reviewing several of the chapter drafts. We are indebted to the various scholarly organizations that allowed us to reproduce figures from their journals, often at little or no charge. The Society for the Experimental Analysis of Behavior was especially generous, waiving all charges for the many figures reproduced from the *Journal of the Experimental Analysis of Behavior*. At West Virginia University, Ann Davis went far beyond the call of duty in assisting with editorial correspondence and the myriad details inherent in preparing an edited volume.

We dedicate this volume to the next generation of behavior analysts, with the hope that the methods described herein will prove useful to them in their efforts to better understand the human animal.

KENNON A. LATTAL
MICHAEL PERONE

Contents

Contents

Handbook of
Research Methods in
Human Operant Behavior

I

Basic Considerations

The Experimental Analysis of Human Operant Behavior

Kennon A. Lattal and Michael Perone

The unprecedented growth in the experimental analysis of human operant behavior has depended on, and been stimulated by, conceptual and theoretical developments in behavior analysis and a corresponding expansion of research methods. Research methods play a key role in scientific development and that is the reason for this volume. The chapters herein review and assess the methods available to researchers interested in the variety of topics that constitute the experimental analysis of human behavior. In so doing, the chapters also provide an overview of important empirical and theoretical issues in this exciting branch of contemporary behavior analysis.

Before turning to the detailed discussions of methods in the chapters, it is useful to review some broader issues in the analysis of human behavior, particularly its place in relation to other experimental and conceptual work in basic and applied behavior analysis. In the material below we consider some basic definitions, the nature of human operant behavior and the development of methods to analyze it experimentally, and the relation of those methods both to basic research with animals and to applied behavior analysis.

WAYS OF STUDYING HUMAN BEHAVIOR

Since the Renaissance, human behavior has constituted much of the subject matter of the arts, the humanities, and the sciences. Whereas the two former methods of knowing contribute significantly to understanding the human condition, the subject matter of this book is that of the methods of science. These methods came to bear on human behavior most directly with the establishment of psychology as a science near the turn of the twentieth century. Refinements over the next 100

Kennon A. Lattal and Michael Perone • Department of Psychology, West Virginia University, Morgantown, West Virginia 26506-6040.

Handbook of Research Methods in Human Operant Behavior, edited by Lattal and Perone. Plenum Press, New York, 1998.

years have left us with a set of procedures that provide a time-tested means of advancing our theoretical and practical understanding of the determinants of human behavior.

To undertake an experimental analysis of human behavior involves several assumptions, beginning with the general axiom that a science's subject matter is reliable and orderly—that is, not capricious—and knowable—that is, determined by variables that can be isolated, studied, and understood. The specific assumptions of the approach to understanding human behavior delineated in this volume are described in detail elsewhere (e.g., Baum, 1994; Skinner, 1974; Zuriff, 1985). These assumptions include the following: (1) Human behavior is of interest as a subject matter in its own right and not merely as a reflection of other processes occurring in other universes of discourse. (2) Human behavior is related functionally to antecedent stimuli and consequences. (3) An explanation of human behavior can be achieved when its controlling environmental variables are identified. (4) The best route to an explanation of human behavior is through the intensive experimental analysis of individual organisms rather than through statistical comparisons across groups of subjects. (5) Humans and other animals often behave similarly because of common behavioral processes. Verbal relations not present in animal behavior often are assumed to play major roles in many behavioral processes operating to determine human behavior. The verbal relations themselves, however, ultimately are accounted for by fundamental behavioral processes that are shared by all living organisms.

Beyond being an invaluable and unique way of understanding human behavior, the methods described in the chapters that follow also lay the foundation for a general paradigm or world-view for conceptualizing human behavior. The behavior analytic paradigm exists concurrently with several alternative world-views that each characterize themselves as rooted in the scientific method. Indeed, several of the chapters in this volume explore the interface between a behavior analytic world-view and alternative or complementary scientific views of human behavior (e.g., Hackenberg, Chapter 17; Higgins & Hughes, Chapter 18; Irwin & McCarthy, Chapter 10; Wixted, Chapter 9). The methods detailed in other chapters are based on behavior analytic accounts of aspects of human behavior that often are seen as antithetical to a behavioral world-view (e.g., Catania, Chapter 13; Critchfield, Tucker, & Vuchinich, Chapter 14; Green & R. Saunders, Chapter 8; Schmitt, Chapter 15; Shimoff & Catania, Chapter 12). The chapters in this volume provide a tapestry of methods used by behavior analysts, woven together to reflect a general conceptual framework for understanding human behavior.

OPERANT BEHAVIOR

Operant behavior is ubiquitous among living organisms, from the rhythmical movements of protozoa to the diverse activities of humans commonly described as cognition and language. Operant behavior may be defined as those actions of organisms that change as a function of their effects on the organism's environment. Operant behavior usually is described in terms of classes of responses, where the members of a class have similar effects on the environment. Furthermore, operants and their constituent responses are defined in the context of antecedent, discriminative stimuli and the consequences of the response. These elements—discriminative stimuli, operant responses, and consequences—constitute the so-called three-term contingency that is central to any experimental analysis of operant behavior.

Operant behavior was distinguished from respondent behavior in the mid-1930s in a series of papers by Skinner (1935b, 1937) and Konorski and Miller (1937; see also Miller & Konorski, 1928/1969). Some of the methods of respondent, or Pavlovian, conditioning were adapted by Skinner in the study of operant behavior, such as precise quantification of the response and physical isolation of the subject from the experimenter to facilitate control over extraneous variables. The methods originally fractured along other well-known dimensions. Foremost among these was the contingency between the response and reinforcer in operant conditioning versus the contingency between the unconditional stimulus and the "reinforcer," or unconditional stimulus, in Pavlovian conditioning:

> Different types of conditioned reflexes arise because a reinforcing stimulus may be presented in different kinds of temporal relations. There are two fundamental cases: in one the reinforcing stimulus is correlated temporally with a response and in the other with a stimulus. For "correlated with" we might write "contingent upon." (Skinner, 1937, p. 272)

Although some of the methodological distinctions, including the nature of response–reinforcer versus stimulus–reinforcer relations, may blur on careful examination (e.g., Hearst, 1975), the distinction between the two learning processes continues to have heuristic value in both research and theory.

HUMAN AND ANIMAL BEHAVIOR

Questions about the relation of human and animal behavior were largely a matter of speculation until the birth of experimental psychology. Pavlov's early work on the conditional reflex included not only experimental studies of humans but also the development of a theory of human functioning based on that body of work (e.g., Pavlov, 1927). The major learning theories of the 1930s assumed a close relation between animal and human behavior, as exemplified by the following remark by Edward Chace Tolman:

> I believe everything important in psychology (except perhaps such matters as the building up of a super-ego, that is, everything save such matters as involve society and words) can be investigated in essence through the continued experimental and theoretical analysis of the determiners of rat behavior at a choice-point in a maze. (1938, p. 34)

The outcome of the early and continued focus on the study of animal behavior was one of retarding the experimental analysis of human behavior. The reasoning seems to have been that, because animal and human behavior fundamentally are similar, one simply could study one or the other, and many psychologists interested in learning theory at the time opted for animals in keeping with the *Zeit-geist*. As a result, although the experimental analysis of human learning was tolerated, it was often a neglected stepchild of mainstream learning theory.

ORIGINS OF THE STUDY OF HUMAN OPERANT BEHAVIOR

Despite the high regard in which animal experimentation was held by early American psychologists, the fundamental and ultimate interest of most psychologists remained firmly that of human behavior. Perhaps this more than any other reason ultimately led to a reemphasis on the study of human behavior, with one offshoot being the development of the experimental analysis of human behavior. Skinner, like other learning theorists of the 1930s, was intent on constructing a general theory of behavior unconstrained by specific environments, classes of responses, or, particularly, species. There were obvious differences, of course, between the behavior of humans and other animals but Skinner kept his focus on the similarities in books like *Science and Human Behavior* (Skinner, 1953), where he extrapolated from basic principles of behavior derived almost exclusively from animal research to interpret many aspects of both human behavior and (the resultant) social institutions. Skinner's concern with human behavior continued to develop along both practical and theoretical lines. His *Verbal Behavior* (Skinner, 1957) was devoid of experimental data but rich in conceptual analysis of the topic in a manner consistent with his general view of behavioral mechanisms. That volume was followed a few years later by one coauthored with Holland, *The Analysis of Behavior,* which put basic research into practice through a college-level textbook designed around the principles of shaping and reinforcement (Holland & Skinner, 1961). Indeed, Skinner's creation of instructional materials and programmed methods for their delivery based on basic behavioral principles was a hallmark of his career. Skinner's work on human behavior remained largely in the arenas of conceptual analysis and education. The *experimental* analysis of human behavior was left largely to others.

By the 1940s, several psychologists had invoked some of the methods derived from the experimental analysis of animal behavior to study human behavior. In one of the earliest demonstrations of applied behavior analysis, for example, Fuller (1949) showed that a "vegetative human organism" could be taught to turn when such turning was followed reliably by food. By the mid-1950s, Lindsley, a student of Skinner, had established a laboratory at Metropolitan State Hospital in Waltham, Massachusetts, for studying the behavior of individuals diagnosed with severe psychiatric disorders (Lindsley, 1960). Much of this work focused on the extension of basic reinforcement effects to a new human population, but it also had a therapeutic orientation. The work with psychotic patients not only suggested that they perform on reinforcement schedules in a manner similar to other humans and animals, but also suggested new ways to gain control over hallucinations and delusions in an era before the widespread use of antipsychotic drugs. For example, while performing on a fixed-ratio schedule, patients were observed to be hallucinating in the period immediately following reinforcement, during the postreinforcement pause, but not during the ratio run (Morse, personal communication,

Nov. 7, 1996). Barrett continued and extended to mentally retarded children this type of laboratory analysis of human behavior (Barrett & Lindsley, 1962).

Along with Baer and Sherman (1964), Cohen (1962), and others, Lindsley expanded the experimental analysis of human operant behavior to include the analysis of social behavior of children, including behavior in natural settings (Azrin & Lindsley, 1956; Lindsley, 1966). This work also was innovative in representing a blend of interests in basic behavioral processes and the amelioration of significant social problems, the latter focus of course ultimately giving rise to the area of applied behavior analysis.

Continuing developments in basic laboratory methods for the analysis of human operant behavior paralleled developments in the analysis of animal behavior. Such was in keeping with the observations of Sidman (1960), who noted both the value of extension through systematic replication and the importance of standardizing laboratory practices as a way of ensuring consistency of findings across laboratories. Human subjects most frequently were studied in small cubicles isolated from extraneous variables, and simple responses and consequences were employed. These methods often were successful in yielding systematic replications of similar procedures with animals despite some obvious, and often unavoidable, differences between the laboratory environments. But the differences between the methods used to study operant behavior in animals and humans demand examination and analysis, as they may affect experimental outcomes and limit our ability to discover principles of behavior that transcend the boundaries of species (Baron, Perone, & Galizio, 1991a,b). Some of the more obvious differences in animal and human methods have involved: (1) the range of events that could be used as potential reinforcers or punishers, and the kinds of processes that could be exploited to establish the effectiveness of those events (Crosbie, Chapter 6; Pilgrim, Chapter 2; Shull & Lawrence, Chapter 4); (2) the number and scheduling of experimental sessions, and, as a consequence, the reliability of any apparent effects (Baron & Perone, Chapter 3); and (3) the degree of control that could be exerted over the variables to which subjects were exposed outside of the laboratory—not only during an experiment, but also before it (the ubiquitous problem of behavioral history). These and related difficulties in extending the concepts and methods of the animal laboratory to the experimental analysis of human behavior continue in contemporary research. As the chapters in this volume attest, however, the problems are not insurmountable, and considerable progress is being made.

Skinner's (1935a) analysis of the operant was central to much of the experimental analysis of human behavior, as it was with animal behavior. A good example of how the response was operationalized can be found in the Lindsley operandum, a solid brass plunger-type device designed to withstand heavy use (and abuse). It could be configured so that it had to be operated by pushing or pulling, and the required force could be adjusted over a wide range. The Lindsley plunger, along with the conventional telegraph key and other push-button operanda, proved as serviceable in operant conditioning studies of humans as was the rat lever or pigeon key with animals. Of course, other devices were used to record human operant behavior, but most of them were variations on the theme of a mechanically defined operant that was easily quantified into discrete units (responses). This particular approach facilitated the establishment of similarities of outcome between animal and human studies. It may have some limitations, however, when the findings derived from such methods are applied to the broad spectrum of human behavior, a point developed in detail by Shull and Lawrence (Chapter 4). Although it is important to recognize potential limitations of the method of studying discrete responses, as Shull and Lawrence note, it also is important to recognize the historical significance of the early studies that employed such methods, and the continued prevalence of the methods in contemporary behavior analysis. Regardless of what future innovations may displace the study of discrete operants, there can be no doubt about the central and enduring significance of applying Skinner's concept of the operant to the analysis of human behavior (e.g., Glenn, Ellis, & Greenspoon, 1992).

Closely related to the potential methodological limitations imposed by the analysis of discrete operant responses of humans, and in fact part of the issue, is the problem of verbal behavior. The consideration of human verbal behavior raises two issues: the analysis of verbal behavior as such and the role of verbal behavior in what might otherwise be the direct control of operant behavior by contingencies. The emerging interest in human operant behavior led investigators quickly to consider the nature and role of human verbal behavior. A few early studies of vocalizations demonstrated that such a response class could be controlled by reinforcement schedules in a manner similar to that of other, nonverbal, operants (e.g., Lane, 1960). Hefferline conducted a series of experiments designed to show that a small-scale muscle twitch of humans could be shaped when the consequence of such twitching was the termination of an unpleasant electrical stimulation and even though the humans could not verbally report that conditioning had taken place (e.g., Hefferline, Keenan, & Harford, 1959). A similar interest in conditioning without awareness led Greenspoon (1955) to study the frequency of human word usage in a conversation as a function of different verbal consequences arranged by an "interviewer" for different classes of verbal responses (e.g., plural nouns). Many of the early studies of operant behavior in humans, including the work on human vocalizations, were systematic replications of effects already demonstrated with animals and particularly of the value of reinforcement contingencies in changing the frequency of targeted responses. The significant feature of the work of Hefferline and Greenspoon was the recognition that the methods also might be used to investigate the role of verbal behavior in conditioning processes at the human level. Progress in this area accelerated when experimenters studied verbal contributions to conditioning by adding verbal stimuli, in the form of instructions, to otherwise conventional schedule arrangements. Classic studies by Allyon and Azrin (1964), Kaufman, Baron, and Kopp (1966), Lippman and Meyer (1967), and Baron, Kaufman, and Stauber (1969) set the stage for an explosion of interest in the late 1970s on the topic of "rule governance" (e.g., Galizio, 1979; Matthews, Shimoff, Catania, & Sagvolden, 1977), an interest that continues through today (Shimoff & Catania, Chapter 12; Shull & Lawrence, Chapter 4).

The analysis of verbal influences focused attention on the challenges of extending the principles and procedures of the animal laboratory to experimentation with human behavior. Another challenge was the appearance of discrepancies in the behavior of humans and animals exposed to putatively similar laboratory arrangements (for a review see Perone, Galizio, & Baron, 1988). As the data base on human operant behavior grew, these discrepancies became increasingly conspicuous, and they had to be addressed. A pioneer in uncovering and addressing human–animal discrepancies was Weiner, who conducted a seminal program of research on the role of behavioral history in schedule performance, beginning in the 1960s and continuing into the 1970s (e.g., Weiner, 1962, 1970). When Weiner observed that human performances on simple schedules sometimes departed from the "characteristic" performances of rats and pigeons, he sought explanations not in the characteristics of the species under investigation, but rather in the different histories of experience that the subjects brought to the experiment. The goal he set for the experimental analysis of human behavior was the identification and control of environmental sources of interspecies variability (Weiner, 1983). This goal is at the foundation of much of the current work on the relations between human verbal behavior and reinforcement schedule performance (e.g., Crosbie, Chapter 6; Mazur, Chapter 5; Pilgrim, Chapter 2; Shimoff & Catania, Chapter 12; Shull & Lawrence, Chapter 4). When the goal is met—that is, when the variables responsible for apparent discrepancies between human and animal performances are identified and controlled—then the generality of the behavioral principles is firmly established.

RELATIONS BETWEEN ANIMAL AND HUMAN RESEARCH

We have seen that the use of animals to study behavioral processes developed from the interest of early psychologists in physiology, evolution, and comparative psychology. Animal experiments often were justified in at least three ways: representativeness, control, and ethical constraints. As the previously cited quotation from Tolman illustrates, many of the early learning theorists asserted that basic behavioral processes were sufficiently general that the study of a few representative species would suffice and might even be preferable to the study of a host of species that characterized the work of earlier comparative psychologists. Animals also were favored because their experiences were more easily controlled than those of humans, an important consideration when trying to isolate basic behavioral principles. In Skinner's words, "We study the behavior of animals because it is simpler. . . . Conditions may be better controlled" (1953, p. 38). Finally, it is obvious that preparations involving animals, although always subject to ethical considerations, offered the possibility of studying a wider range of variables, including physiological manipulations, that were not ethically defensible with human subjects. On the other hand, as Crosbie (Chapter 6) notes, procedures such as aversive control play an important role in much of human behavior in natural settings and behavior analysts would be remiss by not studying it, albeit in ways that meet the ethical standards outlined by Crosbie.

Despite the value, and in some circumstances advantages, of using animals, questions about the generality of discovered behavioral processes to humans are important and inevitable. Furthermore, phenomena involving verbal behavior are precluded in all but a few animal species. Even in apes, verbal behavior cannot yet be assigned any significant role in their behavior in natural settings. Many of the chapters in this volume elaborate on the unique contributions of verbal behavior in humans, both in terms of its relation to nonverbal operant behavior and in terms of its importance as a subject matter in its own right.

Another justification that is sometimes given for studying human behavior is that such behavior is more complex than that of animals. Simplicity and complexity, however, are human verbal creations rather than descriptions of natural phenomena. As a result, such descriptions are overly vague and depend more on the observer's vantage than the phenomenon under investigation. In different circumstances, behavior may be multiply determined or determined by a single variable—and this is true of both humans and animals. Whether a phenomenon is described as simple or complex seems often to depend on how well the controlling variables are understood, rather than on topographical or other features of the behavior under study. The phenomenon is labeled as complex until its controlling variables are understood, at which point it becomes either "simple" or, at least, "simpler." Thus, a justification in terms of human behavior being more complex seems to us to be too vague to be useful.

RELATIONS BETWEEN BASIC HUMAN OPERANT RESEARCH AND APPLIED BEHAVIOR ANALYSIS

The experimental analysis of human operant behavior occupies a unique niche within the discipline of behavior analysis, which concerns itself at the one extreme with articulating basic behavioral mechanisms gleaned from the study of experimental animals and at the other extreme with developing practical solutions to problems of social significance in uniquely human settings (Baer, Wolf, & Risley, 1968). The study of human behavior within the laboratory falls between these two anchor points, with parts falling closer to one extreme than the other. The results of basic research into human behavior often may have greater face validity than animal studies on similar topics simply because the research is conducted on humans and therefore may be easier, particularly for nonlaboratory scientists, to relate to human behavior in natural settings. It is important to remember, however, that face validity is only that. Face validity often represents what Bachrach (1981) called the "analogue error": Similarity of topographical appearance of two phenomena may belie significant differences in controlling variables. To use a well-known example, a child may cry in a similar manner regardless of whether the precipitating event was touching a hot stove or failing to get her way. The behavior looks alike in both circumstances, but its controlling variables are quite different.

The study of human operant behavior in the laboratory also sometimes is viewed as representing an intermediate step between the discovery and articulation of basic behavioral processes with animals and the application of these processes to problems of social significance. This step can be a useful one but it is subject to two caveats. First, the goal of basic research is to understand basic processes, without necessarily giving consideration to direct, or even eventual, application. This is not to say that application is unimportant to basic research, only that application is not the sine qua non of the study of basic behavioral processes. This point holds for basic research with either humans or animals. Second, applied behavior analysis often develops its own concepts and applications independently of basic research and researchers (Lattal & Neef, 1996; Poling, Picker, Grossett, Hall-Johnson, & Holbrook, 1981), thereby obviating the necessity of a linear sequence from animal research to human research to application.

Human operant research borrows and derives concepts and methods from basic animal research and often from applied behavior analysis. In addition, like applied behavior analysis, the experimental analysis of human operant behavior develops concepts that are unique to its subject matter and not typically considered part of animals' natural repertoire, notably verbal behavior and the related topics of equivalence relations and, to some extent, cognitive processes.

CHARACTERISTICS OF THE EXPERIMENTAL ANALYSIS OF HUMAN OPERANT BEHAVIOR

As the chapters demonstrate, the topics investigated under the volume's aegis are wide ranging and diverse, covering at least the same range of topics as is covered by experimental analyses of animal behavior. At the most general level, the methods employed in investigations of the different research topics share two features in common that distinguish them from other psychological approaches to studying human behavior. First, the research is based on analysis of individual subjects studied intensively. Second, the methods involve the assessment of functional relations between environmental variables and behavior. These two features, which are shared with animal research, provide a basis for making strong inferences about causal relations between the experimental variables and behavior (Baron & Perone, Chapter 3). Other features also are shared among the methods, but these features are subject to some qualification depending on such variables as the nature of the subjects (e.g., adults versus infants) and the response class of interest (e.g., verbal versus nonverbal responses). These features include the isolation of the subject from extraneous and potentially confounding variables; the exposure of each subject to each of the experimental conditions (usually, but not always, over multiple sessions); the frequent use of operants defined by discrete, as opposed to continuous, responses; the arranging of discrete consequences in relation to the behavior under study, that is, the use of reinforcement contingencies or schedules; the use of instructions or other verbal prompts in at least parts of the research; and ensuring that appropriate ethical guidelines are followed.

There are, of course, also a number of methodological differences among the research areas that are dictated by the particular problems under study. For example, the investigation of verbal behavior introduces a number of concepts (Catania, Chapter 13) that may require methods not usually associated with some of the other, more traditional research areas such as the analysis of human infant operant behavior (Weisberg & Rovee-Collier, Chapter 11).

A factor that may influence the specific methods to be employed is the investigator's particular approach or conceptual framework for the problem under investigation. Wixted (Chapter 9), for example, has effectively employed the methods of signal detection in the analysis of what has been called human cognition. Yet in that same chapter he outlines several other methodological approaches that also might be used in studying this type of behavior. Green and R. Saunders (Chapter 8) adopt a particular view of stimulus equivalence, based on the work of Sidman (e.g., 1994), that leads to the use of a particular set of methods that are not necessarily used by others conducting research on the problem of equivalence classes in general or the closely related problem of concept learning.

Extant technology also influences methods and the disparity in the technology available from laboratory to laboratory often may dictate procedural variations. Stimulus control is one of the largest areas of human operant research and the procedural details of the stimulus control literature are especially diverse (K. Saunders & Williams, Chapter 7). Yet, despite this diversity, remarkably similar results often are achieved across a range of specific methods.

Still other differences are dictated by the subject population and the environments in which those subjects exist. Weisberg and Rovee-Collier (Chapter 11) suggest the value of studying infants in the home, often with mothers as research participants. At the other extreme, Bernstein (Chapter 16) delineates a useful set of methods for optimizing control over all features of the adult human's environment. The methods of Weisberg and Rovee-Collier and Bernstein are appropriate to the topics under investigation and, at first blush, appear to differ markedly from one another. At a functional level, however, both types of environmental arrangements are designed to optimize the control needed to investigate the behavioral processes of interest. Roberts and Neuringer (Chapter 19) outline their novel ideas about the possibilities and challenges of self-experimentation, thereby expanding the experimental analysis of human behavior to a heretofore overlooked subject, the experimenters themselves. As with the unique methods of Weisberg and Rovee-Collier and Bernstein, using oneself as a subject creates new opportunities and challenges that can only expand the range of questions that can be asked of the behavior of humans and in so doing make a scientific understanding of such behavior more likely.

CONCLUSIONS

This volume is testimony to the host of recent developments in the experimental analysis of human operant behavior. We have selected the authors and the topics to provide a thorough, if not entirely comprehensive, review of both the topical areas of analysis and, most particularly, the research methods currently used to investigate the environmental determinants of human behavior. Some of the areas represented can be traced to the beginnings of experimental psychology (e.g., Irwin & McCarthy, Chapter 10; K. Saunders & Williams, Chapter 7). Some have a rich history within behavior analysis (e.g., Crosbie, Chapter 6; Mazur, Chapter 5; Shull & Lawrence, Chapter 4). Some either explore general methodological issues (e.g., Baron & Perone, Chapter 3; Pilgrim, Chapter 2) or detail methodological applications to specific settings or subjects (e.g., Bernstein, Chapter 16; Roberts & Neuringer, Chapter 19). Others represent the emerging assimilation of behavior analysis with other areas of science (e.g., Hackenberg, Chapter 17; Higgins & Hughes, Chapter 18; Wixted, Chapter 9). Still others describe the applications of operant research methods to areas that have not been investigated by behavior analysts to a degree consistent with their representation in general psychology (e.g., Green & R. Saunders, Chapter 8; Schmitt, Chapter 15; Shimoff & Catania, Chapter 12; Weisberg & Rovee-Collier, Chapter 11) or to which the methods of behavior analysis are just beginning to be applied (e.g., Critchfield, Tucker, & Vuchinich, Chapter 14).

It is our hope that the methods described by the contributors in their respective research areas will both guide and stimulate additional methodological and theoretical developments in the experimental analysis of human behavior. Such an analysis really has only just begun and it would be unfortunate if the methods described in this volume are used as anything more than guidelines for the continued development of the present and future areas of analysis of human behavior. We concur with Shimoff and Catania (Chapter 12) that scientific practices should be more a matter of control by the antecedents and consequences of such practices than it should be a matter of a priori rules laid down by others. The methods proffered by the present authors represent a good starting point for an investigator to enter these areas. Once initiated into the area, perhaps through the methods and ideas presented herein, it is our hope that the natural consequences of the data will guide and control the future research activity of the reader.

REFERENCES

Allyon, T., & Azrin, N. H. (1964). Reinforcement and instructions with mental patients. *Journal of the Experimental Analysis of Behavior, 6,* 477–506.

Azrin, N. H., & Lindsley, O. R. (1956). The reinforcement of cooperation between children. *Journal of Abnormal and Social Psychology, 52,* 100–102.

Bachrach, A. J. (1981). *Psychological research: An introduction* (4th ed.). New York: Random House.

Baer, D. M., & Sherman, J. A. (1964). Reinforcement control of generalized imitation in young children. *Journal of Experimental Child Psychology, 1,* 37–49.

Baer, D. M., Wolf, M. M., & Risley, T. R. (1968). Some current dimensions of applied behavior analysis. *Journal of Applied Behavior Analysis, 1,* 91–97.

Baron, A., Kaufman, A., & Stauber, K. A. (1969). Effects of instructions and reinforcement feedback on human operant behavior maintained by fixed-interval reinforcement. *Journal of the Experimental Analysis of Behavior, 12,* 701–712.

Baron, A., Perone, M., & Galizio, M. (1991a). Analyzing the reinforcement process at the human level: Can application and behavioristic interpretation replace laboratory research? *The Behavior Analyst, 14,* 95–105.

Baron, A., Perone, M., & Galizio, M. (1991b). The experimental analysis of human behavior: Indispensable, ancillary, or irrelevant? *The Behavior Analyst, 14,* 145–155.

Barrett, B. H., & Lindsley, O. R. (1962). Deficits in acquisition of operant discrimination and differentiation shown by institutionalized retarded children. *American Journal of Mental Deficiency, 67,* 424–436.

Baum, W. M. (1994). *Understanding behaviorism: Science, behavior, and culture.* New York: Harper-Collins.

Cohen, D. (1962). Justin and his peers: An experimental analysis of a child's social world. *Child Development, 33,* 697–717.

Fuller, P. R. (1949). Operant conditioning of a vegetative human organism. *American Journal of Psychology, 62,* 587–590.

Galizio, M. (1979). Contingency-shaped and rule-governed behavior: Instructional control of human loss avoidance. *journal of the Experimental Analysis of Behavior, 31,* 53–70.

Glenn, S. S., Ellis, J., & Greenspoon, J. (1992). On the revolutionary nature of the operant as a unit of behavioral selection. *American Psychologist, 47,* 1329–1336.

Greenspoon, J. (1955). The reinforcing effect of two spoken sounds on the frequency of two responses. *American Journal of Psychology, 60,* 409–416.

Hearst, E. (1975). The classical–instrumental distinction: Reflexes, voluntary behavior, and categories of associative learning. In W. K. Estes (Ed.), *Handbook of learning and cognitive processes: Vol. 2. Conditioning and behavior theory* (pp. 181–223). Hillsdale, NJ: Erlbaum.

Hefferline, R. F., Keenan, B., & Harford, R. A. (1959). Escape and avoidance conditioning in human subjects without their observation of the response. *Science, 130,* 1338–1339.

Holland, J. G., & Skinner, B. F. (1961). *The analysis of behavior.* New York: McGraw–Hill.

Kaufman, A., Baron, A., & Kopp, R. E. (1966). Some effects of instructions on human operant behavior. *Psychonomic Monograph Supplements, 1,* 243–250.

Konorski, J., & Miller, S. (1937). On two types of conditioned reflex. *Journal of General Psychology, 16,* 264–272.

Lane, H. (1960). Temporal and intensive properties of human vocal responding under a schedule of reinforcement. *Journal of the Experimental Analysis of Behavior, 3,* 183–192.

Lattal, K. A., & Neef, N. A. (1996). Recent reinforcement-schedule research and applied behavior analysis. *Journal of Applied Behavior Analysis, 29,* 213–230.

Lindsley, O. R. (1960). Characteristics of the behavior of chronic psychotics as revealed by free-operant conditioning methods. *Diseases of the Nervous System Monograph Supplement, 21,* 66–78.

Lindsley, O. R. (1966). Experimental analysis of cooperation and competition. In T. Verhave (Ed.), *The experimental analysis of behavior* (pp. 470–501). New York: Meredith.

Lippman, L. G., & Meyer, M. E. (1967). Fixed-interval performance as related to instructions and to subjects' verbalizations of the contingency. *Psychonomic Science, 8,* 135–136.

Matthews, B. A., Shimoff, E., Catania, A. C., & Sagvolden, T. (1977). Uninstructed human responding: Sensitivity to ratio and interval contingencies. *Journal of the Experimental Analysis of Behavior, 27,* 453–467.

Miller, S., & Konorski, J. (1969). On a particular form of conditioned reflex (B. F. Skinner, Trans.). *Journal of the Experimental Analysis of Behavior, 12,* 187–189. (Originally published in *Les Comptes Rendus des Seances de la Societe de Biologie, Societe Polonaise de Biologie,* 1928, *99,* 1155.)

Pavlov, I. P. (1927). *Conditioned reflexes* (G. V. Anrep, Trans.). London: Oxford University Press.

Perone, M., Galizio, M., & Baron, A. (1988). The relevance of animal-based principles in the laboratory study of human operant conditioning. In G. Davey & C. Cullen (Eds.), *Human operant conditioning and behavior modification* (pp. 59–85). New York: Wiley.

Poling, A., Picker, M., Grossett, D., Hall-Johnson, E., & Holbrook, M. (1981). The schism between experimental and applied behavior analysis: Is it real and who cares? *The Behavior Analyst, 4,* 93–102.

Sidman, M. (1960). *Tactics of scientific research.* New York: Basic Books.

Sidman, M. (1994). *Equivalence relations and behavior: A research story.* Boston: Authors Cooperative.

Skinner, B. F. (1935a). The generic nature of the concepts of stimulus and response. *Journal of General Psychology, 12,* 40–65.

Skinner, B. F. (1935b). Two types of conditioned reflex and a pseudo-type. *Journal of General Psychology, 12,* 66–67.

Skinner, B. F. (1937). Two types of conditioned reflex: A reply to Konorski and Miller. *Journal of General Psychology, 16,* 272–279.

Skinner, B. F. (1953). *Science and human behavior.* New York: Macmillan.

Skinner, B. F. (1957). *Verbal behavior.* Englewood Cliffs, NJ: Prentice–Hall.

Skinner, B. F. (1974). *About behaviorism.* New York: Knopf.

Tolman, E. C. (1938). The determiners of behavior at a choice point. *Psychological Review, 45,* 1–41.

Weiner, H. (1962). Conditioning history and human fixed interval performance. *Journal of the Experimental Analysis of Behavior, 7,* 383–385.

Weiner, H. (1970). Human behavioral persistence. *The Psychological Record, 20,* 445–456.

Weiner, H. (1983). Some thoughts on discrepant human–animal performances under schedules of reinforcement. *The Psychological Record, 33,* 521–532.

Zuriff, G. E. (1985). *Behaviorism: A conceptual reconstruction.* New York: Columbia University Press.

2

The Human Subject

Carol Pilgrim

As the chapters of this volume and others (e.g., Davey & Cullin, 1988; Hayes & Hayes, 1992) attest, there are many important questions to be asked of and about human behavior. And as is the case with questions about animal responding, the natural science strategies of behavior analysis are particularly well-suited to identifying the variables of which human behavior is a function (e.g., Johnston & Pennypacker, 1993). Still, the translation of a research question and a scientific strategy into an actual experiment requires many practical decisions.

Of course, no experiment in which human behavior is the dependent variable can take place in a void. Despite attempts to approximate the arbitrary nature of the animal laboratory, episodes of human responding can be much more difficult to isolate from the ongoing stream of environment–behavior interactions, and the ways in which a researcher attempts to do so can be matters of some consequence. The focus of the present chapter, then, will be on those research tactics that establish the experimental context for human operant research, tactics such as recruiting, scheduling, and compensating subjects, and those involved in designing the laboratory setting and apparatus.

The intent of the chapter will be to promote careful consideration of each of a series of practices that might otherwise receive little thought, because they are rarely central to the experimental question. However, each element of the experimental context rightfully might be considered a variable in and of itself, with potential ramifications for the research outcome, whether practical or functional. Illustrative examples of experimental arrangements will be offered to help underscore the theme that each parameter reflects a choice, to be decided by the particular aims of the research project. Factors that influence these choices will be emphasized, to demonstrate how a research question might drive selection of context variables, rather than the other way around.

In this volume's focus on the methods of human operant research, one potentially important distinction may emerge between the standard experimental arrangements described in this chapter and some of the topic-dependent methods

Carol Pilgrim • Department of Psychology, University of North Carolina at Wilmington, Wilmington, North Carolina 28403.

Handbook of Research Methods in Human Operant Behavior, edited by Lattal and Perone. Plenum Press, New York, 1998.

described in subsequent chapters. The difference is that whereas the latter methods often have been empirically developed, many of the general procedures of human operant research have become established more by convention than by comparative analysis. Certainly our trust in these standard arrangements has grown as evidence of strong experimental control in the studies employing them continues to increase. At the same time, we might do well to recognize that these are not the only possibilities, or even necessarily the best. With respect to general strategies for choosing elements of procedure, there are benefits both to standardization, which allows meaningful comparisons across studies or laboratories, and to creative alternatives, which help to establish generality as lawful relations are demonstrated across a variety of experimental arrangements. Indeed, any number of the elements of procedure described in this chapter are deserving of closer empirical scrutiny, and their experimental analysis would represent a contribution to human operant research methodology.

SELECTING THE SUBJECT POPULATION

When designing an experiment to study human behavior, it makes most sense to begin with a decision about the subject population to be employed. Participant groups can be composed along a myriad of dimensions, and the choice of population will play an important role in determining other critical features of the experimental context (e.g., recruitment strategies, reinforcers, instructional practices). The following discussion will outline the sorts of factors that can serve as guides to optimal selection of experimental participants.

The Research Question

As a first step, researchers should consider carefully any and all implications of their experimental question for choice of the best-suited participants. In some cases, those implications will be obvious; certain research questions dictate the choice of subjects unequivocally. Many clear examples are found in the literature of applied behavior analysis, where experiments are designed frequently to address questions concerning particular behavior deficits or excesses (e.g., self-injurious behavior, eating disorders, absence of functional speech, compliance), and subject populations are necessarily those exhibiting the problems of interest. Similarly, questions about infant or child behavior, or about the variance imposed by other subject variables not amenable to within-subject manipulation, will necessitate selection of particular populations. For example, operant studies with different age groups have been notably influential in demonstrating the contributions of behavior analysis to the understanding of basic developmental processes in children (e.g., Bijou & Bear, 1967; Gewirtz & Pelaez-Nogueras, 1992; Pouthas, Droit, Jacquet, & Wearden, 1990; Weisberg & Rovee-Collier, Chapter 11) and older adults (e.g., Baron & Mattila, 1989; Baron & Menich, 1985).

Another subject variable not easily amenable to direct manipulation is the presence or absence of a verbal repertoire. Choosing subjects on the basis of their verbal ability represents an interesting illustration of the ramifications of some subject-selection decisions. Consider that for researchers investigating the role played by verbal responding in other human behavior patterns (e.g., sensitivity to schedules of reinforcement, the formation of equivalence classes), studies involving subject populations with limited or no verbal abilities (e.g., animals, human infants, individuals with severe developmental disabilities, aphasics) represent an important research strategy. When the performances of nonverbal subjects are functionally similar to those of verbal subjects, clear conclusions about the necessity of verbal behavior can be reached. However, it is important to note that when performances vary across groups, no definitive answers about the role of verbal behavior are provided. Because children and adults, or developmentally delayed and normal individuals, differ along countless dimensions in addition to their verbal repertoires, the determinants of performance differences necessarily remain obscure. Thus, the researcher who selects a particular subject population for reasons of the sort described here must be willing to accept the possibility that some outcomes will be difficult to interpret in terms of the primary experimental question. Group differences may be consistent with a particular theoretical position (e.g., that verbal behavior allows class formation, or decreases schedule sensitivity), but such evidence falls short of the standards generally sought through an experimental analysis of functional relations. Indeed, this example illustrates some of the difficulties inherent in addressing questions about controlling variables by examining differences between fundamentally distinct subject groups (for a further discussion, see Baron & Perone, Chapter 3).

Subject populations also can be well-matched to experimental questions in more subtle ways. Given the range of research questions asked about human behavior, the possibilities here are probably endless, but a few examples will serve to illustrate the point. That some subject populations show greater sensitivity than others to particular manipulations may have important implications for selecting participants. For example, Pilgrim, Chambers, and Galizio (1995) reported that the equivalence performances of young children are more easily disrupted than those of adults when original learning conditions are altered (e.g., Pilgrim & Galizio, 1990, 1995). These findings may suggest that questions about the experiences necessary for long-term maintenance of equivalence patterns could be asked most fruitfully of children, because their baseline performances would allow the functional contribution of experimental manipulations to be observed. Similarly, identifying the factors critical to acquisition of behavior may be approached systematically with subjects who have difficulty mastering a performance. In essence, subject selection provides one strategy by which learning can be slowed sufficiently to allow analysis of the details of development. To illustrate, Saunders and Spradlin's (1989) important analysis of conditional discriminative control in terms of simple successive and sequential discriminations was possible because their subjects failed initially to learn the more complex, conditional arrangements. The effects on acquisition of training each component discrimination could then be demonstrated.

Finally, experimental questions involving certain sorts of independent variables (e.g., psychoactive drugs presented under nontherapeutic protocols, positive punishment contingencies) may require normal, adult populations for ethical reasons. Further discussion of these ethical issues will be found in the last section of this chapter.

Convenience

When the experimental question does not dictate a particular subject population, as is the case for many questions about basic behavioral processes, issues of convenience and practicality become important considerations. Relatively unrestricted access to one's subjects provides an important practical advantage for the researcher, particularly with respect to the repeated testing necessary for implementation of steady-state research strategies (Baron & Perone, Chapter 3). Similarly, financial costs and missed sessions are lessened when participants are in close proximity to their testing environments, and availability for extended durations is more likely. Familiarity with general characteristics of the population also allows the researcher to make reasonable initial predictions about the sorts of events that might function effectively as discriminative or reinforcing stimuli. By way of example, college students represent an ever-popular choice among basic researchers in university settings because they are available on campus and relatively reliable in attendance, histories and deprivations are such that they will often work for signs of progress or accuracy (e.g., points) and almost always for money, and they exhibit few behavior problems (e.g., biting, attention deficits) that would cause a session or experiment to be terminated prematurely.

Generality

It may be noted that a potential long-term drawback of basing choices too frequently on issues of convenience is that the range of subject characteristics represented in our literature could become unnecessarily restricted (e.g., Morris, Johnson, Todd, & Higgins, 1988). Given that interest in species generality inspires some significant portion of human operant research, it follows that researchers should be sensitive to issues of generality in human populations as well. Thus, interest in extending the generality of behavior principles can serve as another important basis for selecting experimental participants, even when basic processes are at issue. Important illustrations can be found in the work of Neef, Mace, and colleagues (Mace, Neef, Shade, & Mauro, 1994, 1996; Neef, Mace, & Shade, 1993; Neef, Mace, Shea, & Shade, 1992; Neef, Shade, & Miller, 1994), who have investigated parameters of the matching law in terms of academic performances by adolescents with severe emotional disturbance and learning difficulties. These studies contribute not only in their applied significance, but also in their successful extension of basic analyses to human populations other than normally capable adults.

Experimental Control

A thoughtful researcher also will want to consider ways in which subject selection might contribute to experimental control. Because human subjects will bring with them into an experiment a range of potentially influential individual characteristics and histories, one strategy is to select participants who are similar along extraexperimental dimensions (e.g., Baron, Perone, & Galizio, 1991a), thus reducing extraneous sources of variability. Just as animal researchers sometimes elect to study subjects from one genetic strain or litter, employing a homogeneous subject population can increase the likelihood that functional relations will be reproducible across subjects. Variables such as age, level of education, or socioeconomic status can be limited to a particular range, even when these factors are not the topic of experimental inquiry in their own right. Although reproduction of functional relations across clearly defined individual differences is itself an important goal, it usually makes sense for initial experiments in a program of study to constrain the range of subject characteristics represented in any single experiment. Selection criteria can contribute to enhanced experimental control by requiring the presence or absence of potentially relevant subject variables. As a classic example, excluding subjects who have completed advanced psychology courses helps to decrease the possibility that performances will be controlled by contact with the experimental literature as opposed to contact with the experimental variables.

Judicious subject selection also can contribute to experimental control by helping to rule out potential alternative explanations of an experiment's outcome. For example, Saunders and Spradlin (1990) argued that institutionalized adults with retardation have advantages over other populations when studying the influence of experimental manipulations on acquisition. Developmental changes and extraexperimental training become unlikely accounts of learning for adults residing in an institutional environment. Confidence about the function of experimental manipulations is increased as such alternative explanations are removed or weakened.

RECRUITING SUBJECTS

Decisions about recruitment strategies will depend largely on the subject population being sought and on the resources available to the researcher. Fortunately, any number of recruitment techniques have proved effective, and most can be fine-tuned to reach the appropriate audience.

College Students and Adults

When college students are the targeted participants, many researchers recruit from a particular course or from a departmental subject pool, typically organized as one option for fulfilling requirements in an introductory psychology course. This tactic rates high on convenience, but the limited number of sessions allowed in most cases can pose a problem for within-subject experimental designs. When individuals complete course requirements but are uninterested in continuing their participation (e.g., for pay), the researcher's time investment yields poor returns. As another observation on using a subject pool, researchers in the human operant laboratory at the University of North Carolina at Wilmington (UNCW) often have noted differences in what might be described as a subject's motivational characteristics as a function of the time of the semester when recruiting takes place. Subjects who volunteer early in the semester are often more conscientious in attending scheduled sessions than those who volunteer late in the semester. One practical solution might be to recruit a number of subjects early on, and then schedule their individual sessions at subsequent points in time.

Making use of the Career Resources Center on campus has proved to be a most effective recruitment technique for the human operant laboratory at UNCW. One service provided by this office is a listing of part-time jobs available to students. Our entry mentions a study of common learning processes and describes a participant's time involvement and the average amount of money earned per hour. The listings are free of charge, the individuals who respond are motivated to find work, and they have tended to approach their participation seriously, perhaps as they would other employment opportunities. Similar services exist at most universities. Closely related practices include posting notices on bulletin boards and placing classified advertisements in university or local newspapers. Newspaper ads typically carry a fee, but they are likely to be seen widely, and can be particularly helpful when large numbers of subjects are required. Obviously, these latter tactics can be effective in locating subjects other than college students as well.

One cautionary note involves the practice of recruiting friends or other personal contacts to serve as experimental subjects. However unlikely, it is possible that the subtleties of social contingencies (e.g., motivation to help the researcher; concerns over appearing foolish) could result in different environment–behavior dynamics for friends versus strangers. Any methodological practice that provides fuel for questions about alternative sources of control is best avoided whenever possible.

Children and Other Special Populations

Recruiting infants or young children to participate in an experiment necessarily begins with their parents. Thus, the most common technique involves sending letters to the parents or guardians of children in a particular nursery, playgroup, preschool, school class, or afterschool program. In many cases, letters can be given directly to parents when they arrive to pick up their child. Because parents will have many concerns about the details of their child's involvement, a successful recruitment letter must provide a comprehensible discussion of the general research issue and a complete description of the experimental task, including exactly what the child will do and what will happen to her or him. An example recruitment letter is provided in Form 2.1 (see also the related discussion of informed consent in the last section of this chapter). It is also good practice for a researcher to familiarize the relevant personnel (e.g., administrators, teachers, careproviders) from the children's programs about the research, so that a parent's questions could be fielded appropriately. Especially when the research will be conducted at the nursery or school, contributions from the researcher to the school (e.g., books, games, playground equipment) can provide an indirect aid to recruitment efforts. Other strategies for recruiting children include direct contact with parents' groups (e.g., Parent–Teacher Association), fliers in pediatricians' offices or maternity wards, and newspaper ads.

When more specialized subject populations are required, the researcher needs to think broadly about strategies that can provide access to the population of interest. For some special groups (e.g., those exhibiting particular medical or behavior problems), contacts with local physicians, therapists, and support groups can prove useful, either in soliciting recruits or in posting advertisements in offices or newsletters. Public service announcements on local radio or television stations also can be arranged. Similarly, studies of behavior-change programs related to health often will receive strong support from local businesses and industries. For example, during a large-scale study of breast self-examination training procedures, a manufacturing plant in Gainesville, Florida, provided on-site access to a nurse's examination room one day a week, and paid time off from work for female employees interested in receiving the training. When institutionalized populations are of interest, each agency will have its own set of practices for determining

FORM 2.1
**Example of an Invitation to Participate and Informed Consent Document
for Parents of Minors**

Dear Parent,

For the past five years, we have been involved in the study of children's learning patterns. One goal of this work has been to develop a group of standard tasks or games that can be used to study learning with children of a wide range of ages. The other goal is to identify the ways in which young children's learning patterns differ from those of older children or adults. Because we are comparing the learning and memory patterns shown by children of different ages, it can be especially useful to work with individual children over an extended period of time, to see if their patterns change.

We feel very fortunate to have been able to conduct some of this project at Wilmington area preschools and after-school child-care programs. A number of parents from our local schools have been most helpful in giving permission for their child to participate. Currently, we are looking for approximately 20 children between 4 and 6 years old to take part in the study. This letter comes as a request for your permission to include your child in this important study of how children learn.

The specifics of your child's participation would be as follows. All study sessions will be held at your child's school during the Afterschool Child Care Program and at times that do not interfere with planned activities for the children. Your child would work with one or two of our advanced, senior students for about 15 minutes a day over a period of time as short as 1 week or as long as 4 to 5 months, depending on your child's interest and learning level.

We tell each child that we are going to play a game with pictures. One of our students sits with the child on one side of a small table. This student "teacher" then shows your child two colorful pictures, presented on a computer screen. Choosing one of these pictures will result in fruit chew or candy being placed in a cup on the table. The child's job is to choose one of the pictures, and over a series of presentations, to learn which of the pictures earns the reward. Different combinations of pictures that have been rewarded and those that have not will be used throughout the study. On any given day, your child would get a maximum of 15–20 pieces of fruit or candy, not enough to spoil the appetite.

Your child may also be asked to play a standardized word game often used in schools. The word game is played with a flip chart, and children are asked to point to the picture that matches a word spoken by the teacher. This word game will allow us to see how language skills are related to other aspects of learning.

These learning games are fun for children. They love to discover the way to earn prizes. Each day's session is short, so they don't get bored. Further, your child is free to decline to participate on any given day, or to withdraw from the study at any time, with absolutely no repercussion. The only possible risk of participation is that for the 15-minute session time, your child will not be engaging in other af-

continued

terschool activities (e.g., playing with friends, working on homework). Benefits of participation include the fact that children seem to enjoy the attention that comes from interacting with our students, and they get some experience working at a structured task. In addition, your child will be contributing to important findings on how learning styles change with age, with possible implications for improving educational practices in the future.

We would like to point out that this project has been approved by the UNCW Institutional Review Board for research with human subjects and by the directors of the Afterschool Child Care Program. Your child's performance will not be compared with that of any other individual child. Instead, we are seeking to find the range of learning patterns that may be shown in specific age groups. At no time will a child's name be used to identify his or her performance. At the end of the project, we will be happy to send you a summary of our findings.

If you have any questions at all about this research, what it means, or how it is handled, please feel free to call us at the University at (phone number). If you have questions about the University's procedures for ensuring the rights of volunteer research participants, please call (name), Dean of Research Administration (phone number). The Site Director of the Afterschool Program is also familiar with the project and could answer questions about its operation. If you would allow your child to participate, please sign the attached permission slip and return it to the Afterschool Child Care Program as soon as is convenient. We appreciate your consideration of this project.

Thank you for your support,

Permission for Participation

I give my permission for my child to participate in the Children's Learning Project being conducted by Drs. (names) at the Afterschool Child Care Program.

Parent's Name . . . . Date . . . .

Child's Name . . . . Child's Birth Date . . . .

---

the individual (e.g., primary therapist or physician) who must be contacted about invitations for experimental participation.

RETAINING SUBJECTS AND MAINTAINING PERFORMANCE: ISSUES OF REINFORCEMENT

Among the most critical of decisions for any operant experiment are those related to methods for ensuring a subject's continued participation and those for consequating the operant(s) of interest. The issues are obviously interrelated, but different sets of factors impinge on the two goals, and it makes sense to consider them separately.

Strategies for Retaining Subjects

Retaining subjects for the duration of an experiment can be a serious challenge for much operant research. Many operant tasks are simple and repetitive, and often described by the subject as boring or uninteresting. Further, the experimental designs employed most frequently necessitate extended participation. Subjects who drop out prior to completing a study represent a loss of significant time and resource investments. Thus, motivational strategies for ensuring completion should be carefully planned and incorporated into the experimental arrangement from beginning to end.

Asking a subject for verbal commitment to completing the study is not only a good idea for behavioral reasons (e.g., Rachlin & Green, 1972), it is also required in the form of informed consent. Particularly for normal adult subjects, the consent document should take the form of a job description, where the required number of hours of participation is specified, and signatures by the participant and experimenter represent a contract of expectations to be fulfilled by both. (An example consent form is provided in Form 2.2; see also the related discussion of informed consent in the final section of this chapter.) A related strategy used in the human operant laboratory at UNCW involves having each subject complete one or two sessions before signing a long-term contract. This practice ensures that subjects are familiar with all dimensions of the task they are promising to complete, and increases the experimenter's confidence that agreement to continue is fully informed.

A more established tactic for retaining subjects involves arranging contingencies specifically for session attendance. This practice has taken a number of forms and must be considered in operant experiments of any significant duration. In any form, the workings of such contingencies must be specified in the informed consent document. In one arrangement, subjects earn a set reinforcer amount (e.g., money, course credit) for each session completed. Sometimes this contingency provides the sole source of remuneration in the experiment; in other cases, reinforcers earned from the attendance contingency are combined with those produced by the operant performances under investigation. Attendance contingencies used in isolation have the practical advantage of allowing total earnings to be controlled and specified in advance. More important, this strategy provides motivation for participation when the experimental question requires an absence of contrived reinforcers for ongoing behavior, as when response deprivation is the manipulation of interest, or when differential feedback would complicate analysis of generalized or emergent response patterns. However, for a majority of experiments targeting operant behavior, explicit contingencies for both attendance and the targeted operant behaviors are in order.

Another effective strategy, used increasingly by operant researchers, involves provisions for a bonus contingency in which reinforcers in addition to those earned throughout the experiment are awarded on completion of all scheduled sessions. Some researchers provide a bonus of some amount for each session completed; others offer one lump sum as incentive for completion. When resources are limited, completion can earn chances in a lottery drawing for a single, sizable prize. With slight modifications the same strategy can be used with a range of sub-

FORM 2.2
Example of Informed Consent Form for College Students

Contract for Experimental Participation and Consent Form

Subject's Name _____

Principal Investigators _____

Date _____

I agree to participate in the research as explained to me below:

    This experiment is designed to investigate how people learn. It is not a psychological test of any kind. Your task will involve making simple choices between abstract, graphic stimuli by touching a computer screen. Any specific questions you have about the task will be answered at the time your experimental instructions are given. In addition, the reasons for this experiment will be described to you fully at the end of your participation.

    Your participation may involve as many as 40 hours of your time. Experimental sessions of approximately 50 minutes in length will be scheduled over the next weeks at times that are convenient to you and your experimenter. In return for your time, you will be paid in cash once a week, at the end of your last session for that week. The amount of money that you earn will be based on two factors. First, you will earn a base rate of $5.00 for every session that you attend. Second, in addition to the $5.00, you can earn more money depending on your performance during the session. (Please note, however, that the amount of extra money may vary from one session to the next.) Each white token that you earn will add 1 cent to your total for the day, while each blue token will subtract 1 cent from your day's earnings. You will be informed of how much money you have earned at the end of each session. Third, in addition to your daily earnings, there will be a bonus of $1.00 for each session attended if you complete all of your scheduled sessions. This bonus will be paid at your final session. If you elect to discontinue your participation prior to completing the experiment, you will be paid for all sessions and work completed but you will not earn the bonus.

    Finally, to protect your privacy, any analysis of data collected from this experiment will be done confidentially and your name will not be associated with the data in any way. In addition, please understand that you are free to withdraw your consent and to discontinue participation in the project at any time without prejudice. You will be paid for all sessions completed.

    If you have any questions or concerns about this research, you should feel free to contact the principal investigator at (phone number and address).

I understand that my participation is voluntary. I have read and I understand the procedure described above. I agree to participate in this experiment and I have received a copy of this description.

Signatures:

Participant _____ Date _____

Experimenter _____ Date _____

---

ject populations. Pilgrim et al. (1995) allowed preschool children to choose a small toy from an array following the last session in each week for which all sessions were completed. The weekly participation contingency was designed to offset the likely impact of long-term contingencies and delayed reinforcers on the behavior of young children.

Such practices carry all of the advantages of arranging explicit contingencies for a desired behavioral outcome. Also important, the positive nature of the arrangement leaves it unlikely to be considered coercive. Federal regulations require that a subject be able to withdraw from an experiment at any time without penalty or coercion (see Ethical Considerations), and the once common stipulation that earned reinforcers would be forfeited when a subject discontinued participation prematurely is now unacceptable. However, bonus contingencies can be used effectively to support completion without repercussions for work already performed.

Relatively unexplored in the operant literature is the impact of designing a more intrinsically interesting experimental task on retaining subjects. By way of example, Leung (1989, 1993) studied choice performances with a video game where subjects earned money by detecting and destroying enemy aircraft. Beardsley and McDowell (1992) studied the matching law in the context of ongoing conversations between subject and experimenter on topics of interest (e.g., current events, campus life, dating, and relationships). Statements of praise from the experimenter were presented contingent on the subject making eye contact during conversation. Hayes, Thompson, and Hayes (1989) studied the formation of equivalence relations among locations on a musical staff, finger placements on a keyboard, and names of musical notes, thereby providing for the emergence of novel, albeit rudimentary, musical performances. Although the degree to which a more interesting task might contribute to retaining subjects is currently unassessed, the possibility has considerable face validity.

In a somewhat similar vein, extraexperimental social contingencies rarely receive explicit attention in accounts of research with human subjects. However, efforts to build and maintain a positive rapport between experimenter and subject can do nothing but increase the probability that participation agreements will be fulfilled. For example, research with children is facilitated when the experimenter spends time interacting with subjects in the classroom or playgroup prior to the start of the study, and time spent playing or reading with a child after each session can provide a potent source of reinforcement for participation.

Strategies for Maintaining Operant Performance

The events programmed to function as reinforcers in operant studies, either for attendance or for within-session performances, have been many and varied (e.g., Galizio & Buskist, 1988). Clearly the most appropriate choice for any given experiment will depend on the population of subjects employed and the research question. With normal adults, unless the research question specifically entails other reinforcers (e.g., drugs, verbal praise, the opportunity to engage in restricted activities), money or points exchangeable for money have been arranged most effectively. Although creative alternatives can prove interesting, money has important advantages in most cases. Compared with other consequent events, a common history establishing money as a potent reinforcer can be assumed for most adults in most cultures, and as a generalized reinforcer, momentary deprivation levels are not a factor in determining the effectiveness of money. The absence of these factors can be observed often in studies where points alone are arranged. Behavior patterns across subjects are frequently variable, indicating an important lack of experimental control. Points and other tokens without backup certainly appear to function as reinforcers with some subjects, but the reasons for this are undoubtedly complex (cf. Shull & Lawrence, Chapter 4). For example, some researchers have cautioned against confusing the influence of instructions (e.g., "Earn as many points as possible") with direct reinforcement effects (e.g., Catania, 1992). At the least, such factors can complicate an analysis of behavior and are probably best avoided whenever possible.

As alluded to above, monetary earnings often are marked by the presentation of points for criterion responses during the course of an experimental session. This practice and other forms of token reinforcement have many advantages, allowing for immediate delivery of individually small reinforcers that can accrue with sustained responding to reinforcers of greater magnitude, delivered at a later time. (This latter effect may be enhanced when cumulative totals can be observed, as on a counter, or when daily earnings are announced at the end of the session.) Satiation during the session is avoided, ongoing operant responding is not disrupted, and the experimenter's resources can be stretched. Decisions must be made, however, about the rate of exchange and the schedule on which it should take place. Both will be determined largely by the subject population. The functional reinforcers for which tokens are traded will be appropriate to the subject's age and personal history. With normal adults, the options for exchange schedules have ranged recently from payment after each 10 minutes of a session to a single payment at the completion of the study. Where extended participation is involved, a strategic medium is to make periodic payments, say once a week. This schedule allows earnings to accrue to functional amounts, and ensures that the benefits of completing multiple sessions will be contacted relatively quickly. Attendance and cooperative session scheduling are likely to improve, particularly when the subject's involvement is motivated primarily by financial need. Periodic exchanges also contribute to the effectiveness of tokens or points as conditioned reinforcers. Thus, exchange procedures may need to be explicitly trained, with the frequency even within a session gradually decreased, as young children or institutionalized individuals learn to work for tokens.

For older children and individuals with moderate levels of developmental disability, the advantages of using money (or points exchangeable for money) as a reinforcer are the same as for adults. However, following approval by parents or guardians, a wide variety of events have proved effective with nonadult populations (cf. Weisberg & Rovee-Collier, Chapter 11). Examples of reinforcers for infants' responses have included consequent presentations of milk, the mother's voice, movements of a mobile, and being held. Reinforcers used with children and developmentally delayed participants have included edibles, tokens exchangeable for commissary goods, access to preferred activities, cartoons, stickers, toys and trinkets, tickles, social attention, and praise, to name a few.

A number of factors can influence decisions about which reinforcers to use and how to present them. When extended participation is required, a practice that can help to prevent or delay boredom and a decline in reinforcer effectiveness is to schedule a variety of reinforcers. A collection of small edibles or trinkets and stickers can be mixed within each session, or tokens can be traded for toys chosen from an array that is replenished frequently with new items. The researcher also should consider (or test) the full range of responses likely to be occasioned by reinforcer presentation. Many of these responses can interfere with the operant of interest or with the progression of an experimental session. For example, edible reinforcers should be ones that can be either picked up and eaten quickly or accumulated for later consumption. In the latter case, or when tokens, trinkets, or small toys are used, reinforcers might be delivered into a clear container where their accumulation can be viewed but manipulation during the session is prevented. Alternatively, the subject might be trained to deposit each reinforcer in a bank or holding device on its delivery.

SESSION NUMBER AND SCHEDULING

Parameters of scheduling experimental sessions also can be related to continued subject participation. When the duration or frequency of scheduled sessions increases to the point of inconvenience or aversiveness, attendance may suffer. Of course, there are important considerations related to session scheduling beyond those of convenience and subject acceptance.

Scheduling Issues

Enhanced experimental control is evident in investigations of animal behavior when time of day and frequency of experimental sessions are held constant. Interestingly, the extent to which standardized schedules are followed across subjects, or to which sessions are conducted at a consistent time of day for individual subjects is difficult to ascertain from the human operant literature. However, sound judgment suggests that such standardization can be valuable and should be approximated to the fullest extent possible. It is the case that some human operant performances have shown surprisingly little disruption following even prolonged absences from the laboratory. For example, Spradlin, Saunders, and Saunders (1992) reported that emergent patterns of stimulus control were maintained after 5 months or more without intervening training or practice for a mildly retarded individual. Thus, the impact of session timing may prove specific to a given experimental arrangement. Still, given the uncontrolled and varied nature of between-session experiences for human subjects, carefully managed scheduling seems especially prudent when control over stable performance is elusive. Routines may be particularly important with certain subject populations (e.g., institutionalized subjects; young children), when primary reinforcers are programmed (e.g., food, drugs), and whenever extended intersession intervals necessitate some amount of reacquisition. An informal convention among human operant researchers, and one with considerable merit, is to schedule sessions for the same time(s) of each day of the workweek. Along with improving experimental control, an indirect advantage of this practice may be to reduce the frequency of appointments forgotten by subjects.

Session duration also can contribute to experimental control because it determines the extent of uninterrupted contact with experimental variables. At a general level, longer sessions are sometimes regarded as superior to shorter ones because the impact of independent variables may be exerted more fully and because the characteristics of a particular repertoire may be sampled more completely (e.g., Bernstein, 1988; Johnston & Pennypacker, 1993). Insufficient amounts of either will severely limit any conclusions that might be made about functional environment–behavior relations. However, decisions about session duration will be based on a number of factors. Session durations for young children and some institutionalized subjects, for example, are necessarily short given limited task persistence and attentional capabilities. Sessions of 5 to 15 minutes may be the maximum possible. Some research questions require more extended session durations, as when a drug's time course is under investigation or when the behavior of interest occurs only in bouts of extended duration. When experimental tasks require focused concentration, such as in some vigilance procedures or when the acquisition of multiple, four- and five-term contingencies is of interest, an extended session may be divided into several shorter segments of responding with breaks in between. Session lengths of 1 to 2 hours may be the norm in human experimental research, but any number of variations can be fit to the needs of a particular research program.

Another issue to capture theoretical attention (Sidman, 1992; Spradlin et al., 1992), and one that may have relevance for decisions about session duration, involves the alleged tendency for human subjects to respond "consistently." If response patterns at one point in a session are even partially determined by the performance shown earlier in the same session, this might imply that shorter sessions could reflect greater sensitivity to experimental manipulations. At issue here is that when patterns of behavior are variable, performances are more likely to include both response units that meet criteria for reinforcement, and responses that do not meet those criteria. Similarly, some responses may meet the reinforcement criteria more efficiently, or with less response cost, than others. In this way, more variable performances may allow the full effects of the differential reinforcement contingency to come to bear (e.g., Chase & Bjarnadottir, 1992; Joyce & Chase, 1990). Thus, if variability is greater at a session's beginning for any reason, the probability of contacting scheduled contingencies may be increased, and numerous short sessions may have their own advantages. As with other features of session scheduling, any functional differences between a few long sessions and a greater number of shorter ones remain to be determined, but may be important to consider relative to particular research questions.

Number of Sessions

Somewhat in contrast to scheduling session duration and frequency, which depend on a number of experimental and subject characteristics, decisions concerning the number of sessions to be conducted per experimental condition can be determined only by the principles of steady-state research strategy (e.g., Baron & Perone, Chapter 3; Johnston & Pennypacker, 1993; Sidman, 1960). A discussion of the many factors that contribute to the production and identification of steady states is beyond the scope of the present chapter. For present purposes, however, the critical point is that none of these factors is altered when humans serve as subjects. Although no formula exists to allow a priori specification of session number, extended exposure to experimental conditions is typically necessary to satisfy steady-state criteria, just as it is for nonhuman behavior. Even where experimental pretraining can be justifiably accelerated by instruction, modeling, and so forth, within-subject comparisons without steady states can address only the most limited questions about behavioral control mechanisms, and results are more likely to reflect extraexperimental history than the full impact of programmed experimental variables (see also Bernstein, 1988, for further discussion).

Studies of human operant behavior that do not include multiple sessions in each of several experimental conditions are likely to involve between-group comparisons. In some cases, effective training procedures can be demonstrated quickly by using mastery criteria to determine progression across training phases, although it should be noted that a demonstration of effective procedures often differs in important ways from a complete analysis of controlling variables in that procedure.

A note of caution also may be called for regarding the tactic of reporting data from a single laboratory visit in the form of multiple "minisessions." Although detailed analysis of within-session patterns is often of legitimate interest, this practice can also present an artificial picture of performance stability if the sample of behavior is too limited. The basis for scientific reasoning provided by steady states requires more than some arbitrary number of data points, and within-session performance may not be a perfect predictor of stability across sessions.

THE APPARATUS AND RESPONSE: ISSUES OF MEASUREMENT

The Nature of the Response

The general criteria for selecting dependent variables in studies of human operant behavior are the same as those for studies with other species. Whatever the response class of interest, it should be defined functionally; that is, response classes are identified in terms of a common relation between each instance of the response and an environmental event, such as a switch closure or an antecedent stimulus presentation (e.g., see Johnston & Pennypacker, 1993). Optimally, the response also should be easy to identify and record, readily repeated and free to vary in rate, and relatively arbitrary in the sense of being independent of controlling variables other than those of experimental concern. When the responses of interest do not meet these characteristics, more complex laboratory arrangements may be required. For example, continuously programmed environments allow for study of response classes that are infrequently repeated, such as bouts of reading, exercise, or playing chess (Bernstein, 1988).

Recent debate has focused on the extent to which even simple responses by human subjects (e.g., a key press) may be free of various extraexperimental constraints (e.g., see Baron, Perone, & Galizio, 1991b; Branch, 1991; Shull & Lawrence, 1991). The concern is that humans, especially adults, are likely to have had experiences with such responses prior to their participation in an experiment, and that these uncontrolled histories may be significant in determining the effectiveness of experimental contingencies. Although these are critical issues, the bottom line is that a great many preparations involving such responses yield functional relations that are reproducible within and across subjects, studies, and, sometimes, species. Indeed, one possibility is that responses that function naturally as a component of multiple operant classes or chains are necessarily sensitive to their contingencies at any given moment. For example, for adult subjects, button presses occur frequently in the course of operating vending machines, video games, computers, doorbells, and so on. The response topography may have an extensive history, but it is arbitrary in the sense of having no fixed relation to environmental events. Experiences then seem likely to have established a response that is free to vary with the situation, a much-sought feature for operant research.

In basic human operant work, responses involving a press, touch, point, or pull have dominated research practice, largely because they satisfy so well the general criteria stated above. However, the data base has not been exclusively restricted to such topographies, and a broader range of experimental questions has been addressed by exploring the operant characteristics of alternative response types. Some novel response adaptations have included (1) wheel turning, which allowed comparison of schedule contingencies with differing relations between duration and count of responses and reinforcers (Williams & Johnston, 1992), and (2) eye contact, which proved sensitive to frequency of reinforcement (Beardsley & McDowell, 1992), perhaps not unlike the nondiscriminated muscle twitches studied by Hefferline and colleagues (e.g., Hefferline & Keenan, 1963) some years ago. In addition to these examples, the study of verbal responses is of increasing interest in human operant research. Methods for dealing with these important response classes are discussed in detail by Shimoff and Catania (Chapter 12) and Critchfield, Tucker, and Vuchinich (Chapter 14). As was the case with previously discussed features of human operant procedure, the dependent measures that can contribute effectively to an experimental analysis are varied and can be designed to match the research question; they need not, and should not, be limited to the topography of pressing.

The Nature of the Apparatus

It is the experimental apparatus that provides the locus for interaction between dependent and independent variables; thus, the primary functions of apparatus design are arranging and detecting environment–behavior relations. Precise and accurate transduction of operant responses is a necessary first step, both for measurement and for purposes of arranging contingencies. Toward this end, computer technology has had a major impact on human operant laboratory procedure, allowing for tremendous flexibility in automated recording. Even relatively inexpensive personal computers allow for a range of response topographies that can be adapted to most any subject population. Responses can be made directly to the computer on either the keyboard or a touchscreen, joystick, or "mouse," or response operanda such as push buttons, panels, response keys, plungers, or drawers may be interfaced. In addition to the many advantages of automatic measurement, on-line data analysis may be possible, allowing the researcher to arrange for changes in experimental conditions to take place automatically when criterion patterns of responding are detected.

In addition to accurate and automatic measurement, computers also provide for flexible experimental control of antecedent and consequent stimuli. Timing and graphics capabilities allow for precise scheduling of varied physical and temporal stimulus properties, whereas randomization capabilities accommodate the necessity of balancing stimulus number, order, and location. These same features can be arranged manually, but doing so is often tedious, and the checks required to prevent and catch errors must be programmed systematically as well. As with interfaced operanda, additional stimulus-presentation mechanisms (e.g., reinforcer delivery systems) can also be arranged.

Particular stimulus needs vary with the behavioral phenomenon under investigation. Lights, sounds, counters, graphics, and instructions are common examples that may require continuous, intermittent, simultaneous, or sequential presentation, in relation to or independent of responding. The particular arrangement will depend, of course, on an experiment's goals. In one interesting example, Belke, Pierce, and Powell (1989; also Pierce & Epling, 1991) designed their apparatus to approximate the configuration of a standard pigeon chamber with respect to subject size. Reinforcer delivery mechanisms can also be variously adapted to accommodate points, coins or tokens, edibles, visual displays such as reading material (Williams & Johnston, 1992) or videos (e.g., Darcheville, Riviere, & Wearden, 1993), social reinforcers such as tickles from a child's mother (Reeve, Reeve, Brown, Brown, & Poulson, 1992; Reeve, Reeve, & Poulson, 1993), and presentation of heat (Silberg, Thomas, & Berendzen, 1991). Once again, particulars of the experimental apparatus can and should follow from the research question.

When Automation Is Not Possible

The precision, accuracy, and control provided by automated experimental procedures are to be sought whenever possible. However, some research questions or environment–behavior interactions make automation impractical or even impossible, and human experimenters are required to either measure behavior, implement procedures, or both. Some response classes, particularly those involving more naturalistic behaviors, may be difficult to measure in the absence of a human observer. The difficulties may arise either from dimensions of the response topography (e.g., the behavior involves manipulation of various objects, as in classroom or work activities, or could occur in numerous locations) or from the nature or number of the criteria used to define the response operationally (e.g., correct responses on a musical keyboard, eye contact, play). In other cases, functional antecedents or consequences of interest may be difficult to automate (e.g., social stimuli, such as a mother's presence or her tickles).

The importance of closely monitoring the reliability of human observers is widely and formally acknowledged (e.g., Johnston & Pennypacker, 1993). Regular calibration is sound practice for any procedure or measurement system. Methods for establishing reliable observers have been described in detail elsewhere (Johnston & Pennypacker, 1993), and the same practices hold for ensuring that experimenters present stimuli and reinforcers reliably. The most important step involves rigorous training prior to the start of the experiment. Training might include modeling or role-play with feedback; videotapes can be used for practice with measurement or with identifying occasions for reinforcement. Training should continue until the trainee consistently meets predetermined accuracy criteria under conditions as similar to those of the experiment as possible. Periodic reevaluation in terms of the training criteria throughout the duration of the experiment also is a wise convention to prevent drifts in accuracy or precision. Sessions may be videotaped or visited by an observer, to assess the reliability of implementation and measurement. Of course, the observer should have completed successfully the same training regimen as the experimenter. Documentation of interobserver agreements and accuracy in implementing procedures will strengthen reports of experiments involving human observers; some publication outlets require this practice. If training procedures are unsuccessful in remediating poor interobserver agreement, researchers will need to reevaluate and refine their response definitions.

ESTABLISHING A CONTEXT: INSTRUCTIONS AND LABORATORY SETTINGS

Investigations of environment–behavior interactions necessarily occur within a context that includes features in addition to those under study. These elements of the experimental setting can either contribute to or interfere with experimental control, and so require attention.

Experimental Instructions

For many research scenarios involving human subjects, the combination of social contingencies and practical needs dictates that some form of instructions be provided by the experimenter as a starting point in a subject's participation. Although practices vary widely in the human operant literature (see Pilgrim & Johnston, 1988, for review), from the minimalist "Try anything" to literally pages of description, there is general appreciation that instructions can have a potent effect on experimental outcomes. Shimoff and Catania (Chapter 12) and Shull and Lawrence (Chapter 4) provide a review of such issues, but for present purposes, a general caution is in order. When an experiment is conducted to identify relations between behavior and (the noninstructional) environment, the wise researcher will avoid instructions that could provide an alternative account of performance. This adage in no way implies a reactionary omission of all instructions, but simply underscores the nature of the research agenda in behavior analysis. Statements about functional relations are compromised when control by independent variables is confounded with the content of experimental instructions. A good rule is to design instructions with parsimony as a goal.

That said, it is clear that the content of instructions will vary with factors like task complexity and subject population, as will the mode of presentation. With children, for example, oral instructions and modeling appear similarly effective (Michael & Bernstein, 1991). A written format may be preferred with normal adults, particularly when the instructions describe a complex task, but having an experimenter read aloud as the subject views his or her own copy allows key points to be emphasized as well. Leaving a copy of the instructions in sight allows the subject to review. In some cases, instructed elements may not become salient until certain events take place in the experiment, and the instructions should be allowed to have their full effects, once presented. To help ensure this, some researchers quiz their subjects about the instructions prior to starting the experiment. Others arrange pretraining periods in which misunderstandings can be corrected. Either practice can be worthwhile when there is reason to doubt that the subject has made full contact with the instruction set (e.g., when there are language difficulties or when inattention is at issue). Regardless of mode or complexity, a standardized instruction script should be used to ensure consistency, and the script should appear verbatim in any published report of the work.

The Physical Context

The physical setting in which a human operant study takes place should be designed primarily with the goal of eliminating, or at least limiting, distractions that could compete with control by experimental conditions. For general purposes, optimal conditions might include an experimental space that is quiet, well lit, and physically comfortable in terms of temperature and seating, free of visually interesting stimuli unrelated to the research (e.g., open windows, magazines), regularly available for as long as needed without disruption from other individuals, and equipped such that the experimenter has visual access to the subject's behavior, but not vice versa. Of course, many perfectly serviceable settings have lacked one or more of these characteristics, but approximation of them is a step toward experimental control. At the same time, we may do well to recognize that the austere settings typical of much human operant research are likely to engender complex social repertoires related to "psychologists" and appropriate patterns of conduct in monitored situations (i.e., demand characteristics; Orne, 1962). More naturalistic experimental settings may decrease this possibility, but extended exposure to the simpler conditions, as in steady-state research designs, also allows demand effects to diminish.

In contrast to the typical, spartan arrangements described above, alternatives can be designed to explore particular types of research questions without sacrificing experimental control. Studies such as those described here inspire consideration of a broader range of possibilities for laboratory settings. Residential laboratory facilities, for example, have the important advantage of control over conditions even when data are not being collected and can also allow for experimental contingencies to be continuously programmed (Bernstein, Chapter 16).

Live-in settings have been used to study issues such as the distribution of time spent on leisure (e.g., Bernstein & Ebbesen, 1978; Bernstein & Michael, 1990) or work activities (Foltin et al., 1990), patterns of drug intake (e.g., Griffiths, Bigelow, & Liebson, 1989), and effects of drugs over extended periods (e.g., Bickel, Higgins, & Griffiths, 1989; Foltin et al., 1990; Higgins, Woodward, & Henningfield, 1989). The live-in arrangements typically consist of comfortable and even homey bedrooms with baths, recreation and dining areas, materials for recreational activities, and other amenities for physical comfort. In most cases, specialized equipment for operant measurement is also present. Typically, multiple subjects participate simultaneously, but not always (e.g., Bernstein & Michael, 1990), and contact with events outside of the experimental setting is explicitly prevented in some cases (no newspapers, television, or telephones; e.g., Bernstein & Michael, 1990; Foltin et al., 1990).

Much of the literature of applied behavior analysis has been conducted in natural settings (e.g., schools, communities, the workplace, residential institutions). This has been a less frequent strategy in investigations focused on basic principles of behavior, but one that also has a longstanding tradition within behavior analysis (e.g., Ayllon & Michael, 1959). More recent examples include (1) tests of fit between Herrnstein's equation and the allocation of a retarded girl's classroom behaviors as a function of naturally occurring social consequences (Martens & Houk, 1989), (2) demonstration of behavioral momentum when a distracting videotape was presented to institutionalized subjects at work in their group home (Mace et al., 1990), and (3) an analysis of children's self-talk during private play in their own homes, which showed that frequency and type of verbal behavior varied as a function of the toy in play (Lodhi & Greer, 1989). By choosing the setting for data collection carefully, studies such as these are able to reveal stable functional relations while simultaneously examining the generality of basic behavioral processes.

In addition to the physical laboratory space, certain setting variables may be chosen for their motivational functions. Such variables, or establishing operations (e.g., Michael, 1982), are important in increasing the effectiveness of programmed consequences. For example, the context of a video game or of competition with another individual may increase the value of points as consequences when compared with nongame situations. Similarly, illuminations of a heat lamp have been established as reinforcers by maintaining an environmental chamber at low temperatures (Silberberg et al., 1991). In a related manner, statements like "uh-huh" or "that's right" may have been more effective reinforcers when delivered by a listener during a conversation (Beardsley & McDowell, 1992), than if they had been presented on a computer screen. Finally, young children may work harder for tokens, exchangeable for prizes, when those prizes are visible throughout the experimental session. These examples serve to illustrate how creative arrangements of setting features can be used to enhance control by experimental conditions.

ETHICAL CONSIDERATIONS

As evidenced by their frequent mention throughout this chapter, ethical considerations play a role in every dimension of conducting research with human subjects. A successful researcher will be one who is committed to the ethical practices described by both formal and informal rules. The practice of ethics is based on the principle of treating all others with respect and dignity. Nowhere is this more important than in the relationship between experimenter and subject. Perhaps the best way to begin any research project is with the attitude that our subjects are our partners in asking questions about behavior. As researchers, we are privileged to have their help, we owe them every courtesy, and we must behave accordingly when making experimental decisions.

Basic Issues

In addition to basic professional civilities such as being polite, prompt, and prepared in dealings with research participants, experimenters also have more formal obligations to their subjects. One is providing for the subject's safety and comfort, both physical and psychological. Another is ensuring that all information and data obtained are treated confidentially, including the fact that a particular individual participated. An additional, critical obligation concerns the importance of arranging for voluntary participation, without coercion, under conditions that the subject explicitly has agreed to experience.

Methods for fulfilling these obligations necessarily will vary with the subject population and the research question. Still, certain practices are important for use in most or all studies with human subjects. Requirements for obtaining informed consent from normally capable adults, or parents or legal guardians of other populations, are spelled out explicitly (see later discussion). Alternatives to research participation must be provided when serving as a subject earns course credit or access to otherwise restricted activities. Data should be recorded and stored anonymously, for example, by subject number, and consent forms should be stored separately from the data. Discomfort and inconvenience are minimized by careful attention to the details of the experimental setting and the testing schedule. The necessity of any potential risk is scrutinized at multiple levels (e.g., by the researcher and IRB) and fully described to the subject, with precautions arranged in case of problems (e.g., medical personnel may be present or on-call when drug effects are investigated).

One particularly troublesome ethical issue in research with human subjects concerns the deliberate use of deception. Deception differs from the practice of omitting detailed descriptions; it involves the presentation of patently false information. It is easy to advise that deception should be considered a practice of last resort. Still, some investigations would be difficult to conduct without deception. Important examples include studies of cooperation, competition, or verbal interactions. Putative "decisions," programmed by the experimenter but said to be made by another subject in an adjoining room, are conveyed via computer and serve as antecedent or consequent stimuli for the true subject's performance. Experimental analyses of such interactions would be difficult or impossible without control over the "social" stimuli of interest. Nevertheless, practices involving deception should be considered only when risk to the subject is minimal and when an important research question demands it.

Whenever deception is used, and often when it is not, debriefing the subject about the experiment will help to fulfill ethical obligations. Simply put, participants who have invested their time and energy deserve to have their questions answered. In most cases, the extent of the debriefing can be driven by the subject's level of interest, although the researcher should be careful not to neglect quiet subjects. Elaborate descriptions are rarely appropriate. Theoretical contexts will mean little to most participants, and clear statements of the experimental question (e.g., "We wondered how X would affect the way you did Y") are typically of primary interest. When the researcher has concerns that other subjects could learn about the experimental issues under investigation, it may be appropriate to schedule an appointment for debriefing on completion of the entire study. Formalized debriefing scripts also can be useful when the researcher wishes to have some control over the information that becomes available about an experiment, particularly when the study requires a large number of subjects (e.g., from a departmental subject pool). Debriefing scripts may be requested by an Institutional Review Board (IRB), particularly when studies involve deception.

Institutional Review Boards

Every research project involving human subjects must be submitted for approval to an IRB, the function of which is to ensure that researchers have provided sufficient protection of subjects' "rights and welfare" (Office for Protection from Research Risks, 1979, 1989). Without approval, an experiment cannot be conducted, and if researchers are collecting data away from their home institution, approval may be needed from review boards at every institution involved. In addition, continuing research projects must be reapproved at least once a year.

Dimensions of research proposals involving human operant behavior that are likely to receive scrutiny include use of subject populations other than normally capable adults; potentially harmful (e.g., drugs) or aversive (e.g., shock) independent variables; unusual settings (e.g., cold) or scheduling (e.g., continuous residence); participation contingencies (particularly those in which bonuses are forfeited if participation is discontinued); deception; and informed consent procedures. The committee's charge is to ensure that the subjects' interests have been safeguarded with respect to each of these practices. It may be important to note that review boards are *not* charged with evaluating the scientific merits of a proposal. However, one of the stated criteria for IRB approval is that any risks to subjects be considered in relation to anticipated benefits, which include "the importance of the knowledge that may reasonably be expected to result" from the research. Thus, discussion of scientific contributions certainly can take place during IRB deliberations. The best advice is for the researcher to consider all steps of the review process carefully.

Sound preparation of the IRB document should take the composition of the committee into account. Although committee members usually do not mean to obstruct research, they are diverse in their opinions as to how research should be conducted and how subjects' rights should be protected. Federal guidelines specify that the IRB be composed of members from scientific and nonscientific backgrounds, with at least one member from outside of the institution. For a university IRB, even the scientist members are likely to represent a range of academic dis-

TABLE 2.1

Information Requested by Institutional Review Board for Consideration of Research Projects with Human Participants

1. Describe the population of participants.
2. If the population includes individuals other than healthy, normally capable adults, state the necessity for your choice.
3. Briefly describe what you propose to do and why.
4. List all procedures to be used with human participants, with a description of those you consider beyond already established and accepted techniques.
5. State the potential risks—for example, physical, psychological, financial, social, legal, or other—connected with the proposed procedures.
6. Describe procedures (including methods to assure confidentiality) for protecting against, or minimizing, potential risks. Assure their effectiveness. If you consider the participant to be "at risk," in what respect do the potential benefits to the participant or contributions to the general body of knowledge outweigh the risks?
7. State how you will obtain documentation of informed consent. Answer even if you consider participants not at risk. (You must retain the signed consent forms for *at least three years* after the completion of the research.)
8. If you consider the subject to be "at risk," state exactly what you tell him/her in lay language to obtain informed consent relative to each procedure wherein he/she is "at risk."
9. Attach a copy of the informed consent form you plan to use.

Note. Taken from the form, *Documentation of Review and Approval of Research Projects Utilizing Human Subjects,* used by the Institutional Review Board for the Protection of Human Subjects at the University of North Carolina at Wilmington.

ciplines, as well as most professional schools. Thus, the challenge becomes one of describing research activities concisely, in nontechnical language, with an eye toward justifying those practices that impinge most directly on the subject. Table 2.1 provides examples of questions that are commonly asked on project-approval forms from a university IRB.

When appropriate, descriptions that emphasize the standard nature of an experimental arrangement can provide a useful context for judging relative risk to subjects, particularly for committee members unfamiliar with operant research. Similarly, providing a debriefing statement and protocol can help allay concerns of IRB members over issues of deception or the omission of information about an experimental hypothesis. Choosing words carefully also can help to avoid concerns. *Manipulation* and *control,* for example, are particularly loaded terms. Standardized conditions and changes in an independent variable all can be described without reference to manipulation or control; potential confusion of an experiment's defining features with implications of coercion may thus be prevented.

When a researcher has concerns about how a proposal will be received, feedback from the IRB chair or an IRB representative from one's home department prior to submission can be useful. Because the IRB may meet only at set times during the calendar or academic year, it also can be important to determine scheduled dates in advance, to allow sufficient time for proposal distribution. In some cases, the principal investigator may be asked to attend the committee meeting, to provide details about any issues of concern. For any proposal, careful adherence to the American Psychological Association's ethical principles (reprinted in the Appendix to this volume) is the surest route to approval by an IRB.

Informed Consent

The key ethical principle underlying informed-consent requirements is that participants in an experiment should be exposed to only those experiences and conditions that they agree to, beforehand. To help ensure that this important standard of practice is observed, federal regulations require that every human subject (or legal representative) participating in nonexempted research provide uncoerced and fully informed consent, documented by either a signed written form or a signed and witnessed summary of an oral presentation. (Exempted status must be determined by the IRB; it covers studies involving "normal" educational practices, survey procedures on nonsensitive topics where respondents cannot be identified, or observation of nonsensitive public behavior where subjects cannot be identified. See OPRR, 1989, for further description.) As implementers of this regulation, the IRB will review consent procedures carefully in terms of the degree to which experimental procedures are characterized accurately. Table 2.2 outlines the information to be provided to each subject, although exceptions can be considered by the IRB when the research would be compromised without some alteration. Examples of consent forms designed for the parents of young children and for college students are provided in Forms 2.1 and 2.2, respectively. (Both examples have been approved by a university IRB and by the Office for Protection from Research Risks of the National Institutes of Health.) Even when a parent or other legal guardian must sign the consent form, some indication of agreement to participate should be obtained from the subject as well, to the extent that this is feasible (e.g., with young, verbal children but not infants). Indeed, IRBs increasingly require this. An example script used to request consent from 4- to 6-year-olds at the start of a study is presented in Form 2.3.

With respect to informed consent, several common issues for operant researchers warrant comment, although some of these hold for scientists in other areas of human research as well. One question concerns the amount of information that must be provided to allow for informed consent, particularly with respect to the experimental manipulation. Here it is important to note that adequate descriptions need not specify the experimental question or the functional relation under investigation. The consent document needs to provide basic descriptions of what the subject will be asked to do (e.g., press a key, fill out a questionnaire, "see if you can figure out how . . ."), and the generic sorts of experimental stimuli to which subjects will be exposed (e.g., a computer game or abstract, graphic stimuli). An exception is when experimental variables could be described as unusual or aversive (e.g., sexually graphic stimuli, shock presentations, psychoactive drugs and placebo conditions); typically these will require more complete descriptions. However, when well crafted, rather general statements about most of the contingency arrangements used in operant research often will suffice. For example, "Some choices will earn points worth 5 cents each" can provide an adequate summary of discrimination-training procedures and generalization tests, even when discrimination reversals are planned, and "The number of tokens earned in each session may vary" usually is sufficient when experiments involve manipulation of reinforcement schedules.

Operant researchers also must grapple with how to inform subjects about the

TABLE 2.2
Guidelines for Composing Informed Consent Statements

1. Use wording understandable to the participants.
2. Tell participants that the study involves research and describe:
   a. procedures
   b. purpose
   c. risks and side effects
   d. possible benefits to the subject or other individuals
   e. safeguards to be used
   f. expected duration of participation
3. Discuss alternative procedures or course of treatment, if applicable.
4. Include an invitation for participants to ask questions about the study and its procedures. Include the investigator's name, address, and telephone number. Include a statement that if there are questions regarding the study, the subject should feel free to contact the investigator.
5. State the terms of compensation for study participants, if any. State how and when participants will receive payment or compensation.
6. Tell subjects that participation is voluntary, that they may decline to participate, and that they may withdraw from the study at any time without prejudice, or if applicable, loss of benefits.
7. State the intention to keep the participant's identity in confidence, and explain how the confidentiality of the data collected will be protected.
8. If deception is used, include a statement to the effect that the research cannot be fully described at this time, but that an explanation will be provided at the conclusion of participation.
9. Where appropriate, describe anticipated circumstances under which the subject's participation may be terminated by the investigator.
10. State the approximate number of participants to be included in the study.
11. If participants are to be audio-taped, videotaped, or filmed, request permission to do so in writing and indicate how the materials will be used.
12. Include a statement of consent to participate in the study.
13. If the participant and/or their parent(s)/guardian consent to participation, provide two copies of the Consent Form, one to be retained by the participant and one to be signed and returned to the investigator.
14. If participants are minors, their verbal consent is required whenever possible. Use the following guidelines for obtaining signed consent:
   6 years old and younger—only parent/guardian need sign;
   7–8 years old—signature of minor is optional, signature of parent/guardian is required;
   9 years old or older—signature of both minor and parent/guardian is required.
15. If the participant or legal representative is unable to read and understand the written consent, it may be verbally presented in an understandable manner and witnessed (with signature of witness).

Note. Guidelines taken from OPRR (1989) and from the requirements for informed consent used by the Institutional Review Board for the Protection of Human Subjects at the University of North Carolina at Wilmington.

time requirements of an experiment when its duration is dependent on the subject's performance and cannot be predetermined precisely. Relatedly, researchers are obliged to provide some information on the conditions under which a subject's participation could be terminated, when relevant for a study. One solution to this problem is for the researcher to estimate an approximate number of hours required and then request consent with respect to "a maximum possible duration" that exceeds the estimate by some margin of safety. It should be clear that the exact number of sessions is not fixed, but any information that would lead a subject to perceive the duration of participation as an indication of successful or unsuccessful

FORM 2.3
Example of a Script for Obtaining Informed Consent from Minors (Aged 4–6)

Hi (Child's name),

My name's_____. I have a game here that uses toys and pictures. Would you like to play this game with me?

(If no) That's OK. Maybe we can play tomorrow.

(If no after three or four requests, requests will stop.)

(If yes) Let me show you how this game works. There are some pictures here for you to choose from (show stimulus presentation). You should choose only one at a time. Sometimes your picks will earn prizes like these (show fruit bits). Sometimes your picks will not earn prizes. You can try to get as many prizes as you can while you play this game. Would you like to play?
I like to play this game for about 15 minutes, but if you want to stop before that, just tell me, OK? I'll be visiting your school in the afternoons for a while, to play this game with some of the children. You and I can play this game as many afternoons as you'd like. This game is fun and you can get prizes. Of course, you can't be doing other things while you're playing. You can just tell me if you want to play or not—no problem. Do you have any questions?

---

performance should be avoided (e.g., "The exact number of sessions will depend on the particular experimental conditions that you are selected to receive, but as many as X hours of your time may be required").

Explaining bonus contingencies also requires some thought, because any connotations of coercion are inappropriate. A subject must be able to discontinue participation in an experiment at any time without penalty. The best approach is to describe the bonus arrangement as positively as possible, but the conditions under which the bonus will and will not be provided both should be specified (e.g., "In addition to your daily earnings, you will earn a bonus of $50 if you complete all of your scheduled sessions. If you elect to discontinue your participation prior to completing the experiment, you will be paid for all sessions and work completed up to that point, but you will not earn the bonus").

It is interesting that the content of consent forms rarely receives comment in published accounts of human operant research, whereas verbatim transcriptions of experimental instructions have become standard. To give consent, subjects must be told something of what they will be doing, and a general context for the research often is provided as well (e.g., "This is an experiment on human learning"). Thus, statements made on the consent form may play a role in the subject's subsequent performance, much as do experimental instructions. Where the consent form presents task-relevant information that is not repeated in the instructions, some mention in the final report might be considered.

FINAL CONSIDERATIONS

It seems appropriate to outline here a few general considerations for selecting parameters of the experimental arrangement. A starting principle is that the procedural arrangement should be no more complex (contain no more elements) than necessary to address the research question. Although the use of human subjects often may seem to justify (or even require) involved preparations, a parsimonious approach proves as well-suited for designing procedures as for theoretical interpretation.

Another general consideration involves the essential role of the subject's performance in evaluating the adequacy of an experimental arrangement. As in the study of any species, the benchmark of an effective experimental preparation is its ability to reveal orderly relations between behavior and environmental manipulations. Indeed, even when order is elusive, subjects' responses may prove instructive. Some researchers report using exit interviews, not as a means of generating dependent measures, but rather as one tactic for suggesting possible sources of competing control. Such reports cannot be accepted simply at face value, given the multiple sources of control over verbal behavior (Critchfield et al., Chapter 14), but they may be useful in identifying variables to be subjected to empirical test (see Wulfert, Dougher, & Greenway, 1991, for example).

Finally, a reminder to let one's research question determine choice of procedural arrangements, rather than vice versa, will be reiterated. Research now has demonstrated convincingly that any number of experimental arrangements can be fit to the natural science strategies of behavior analysis. At the same time, human operant research is undergoing a period of tremendous growth and development, inspiring, and inspired by, new perspectives on the empirical foundation that has been laid. If our field is to make progress, research practices must draw on experimental arrangements that have already proved effective, as well as the novel variations that will inevitably emerge to address new issues.

REFERENCES

Ayllon, T., & Michael, J. (1959). The psychiatric nurse as a behavioral engineer. *Journal of the Experimental Analysis of Behavior, 2,* 323–334.

Baron, A., & Mattila, W. R. (1989). Response slowing of older adults: Effects of time-limit contingencies on single- and dual-task performances. *Psychology and Aging, 4,* 66–72.

Baron, A., & Menich, S. R. (1985). Age-related effects of temporal contingencies on response speed and memory: An operant analysis. *Journal of Gerontology, 40,* 60–70.

Baron, A., Perone, M., & Galizio, M. (1991a). Analyzing the reinforcement process at the human level: Can application and behavioristic interpretation replace laboratory research? *The Behavior Analyst, 14,* 95–105.

Baron, A., Perone, M., & Galizio, M. (1991b). The experimental analysis of human behavior: Indispensable, ancillary, or irrelevant? *The Behavior Analyst, 14,* 145–155.

Beardsley, S. D., & McDowell, J. J. (1992). Application of Herrnstein's hyperbola to time allocation of naturalistic human behavior maintained by naturalistic social reinforcement. *Journal of the Experimental Analysis of Behavior, 57,* 177–185.

Belke, T. W., Pierce, W. D., & Powell, R. A. (1989). Determinants of choice for pigeons and humans on concurrent-chains schedules of reinforcement. *Journal of the Experimental Analysis of Behavior, 52,* 97–109.

Bernstein, D. J. (1988). Laboratory lore and research practices in the experimental analysis of human behavior: Designing session logistics—how long, how often, how many? *The Behavior Analyst, 11,* 51–58.

Bernstein, D. J., & Ebbesen, E. B. (1978). Reinforcement and substitution in humans: A multiple-response analysis. *Journal of the Experimental Analysis of Behavior, 30,* 243–253.

Bernstein, D. J., & Michael, R. L. (1990). The utility of verbal and behavioral assessments of value. *Journal of the Experimental Analysis of Behavior, 54,* 173–184.

Bickel, W. K., Higgins, S. T., & Griffiths, R. R. (1989). Repeated diazepam administration: Effects of the acquisition and performance of response chains in humans. *Journal of the Experimental Analysis of Behavior, 52,* 47–56.

Bijou, S. W., & Baer, D. M. (Eds.). (1967). *Child Development: Readings in experimental analysis.* New York: Appleton–Century–Crofts.

Branch, M. N. (1991). On the difficulty of studying "basic" behavioral processes in humans. *The Behavior Analyst, 14,* 107–110.

Catania, A. C. (1992). *Learning* (3rd ed.). Englewood Cliffs, NJ: Prentice–Hall.

Chase, P. N., & Bjarnadottir, G. S. (1992). Instructing variability: Some features of a problem-solving repertoire. In S. C. Hayes & L. J. Hayes (Eds.), *Understanding verbal relations* (pp. 181–193). Reno, NV: Context Press.

Darcheville, J. C., Riviere, V., & Wearden, J. H. (1993). Fixed-interval performance and self-control in infants. *Journal of the Experimental Analysis of Behavior, 60,* 239–254.

Davey, G., & Cullen, C. (Eds.). (1988). *Human operant conditioning and behavior modification.* New York: Wiley.

Foltin, R. W., Fischman, M. W., Brady, J. V., Bernstein, D. J., Capriotti, R. M., Nellis, M. J., & Kelly, T. H. (1990). Motivational effects of smoked marijuana: Behavioral contingencies and low-probability activities. *Journal of the Experimental Analysis of Behavior, 53,* 5–19.

Galizio, M., & Buskist, W. (1988). Laboratory lore and research practices in the experimental analysis of human behavior: Selecting reinforcers and arranging contingencies. *The Behavior Analyst, 11,* 65–69.

Gewirtz, J. L., & Pelaez-Nogueras, M. (1992). B. F. Skinner's legacy to human infant behavior and development. *American Psychologist, 47,* 1411–1422.

Griffiths, R. R., Bigelow, G. E., & Liebson, I. A. (1989). Reinforcing effects of caffeine in coffee and capsules. *Journal of the Experimental Analysis of Behavior, 52,* 127–140.

Hayes, L. J., Thompson, S., & Hayes, S. C. (1989). Stimulus equivalence and rule following. *Journal of the Experimental Analysis of Behavior, 52,* 275–291.

Hayes, S. C., & Hayes, L. J. (Eds.). (1992). *Understanding verbal relations.* Reno, NV: Context Press.

Hefferline, R. F., & Keenan, B. (1963). Amplitude-induction gradient of a small-sale (covert) operant. *Journal of the Experimental Analysis of Behavior, 6,* 307–315.

Higgins, S. T., Woodward, B. M., & Henningfield, J. E. (1989). Effects of atropine on the repeated acquisition and performance of response sequences in humans. *Journal of the Experimental Analysis of Behavior, 51,* 5–15.

Johnston, J. M., & Pennypacker, H. S. (1993). *Strategies and tactics of human behavioral research* (2nd ed.). Hillsdale, NJ: Erlbaum.

Joyce, J. H., & Chase, P. N. (1990). The effects of response variability on the sensitivity of rule-governed behavior. *Journal of the Experimental Analysis of Behavior, 54,* 251–262.

Leung, J. P. (1989). Psychological distance to reward: A human replication. *Journal of the Experimental Analysis of Behavior, 51,* 343–352.

Leung, J. P. (1993). Psychological distance to reward: Segmentation of aperiodic schedules of reinforcement. *Journal of the Experimental Analysis of Behavior, 59,* 401–410.

Lodhi, S., & Greer, R. D. (1989). The speaker as listener. *Journal of the Experimental Analysis of Behavior, 51,* 353–359.

Mace, F. C., Lalli, J. S., Shea, M. C., Lalli, E. P., West, B. J., Roberts, M., & Nevin, J. A. (1990). The momentum of human behavior in a natural setting. *Journal of the Experimental Analysis of Behavior, 54,* 163–172.

Mace, F. C., Neef, N. A., Shade, D., & Mauro, B. (1994). Limited matching on concurrent-schedule reinforcement of academic behavior. *Journal of Applied Behavior Analysis, 27,* 585–596.

Mace, F. C., Neef, N. A., Shade, D., & Mauro, B. (1996). Effects of problem difficulty and reinforcer quality on time allocated to concurrent arithmetic problems. *Journal of Applied Behavior Analysis, 29,* 11–24.

Martens, B. K., & Houk, J. L. (1989). The application of Herrnstein's Law of Effect to disruptive and on-task behavior of a retarded adolescent girl. *Journal of the Experimental Analysis of Behavior, 51,* 17–27.

Michael, J. (1982). Distinguishing between discriminative and motivational functions of stimuli. *Journal of the Experimental Analysis of Behavior, 37,* 149–155.

Michael, R. L., & Bernstein, D. J. (1991). Transient effects of acquisition history on generalization in a matching-to-sample task. *Journal of the Experimental Analysis of Behavior, 56,* 155–166.

Morris, E. K., Johnson, L. M., Todd, J. T., & Higgins, S. T. (1988). Laboratory lore and research practices in the experimental analysis of human behavior: Subject selection. *The Behavior Analyst, 11,* 43–50.

Neef, N. A., Mace, F. C., & Shade, D. (1993). Impulsivity in students with serious emotional disturbance: The interactive effects of reinforcer rate, delay and quality. *Journal of Applied Behavior Analysis, 26,* 37–52.

Neef, N. A., Mace, F. C., Shea, M. C., & Shade, D. (1992). Effects of reinforcer rate and reinforcer quality on time allocation: Extensions of matching theory to educational settings. *Journal of Applied Behavior Analysis, 25,* 691–699.

Neef, N. A., Shade, D., & Miller, M. S. (1994). Assessing influential dimensions of reinforcers on choice in students with serious emotional disturbance. *Journal of Applied Behavior Analysis, 27,* 575–583.

Office for Protection from Research Risks, The National Commission for the Protection of Human Subjects of Biomedical and Behavioral Research. (1979). *The Belmont report* (FR Doc. 9-12065). Washington, DC: U.S. Government Printing Office.

Office for Protection from Research Risks, National Institutes of Health, Department of Health and Human Services. (1989). *Protection of human subjects.* Code of Federal Regulations (Title 45—Public Welfare; Part 46). Washington, DC: National Institutes of Health.

Orne, M. T. (1962). On the social psychology of the psychological experiment: With particular reference to demand characteristics and their implications. *American Psychologist, 17,* 776–783.

Pierce, W. D., & Epling, W. F. (1991). Can operant research with animals rescue the science of human behavior? *The Behavior Analyst, 14,* 129–132.

Pilgrim, C., Chambers, L., & Galizio, M. (1995). Reversal of baseline relations and stimulus equivalence: II. Children. *Journal of the Experimental Analysis of Behavior, 63,* 239–254.

Pilgrim, C., & Galizio, M. (1990). Relations between baseline contingencies and equivalence probe performances. *Journal of the Experimental Analysis of Behavior, 54,* 213–234.

Pilgrim, C., & Galizio, M. (1995). Reversal of baseline relations and stimulus equivalence: I. Adults. *Journal of the Experimental Analysis of Behavior, 63,* 225–238.

Pilgrim, C., & Johnston, J. M. (1988). Laboratory lore and research practices in the experimental analysis of human behavior: Issues in instructing subjects. *The Behavior Analyst, 11,* 59–64.

Pouthas, V., Droit, S., Jacquet, A.-Y., & Wearden, J. H. (1990). Temporal differentiation of response duration in children of different ages: Developmental changes in relations between verbal and nonverbal behavior. *Journal of the Experimental Analysis of Behavior, 53,* 21–31.

Rachlin, H., & Green, L. (1972). Commitment, choice, and self-control. *Journal of the Experimental Analysis of Behavior, 17,* 15–22.

Reeve, L., Reeve, K. F., Brown, A. K., Brown, J. L., & Poulson, C. L. (1992). Effects of delayed reinforcement on infant vocalization rate. *Journal of the Experimental Analysis of Behavior, 58,* 1–8.

Reeve, L., Reeve, K. F., & Poulson, C. L. (1993). A parametric variation of delayed reinforcement in infants. *Journal of the Experimental Analysis of Behavior, 60,* 515–527.

Saunders, K. J., & Spradlin, J. E. (1989). Conditional discrimination in mentally retarded adults: The effect of training the component simple discriminations. *Journal of the Experimental Analysis of Behavior, 52,* 1–12.

Saunders, K. J., & Spradlin, J. E. (1990). Conditional discrimination in mentally retarded adults: The development of generalized skills. *Journal of the Experimental Analysis of Behavior, 54,* 239–250.

Shull, R. L., & Lawrence, P. S. (1991). Preparations and principles. *The Behavior Analyst, 14,* 133–138.

Sidman, M. (1960). *Tactics of scientific research.* New York: Basic Books.

Sidman, M. (1992). Equivalence: Some basic considerations. In S. C. Hayes & L. J. Hayes (Eds.), *Understanding verbal relations* (pp. 15–27). Reno, NV: Context Press.

Silberberg, A., Thomas, J. R., & Berendzen, N. (1991). Human choice on concurrent variable-interval variable-ratio schedules. *Journal of the Experimental Analysis of Behavior, 56,* 575–584.

Spradlin, J. E., Saunders, K. J., & Saunders, R. (1992). The stability of equivalence classes. In S. C. Hayes & L. J. Hayes (Eds.), *Understanding verbal relations* (pp. 29–42). Reno, NV: Context Press.

Williams, D. C., & Johnston, J. M. (1992). Continuous versus discrete dimensions of reinforcement schedules: An integrative analysis. *Journal of the Experimental Analysis of Behavior, 58,* 205–228.

Wulfert, E., Dougher, M. J., & Greenway, D. E. (1991). Protocol analysis of the correspondence of verbal behavior and equivalence class formation. *Journal of the Experimental Analysis of Behavior, 56,* 489–504.

3

Experimental Design and Analysis in the Laboratory Study of Human Operant Behavior

Alan Baron and Michael Perone

Research methods play an essential role in efforts to describe, understand, and control nature. Consensus about appropriate procedures and practices allows researchers to compare and integrate their observations with those of others. On a deeper level, a researcher's methods express what is regarded as important in the field under study—and what is not. Consider, for example, the earliest experiments of psychologists in which subjects were asked to report on the contents of their consciousness as they engaged in various activities (Boring, 1950, Chapter 16). This "method of introspection" reflected the conviction that the important questions of psychology pertained to the individual's mental life. Behavior was of interest, but only insofar as it shed light on consciousness and the like. Later psychologists led by Watson and Skinner came to regard behavior as interesting and important in its own right. This emphasis is reflected in the label attached to the methods originated in Skinner's seminal work on operant conditioning in rats (Skinner, 1938) and pigeons (Ferster & Skinner 1957): the *experimental analysis of behavior.*

Skinner's methods have gained wide acceptance within the animal laboratory, not only for research on issues of learning and conditioning but also in a range of other areas including behavioral pharmacology, behavioral neurochemistry, and behavioral ecology (Iversen & Lattal, 1991). The critical features have remained more or less unchanged since their inception. The experimental subject is observed in an environment designed with the following ends in view: the measurement of a clearly defined response, the control of contingencies involving discriminative and reinforcing stimuli, and the elimination of unwanted influences.

Alan Baron • Department of Psychology, University of Wisconsin–Milwaukee, Milwaukee, Wisconsin 53201.   **Michael Perone** • Department of Psychology, West Virginia University, Morgantown, West Virginia 26506-6040.

Handbook of Research Methods in Human Operant Behavior, edited by Lattal and Perone. Plenum Press, New York, 1998.

Although the implications of behavior analysis for human behavior were recognized quickly (Keller & Schoenfeld, 1950; Skinner, 1953, 1957), actual use of Skinner's procedures for laboratory study of human behavior was more the exception than the rule for many years (Buskist & Miller, 1982). The situation is changing rapidly. About one-third of the articles published in the *Journal of the Experimental Analysis of Behavior* from 1988 to 1992 reported experiments with human subjects (Dougherty, Nedelman, & Alfred, 1993).

This chapter addresses the issues that arise when the methods of experimental analysis are extended to the human subject. Our goal is to provide information that will be of practical use to the laboratory worker. But questions of methodology cannot be divorced from underlying conceptual issues, many of which remain unresolved. We must consider them as well at each step of the way.

The behavior analyst's commitment to the study of behavior is accompanied by the conviction that the controlling variables should be sought in the organism's environment rather than in other realms. To the extent that either of these values, axiomatic to the experimental analysis of behavior, also may be found in the value systems of other behavioral, social, and biological sciences, they provide a basis for integrating research outcomes with knowledge from other disciplines. But divisions are apparent as well. For example, other experimental approaches may seek the determinants of behavior in different domains (e.g., neurological or genetic rather than environmental) or take a different view of the phenomenon to be explained (e.g., cognition rather than behavior).

Perhaps the most intractable divergence is at the level of research design. Which arrangement of experimental procedures best advances our understanding of behavior? The behavior analyst's commitment to the direct study of behavior requires procedures that will reveal experimental effects in the behavior of the individual organism—the single subject. This emphasis, although perhaps obvious and reasonable, is at odds with the conventional view that properly designed experiments involve group comparisons and statistical tests. Many of the issues discussed in this chapter hinge on the tension that exists between these two approaches.

Group-Statistical Methods

The elements of conventional group-statistical experiments are familiar to students of psychology. The procedures are designed to compare the average performances of subjects exposed to different levels of the treatment under study. In a simple two-group experiment, for example, the experimental group encounters the treatment whereas the control group does not. Preexisting differences from subject to subject ("individual differences") are addressed by randomly assigning the subjects to the groups and by including enough subjects to average out deviant cases. In the final step, inferential statistics such as the t or F-ratio are used to decide whether between-group variation (differences between the averages of the treatment groups) exceeds within-group variation (differences among the subjects within each treatment group). If the ratio is large enough, the results are deemed "statistically significant" and are taken to support the conclusion that the experimental treatment had an effect.

Group-statistical methods frequently rely on *between-group* comparisons in which a different group of subjects is assigned to each experimental condition. With some adjustment in the assumptions of the associated statistics, the approach also can accommodate *within-group* experiments in which the researcher observes the same group of subjects under the various conditions. In the latter case, the designs bear some similarity to the single-subject methods favored by behavior analysts; indeed, both within-group and single-subject experiments may be classified as within-subject designs. But within-group experiments retain the principal features of the group-statistical approach. Like their between-group counterparts, they continue to analyze performances averaged across a number of subjects and to infer the operation of experimental effects by way of statistical tests.

The strength of the scientific community's commitment to the design of experiments within the group-statistical framework is difficult to overestimate. Perhaps because of Campbell and Stanley's (1963) influence, only experiments within this framework qualify as "true experiments" in the eyes of many psychologists and social scientists. Other research designs, including the single-subject methods favored by behavior analysts, are relegated to the dubious status of "quasi-experiments."

The group-statistical approach leaves essential questions unresolved. Even when differences between subjects exposed to different treatments are statistically significant at the group level, the averages conceal exceptions at the individual level. Functional relations derived from group averages may have no counterpart in the behavior of any particular organism. Finally, group-statistical approaches may divert the researcher from a full experimental analysis. The hallmark of the scientific experiment is the manipulation and control of variables. Although group-statistical researchers no doubt are as committed to this ideal as behavior analysts, they must be prepared to tolerate uncontrolled differences among subjects as an inherent feature of their experimental procedures. This concession can only undermine the reasons for conducting experiments in the first place.

Single-Subject Methods

To circumvent the limitations of the group-statistical approach, the experimental analysis of behavior favors designs that focus on the behavior of individual organisms. A small number of subjects are studied at length under several experimental conditions, rather than a large number of subjects for brief durations, as in group-statistical arrangements. Although the experiment usually involves more than one subject, each subject's data are treated as an independent replication. Because data are not averaged across subjects, the behavior of the individual organism remains the unit of analysis. Behavior is observed repeatedly, and conditions are imposed until the behavior of interest stabilizes from one observation to the next—a behavioral *steady state* (Sidman, 1960). Extraneous variables are controlled rather than averaged out statistically, and effects of variables across their range of influence—functional relations—are examined as they naturally occur within the same organism rather than as a construction from the average performances of several groups. Finally, the need for inferential statistics is obviated because the high degree of control makes differences and relations self-evident from steady-state performance under each condition of the experiment.

The essential difference between individual and group methods hinges on the way behavioral variation is approached. The study of behavior as a subject matter in its own right requires identification of order at the level of the individual organism within some specified environment, and such order is accomplished by experimentally isolating sources of environmental influence. Although some behavioral variation may be tolerated as a practical matter, little is to be gained by concealing irregularities within the average performances of different subjects. The success of a single-subject experiment, therefore, is gauged in terms of the researcher's ability to reduce irregularities through improved experimental control. By comparison, group-statistical researchers certainly benefit from control over variation, but they need not rely on it. Instead, they may reduce the impact of variation on the results by way of averaging and interpretations based on inferential statistics.

Can the Approaches Be Reconciled?

The philosophical underpinnings of the single-subject and group-statistical approaches have created a gap within the behavioral sciences that is difficult to bridge. Writing from a behavior-analytic perspective, Sidman (1960) argued that the data generated by the two methods are not only different but incommensurable: The data "represent in a very real sense, two different subject matters," he wrote, so that researchers must take a stand "as to which of these types of data, individual or group, will form the basis of the science they are trying to build" (p. 54). This is not to say that the group approach is completely without utility. According to Sidman, group-statistical methods are appropriate when the behavior of the individual is of no concern, as may be the case in some practical applications of behavioral principles or, perhaps, in cases when concern is with the total behavioral output of a group without regard for the behavior of its members (Antonitis, Frey, & Baron, 1964). From the standpoint of basic knowledge, however, it is essential that the analysis be conducted at the level of the individual.

Both individual and group-statistical strategies are well-represented within the research literature, to the extent that experiments from the two traditions now appear side by side in some journals (consider recent issues of *Animal Learning and Behavior, Learning and Motivation,* and the *Journal of Experimental Psychology: Animal Behavior Processes*). This seems remarkable in the light of the aforementioned differences in the logic, if not the underlying philosophy, of the two approaches. Even more remarkable is that the discrepancy has been acknowledged so rarely, let alone critically discussed, since Sidman's (1960) original statement. Important issues need to be addressed. Should Sidman's view—that the approaches are fundamentally incompatible—prevail, or can the results be compared directly and even interchanged? Can equal confidence be placed in the outcomes?

Although we confess a strong sympathy for the single-subject designs of behavior-analytic research (and this is the theme of this volume), we do not want to leave the reader with the impression that single-subject methods are without flaw.

The limitations become especially evident when the research is conducted with human subjects rather than animals. When the subjects are human, the researcher must come to grips with a range of variables that cannot be brought under direct experimental control. In some instances, the constraints are ethical. The subject must be asked to consent to participate in the experiment, must be protected from unnecessary risk, and must be allowed to terminate participation at any time. In addition, some variables defy experimental analysis because they cannot be manipulated. The study of age and gender, for example, as well as less accessible ontogenic factors such as socioeconomic status, intellectual level, and educational attainment, pose formidable barriers to experimental control. In the eyes of many, variables such as these represent important elements of the context of human behavior. They can hardly be ignored if behavior-analytic knowledge, gathered with the procedures of the single-subject approach, is to be integrated with knowledge from the other behavioral, social, and biological sciences (cf. Baron, 1990).

These issues converge on the central themes of this chapter: How can the single-subject methods that have been so successful with animals be adapted for use with humans? Under what circumstances might deviations be needed or at least justified? In the sections that follow, we show that single-subject methods are uniquely suited for the study of human operant behavior (Baron & Perone, 1982; Perone, Galizio, & Baron, 1988). Although a range of practical and ethical considerations make it hard for researchers to conduct human experiments with the rigor of the animal laboratory, we believe that concerted efforts in this direction should be encouraged. Indeed, the scientific community's acceptance of behavior-analytic theory at the human level may well depend on the success of such efforts (Baron, Perone, & Galizio, 1991a,b). In the end, however, we must acknowledge that not all questions about human behavior may be amenable to single-subject methods, even if we restrict ourselves to questions posed by behavior analysts. As we will see, some research goals dictate the need for between-group comparisons and, along with them, development of an uneasy alliance of individual and group strategies (e.g., as in Baron, Menich, & Perone, 1983).

THE STEADY-STATE STRATEGY

The goal of an experiment is to determine whether manipulating some variable—the independent variable—produces a change in behavior represented by the dependent variable. At a minimum, behavior must be compared across two levels of the independent variable. In single-subject experiments, these levels or experimental conditions are imposed on an individual organism, often over some extended period. Within each condition, behavior is measured repeatedly until it reaches a steady state, that is, until there is minimal variation across the most recent set of successive measurements. If behavior is stable *within* conditions but changes substantially and systematically *between* conditions, then there is a good basis for attributing the changes to the manipulation of the independent variable.

This logic may be compared with group-statistical approaches, which also judge the effect of the independent variable by comparing behavioral variation within and between conditions (note that the ubiquitous F statistic is calculated by forming a ratio of estimates of these two types of variation). But single-subject research goes beyond merely assessing variation in behavior. Variation must be eradicated through experimental *control*. The guiding principle is that when control is complete, within-condition variability will be reduced to essentially zero. Such a high degree of control is, of course, more ideal than real given our present understanding of behavior, and a certain amount of unexplained variation must be tolerated. Still, stability is at the foundation of single-subject research, and the evaluation of single-subject data depends on agreement that some reasonable degree of stability has been attained.

Agreement is fostered by decision rules called *stability criteria* that specify standards for judging steady states. Viewed broadly, stability criteria set limits on two types of variability over time: systematic increases and decreases as well as unsystematic changes. Following Perone (1991), we will refer to these changes as *trend* and *bounce*. Although the researcher has considerable leeway about how stability will be assessed, several factors must be considered: when the criterion will be applied, how it will be defined, and how much and what kind of data will be included. We refer the reader to Sidman's (1960, pp. 234–280) classic discussion of these and related issues. Although Sidman focused on work in the animal laboratory, the researcher interested in the study of human subjects will profit from his comments.

When to Apply a Stability Criterion

A key issue is the point at which the criterion should be applied. Human behavior is not likely to change much immediately on introduction of an experimental manipulation; indeed, behavior at high strength may have considerable momentum (Nevin, 1992), and may tenaciously resist modification by a change in experimental conditions (e.g., Mace et al., 1990). Moreover, the persistence of the subject's initial response pattern may falsely suggest stable terminal performance, with the risk that premature termination of a condition may underestimate the effect of the experimental variable.

Practical considerations understandably will lead researchers to seek stability in their human subjects in the shortest possible time. Our experience, however, has been that this can be a tactical error. Adult humans bring a complicated verbal and social history to the laboratory that renders them highly susceptible to control by instructions, rules, social demand characteristics, and the like, rather than by the contingencies imposed within the experimental environment (Baron & Perone, 1982; Bernstein, 1988). Extended exposure is needed to allow experimental variables to compete with previously established forms of social and verbal control. We cannot specify the timing in general terms. It must depend on the goals of the research as well as the researcher's judgment about the size of the anticipated effects and the speed of their onset (Sidman, 1960, offered a similar conclusion).

Our advice is that researchers might best err in the direction of longer exposures. As an example of the hazards of brevity, consider the common finding that humans are insensitive to large shifts in rates of reinforcement. Figure 3.1 shows college students' responding on a multiple schedule in which a variable-interval

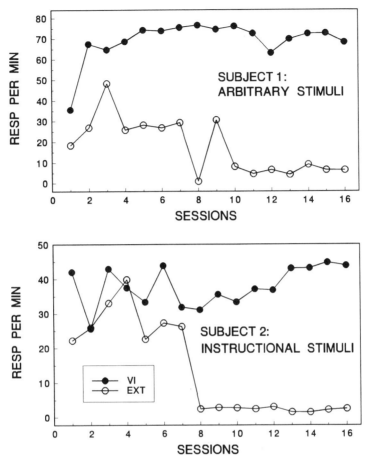

FIGURE 3.1. Response rates of two college students on a multiple VI EXT schedule of monetary reinforcement. For Subject 1 the schedule components were accompanied by arbitrary verbal labels; for Subject 2 the labels were instructions about the likelihood of reinforcers.

(VI) component that provided 5-cent reinforcers about twice per minute alternated with an extinction (EXT) component (Perone & Kaminski, 1992). For Subject 1 the discriminative stimuli were arbitrary verbal labels; a video monitor identified one component as *A* and the other as *B*. Despite the sizable difference in reinforcement rates across the two schedule components, the subject responded at substantial rates in the EXT component until the tenth half-hour session (upper panel of Figure 3.1). For Subject 2, by comparison, the stimuli were instructional: During the VI component the video monitor indicated that "*At this time scores are TWICE AS LIKELY as normal*" and during EXT that "*At this time NO SCORES can be earned.*" Given the established power of instructions in laboratory settings (Baron & Galizio, 1983), one might expect the discrimination to be virtually instantaneous, but high rates continued in the EXT component until the eighth session.

The lesson is straightforward. Had the condition been terminated after a few sessions with no apparent trend in behavior (say, after the sixth session), the results would have been seen as failing to establish adequate levels of discriminative control. This, in turn, might raise the familiar questions about the relevance of reinforcement to the analysis of human behavior (Lowe, 1979). A few additional sessions, however, virtually eliminated responding in the EXT component while maintaining it in the VI component. In this experiment, at least, there was no substitute for prolonged exposure to the contingencies.

Kinds of Stability Criteria

Once the criterion is instituted, the researcher must decide what span of time—how many sessions or trials—will constitute the basis for assessing stability. Experiments with rats and pigeons usually consider the most recent several sessions (about 4–10); when this sample of behavior meets the criterion the condition is ended, and the data from the terminal sessions are taken as representing the steady state. The approach with human subjects is similar, but, as might be expected from the discussion above, the sample of behavior sometimes is smaller. An idea of current practices can be gained from a special issue of the *Journal of the Experimental Analysis of Behavior* devoted to human behavior (November 1990). Seven of ten experiments specified stability criteria with samples ranging from two to five sessions (in one case, only responding during the last 2 min of the most recent three sessions was considered).

Researchers need to consider not only the number of sessions included in the sample, but also the duration and scheduling of the sessions. These matters are not often discussed in treatments of animal research, perhaps because practices in that arena have become fairly standardized. Sessions with animals tend to be long and widely separated: One hour per day is typical. When the animal's behavior is similar across a number of such sessions, it shows that the researcher can produce a particular outcome at will. But, as Pilgrim (Chapter 2) and Bernstein (Chapter 16) have noted, research practices with humans are much more variable, and some demonstrations of stability fall short of the standards of the animal laboratory. We are especially worried about the demonstrations when sessions are brief and close together. In the limiting case, some researchers have treated a stream of temporally contiguous observations as if they were separate sessions—for example, by dividing a single exposure to a schedule into a set of 2-min periods. The fact that behavior changes little over such a short time may say more about limitations on the opportunity for manifestations of variability than about the degree of control exerted by the experimental variables. But we also can envision circumstances under which the decision to use brief behavioral samples may be justified. In the end, the decision must hinge on the researcher's best judgment about the likely time course of the processes under study. Here, as in other aspects of steady-state methods, we encourage researchers to explain the basis for their judgments in reports of their work.

Regardless of sample size, repeated measures of the dependent variable should reveal an absence of trend and minimal bounce. Eliminating trend is not too difficult in well-controlled laboratory settings, at least in theory: One has merely to impose each experimental condition long enough for behavior to adjust. Bounce, however, is a direct function of the researcher's success in controlling relevant variables, and almost never can be eliminated completely. Sidman (1960) offered researchers practical advice about this. If the stringency of their criterion does not fit the level of control within their laboratory, "the variability which they observe will otherwise be so great as to cause them to spend a lifetime, if they are that stubborn, on the same uncompleted experiment" (p. 260).

Communication is improved when the researcher can express the degree of trend and bounce in quantitative terms. But the tradition in behavior analysis is also to accept criteria that depend exclusively on the researcher's judgment as the subject's performance is monitored from session to session. In the end, the adequacy of the criterion lies in the data. If decisions about stability have been faulty— be they based on quantitative or qualitative assessments—the researcher will have to live with the consequences.

Quantitative Criteria

Limits on variation can be expressed in absolute or relative terms. Perhaps the most common application of absolute criteria is for acquisition of behavior, where training conditions may be imposed until the subject performs at a predefined level of mastery over some specified period of time. For example, in a study of conditional discrimination, Harrison and Green (1990) continued training until the subject responded correctly on 30 of 32 consecutive trials. In many studies, however, "correct" responding cannot be defined, or at least not in any obvious way. What, for example, is the correct rate of responding on a VI schedule? In cases such as these, stability criteria are designed to assess whether behavior is consistent across the sample period.

Although behavioral consistency can be expressed in absolute terms (e.g., response rates may not vary by more than two responses per min across the last five sessions), the more common approach specifies acceptable variation in terms of percentage change across the sample period. For example, in a study of avoidance behavior maintained by schedules in which responding postponed signaled periods of monetary loss (Galizio, 1979), the criterion depended on response rates from the most recent four sessions. Means were calculated on the basis of the first pair of sessions, the second pair, and the entire set of four. Behavior was judged stable when the difference between the submeans was within 15% of the overall mean.

The stringency of a quantitative criterion is affected by factors in and out of the researcher's direct control. Raising the absolute or relative limits on bounce will relax the criterion, as will increasing the number of sessions or trials in the sample period. Enlarging the behavioral sample reduces the influence of short-term (e.g., session-to-session) fluctuations, so that the long-term bounce assessed by comparisons across large blocks of sessions can be small even while short-term bounce is large.

A less-obvious influence is exerted by the prevailing levels of behavior. As response rates decrease, relative criteria become stricter in absolute terms (smaller and smaller absolute variations will be tolerated), while absolute criteria relax in relative terms (larger and larger percentage variations will be tolerated). The converse is true as response rates increase, that is, relative criteria relax and absolute criteria become stricter.

As an illustration, consider again the data in Figure 3.1. Over 16 sessions, Subject 1's EXT rates dropped from a mean of about 29 responses per min (Sessions 1–6) to about 6 responses per min (Sessions 11–16). What happens when stability is assessed in relative terms? If the difference between the mean of Sessions 11 through 13 versus the mean of Sessions 14 through 16 are expressed as a percentage of the overall mean, the result exceeds 35%—this despite an absolute difference between the submeans of only 2 responses per min. By comparison, if the calculations are based on Sessions 1 through 6, when prevailing rates were substantially higher, the relative value is less than 15%, even though the absolute differences are roughly double. Clearly, then, researchers need to consider the response rates likely to be generated by their procedures when they establish standards for detecting stability. When a range of rates is generated, it may be wise to assess stability in both relative and absolute terms. For example, a researcher might decide that rates are stable when submeans are within 15% of the grand mean *or* when the absolute difference is within 2 responses per min. (For a fuller discussion of this issue, see Perone, 1991, pp. 141–144.)

Fixed-Time Criteria

One approach simply specifies the overall duration of the experimental conditions and the size of the sample to be considered as representing the steady state. In Horne and Lowe's (1993) study of choice on concurrent schedules, for example, the conditions were imposed for 16 sessions, each lasting 90 min, and the analysis was based on results from the last 3 sessions.

Fixed-time criteria excuse the researcher from closely monitoring each individual for signs of stability and simplify the task of planning and scheduling sessions. In addition, the fact that exposure to the various conditions is equalized within and across subjects may be an advantage in some areas of research. By comparison, criteria based on session-to-session performances make the duration of an experiment uncertain, and the duration will differ for different subjects. The resulting logistical problems are difficult enough when the subjects are rats and pigeons; the problems are compounded with human subjects who generally insist on information about the duration of the experiment before agreeing to participate. The popularity of fixed-time criteria is easy to understand: They make life easier for researchers and subjects alike.

But convenience comes at a price. As Sidman (1960) envisioned it, a fixed-time criterion is most effective when the researcher can afford a leisurely pace. If the terminal data are to represent a steady state, the duration of the experiment must be extended to accommodate the slowest subject. As noted above, lengthy experimental conditions are difficult to arrange in human research and decisions about the duration of the conditions may have to be based on experience as well as careful deliberations about the time course of the behavioral processes under investigation.

Moreover, regardless of the pains taken by the researcher, there is no guarantee that the terminal fixed-time data will be stable. At the least, researchers must report their results in enough detail to allow readers to judge the level actually attained. In the study mentioned above, Horne and Lowe (1993) augmented their fixed-time criterion by reporting a post-hoc assessment of stability over the last five sessions. In most, but not all, cases, the terminal behavior was reported to be stable.

Visual Criteria

The last method involves qualitative assessments of stability from visual examination of the results, usually session-by-session graphs of the dependent variable. Presumably, researchers consider both trend and bounce in such judgments. Most published reports are vague on this point, however, and indicate simply that stability was judged "visually." The development and maintenance of sound methods would be facilitated if researchers routinely reported the basis for their conclusion that performance indeed was stable.

Sidman (1960, p. 268) suggested that visual criteria be restricted to the study of variables expected to have obvious effects. The implication is that visual criteria are more tolerant of bounce, and perhaps trend, than the criteria outlined above. Whether this is so remains to be shown. Still, as with fixed-time criteria, the cautious researcher will follow the use of visual criteria with a report of the results that allows the reader to see the levels of stability actually attained.

Which Data to Consider

Researchers usually measure several aspects of behavior, and this raises an important question: Which must meet the stability criterion? The easy answer— "all of them"—may prove impractical. If the number of dependent measures is large, and if the stability criterion is stringent, random fluctuations are likely to prevent all of them from meeting the criterion simultaneously. Some flexibility is needed. In Galizio's (1979) experiment on avoidance of monetary loss, subjects responded on a multiple schedule with four components, and the objective was for response rates in each component to meet a 15% stability criterion. But Galizio planned two exceptions: First, rates in an EXT component were judged visually because they were too low to meet the percentage criterion. Second, a maximum of 15 hours was allowed per condition, effectively replacing the visual and percentage criteria with a fixed-time criterion as a stop-gap measure. In practice, then, failure to meet the stability criteria (visual or quantitative) in all four components simultaneously could not bring the experiment to a halt. In line with the recommendations offered above, Galizio provided a comprehensive report of his results, and the stability of his subjects' behavior was evident despite occasional departure from the standard decision rule.

A different solution is to combine several dependent variables into a single composite measure. In the condition depicted in Figure 3.1, for example, concern was with the discrimination between the VI and EXT components rather than the absolute rate of responding in each. Consequently, stability was judged on the basis of the ratio formed by dividing the VI response rates by the sum of the VI and EXT rates. These results are in Figure 3.2. Over the last six sessions, the ratios of both subjects show no trend and the difference between submeans based on the

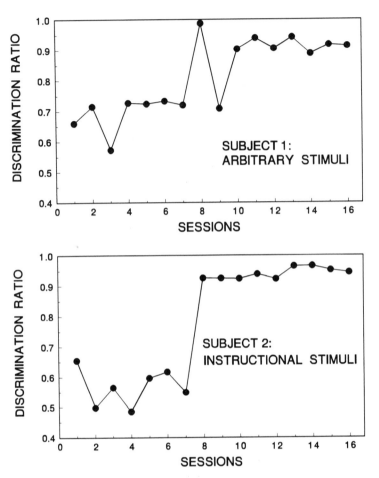

FIGURE 3.2. Discrimination ratios of two college students responding on a multiple VI EXT schedule of monetary reinforcement. The ratios, based on the data presented in Figure 3.1, were calculated by dividing the response rate in the VI component by the sum of rates in the VI and EXT components. Other details as in Figure 3.1.

first three and last three sessions is within 3% of the grand mean. Interestingly, the discrimination ratios are more stable than the component rates on which they are based (Figure 3.1), suggesting that the ratios capture an aspect of the subjects' performances—the discrimination per se—that was more reliable than the absolute response rates themselves. Indeed, our experience suggests that human subjects often show stable performances measured in relative terms such as discrimination ratios and choice proportions even when the absolute rates in the individual components or concurrent schedules are characterized by substantial bounce (e.g., Perone & Baron, 1980; Perone & Kaminski, 1992). Evidently, the factors affecting the absolute rate at which responses are emitted do not have as much influence on the distribution of those responses across schedules.

In deciding which aspects of behavior must stabilize, the researcher should weigh carefully the aims of the experiment. A common practice is to define the steady state in terms of some global measure (e.g., overall response rate) and then go on to include analyses of more molecular measures that might be regarded as reflections of the underlying structure of the steady state (e.g., interresponse time distributions; see Perone, 1991, pp. 146–147). Often this is a practical matter: It is not obvious how one might measure the stability of, say, an interresponse time distribution. Ultimately, however, the researcher is obligated to demonstrate that the analyses supporting the major interpretations are based on stable data.

Stability Criteria in the Context of Replication and Control

Researchers enjoy considerable latitude in defining stability criteria for single-subject experiments (as they do in selecting statistical tests for group experiments). This state of affairs can be evaluated in different ways. On the one hand, the availability of several ways to identify steady states can be seen as providing the researcher with the flexibility needed to study a range of issues. On the other, critics may wonder whether such latitude provides an easy way for researchers to delude themselves—to see what they want to see, or to otherwise reinforce a confirmatory bias (one can see counterparts in the way statistical tests sometimes are selected).

The remedy, according to Sidman (1960), is replication. If marked differences are observed when conditions are replicated, either the stability criterion is inadequate or the researcher's control over relevant variables is efficient. But if everything falls into place—if the observed relations between the independent and dependent variables are orderly and reproducible—then the researcher can be assured not only of the adequacy of the criterion used to identify the steady state, but also of the experimental methods used to engender it.

Note that legislating the use of particular criteria is not a satisfactory alternative. Even the most stringent criteria may be met by chance, just as statistical tests may erroneously indicate the presence of significant results. Replication alone can reveal such coincidences, regardless of whether single-subject or group-statistical designs are used.

In summary, stability criteria constitute an indispensable element of the single-subject research strategy, a strategy that emphasizes the identification of variables relevant to the processes under study, the exercise of rigorous control over those variables, and the use of experimental designs that incorporate replication. We now turn to a consideration of the issues that researchers must confront in designing experiments that will properly answer the question that prompted the research.

FINDING VALID ANSWERS

Despite the fundamental differences between single-subject and group-statistical approaches to experimentation, they share a common goal: that of making valid inferences about the consequences of manipulating the independent variable. The question of validity has been discussed extensively by workers within the group tradition. If behavior analysts are willing to look away from their over-reliance on statistical decision rules and to make some adjustments in the language, much of value can be learned.

Influential books by Campbell and Stanley (1963) and Cook and Campbell (1979) have led the way in identifying four fundamental types of validity. Each can be illustrated by a different question that researchers hope to answer through their data: Do the independent and dependent variables covary (*statistical conclusion validity*)? Does the covariation indicate a causal relation between the independent and dependent variables (*internal validity*)? In what abstract terms should the causal relation be understood (*theoretical validity*)? Does the causal relation generalize across subject populations, times, and environmental settings (*external validity*)?

The first two questions are closely connected (a negative answer to the first obviates the second) and they have direct implications for experimental design and analysis. The remaining questions are at a different level. They address strategies for planning entire programs of research and for integrating data from different studies—broad issues whose scope extends well beyond the technical requirements of a particular experiment. Below we consider these four questions within the context of single-subject experiments with human subjects. Additional discussions that are slanted toward behavior analysis, including reviews of specific research problems and experimental designs, may be found in a number of sources (Barlow & Hersen, 1984; Johnston & Pennypacker, 1993; Kazdin, 1982, 1992; Kratochwill, 1978; Kratochwill & Levin, 1992; Perone, 1991; Poling & Fuqua, 1986; Sidman, 1960).

Statistical Conclusion Validity

Experiments must be designed so that they are sensitive enough to detect systematic relations between the independent and dependent variables. The evidence for such covariation is essentially statistical (note that the term *statistics* is used here in the broad sense). Systematic relations are demonstrated when behavior changes more across experimental conditions than within them, and when these changes can be repeated in an individual subject as well as from one subject to the next. In both single-subject and group approaches, therefore, statistical conclusion validity is increased by procedures that reduce the unsystematic variability that may obscure the relation—in other words, by the exercise of experimental control.

The researcher can pursue the goal of increased control with a number of techniques. All are straightforward, so it will suffice simply to list them: (1) by standardizing experimental manipulations, (2) by using reliable measures of behavior, (3) by restricting the influence of extraneous variables, (4) by employing homogeneous samples of subjects, and (5) by changing conditions only when behavior meets appropriate stability criteria. The last of these techniques underscores a special strength of long-term, steady-state designs. The fact that the stability criterion has been met is good evidence that unsystematic variability has been reduced to tolerable levels, and the evidence is even stronger when the criterion is applied to replications of a procedure imposed at different times within the experiment (the researcher attempts to "recover" a data point). Replications can be arranged within each individual subject or between subjects; the most convincing experiments include both.

Although strong experimental control is the most direct way to enhance statistical conclusion validity, the group-statistical researcher often adopts an alternative strategy, that of trying to boost an experiment's sensitivity (or *statistical power;* e.g., Cohen, 1988) by increasing the number of subjects per group. The net effect is to allow even small differences to be detected as statistically significant when inferential tests are applied. As we have noted elsewhere in this chapter, the fundamental problem with this strategy is that the relations that emerge for groups of subjects may be absent in the performances of one or more individual members of the group.

Internal Validity

Experiments also must be designed so that any systematic variation in behavior can be attributed to the manipulation of the independent variable. To the extent that this requirement is met, internal validity has been achieved. Campbell and Stanley (1963) and Cook and Campbell (1979) identified several classes of extraneous variables that can become confounded with the independent variable and thus compromise internal validity. Experimental designs can be judged in terms of their success in overcoming these "threats to internal validity." Here we consider those of special relevance to single-subject experiments with humans.

Within-Subjects Threats

Several threats originate in variables that operate as a function of time or repeated exposure to laboratory procedures: *historical variables* such as previous experimental conditions or extralaboratory experience; *maturational variables* including long-term effects associated with biological aging and short-term effects such as fatigue; and *testing* procedures that may come to influence behavior when administered more than once. The possibility that these variables are operating within an experiment opens the door to conflicting interpretations of the results: Was the apparent experimental effect truly a consequence of the experimental manipulation?

Confounds from within-subject variables may originate in the experimental procedures themselves or in carryover effects from one condition to the next. Factors outside the laboratory become an additional concern in long-term human experiments. As time passes, it becomes more likely that a subject will encounter life events that will influence behavior in the experimental setting—semester examinations, illness, family crises, and so on. Because these events are beyond the experimenter's control, they cannot be eliminated or even held constant. The remedy is to design the experiment so that the effects of such factors can be distinguished from those of the independent variable. This is not always an easy job.

A distinct advantage of a steady-state approach is that it includes some built-in checks for within-subject confounds. Possible effects of testing, for example, should stabilize as the subject is repeatedly exposed to the procedures, and short-term historical or maturational effects will make themselves known insofar as they interfere with the attainment of stability. In addition, the researcher's success in recovering previous performances when replicating conditions makes these confounds less plausible. The recovery-of-performance strategy was used in a signal-detection analysis of recognition memory in older men (Baron & Surdy, 1990). The reinforcement contingencies were varied from a neutral arrangement to arrangements that encouraged more liberal or more conservative recognition patterns, and performances changed accordingly. Confidence in these results was enhanced by the further finding that performances also reverted to original levels when the neutral condition was reinstated.

The key, therefore, is replication. Consider, for example, an experiment in which Condition A is followed by Condition B (an *A-B design*). Any change in behavior from A to B might be related to the experimental manipulation, but it also could be attributed to history, maturation, or testing effects. Replicating the initial condition in an *A-B-A design* puts these rival accounts to the test. If behavior returns to its initial state, as in Baron and Surdy's study, then the experimental manipulation is probably responsible. Each additional replication (e.g., *A-B-A-B designs*), if accompanied by appropriate shifts in behavior, makes it less plausible that factors besides the independent variable could be responsible for any observed differences across the conditions.

What happens if the replication fails? Sometimes all that is needed is another set of replications. Suppose, for example, that low response rates are obtained in a baseline phase—Condition A—and moderately higher rates in an experimental phase—Condition B. Unfortunately, the moderate rates are maintained on returning to Condition A. Perhaps another phase of Condition B may lead to even further increases in responding, whereas another Condition A may yield decreases at last. Such a pattern suggests attributing the initial failure to recover low rates in Condition A to a shift in the behavioral baseline.

Inevitably, the researcher working with human subjects will have to confront findings that cannot be replicated within the bounds of the existing experimental procedures. Under these circumstances, there is little choice but to recognize the limits of the data at hand and suspend final judgment until more work has been done. Figure 3.3 illustrates results from an experiment in which college students could avoid monetary loss by responding on a multiple schedule; the schedule components differed in terms of the programmed rate of loss in the absence of responding (Galizio, 1979, Experiment 1). Initially, response rates of most subjects were not well differentiated, indicating a lack of sensitivity to the schedule parameter. The procedure then was altered so that the components were accompanied by instructional labels about the loss rates, and response rates were found to vary systematically. Finally, the initial condition was reinstated by removing the labels. Only one subject reverted to the initial pattern. What interpretation should be placed on the results from the other two? Galizio suggested that the instructional condition sensitized behavior to subsequent schedules (a sort of carryover effect). Also possible is that the sensitivity might have emerged without the specific experience with instructions—perhaps any continued exposure to the schedules would have been sufficient. Further research is needed to decide the issue and, to his credit, Galizio followed up his initial experiment with three others.

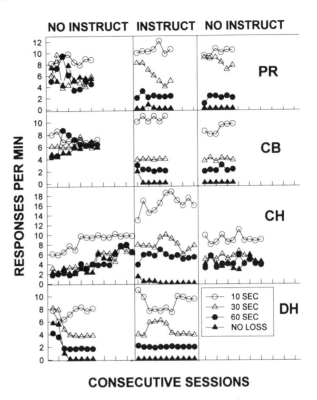

FIGURE 3.3. Response rates of college students in Galizio's (1979) Experiment 1. The students responded on a multiple schedule in which pulling a lever postponed monetary loss for 10, 30, or 60 s, across components. No loss was programmed in a fourth component. In the first and third phases of the experiment, the schedule components were accompanied by colored lights. In the second phase, the lights were paired with instructional labels indicating the response-loss interval.

Irreversible effects of the sort encountered by Galizio (1979) can also be identified and studied with *multiple-baseline designs* (Barlow & Hersen, 1984). Two or more independent behaviors are investigated simultaneously, and the experimental manipulation is applied to these baselines at different times. For example, the instructional condition might be imposed at staggered intervals across the three subjects (a *multiple-baseline across-subjects design*). If each subject's behavior changed only on introduction of the instructions, it would be possible to attribute the change to the manipulation rather than time-related extraneous factors.

The multiple-baseline strategy is useful not only for irreversible effects but also as a general practice in single-subject research. The procedure of initiating the experiment at different times for different subjects is a tried-and-true way of avoiding systematic confounds between the experimental variables and extraneous factors that may impinge on a particular individual (perhaps the semester exam we mentioned previously).

Between-Group Threats

Additional threats are created when different subjects are exposed to different experimental treatments. Although this problem might seem limited to group-statistical designs, and thus outside the scope of this chapter, there are good reasons for behavior analysts to heed these threats. One reason is pragmatic: Behavior analysts occasionally depart from a purely within-subject analysis—sometimes as a matter of expedience and sometimes by design. We might question the desirability of such departures, but we must recognize their existence. Under such circumstances, like it or not, the researcher has adopted a group-statistical strategy and can hardly ignore the pitfalls that come as a consequence.

When comparisons are made of different subjects assigned to different conditions, the central issue concerns how the subjects are assigned to the groups. Random assignment is generally regarded as an effective way of reducing group differences on factors besides the independent variable—an essential requirement for valid group comparisons. When there is reason to question the equivalence of the groups, *selection bias* is said to threaten the internal validity of the experiment. The issue of selection bias is related to the broad topic of individual differences, which we discuss later. Here it will be sufficient to note that the reduction in bias produced by random assignment can be raised by increasing the number of subjects (so that individual differences are more likely to "average out" in the group comparisons) and by drawing the subjects from relatively homogeneous populations (so that individual differences will tend to be small).

Our reading of the literature is that when behavior analysts have recourse to group comparisons, they need to exercise greater care in forming the groups. Consider, for example, the widely accepted claim that behavior shaped by the method of successive approximations is more sensitive to schedule effects than behavior prompted by modeling. The research providing the major impetus for this view did not randomly assign the subjects to the shaping and modeling conditions (Matthews, Shimoff, Catania, & Sagvolden, 1977). The researchers tried to shape the target response in every subject; some were assigned to the modeling condition after a brief attempt at shaping failed and "time constraints precluded extensive preliminary training" (Matthews et al., 1977, p. 456). Why, then, did these latter subjects fail to show schedule sensitivity? It may well have been because of the way the target response was established. But it may have been because they were relatively insensitive to the contingencies, or some aspect of them (e.g., the reinforcer selected by the researchers) at the outset. Perhaps the time constraints peculiar to these subjects affected their performance throughout. It would be interesting to repeat the experiment with random assignment of the subjects to the shaping and modeling conditions.

Even when the groups are equivalent at the outset of an experiment, they might not be at the end if some drop out along the way. When the drop-out rate is systematically related to the experimental treatments, one is faced with the threat to internal validity dubbed *mortality* by Campbell and Stanley (1963). The best remedy is prevention: Contingencies should be arranged to foster the subject's continued participation (for specific suggestions, see Pilgrim's advice in Chapter 2). Unfortunately, once the problem has occurred, the researcher can do little else but acknowledge the damage.

Researchers who adhere to single-subject designs avoid the threats described above, but there still are some between-group threats to worry about when the subjects have contact with one another outside the experiment. The problem is that subjects in one experimental condition may learn about the conditions of others who have reached a more advanced stage, and their behavior may be affected as a consequence. Perhaps they will resent their current experimental status as a consequence (Cook & Campbell, 1979, called this *resentful demoralization*). Or they may treat the experiment as a competition and try to work against the odds (*compensatory rivalry*). The net result is that behavioral differences between the subjects may be attributed to something other than the independent variable.

Communication among subjects also can contribute to a loss of control over the independent variable (*diffusion or imitation of treatments*). Consider an experiment in which subjects are scheduled to receive an instructional manipulation after a baseline is established. Imagine the havoc that could be wreaked if a subject in the instructional condition passed the information on to a subject in the baseline condition. Such possibilities are not far-fetched; Horne and Lowe (1993, Experiment 3) reported a dramatic change in a subject's performance after a conversation with another subject ("I cheated," she admitted).

Overcoming these between-group threats is not so much a matter of experimental design per se as of the logistics of implementing the design. The prudent researcher will take steps to minimize contact among subjects, for example, by drawing subjects from different sources (different courses or classrooms in the case of students). Another possibility is to conduct more than one experiment at the same time so that information one subject might provide another is irrelevant. It also may help to educate subjects about the problems caused by unauthorized communication. We have used the procedure of requiring subjects to sign oaths to refrain from discussing the nature of the experiment, but we have no evidence that this procedure has the desired effect. See Pilgrim's advice (Chapter 2) for a fuller consideration of this general issue.

We conclude our discussion of validity by turning to the last two types—those that pertain to the broad implications of experimental data.

Theoretical Validity

An internally valid experiment allows the researcher to conclude that some particular set of manipulations produced the changes observed in some particular measure of behavior. But in the experimental analysis of behavior as well as in other branches of psychology, researchers typically express their findings in more abstract terms. Features of an experimental manipulation may be described as "discriminative stimuli" instead of lights, as "reinforcers" instead of money, or as "rules" instead of specific verbalizations. Although behavior is likely to be measured in terms of button presses per unit time, it is likely to be described in such terms as "response strength," "self-control," "rule-governed behavior," and so on.

In designing experiments, the practical issue for the researcher is whether a set of operations captures the process of interest. For example, it may seem reasonable to label a stimulus that is contingent on responding as a reinforcer or punisher, but such a designation requires empirical evidence that the event actually serves the ascribed functions (see Wearden, 1988, for a discussion of this issue). Moreover, the outcome is sometimes difficult to anticipate. To illustrate: One experiment with nursery school children used tape-recorded verbal messages to reinforce and punish lever pressing. Unexpectedly, "That's bad!" served as a positive reinforcer, not a punisher, and it was about as effective as "That's good!" (Antonitis et al., 1964). And one of us was surprised to discover in his research that, reputation to the contrary, M&M's are not necessarily reinforcing (several children explained that their mothers did not allow them to take candy from strange men).

An important issue, therefore, concerns the validity of generalizations from particular operations of manipulation and measurement to higher-order abstractions—what is termed in the Campbell–Stanley–Cook analysis the *theoretical or construct validity* of a body of data from a group of experiments. Our impression is that behavior analysts have not given this issue its due, perhaps because discussion of constructs is discredited by an association with methodological, as opposed to radical, behaviorism.

Assessing theoretical validity is difficult. Consider the common claim that rules render human behavior less sensitive to schedules of reinforcement than behavior that is not susceptible to rule governance (e.g., the behavior of preverbal children or of animals). What would it take to justify this claim? A wide variety of operations can be used to manipulate rules (e.g., content of verbal stimuli, methods of delivery) and measure sensitivity (e.g., resistance to extinction, multiple schedules favoring high- and low-rate behavior in different components, concurrent schedules providing a range of reinforcement rates). Before consensus is reached about broad generalizations, it is necessary to demonstrate that the functional relation is not bounded by a specific set of operations. In brief, the process is inductive. Functional relations need to be replicated under circumstances that differ from those under which the relation was originally discovered—specifically, with the major constructs operationalized in different ways. This strategy, called *constructive replication* by Lykken (1968), is one of several types of *systematic replication* described by Sidman (1960).

External Validity

Although we regard the Campbell–Stanley–Cook analysis of the first three types of validity as quite cogent, we are uneasy about the last. The external validity of an experiment pertains to the extent to which sample results can be generalized across subject populations and environmental settings. Failure to attain external validity is the most common (and perhaps obvious) complaint about the single-subject approach. After all, it is said, data from a few individuals observed under highly controlled laboratory conditions can hardly be representative of people in general as they behave in their natural environments. This criticism is misguided for several reasons.

The emphasis on samples and populations is borrowed from the logic of inferential statistical analysis, the goal of which is to infer population parameters (usually means and variances) from the scores of a representative sample of subjects. Remarkably, and despite the emphasis placed on this point by traditional psychology, the goal of generality is one that has been more honored in the breach. To be sure, certain forms of descriptive and correlational research (e.g., survey and consumer research, polls of voter preferences, test development) take seriously the strictures of the inferential model, and considerable care is exerted to ensure that research samples properly represent the population under study. Everyone is aware of the trouble that election-year pollsters encounter if they neglect to restrict their sample to individuals likely to vote in the coming election.

Experimental research, however, almost always uses samples that do not appear to represent very well the populations about which generalizations are made. This fact has not gone unnoticed. A perennial complaint within psychology is that experiments rely too much on observations of college sophomores (sometimes the complaint is extended to include the laboratory rat) within sterile laboratory settings that are not properly representative of the everyday world. Despite the expression of such concerns, remedial procedures are not often specified, and for good reason. The questions to be addressed are formidable. Should experimental psychology rely on the study of the *average* college sophomore? The *average* young adult? Or, for that matter, the *average* human being? Equally puzzling is what answer might be given to the accompanying question of which laboratory environments should be regarded as properly representative of the settings of everyday life (see Brunswick, 1955, for an effort in this direction).

It may not take a deep analysis to recognize that a psychology that focuses exclusively on representative populations of subjects and settings is not practical. Moreover, such an approach, although perhaps useful for certain types of social science research, is not particularly desirable if the goal is to attain a science of psychology. Better models can be found in the natural sciences where experiments are construed not so much as representations of nature as ways of testing theoretical formulations about nature.

The work of the chemist can serve as a guide. The chemical researcher usually conducts experiments on refined substances without normal impurities, to study their properties in isolation from confounding influences. The results contribute to a theory of chemical action, and thus to basic understanding of chemical processes. Once validated, the theory can be extended (applied) to deal with the chemical elements in their impure forms. By the same token, a psychology whose goal is the development of theoretical formations about behavior must choose as its subjects and settings those organisms and laboratory environments that provide the best preparations for gaining such understanding. Thus, single-subject methods, with their emphasis on steady states, controlled environments, and experimental manipulation of variables, exemplify the spirit of a natural science approach to behavioral processes.

As we have noted, the experimental analysis of behavior originated in the animal laboratory, and the approach continues to rely heavily on animal models for the development of broad theories of human conduct. Questions about the generality of the principles (their external validity) usually are answered by referring to successful practical applications (often in the classroom and clinic), and by offering interpretations (the principles are used to account for human behavior within natural environments). Both methods have provided considerable support for the external validity of the principles discovered with animals. They often rest, however, on information obtained under uncontrolled circumstances. A third alternative, still much neglected, is the direct study of human behavior within the controlled conditions of the laboratory, using the methods described in this chapter.

BEHAVIORAL HISTORIES

Historical variables deserve special attention in the design of human experiments because they represent such an intractable problem (for a discussion of behavioral histories see Wanchisen, 1990). Indeed, the problem has led some behavior analysts to raise doubts about whether research with humans has much to contribute to the experimental analysis of fundamental behavioral processes (cf. Branch, 1991; Palmer & Donahoe, 1991). We must acknowledge that the obstacles posed by historical variables are formidable. Although the primary concern of an experiment is with the variables manipulated as part of the procedure, the outcomes also are influenced by variables in the organism's past. The researcher usually cannot ascertain with any accuracy the human subject's previous environments, and the possibility of experimentally controlling them is even more remote. Nevertheless, we believe that the methods of research available to behavior analysts are up to the challenge. In this section, we provide our assessment of the scope of the problem and then offer some remedies.

History Effects

A realistic view of history effects might begin with the recognition that they are by no means unique to human research. The rat's experiences before its arrival at the animal laboratory also are not known with any certainty, and the researcher is confronted with the possibility that a particular history (perhaps one more characteristic of one animal supplier than another) may interact in special ways with the experimental variable. The research literature on environmental enrichment is instructive here. In a classic experiment, Hebb (1949) found that rats raised as pets by his daughter were more accomplished maze learners than his usual laboratory rats; with such results in view, Christie (1951) proposed that the theoretical controversy between Spence and Tolman stemmed from the way they cared for their animals (the laboratories of Tolman's group provided richer environments). Since then, numerous experiments have established the importance of housing and rearing conditions in the behavioral development of the rat, and this by no means exhausts the range of potential confounding variables. Other lines of research have studied the impact of such historical variables as exposure to aversive events, schedules of deprivation, and effects of stimulus restriction and deprivation in general.

Although histories must be reckoned with in the animal laboratory, a straightforward remedy is available. As illustrated by the enrichment research, rats and other animal subjects can be reared within controlled environments, and thus given more or less similar preexperimental histories. Availability of this strategy constitutes a major advantage of conducting research with animals. But the double-edged nature of the control procedures should not be overlooked. The advantage is that the power of the experiment is increased because variation related to histories is reduced and more sensitive tests of the experimental variables are possible. The disadvantage is that too-strict control of historical variables conceals the contribution of the particular history that has been arranged. If all of the rats were housed individually in laboratory cages, the conclusions must be limited to subjects with such a history. And should it be the case that animals raised in large pens with cagemates perform more capably, then the findings can be misleading as well.

These pros and cons of controlling histories suggest the wisdom of a balanced approach. Even when strict control of histories is technically possible, the animal researcher may relax standards so as to establish that a contemporary variable has its characteristic effect when histories are disregarded. Turning to the human subject, the fact that manipulation of preexperimental histories is out of reach some-times can be regarded as a blessing in disguise. When orderly findings emerge de-spite the subjects' varied behavioral histories, the researcher gains confidence that essential controlling variables have been identified.

Closely allied with the problem of uncontrolled behavioral histories are so-called "individual difference" or "subject" variables. On the human level, these include not only such personal characteristics as age and gender, but also differ-ences less easy to specify, such as the individual's intellectual ability, education-al level, or socioeconomic status. The study of individual differences has not been popular among behavior analysts, perhaps because of research in the areas of per-sonality and social psychology where group-statistical methods and mentalistic theories hold sway. Nevertheless, individual differences play important roles within the broad field of psychology, to the extent that they are commonly used to define entire areas of inquiry (e.g., "the psychology of aging," "the psychology of gender").

From a behavioral-analytic standpoint, individual differences may be charac-terized as imperfect ways of characterizing past environments. This is the reason we are subsuming them under history effects. The important consideration for the present discussion is that individual differences and histories in general designate variables that, on the one hand, defy manipulation within the context of human experiments, but, on the other, are important correlates of human behavior. Histo-ry effects in humans, therefore, play contradictory roles. Although they pose an obstacle to experimental control, they also constitute a phenomenon worthy of study in its own right. Indeed, many of the classic issues within human psychol-ogy can be couched in terms of interactions between historical and contemporary influences. In the case of so-called "pathological" behaviors, for example, a person is said to be acting in ways that are contrary to his or her psychological needs—the behavior is not in the person's best interest, so to speak. A behavioral account removes the mystery by pointing to the possibility that previously encountered schedules of reinforcement are leading the person to respond inappropriately un-der current circumstances.

Procedures

We now turn to specific control procedures, several of which flow from an analysis of history effects as a competition between past and present influences. As with competitions in general (e.g., choice), the outcome hinges on the relative strength of the influences, and procedures that aid one or the other will sway the interaction in that direction. The researcher's task is to adjust the competing fac-tors to fit the goals of the research. Most often, primary concern is with contem-porary variables, in which case the key is to weaken historical influences and to strengthen contemporary ones. The opposite strategy is in order for those inter-ested in studying behavioral histories per se.

Repeated Observations

In the animal laboratory, the standard procedure for weakening history effects is long-term exposure to the experimental procedures. Of necessity, performances at the start are much more a function of preexperimental influences than whatever conditions are in the process of being imposed, and the emotional and other responses that the rat or pigeon brings to the experiment can overwhelm the conditions of interest. It is therefore standard practice to begin an experiment by taming the animal, habituating it to the apparatus, and acclimating it to the particular contingencies under investigation. Serious data collection only begins as a steady state emerges, that is, with the emergence of response patterns that are strongly controlled by the current contingencies.

Not surprisingly, the human subject's history, which includes a myriad of verbal and social influences, also can affect performances within an experiment. Indeed, human performances sometimes are said to be more a function of the so-called "demand" characteristics of the experiment—the subject's roles and expectations about being a subject—than of the current experimental conditions. Nevertheless, the human researcher can be optimistic that the series of sessions needed for a steady-state experiment can only serve to diminish history effects, as earlier contingencies become more remote in time and new ones have a chance to gain control over behavior. Certainly, the notion that history effects arising from past contingencies cannot be displaced by new contingencies is contrary to established principles of behavior. The best way to confront these effects (if not the only way) is to provide subjects with sufficient exposure to the experimental condition.

Especially Forcing Procedures

There is no guarantee, of course, that extended exposure will, in the end, counteract history effects. In their review of reinforcement and punishment, Morse and Kelleher (1977) noted that historical variables are overridden by experimental procedures that are "especially forcing." This principle is frequently put to use in the animal laboratory, as when a researcher increases the vigor of responding for a food reinforcer by increasing the level of deprivation or the palatability of the food.

History effects may bedevil the researcher of human behavior because the experimental variables are at low levels—not especially forcing. The obvious antidote is to seek stronger versions. Although ethical as well as practical considerations constrain what the human researcher can do, the remedies sometimes are within reach. Consider the extensive use of points as reinforcers: a counter advances contingent on responding and the subject is instructed to earn as many points as possible. Although earning points usually maintains responding to some extent, the basis of this reinforcing function is obscure (see Shull & Lawrence's discussion in Chapter 4). The researcher stands a better chance of insulating current effects from historical influences by using stimuli with clearer and better established links to deprivation conditions (such as monetary payment—or points that signify such payment).

A failing of human research is the limited attention paid to the deprivation–incentive relations that control the properties of reinforcing and aversive events. Conditions that are especially forcing for the human subject are those from which the subject can be effectively deprived or those whose incentive properties can be increased to higher levels. Worth exploring are procedures that capitalize on the human subject's stimulus-seeking tendencies, as may be tapped by computer games, complex visual material, and the like (a common complaint from subjects is that the experiment is "boring"). Some interesting possibilities can be found in the literature, as witnessed by experiments in which infants produced brief clips of a cartoon (Darcheville, Riviere, & Wearden, 1993); children avoided termination of a cartoon movie (Baer, 1960); adults changed and focused projector slides (Benton & Mefferd, 1967); college students illuminated the experimental room and thereby permitted reading (Shipley, Baron, & Kaufman, 1972); students displayed textual material about which they were quizzed later (Williams & Johnston, 1992); and students engaged in computer games (Baum, 1975; Case, Ploog, & Fantino, 1990). More ingenuity along the lines of these procedures would be welcome.

Control through Selection

The potential influences of subject characteristics (such as age or gender) are reduced in the animal laboratory by selecting subjects from circumscribed groups. A similar strategy is available in research with human subjects where the prudent researcher can seek uniformity by studying individuals of the same age, gender, educational background, and so forth. Fortunately for the present discussion, the exact origin of the potential influence is not critical, and even such characteristics as age or sex, often viewed loosely as expressing biological determinants, incorporate historical factors. Such links are well-recognized in the field of gerontology (Schaie, 1994). A group of 70-year-olds (a cohort), for example, not only share the same chronological age but also a set of similar life experiences that differentiate them from individuals born 10 years earlier or 10 years later.

By studying individuals who are homogeneous in terms of personal characteristics, whatever these characteristics may be, the researcher reduces the likelihood that historical factors will confound the results. Our impression from published research is that more care could be exerted in this regard (we have been disconcerted by journal articles that reveal neither the age nor the gender of human subjects). Three caveats about subject selection warrant mention: (1) As implied by our earlier comments, too-close selection will limit the findings to the particular type of subject chosen for study. (2) A related practical consideration is that the chances of publishing the findings may be reduced (e.g., for a number of years, the journal *Developmental Psychology* has only considered research using children of both sexes) and the possibility of gaining grant support jeopardized (federal guidelines now require that attention be paid to populations that have been underrepresented in biomedical research, i.e., minorities and women). (3) The researcher must not make the mistake of drifting into the practice of attributing causal significance to historical variables identified through selection. Any differences are, at best, correlational.

Beyond pointing out that individual difference variables can be approached using selection procedures, we cannot offer specific guidelines about which variables should be or need be controlled. A host of such variables have been studied on the human level since the early days of psychology, and each has had its champions as a critical factor in behavior (some extreme examples, for the behavior analyst, at least: body type, Sheldon 1954; introversion–extroversion, Eysenck,

1953). Common observation, at least, would suggest that a person's age and sex might head any list; consider how much we know about a stranger's behavioral capabilities solely from this information. Whether these variables truly are critical for fundamental processes of behavior, however, remains to be determined.

Experimental Control of History Effects

Histories can be both controlled and studied within the laboratory by creating the history within the confines of the experiment and then calculating its subsequent effects. Two options are available to the researcher who pursues this strategy: the between-group design and the within-subject design.

A between-group approach to human histories may be seen in Weiner's (1964, 1969) classic research on human responses to fixed-interval (FI) schedules of reinforcement. In one experiment, different individuals were trained initially under schedules that controlled either high or low response rates: fixed ratio (FR) or differential reinforcement of low rates (DRL). The conditions for all subjects then were changed to a common FI schedule. Figure 3.4 shows the results in the form of cumulative records collected during the 15th hour of exposure to the FI test schedule (Weiner, 1964, Figure 1). It is apparent that despite the changed contingencies, the FR history led to high response rates whereas rates were much lower after the DRL history.

The between-group design for studying history effects constitutes an obvious departure from single-subject methods. The shortcoming is illustrated by Weiner's results. Although no overlap can be seen between the performances of the subjects

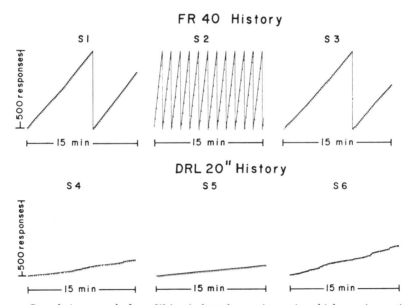

FIGURE 3.4. Cumulative records from Weiner's (1964) experiment in which nursing assistants responded on an FI 10-s schedule of points after a history with either an FR 40 schedule (top records) or a DRL 20-s schedule (bottom records).

with high- and low-rate histories, the comparison of two groups of three subjects raises the question of whether the difference actually is a reliable one. When the outcome is addressed using the conventional rules of inferential statistics—there is nothing in the logic of the single-subject method to provide an alternative—it turns out that the split illustrated in Figure 3.4 does not attain significance at the customary .05 probability level, that is, $t(4) = 1.33$, $p = .25$ (Weiner did not report such a test). The sad lesson, therefore, is that this degree of variation in a between-group design calls for a larger sample than the one studied in the experiment.

History effects also can be studied using within-subject designs, but not without a different set of complications. In other experiments, Weiner (1969) sequentially imposed high- and low-rate schedules on the same subject. One experiment investigated FR and DRL histories with a sequence of three pairs of schedules: (1) FR followed by FI; (2) DRL followed FI; and (3) replication of the FR–FI sequence. During the first phase, the FR history led to high FI rates, but this effect was absent in the last phase. Weiner attributed the difference to the intervening experience with the DRL schedule, and he concluded that a low-rate history (DRL) perseverated despite exposure to a later FR schedule. But also possible is that the effect was a consequence of some variable other than the intervening schedules. Strong support for Weiner's conclusion requires comparisons with subjects exposed to sequences in which the intermediate phase is omitted, in other words, a between-group design.

A procedure developed by Freeman and Lattal (1992), although not used to our knowledge in experiments with humans, promises a more adequate within-subject approach to history effects. The novel feature of their pigeon experiments was the establishment of parallel rather than sequential histories. Each of two reinforcement schedules was correlated with a different stimulus during the first phase of the study. The subsequent influences of the two histories then were assessed by introducing the stimuli while the subjects responded under a third schedule. For example, in one experiment the birds responded under VR and DRL schedules during the first phase and then were observed under an FI schedule. Each subject provided clear evidence of the different effects of the two histories in that they persisted in responding on the FI at high rates in the presence of the VR stimulus and at low rates in the DRL stimulus. Reversibility also was shown. With continued training, rates on the FI schedule converged to common levels regardless of which stimulus was present.

ANALYSIS

Experimental design is only half the story. Scientists conduct experiments to ask questions of nature, and the answers depend not only on how the questions are phrased—the experimental design—but also on how the data are analyzed. The relevant issues cut across many disciplines, research areas, and traditions, and they have been discussed by psychologists under such headings as psychometric and quantitative methods, psychophysics, measurement and scaling theory, test theory, and, of course, statistics in general. All of these topics are part of the context in which behavior-analytic research is conducted, and they demand careful study in their own right. For better or worse, such attention can hardly be avoided by the student—a heavy dose of statistics and measurement theory continues to be a standard part of the curriculum in psychology.

But the case also has been made that the extensive literature on data analysis, with its numerous directives, restrictions, and prohibitions, constitutes a burden as well as a boon for the working researcher (Baer, 1977; Michael, 1974). The conventional wisdom is that safeguards are needed to ensure the researcher's consistency and objectivity, and statistical analysis with its formal rules of inference is offered as the proper way to do this. We will present an alternative view. The ultimate responsibility for treatment and interpretation of data must rest on the researcher's judgment, not any particular set of rules to be mechanically applied. Freedom is accompanied by responsibility, of course. The researcher also must be prepared to defend the wisdom of his or her decisions in terms of agreed-upon principles of data analysis and measurement theory.

Measurement Scales

Accurate measurement is an essential part of empirical research, and an obvious point is that the researcher must follow a consistent and specifiable system of assigning the numbers to the measured events. A useful approach is Stevens's (1951) well-known taxonomy that orders the scales in terms of the amount of information provided by each (he called them *nominal, ordinal, interval,* and *ratio* scales). For example, the numbers can be used to rank the magnitude of the events (ordinal), or they can be arranged so that, in addition, equal numerical intervals match equal magnitude differences (interval).

Details of Stevens's system can be found in most texts on research methods where it will be seen that they involve not only classification but also specification of permissible mathematical and statistical operations. The aforementioned ordinal–interval difference, for example, is said to determine the proper measure of central tendency. If the scale was ordinal, the median is the proper measure; the mean will not do because it requires a scale in which the numerical and magnitude differences match (as on interval and ratio scales). The restrictions extend to many other calculations including indices of variation and correlation and the whole gamut of significance tests (e.g., whether the analysis can be parametric or nonparametric; Siegel & Castellan, 1988).

Should such strictures be taken seriously by the behavior-analytic researcher? We think not. Although Stevens's dictates about "permissible" measurement operations are treated as dogma within some circles—many texts represent them as an essential feature of data analysis—they have not gained much acceptance among statisticians (cf. Gaito, 1980; Howell, 1995; Mitchell, 1986; Nunnally, 1978; Velleman & Wilkinson, 1993). Critics have objected that the restrictions presuppose a real scale for each phenomenon for which the measures are only an imperfect approximation, in other words, a necessary connection between the activities involved in measuring things and subsequent activities when the numbers are manipulated.

A better description of the work of the scientist—one more consistent with a behavioral view—is that a measurement scale is "a convention, an agreement among scientists that a particular scaling of an attribute is a 'good' scaling" (Nunnally, 1978, p. 30). No doubt, *interpretations* of the data as they relate to the behavioral phenomenon under study must reckon with the measurement procedure along with many other features of the experiment. But the statistical or mathematical operations that intervene between measurement and interpretation are governed only by the rules of mathematics. To return to our previous example, the research is quite correct to calculate the mean of a set of ranks, as long as the outcome serves some useful purpose. Lord (1953) captured our point well by observing that "the numbers don't remember where they came from" (p. 751).

This is not to say that things can be measured and calculations made willy-nilly. In the end, the researcher must face the challenge of making sense out of the numbers (in other words, it is the *researcher* who must remember where the numbers came from). Interpreting data is hardly a simple matter, and different measurement scales can lead to diverse conclusions.

To illustrate: A popular theory in behavioral gerontology is that age-related deficits on speeded tasks increase as a function of task complexity, and most writers (e.g., Salthouse, 1985) have concluded that the literature overwhelmingly supports such a relationship. But experiments on this question generally use response *latencies* to describe performance; when the data are rescaled in terms of response *speeds* (the inverse of latency), the theoretically expected interaction between age and complexity is substantially reduced, and the conclusions must be changed. Figure 3.5 shows some of the results from an experiment in which younger and older men worked on a matching-to-sample task (Baron, 1985). Complexity was varied by using compound stimuli as the samples with either one, two, or three elements. When the men had unlimited time to respond (left panels), the three older ones generally were slower and the age-by-complexity interaction is apparent when the data are scaled according to latencies (top left; compare the slopes of the functions obtained from the young and old subjects). But the interaction is more or less absent when performances were scaled as speeds (bottom left). Interestingly, both the interaction and the age difference itself were substantially attenuated, regardless of measure, when time limits were placed on responding (right panels).

Alternative outcomes from different scaling of the same data certainly pose a puzzle. Whatever the resolution, we expect that it will depend more on the contribution that one or the other depiction makes to understanding the phenomenon than on axiomatic claims that either one somehow represents the essence of the behavior that is measured.

What Should Be Measured?

We noted earlier that behavior analysis places no real limits on which responses should be studied, so long as the behavior can be objectively measured. In practice, however, experiments have studied relatively few responses; in most cases, the human subject pushes a button or pulls a plunger. These operanda are in the spirit of Skinner's studies of lever pressing and key pecking by rats and pigeons. Such responses can be recorded automatically and their momentary character makes them appropriate for analysis in terms of both rate and latency. A special benefit is that the response does not alter the organism's environment to any

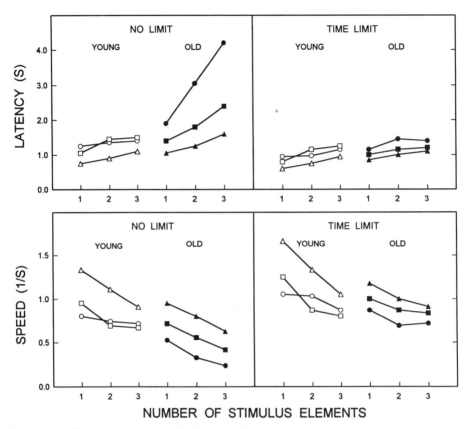

FIGURE 3.5.   Choice response latencies (top panels) and speeds (the inverse of the latencies; bottom panels) of three young men (aged 18–23) and three old men (aged 65–73) working a delayed match-to-sample task (the comparison stimuli were presented 15 s after the sample). The results are shown as a function of the complexity of the sample stimulus (1, 2, or 3 stimulus elements) and the presence or absence of a time limit on responding; when the limit was in effect, only matching responses occurring within 2 s of the comparison stimuli could earn monetary reinforcers. Figure redrawn from data presented by Baron (1985).

great extent, thus giving the researcher considerable control over the consequences of responding.

The rationale for studying so few responses hinges on the assumption that topography is not critical in the analysis of operant performances. This assumption has been questioned, however, most frequently in the area of animal learning (for a recent review, see Mazur, 1994; Chapter 5). In avoidance conditioning, for example, the rat's species-specific defense reactions are said to lead to more rapid acquisition of a running response than a lever-press response. Parallel concerns about responses in human experiments were raised by Gonzalez and Waller (1974) who proposed that improved schedule control might result if rather than "button pushing or lever pulling . . . a typically *human* response was used" (p. 165, their italics). This led them to study handwriting. Other writers also have expressed doubts about whether button pressing in the laboratory actually is a functional unit of human behavior, that is, an operant controlled by its consequences (Branch, 1991).

Despite these reservations, we see little justification for abandoning the button press (or similar responses) as a vehicle for studying human behavior. For one thing, button pressing indeed *is* a "typically human response." It is common in everyday life: We press buttons when we phone friends, use computers, or withdraw cash from automatic teller machines. The ubiquity of finger-operated switches in our natural environments should not surprise us; these devices have been explicitly designed with the prehensile ability of the human organism in view.

Perhaps concerns about the status of the button press will be allayed by noting the range of human behavioral functions that have been studied with this response. In the laboratory, human subjects have pressed buttons for a variety of reasons: to see a meter (*vigilance,* Holland, 1958); to identify a stimulus that was previously presented (*matching-to-sample,* Sidman, 1969); to prevent occurrence of a signal correlated with loss of money (*avoidance,* Baron & Kaufman, 1966); to produce stimuli correlated with the components of a compound schedule of positive reinforcement (*observing,* Perone & Baron, 1980); to review scores reflecting a fellow subject's performance (*auditing,* Hake, Vukelich, & Kaplan, 1973); or to answer "yes" or "no" to questions about recent behavior on a conditional discrimination task (*self-reports,* Critchfield & Perone, 1990). The act of button pressing, despite its apparent simplicity, has served as a powerful tool in the laboratory analysis of human behavior.

The fact that complex behavioral functions can be studied with simple, repetitive responses does not mean that the role of the response in human behavior is unimportant. Bijou and Baer (1966) distinguished between the laboratory study of "convenient" responses and "interesting" responses. Responses such as button pressing and plunger pulling are in the former category. The variety of human behaviors encompassed by the latter—social behaviors, complex motor patterns, handwriting, vocal responses, and verbal behavior in general—constitute interesting and challenging aspects of human activity that we need to know more about through laboratory research. Other chapters in this volume point the way.

The Role of Verbal Processes

At the top of the list of interesting human responses are verbal ones. Perhaps it goes without saying that the human subject's verbal ability must be reckoned with in designing experiments. But does this call for major deviations from usual methods of experimental analysis? Because verbal processes are treated at length in other parts of this book, we will limit our comments to issues with a direct bearing on matters of design and data analysis. The principle that emerges is that the methodological framework that we have outlined in this chapter appears up to the job.

Verbal Responses

We noted that experiments can be designed so that a verbal response (such as talking or writing) is the target behavior. Special problems are created, however, by the need for a steady-state approach. The research initiated by Greenspoon's

(1962) work on verbal conditioning is instructive. In his well-known experiment, subjects were asked to say words and reinforcers were delivered for each word in a particular class (plural nouns). Although this and similar experiments helped establish that verbal behavior is controlled by operant conditioning variables, steady-state analyses were impractical. Without automated equipment, a continuously present observer is required to identify and appropriately reinforce the subject's responses.

Over the years, solutions have been sought through voice-activated relays (e.g., Miller, 1968), and, more recently, microcomputer-controlled speech recognition devices (Baron & Journey, 1989). A flexible method remains to be developed, however, and steady-state investigations undoubtedly will be furthered by future availability of affordable devices that can rapidly and reliably identify human speech. An approach presently within reach is to have verbal responses take the form of entries on the keyboard of a computer (button pressing again!), which then provides the desired instrumentation (Hyten & Chase, 1991).

Control by Instructions and Rules

Verbal processes also enter into the study of stimulus functions. The involvement of verbal stimuli in human experiments is virtually unavoidable, if only because of the exchanges needed to recruit the subject into the experiment and to initiate the procedures. Some researchers (perhaps making a virtue out of necessity) have used instructions as a vehicle for the study of verbal control (Baron & Galizio, 1983). For example, subjects may be provided with instructions about one or another aspect of the procedure (e.g., the schedule of reinforcement) with the objective of determining effects on subsequent responding (e.g., under avoidance schedules; Galizio, 1979).

As noted by Hayes and Brownstein (1984), manipulation of instructional stimuli provides an operant framework for the study of rule-governed behavior ("we . . . follow rules because of reinforcing consequences," Skinner, 1984, p. 577). For the present discussion, the important consideration is that instructions represent a form of external control amenable to experimental manipulation, in which case the design of experiments can proceed along the same lines as when control by other (nonverbal) stimuli is studied (interested readers should consult Shimoff & Catania's discussion of verbally governed behavior in Chapter 12).

Self-Instructions

But human performances also have been described as under the control of self-instructions (Lowe, 1979). By comparison with control by experimenter-provided instructions, such accounts regard the subject as the speaker—the source of the instructions—as well as the listener. Put simply, subjects are envisioned as telling themselves what to do, listening to the commands, and then proceeding to obey (or perhaps disobey) them.

To study these hypothetical interactions, the researcher must somehow gain access to the self-instructions. The usual approach has been to question the subject at the end of the experiment; correlations between the answers and actual performances then are taken to indicate the extent of verbal control during the experiment (e.g., Horne & Lowe, 1993). Shimoff (1984), Hayes (1986), and others have noted problems with this approach. What a subject might say after an experiment can be completely unrelated to any verbal behavior that actually occurred during the sessions. Many variables control answers to the researcher's questions: the stimuli and reinforcers at work during the interview, as well as complex features of the subject's preexperimental and experimental histories. Of course, postsession reports may be veridical with previous verbalizations, but, alternatively, the subject may never have spoken about the procedure until prompted to do so.

An improved method solicits the subject's verbal reports *during* the sessions rather than afterward (e.g., Matthews, Catania, & Shimoff, 1985; Wulfert, Dougher, & Greenway, 1991). Nevertheless, the researcher must tread cautiously because the procedures used to measure verbal responses—to prompt and record them—can have potent behavioral effects of their own. The potential for confusion is demonstrated in an illuminating study by Rosenfarb, Newland, Brannon, and Howey (1992). When college students responded on a multiple schedule with DRL and FR components, those subjects who were prompted to generate task instructions every 2 min responded differently than unprompted subjects. It seems unlikely that the self-instructions of the prompted subjects corresponded to whatever unprompted verbal behavior may have occurred among the control subjects.

Circumventing an Operant Analysis

Although the studies by Matthews et al. (1985), Rosenfarb et al. (1992), and Wulfert et al. (1991) are welcome exceptions, the fact remains that many researchers are inclined to rely on verbal communications between subject and experimenter as a substitute for objective records of the behavior of interest. A variant on this approach is to use verbal communication as a substitute for the explicit arrangement of contingencies of reinforcement. For example, as an alternative to repeated exposure to the contingencies, subjects may be given verbal descriptions of the contingencies (e.g., Fantino & Case, 1983).

Although both of these practices are common in psychological research, Skinner (1966, pp. 22–23) decried them as "the circumvention of an operant analysis." He noted that the procedure of substituting verbal communications for direct manipulation and observation has come to be used "as if it were a labor-saving device in many essentially behavioristic formulations," this despite the fact that "there is no reason why a description of contingencies of reinforcement should have the same effect as exposure to the contingencies" and the fact that "only in the simplest cases can a person correctly describe his ongoing behavior."

The human research program envisioned by Skinner (the one advocated in this chapter) called for the direct control of experimental variables by the researcher and direct observation of the subject's responses to them—the same procedures that are unavoidable in the study of nonverbal organisms. But the reader should take careful note that it was hardly Skinner's intention (nor is it ours) to inhibit the study of verbal behavior—to the contrary, the objection is strictly to the practice of using verbal behavior as a *substitute* for events that should be manipulated and observed directly. Movement away from Skinner's ideal sometimes is seen as a way of expanding the horizons of behavior analysis. The obvious gain is that human data can be collected rapidly in less intrusive ways. The downside is that such "advances" usually are accompanied by the adoption of nonbehavioral methods of design and data analysis.

EVALUATING DATA

When the data collection phase is over, the researcher must put the data—sets of numbers—into a form that will allow answers to whatever questions were posed by the experiment. In this area as well, group-statistical and single-subject researchers proceed differently, each with their favored way of treating data: inferential statistics versus what we will term *graphic analysis.* We touched on these differences in earlier sections. In this section we consider their respective strengths and weaknesses in more detail. At the outset, however, it is important to reiterate that, as with other aspects of design and analysis, the most important factor in evaluating data is the judgment of the researcher. Analytic tools, whether statistical or graphic, are aids to good judgment, not substitutes for it.

Inferential Statistics

Although behavior-analytic researchers have long had an antipathy to *inferential* statistics, the value of *descriptive* statistics has never been in doubt. Experimental data must be organized and summarized, and the same descriptive tools are used by workers in all traditions: measures of central tendency (e.g., median, mean), variation (e.g., interquartile range, standard deviation), and association (e.g., correlation, linear regression).

Inferential statistics play a different role. Put in simple terms, the goal of an inferential statistical analysis is to infer the parameters of some hypothetical aggregation (a population) from a limited set of observations (a sample). Within the behavioral sciences, the population is usually construed as a large, frequently inaccessible, group of observations. The sample is a subset of the potential observations, and the significance test expresses in probabilistic terms the researcher's confidence in the accuracy of population estimates (such as the mean) from the sample values. The analysis of experimental results is a special case of this logic. When data are from two or more samples (e.g., performances of experimental and control subjects), the question is whether the means were drawn from different populations, in other words, whether the experimental variable had an effect. Because the decision rests on the size of the ratio of the variance across the sample means to the pooled variance within the samples, the method is referred to broadly as *analysis of variance.*

We observed earlier that the methods of inferential statistics have come to be regarded as indispensable within the behavioral, social, and biological sciences—an experiment is not an experiment if randomly assigned groups are not compared by analysis of variance. But even within traditional circles, there has been considerable uneasiness about using significance tests to make decisions about data, most notably the incorrect practice of regarding the results of the test as directly verifying or refuting the hypotheses that generated the research (e.g., Bakan, 1966; Bolles, 1962; Cohen, 1994; Lykken, 1968; Meehl, 1967).

The larger problem, however, is that the logic of the inferential method is at odds with the objectives of behavior analysis. Recall that the behavior analyst seeks *direct* evidence that the performance of the *individual* is under the *control* of the experimental variable. Statistical approaches reduce the need for strong forms of control, and the focus on group means raises the possibility that the resulting functions may not represent behavioral processes as they occur within any particular individual.

Graphic Analysis

The single-subject alternative places the burden of evaluating the data directly on the researcher's shoulders. In lieu of presenting the results of statistical tests, the experimental findings are displayed in a series of graphs (tables of data may be used as well). These displays then are referred to in the research report as needed to support and justify the conclusions. Of course, graphs also can be found in reports of group-statistical experiments but the difference is that their role is a secondary one: to illustrate the data on which the statistical conclusions are based. By comparison, the graphic analyses of the single-subject researcher tell the whole story. They must stand on their own.

Parsonson and Baer (1986) attributed the popularity of graphic methods to the records produced by Skinner's cumulative recorder. This ingenious device depicts the behavior of individual subjects in such a way that "the rate of responding, and the pattern over time of the rate of responding, could be seen instantly, sensitively, and directly" (p. 157). Although cumulative records continue to provide valuable information, contemporary single-subject researchers employ a much wider range of graphic techniques. Representations need not be limited to momentary changes in rate; depending on the purposes of the experiment, graphs and tables may show performances averaged over one or more sessions. Dimensions other than response rate are displayed as well, such as response latencies, interresponse times, and measures of response force and duration. A variety of derived measures may be found: choice proportions, discrimination ratios, and conditional response probabilities. Regression analysis also is common: In studies of choice, for example, behavioral measures (e.g., relative response rate) are expressed as a function of the alternative reinforcement schedules (e.g., relative reinforcement rate), and linear regression is used to fit the function (e.g., Bradshaw & Szabadi, 1988). The guiding principle in all of these instances is that the research report must provide sufficient exposure to the data to convince the reader that the conclusions offered in the text are valid, and that they apply to the results observed at the level of the individual subject.

Clearly, then, the graph bears a heavy burden in the analysis of single-subject data. The theory and practice of graph construction must be taken seriously by single-subject researchers. Fortunately for the student, systematic treatments can be found in a number of references. Some have been written by statisticians and consider graphic analysis in general: Cleveland (1985), Tufte (1983; reviewed by Iversen, 1988), and Tukey (1977; reviewed by Church, 1979). Others are directed toward behavioral data in particular: Iversen (1988), Johnston and Pennypacker (1993), Kazdin (1982), and Parsonson and Baer (1992). Particularly noteworthy is a series of tutorial articles by Parsonson and Baer (1978, 1986). These writers not only explain how to prepare graphs that will meaningfully depict single-subject data, but they also show how to use the methods to identify similarities and differences in patterns and trends.

It may come as no surprise that objections to inferential statistics from the behavior-analytic camp have been more than matched by objections to graphic data analysis from traditional quarters. The dominating presence of inferential methods has created suspicion of any scientific conclusion not accompanied by such proof. Indeed, this state of affairs led Huitema (1986) to offer special advice to researchers who must deal with nonbehavioral audiences (especially granting agencies, journal editors, and program evaluators): Always remember to include results of statistical test results regardless of whether they actually are needed for the analysis.

Kazdin (1982) summarized some common criticisms of graphic analysis. Leading the list is the specter of experimenter bias:

> Perhaps the major issue pertains to the lack of concrete decision rules for determining whether a particular demonstration shows or fails to show a reliable effect. The process of visual inspection would seem to permit, if not actively encourage, subjectivity and inconsistency in the evaluation of intervention effects. (p. 239)

In addition, both Kazdin (1992) and Parsonson and Baer (1986) argued that the graphic method suffers from the researcher's insensitivity to reliable effects. Thus, potentially important differences may be overlooked because they are small or because they are superimposed on irregular performances. Such problems are exacerbated when performances are unstable, when variation produces overlap between values obtained from difference conditions, or when baselines are systematically increasing or decreasing. Interestingly, Matyas and Greenwood (1990) suggested that the problem with graphic analysis is just the opposite—that it leads behavior analysts to see effects when they are absent, particularly when the data are characterized by substantial degrees of serial dependence (see below).

These criticisms of graphic analysis seem misguided to us because they point more to the behavior of the researcher who interprets the data than to the underlying logic of the analysis itself. Consider that errors of interpretation also occur in the case of statistical analysis. There is consensus, however, that the remedy lies in improved education of researchers and consumers of group-statistical research, not the abandonment of inferential statistics as an analytic tool. A similar view is in order for graphic analysis. Insofar as the method sometimes allows subjective, inconsistent, or insensitive data-analytic behavior, the remedy lies in more systematic and rigorous training of those who use the method.

Statistical Analysis of Single-Subject Data

Some have suggested that the established decision rules of statistics can serve as the remedy for the aforementioned ills of single-subject designs, thus producing a happy marriage of these antagonistic views. As pointed out by Huitema (1986), there is no *necessary* connection between the way an experiment is designed and the way the results are analyzed, in which case one should not reject such a linkage out of hand (or, alternatively, a wedding of group designs and non-statistical data analysis). We suggest caution in these regards lest the offspring of such unions include the worst features rather than the best ones from each approach. In this section we address some of the problems and prospects for the behavior analyst considering inferential statistics. To forestall confusion, it is well to summarize our position at the outset: Whatever attraction there may be in inferential statistics, the need for them is obviated when the full power of an experimental analysis can be exercised.

Serial Dependencies

The fundamental problem is that analysis of variance was not developed for single-subject data (the method emerged from agricultural research). According to statistical theory, the data points need to be independent of one another, and to meet this assumption, subjects are randomly assigned to experimental conditions so that the value produced by one subject does not determine that for another. Although this strategy makes good sense in the case of group designs, it can hardly work for single-subject designs in which the same subject is exposed to the different experimental conditions. If the subject's behaviors on the different occasions are correlated (serially dependent), interpretations of significance tests will be compromised.

The issue of serial dependencies in single-subject data has been the subject of considerable debate. One view is that serial dependencies do not ordinarily occur, in which case concerns about analysis of variance are not well-founded (see Huitema, 1988, and Busk & Marascuilo, 1988, for opposing positions on this). Then there is the question of what to do when dependencies are known to occur. Perhaps the most widely used method is interrupted time-series analysis, a procedure that statistically extracts the dependencies (autocorrelations) from the data (Kazdin, 1982; Kratochwill, 1978). A potential limitation of some versions of time-series analysis is that large numbers of data points are needed (for one exception see Crosbie, 1993). Another is that unlike conventional analysis of variance, time-series analysis cannot deal in simple ways with the interactive effects of factorial experiments.

Baer (1988) argued that serial dependencies are an integral property of behavior. On this view, little is gained by trying to remove them statistically when they occur. To the contrary, they should be studied in their own right. But not much is known about the conditions that may produce dependencies. From the perspective of design and analysis, the important point is that dependencies are much less likely to distort conclusions about the effects of an independent variable when the goals of experimental analysis are met, that is, when behavior reaches a steady state within each level of the variable and changes reliably across levels. Recall the two sources of instability we described earlier: trend (systematic increases or decreases) and bounce (unsystematic variations). In the limiting case (a perfect steady state), the absence of these patterns of variation would indicate that serial dependencies also are absent (correlation requires variation). The fact that conventional analysis of variance procedures may be permitted in such cases does not, however, make them particularly desirable.

Applied Research

The case for inferential statistics is easiest to make when data are collected in applied settings. Numerous obstacles, ethical as well as practical, confront workers who collect their data in the field—schools, clinics, industrial settings, public places, and the like. Within these environments, the researcher does not have the luxury of the control procedures routinely available within the laboratory. Sound principles of experimental design must give way to the social constraints of the research setting (Baer, Wolfe, & Risley, 1968), and the applied researcher often is faced with data that do not reveal clear effects through graphic methods of analysis. The choice is a stark one: Either the data must be abandoned or a last-ditch effort made to clarify them through statistical tests. Researchers who make the latter decision must anticipate the questions that reviewers and journal editors will ask: Is the research question sufficiently important to tolerate the irregularities? Were all reasonable control procedures employed? Affirmative answers help justify a statistical analysis.

Our best advice to researchers who choose this route is to use the statistics reluctantly and sparingly. To do otherwise can only raise questions about their choice of a single-subject approach to the research question. But we much prefer a different solution: more intensive training of applied researchers in behavior-analytic research methods, so that the need for statistics will be reduced (see Parsonson & Baer, 1978, 1986, for a program designed to accomplish this).

Basic Research

Whatever the justifications that can be marshaled for statistical analysis of applied single-subject data, they lose force when human research is conducted within the laboratory. The slippery slope we described for applied research becomes even more treacherous. The door is opened to two standards of evidence within the experimental analysis of behavior: one for the animal laboratory (where, for all the reasons we have given, inferential statistics are rare) and the other for laboratory experiments with human subjects. The corollary to this division about standards of evidence is the view that humans simply are unsuitable subjects for the analysis of fundamental behavioral processes. We have argued the contrary view (Baron & Perone, 1982; Baron et al., 1991a,b). The human laboratory provides an essential bridge between the models developed in the animal laboratory and interpretations of behavior within the world of human affairs. The absence of this link can only fuel conventional doubts about whether behavior-analytic principles have much relevance for complex human behavior.

Admittedly, the laboratory study of human subjects is accompanied by formidable problems of control and analysis. We do not mean to minimize their seriousness. But it is well to remember that equally serious problems confront the researcher within the animal laboratory—the setting usually held out as the epitome of experimental control. There, the novice researcher is prone to a variety of errors when arranging deprivation levels, shaping responses in the experimental chamber, or controlling extraneous variables. The important difference from human research is that many of the solutions are known—those developed during the history of the experimental analysis of animal behavior—and they now constitute standard laboratory practice. The case can be made that these same methods, if taken seriously and if properly extended, can provide the methods needed for a single-subject analysis of human behavior. Procedures for analyzing single-subject data are closely linked to the apparatus and accompanying methods developed by Skinner to study operant conditioning. In our view, the success of a nonstatistical analysis of the data on the human level depends directly on the extent to which this framework is maintained.

Between-Group Comparisons

Despite the fact that inferential statistics and single-subject research do not mix very well, a special need is created when the researcher compares data from different subjects who have been exposed to different conditions. Given the aforementioned requirements of a single-subject analysis, why should the researcher be in this position? Two behavioral phenomena that we have touched on already are the culprits: *irreversible effects* and *individual differences.* Because of these problems, it may not be possible to exercise the full power of an experimental analysis, and the researcher may justifiably, if reluctantly, adopt inferential statistics as an aid to judgment.

Irreversible effects are well known in the animal laboratory, most notably in the study of aversive control. Severe punishment, for example, may permanently suppress responding by rats and pigeons, thus prohibiting subsequent study of lesser intensities in the same animal. Whether an effect is permanent is always open to question, of course; further exposure to new conditions might eventually weaken previously established responses. On the human level, especially, extended training cannot be held out as a panacea. Human subjects are reluctant to participate in unduly prolonged experiments. In addition, the reversal of experimental effects may, for unclear reasons, be extremely slow for humans. A case in point is one experiment on aversive control in humans (the subjects responded to avoid loss of money); once established, responding perseverated more or less indefinitely despite omission of the aversive event (Kaufman & Baron, 1969). The options for the single-subject researcher are limited when irreversible effects are encountered. Either a multiple-baseline design must be used, further study of the variable must be abandoned, or the research must fall back on the traditional procedure of contrasting subjects exposed to the variables with those who were not, and this in turn may require statistical justification.

A different need for statistics arises when the research is concerned with variables simply not subject to manipulation. Examples already discussed are the human subject's gender and age. Selecting subjects in terms of individual-difference variables represents a way of reducing subject-to-subject variability. But another possibility is that the researcher may have an interest in the variable in its own right. The parallel to research in comparative psychology is apparent, as when experiments are concerned with constraints that phylogenic status place on conditioning. Insofar as such variables as human gender and age have similar potential for interactions, they also are deserving of experimental study (Baron, Myerson, & Hale, 1988). Age has a special status in this regard in that researchers with the patience and time can examine short-term developmental changes on a single-subject (*longitudinal*) basis. As a practical matter, however, the study of human development across widely different developmental stages calls for between-group (*cross-sectional*) designs involving subjects of different ages. In the case of gender differences, of course, between-group designs are unavoidable.

When different subjects are compared, the single-subject researcher is confronted with the problem of determining whether the differences are, in fact, reliable. Such a decision hinges on considerations mentioned earlier: The average variation between conditions is compared with subject-to-subject variation within conditions. As the former source of variation increases and the latter decreases, the researcher gains increasing confidence in the reliability of the difference. We are describing, of course, the decision rules of inferential statistics. The single-subject researcher who uses group designs would appear to have no choice but to follow these rules. The rules that govern assessment of steady-state differences in the performance of the same individual simply are not appropriate for comparisons of the performances of different subjects.

The recognition that between-group comparisons sometimes are unavoidable does not mean that researcher should abandon the other strengths of a single-subject approach (Perone, 1994). A saving grace is that concern often is with interactions between individual difference variables and those that can be manipulated (termed *mixed designs* in analysis-of-variance classifications). Close attention to variables that can be controlled can only reduce subject-to-subject variation within groups and thus make between-group differences more apparent. If the researcher has studied a reasonable number of subjects, reliable differences may, in fact, be self-evident if and when they occur, and only die-hard advocates of inferential statistics (perhaps those envisioned by Huitema, 1986) might insist on statistical tests. Finally, a point worth reiterating is that when comparisons are made of variables defined by selection (rather than manipulation), the results are at best correlational; the researcher must not make the unfortunate mistake of attributing causal significance to such variables as age and gender.

CONCLUSIONS

In the end, both single-subject and group-statistical researchers must rely on their judgment, not only about what the results show but also about their worth as a contribution to knowledge. The ultimate jury is the scientific community—the reactions of one's colleagues and others to the experiment. A special role is played by those individuals involved in the publication process (journal editors and reviewers; a close second are members of grant review panels). Their approval or disapproval constitutes a powerful force in the shaping of most researchers' skills.

The Scientist as Trial Attorney

It may be useful to pursue the parallel between what goes on when an experiment is conducted, and what transpires within the courtroom—a trial in which an individual is judged by a jury of peers. As with the trial attorney, the researcher also has a case to present. Using the data from the experiment (the attorney's courtroom exhibits and relevant testimony), the researcher attempts to convince the scientific community (the jury) of the reasonableness of the conclusions provided in the research report (whatever legal theory is being propounded). If the researcher's judgment is sound, the presentation should convince the scientific audience that the experimental variables did or did not have an effect (that the client is innocent or guilty).

Within the law, there is considerable reliance on the concept of "the reasonable person" in the jury process. Given the facts presented as evidence, what would a reasonable person conclude? The scientific counterpart is peer review, and the task for the researcher is to gain assent from reasonable scientists that knowledge has been advanced by the research. Prediction and probabilities play essential roles in this effort. Bachrach (1981) noted that the test of scientific knowledge is the scientist's success in making accurate predictions from experimental results.

> When we talk about the probabilities of an event occurring, we are, in a sense, giving odds, saying that the chances are that if X is manipulated in a certain fashion, Y will change in a certain way. Experimentation is clearly a method for increasing the likelihood of the prediction being correct. (p. 49)

The trial metaphor nicely brings out the similarities and differences between statistical and nonstatistical approaches. The evidence provided by the group researcher is largely the outcome of statistical tests performed on the data. (To be sure, the group researcher may also include depictions of the data, but the case stands or falls with the tests.) The single-subject researcher, by comparison, having disdained statistical support, must make the case strictly on the basis of the data and supporting graphic analyses. Thus, the goals of the two approaches are the same but different means are used to attain them.

The concept of probability provides a bridge of sorts between the methods of statistical inference and graphic analysis. The key to inferential statistics is the significance level expressed as a probability: If the level is attained, the researcher is confident that the difference is "real." But where should the cutoff point be located? Fisher, who originated the analysis of variance, indicated that his choice of $p = .05$ was no more than a matter of his own opinion of what is or is not coincidental, and he invited choice of other values (Moore, 1979). As it turns out, most of us would agree that the appearance of something that ordinarily happens no more than once in 20 times *is* sufficiently unusual to attract attention, regardless of whether this conclusion is reached from the method of inferential statistics or on other grounds. These other grounds are the behavior analyst's responses to the data—his or her judgment about whether a particular effect has been convincingly demonstrated.

We now can summarize the nature of the interactions that ensue between the single-subject researcher and the data from his or her experiment. We emphasized the great value placed on the experimental control of variability and on the attainment of steady states. But these goals are not ends in themselves. To the contrary, they constitute a means of increasing the likelihood that the data will evoke appropriate discriminative behavior, in particular, a set of common responses on the part of the researcher and the other members of the scientific community.

Skinner (1959) identified the process whereby these responses are developed in his "case history in scientific method." Having been asked to provide a systematic formulation of his theory and method (Koch, 1959), Skinner responded by recounting his own behavioral development as a researcher, thus making the point that the key feature as not "formalized constructions of statistics and scientific method" (p. 369), but, rather, direct exposure to the contingencies of the laboratory. In Skinner's view, this is what shaped his own data-analytic skills as well as the direction of his research ("When you run onto something interesting, drop everything and study it" [p. 363]).

The difficult task for the researcher is to acquire the needed discriminative repertoire, and this suggests a role for inferential statistics. Perhaps statistical treatment of data can be regarded as an intermediate step in the behavioral development of the single-subject researcher—a training tool, so to speak (Parsonson & Baer, 1978, 1986). Through its use, the student can learn to identify what is and is not important in the data. As the discriminations are formed (as the contingencies from the scientific community take hold), the need for the statistical aid is reduced. Eventually, statistical tests become a superfluous exercise because the experienced researcher can anticipate the outcome by simply inspecting the data. To continue the legal metaphor, the researcher has reached the position of former justice Potter Stewart of the Supreme Court. In a famous decision he admitted considerable difficulty in precisely defining "pornography." Nevertheless, he insisted that "I know it when I see it."

ACKNOWLEDGMENTS. We thank John Crosbie for illuminating discussions of various matters in the design and analysis of single-subject experiments, and for his constructive criticism of a previous draft of the section on serial dependencies.

REFERENCES

Antonitis, J. J., Frey, R. B., & Baron, A. (1964). Group operant behavior: Effects of tape-recorded verbal reinforcers on the bar-pressing behavior of preschool children in a real-life situation. *Journal of Genetic Psychology, 105,* 311–321.

Bachrach, A. J. (1981). *Psychological research* (4th ed.). New York: Random House.

Baer, D. M. (1960). Escape and avoidance response of pre-school children to two schedules of reinforcement withdrawal. *Journal of the Experimental Analysis of Behavior, 3,* 155–159.

Baer, D. M. (1977). "Perhaps it would be better not to know everything." *Journal of Applied Behavior Analysis, 10,* 167–172.

Baer, D. M. (1988). An autocorrelated commentary on the need for a different debate. *Behavioral Assessment, 10,* 295–297.

Baer, D. M., Wolfe, M. M., & Risley, T. R. (1968). Some current dimensions of applied behavior analysis. *Journal of the Applied Analysis of Behavior, 1,* 91–97.

Bakan, D. (1966). The test of significance in psychological research. *Psychological Bulletin, 66,* 423–437.

Barlow, D. H., & Hersen, M. (1984). *Single case experimental designs: Strategies for studying behavior change* (2nd ed.). New York: Pergamon Press.

Baron, A. (1985). Measurement scales and the age–complexity hypothesis. *Experimental Aging Research, 11,* 193–199.

Baron, A. (1990). Experimental designs. *The Behavior Analyst, 13,* 167–171.

Baron, A., & Galizio, M. (1983). Instructional control of human operant behavior. *The Psychological Record, 33,* 495–520.

Baron, A., & Journey, J. W. (1989). Reinforcement of human reaction time: Manual–vocal differences. *The Psychological Record, 39,* 285–296.

Baron, A., & Kaufman, A. (1966). Human free-operant avoidance of "time-out" from monetary reinforcement. *Journal of the Experimental Analysis of Behavior, 9,* 557–565.

Baron, A., Menich, S. R., & Perone, M. (1983). Reaction times of younger and older men and temporal contingencies of reinforcement. *Journal of the Experimental Analysis of Behavior, 40,* 275–287.

Baron, A., Myerson, J., & Hale, S. (1988). An integrated analysis of the structure and function of behavior: Aging and the cost of divided attention. In G. Davey & C. Cullen (Eds.), *Human operant conditioning and behavior modification* (pp. 139–166). New York: Wiley.

Baron, A., & Perone, M. (1982). The place of the human subject in the operant laboratory. *The Behavior Analyst, 5,* 143–158.

Baron, A., Perone, M., & Galizio, M. (1991a). Analyzing the reinforcement process at the human level: Can application and behavioristic interpretation replace laboratory research? *The Behavior Analyst, 14,* 95–105.

Baron, A., Perone, M., & Galizio, M. (1991b). The experimental analysis of human behavior: Indispensable, ancillary, or irrelevant? *The Behavior Analyst, 14,* 145–155.

Baron, A. & Surdy, T. (1990). Recognition memory in older adults: Adjustment to changing contingencies. *Journal of the Experimental Analysis of Behavior, 54,* 201–212.

Baum, W. M. (1975). Time allocation in human vigilance. *Journal of the Experimental Analysis of Behavior, 23,* 45–53.

Benton, R. G., & Mefferd, R. B., Jr. (1967). Projector slide changing and focusing as operant reinforcers. *Journal of the Experimental Analysis of Behavior, 10,* 479–484.

Bernstein, D. J. (1988). Laboratory lore and research practices in the experimental analysis of human behavior: Designing session logistics—How long, how often, how many? *The Behavior Analyst, 11,* 51–58.

Bijou, S. W., & Baer, D. M. (1966). Operant methods in child behavior and development. In W. K. Honig (Ed.), *Operant research: Areas of research and application* (pp. 718–789). New York: Appleton–Century–Crofts.

Bolles, R. C. (1962). The difference between statistical hypotheses and scientific hypotheses. *Psychological Reports, 11,* 639–645.

Boring, E. G. (1950). *A history of experimental psychology* (2nd ed.). New York: Appleton–Century–Crofts.

Bradshaw, C. M., & Szabadi, R. (1988). Quantitative analysis of human operant behavior. In G. Davey & C. Cullen (Eds.), *Human operant conditioning and behavior modification* (pp. 225–259). New York: Wiley.

Branch, M. (1991). On the difficulty of studying "basic" behavioral processes in humans. *The Behavior Analyst, 14,* 107–110.

Brunswick, E. (1955). Representative design and probabilistic theory in a functional psychology. *Psychological Review, 62,* 193–217.

Busk, P. L. & Marascuilo, L. A. (1988). Autocorrelation in single-subject research: A counterargument to the myth of no autocorrelation. *Behavioral Assessment, 10,* 229–242.

Buskist, W., & Miller, H. L. (1982). The study of human operant behavior, 1958–1981: A topical bibliography. *The Psychological Record, 32,* 249–268.

Campbell, D. T., & Stanley, J. C. (1963). *Experimental and quasi-experimental designs for research.* Chicago: Rand McNally.

Case, D. A., Ploog, B., & Fantino, E. (1990). Observing behavior in a computer game. *Journal of the Experimental Analysis of Behavior, 54,* 185–199.

Christie, R. (1951). Experimental naivete and experiential naivete. *Psychological Bulletin, 48,* 327–339.

Church, R. M. (1979). How to look at data: A review of John W. Tukey's *Exploratory Data Analysis. Journal of the Experimental Analysis of Behavior, 31,* 433–440.

Cleveland, W. S. (1985). *The elements of graphing data.* Monterey, CA: Wadsworth.

Cohen, J. (1988). *Statistical power analysis for the behavioral sciences* (2nd ed.) Hillsdale, NJ: Erlbaum.

Cohen, J. (1994). The earth is round (p < .05). *American Psychologist, 49,* 997–1003.

Cook, T. D., & Campbell, D. T. (1979). *Quasi-experimentation: Design and analysis issues for field settings.* Chicago: Rand McNally.

Critchfield, T. S., & Perone, M. (1990). Verbal self-reports of delayed matching to sample by humans. *Journal of the Experimental Analysis of Behavior, 53,* 321–344.

Crosbie, J. (1993). Interrupted time-series analysis with brief single-subject data. *Journal of Consulting and Clinical Psychology, 61,* 966–974.

Darcheville, J. C., Riviere, V., & Wearden, J. H. (1993). Fixed-interval performance and self-control in infants. *Journal of the Experimental Analysis of Behavior, 60,* 239–254.

Dougherty, D. M., Nedelman, M., & Alfred, M. (1993). An analysis and topical bibliography of the last ten years of human operant behavior: From minority to near majority (1982–1992). *The Psychological Record, 43,* 501–529.

Eysenck, H. J. (1953). *The structure of human personality.* New York: Wiley.

Fantino, E., & Case, D. A. (1983). Human observing: Maintained by stimuli correlated with reinforcement but not extinction. *Journal of the Experimental Analysis of Behavior, 40,* 193–210.

Ferster, C. B., & Skinner, B. F. (1957). *Schedules of reinforcement.* Englewood Cliffs, NJ: Prentice–Hall.

Freeman, T. J., & Lattal, K. A. (1992). Stimulus control of behavioral history. *Journal of the Experimental Analysis of Behavior, 57,* 5–15.

Gaito, J. (1980). Measurement scales and statistics: Resurgence of an old misconception. *Psychological Bulletin, 87,* 564–567.

Galizio, M. (1979). Contingency-shaped and rule-governed behavior: Instructional control of human loss avoidance. *Journal of the Experimental Analysis of Behavior, 31,* 53–70.

Gonzalez, F. A., & Waller, M. B. (1974). Handwriting as an operant. *Journal of the Experimental Analysis of Behavior, 21,* 165–175.

Greenspoon, J. (1962). Verbal conditioning and clinical psychology. In A. J. Bachrach (Ed.), *Experimental foundations of clinical psychology* (pp. 510–552). New York: Basic Books.

Hake, D. F., Vukelich, R., & Kaplan, S. J. (1973). Audit responses: Responses maintained by access to existing self or coactor scores during non-social, parallel work, and cooperation procedures. *Journal of the Experimental Analysis of Behavior, 19,* 409–423.

Harrison, R. J., & Green, G. (1990). Development of conditional and equivalence relations without differential consequences. *Journal of the Experimental Analysis of Behavior, 54,* 225–237.

Hayes, S. C. (1986). The case of the silent dog—Verbal reports and the analysis of rules: A review of Ericsson and Simon's *Protocol Analysis: Verbal Reports as Data. Journal of the Experimental Analysis of Behavior, 45,* 351–363.

Hayes, S. C., & Brownstein, A. J. (1984). Verbal behavior: Is the human operant lab an ideal place to begin? *Experimental Analysis of Human Behavior Bulletin, 2,* 11–13.

Hebb, D. O. (1949). *The organization of behavior: A neuropsychological theory.* New York: Wiley.

Holland, J. G. (1958). Human vigilance. *Science, 128,* 61–63.

Horne, P. J., & Lowe, C. F. (1993). Determinants of human performance on concurrent schedules. *Journal of the Experimental Analysis of Behavior, 59,* 29–60.

Howell, D. C. (1995). *Fundamental statistics for the behavioral sciences* (3rd ed.). Belmont, CA: Duxbury Press.

Huitema, B. E. (1986). Statistical analysis and single-subject designs: Some misunderstandings. In A. Poling & R. W. Fuqua (Eds.), *Research methods in applied behavior analysis: Issues and advances* (pp. 209–232). New York: Plenum Press.

Huitema, B. E. (1988). Autocorrelation: 10 years of confusion. *Behavioral Assessment, 10,* 253–294.

Hyten, C., & Chase, P. N. (1991). An analysis of self-editing: Method and preliminary findings. In L. J. Hayes & P. N. Chase (Eds.), *Dialogues on verbal behavior* (pp. 67–81). Reno, NV: Context Press.

Iversen, I. H. (1988). Tactics of graphic design. A review of Tufte's *The Visual Display of Quantitative Information. Journal of the Experimental Analysis of Behavior, 49,* 171–189.

Iversen, I. H., & Lattal, K. A. (Eds.). (1991). *Techniques in the behavioral and neural sciences: Vol. 6. Experimental analysis of behavior.* Amsterdam: Elsevier.

Johnston, J. M. & Pennypacker, H. S. (1993). *Strategies and tactics of behavioral research.* Hillsdale, NJ: Erlbaum.

Kaufman, A., & Baron, A. (1969). Discrimination of periods of avoidance-extinction by human subjects. *Psychonomic Science Monographs Supplements, 3,* (Whole No. 37), 53–60.

Kazdin, A. E. (1982). *Single-case research designs: Methods for clinical and applied settings.* London: Oxford University Press.

Kazdin, A. E. (1992). *Research design in clinical psychology* (2nd ed.). New York: Macmillan Co.

Keller, F. S., & Schoenfeld, W. N. (1950). *Principles of psychology.* New York: Appleton–Century–Crofts.

Koch, S. (1959). Appendix: Suggested discussion topics for contributors of systematic analyses. In S. Koch (Ed.), *Psychology: A study of a science* (Vol. 2, pp. 653–673). New York: McGraw–Hill.

Kratochwill, T. R. (1978). Foundations of time-series research. In T. R. Kratochwill (Ed.), *Single subject research. Strategies for evaluating change* (pp. 1–100). New York: Academic Press.

Kratochwill, T. R., & Levin, J. R. (1992). *Single-case research design and analysis: New directions for psychology and education.* Hillsdale, NJ: Erlbaum.

Lord, F. (1953). On the statistical treatment of football numbers. *American Psychologist, 8,* 750–751.

Lowe, C. F. (1979). Determinants of human operant behavior. In M. D. Zeiler & P. Harzem (Eds.), *Advances in analysis of behaviour: Vol. 1. Reinforcement and the organization of behaviour* (pp. 159–192). New York: Wiley.

Lykken, D. T. (1968). Statistical significance in psychological research. *Psychological Bulletin, 70,* 151–159.

Mace, F. C., Lalli, J. S., Shea, M. C., Lalli, E. P., West, B. J., Roberts, M., & Nevin, J. A. (1990). The momentum of human behavior in a natural setting. *Journal of the Experimental Analysis of Behavior, 54,* 163–172.

Matthews, B. A., Catania, A. C., & Shimoff, E. (1985). Effect of uninstructed verbal behavior on nonverbal responding: Contingency descriptions versus performance descriptions. *Journal of the Experimental Analysis of Behavior, 43,* 155–164.

Matthews, B. A., Shimoff, E., Catania, A. C., & Sagvolden, T. (1977). Uninstructed human responding: Sensitivity to ratio and interval contingencies. *Journal of the Experimental Analysis of Behavior, 27,* 453–467.

Matyas, T. A., & Greenwood, K. M. (1990). Visual analysis of single-case time series: Effects of variability, serial dependence, and magnitude of intervention effects. *Journal of Applied Behavior Analysis, 23,* 341–351.

Mazur, J. E. (1994). *Learning and Behavior* (3rd ed.). Englewood Cliffs, NJ: Prentice–Hall.

Meehl, P. E. (1967). Theory-testing in psychology and physics: A methodological paradox. *Philosophy of Science, 34,* 103–115.

Michael, J. (1974). Statistical inference for individual organism research: Mixed blessing or curse? *Journal of Applied Behavior Analysis, 7,* 647–653.

Miller, L. K. (1968). Escape from an effortful situation. *Journal of the Experimental Analysis of Behavior, 11,* 619–627.

Mitchell, J. (1986). Measurement scales and statistics: A clash of paradigms. *Psychological Bulletin, 100,* 398–407.

Moore, D. S. (1979). *Statistics: Concepts and controversies.* San Francisco: Freeman.

Morse, W. H., & Kelleher, R. T. (1977). Determinants of reinforcement and punishment. In W. K. Honig & J. E. R. Staddon (Eds.), *Handbook of operant behavior* (pp. 174–200). Englewood Cliffs, NJ: Prentice–Hall.

Nevin, J. A. (1992). An integrative model for the study of behavioral momentum. *Journal of the Experimental Analysis of Behavior, 57,* 301–316.

Nunnally, J. C. (1978). *Psychometric theory* (2nd ed.). New York: McGraw–Hill.

Palmer, D. C., & Donahoe, J. W. (1991). Shared premises, different conclusions. *The Behavior Analyst, 14,* 123–127.

Parsonson, B. S., & Baer, D. M. (1978). The analysis and presentation of graphic data. In T. R. Kratochwill (Ed.), *Single-subject research: Strategies for evaluating change* (pp. 101–165). New York: Academic Press.

Parsonson, B. S., & Baer, D. M. (1986). The graphic analysis of data. In A. Poling & R. W. Fuqua (Eds.), *Research methods in applied behavior analysis* (pp. 157–186). New York: Plenum Press.

Parsonson, B. S., & Baer, D. M. (1992). The visual analysis of data, and current research into the stimuli controlling it. In T. R. Kratochwill & J. R. Levin (Eds.), *Single-case research design and analysis: New directions for psychology and education* (pp. 15–40). Hillsdale, NJ: Erlbaum.

Perone, M. (1991). Experimental design in the analysis of free-operant behavior. In I. Iversen & K. A. Lattal (Eds.), *Techniques in the behavioral and neural sciences: Vol. 6. Experimental analysis of behavior, Part 1* (pp. 135–171). Amsterdam: Elsevier.

Perone, M. (1994). Single-subject designs and developmental psychology. In S. H. Cohen & H. W. Reese (Eds.), *Life-span developmental psychology: Methodological contributions* (pp. 95–118). Hillsdale, NJ: Erlbaum.

Perone, M., & Baron, A. (1980). Reinforcement of human observing behavior by a stimulus correlated with extinction or increased effort. *Journal of the Experimental Analysis of Behavior, 34,* 239–261.

Perone, M., Galizio, M., & Baron, A. (1988). The relevance of animal-based principles in the laboratory study of human operant conditioning. In G. Davey & C. Cullen (Eds.), *Human operant conditioning and behavior modification* (pp. 59–85). New York: Wiley.

Perone, M., & Kaminski, B. J. (1992). Conditioned reinforcement of human observing behavior by descriptive and arbitrary verbal stimuli. *Journal of the Experimental Analysis of Behavior, 58,* 557–575.

Poling, A., & Fuqua, R. W. (Eds.). (1986). *Research methods in applied behavior analysis: Issues and advances.* New York: Plenum Press.

Rosenfarb, I. S., Newland, M. C., Brannon, S. E., & Howey, D. S. (1992). Effects of self-generated rules on the development of schedule-controlled behavior. *Journal of the Experimental Analysis of Behavior, 58,* 107–121.

Salthouse, T. A. (1985). Speed of behavior and its implications for cognition. In J. E. Birren & K. W. Schaie (Eds.), *Handbook of the psychology of aging* (2nd ed., pp. 400–426). New York: Van Nostrand Reinhold.

Schaie, K. W. (1994). Developmental designs revisited. In S. H. Cohen & H. W. Reese (Eds.), *Life-span developmental psychology: Methodological contributions* (pp. 45–64). Hillsdale, NJ: Erlbaum.

Sheldon, W. H. (1954). *Atlas of men: A guide for somatotyping the adult male at all ages.* New York: Harper Bros.

Shimoff, E. (1984). Post-session questionnaires. *Experimental Analysis of Human Behavior Bulletin, 2,* 1.

Shipley, C. R., Baron, A., & Kaufman, A. (1972). Effects of time-out from one reinforcer on human behavior maintained by another reinforcer. *Psychological Record, 22,* 201–210.

Sidman, M. (1960). *Tactics of scientific research: Evaluating experimental data in psychology.* New York: Basic Books.

Sidman, M. (1969). Generalization gradients and stimulus control in delayed matching-to-sample. *Journal of the Experimental Analysis of Behavior, 12,* 745–757.

Siegel, S., & Castellan, N. J. ,Jr. (1988). *Nonparametric statistics for the behavioral sciences* (2nd ed.). New York: McGraw-Hill.

Skinner, B. F. (1938). *The behavior of organisms.* New York: Appleton–Century–Crofts.

Skinner, B. F. (1953). *Science and human behavior.* New York: Macmillan Co.

Skinner, B. F. (1957). *Verbal behavior.* Englewood Cliffs, NJ: Prentice–Hall.

Skinner, B. F. (1959). A case history in the scientific method. In S. Koch (Ed.), *Psychology: A study of a science* (Vol. 2, pp. 359–370). New York: McGraw–Hill.

Skinner, B. F. (1966). Operant behavior. In W. K. Honig (Ed.), *Operant research: Areas of research and application* (pp. 12–32). New York: Appleton–Century–Crofts.

Skinner, B. F. (1984). Coming to terms with private events. *Behavioral and Brain Sciences, 7,* 572–581.

Stevens, S. S. (1951). Mathematics, measurement, and psychophysics. In S. S. Stevens (Ed.), *Handbook of experimental psychology* (pp. 1–49). New York: Wiley.

Tufte, E. R. (1983). *The visual display of quantitative information.* Cheshire, CN: Graphics Press.

Tukey, J. W. (1977). *Exploratory data analysis.* Reading, MA: Addison–Wesley.

Velleman, P. F., & Wilkinson, L. (1993). Nominal, ordinal, interval, and ratio typologies are misleading. *The American Statistician, 47,* 65–72.

Wanchisen, B. A. (1990). Forgetting the lessons of history. *The Behavior Analyst, 13,* 31–38.

Wearden, J. H. (1988). Some neglected problems in the analysis of human operant behavior. In G. Davey & C. Cullen (Eds.), *Human operant conditioning and behavior modification* (pp. 187–224). New York: Wiley.

Weiner, H. (1964). Conditioning history and human fixed-interval performance. *Journal of the Experimental Analysis of Behavior, 7,* 383–385.

Weiner, H. (1969). Controlling human fixed-interval performance. *Journal of the Experimental Analysis of Behavior, 12,* 349–373.

Williams, D. C., & Johnston, J. M. (1992). Continuous versus discrete dimensions of reinforcement schedules: An integrative analysis. *Journal of the Experimental Analysis of Behavior, 58,* 205–228.

Wulfert, E., Dougher, M. J., & Greenway, D. E. (1991). Protocol analysis of the correspondence of verbal behavior and equivalence class formation. *Journal of the Experimental Analysis of Behavior, 56,* 489–504.

II

Reinforcement and Punishment

4

Reinforcement
Schedule Performance

Richard L. Shull and P. Scott Lawrence

The simplest reinforcement procedure to arrange is one where each instance of a class of response is reinforced; such a procedure is called *continuous reinforcement*. It is also possible to arrange procedures so that some instances of the response class are reinforced and other instances are not (i.e., intermittent reinforcement procedures). The various procedures for arranging reinforcers in relation to behavior and to other events are known collectively as *schedules of reinforcement*.

An enormous body of empirical research (mostly with animals) and theoretical commentary exists concerning schedules of reinforcement and their effects (for reviews see Ferster & Skinner, 1957; Lattal, 1991; Morse, 1966; Nevin, 1973; Zeiler, 1977, 1984). The topic has attracted attention for several reasons. First, many everyday situations appear to involve intermittent reinforcement of a response rather than continuous reinforcement. It might be important, therefore, (say, for applied work) to better understand the effects of such intermittency on the generation, maintenance, and persistence of operant behavior. The topic has attracted attention also because seemingly subtle differences in the schedule can produce large differences in the rate and the temporal pattern of responding. These differences often are substantially larger than those produced by changes in motivational or incentive variables (e.g., deprivation or the size of the reinforcer). Moreover, the performance baselines generated by different schedules of reinforcement can determine the effects that other variables (e.g., drugs) have on behavior.

The performances engendered by various schedules of reinforcement have proven to be reproducible and remarkably general across species of nonhuman animals. They have provided challenging material for theoretical analyses of behavioral phenomena. Also, the study of schedules of reinforcement has revealed or clarified some basic principles—concerning, for example, the role of relative time intervals in determining the likelihood of responding and the effect of relative rate

Richard L. Shull and P. Scott Lawrence • Department of Psychology, University of North Carolina at Greensboro, Greensboro, North Carolina 27402-6164.
Handbook of Research Methods in Human Operant Behavior, edited by Lattal and Perone. Plenum Press, New York, 1998.

of reinforcement on the likelihood and persistence of operant behavior (for a review see Williams, 1988).

Understandably, then, investigators have been interested in developing techniques for studying the behavior of humans under various schedules of reinforcement. The goals of such research are diverse (see Baron, Perone, & Galizio, 1991) and include the following: (1) establishing behavioral baselines with particular properties against which to examine the effects of other variables, (2) assessing the degree to which the effects of schedule type and value are general between animals and humans, (3) using human subjects in experiments designed to test general theories or reveal general functional relations, and (4) using schedules to study complex human behavioral phenomena such as problem solving, learning by instruction, optimal behavioral adjustments, and perception of causality.

The present chapter is written, largely, as a two-part cautionary note—one that is more relevant to the first three goals listed immediately above than to the fourth goal. The first caution is that procedures involving schedules of reinforcement that appear similar between human and animal experiments are not necessarily functionally similar. The second caution is that the most common taxonomy of schedules of reinforcement—a taxonomy based on the conception of intermittent reinforcement of equivalent instances of a response class—might not be the most productive one for revealing and clarifying general principles. This second caution might apply to research with animals as well as with humans.

We begin by discussing some of the considerations that could justify the features of the experimental preparations that are commonly used in reinforcement-schedule work with animals. We then review critically some of the efforts to arrange analogous procedures with humans. Finally, we consider some alternative ways to conceptualize schedules of reinforcement other than as procedures for arranging intermittent reinforcement of instances of a response class.

SKINNER'S EXPERIMENTAL PREPARATION

Skinner wanted to identify general principles pertaining to the reinforcement of operant behavior, and he developed an experimental preparation that he hoped would be suitable for this purpose (Skinner, 1938, pp. 44–60). Although the preparation was developed initially for research with rats, its features, and the reasons for selecting them, are worth considering here because preparations developed to study the operant behavior of humans are often modeled after those developed for studying the operant behavior of animals.

First, a response had to be selected, and doing so required confronting some fundamental questions. Should the response be a complex act that takes a lot of time to execute or a brief one? Should the response be a part of the subject's normal behavioral repertoire or should it be one relatively free of such history? Skinner opted for a response—pressing a lever—that is brief and not something that rats normally do.

Choosing that kind of response has both advantages and disadvantages. A disadvantage is that lever pressing does not appear on the surface to resemble the kinds of acts most people find interesting (e.g., problem solving, interacting with others). That is, it lacks face validity. Consequently, people often have difficulty seeing the relevance of lever pressing data to broadly significant behavioral phenomena.

Skinner believed, however, that the advantages of the lever-press response more than compensated for its disadvantages. To appreciate the advantages it is important to remember that Skinner's goal was to discover laws that apply to operant behavior in general, not just to particular interesting responses. Even though the laws might apply generally, it would have been difficult to extract those laws from experimental data unless the response and other elements of the preparation had been chosen so as to reduce the influence of extraneous variables. The law of gravity applies to the trajectory of a falling leaf on a windy day. But it is hard to detect that invariant law except under the simplified preparation of a vacuum chamber that eliminates the effects of air resistance and wind forces.

For Skinner, the purpose of an experimental preparation was to isolate relevant variables so that their effects could be determined with minimal contamination by uncontrolled influences. If a naturally occurring response had been selected, it would have been difficult to separate the effects of the experimentally arranged variables from the effects of variables operating outside the experiment. Thus, the "unnaturalness" of the lever press seemed a virtue, given the goal of discovering general laws. It is in this sense that the lever press is said to be an arbitrary response.

There are reasons, too, for selecting a response that is brief and easy to execute. The fundamental dependent variable for operant behavior is its likelihood of occurrence, expressed as its emission rate (i.e., responses per unit of time). If one is trying to discover the general effects of some independent variable on response rate, one would like a response that can vary widely in rate. To the extent that the response is effortful or takes time to execute, there will be a ceiling on the maximum rate that can be observed. This constraint on response rate would be a specific effect of the properties of the particular response chosen for study rather than a general effect of the independent variable of interest. Any such constraint, therefore, will limit the generality of the experimental results. Although it might be possible to remove the effects of the constraint statistically—for example, by subtracting the duration of each response from the time base for calculating the response rate—such treatments may require making assumptions about response properties that are hard to verify. A simpler solution would be to use a response like the lever press that takes very little time and that is easy to execute.

Experimentally established relations, then, might have greater generality if they have been obtained with a response like the lever press than if they have been obtained with a response having greater face validity. As noted by Sidman (1989, p. 52), "Using face validity as the criterion for deciding what to observe and measure inhibits the development of a science of behavior by creating independent minisciences."

A similar set of issues surrounds the decision of what reinforcer to select for the experimental preparation. The reinforcer that Skinner selected was a small pellet of food delivered into a cup located near the lever. Again, this selection carries both advantages and disadvantages, with the advantages coming mainly from enhanced experimental control. One can say with confidence precisely when a food pellet was delivered. And one can be fairly sure that each pellet was consumed quickly and completely after it was delivered. Thus, reinforcement can be represented as a brief, discrete event that occurs at a particular point in time. This property is important because the time intervals between reinforcement and other events—such as the time between the response and the reinforcer—are critically important variables, and so it is important to be able to control and measure them precisely (for a review see Lattal, 1995). Brevity is important also so that the time taken to consume or otherwise contact the reinforcer does not interfere appreciably with the operant behavior and thus constrain its rate.

An additional advantage of using small food pellets is that their effectiveness as reinforcers can be fairly stable over the course of an experimental session. Food is an effective reinforcer because of food deprivation. In other words, food deprivation is an establishing operation (or motivational operation) for food (Malott, Whaley, & Malott, 1997, pp. 143–162; Meehl, 1992; Michael, 1982, 1993a,b; Vollmer & Iwata, 1991). Thus, any operation that caused the level of deprivation to change substantially during the session could cause a corresponding change in the effectiveness of the reinforcer. Delivering a food pellet has two opposing effects: It reinforces the behavior that it follows, but it also reduces the level of deprivation thereby reducing the likelihood of the response and reducing the ability of subsequent pellets to reinforce behavior. If the pellets are large in relation to the rat's normal daily food intake, the satiation effect may be substantial. Under such conditions, response rates taken at different points during a session will be based on different motivational levels (or on different levels of reinforcer effectiveness), and so data averaged over the whole session will be of limited generality. The problem may be reduced (although not entirely eliminated; see McSweeney & Roll, 1993) by using pellets that are small in relation to the rat's normal daily food intake. Each small pellet will have only a small satiating effect, and so each consecutive pellet during a session will be about as reinforcing as the last one. The troublesome effects of satiation can be further reduced by ending the session before too many pellets have been delivered to produce significant satiation (Dougan, Kuh, & Vink, 1993).

A disadvantage of using food pellets as reinforcers is that the properties that make them useful in an experimental preparation make them different from many of the events that seem likely to function as reinforcers in the everyday life of animals and humans. Such events are often extended in time and have gradual, ambiguous onsets and offsets. For rats potent reinforcers presumably result from such activities as nest building, running, curling up in a warm spot, and sniffing food. Similarly, for humans reinforcers likely arise from playing with a toy, engaging in a lively conversation, sitting in the warm sun, or listening to music. Yet it is hard to imagine such reinforcers as being brief, discrete events.

Furthermore, many events function as reinforcers (for humans and animals) only under limited circumstances. The occurrence of the reinforcer might produce rapid satiation (e.g., copulation). Or the relevant motivational (or establishing) operations may be short-acting. For example, the opportunity to hurt another person is not normally an effective reinforcer, but certain inducing conditions can make it so. If you stub your toe, you may feel momentarily inclined to lash out, and the opportunity to do so might be capable of functioning as a reinforcer (Azrin, Hutchinson, & Hake, 1966; Skinner, 1953, pp. 160–170). But the mood quickly passes. That is, the effects of the establishing operation (having your toe smashed) dissipate quickly, because of either the passage of time or the occurrence of lash-ing out, and so the opportunity to act aggressively quickly loses its reinforcing value. In a similar way, the opportunity to scratch your arm, the opportunity to listen to certain music, or the opportunity to watch a horror movie may be capable of functioning as a reinforcer, but only under special circumstances that may be short-acting. Such short-acting effects are unlike the relatively stable, persisting effects of food deprivation.

A disadvantage, then, of using food pellets as reinforcers is that people can easily, but mistakenly, come to equate the specific properties of food pellets and food deprivation with the general properties of reinforcers and establishing operations. If one thinks that reinforcers have to be brief, discrete events that are relatively stable in their effectiveness, one will likely overlook many opportunities for reinforcement by subtler kinds of events and will, therefore, underestimate the role of reinforcement in everyday life. Despite these problems, however, Skinner again opted for experimental rigor and analytic convenience over face validity.

Skinner's experimental preparation with rats (and a similar one for pigeons) was successful in yielding orderly, reliable, and general relations between various classes of independent variables (including the type and value of the schedule of reinforcement) and the rate and temporal patterning of responding. Typically, these relations are demonstrated in the behavior of the individual subjects and not just in the average performance of a group of subjects. Such demonstrations indicate a high degree of experimental control (Sidman, 1960, 1990).

Despite this success, there are grounds for suspecting that these experimental preparations do not necessarily achieve fully the intended simplification of the phenomena of interest. For example, under schedules of intermittent reinforcement the response unit may change from a single instance of the measured response to structured groupings of responses (for reviews and theoretical treatment see Arbuckle & Lattal, 1988; Killeen, 1994; Shimp, 1975, 1976). Moreover, exposure to schedules of reinforcement can lead to discriminations based on subtle features such as elapsed time since various events, response-reinforcer contiguities, and the organism's own ongoing behavior (e.g., Anger, 1956; Catania & Reynolds, 1968; Davis, Memmott, & Hurwitz, 1975; Ferster & Skinner, 1957; Ray & Sidman, 1970). Although certainly interesting—and perhaps even useful for some purposes—such complexities make the task of clarifying elementary principles more difficult.

Further complications arise when the subjects are verbally competent humans and add to the challenge of deriving general principles from schedule work. We consider in the next section some of the efforts to develop procedures to study the effects of reinforcement schedules with human subjects.

PROCEDURES FOR HUMANS DESIGNED TO RESEMBLE THOSE FOR ANIMALS

In one common version (see Galizio & Buskist, 1988) the human subject works alone in a small, nearly barren room. Just as the rat obtains food pellets by pressing a lever, the human subject obtains tokens or points by pressing a button, tapping a telegraph key, or pulling a plunger. The points may be exchangeable for money or prizes after the end of the session. The response for the human is brief and discrete, much like the lever press. And the tokens or points delivered as a consequence of responding are brief, discrete events just as food pellets are.

This preparation does, indeed, appear similar in form to the ones used with rats and pigeons. But is it functionally similar? That is, do variations in the contingencies of reinforcement affect the behavior of humans and animals through similar processes?

The question is a familiar one in comparative psychology (e.g., Bitterman, 1960). And it has always been hard to answer. Similar results between species can occur through different processes, and different results can reflect rather trivial procedural factors having little significance for general principles. Thus, interpreting either similarities or differences requires care.

Sensitivity to VR and VI Schedules

Some of the problems can be illustrated by considering research on "schedule sensitivity" involving variable-ratio (VR) and variable-interval (VI) schedules. Under a VR schedule, a certain number of unreinforced responses is required before the next response can be reinforced. But the number varies from one reinforcer to the next around some average (mean) value. For example, under a VR 50 schedule the required number of responses might be 40 for the first reinforcer, 10 for the second, 60 for the third, 90 for the fourth, and so forth. A feature of VR schedules is that the rate of reinforcers is proportional to the rate of responding. If 1 in 50 responses are reinforced on average and if responding occurs at a rate of 1 response/s, reinforcers will be obtained, on average, at a rate of 1 every 50 s. If, instead, responses occur at a rate of 2/s reinforcers will be obtained at an average rate of 1 every 25 s.

Under a VI schedule, a response will be reinforced only after an interval of time has elapsed. Responses during the interval have no particular consequence. The intervals vary from one reinforcer to the next. The value of the VI schedule is the mean of a long series of intervals. Thus, a VI 60-s schedule indicates that the mean elapsed time interval from one reinforcer to the next reinforcement opportunity is 60 s. A feature of VI schedules is that the rate of responding has relatively little effect on the rate of reinforcement as long as the subject responds often enough to obtain the reinforcer soon after the interval elapses. No matter how fast the subject responds, reinforcement will not occur until after the interval elapses.

The most useful comparisons are conducted with yoking procedures that ensure roughly equivalent rates of reinforcement under the two schedules. The time taken by one subject to obtain a reinforcer under the VR schedule is then "played back" as the elapsed time interval of a VI schedule for a different subject. With this comparison, one can compare the effects of the two different kinds of schedules (VR versus VI) knowing that the rate and temporal distribution of reinforcers are similar. The results of this kind of comparison are clear: Animals respond at higher rates under the VR schedule than under the VI schedule (Catania, Matthews, Silverman, & Yohalem, 1977; see also Zuriff, 1970).

It is also possible to expose the same subject to both a VR and a VI schedule within a single session. One way is to have the two schedules alternate, with a signal indicating which one currently is in effect. That is, the VR schedule might operate for a while, signaled by the illumination of a light. Then the VI schedule operates for a while, signaled by the illumination of a different light, and so forth. Technically, this is a multiple VR VI schedule.

Humans exposed to this kind of schedule appear to behave similarly to the way animals behave: higher response rates under VR than under comparable VI schedules (Baxter & Schlinger, 1990; Matthews, Shimoff, Catania, & Sagvolden, 1997; see also McDowell & Wixted, 1986). But are the processes responsible for the response-rate differences the same for human and animal subjects?

Suppose during some relatively short period of time we observe higher response rates when a VR schedule is in effect than when a VI schedule is in effect. There are at least three different kinds of processes that could produce such response-rate differences. First, we might be observing a direct differential reinforcement effect of the schedule on response rates (e.g., a shaping or a strengthening effect of the reinforcement contingencies). Second, we might be observing an effect of the signal on response rates (i.e., a discriminative stimulus effect). That is, in the past one cue light has been correlated with the VR schedule and the other cue light has been correlated with the VI schedule. As a result of that correlation, the cue lights will come to evoke the response rates appropriate to the correlated schedule. We can be confident that the control is by the discriminative stimulus, rather than a result of current differential reinforcement by the schedule contingencies, if we observe the subject responding immediately at the appropriate rate when the cue light comes on, before a reinforcer has been obtained in that component. We also demonstrate a discriminative effect by switching the signal–schedule correlation and noting that the response rates persist for some time consistent with the previous signaling correlation.

The third possible reason for the different response rates is that the subject has formulated descriptions, rules, strategies, or hypotheses related to the schedules. Humans can instruct themselves, either overtly or covertly. Aspects of the task might prompt the subject to construct rules or hypotheses about how to "solve the problem," and such verbal constructions (whether overt or covert) can act, in turn, as stimuli to influence other verbal and nonverbal behavior including the response being measured (Catania, Matthews, & Shimoff, 1982, 1990; Cerutti, 1989; Hayes, 1986; Keller & Schoenfeld, 1950; Perone, 1988; Schlinger, 1993; Skinner, 1969).

VR and VI schedules differ in what is required to obtain the highest possible rate of reinforcers (i.e., the largest number of reinforcers per unit of session time). The VR schedule requires responding as fast as possible whereas the VI schedule requires only a moderate rate of responding. An individual who has constructed a rule that specifies these dependencies between response rate and reinforcer rate may come to respond "efficiently" in the sense of obtaining the highest rate or amount of reinforcement for the least amount of responding.

Thus, sensitivity of behavior to changes in contingencies can result from one or more of the following: (1) direct shaping by the currently operating schedule, (2) discriminative control by a stimulus previously correlated with the schedule, or (3) discriminative control mediated by rules, hypotheses, conceptualizations, and so forth.

Despite the greater complexity inherent in the third kind of sensitivity, a good case can be made that the relevant phenomena can be explained in terms of more

elementary processes (e.g., Skinner, 1957, 1969). For example, any relevant discriminative and verbally mediated control presumably developed through a history of differential reinforcement within the experiment or in the subject's so-
cial/verbal environment outside the experiment. Thus, the different kinds of
sensitivity to contingencies may be traceable to common fundamental processes.
But the immediate controlling variables are nonetheless different at the time they
operate in the experiment to produce different response rates.

Assessing the possible role of self-instructions poses methodological challenges (Shimoff & Catania, Chapter 12). The important events are often covert, and
there are at least two different links to consider: the link between the task and the
verbal behavior that it evokes and the link between such self-talk and other behavior. The linkages in neither case occur automatically but instead depend on a
social/verbal history which can differ among subjects. Moreover, it is difficult to
determine whether particular verbal behavior is part of a causal sequence with other behavior or merely part of a pattern of correlated actions resulting from environmental variables (e.g., Hineline & Wanchisen, 1989).

Techniques are available, however, that can provide indirect evidence of such
influences. In one study (Shimoff, Matthews, & Catania, 1986) the training schedule
was a multiple schedule as described above (multiple VR VI). That is, two different
cue lights were illuminated in alternating sequence. In the presence of one, a VR 10
schedule for points was in effect; in the presence of the other, a VI 5-s schedule was
in effect. The results were consistent with those previously reported with humans
and animals as just described: higher response rates under the VR than under the VI
schedule. Furthermore, when the experimenters reversed the schedule–cue light
correlation, response rates quickly switched in corresponding fashion.

Indeed, response rates switched so quickly that the experimenters began to
wonder if contact with the contingencies was actually responsible for shaping and
reshaping the different response rates. Although no explicit cue indicated that the
schedules had been reversed between the cue lights, could there have been some
nonobvious cue? Indeed, there was. Imagine that you are a subject. You could find
out what schedule is in effect for a particular cue light in the following way. Pause
for a short period of time at the beginning of a cue-light period (5–10 s), and then
respond. If your first response is reinforced, then the schedule is probably the VI
5-s; otherwise it is probably the VR. The reason is that the VI interval will time
during the pause. If the pause is long relative to the average elapsed time interval,
the probability is high that the interval will have elapsed by the end of the pause,
making the first response eligible for reinforcement. Pausing does not reduce the
response requirement under the VR schedule, and so the response count will need
to be completed after the pause no matter how long the pause is. In short, the outcome of a single response after a pause at the beginning of a cue light could come
to indicate which kind of schedule is in effect during that cue light.

The experimenters arranged a test to see if the response–outcome occurrence
actually functioned as a signal. After several reversals of the schedules, they
added a contingency to the VI component so that reinforcement could not be obtained until six unreinforced responses had occurred after the start of the cue
light. Thus, if the subject paused for 5 or 6 s and then responded, even if the in-

terval had elapsed, the first response would not be reinforced. The outcome of responding after the initial pause was thus made similar to what had indicated the VR schedule.

The result of this manipulation was that subjects responded during the VI schedule at a high rate characteristic of their performance under the VR schedule. Other tests that followed a similar logic produced similar results. Apparently, the outcome of a response following an initial pause functioned as signal for the schedule in effect.

Events involving response-outcome relations can come to function as discriminative stimuli for animal subjects as well (e.g., Davis et al., 1975). Shimoff et al. (1986) suggested that these events played a more complex role in the behavior of their human subjects, namely, evoking verbal rules or hypotheses of the sort: "To respond most efficiently (i.e., to get the most points for the least work), pause at the start, and if the first response gets points, then respond slowly throughout the component; otherwise respond fast." Indirect evidence for such verbal influence came from analyzing descriptions of the schedule that the subjects made periodically throughout the experimental sessions.

Whether or not verbal rules in fact played a role, the data show that local correlates of the schedules can come to function as signals (or discriminative stimuli). Control by such events indicates a kind of sensitivity to the contingencies, but it is a different kind of sensitivity from adjustments related to direct strengthening of the response or shaping of response rates by the schedule contingencies.

The significance of these data is that even when responding adjusts in correspondence to changes in the schedules, the reasons for the changes—i.e., the controlling variables—might be different from those responsible for the similar-appearing changes in the behavior of animal subjects under conditions that appear analogous. Similar results can occur for different reasons and so do not necessarily imply that similar controlling relations are at work.

There is little evidence, for example, that overall efficiency or verbal-like rules are responsible for the schedule effects with animal subjects. If the behavior of animal subjects is efficient, it is most likely so only as an incidental by-product of other processes (e.g., Galbicka, Kautz, & Jagers, 1993; Mazur, 1981; Mazur & Vaughan, 1987; Vaughan, 1981; Vaughan & Miller, 1984). The requirements for efficiency, however, may be part of a rule or strategy relevant to human performance.

There are methodological implications. Suppose an experimenter uses schedules under which rules (based, say, on "efficiency" criteria) and nonverbal processes produce similar outcomes. If so, finding similar outcomes between human and animal subjects would be ambiguous as to what processes are involved. If one suspects different processes, one might be wise to select schedules under which the performances would differ depending on whether or not verbal-like processes were playing a role. If humans were to respond contrary to efficiency criteria but similar to the way animals respond, the case for similar processes would be stronger. Schedules with those properties are easy to arrange with computers, and they have been used with good effect in work both with animal subjects (e.g., Mazur, 1981; Vaughan, 1981; Vaughan & Miller, 1984) and with humans (e.g., Hackenberg & Axtell, 1993; Jacobs & Hackenberg, 1996).

Performance under Fixed-Interval Schedules

Probably the most extensively documented performance difference between humans and animals occurs under fixed-interval (FI) schedules. Under FI schedules, a response is reinforced only after an interval of time has elapsed; the duration of the time interval is the same from one reinforcer to the next. With animals given extensive exposure to the schedule, each interval begins with a pause averaging between a third and a half of the interval. Then response rate accelerates either gradually (the FI scallop) or abruptly to a moderately high rate until reinforcement. Other patterns that are less easily characterized occasionally appear (see Lattal, 1991; Perone, Galizio, & Baron, 1988). This pattern is efficient in the sense that response rate is lowest at the start of the interval when reinforcement is unlikely and highest toward the end. It is also true, however, that the subject makes many more responses per reinforcer than is required. If the subject paused for exactly the duration of the interval and then responded once, it would obtain reinforcers at the highest possible rate with the fewest possible responses.

Human subjects under FI schedules commonly display one of two different patterns, neither of which resembles those generated most frequently by animal subjects (Hyten & Madden, 1993; Weiner, 1983). They either pause for the full interval and then make a single reinforced response or they respond throughout the interval at a high constant rate. The first pattern seems maximally efficient and the second seems maximally inefficient on the assumption that responding is costly or aversive.

It appears, then, that the performance of adult humans differs from that of animal subjects under FI and other schedules (but see Perone et al., 1988, for some qualifications). An important question then becomes: What factors are responsible for these differences? In the next section we consider some possible candidates.

DIFFERENCES RELATED TO RESPONSE UNITS AND REINFORCERS

One would expect similar performances between human and animal subjects under formally equivalent schedules only if the experimental preparations are, indeed, functionally analogous. But is the button press by a human functionally analogous to a lever press by a rat or a key peck by a pigeon? And are points as reinforcers analogous to food pellets and grain? We will consider some of the relevant issues in the following subsections.

Response Unit

Formal versus Functional Unit

A key problem is that the functional behavioral unit might not correspond to the segment of behavior that the experimenter has chosen to measure (Arbuckle & Lattal, 1988; Bernstein, 1987; Catania, 1973; Hineline, 1981; Killeen, 1994; Levine, 1971; Schoenfeld, 1972; Shimp, 1975, 1976; Thompson & Lubinski, 1986; Thompson & Zeiler, 1986; Zeiler, 1977). Suppose, for example, that a button press by a particular individual is part of a more complex act such as a problem-solving strategy that developed through experiences outside the experiment. If some independent variable during the experiment changed the strategy, the frequency of button pressing might change as well. But it would be a mistake to interpret that change as a direct effect of the independent variable on the likelihood of button pressing as a unit of behavior. The formal similarities between, say, a human's button press and a rat's lever press do not guarantee that the two responses are functionally similar as behavioral units or as parts of units.

An anecdote may illustrate the problem. Some years ago, one of us served as a subject in a study of the conditioned emotional response. The sessions took place in a small isolation booth and lasted an hour or so. The measured response (operant) was pressing a telegraph key, and the nominal reinforcers were points added to a counter visible to the subject. The subject was permitted to bring textbooks and other study material into the session. During the session, the subject spent most of his time reading while absent-mindedly pressing the key at a moderate rate and occasionally glancing at the console. Occasionally a stimulus (the number "8") would appear on the console display, and a minute or so later the subject received a rather unpleasant electric shock through electrodes taped to his arm.

Analogous procedures with rats as subjects demonstrate a conditioned suppression effect. That is, the rat obtains food pellets by lever pressing until the stimulus comes on that signals unavoidable shock. At that point the rat stops lever pressing until the shock occurs and the warning stimulus goes off. The suppression of productive operant behavior has been called a conditioned emotional reaction.

The human subject's results, however, appeared quite different: The rate of key pressing remained the same or even increased during the warning stimulus. Here is what was going on. When the warning stimulus came on, the subject stopped reading and began silently (and anxiously) to hum a little tune, pressing the key at certain beats in the rhythm:

ta-de-da-ta-de-da-press-press-ta-de-da-press-press-ta-de-da-ta-de-da-press-press . . .

Productive operant behavior (reading) was indeed suppressed during the warning stimulus, but the rate of the measured response was not. Key pressing was part of a larger unit of behavior (the little tune) evoked by the warning stimulus, and its rate was constrained by the occurrence and structure of that larger unit.

With verbally competent human subjects differences between the formal and functional response may be especially troublesome. There is always the strong possibility that instructions, stated or implied, will evoke chains or other complex behavioral units.

In light of these possibilities, it seems risky to assume that a button press by a human and a lever press by a rat will necessarily function equivalently as units of behavior. Indeed, it might be risky to assume that either functions generally as an independent unitary response.

Points as Reinforcers

A common practice is for the number of points to be displayed on a counter located in plain view of the subject. When the appropriate response occurs, the counter is incremented. Sometimes a light flashes or a tone sounds briefly, indi-

cating the delivery of the points. A variation of this procedure is simply to indicate when points have been obtained but to not make the point total visible to the
subject. (See Galizio & Buskist, 1988, for a review.)

Points as Conditioned Reinforcers: The Role of Instructions

Whereas food pellets are primary reinforcers, points are conditioned reinforcers as a result of being correlated with other reinforcers. With animal subjects
conditioned reinforcers are created by directly correlating a neutral stimulus (e.g.,
a light flash or a token) with an effective reinforcer (e.g., a food pellet) or by making the neutral stimulus a discriminative stimulus in a chain (for reviews see
Dinsmoor, 1983; Fantino, 1977; Gollub, 1977). With human subjects, instructions
often are used to produce the same effect indirectly. That is, the subject may be
told at the beginning of the experiment that he or she will be able to earn points
that can be exchanged for prizes or money at the end of the experiment.

Actually, prizes or money may be unnecessary as backup reinforcers. Sometimes it has been sufficient merely to tell subjects to try to earn points without suggesting that points can be exchanged for anything (Galizio & Buskist, 1988). Apparently points can derive their reinforcing effectiveness from being correlated
with other reinforcers arranged incidentally in the experiment or outside the experiment.

One such reinforcer could be escaping from the experimental session. The task
is likely to be boring, and the subject may have volunteered to participate only to
satisfy a course requirement. In such circumstances, the opportunity to leave the
task might be able to function as a potent reinforcer. Gaining points, then, might
become a conditioned reinforcer simply because the growing point total signals
progress toward the end of the session and thus the opportunity to leave. It may
be worth noting that the opportunity to escape from some experimental tasks has
been shown to function as a reinforcer for developmentally disabled human children (Iwata, Pace, Kalsher, Cowdery, & Cataldo, 1990) and pigeons (Creed & Ferster, 1972).

Another possibility is that points are reinforcing because they have signaled
success in a variety of situations prior to the experiment. Most normal adult humans have had experience earning points in games and in academic settings. In
such settings accumulating points are often signs of achievement and success, so
points might become conditioned reinforcers on that account. Indeed, points, like
money, may be generalized conditioned reinforcers for many individuals. Points
would be especially likely to function this way to the extent that the experimental task resembles a game or an academic test.

Difficult issues are raised also when instructions are used to establish points
as reinforcers. Suppose points become effective as reinforcers when a subject has
been told that points can be used after the end of the session to buy prizes. What
competencies must the subject have for that to happen? Clearly, the subject must
be able to be influenced by descriptions of contingencies involving events that are
remote in time. Might such competencies contribute to performance differences
between human and animal subjects under schedules of reinforcement?

Consummatory Behavior

Most of the reinforcers used with animal subjects evoke consummatory behavior or some other sort of contact behavior. Such behavior guarantees that the operant behavior will be interrupted, at least briefly. When points are delivered, in contrast, the operant behavior can continue uninterrupted. Indeed, the subject may not even look at the point counter (Matthews et al., 1977). Perhaps the interruption of operant behavior by consummatory or contact behavior contributes to the effect that reinforcers have (Guthrie, 1940; Matthews et al., 1977; Sheffield, 1966).

If, for whatever reason, points are not particularly effective reinforcers for humans, it probably should not be surprising that the performance of humans and animals differs under schedules that are formally similar. Techniques designed to achieve greater similarity in the reinforcer potency between animals and humans are described in the latter part of the next section.

TECHNIQUES TO MAKE THE HUMAN AND ANIMAL PROCEDURES ANALOGOUS

In the following subsections we will describe several different approaches experimenters have taken in an effort to overcome the problems that limit the comparability of results between human and animal subjects. The first subsection will summarize procedures designed to reduce the influence of verbal and other complex behavior, thereby making the behavior of humans functionally more like that of animal subjects. The second subsection will summarize procedures designed to make the reinforcers more comparable.

Reducing the Influence of Verbal and Other Repertoires

Undetected Responses

Some investigators have tried to reduce the impact of verbal influences by using a response that the subject cannot report making. Hefferline's work provides a useful example. In one study (Hefferline, Keenan, & Harford, 1959) the response was a muscle twitch in the thumb that was too small to be detected either by the subject or by the experimenter except by special instruments. In everyday terms, we would say that the subject was unaware of making the response. Nonetheless, when a reinforcer (the removal of noise superimposed on music) was made contingent on the muscle twitch, the rate of those twitches increased. This reinforcement effect was demonstrated in subjects who were told how to turn off the noise as well as in subjects who were given no particular information about the contingencies. Indeed, the latter subjects reported amazement that their behavior changed and that their behavior had an effect on the noise.

Hefferline (1962, p. 129) saw great potential for this technique:

> The theoretical and practical importance which we attribute to conditioning under this technique is that it enables us to approach the adult human subject

just as we would an animal of another species. Since he does not discriminate
his own behavior in the manner called conscious, he is not in a position to introduce the confusing array of variables which are the product of the socializa-
tion process. It is as if his "human" behavior has been functionally dissected
out of the repertoire, leaving his "animal" behavior to be independently manipulated.

Whether the muscle twitch indeed functions like a rat's lever press under different schedules of reinforcement remains an untested possibility.

Other techniques, based on a similar logic, have provided evidence of an effect of contingencies without the human subject being able to describe the contingencies (e.g., Rosenfeld & Baer, 1970; Svartdal, 1995).

Nonverbal Human Children

Another approach has been to use human subjects who have not learned to
speak. In one study (Lowe, Beasty, & Bentall, 1983), for example, the subjects were
two children, one 9 months old and the other 10 months. The response was touching a metal cylinder. For one child the reinforcers were small snack items; for the
other the reinforcers were brief (4 s) sounds of music played from various music
boxes. Each child was exposed to several different FI durations, ranging from 10 s
to 50 s, over successive blocks of sessions.

The interesting result was that the children behaved much like animals do under FI schedules and unlike the way older children and adults behave. The inference Lowe et al. drew was that verbal events probably played a role in producing
these age-related differences. (Obviously, however, there are differences between
the young children and older children other than language proficiency that could
have contributed to the performance differences.)

Concurrent Tasks (Masking Procedures)

Another technique is to have the subject engage in some task that interferes
with the performance of verbal and other complex behavior relevant to the task
(e.g., Laties & Weiss, 1963; Lowe, 1979; Svartdal, 1992). For example, the subject
might be asked to repeat, word for word, a passage of text presented to the subject
through earphones (i.e., to "shadow" the heard text). The reasoning is that this task
is sufficiently demanding that the subject will not be able to construct or follow
verbal rules or hypotheses, keep close track of time intervals, and so forth. By having the subject repeat the words aloud, the experimenter can determine that the
subject is actually performing the shadowing task.

This technique sometimes seems to work. That is, the competing task leads to
performance by humans that sometimes looks much like the performance of animals under analogous schedules of reinforcement.

Is it still possible, however, that the schedule performance of the humans was
influenced by verbal rules and other complex repertoires despite the competing
task? At the risk of appearing churlish, we suggest that it might be. Perhaps the
competing tasks did not eliminate the complex repertoires but merely made them
less complex. If so, the altered schedule performance might reflect the altered rules

instead of revealing performance free of such rules. People can become increasingly proficient at "divided attention"—doing two different tasks at the same time. Parents may be familiar with the phenomenon of reading to a young child while daydreaming. (See also Skinner, 1957, pp. 384–402.) Thus, to assume that the competing tasks totally eliminate the influences of verbal and other complex repertoires strikes us as unwarranted. (If the nature of the masking task were changed frequently during the experiment, subjects might be less likely to develop proficiency, and the masking tasks might be more effective in interfering with verbal functioning.)

Whether or not competing (concurrent) tasks eliminate mediating or correlated covert activity, the fact that they alter performance on the schedule of reinforcement of interest provides at least suggestive evidence for the influence of such activity. As Laties and Weiss (1963, p. 435) put it,

> We have noted . . . that [human subjects] working on such schedules usually count or recite, and it seems likely that the effect of concurrent activity is due to interference with such mediating responses. . . . The present observations . . . again point up both the ubiquity and the importance of covert mediating behavior in the operant behavior of man.

Shaped versus Instructed Responses

In many studies, the subjects are instructed about what response to make (Pilgrim & Johnston, 1988; Shimoff & Catania, Chapter 12). Matthews et al. (1977) reasoned that such instructions might be especially likely to engender covert rules and hypotheses. If so, verbal processes would be less likely to occur if the response were shaped by reinforcing successive approximations. To test this hypothesis, Matthews et al. used a shaping procedure with some subjects to establish button pressing and used instructions with other subjects. The results were clear. The subjects whose button pressing responses were shaped behaved more like animal subjects under formally similar schedules.

Whether shaping led to button-pressing behavior that was really free of verbal influences remains an open question, however. As described above, these same authors later demonstrated that behavior could appear sensitive to schedule changes but as a result of discriminations based on subtle features of response-outcome events and possibly involving rules about the contingencies (Shimoff et al., 1986).

Stability

When a subject is first exposed to an experimental procedure, any behavior that occurs initially must reflect dispositions established by variables that operated prior to the experiment. Such variables may have persisting effects, so extensive contact with the experimental procedures might be required for the currently arranged variables to gain full control. In research with animals, it is common to expose the subjects to each experimental condition for some fairly large number of consecutive daily sessions (perhaps 20 or 30) of an hour or so each until responding is judged to be stable (Killeen, 1978; Sidman, 1960). In judging stability one looks for the absence of any systematic trend in the measure of responding over sessions—for example, no upward or downward trend in response rate—and a reasonable degree of consistency in the measure of responding from session to session (see Baron & Perone, Chapter 3). A systematic trend in the data indicates that there are persisting, residual effects of variables from prior conditions or from conditions outside the experiment and that variables arranged by the current condition have not yet gained complete control. Too much session-to-session variability in the measure of responding indicates that some influential variables have not been identified or controlled sufficiently.

Often in research with humans the whole experiment is completed in a few sessions. Indeed, it is not unusual for several different conditions to be imposed for periods of only 10 or 15 min each during a single session. The reasons for such brief exposure are understandable. It is often difficult to get human subjects to spend more than an hour or so in an experiment. But the fact remains that such brief exposure precludes assessing stability and virtually guarantees that performance in the experiment will reflect residual effects of prior variables (see discussion by Bernstein, 1988).

Baron et al. (1991) therefore reasoned that the effects of verbal/social histories might be weakened by giving the human subjects substantially more exposure to the experimental conditions than is typical and by establishing stable baselines. Such procedures make severe practical demands, but doing so may be necessary for the current variables to produce effects like those obtained with animal subjects.

It is, however, an open question whether or not such procedures will generally minimize the effects of variables outside the experiment (Branch, 1991; Wanchisen & Tatham, 1991). For example, although trends in the data indicate persisting effects of prior variables, stability does not necessarily indicate an absence of such effects. Stability can occur for a variety of reasons. Is it possible, for example, that invariant conditions in a game like task could provoke hypotheses and reminiscences that encourage stereotyped responding? Also, it may be relevant that with only rare exceptions the experimental session occupies a small portion of most human subjects' daily activities.

Making the Reinforcers Analogous

Consummatory Response

If a consummatory or contact response plays an important role in reinforcement, then points might function more like food pellets if a consummatory-like response were required. Matthews et al. (1977) created a consummatory-response analogue by requiring human subjects to make a second response to obtain the points after the schedule requirement had been satisfied. Under this procedure, the behavior of humans did indeed more closely resemble the behavior of animal subjects under analogous schedules.

Food as Reinforcement

One might suppose that the simplest and most straightforward way to create functionally similar reinforcers would be to use small bits of food as reinforcers for human subjects. But it must be remembered that food functions in various ways in the culture of most humans—especially given the practical impossibility of depriving human subjects to the level typical with animal subjects (e.g., Harris, 1974; Logue, 1991). For example, eating candy before lunch might be frowned on in a health-conscious culture as is sometimes found on college campuses. For people the reinforcing effects of an item of food depend on a variety of factors other than deprivation level, its taste, and its caloric content.

Galizio and Buskist (1988) described some relevant anecdotal evidence. Female students, working individually, could obtain bits of tasty snack food by button pressing, and button pressing typically occurred at high rates. One might suppose that the snacks were potent reinforcers. The experimenter discovered, however, that the subjects often were not eating the snacks but instead were hiding them or throwing them out of the window. Apparently the snacks—if they were functioning as reinforcers at all—were acting like points, perhaps as a token of success or of progress toward the end of the session rather than as consumable reinforcers.

Natural Reinforcers

It may be possible to select reinforcers for research that more closely approximate reinforcers encountered in the person's normal environment (see Galizio & Buskist, 1988). The aim would be to select reinforcers that are reinforcing when they occur, in contrast to points where the reinforcing effect may come from accumulating a large number. Some researchers, for example, have used access to a computer game or have even embedded the operant task into a computer video game (Case, Ploog, & Fantino, 1990). Destroying a "Klingon" might have an immediate reinforcing effect that is largely independent of its signaling progress toward winning the game. Other examples include access to a movie, television show, conversation, music, toys, and reading material.

These sorts of everyday reinforcers are commonly used in applied work (e.g., see Martin & Pear, 1996, pp. 30–35) but are less often used in basic research preparations, probably because their use appears to sacrifice some experimental control. As discussed earlier, such reinforcers may have ambiguous onsets and offsets, they may lead to rapid satiation, and there is likely to be wide individual differences in their effectiveness. But the apparent gain in experimental control through using points or small bits of food may be illusory for the reasons discussed above. Neither kind of reinforcer seems likely to have the advantageous properties of food pellets for a food-deprived rat. On balance, then, the advantages from using a potent reinforcer might offset the disadvantages from using reinforcers whose potency may be weak, inconstant, and derived from events in and outside the experiment that are hard to specify.

Certain precautions can be taken to enhance the level of control. For example, when the operant behavior occurs that is to be reinforced, a stimulus can be presented immediately that signals the opportunity to contact the reinforcer or engage in the reinforcing activity. Access to the activity would be provided at that time rather than after the end of the session. (See, for example, Iversen, 1993, for an effective use of this technique with wheel running as a reinforcer for lever pressing by rats.)

Suppose, for example, that the reinforcer were access to a movie. The designated response might turn on a light signaling that the movie machine is now operative. The subject would then turn on the movie and watch it for a period of time at the end of which the movie machine would turn off and additional operant behavior would be required to gain access again. It would be important to realize that the amount of time the subject can watch the movie per access is likely to influence its reinforcing effectiveness. If the access periods are brief (e.g., 30 s), they might be aversive rather than reinforcing. There may be optimal durations or natural breaks that produce an optimal reinforcing effect (see Bernstein, 1988; Dunham, 1977).

Discovering effective reinforcers for individuals may require some trial and error. One might be tempted simply to ask the subject. Sometimes the answer will prove useful (Bernstein & Michael, 1990). But it must be remembered that reinforcers are defined by their effect on behavior, not by what people say about them. People may or may not be able to identify important reinforcers depending on a variety of complex factors including their social/verbal experiences outside the experiment related to describing reinforcing effects. The variables influencing such self-reports can be examined (e.g., Critchfield & Perone, 1993; Critchfield, Tucker, & Vuchinich, Chapter 14; Lubinski & Thompson, 1993; Nisbett & Wilson, 1977). It is risky merely to assume that such reports are valid guides to the controlling variables (Skinner, 1953, pp. 257–282).

Efforts have been made to develop predictive theories about what events will function as reinforcers based on observations of behavior made prior to arranging a contingency. For example, access to high-frequency activities often can function as reinforcers for lower-frequency activities (Premack, 1965). Related proposals are discussed in Allison (1993), Bernstein (Chapter 16), Bernstein and Ebbesen (1978), Dunham (1977), and Timberlake (1993).

Using Weak Conditioned Reinforcers with Animals

The techniques just described are based on the assumption that the performance of humans might come to resemble that of animals under similar schedules if the reinforcers used with humans are sufficiently effective. By the same reasoning, the performance of animals might more closely resemble that of humans under schedules of reinforcement if the reinforcers were conditioned reinforcers analogous to those used with humans. Some evidence supporting the latter possibility has been reported by Jackson and Hackenberg (1996).

ALTERNATIVES TO INTERMITTENT-REINFORCEMENT CONCEPTION

As discussed at the beginning of this chapter, the usual practice is to classify reinforcement schedules on the basis of how the schedule arranges intermittent reinforcement of instances of a response class. Such a classification, and the conception from which it derives, might be unnecessarily limiting, however. Suppose, for example, that the measured instances are parts of larger behavioral units—perhaps a temporal pattern or a burst of responding (e.g., Arbuckle & Lattal, 1988). Which instances, then, are reinforced and which are not?

Indeed, it might be misleading (or at least limiting) to think of schedules as determining which instances of a response class are to be reinforced and which are not. Schedules might be usefully conceptualized as arranging reinforcement to follow, more or less reliably, sequences of responses and correlated stimulus events, thereby creating new behavioral structures—new units (see Marr, 1979). Some theorists have proposed that the effects of reinforcement are on the contents of working memory (Killeen, 1994; Shimp, 1976), which may include measured and unmeasured behavioral events. A theory of working memory would be needed to predict the functional behavioral unit. In such conceptions, the functional unit of behavior would seldom correspond to the unit specified by the intermittent-reinforcement procedure. (One might even question the necessity or utility of conceptualizing behavior under schedules of reinforcement in terms of repeatable units.)

Catania (1971) made a related point, although from a different theoretical perspective. He noted that even though the reinforcer is produced by one particular brief response, the reinforcer follows all of the preceding behavior and ought to strengthen all such behavior. The magnitude of the strengthening effect presumably diminishes as a function of the delay between the particular response and the reinforcer. Catania reported evidence in support of this proposal. This conception is reminiscent of Schoenfeld's metaphor—that behavior should be viewed as a stream (Schoenfeld, 1972; Schoenfeld & Farmer, 1970).

Investigations of schedule-of-reinforcement effects have often focused on the various response patterns observed at the level of individual interreinforcement intervals. It may be, however, that the fine details of such patterns depend on highly particular and relatively technical features of schedule control. They may depend, for example, on details of the functional response unit and on the influence of proprioceptive stimulation (Ferster & Skinner, 1957; Ray & Sidman, 1970). Because of the network of idiosyncratic relations involved, providing a thorough account of such effects has proven to be difficult (Zeiler, 1977, 1984), and the effort will not necessarily yield information of general significance (Jenkins, 1970).

A different approach to studying schedule effects would be to focus on functional relations between dimensions of the schedule and dimensions of behavior that are less dependent on the intermittent-reinforcement conception of schedules and their effects. Sometimes characteristics of such functions are general over a range of particular procedures, less tied, that is, to particular properties of the response unit and preparation (cf. Nevin, 1984; Sidman, 1960), and so they might be demonstrated more easily in the behavior of humans. We offer a few examples below—tentatively and speculatively—to suggest some possible directions. Although the phenomena to be described may be relatively independent of particular response units, it still would be important to give due consideration to the possible influence of verbal and other complex repertoires as well as to the other factors discussed above.

Temporal Control Gradient

With animal subjects, a remarkable invariance emerges when performance is compared across a wide range of FI schedules. The procedure involves exposing the subject to different FI durations, with each one in effect for a sufficient number of sessions to achieve stability. For purposes of data analysis, each FI duration is divided into equal parts, called *bins,* and the responses occurring in each bin are accumulated over the session. From those response totals one then calculates the average response rate in each bin. If the FI is divided into five bins, then the calculation gives the average response rate in consecutive fifths of the FI. Typically, these calculations are based on response totals over the last five or so sessions of a condition and represent stable performance.

The common result is that average response rate increases over consecutive bins, thus revealing an orderly temporal control gradient. The really striking result appears, however, when the temporal control functions from different FI values are compared. For this comparison, the x-axis shows elapsed time as a proportion of the interval rather than absolute elapsed time. And the y-axis shows response rate as a proportion of the response rate in the last bin. Thus, the plots show relative rate of responding as a function of relative elapsed time in the FI. For FI durations ranging from 30 s to 3000 s these functions virtually superimpose (Dews, 1970). This and similar invariant effects of relative elapsed time have served as foundational facts for the construction of some powerful and general theories of temporal control (Gibbon, 1977; Gibbon & Church, 1992; Killeen, 1975; Killeen & Fetterman, 1988).

Moreover, this invariant temporal relation does not depend on using literally a FI schedule—that is, it does not depend on the occurrence and intermittent reinforcement of identical, brief, discrete responses. Similar temporal control functions occur even when food reinforcers are presented at fixed time intervals independently of any particular response. The measures of behavior include the temporal distribution of activity (Killeen, 1975) and the temporal distribution of time spent in the location where food is presented (Staddon, 1977). Even though the FI schedule has been defined in terms of the intermittent reinforcement of a response unit, that specification might be incidental to certain scientifically significant effects of the schedule.

The most general effect of FI schedules might be the generation of a temporal gradient in the disposition to respond in various ways (an "anticipation gradient") as a function of relative elapsed time. The important property of the schedule for producing this effect might be the temporal regularity of significant events. For reasons discussed earlier, points as reinforcers for people might not be nearly as significant as the end of the session, and the human's button press might not function as a unit of behavior like the rat's lever press reflecting changing dispositions. Thus, the scheduling of other kinds of events and other measures of behavior might reveal anticipation gradients whose relation to the scheduled intervals more closely resembles those obtained with animal subjects.

Malott et al. (1997, pp. 263–266) wisely urged caution in applying schedule names to everyday situations when only some features of the everyday situations are analogous to those of the schedule as arranged in the laboratory. For example, a paycheck given at the end of each week might be described as an FI schedule, and that description might be the basis of interpreting an acceleration in productive work as the week progresses. Malott et al. suggested, however, that such an identification would be misleading. For one thing, the receipt of the paycheck is not contingent on the first episode of productive work that occurs after the end of the interval. For another thing, external cues are available that signal the passage of time. Finally, other contingencies are most likely in effect to provide more immediate consequences for various aspects of productive work. We agree completely with the thrust of Malott and colleagues' caution for this particular example and in general. It may be worth noting, however, that deciding what everyday situations might be analogous to particular schedules of reinforcement in the laboratory depends on one's view about what the critical aspects of the schedules are and what aspects of behavior are most useful to attend to.

Procrastination under FR Schedules

Under fixed-ratio (FR) schedules, a response is reinforced only after a specified number of prior unreinforced responses have been emitted. With animals under FR schedules the subject pauses for a period of time after each reinforcement and then responds at a high and fairly constant rate until the next reinforcement. Moreover, the duration of the pause varies from one reinforcer to the next, but its average value increases as a function of the FR size (Felton & Lyon, 1966).

The pause seems counterproductive on a commonsense view of what would be most adaptive or rational. Because the reinforcer depends on completing the fixed number of required responses, the reinforcer will come most quickly if the subject emits those responses as quickly as possible. Any pausing delays the reinforcer and does not diminish the remaining work to be done. In this sense, the pause seems similar to procrastination.

What aspect of the FR schedule might be responsible for this relation? It turns out that the repetition of N brief identical responses is unimportant. The relation is similar (although perhaps not identical) if the schedule is changed so that the first response changes the prevailing stimulus (e.g., turns on a light) and then the reinforcer is delivered after a time interval elapses that approximates the time usually taken to complete the FR (see Grossbard & Mazur, 1986; Shull, 1979). The pause, then, might exemplify a more general principle that behavior tends to be weak at relatively early points in a chain (see Fantino, 1977; Kelleher & Gollub, 1962).

The FR schedule was originally defined in terms of the intermittent reinforcement of identical members of a response class. But that property may be only incidental to the general effect that the relative distance to the end of a chain has on the disposition to initiate responding. Research seeking general principles might be more successful if the focus is on the relation between disposition to initiate a chain and the length of the chain rather than on the rate and temporal pattern of the intermittently reinforced response.

Relative Resistance to Change

Suppose responding is maintained under two different VI schedules, each correlated with a different stimulus. The stimuli, and their correlated schedules, alternate every minute or so throughout the session (i.e., the schedule is a multiple VI VI schedule). Now suppose that conditions are introduced or changed that will tend to reduce the rate of responding in the presence of both stimuli. Such conditions might include satiating the subject so that the maintaining reinforcer is no longer effective, withholding the reinforcer (i.e., extinction), or introducing a stimulus that previously has signaled unavoidable shock. Such conditions will cause response rates to decline, and the rapidity and extent of the decline is a potentially important property of behavior.

Resistance-to-change functions have proven to be most orderly and general when response rates recorded during the change operation are expressed as proportions of each response's baseline rate (Nevin, 1974, 1988). That is, how much does the response rate decline relative to its initial, or baseline, value? One factor that determines a response's resistance to change is the rate at which the response was reinforced in the presence of its stimulus during baseline training. The higher the rate of reinforcement, the more resistant the response's rate is to the decremental effects of the change operation. (Studies of this effect commonly use VI schedules because such schedules effectively control the reinforcement rate; that is, the rate of reinforcement is kept close to that specified by the VI schedule despite fluctuations in response rate.)

Different baseline response rates can be produced by requiring different response units in the presence of the stimuli (e.g., by requiring pauses of different durations before the reinforced response). In absolute terms the resistance-to-change functions for the different response units differ even if the rate of reinforcement is the same. But if the resistance-to-change functions are expressed relative to baseline response rates, a remarkable invariance emerges. The functions are the same, provided the rate of reinforcement during baseline was the same, regardless of the response unit. Thus, relative resistance to change appears to be an orderly function of the baseline rate of reinforcement independent of the response unit (see Nevin, 1988; but see Lattal, 1989, for some contrary evidence).

It may be possible, then, to investigate the factors determining resistance to change (or persistence) without having to be much concerned about the response unit. There is evidence, for example, that the persistence of operant behavior in a particular stimulus setting depends more on the relative rate of reinforcement received in that setting than on the relative rate of reinforcement for the particular response. That is, persistence seems to depend more on stimulus–reinforcer (i.e., Pavlovian) contingencies than on operant contingencies (see Nevin, 1992, 1996; Nevin, Tota, Torquato, & Shull, 1990). The effect of schedule on persistence, then, does not seem to depend critically on the behavioral unit or on dimensions of the schedules that are based on the intermittent-reinforcement conception.

Most of the relevant research has been conducted with animal subjects. There has, however, been some research with human subjects, and the results are at least suggestive that these determinants of persistence might generalize to humans (Mace, 1994; Mace et al., 1990; Tota-Faucette, 1991). It may be worthwhile, nonetheless, to consider more fully the possible influence of verbal and other complicating variables of the sort discussed above.

The Modulating Effects of Schedules

An important effect of schedules of reinforcement is that they determine, or modulate, the effects that other variables have on behavior. The effects of drugs, deprivation, emotional operations, or the presentation of stimuli can be different depending on the schedule of reinforcement maintaining the behavior. For example, the effect that an electric shock has on behavior depends on the behavioral baseline, which, in turn, depends on the current and previously operative schedules of reinforcement. Under some arrangements, shock can even appear to function as reinforcement (see Guthrie, 1963; Morse & Kelleher, 1970). The powerful role of behavioral context led Morse and Kelleher (1970) to speak of schedules as "fundamental determinants of behavior."

Psychologists have long known that the behavioral (or psychological) context can determine the effects of other variables (e.g., Guthrie, 1963; Hefferline, 1962; Kuo, 1967; Schoenfeld, 1971, 1972; Smith, 1967). For example, reaction times to the same physical stimulus differ depending on whether the person has received a ready signal. The concept of "attentional set" acknowledges that and related facts. The instructions or ready signal often do not appear to evoke phasic instances of behavior, but rather produce a tonic adjustment that alters the disposition to react to other events when they occur (Davis, 1957; Hefferline, 1962). It may be that the modulating effects of schedules can be viewed as analogues of phenomena like those classed as "set."

If so, it might prove useful to reconceptualize schedules in ways that are less tied to intermittent reinforcement of a discrete response. The modulating effects of schedules of reinforcement might be viewed as special cases of more general relations involving the modulating effects of behavioral baselines (perhaps viewed as tonic adjustments affecting dispositions). Schedules as usually conceptualized might or might not provide the most useful experimental preparation for research relevant to the topic.

Adjunctive Dispositions

Schedules of reinforcement can alter the disposition to engage in behavior and obtain reinforcers that are not specified by the contingency. For example, a food-deprived rat given a food pellet every 60 s will drink water after most pellets. Over the course of a session, the amount of water drunk can be enormous—as much as a third of the rat's body weight in a 3-hr session (Falk, 1971, 1977).

Other examples of schedule-induced behavior (also called *adjunctive* or *interim behavior*) have been observed. For example, pigeons will attack another pigeon or a mirror reflection; and rats will run in a wheel or gnaw a wood block (for reviews see Falk, 1971, 1977, 1981, 1986; Killeen, 1975; Segal, 1972; Staddon, 1977; Staddon & Simmelhag, 1971; Thompson & Lubinski, 1986; Wetherington, 1982).

The intermittent delivery of the food pellet does not simply induce adjunctive activity; it makes the opportunity to engage in the adjunctive activity momentarily effective as a reinforcer (Falk, 1966; Herrnstein, 1977; Staddon, 1977; see Michael, 1993a). That is, the scheduled pellet induces a short-duration motivational state. For example, one can make access to water contingent on pressing a lever. Because the rat is not water-deprived, it normally will not often press the lever. But for a short time after receiving the scheduled food pellet, the rat will press the lever at a high rate (Falk, 1966). The opportunity to run in a wheel or gnaw a block of wood can be made momentarily effective as a reinforcer the same way (Reid, Bacha, & Moran, 1993).

A variety of schedules seem capable of generating adjunctive behavior (Falk, 1971; Staddon, 1977). For example, such behavior is likely during the initial pause under FR schedules. But it is also likely when the scheduled reinforcer is delivered independently of responding after fixed or variable intervals of time. Thus, the intermittent reinforcement of a discrete response is an unimportant property of schedules for generating adjunctive behavior.

The intermittency of reinforcement in time, however, is important. If the inducing reinforcer (e.g., the pellet) is presented either very frequently or very infrequently, little adjunctive behavior occurs. The largest amount of adjunctive behavior per reinforcer occurs when the level of intermittency is intermediate (Falk, 1977; Flory, 1971).

It is also critical that the inducing reinforcer be a potent one. If, for example, the level of food deprivation is mild, the food-delivery schedule will induce little adjunctive drinking (Falk, 1971, 1977; Staddon, 1977).

Falk (1977) took the bitonic (inverted-V) function between the amount of adjunctive behavior and the average time between the inducing reinforcers as fundamental. He argued that intermittent reinforcement generates conflicting dispositions: to stay because significant reinforcers are delivered and to leave because the intermittency itself is aversive. Adjunctive behavior is most likely, Falk suggested, when these dispositions are in approximate balance so that neither wins out. In that respect, he noted, adjunctive behavior is like displacement activities studied by ethologists, activities that are thought to function to keep the organism in a situation until circumstances change so as to resolve the conflict one way or the other. The dispositions are most nearly in balance when the level of intermittency is intermediate, and so the level of adjunctive behavior is greatest. (Staddon and Simmelhag, 1971, offered an account of adjunctive behavior that is different in detail and based on different analyses of the data but that is similar in interpreting adjunctive behavior as the result of conflicting dispositions to stay and leave. A different account—one based on arousal induced by the scheduled reinforcer—is summarized by Killeen, 1975.)

Falk (1977, 1981, 1986, 1994) suggested that certain rituals and obsessive-like behavior (e.g., smoking cigarettes, drinking at a cocktail party, straightening one's desk at the start of writing a paper) might be instances of adjunctive behavior. Although there have been experimental demonstrations of schedule-induced behavior with human subjects, the phenomenon has not been explored extensively (Falk, 1994).

Feedback Functions

Schedules of reinforcement are usually conceptualized in terms of the intermittent reinforcement of a brief, discrete response. But there are some important everyday examples of reinforcement schedules that do not easily fit the intermittent-reinforcement scheme. Alternative conceptualization of reinforcement schedules might prove useful in such cases. One such alternative is to represent reinforcement schedules as continuous feedback functions. That is, some dimension of reinforcement (e.g., its amount, immediacy, or rate) varies as a continuous function of some dimension of a response (e.g., its force, speed, or rate). For example, the faster one walks, the sooner one gets to one's destination. The more loudly one complains, the greater the attention one may receive. Variations in the way one chews food or sips wine produce corresponding variations in the sensory impact of the stimuli for taste. Such feedback functions may play an important role in shaping and refining skilled performances (Malott et al., 1997, pp. 137–139; see also discussions of what are sometimes called *conjugate schedules* [e.g., Lindsley, 1957; Rovee-Collier & Capatides, 1979]).

Predicting the results of such schedules involves, first, specifying the feedback function, which, in turn, requires identifying the relevant dimensions of behavior and of the reinforcer. That is, one needs to know what dimensions of the reinforcer matter. And one needs to know what values along the reinforcer dimensions will be produced by particular values along the dimension of responding. For example, one might propose (perhaps on the basis of prior research) that the rate of the reinforcer is a critical dimension of reinforcement. One would then determine for the particular schedule, what rates of reinforcement will be produced by different rates or patterns of responding. Specifying the feedback function is often not a simple task (e.g., Baum, 1992). Additionally, responding may incur a cost that will need to be taken into account (Allison, 1993; Baum, 1973). Walking faster, for example, may get you to your destination sooner, but it will also generate more fatigue and perspiration.

The feedback function is strictly a description of the environment (i.e., of the schedule). That is, it specifies what will occur if a certain value of responding occurs. The next step in the analysis, then, is to determine what effect the occurrence of different values of the reinforcer will have on the future occurrence of responding. This relation is the behavior function.

The resulting behavior is thus conceptualized as the product of two functions, one specifying what reinforcer values are produced by behavior and the other specifying how those reinforcer values affect future responding. Behavior, in other words, is treated as an equilibrium solution. Mathematical and graphical techniques are available to derive such solutions (Allison, 1993; Baum, 1973, 1989; Logan, 1960; McDowell & Wixted, 1986; Shull, 1991).

Conventional intermittent schedules of reinforcement can be reconceptualized as feedback functions. Interval and ratio schedules are particularly interesting, in this view, because they represent extreme cases of feedback functions. Under ratio schedules, the rate of reinforcement is directly proportional to the rate of responding; under interval schedules the rate of reinforcement is to a large degree independent of the rate of responding. They thus exemplify the more general case in which the reinforcement one receives either does or does not depend closely on what one does (Baum, 1992). That response rate is higher under ratio than under interval schedules is consistent with this view. But whether, or to what extent, such feedback functions actually influence behavior under interval and ratio schedules remains an important but unresolved and controversial issue (e.g., Galbicka et al., 1993; Mazur, 1981; Rachlin, Battalio, Kagel, & Green, 1981; Vaughan & Miller, 1984; Williams, 1988).

CONCLUSION

It seems self-evident that the behavior of humans is sensitive to its consequences, that is, to contingencies of reinforcement. One goal of research is to clarify the nature of this sensitivity.

The phrase, *sensitivity of behavior to contingencies,* can mean different things, and the *sensitivity* referred to can arise for different reasons. Sensitivity could be taken to imply detection or discrimination, as when one speaks of someone being very sensitive to the taste qualities of wine or to the tonal quality of the violins in an orchestra. Usually when one speaks of the sensitivity of behavior to contingencies, however, one is using the term less restrictively. One means simply that some aspect of behavior varies as a function of some aspect (or aspects) of the contingency. Insensitivity in that sense means simply that the aspect of behavior does not vary as a function of variations in the contingency. A high degree of sensitivity, then, means that relatively small changes in the contingency produce large changes in behavior. There is no implication one way or the other that discrimination or detection of the contingency is involved.

Different kinds of processes can result in sensitivity to contingencies of reinforcement. First, the consequences of behavior can have a direct strengthening or weakening effect on the behavior that they follow, that is, a genuine reinforcement (or punishment) effect (see Williams, 1988). Changing the contingencies could also directly affect behavior by changing the response units, by changing the potency of the reinforcer, and by changing the contingent relationship between aspects of behavior and the consequences.

Second, the consequences of behavior or the behavior–consequence contingencies per se can function as cues or as discriminative stimuli. For example, receipt of a reinforcer at one time (perhaps in a particular relation to preceding behavior) can come to signal what contingencies are next in effect. To take a simple example, imagine that some consequence will be delivered according to a VR schedule for pressing one of two buttons. Imagine, further, that the "hot" button is determined randomly at the start of each block of trials but that there is no obvious signal indicating which one is hot. There is, however, a nonobvious signal, namely, the occurrence of the consequence following a press on a particular button (a win–stay contingency). The subject might sample both buttons at the beginning of a session and then stick with whichever button paid off. These results might look like a pure reinforcement effect (persisting in the behavior that produced the reinforcer), but an important controlling variable may be the history in which response-outcome events have signaled subsequent response-outcome events (i.e., a history with three-term contingencies). That is, the behavioral adjustment reflecting sensitivity to contingencies may be based at least partly on discriminative control by contingency events functioning as discriminative stimuli. The reinforcing and discriminative roles could be demonstrated by having a response-outcome event on one button signal that the next reinforcer will occur for pressing the other button (win–shift contingency). More generally, correlates of contingencies can function as discriminative stimuli for additional behavior that may or may not be efficient but that may, nevertheless, vary in accordance with the contingencies.

Third, sensitivity to contingencies can be mediated by verbal rules, instructions, strategies, hypotheses, and so forth. That is, contact with the contingencies or aspects of the task can evoke constructing rules, visualizing aspects of the task, and other complex behavioral phenomena both covert and overt. Such behavior can, in turn, evoke additional verbal and nonverbal behavior including the behavior that is measured in the experimental task. Accounting for the sensitivity of behavior on such tasks, then, would require accounting for at least two intervening links: the relationship between aspects of the task and the complex behavior (i.e., the rules, strategies, and so forth) and the relationship between that behavior and the behavior measured in the experiment. Such accounts will almost certainly need to point to social/verbal histories prior to the experiment.

Each of these sources of sensitivity to contingencies is significant for human functioning. But the third type may be the basis of what is most distinctively human. Some years ago, Keller and Schoenfeld (1950, pp. 368–370) expressed the matter this way:

> Of great importance to the formation of personality, is the fact that human beings can discriminate their own actions, appearance, feelings, and successfulness. In the course of growing up, the child comes to 'know' about himself; he becomes at least partially 'aware' of his capacities and weaknesses, his likelihood of winning or losing in given situations, his physical and social attractiveness, his characteristic reactions. This is sometimes spoken of as the development or emergence of the "Self," a word that is meant to designate the ability to speak of (be "aware" of) one's own behavior, or the ability to use one's own behavior as the S^D for further behavior, verbal or otherwise. . . . [Those events] are made discriminative for him by his social community, as it teaches him his language. . . . [A] person possessing no verbal behavior of any sort would not have a "Self," or any 'consciousness.' His reactions to the world would be like those of any animal. . . . He would go after positive reinforcements, and would avoid negative reinforcements, but would do so directly, without "reflection."

There is an implication: If one is to study pure reinforcement effects with human subjects, one will need somehow to eliminate the "Self," that is, eliminate the effects of the relevant social/verbal contingencies in the subject's history. Obviously, this is not a simple thing to do, and it is not surprising that the efforts have been viewed with some skepticism (e.g., Branch, 1991; Dinsmoor, 1991). Several approaches were described above. One can, for example, study the behavior of preverbal infants. Alternatively, one can study the behavior of adult humans but use a response that the adult cannot detect making. But even here, the adult human may be prompted to formulate hypotheses and engage in other complex behavior, especially if the task is identified as an experiment or game. And these activities may influence the measured responding even if the subject is unaware of them. The various concurrent responses of an organism are not, in reality, isolated independent systems even though we may treat them as such for analytic and experimental convenience (Hefferline, 1962; Kuo, 1967; Schoenfeld, 1971, 1972; Smith, 1967).

Acknowledging the probable role of verbal and other complex activities in experimental procedures with humans in no way implies a fundamental discontinuity in behavioral processes between humans and animals. Skinner, for example, did not disagree that humans function differently from other species in these respects. But he proposed that these very important complex activities and dispositions develop through processes that humans *do* share with other species (e.g., Skinner, 1953, 1957, 1969). He showed in detail how processes demonstrated experimentally with nonhuman animals could, in principle, account for much complex human functioning including verbal behavior and instruction-following. That is, he offered an *interpretation* of complex human behavior in terms of a small set of fundamental, general principles derived mostly from experimental work with animals (see also Donahoe & Palmer, 1994; Keller & Schoenfeld, 1950). Interpretation, when appropriately disciplined and principled, has played key roles in the development of behavioral and other sciences (Donahoe & Palmer, 1994; Palmer & Donahoe, 1991; Skinner, 1957, 1960).

One can, of course, study the sensitivity of human behavior to variations in contingencies without regard for whether the processes are the same as or different from those operating with animals under formally similar schedules. One can be interested, for example, in how the verbal and nonverbal behavior of humans adjusts to certain types of contingencies that are prominent in the normal environment. To investigate such adjustments one need not feel constrained to use experimental preparations that resemble those designed for research with animals to reveal the fundamental effects of reinforcement and other independent variables on the likelihood of operant behavior. Those preparations were developed to address a particular set of experimental questions (see section Skinner's Experimental Preparation), and it would be a remarkable coincidence if they were optimal for addressing different kinds of questions.

For example, one might be interested in analyses of problem solving or remembering. Research on these topics, much of which has been conducted by nonbehavioral researchers, has addressed such questions as how various kinds of experiences, measurable individual characteristics, or aspects of the task influence success. Mediating rules, strategies, or hypotheses are sometimes inferred from patterns of performance, from verbal protocols, or both. From the perspective of behavior analysis, such research falls under the rubrics of complex stimulus control, instructional control, and complex behavioral units. Experimental and analytical techniques for such phenomena are described elsewhere in this book.

At the beginning of this chapter we summarized two cautionary themes around which the chapter is organized. We end with a cautionary note of a different sort. Our working assumption has been that the strengthening effects of reinforcement reflect a relatively primitive process. Discriminations based on subtle features of the schedule and verbal-like phenomena are viewed, then, as complicating factors if the goal is to study reinforcement in its most elementary form. It may be worthwhile remembering, however, that the empirical-based principle of reinforcement is silent about the processes that are responsible for the reinforcement effect, and, in fact, those processes might be rather complicated and rich in potential. Indeed, there is a long and venerable tradition of theorizing in which phenomena that are aptly described as cognitive are assumed to be evoked by and developed through contact with contingencies. In some accounts, these phenomena are critical, fundamental parts of the effects of contingencies (see Colwill, 1994; Tolman & Krechevsky, 1933; Williams, 1983, 1997). The present chapter would have had a different thrust if it had been written from the perspective of such theories.

ACKNOWLEDGMENT. Preparation of this chapter was supported, in part, by NSF Grant IBN-9511934 to UNCG.

REFERENCES

Allison, J. (1993). Response deprivation, reinforcement, and economics. *Journal of the Experimental Analysis of Behavior, 60,* 105–128.

Anger, D. (1956). The dependence of interresponse times upon the relative reinforcement of different interresponse times. *Journal of Experimental Psychology, 52,* 145–161.

Arbuckle, J. L., & Lattal, K. A. (1988). Changes in functional response units with briefly delayed reinforcement. *Journal of the Experimental Analysis of Behavior, 49,* 249–263.

Azrin, N. H., Hutchinson, R. R., & Hake, D. F. (1966). Extinction-produced aggression. *Journal of the Experimental Analysis of Behavior, 9,* 191–204.

Baron, A., Perone, M., & Galizio, M. (1991). Analyzing the reinforcement process at the human level: Can application and behavioristic interpretation replace laboratory research? *The Behavior Analyst, 14,* 95–105.

Baum, W. (1973). The correlation-based law of effect. *Journal of the Experimental Analysis of Behavior, 20,* 137–153.

Baum, W. M. (1989). Quantitative prediction and molar description of the environment. *The Behavior Analyst, 12,* 167–176.

Baum, W. M. (1992). In search of the feedback function for variable-interval schedules. *Journal of the Experimental Analysis of Behavior, 57,* 365–375.

Baxter, G. A., & Schlinger, H. (1990). Performance of children under a multiple random-ratio random-interval schedule of reinforcement. *Journal of the Experimental Analysis of Behavior, 54,* 263–271.

Bernstein, D. J. (1987). A volume in honor of Kenneth MacCorquodale: A review of *Analysis and Integration of Behavioral Units. The Behavior Analyst, 10,* 89–94.

Bernstein, D. J. (1988). Laboratory lore and research practices in the experimental analysis of human behavior: Designing session logistics—how long, how often, how many? *The Behavior Analyst, 11,* 51–58.

Bernstein, D. J., & Ebbesen, E. (1978). Reinforcement and substitution in humans. *Journal of the Experimental Analysis of Behavior, 30,* 243–253.

Bernstein, D. J., & Michael, R. L. (1990). The utility of verbal and behavioral assessment of value. *Journal of the Experimental Analysis of Behavior, 54,* 173–184.

Bitterman, M. E. (1960). Toward a comparative psychology of learning. *American Psychologist, 15,* 704–712.

Branch, M. N. (1991). On the difficulty of studying "basic" behavioral processes in humans. *The Behavior Analyst, 14,* 107–110.

Case, D. A., Ploog, B. O., & Fantino, E. (1990). Observing behavior in a computer game. *Journal of the Experimental Analysis of Behavior, 54,* 185–199.

Catania, A. C. (1971). Reinforcement schedules: The role of responses preceding the one that produces the reinforcer. *Journal of the Experimental Analysis of Behavior, 15,* 271–287.

Catania, A. C. (1973). The concept of the operant in the analysis of behavior. *Behaviorism, 1,* 103–116.

Catania, A. C., Matthews, B. A., & Shimoff, E. (1982). Instructed versus shaped human verbal behavior: Interactions with nonverbal responding. *Journal of the Experimental Analysis of Behavior, 38,* 233–248.

Catania, A. C., Matthews, B. A., & Shimoff, E. (1990). Properties of rule-governed behavior and their implications. In D. E. Blackman & H. Lejeune (Eds.), *Behavior analysis in theory and practice: Contributions and controversies* (pp. 215–230). Hillsdale, NJ: Erlbaum.

Catania, A. C., Matthews, B. A., Silverman, P. J., & Yohalem, R. (1977). Yoked variable-ratio and variable-interval responding in pigeons. *Journal of the Experimental Analysis of Behavior, 28,* 155–161.

Catania, A. C., & Reynolds, G. S. (1968). A quantitative analysis of the responding maintained by interval schedules of reinforcement. *Journal of the Experimental Analysis of Behavior, 11*, 327–383.

Cerutti, D. T. (1989). Discrimination theory of rule-governed behavior. *Journal of the Experimental Analysis of Behavior, 51*, 259–276.

Colwill, R. M. (1994). Associative representation of instrumental contingencies. In D. L. Medin (Ed.), *The psychology of learning and motivation: Advances in research and theory. Vol. 31* (pp. 1–72). New York: Academic Press.

Creed, T. L., & Ferster, C. B. (1972). Space as a reinforcer in a continuous free-operant environment. *Psychological Record, 22*, 161–167.

Critchfield, T. S., & Perone, M. (1993). Verbal self-reports about matching to sample: Effects of the number of elements in a compound sample stimulus. *Journal of the Experimental Analysis of Behavior, 59*, 193–214.

Davis, H., Memmott, J., & Hurwitz, H. M. B. (1975). Autocontingencies: A model for subtle behavioral control. *Journal of Experimental Psychology: General, 104*, 169–188.

Davis, R. C. (1957). Response patterns. *Transactions of the New York Academy of Science* (Ser II), *19*, 731–739.

Dews, P. B. (1970). The theory of fixed-interval responding. In W. N. Schoenfeld (Ed.), *The theory of reinforcement schedules* (pp. 43–61). New York: Appleton–Century–Crofts.

Dinsmoore, J. A. (1983). Observing and conditioned reinforcement. *Behavioral and Brain Sciences, 6*, 693–728 (includes commentary).

Dinsmoore, J. A. (1991). The respective roles of human and nonhuman subjects in behavioral research. *The Behavior Analyst, 14*, 117–121.

Donahoe, J. W., & Palmer, D. C. (1994). *Learning and complex behavior.* Boston: Allyn & Bacon.

Dougan, J. D., Kuh, J. A., & Vink, K. L. (1993). Session duration and the VI response function: Within-session prospective and retroactive effects. *Journal of the Experimental Analysis of Behavior, 60*, 543–557.

Dunham, P. (1977). The nature of reinforcing stimuli. In W. K. Honig & J. E. R. Staddon (Eds.), *Handbook of operant behavior* (pp. 98–124). Englewood Cliffs, NJ: Prentice–Hall.

Falk, J. L. (1966). The motivational properties of schedule-induced polydipsia. *Journal of the Experimental Analysis of Behavior, 9*, 19–25.

Falk, J. L. (1971). The nature and determinants of adjunctive behavior. *Physiology and Behavior, 6*, 577–588.

Falk, J. L. (1977). The origin and functions of adjunctive behavior. *Animal Learning and Behavior, 5*, 325–335.

Falk, J. L. (1981). The environmental generation of excessive behavior. In S. J. Mule (Ed.), *Behavior is excess: An examination of the volitional disorders* (pp. 313–337). New York: Free Press.

Falk, J. L. (1986). The formation and function of ritual behavior. In T. Thompson & M. D. Zeiler (Eds.), *Analysis and integration of behavioral units* (pp. 335–355). Hillsdale, NJ: Erlbaum.

Falk, J. L. (1994). Schedule-induced behavior occurs in humans: A reply to Overskeid. *Psychological Record, 44*, 45–62.

Fantino, E. (1977). Conditioned reinforcement: Choice and information. In W. K. Honig & J. E. R. Staddon (Eds.), *Handbook of operant behavior* (pp. 313–339). Englewood Cliffs, NJ: Prentice–Hall.

Felton, M., & Lyon, D. O. (1966). The post-reinforcement pause. *Journal of the Experimental Analysis of Behavior, 9*, 131–134.

Ferster, C. B., & Skinner, B. F. (1957). *Schedules of reinforcement.* New York: Appleton–Century–Crofts.

Flory, R. K. (1971). The control of schedule-induced polydipsia: Frequency and magnitude of reinforcement. *Learning and Motivation, 2*, 215–227.

Galbicka, G., Kautz, M. A., & Jagers, T. (1993). Response acquisition under targeted percentile schedules: A continuing quandary for molar models of operant behavior. *Journal of the Experimental Analysis of Behavior, 60*, 171–184.

Galizio, M., & Buskist, W. (1988). Laboratory lore and research practices in the experimental analysis of human behavior: Selecting reinforcers and arranging contingencies. *The Behavior Analyst, 11*, 65–69.

Gibbon, J. (1977). Scalar expectancy theory and Weber's law in animal timing. *Psychological Review, 84*, 279–325.

Gibbon, J., & Church, R. M. (1992). Comparison of variance and covariance patterns in parallel and serial theories of timing. *Journal of the Experimental Analysis Behavior, 57,* 393–406.

Gollub, L. (1977). Conditioned reinforcement: Schedule effects. In W. K. Honig & J. E. R. Staddon (Eds.), *Handbook of operant behavior* (pp. 288–312). Englewood Cliffs, NJ: Prentice–Hall.

Grossbard, C. L., & Mazur, J. E. (1986). A comparison of delays and ratio requirements in self-control choice. *Journal of the Experimental Analysis of Behavior, 45,* 305–315.

Guthrie, E. R. (1940). Association and the law of effect. *Psychological Review, 47,* 127–148.

Guthrie, E. R. (1963). Association by contiguity. In S. Koch (Ed.), *Psychology: A study of a science: Vol. 2. General systematic formulations, learning, and special processes* (pp. 158–195). New York: Mc-Graw–Hill.

Hackenberg, T. D., & Axtell, S. A. M. (1993). Humans' choices in situations of time-based diminishing returns. *Journal of the Experimental Analysis of Behavior, 59,* 445–470.

Harris, M. (1974). *Cows, pigs, wars, and witches: The riddles of culture.* New York: Random House.

Hayes, S. C. (1986). The case of the silent dog—Verbal reports and the analysis of rules: A review of Ericsson and Simon's *Protocol Analysis: Verbal Reports as Data. Journal of the Experimental Analysis of Behavior, 45,* 351–363.

Hefferline, R. F. (1962). Learning theory and clinical psychology—An eventual symbiosis? In A. J. Bachrach (Ed.), *Experimental foundations of clinical psychology* (pp. 97–138). New York: Basic Books.

Hefferline, R. F., Keenan, B., & Harford, R. A. (1959). Escape and avoidance conditioning without their observation of the response. *Science, 130,* 1338–1339.

Herrnstein, R. J. (1977). The evolution of behaviorism. *American Psychologist, 32,* 593–603.

Hineline, P. N. (1981). The several roles of stimuli in negative reinforcement. In P. Harzem & M. D. Zeiler (Eds.), *Predictability, correlation, and contiguity* (pp. 203–246). New York: Wiley.

Hineline, P. N., & Wanchisen, B. A. (1989). Correlated hypothesizing and the distinction between contingency-shaped and rule-governed behavior. In S. C. Hayes (Ed.), *Rule-governed behavior: Cognition, contingencies, and instructional control* (pp. 221–268). New York: Plenum Press.

Hyten, C., & Madden, G. J. (1993). The scallop in human fixed-interval research: A review of problems with data description. *Psychological Record, 43,* 471–500.

Iversen, I. H. (1993). Techniques for establishing schedules with wheel running as reinforcement in rats. *Journal of the Experimental Analysis of Behavior, 60,* 219–238.

Iwata, B. A., Pace, G. M., Kalsher, M. J., Cowdery, G. E., & Cataldo, M. F. (1990). Experimental analysis and extinction of self-injurious escape behavior. *Journal of Applied Behavior Analysis, 23,* 11–27.

Jackson, K., & Hackenberg, T. D. (1996). Token reinforcement, choice, and self-control in pigeons. *Journal of the Experimental Analysis of Behavior, 66,* 29–49.

Jacobs, E. A., & Hackenberg, T. D. (1996). Humans' choices in situations of time-based diminishing returns: Effects of fixed-interval duration and progressive-interval step size. *Journal of the Experimental Analysis of Behavior, 65,* 5–19.

Jenkins, H. M. (1970). Sequential organization in schedules of reinforcement. In W. N. Schoenfeld (Ed.), *The theory of reinforcement schedules* (pp. 63–109). New York: Appleton–Century–Crofts.

Kelleher, R. T., & Gollub, L. R. (1962). A review of positive conditioned reinforcement. *Journal of the Experimental Analysis of Behavior, 5,* 543–597.

Keller, F. S., & Schoenfeld, W. N. (1950). *Principles of psychology: A systematic text in the science of behavior.* New York: Appleton–Century–Crofts.

Killeen, P. (1975). On the temporal control of behavior. *Psychological Review, 82,* 89–115.

Killeen, P. R. (1978). Stability criteria. *Journal of the Experimental Analysis of Behavior, 29,* 17–25.

Killeen, P. R. (1994). Mathematical principles of reinforcement. *Behavioral and Brain Sciences, 17,* 105–172 (with peer commentary).

Killeen, P., & Fetterman, G. (1988). A behavioral theory of timing. *Psychological Review, 95,* 274–295.

Kuo, Z.-Y. (1967). *The dynamics of behavior development: An epigenetic view.* New York: Random House.

Laties, V. G., & Weiss, B. (1963). Effects of a concurrent task on fixed-interval responding in humans. *Journal of the Experimental Analysis of Behavior, 6,* 431–436.

Lattal, K. A. (1989). Contingencies on response rate and resistance to change. *Learning and Motivation, 20,* 191–203.

Lattal, K. A. (1991). Scheduling positive reinforcers. In I. H. Iversen & K. A. Lattal (Eds.), *Techniques in the behavioral and neural sciences: Vol. 6. Experimental analysis of behavior, Part 1* (pp. 87–171). Amsterdam: Elsevier.

Lattal, K. A. (1995). Contingency and behavior analysis. *Mexican Journal of Behavior Analysis, 21,* 47–73.

Levine, M. (1971). Hypothesis theory and nonlearning despite ideal S-R-reinforcement contingencies. *Psychological Review, 78,* 130–140.

Lindsley, O. R. (1957). Operant behavior during sleep: A measure of depth of sleep. *Science, 126,* 1290–1291.

Logan, F. A. (1960). *Incentive: How the conditions of reinforcement affect the performance of rats.* New Haven, CT: Yale University Press.

Logue, A. W. (1991). *The psychology of eating and drinking* (2nd ed.). San Francisco: Freeman.

Lowe, C. F. (1979). Determinants of human operant behavior. In M. D. Zeiler & P. Harzem (Eds.), *Advances in analysis of behaviour: Vol. 1. Reinforcement and the organization of behaviour* (pp. 159–192). New York: Wiley.

Lowe, C. F., Beasty, A., & Bentall, R. P. (1983). The role of verbal behavior in human learning: Infant performance on fixed-interval schedules. *Journal of the Experimental Analysis of Behavior, 39,* 157–164.

Lubinski, D., & Thompson, T. (1993). Species and individual differences in communication based on private states. *Behavioral and Brain Sciences, 16,* 627–680 (includes commentaries).

Mace, F. C. (1994). Basic research needed for stimulating the development of behavioral technologies. *Journal of the Experimental Analysis of Behavior, 61,* 529–550.

Mace, F. C., Lalli, J. S., Shea, M. C., Lalli, E. P., West, B. J., Roberts, M., & Nevin, J. A. (1990). The momentum of human behavior in a natural setting. *Journal of the Experimental Analysis of Behavior, 54,* 163–172.

Malott, R. W., Whaley, D. L., & Malott, M. E. (1997). *Elementary principles of behavior* (3rd ed.). Englewood Cliffs, NJ: Prentice–Hall.

Marr, M. J. (1979). Second-order schedules and the generation of unitary response sequences. In M. D. Zeiler & P. Harzem (Eds.), *Advances in analysis of behaviour: Vol. 1. Reinforcement and the organization of behaviour* (pp. 223–260). New York: Wiley.

Martin, G., & Pear, J. (1996). *Behavior modification: What it is and how to do it* (5th ed.). Englewood Cliffs, NJ: Prentice–Hall.

Matthews, B. A., Shimoff, E., Catania, A. C.,& Sagvolden, T. (1977). Uninstructed human responding: Sensitivity to ratio and interval contingencies. *Journal of the Experimental Analysis of Behavior, 27,* 453–467.

Mazur, J. E. (1981). Optimization theory fails to predict performance of pigeons in a two-response situation. *Science, 214,* 823–825.

Mazur, J. E., & Vaughan, W., Jr. (1987). Molar optimization versus delayed reinforcement as explanations of choice between fixed-ratio and progressive-ratio schedules. *Journal of the Experimental Analysis of Behavior, 48,* 251–261.

McDowell, J. J., & Wixted, J. T. (1986). Variable-ratio schedules as variable-interval schedules with linear feedback loops. *Journal of the Experimental Analysis of Behavior, 36,* 315–329.

McSweeney, F. K., & Roll, J. M. (1993). Responding changes systematically within sessions during conditioning procedures. *Journal of the Experimental Analysis of Behavior, 60,* 621–640.

Meehl, P. E. (1992). Needs (Murray, 1938) and state-variables (Skinner, 1938). *Psychological Reports, 70,* 407–450.

Michael, J. (1982). Distinguishing between discriminative and motivational functions of stimuli. *Journal of the Experimental Analysis of Behavior, 37,* 149–155.

Michael, J. (1993a). Establishing operations. *The Behavior Analyst, 16,* 191–206.

Michael, J. (1993b). *Concepts and principles of behavior analysis.* Kalamazoo, MI: Society for the Advancement of Behavior Analysis.

Morse, W. H. (1966). Intermittent reinforcement. In W. K. Honig (Ed.), *Operant behavior: Areas of research and application* (pp. 52–108). New York: Appleton–Century–Crofts.

Morse, W. H., & Kelleher, R. T. (1970). Schedules as fundamental determinants of behavior. In W. N. Schoenfeld (Ed.), *The theory of reinforcement schedules* (pp. 139–185). New York: Appleton–Century–Crofts.

Nevin, J. A. (1973). The maintenance of behavior. In J. A. Nevin & G. S. Reynolds (Eds.), *The study of behavior: Learning, motivation, emotion, and instinct* (pp. 200–236). Glenview, IL: Scott, Foresman.

Nevin, J. A. (1974). Response strength in multiple schedules. *Journal of the Experimental Analysis of Behavior, 21*, 389–408.

Nevin, J. A. (1984). Quantitative analysis. *Journal of the Experimental Analysis of Behavior, 42*, 421–434.

Nevin, J. A. (1988). Behavioral momentum and the partial reinforcement effect. *Psychological Bulletin, 103*, 44–56.

Nevin, J. A. (1992). An integrative model for the study of behavioral momentum. *Journal of the Experimental Analysis of Behavior, 57*, 301–316.

Nevin, J. A. (1996). The momentum of compliance. *Journal of the Experimental Analysis of Behavior, 29*, 535–547.

Nevin, J. A., Tota, M. E., Torquato, R. D., & Shull, R. L. (1990). Alternative reinforcement increases resistance to change: Pavlovian or operant contingencies? *Journal of the Experimental Analysis of Behavior, 53*, 359–379.

Nisbett, R. E., & Wilson, T. D. (1977). Telling more than we can know: Verbal reports on mental processes. *Psychological Review, 84*, 231–259.

Palmer, D. C., & Donahoe, J. W. (1991). Shared premises, different conclusions. *The Behavior Analyst, 14*, 123–127.

Perone, M. (1988). Laboratory lore and research practices in the experimental analysis of human behavior: Use and abuse of subject's verbal reports. *The Behavior Analyst, 11*, 71–75.

Perone, M., Galizio, M., & Baron, A. (1988). The relevance of animal-based principles in the laboratory study of human operant conditioning. In G. Davey & C. Cullen (Eds.), *Human operant conditioning and behavior modification* (pp. 59–85). New York: Wiley.

Pilgrim, C., & Johnston, J. M. (1988). Laboratory lore and research practices in the experimental analysis of human behavior: Issues in instructing subjects. *The Behavior Analyst, 11*, 59–64.

Premack, D. (1965). Reinforcement theory. In D. Levine (Ed.), *Nebraska symposium on motivation, 1965* (pp. 123–180). Lincoln: University of Nebraska Press.

Rachlin, H., Battalio, R., Kagel, J., & Green, L. (1981). Maximization theory in behavioral psychology. *Behavioral and Brain Sciences, 4*, 371–417 (includes peer commentary).

Ray, B. A., & Sidman, M. (1970). In W. N. Schoenfeld (Ed.), *The theory of reinforcement schedules* (pp. 187–214). New York: Appleton–Century–Crofts.

Reid, A. K., Bacha, G., & Moran, C. (1993). The temporal organization of behavior on periodic food schedules. *Journal of the Experimental Analysis of Behavior, 59*, 1–27.

Rosenfeld, H. M., & Baer, D. M. (1970). Unbiased and unnoticed verbal conditioning: The double agent robot procedure. *Journal of the Experimental Analysis of Behavior, 14*, 99–107.

Rovee-Collier, C. K., & Capatides, J. B. (1979). Positive behavioral contrast in 3-month-old infants on multiple conjugate reinforcement schedules. *Journal of the Experimental Analysis of Behavior, 32*, 15–27.

Schlinger, H. D., Jr. (1993). Separating discriminative and function-altering effects of verbal stimuli. *The Behavior Analyst, 16*, 9–23.

Schoenfeld, W. N. (1971). Conditioning the whole organism. *Conditional Reflex, 6*, 125–128.

Schoenfeld, W. N. (1972). Problems of modern behavior theory. *Conditional Reflex, 7*, 33–65.

Schoenfeld, W. N., & Farmer, J. (1970). Reinforcement schedules and the "behavior stream." In W. N. Schoenfeld (Ed.), *The theory of reinforcement schedules* (pp. 215–245). New York: Appleton–Century.

Segal, E. F. (1972). Induction and the provenance of operants. In R. M. Gilbert & J. R. Millenson (Eds.), *Reinforcement: Behavioral analysis* (pp. 1–34). New York: Academic Press.

Sheffield, F. D. (1966). New evidence on the drive-induction theory of reinforcement. In R. N. Haber (Ed.), *Current research in motivation* (pp. 111–122). New York: Holt, Rinehart, & Winston.

Shimoff, E., Matthews, B. A., & Catania, A. C. (1986). Human operant performance: Sensitivity and pseudosensitivity to contingencies. *Journal of the Experimental Analysis of Behavior, 46*, 149–157.

Shimp, C. P. (1975). Perspectives on the behavior unit: Choice behavior in animals. In W. K. Estes (Ed.), *Handbook of learning and cognitive processes: Vol. 2. Conditioning and behavior theory* (pp. 225–268). Hillsdale, NJ: Erlbaum.

Shimp, C. P. (1976). Organization in memory and behavior. *Journal of the Experimental Analysis of Behavior, 26,* 113–130.

Shull, R. L. (1979). The postreinforcement pause: Some implications for the correlational law of effect. In M. D. Zeiler & P. Harzem (Eds.), *Advances in analysis of behaviour: Vol. 1. Reinforcement and the organization of behaviour* (pp. 193–221). New York: Wiley.

Shull, R. L. (1991). Mathematical description of operant behavior: An introduction. In I. H. Iversen & K. A. Lattal (Eds.), *Techniques in the behavioral and neural sciences: Vol. 6. Experimental analysis of behavior. Part 2* (pp. 243–282). Amsterdam: Elsevier.

Sidman, M. (1960). *Tactics of scientific research.* New York: Basic Books.

Sidman, M. (1989). *Coercion and its fallout.* Cambridge, MA: Authors Cooperative.

Sidman, M. (1990). *Tactics:* In reply. *The Behavior Analyst, 13,* 187–197.

Skinner, B. F. (1938). *The behavior of organism: An experimental analysis.* New York: Appleton–Century–Crofts.

Skinner, B. F. (1953). *Science and human behavior.* New York: Macmillan Co.

Skinner, B. F. (1957). *Verbal behavior.* New York: Appleton–Century–Crofts.

Skinner, B. F. (1960). Concept-formation in philosophy and psychology. In S. Hook (Ed.), *Dimensions of mind: A symposium* (pp. 204–207). New York: Collier.

Skinner, B. F. (1969). An operant analysis of problem solving. In B. F. Skinner, *Contingencies of reinforcement* (pp. 133–171). New York: Appleton–Century–Crofts.

Smith, K. (1967). Conditioning as an artifact. In G. A. Kimble (Ed.), *Foundations of conditioning and learning* (pp. 100–111). New York: Appleton–Century–Crofts. (Original work published 1954)

Staddon, J. E. R. (1977). Schedule-induced behavior. In W. K. Honig & J. E. R. Staddon (Eds.), *Handbook of operant behavior* (pp. 125–152). Englewood Cliffs, NJ: Prentice–Hall.

Staddon, J. E. R., & Simmelhag, V. L. (1971). The "superstition" experiment: A reexamination of its implications for the principles of adaptive behavior. *Psychological Review, 78,* 3–43.

Svartdal, F. (1992). Sensitivity to nonverbal operant contingencies: Do limited processing resources affect operant conditioning in humans? *Learning and Motivation, 23,* 383–405.

Svartdal, F. (1995). When feedback contingencies and rules compete: Testing a boundary condition for verbal control of instrumental performance. *Learning and Motivation, 26,* 221–238.

Thompson, T., & Lubinski, D. (1986). Units of analysis and kinetic structure of behavioral repertoires. *Journal of the Experimental Analysis of Behavior, 46,* 219–242.

Thompson, T., & Zeiler, M. D. (Eds.). (1986). *Analysis and integration of behavioral units.* Hillsdale, NJ: Erlbaum.

Timberlake, W. (1993). Behavior systems and reinforcement: An integrative approach. *Journal of the Experimental Analysis of Behavior, 60,* 105–128.

Tolman, E. C., & Krechevsky, I. (1933). Means-end-readiness and hypothesis—A contribution to comparative psychology. *Psychological Review, 40,* 60–70.

Tota-Faucette, M. E. (1991). *Alternative reinforcement and resistance to change.* Doctoral dissertation, University of North Carolina at Greensboro.

Vaughan, W., Jr. (1981). Melioration, matching, and maximizing. *Journal of the Experimental Analysis of Behavior, 36,* 141–149.

Vaughan, W., Jr., & Miller, H. L. (1984). Optimization versus response-strength accounts of behavior. *Journal of the Experimental Analysis of Behavior, 42,* 337–348.

Vollmer, T. R., & Iwata, B. A. (1991). Establishing operations and reinforcement effects. *Journal of Applied Behavior Analysis, 24,* 279–291.

Wanchisen, B. A., & Tatham, T. A. (1991). Behavioral history: A promising challenge in explaining and controlling human operant behavior. *The Behavior Analyst, 14,* 139–144.

Weiner, H. (1983). Some thoughts on discrepant human–animal performances under schedules of reinforcement. *Psychological Record, 33,* 521–532.

Wetherington, C. L. (1982). Is adjunctive behavior a third class of behavior? *Neuroscience and Biobehavioral Reviews, 6,* 329–350.

Williams, B. A. (1983). Revising the principle of reinforcement. *Behaviorism, 11,* 63–88.

Williams, B. A. (1988). Reinforcement, choice, and response strength. In R. C. Atkinson, R. J. Herrnstein, G. Lindzey, & R. D. Luce (Eds.), *Stevens' handbook of experimental psychology: Vol. 2. Learning and cognition* (2nd ed., pp. 167–244). New York: Wiley.

Williams, B. A. (1997). What is learned? Revisiting an old issue. *Analysis of Behavior, 67,* 255–258.

Zeiler, M. D. (1977). Schedules of reinforcement: The controlling variables. In W. K. Honig & J. E. R. Staddon (Eds.), *Handbook of operant behavior* (pp. 201–232). Englewood Cliffs, NJ: Prentice–Hall.

Zeiler, M. D. (1984). The sleeping giant: Reinforcement schedules. *Journal of the Experimental Analysis of Behavior, 42,* 485–493.

Zuriff, G. E. (1970). A comparison of variable-ratio and variable-interval schedules of reinforcement. *Journal of the Experimental Analysis of Behavior, 13,* 369–374.

5

Choice and Self-Control

James E. Mazur

For several decades, choice has been the focus of considerable research by those who study operant behavior. This is not surprising, because the topics of choice and operant behavior are intimately intertwined. In everyday life, people can choose among a large, almost infinite set of operant behaviors, and they can choose not only which behaviors to perform, but under what conditions, at what rate, and for how long. Because choice is an essential part of human (and animal) life, it has been studied with great interest not only by behavioral psychologists, but also by decision theorists, economists, political scientists, biologists, and others. The research methods used in these different disciplines vary widely, and a review of all of the different methods for studying choice is well beyond the scope and purpose of this chapter. Instead, the chapter will focus on the techniques most frequently used in operant research—techniques that involve single-subject designs, that allow precise control of the reinforcement contingencies, and that produce (in most cases) large and clear effects on each subject's behavior.

The chapter is divided into three major sections. The first section examines research with concurrent schedules; that is, situations in which two or more reinforcement schedules are simultaneously available. The next section will examine the techniques used to study *self-control* choice, which can be defined as a choice between a small, fairly immediate reinforcer and larger, more delayed reinforcer. Operant researchers have been interested in this topic because many common behavior problems (e.g, overeating, smoking, impulsive spending, unsafe sexual practices) can be viewed as problems of self-control. The third section will cover a few other techniques that do not fit easily into either of the first two categories.

The researcher planning an experiment on human choice can choose from a much wider range of options and must therefore make more critical decisions than the researcher working with animal subjects. In most of the research on choice with animals, the subjects are rats pressing levers or pigeons pecking response keys, the discriminative stimuli are lights or physical locations, and the reinforcers are food.

James E. Mazur • Psychology Department, Southern Connecticut State University, New Haven, Connecticut 06515.

Handbook of Research Methods in Human Operant Behavior, edited by Lattal and Perone. Plenum Press, New York, 1998.

The sessions take place in standard operant conditioning chambers, last perhaps an hour, and are repeated day after day, often for many months. As we will see, however, the research with human subjects has utilized a much greater variety of operant responses, discriminative stimuli, and reinforcers. The amount of pre-training (if any), the duration and number of sessions, and the instructions given to subjects have also been quite variable. This chapter will attempt to survey the various methods used and, where possible, evaluate the advantages and disadvantages of different research strategies.

CONCURRENT REINFORCEMENT SCHEDULES

Background

Two Prominent Theories

Although the emphasis of this chapter is primarily on methodology, not theory, no description of operant research on choice would be complete without some mention of the theories that have served as an impetus for much of this research. One major theory of choice is Herrnstein's (1961, 1970) *matching law,* which states that in a choice situation, subjects' response proportions will equal or match the reinforcement proportions. The basic form of the matching law can be written as follows:

$$\frac{B_1}{B_1 + B_2} = \frac{R_1}{R_1 + R_2} \tag{1}$$

where B_1 and B_2 are the response rates for two alternative responses, and R_1 and R_2 are the reinforcement rates for these two alternatives. Herrnstein (1961) initially tested this equation with pigeons responding on concurrent variable-interval (VI) schedules: Each of two response keys delivered food reinforcers on separate VI schedules. Since then, the matching law has been tested in many experiments with a variety of species, including humans, and the results have often conformed fairly well to Equation 1 (see Davison & McCarthy, 1988; de Villiers, 1977; McDowell, 1988). In essence, the matching law states that subjects will distribute their behaviors among alternative responses in proportion to the reinforcers received from these alternatives.

The best-known alternative to the matching law is *optimization theory,* also called *molar maximizing theory* or other similar names (e.g., Rachlin, 1978; Rachlin, Battalio, Kagel, & Green, 1981; Schoener, 1971). This theory states that in a choice situation, subjects tend to distribute their choices in a way that maximizes the *total* rate of reinforcement (summed across all of the choice alternatives). According to optimization theory, the reason subjects exhibit matching with concurrent VI schedules is that this distribution of responses produces a higher overall rate of reinforcement than any other distribution (Rachlin, Green, Kagel, & Battalio, 1976). The extensive and continuing debate over the merits of these two theories will not be reviewed here (see Commons, Herrnstein, & Rachlin, 1982; Heyman & Herrnstein, 1986; Rachlin, Green, & Tormey, 1988). Both matching and optimization theories are *molar* theories because the important variables in these theories (reinforcement rates) must be measured over fairly long periods of time. A variety of *molecular theories* have also been developed, which emphasize the important influence of short-term variables on choice responses (e.g., Mazur, 1984, 1993; Shimp, 1969; Shull & Spear, 1987). The molecular theories are especially relevant to the research on self-control described later in this chapter.

Deviations from Matching

Whereas some studies have obtained results that conformed closely to Equation 1, others have found systematic deviations from this basic matching relation. Baum (1974, 1979) identified three common deviations from matching: bias, undermatching, and overmatching. Bias occurs if a subject consistently makes more responses on one alternative than predicted by Equation 1, perhaps because of a position preference, a color preference, or some other difference between the two alternatives. Undermatching occurs when a subject's response ratios are not as extreme as the reinforcement ratios. For example, if response key 1 delivers three times as many reinforcers as response key 2, a subject might make only twice as many responses on key 1, not three times as many. The opposite of undermatching is overmatching, in which response ratios are more extreme than the reinforcement ratios.

Baum (1974) suggested that these deviations can be encompassed by a more general equation called the *generalized matching law:*

$$\frac{B_1}{B_2} = b \left(\frac{R_1}{R_2}\right)^a \tag{2}$$

In this equation, the parameter b is a measure of bias: A subject has a bias for alternative 1 if $b > 1$, a bias for alternative 2 if $b < 1$, and no bias if $b = 1$. The parameter a is included to accommodate cases of undermatching or overmatching. Undermatching results in values of $a < 1$, and overmatching results in values of $a > 1$.

Baum (1974) also showed that a convenient way to analyze the results from studies in which the two reinforcement rates, R_1 and R_2, are varied is to plot the logarithm of the ratio R_1/R_2 on the abscissa and the logarithm of B_1/B_2 on the ordinate. This method is useful because in log–log coordinates, Equation 2 predicts that the data points should approximate a linear function with a y-intercept equal to the log of b, and a slope equal to the exponent a. In these coordinates, matching of response proportions to reinforcement proportions will produce a slope of 1, undermatching will produce a slope less than 1, and overmatching will produce a slope greater than 1.

As an example, Figure 5.1 shows the results from a study by Bradshaw, Ruddle, and Szabadi (1981), in which six female subjects earned pennies by pressing either of two levers, which delivered the reinforcers according to five different

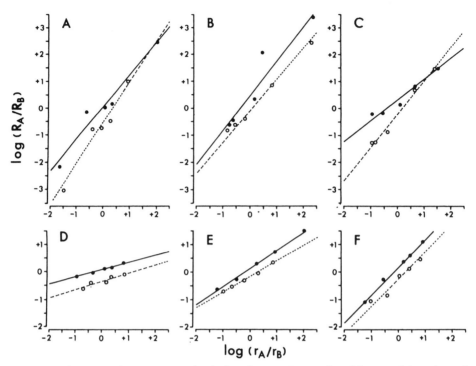

FIGURE 5.1. The ratios of response rates (R_A/R_B) in the experiment of Bradshaw et al. (1981) are plotted as a function of the ratios of the reinforcement rates (r_A/r_B). Filled circles are from conditions with equally weighted levers, and open circles are from conditions in which lever A required more force to operate. The lines are the best-fitting regression lines.

pairs of VI schedules. Each panel in Figure 5.1 shows the results from one subject. The filled circles are the results from conditions in which the levers both required little effort to operate, and the solid lines are regression lines fitted to these data. The slopes of these functions vary substantially: Subjects A and B exhibited some overmatching, Subjects C, D, and E exhibited substantial undermatching, and Subject F exhibited approximate matching. This type of variability among subjects is not unusual, but it certainly makes the researcher's job of interpreting the results more challenging.

The open circles in Figure 5.1 are from conditions in which much more effort was needed to operate one of the two levers (labeled response A in the figure). For most subjects, this change produced a downward shift in the data points with little change in slope, which is consistent with the interpretation that the increased effort requirement produced a bias against lever A. What Figure 5.1 does not show, however, is that the increased effort requirement produced about a 50% decrease in response rates on lever A, whereas response rates on lever B remained roughly the same for most subjects. The point is that although plots such as those in Figure 5.1 are commonly used to summarize the results from experiments with concurrent schedules, there are many other useful ways to analyze and report the data. For example, Bradshaw et al. also presented a figure with the actual response rates (responses per minute) plotted for each of the two levers as a function of reinforcement rate. In some studies, time ratios (e.g., T_1/T_2), or their logarithms, are plotted as a function of reinforcement ratios, just as response ratios are plotted in Figures 5.1. T_1 and T_2 are the cumulative times spent responding on each of the two schedules, usually measured from one changeover to the next. That is, the clock for response 2 would start to operate when the subject switched from schedule 1 to schedule 2, and would continue to run (excluding reinforcement periods) until the subject made another response on schedule 1. Time ratios often exhibit closer matching to reinforcement ratios than do response ratios. These times can also be used to calculate *local response rates,* which are defined as the number of responses on one schedule divided by the time spent on that schedule. Local response rates can indicate whether subjects responded faster on one schedule than on another. Each of these methods of reporting the data provides additional information, and no single analysis can give a complete picture of a subject's performance.

Procedural Details

Most experiments with human subjects and concurrent schedules have employed several features inherited from earlier work with animal subjects. First, the most common procedure with human subjects has been to use two VI schedules. One advantage of concurrent VI schedules is that they tend to produce fairly steady responding. Another advantage is that approximate matching often results, thus providing a predictable baseline from which the effects of other variables (e.g., reinforcer magnitudes, delays, punished responding) can be assessed. Although the two VI schedules usually store and deliver reinforcers independently, many experiments have included a *changeover delay* (COD). For instance, in his initial study with pigeons, Herrnstein (1961) included a 1.5-s COD, which meant that each time a subject switched from one key to the other, at least 1.5 s had to elapse before a response could be reinforced. Suppose the VI schedule for the right key stored a reinforcer while a pigeon was pecking on the left key. The pigeon's next response on the right key would not be reinforced, and 1.5 s would have to elapse before a right-key response would be reinforced. Herrnstein suggested that the use of a COD helps to avoid the accidental reinforcement of switching behavior. With human subjects, there is evidence that the use of a COD can reduce or eliminate such superstitious responses (Catania & Cutts, 1963). Some studies with human subjects have included CODs and others have not. A few found substantial undermatching when no COD was used, but when a COD of several seconds' duration was added, the same subjects exhibited approximate matching (Baum, 1975; Schroeder & Holland, 1969).

It is clear that the presence and duration of a COD can have a major effect on concurrent-schedule performance. In deciding whether or not to use a COD, the researcher might consider the following trade-offs. Without a COD, rapid switching between alternatives may be adventitiously reinforced, response ratios (B_1/B_2) may be close to 1, and as a result, any preference for one schedule over the other may be obscured. At the other extreme, if a very long COD is used, the result may be overmatching, with little switching between the alternatives. Using a COD of

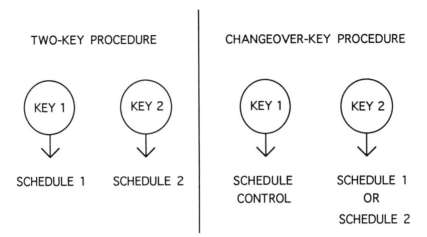

TWO-KEY PROCEDURE   CHANGEOVER-KEY PROCEDURE

KEY 1   KEY 2   KEY 1   KEY 2

SCHEDULE 1   SCHEDULE 2   SCHEDULE   SCHEDULE 1
                                CONTROL   OR
                                                SCHEDULE 2

FIGURE 5.2.   A two-key procedure for concurrent schedules (e.g., Herrnstein, 1961) versus a changeover-key procedure (e.g., Findley, 1958).

moderate size may be the best compromise. In studies with human subjects, CODs of about 2 to 3 s have been typical.

Another variation that was first used with animal subjects and later with human subjects is the *changeover-key* procedure (Findley, 1958). Figure 5.2 shows the changeover-key procedure versus the two-key procedure used by Herrnstein (1961). As already explained, in the two-key procedure, each key is associated with its own reinforcement schedule. In the changeover-key procedure, one key (the *changeover key*) delivers no reinforcers, but it controls which of two reinforcement schedules is in effect on the other key (the *schedule key*). Each of the two reinforcement schedules is associated with a different discriminative stimulus, and every response on the changeover key changes both the discriminative stimulus and the reinforcement schedule currently in effect on the schedule key. In studies with pigeons, the discriminative stimuli are usually two different colors on the schedule key, and in studies with humans the discriminative stimuli might be two different lights on a response panel. In both cases, only the schedule currently in effect can deliver reinforcers. However, with interval schedules, the clocks for both schedules continue to operate (and store reinforcers) regardless of which schedule is currently in effect.

An advantage of the changeover-key procedure is that it provides a simple way to measure how much time the subject spends on each schedule: One can simply record the amount of time spent in the presence of each discriminative stimulus. Another advantage is that it clearly distinguishes between switching responses and schedule-controlled responses, whereas the two-key procedure does not. In some studies, a COD has been used with the changeover-key procedure: After each changeover response, a certain number of seconds must elapse before a response on the schedule key can be reinforced (e.g., Ruddle, Bradshaw, Szabadi, & Foster, 1982; Wurster & Griffiths, 1979). In other studies, the changeover-key procedure has been used without a COD (e.g., Bradshaw, Szabadi, & Bevan, 1979; Bradshaw,

Szabadi, Bevan, & Ruddle, 1979). The success of these studies, plus additional data from animal subjects (e.g., Heyman, 1979), suggests that the presence of a COD may be less important in a changeover-key procedure than in a two-key procedure.

One other general feature of both animal and human studies on choice should be mentioned. The vast majority of all studies with concurrent schedules have reported only "steady-state" behavior (see Baron & Perone, Chapter 3). That is, most studies have provided little or no information about the acquisition of choice behavior, or about behavior during periods of transition, when one condition has ended and a new condition with different reinforcement schedules has begun. Rather, researchers have usually waited until the subjects' choice responses met certain stability criteria (e.g., five consecutive sessions with no more than a 10% variation in choice proportions), and only the data from the end of the condition (e.g., the mean choice proportion from the last five sessions) are then reported. The intent of this strategy is clearly to study subjects' choices only after they have come under control of the reinforcement schedules currently available. One experimental condition is not terminated until the stability criteria are satisfied. With animal subjects this often requires 20 or more sessions per condition, and a complete experiment can last a year or more. Studies with human subjects have generally been much shorter in duration. Some have involved a few weeks of daily sessions, whereas a few have included only one session per subject (e.g., Berlyne, 1972; Conger & Killeen, 1974).

To illustrate the variety of procedures that can be used to study choice with concurrent schedules, two fairly different experiments will be described in detail.

An Early Study: Schroeder and Holland (1969)

Schroeder and Holland conducted one of the first experiments on concurrent VI schedules with human subjects. A subject sat in front of a display panel that had a dial in each of four corners, and the subject's task was to detect needle deflections in any of the dials. One VI schedule controlled needle deflections for the two dials on the left, and another VI schedule controlled needle deflections for the two dials on the right. There was one response button for the two left dials and another for the two right dials, and subjects were told to press the appropriate button whenever they detected a needle deflection, which in turn reset the needle to its initial position. These needle deflections served as the reinforcers: Subjects were told that this was a game in which the goal was to detect as many needle deflections as possible.

The operant responses in this experiment were the subject's eye movements. Throughout the experiment, a subject sat with her mouth in a bite plate made of dental wax, which kept her head steady so that a camera could record all eye movements. Eye movements toward either of the left dials constituted one response class, and eye movements toward either of the right dials constituted the other response class. In some conditions, a COD of either 1 or 2.5 s was imposed, such that no needle deflections could occur after a subject's fixation point switched from the left side to the right side, or vice versa, until the COD had elapsed.

Six subjects each participated in up to ten 25-min sessions, in which they were exposed to two or more conditions. Each condition lasted from one to five sessions, and each featured a different pair of VI schedules. Only the data from the last session of each condition were analyzed. Schroeder and Holland reported that subjects were not tested longer because they found the task "very uncomfortable and boring." Yet although the subjects may not have enjoyed the experiment, their responses followed a systematic pattern. With a 2.5-s COD, all subjects exhibited excellent matching; that is, the proportion of eye movements directed toward the two left dials was always very close to the proportion of needle deflections on those two dials. With a 1-s COD, one subject exhibited undermatching, but the others still exhibited matching. With no COD, fairly extreme undermatching was observed in all cases. This study therefore illustrates the major effects a COD can have on choice responses.

Several features of this experiment are worth emphasizing. First, the results demonstrate that, at least under certain conditions, the choice responses of human subjects can show the same type of matching that has been observed with animals. Second, these results were obtained after only a few sessions of exposure to each new pair of VI schedules, which contrasts with the numerous sessions that must be used before animal subjects exhibit such stable responding. Third, the subjects were paid on an hourly rate for their participation, but they earned no additional money by detecting needle deflections. And although they were told to try to observe as many needle deflections as possible, neither during nor after a session were they told how many deflections they had detected. Thus, these orderly results were obtained despite the use of seemingly very weak reinforcers in a boring and repetitive task.

A Changeover-Key Experiment: Bradshaw, Szabadi, and Bevan (1979)

Bradshaw and his colleagues (Bradshaw, Szabadi, & Bevan, 1976, 1977, 1978, 1979; Bradshaw, Szabadi, Bevan, & Ruddle, 1979) have conducted a series of experiments in which the discriminative stimuli were colored lights on a control panel, the operant responses were presses on either of two buttons, and the reinforcers were points on a counter that were worth one penny each. Their subjects were university employees who had never taken a course in psychology and had never previously participated in a psychological experiment. Each experimental session lasted approximately 1 hour, and each subject usually participated in one session a day, about 5 days a week, for several weeks. To increase the likelihood that subjects would continue until the end of the experiment, they were informed at the start that the amount of money they earned each day would be recorded, but they would be paid in one lump sum at the end of the experiment. In studies where subjects receive many sessions over a period of weeks, it is a common practice to withhold at least part of their earnings, which are forfeited if the subject does not complete the experiment (e.g., Baum, 1975; Kelly, Fischman, Foltin, & Brady, 1991; Logue, Forzano, & Tobin, 1992; see Pilgrim, Chapter 2, for a discussion).

Figure 5.3 shows the apparatus used by Bradshaw et al. (1979). A subject sat at a table facing this apparatus in a small room. The experiment was controlled by electromechanical relay equipment that was located outside the room and far enough away that the subject could not hear the sounds of the equipment. In Phase I of the experiment, the auxiliary box was not present, and responses on the sin-

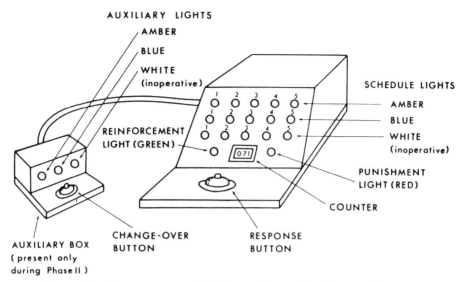

FIGURE 5.3.   The apparatus used in the experiment of Bradshaw et al. (1979).

gle response button were reinforced according to several different VI schedules. Although this phase was not a choice procedure, it is important to examine both this initial training and the initial instructions given to the subjects. At the start of the first session, subjects were told that they could earn money by pressing the response button. Each time a penny was earned, the green reinforcement light flashed and the counter was incremented to show the total amount earned during the session. The subjects were also informed that each of the five amber lights would be turned on for one 10-min period during the session, and when an amber light was on they could earn money. Between each 10-min period was a 5-min rest period in which no panel lights were on and no money could be earned.

Although the subjects were not told this, the five amber lights were associated with five different VI schedules, ranging from VI 8-s to VI 720-s. In other words, during a single session, a subject responded in turn on five different VI schedules, each associated with a different discriminative stimulus (a different amber light) and each lasting 10 min. This procedure (along with a variation that will not be discussed here) continued for 30 sessions. As in studies with animal subjects (Catania & Reynolds, 1968; de Villiers & Herrnstein, 1976), response rates were higher on the richer VI schedules, and they approached an asymptote as reinforcement rates increased.

The procedure in Phase II of the experiment was similar in most ways, for the same five VI schedules were used, each for one 10-min period. The main difference was that each of the five schedules now ran concurrently with a VI 171-s schedule. Regardless of which VI schedule was operating, subjects could switch to the VI 171-s schedule (or vice versa) by pressing a changeover button. As in the usual changeover-key procedure, two different stimuli indicated which of the two VI schedules was currently in effect. Whenever an amber light on the auxiliary box was lit (see Figure 5.3), the VI 171-s schedule was in effect. Whenever one of the amber lights on the main box was lit, one of the five original VI schedules was in effect. Each response on the changeover button switched from one amber light (and one schedule) to the other. Subjects were told only that the changeover button was for changing from an amber light on the main box to the amber light on the auxiliary box (or vice versa); they were not told anything about the nature of the reinforcement schedules for either light. In summary, each session consisted of five segments in which each of the five original VI schedules ran concurrently with a VI 171-s schedule. Phase II continued for a total of 20 sessions.

In their presentation of the results, Bradshaw et al. referred to each schedule associated with a light on the main box as Schedule A, and to the schedule associated with the light on the auxiliary box as Schedule B. Figure 5.4 shows the response rates on Schedule A (filled circles) and Schedule B (filled triangles) as a function of the number of reinforcements per hour delivered by Schedule A. All calculations were based on the data from the last three sessions of each condition. As the rate of reinforcement increased on Schedule A, response rates increased on Schedule A and decreased on Schedule B for all three subjects. The results conformed well to the predictions of the matching law. The solid curves were derived from a variation of the matching equation that includes two free parameters (Herrnstein, 1970).

The open circles and triangles in Figure 5.4 show the results from the last condition of the experiment, in which responses on Schedule B were punished according to a variable-ratio (VR) 34 schedule: Each punishment consisted of subtracting one point from the reinforcement counter (i.e., one penny from the subject's earnings). Under these conditions, responding on Schedule B dropped to a very low rate, and response rates on Schedule A approached their asymptotic levels more quickly as the reinforcement rate increased.

This detailed examination of the Bradshaw et al. (1979) experiment has presented one research group's decisions about what instructions to give subjects, what types of responses, reinforcers, and discriminative stimuli to use, and how long each session and each condition should last. It also demonstrates their unique strategy of presenting five different schedule combinations within a single session. Finally, this study shows how, once stable responding has been obtained, a procedure with concurrent schedules can be used to test the effects of additional variables, such as a punishment contingency.

Different Responses and Different Reinforcers

Most of the human research with concurrent schedules has used simple responses such as key or button presses or lever pulls, probably because these responses are easy for the subject to make and for the experimenter to record (see Pilgrim, Chapter 2, and Shull & Lawrence, Chapter 4). However, a few other response types have been used successfully. As already discussed, Schroeder and Holland (1969) used eye movements as operant responses. In some studies, students with learning difficulties worked on simple arithmetic problems from two different sets, and correct solutions were reinforced according to two different VI schedules (Mace, Neef, Shade, & Mauro, 1994; Neef, Mace, Shea, & Shade, 1992).

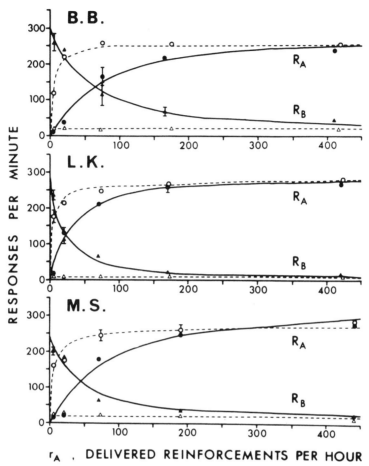

FIGURE 5.4.   For the experiment of Bradshaw et al. (1979), response rates are shown for Schedule A (filled circles) and Schedule B (filled triangles) as a function of the rate of reinforcement for Schedule A. The open circles and triangles are from a condition in which Schedule B responses were punished. The curves were derived from the matching law. The solid curves were fit to the filled data points, and the dashed curves were fit to the open data points. The error bars show standard errors around the means of the last three sessions of each condition.

In two experiments on social interactions, the operant response was defined as the amount of time a subject spent talking to two other individuals during group discussions (Conger & Killeen, 1974; Pierce, Epling, & Greer, 1981). The reinforcers in these studies were also unusual: Besides the one true subject, the other members of the discussion group were confederates who delivered verbal reinforcers to the subject according to independent VI schedules. For example, a confederate might deliver a verbal reinforcer to the subject at the appropriate time by saying, "That's a good point." Although these two studies were similar in general design, they obtained very different results: Conger and Killeen found that the proportions of time subjects spent talking to the different confederates approximately matched the proportions of verbal reinforcers delivered by these confederates. In contrast,

Pierce et al. found major departures from matching, and in some cases subjects actually spent less time talking to confederates who delivered more social reinforcers. The reasons for these different results are not known, but it should be clear that in such complex social situations, many factors besides the sheer number of reinforcers can influence a subject's behavior.

The most common reinforcers in human research on concurrent schedules have been points that are exchanged for money at the end of the experiment. In other cases, subjects have been instructed to try to earn as many points as possible, but the points were not exchanged for money. A few other types of reinforcers have also been used with good results. Buskist and Miller (1981) used a modified vending machine to deliver food reinforcers to college students. With special education students, both snack foods and social reinforcers (praise and encouragement from the teacher) have been delivered on concurrent schedules (Mace, McCurdy, & Quigley, 1990). Silberberg, Thomas, and Berendzen (1991) had subjects sit in a cold room (4°C), and the reinforcers consisted of 10-s periods during which six heat lamps were turned on.

Reinforcer type can also be manipulated as an independent variable to evaluate subjects' preferences. For example, Berlyne (1972) had subjects respond on concurrent VI 20-s schedules, and the reinforcers were 5-s presentations of slides of different black-and-white patterns. (Subjects were told that the purpose of the experiment was to measure physiological responses to visual stimuli.) The slides for one schedule were complex visual patterns, and for the other schedule they were simpler patterns. Berlyne found higher response rates on the schedule that delivered the slides of greater visual complexity.

Notice that, in different studies, the reinforcers have ranged from weak conditioned reinforcers (e.g., detection of needle deflections) to delayed conditioned reinforcers (e.g., money delivered at the end of the experiment) to immediate primary reinforcers (e.g., warmth, food). If the researcher's selection of reinforcer type has any major effect on the patterns of behavior subjects exhibit under concurrent schedules, it is not apparent from these studies. This contrasts with the situation in self-control choice, where there is evidence that different choice patterns may emerge with different reinforcer types, as discussed later in this chapter.

The Role of Rule-Governed Behavior

Although we have examined several studies in which the results conformed fairly well to the predictions of the matching law, this is not a universal finding. Some experiments with concurrent VIs and human subjects have obtained gross departures from matching, such as severe undermatching, or little sensitivity to the relative rates of reinforcement (e.g., Navarick & Chellsen, 1983; Pierce et al., 1981; Takahashi & Iwamoto, 1986). Lowe and his colleagues have conducted a number of these studies, and Lowe has concluded that human behavior in these situations is not governed by the same matching principle that has worked fairly well with animals (Horne & Lowe, 1993; Lowe & Horne, 1985). Lowe's analysis and his conclusions should be given serious consideration, not just by those interested in the matching law, but by anyone planning an experiment on human choice.

Horne and Lowe (1993) conducted a series of experiments with concurrent VI schedules that were patterned after the research of Bradshaw and colleagues, such as the Bradshaw et al. (1979) study described above. Many of their subjects exhibited gross deviations from matching, such as severe undermatching or exclusive preference for the richer schedule. After the experiment, subjects were asked a series of questions about their views of the experiment, their behaviors, and their hypotheses. In general, there was substantial correspondence between a subject's hypotheses about the optimal way to earn points and his or her actual choice behavior. For example, a subject who responded exclusively on the richer schedule stated, "I decided that I could get more points by only pressing the key giving more points" (p. 34). A subject whose choice responses were close to indifference in all conditions reported, "I tried several strategies. . . . This did not seem to produce more points than if I pressed them randomly. So, after experimenting with the aforesaid ideas I continued to press randomly" (p. 34).

Horne and Lowe concluded that the choice behavior of human subjects (except very young children) is to a large extent "rule governed" rather than "contingency shaped." If the subject's verbal rule about how to respond in the experiment happens to be consistent with a matching principle, then matching will be observed; if not, then matching behavior will not be observed regardless of the prevailing reinforcement contingencies. This conclusion is similar to Lowe's analysis of human performance on single reinforcement schedules: Because human behavior is to a large extent rule governed, human response patterns on standard reinforcement schedules are often quite different from those of animals (e.g., Bentall, Lowe, & Beasty, 1985; Lowe, 1979; Lowe, Beasty & Bentall, 1983; also see Shimoff & Catania, Chapter 12; Shull & Lawrence, Chapter 4).

Lowe and Horne (1985) also concluded that the approximate matching obtained in many of the experiments of Bradshaw and his colleagues may have reflected their use of a specific configuration of discriminative stimuli. In these experiments, one constant VI schedule was paired, in turn, with each of five different VI schedules, and each schedule was associated with one of five amber lights (see Figure 5.3). The positions of the lights were ordinally related to the sizes of the VI schedules (i.e., light 1 was the stimulus for the shortest VI schedule, and light 5 was the stimulus for the longest VI schedule). Lowe and Horne conducted a series of experiments similar to those of Bradshaw and colleagues, except that this ordinal relationship between stimulus location and VI size was eliminated—the discriminative stimuli for the five VI schedules were five different geometric shapes, each presented in the same location. With ordinal position eliminated as an additional cue, the subjects showed virtually no sensitivity to the size of the VI schedule, and response proportions were close to indifference with all five schedules. Lowe and Horne concluded that the matching behavior obtained by Bradshaw and colleagues was a fortuitous result of their particular arrangement of stimuli, but that matching is by no means a general outcome with human subjects.

The research of Lowe and his colleagues has shown that rule-governed behavior can play an important role in human choice behavior. Their studies also demonstrated, once again, that small procedural differences can sometimes produce large differences in performance. However, their more general conclusion— that principles of behavior discovered with animal subjects have little or no applicability to human behavior—seems unfounded. Whereas some of their subjects showed little sensitivity to the relative rates of reinforcement, this chapter has list-ed many other studies in which human subjects have shown such sensitivity (and exhibited approximate matching of response proportions to reinforcement pro-portions). The issue for future research is not whether human choice behavior is sensitive to reinforcement rate, but under what conditions this sensitivity can be overshadowed by other factors, such as an individual's verbal rules about when and how to respond.

Types of Instructions Given to Subjects

Considering the potentially major role of rule-governed behavior in choice situ-ations, it follows that the types of instructions subjects are given might also affect their performance. A few studies with single reinforcement schedules found that the schedules exerted more control over behavior if subjects were given very min-imal instructions, and if the operant response itself was taught by a shaping pro-cedure rather than by verbal or written instructions (Matthews, Shimoff, Catania, & Sagvolden, 1977; Shimoff, Catania, & Matthews, 1981). Based on these findings, Logue and her colleagues (e.g., Forzano & Logue, 1992; Logue et al., 1992) have used minimal instructions in their research on choice, simply informing subjects that they could earn the reinforcers by touching some parts of the apparatus.

The strategy of giving minimal instructions is by no means a universal prac-tice in choice experiments, however. As we have seen, Bradshaw and colleagues routinely gave subjects detailed instructions about how and when to press the re-sponse buttons. Similarly explicit instructions have been used in other research with concurrent schedules (e.g., Baum, 1975; Frazier & Bitetto, 1969). Yet despite the potential importance of this factor, there has been little systematic research on the effects of different amounts and types of instructions. In a study by Hacken-berg and Joker (1994), subjects were sometimes given incorrect instructions, which did not actually describe the best way to earn points. Subjects initially followed the instructions, but over time their choice responses gradually shifted toward a pattern that allowed them to earn more points. Takahashi and Iwamoto (1986) gave all subjects instructions about how to press two levers to earn money, but only some subjects were given additional instructions stating that the two levers oper-ated independently, and that "you can choose between them freely" (p. 260). Taka-hashi and Iwamoto found some evidence that these additional instructions (when combined with other factors such as a distinctive stimulus for each schedule) pro-duced greater sensitivity to the reinforcement contingencies. The results are not clear-cut, however, and more research on the effects of instructions on choice be-havior is certainly needed.

Varying Reinforcer Amount

Reinforcer amount is another variable that has been manipulated in studies with concurrent VI schedules. Baum and Rachlin (1969) proposed a variation of the matching law in which reinforcer amount replaces reinforcement rate. For ex-ample, suppose a subject is presented with two identical VI schedules, except that each reinforcer on one schedule is worth three times as much money as each reinforcer on the other schedule. According to Baum and Rachlin's analysis, the subject should make three times as many responses on the first schedule, thus matching response rates to reinforcer amounts. However, in two studies in which the number of cents per reinforcer was varied, Schmitt (1974) and Wurster and Griffiths (1979) found little sensitivity to the amount of reinforcement. In a similar study, Fukui and Kimura (1988) found large individual differences in sensitivity to reinforcer amount.

One factor that may have an important effect on the sensitivity of human subjects to reinforcer amount is the manner in which the reinforcers are delivered. Sensitivity may be greater if subjects are required to perform some "consummatory response" to obtain the reinforcer than if the reinforcer is delivered automatically once the schedule requirements have been met (King & Logue, 1990; Matthews et al., 1977). In previous studies with single reinforcement schedules, the schedule contingencies appeared to exert greater control over subjects' responding when the subjects were required to perform such a consummatory response (Hawkins & Pliskoff, 1964; Matthews et al., 1977). King and Logue compared two different methods of delivering reinforcers (points on a counter, worth 0.10 cent each). In one experiment, points were delivered automatically during each reinforcement period. In a second experiment, subjects had to turn a knob during the reinforcement period to obtain their points; each 90-degree turn of the knob earned one point. King and Logue found that choice responses were much more sensitive to variations in the amount of reinforcement when subjects had to make a response during the reinforcement period. These findings suggest that it may be a good practice to require subjects to perform some sort of response to collect reinforcers during each reinforcement period, as has been done in a number of experiments (e.g., Bangert, Green, Snyderman, & Turow, 1985; Logue, Pena-Correal, Rodriguez, & Kabela, 1986; Logue, King, Chavarro, & Volpe, 1990).

Other Concurrent Reinforcement Schedules

Compared with the many studies that have used concurrent VI schedules, there has been relatively little research on other combinations of concurrent schedules. Some of this research has addressed the same theoretical issues that have motivated much of the work with concurrent VIs. For example, Silberberg et al. (1991) had adult males respond on concurrent VI and VR schedules, with the warmth from heat lamps as a reinforcer. The experiment was designed to test the different predictions made by the matching and maximizing theories. According to maximization theory, subjects should respond mainly on the VR schedule and only occasionally on the VI schedule, because this manner of responding would maximize the overall rate of reinforcement. In contrast, matching theory predicts that subjects will make enough responses on the VI schedule so that the response proportion equals the reinforcement proportion (see Equation 1). Silberberg et al. reported that in many conditions, response proportions deviated from matching in the direction of reinforcement maximization. However, the choice proportions of individual subjects varied as a function of whether or not a subject had received prior discrimination training with the VI and VR schedules presented separately. After receiving this training, subjects showed (1) faster responding on the VR schedules than on the VI schedules and (2) closer approximations to reinforcement maximization. Besides its theoretical implications, this study demonstrates that pretraining or previous experience with single reinforcement schedules can have important effects on choice behavior under concurrent schedules (cf. Takahashi & Iwamoto, 1986).

Other research has examined the response patterns produced by different concurrent schedules. For example, Frazier and Bitetto (1969) used a vigilance task in which there were three response buttons and three dials to monitor for needle deflections. Each button press briefly illuminated the corresponding dial, thus allowing the subject to detect any needle deflection. Needle deflections on the three dials were programmed according to three different reinforcement schedules. For half of the subjects, needle deflections on the three dials were arranged according to fixed-ratio (FR), fixed-interval (FI), and differential-reinforcement-of-low-rates (DRL) schedules, respectively. Figure 5.5 presents cumulative records from two subjects, which show different response patterns for the three schedules. Frazier and Bitetto reported that for this group of subjects, the response patterns resembled, at least in some ways, the response patterns of nonhuman subjects on these schedules. However, for a second group of subjects, a VI schedule was used instead of the FR schedule, and these subjects tended to show the same response patterns on all three schedules. Perhaps the use of three time-based schedules (VI, FI, and

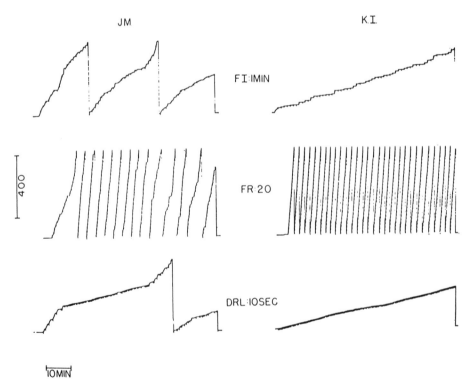

FIGURE 5.5. Cumulative records from two subjects in the experiment of Frazier and Bitetto (1969), showing their response patterns on three concurrent reinforcement schedules.

DRL) made their different contingencies more difficult to discriminate; two sub-jects who received extensive training and instructions about the nature of the schedules did eventually exhibit different response patterns on the three sched-ules. In any case, these results illustrate, once again, how slight changes in proce-dure can lead to dramatically different results in this type of research.

A few studies have examined other combinations of FI, FR, VI, VR, and DRL schedules, with normal adults (e.g., Poppen, 1972; Rosenberger, 1973; Sanders, 1969; Spiga, Cherek, Grabowski, & Bennett, 1992) and with retarded or abnormal subjects (Oscar-Berman, Heyman, Bonner, & Ryder, 1980; Schroeder, 1975). The results of these studies were quite variable, but one recurrent theme is that factors such as instructions, amount of training, and context can have major effects on per-formance. For example, Poppen (1972) found more evidence of "scalloping" on an FI 1-min schedule (i.e., an acceleration in responding as the minute elapsed) if the alternative was an FR schedule than if it was a DRL schedule.

In summary, many procedural details, some of them seemingly minor, can have large effects on human performance on concurrent reinforcement schedules. The effects of some of these factors are still not well understood. Nevertheless, the researcher is well advised to consider carefully all procedural details before be-ginning an experiment on human choice.

SELF-CONTROL CHOICE PROCEDURES

As explained in the introduction, the term *self-control choice* usually refers to a choice between a small, fairly immediate reinforcer and a larger, more delayed reinforcer. Some studies on self-control have used procedures similar to those al-ready described, in which concurrent VI schedules are used to measure preference. Other studies have used discrete-trial procedures, in which a subject makes only one response per trial, thereby choosing either the smaller or the larger reinforcer. Examples of both procedures are described in this section.

A Discrete-Trial Study: Darcheville, Riviere, and Wearden (1992)

The subjects in this study were 16 children between 5 and 7 years old, re-cruited from an elementary school. The experiment was conducted in an empty classroom at the school. In each session (which lasted about half an hour), a child sat at a table that held a color TV monitor, a set of headphones, a button at the end of a long cable, and a panel with three response buttons and two circular disks that could be illuminated with different colors. The children were given fairly mini-mal instructions: They were told that the apparatus was a "robot" that could show cartoons to them. They were instructed to put on the headphones, and to try to press the buttons until they succeeded in getting to see the cartoon.

In one phase of the experiment, the children received several different condi-tions of a discrete-trial procedure in which each trial consisted of making a single response (on either the left or the right button), a delay, and then reinforcement (presentation of a cartoon). Figure 5.6 diagrams the procedure for one condition in which the children had to choose either (1) a short delay and a small reinforcer or

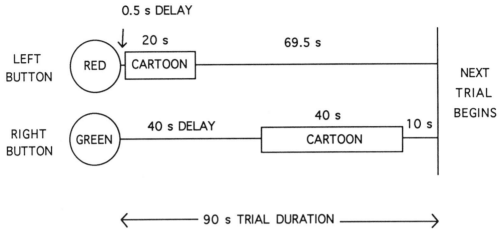

FIGURE 5.6. The sequence of events that followed presses on the left and right buttons in one condition used by Darcheville et al. (1992).

(2) a longer delay and a larger reinforcer. At the start of each choice trial, the left disk on the response panel was red, and the right disk was green. If the child pressed the left button, these colored lights were turned off for a delay of 0.5 s, and then a cartoon was presented for 20 s (the small reinforcer). If the child pressed the right button, the colored lights were turned off for a delay of 40 s, and then a cartoon was presented for 40 s (the large reinforcer). Throughout the experiment, a consummatory response was required to obtain the reinforcer: To see the cartoon, the child had to press the center button and continuously depress the button on the cable. At the end of each reinforcement period, there was an intertrial interval (ITI), during which the two disks on the response panel were yellow, and all responses were ineffective.

Note that the durations of the ITIs differed for the two alternatives: On all trials, ITI duration was adjusted so that the total time from the start of one trial to the start of the next was 90 s. This was done so that the subject's choices did not affect the overall rate of reinforcement, or the rate at which trials were presented. Holding total trial duration constant is a common strategy in studies on self-control. If ITI duration is equal for the two alternatives, *total* trial duration will be shorter for the alternative with the smaller, more immediate reinforcer, and a subject may choose this alternative because reinforcers are delivered at a higher rate.

Another common design feature used by Darcheville et al. was the inclusion of forced trials, in which only one disk (red or green) was illuminated, and only one alternative was available. The purpose of forced trials is to ensure that a subject has at least some exposure to both alternatives. Without forced trials, it would be possible for a subject to choose one alternative exclusively, and thus never experience the consequences of choosing the other alternative. Each session in the Darcheville et al. experiment began with 4 forced trials (2 for each alternative), followed by 20 choice trials. Each condition of the self-control phase of the experiment lasted from two to six sessions, and a condition was ended when certain stability criteria were met. Besides the condition illustrated in Figure 5.6, this part of the experiment included five other conditions with different delays and reinforcer durations.

Darcheville et al. (1992) found large individual differences in the children's choice responses. Based on their responses, seven of the children were classified as "impulsive" (tending to choose the small, less delayed reinforcer), and the other nine were classified as "self-controlled" (tending to choose the large, more delayed reinforcer). Remarkably, Darcheville et al. found a high degree of correspondence between these classifications and the children's performances in the other phase of the experiment, in which the cartoons were presented on single FI schedules. In different conditions, the schedules ranged from FI 20-s to FI 40-s, and only one response button was operative. For each subject, Figure 5.7 shows the mean postreinforcement pause durations and running response rates (response rates in the time after the postreinforcement pause). Postreinforcement pauses were much longer and running rates much slower for all nine "self-controlled" subjects than for the seven "impulsive" subjects. Whereas large individual differences are common in research on human choice, the consistency of these individual differences across two fairly different tasks is quite unusual. Darcheville et al. suggest that impulsive and nonimpulsive children may behave differently on many tasks in which the passage of time is an important factor, and performance on one task might be used to predict performance on others.

Darcheville, Riviere, and Wearden (1993) demonstrated that their procedure, with cartoon presentations as the reinforcer, could be used to measure self-control choices in infants as young as 3 months of age. Discrete-trial procedures have been used in quite a few other studies on self-control with both children (e.g., Eisenberger & Adornetto, 1986; Schweitzer & Sulzer-Azaroff, 1988) and adults (e.g., Flora, Schieferecke, & Bremenkamp, 1992; Forzano & Logue, 1995; Navarick, 1985).

The study of Darcheville et al. (1992) illustrates many of the typical features of a discrete-trial experiment: a mixture of forced trials and choice trials, the requirement of just one response on each trial, the presence of an ITI, and the use of several sessions per condition. Although this section has focused on self-control, discrete-trial choice procedures have many other applications. They have been used in research on the effects of pharmacological agents (Chait & Zacny, 1992; Stern, Chait, & Johanson, 1989), on infants' choices of reinforcement schedules (Bailey, Deni, & Finn-O'Connor, 1988), on adults' choices between fixed and variable reinforcer amounts (Kohn, Kohn, & Staddon, 1992), and in many other situations.

Concurrent-Chain Schedules

In a *chain schedule,* two or more reinforcement schedules (called the *links* of the chain) must be completed in succession, and a reinforcer is delivered only after the last link of the chain is completed. Each schedule is associated with its own discriminative stimulus, so the subject can discriminate when one link has been completed and the next link has begun. If two chain schedules are presented simultaneously, the result is a *concurrent-chain schedule* (Autor, 1960).

The most common type of concurrent-chain schedule used in choice research

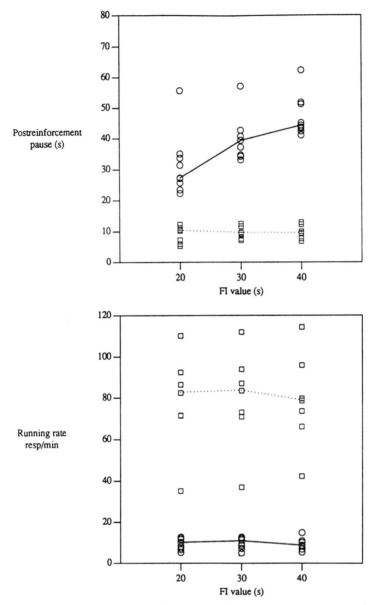

FIGURE 5.7. Mean postreinforcement pause durations and running response rates on three FI schedules are shown for all subjects in the experiment of Darcheville et al. (1992). The children were classified as "self-controlled" (circles) or "impulsive" (squares), based on their responses in a self-control choice situation. The lines connect the medians for each of the two classifications.

includes two links for each chain schedule, which are called the *initial links* and the *terminal links*. The initial links often consist of two equal VI schedules, so this phase of the procedure is the same as a typical concurrent VI schedule (as described in the first part of this chapter). The terminal links can be any type of reinforcement schedule, but in self-control experiments the two terminal links are usually just delays (sometimes called *fixed-time* schedules) of different durations, terminating with reinforcers of different amounts.

A typical experiment on self-control involving a concurrent-chain procedure was conducted by Sonuga-Barke, Lea, and Webley (1989a). Their subjects were 16 girls of four different ages (4, 6, 9, and 12 years). Each subject worked on an apparatus that included a computer monitor, two response panels (one red and one blue), and a token dispenser. The tokens a child earned could be exchanged for sweets or toys. During each initial link, red and blue arrows on the monitor pointed to the red and blue response panels, and two independent VI 10-s schedules were in effect. Whenever one of the VI schedules was completed, the arrows disappeared and the terminal link for that schedule began. The red terminal link was signaled by a red square on the monitor, and the blue terminal link by a blue square. The terminal link for one alternative (with color counterbalanced across subjects) was a 10-s delay followed by a the delivery of one token. The terminal link for the other color was a longer delay followed by the delivery of two tokens. In different sessions, the long delay was either 20, 30, 40, or 50 s. After the delivery of the token(s), the arrows reappeared and the next initial links began. Each session lasted for 15 min.

As is commonly done in concurrent-chain schedules, Sonuga-Barke et al. used the relative response rates in the initial links as a measure of preference. Figure 5.8 presents these results for the four age groups and the four large-reinforcer delays, where R_L and R_S are the initial-link response rates for the large and small reinforcers, respectively. It is seen that the 4-year-olds tended to choose the smaller, more immediate reinforcer, whereas the 6- and 9-year-olds showed a preference for the larger, more delayed reinforcer. The 12-year-olds showed a more complex pattern. They showed a preference for the large reinforcer when its delay was only 20 or 30 s, but they avoided this alternative when its delay was 40 or 50 s. The authors offered the following interpretation of their results: The 4-year-olds' choices were mainly controlled by the delay to reinforcement, and those of the 6- and 9-year-olds were mainly controlled by the amount of reinforcement. The 12-year-

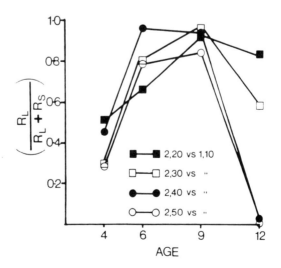

FIGURE 5.8. The proportion of choices of the larger, more delayed reinforcer by children of four age groups in the experiment of Sonuga-Barke et al. (1989a). The numbers in the legend give the number of tokens and the delay for each alternative (e.g., "2, 20" signifies 2 tokens after a 20-s delay).

olds' choices were more sensitive to the overall rate of reinforcement (number of tokens earned per session), so they avoided the large reinforcer only when its delay was so long that it was more profitable to choose the smaller, more immediate reinforcer.

Whether or not this interpretation is correct, this experiment illustrates a complication that may be found in many studies with concurrent-chain schedules: If the terminal links are unequal in duration, and if the initial links resume immediately after each terminal link, the rates of reinforcement for the two schedules will not be identical. This design therefore confounds delay to reinforcement and rate of reinforcement. For example, when the delay for 2 tokens was 50 s, exclusive choice for this alternative would yield about two tokens every 60 s (because the average initial link was 10 s, the terminal link was 50 s, and the reinforcer was two tokens). In comparison, exclusive choice of the smaller reinforcer would yield about 3 tokens every 60 s (because the average initial link was 10 s, every terminal link was 10 s, and the reinforcer was one token). Therefore, in this case, the optimal behavior is to show exclusive preference for the smaller, more immediate reinforcer, because this behavior will maximize the total number of tokens received.

Of course, the potential conflict between delay and rate of reinforcement can be eliminated in a concurrent-chain schedule just as it can be in discrete-trial procedures—by including postreinforcer delay periods (or ITIs) that are adjusted to keep the total durations of both terminal links the same. This simple step has been taken in some concurrent-chain research with animal subjects (Snyderman, 1983), but not in studies with human subjects.

Reinforcer Types: Primary and Conditioned, Positive and Negative

Many studies on self-control with human subjects have used conditioned reinforcers—points exchangeable for money, or money itself (e.g., Burns & Powers, 1975; King & Logue, 1987; Logue et al., 1986, 1990; Sonuga-Barke, Lea, & Webley, 1989b). However, other studies on self-control have used primary reinforcers, such as food or drink, instead of conditioned reinforcers (e.g., Forzano & Logue, 1992, 1995; Ragotzy, Blakely, & Poling, 1988). There is some evidence that adults may exhibit more impulsive behavior (choosing the smaller, more immediate reinforcer) if primary reinforcers are used. For example, Logue and King (1991) used different quantities of fruit juice as the large and small reinforcers with college students who had not consumed food or liquid for several hours before each experimental session. A session included 4 forced trials followed by 15 choice trials, which occurred at a constant pace of one every 3 min. On every choice trial, a subject chose between a small amount of juice after 1 s or a larger amount after 60 s. Logue and King obtained large individual differences: One subject chose only the large reinforcer, one subject chose only the small reinforcer, and the other subjects made some choices of each. Eight of their nineteen subjects chose the small reinforcer more than half of the time.

Some studies on self-control have successfully used a negative primary reinforcer—escape from loud noise (Navarick, 1982; Solnick, Kannenberg, Eckerman, & Waller, 1980). In the experiments of Solnick et al., college students were told to work on math problems as quickly and accurately as possible in the presence of a 90-dB white noise. During the 1-hour sessions, they were presented with a series of choice trials in which they could temporarily stop the noise. In one condition, pressing one button produced quiet for 90 s, then noise for 90 s. Pressing the other button produced noise for 60 s, then quiet for 120 s. (Note that the total trial duration was equal for the two alternatives.) Solnick et al. found that, under some conditions, subjects showed almost exclusive preference for the shorter but more immediate period of quiet.

The distinction between primary and conditioned reinforcers is not always easy to make. However, several other studies on self-control have used what appear to be primary reinforcers, in the sense that the reinforcers delivered on each trial were not exchanged for something else at the end of the session. With college students, Millar and Navarick (1984) used the opportunity to play a video game as a reinforcer, and Navarick (1986) used slides of sports and entertainment personalities. With young children, Logue and Chavarro (1992) used peel-off pictures (stickers) as reinforcers, and Schweitzer and Sulzer-Azaroff (1988) used stickers and a variety of snack items (e.g., raisins, crackers).

Some writers have suggested that primary and conditioned reinforcers have different effects in self-control situations. For example, Flora and Pavlik (1992) concluded that when primary (and immediately "consumable") reinforcers are used in self-control studies, both adults and children usually make at least some "impulsive" choices, although these choices do not maximize the amount of reinforcement in the long run. In some cases, subjects may show a clear preference for the smaller, more immediate reinforcers. In contrast, when conditioned reinforcers are used, adults and older children tend to approximate a maximizing strategy— they show a preference for the larger, more delayed reinforcer (unless the smaller, more immediate alternative produces a more rapid rate of trials that is actually advantageous in the long run, as discussed in the previous section). This finding is not surprising: Why should a subject choose the alternative that delivers fewer points a few seconds earlier, when these points cannot be exchanged for money (and the money cannot be spent) until after the session is over? Consistent with this line of reasoning, Hyten, Madden, and Field (1994) found that subjects were more likely to choose an alternative that delivered a smaller number of points exchangeable for money immediately after the session, rather than an alternative that delivered more points that could not be exchanged for several weeks.

In summary, the available data suggest that delaying a conditioned reinforcer such as points or money has little effect on the choice responses of adults or older children as long as the overall rate of reinforcement is controlled. If the purpose of an experiment is to obtain clear effects of delayed reinforcement, the researcher should probably choose a primary reinforcer that the subject must consume or use as soon as it is delivered.

OTHER CHOICE PROCEDURES

This section will briefly describe several other procedures that have been used to study choice with human subjects. Although these procedures have been used less frequently than those already described, they are nevertheless well worth examining, for they illustrate the diversity of techniques available to those who study choice behavior.

An Adjusting Procedure

Rodriguez and Logue (1988, Experiment 2) used an *adjusting procedure* (also called a *titration procedure*) to study the self-control choices of four female undergraduates, who earned points exchangeable for money. Their experiment was patterned after a procedure for pigeons developed by Mazur (1987). In the Rodriguez and Logue experiment, there were 12 blocks of four trials each, and each trial was followed by a 10-s ITI. The first two trials of each block were forced trials, in which only one alternative was available, and a rod-push in the appropriate direction started the trial. The other two trials of each block were choice trials, in which subjects could push a metal rod either to the left or to the right, to choose either a small reinforcer after a short delay or a larger reinforcer after a longer delay.

For example, in one condition, a left push produced a 10-s delay followed by a 4-s reinforcement period, and a right push produced an adjusting delay followed by an 8-s reinforcement period. During each reinforcement period, each press on a button earned one point (worth 1/15 cent). The procedure also included a penalty during the delays—one point was lost for every 0.4 s of delay. After each block of four trials, the duration of the adjusting delay might be changed, as follows: If the large reinforcer was chosen on both choice trials, the adjusting delay was increased by 2 s. If the small reinforcer was chosen on both choice trials, the adjusting delay was decreased by 2 s. If each reinforcer was chosen once, the adjusting delay was not changed. The purpose of these adjustments was to estimate an *indifference point,* or a delay at which both alternatives were chosen about equally often. With both pigeon and human subjects, after a number of sessions, the variations in the adjusting delay usually settle into a relatively narrow range, and the middle of this range can be treated as an estimate of the indifference point. Rodriguez and Logue used a predetermined set of criteria to decide when this stability in the adjusting delay was reached in each condition.

In five different conditions, the delay for the 4-s reinforcer was set at 2, 4, 6, 8, and 10 s, and an indifference point (delay for the 8-s reinforcer) was estimated. Figure 5.9 shows the results for each subject, with regression lines fitted to the data points. Each regression line estimates combinations of reinforcer magnitude and delay that should be chosen equally often. For example, the line for Subject S6 predicts that this subject would choose the two alternatives equally often if the small reinforcer was delayed by 6 s and the large reinforcer was delayed by 14.6 s. Although one subject's data points were quite variable, the results from the other subjects were fairly well approximated by the linear functions. This pattern of results is quite similar to that obtained with pigeon subjects (Mazur, 1987; Rodriguez & Logue, 1988, Experiment 1).

Interpretation of this similarity between the human and pigeon results is complicated by several differences in procedure, including the use of conditioned reinforcers (points) rather than primary reinforcers (food), and the loss of points that the human subjects incurred during the delays. Nevertheless, the Rodriguez and

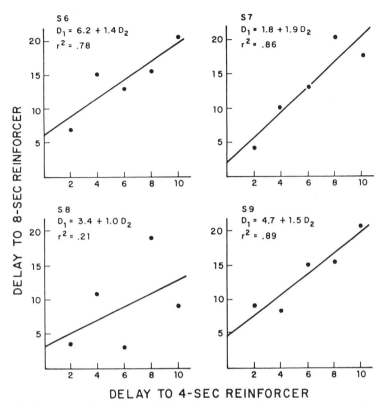

FIGURE 5.9.   The durations of the (adjusted) delay for an 8-s reinforcer are shown as a function of the (fixed) delay for a 4-s reinforcer, for the four subjects of Rodriguez and Logue (1988, Experiment 2). Regression lines are plotted for each subject, and the equations for these lines are shown.

Logue experiment demonstrates the feasibility of using an adjusting procedure to obtain indifference points with human subjects. Such indifference points can be valuable in comparing the quantitative predictions of different theoretical models of choice (see Mazur, 1984, 1986, 1987, for some examples of how indifference points can be used for this purpose).

Dynamic Contingencies

In research designed to distinguish between different theories of choice, Herrnstein and his associates used discrete-trial procedures in which some reinforcement parameter (delay, amount, or rate) varied continuously as a function of the subject's last few responses. This research exemplifies the complex contingencies that have been arranged in some recent experiments on choice. For example, in one experiment, college students sat in front of a computer screen and earned money by pressing either of two keys (Herrnstein, Loewenstein, Prelec, & Vaughan, 1993, Experiment 3). A subject had 15 min to complete as many trials as possible. After each key press, the screen would show a coin dropping into a can.

As soon as one coin finished dropping, the subject could make another response. What varied continuously during this experiment was the delay for each alternative—the amount of time needed for each coin to drop. In one condition, the delay for the right key was always 2 s less than the delay for the left key, so in the short run it was advantageous to choose the right key. However, the actual size of the delays depended on the subject's last 10 responses: If all 10 responses were made on the right key, the delays for the left and right keys were 8 and 6 s, respectively. But for every left response in the last 10, the delays for *both* alternatives were decreased by 0.4 s (so if all 10 responses were on the left key, the delays for the left and right keys were reduced to 4 and 2 s, respectively).

Under these specific conditions, the way to optimize one's earnings was to choose the left key exclusively. However, the subjects' actual choice responses were far from optimal. About two-thirds of the subjects made over 90% of their responses on the right key, thereby virtually *minimizing* their winnings. Only 2 of 24 subjects even came close to the optimal strategy of choosing the left key exclusively. The authors concluded that, under these conditions, choices were not controlled by the overall rate of reinforcement, but by a principle called *melioration,* which is closely related to the matching law (Herrnstein, 1991; Herrnstein & Prelec, 1991; Herrnstein & Vaughan, 1980). However, in other variations of this procedure (for instance, when amount of reinforcement was varied rather than delay), Herrnstein et al. found behavior that was more nearly optimal. They suggested that an important goal for future research is to determine when human choices will approximate an optimal solution and when they will not.

Other fairly complex schedules have been used to address theoretical issues about choice. For instance, Hackenberg and Axtell (1993) gave adults repeated choices between fixed-interval and progressive-interval (PI) schedules to determine whether their choices would be controlled by short- or long-term consequences. In one condition, subjects chose between an FI 30-s schedule and a PI schedule that increased by 5 s after each reinforcer. That is, the interval was 0 s for the first reinforcer, 5 s for the second reinforcer, 10 s for the third, and so on. In "no-reset" conditions, the PI continued to increase throughout a session. To maximize the overall rate of reinforcement, a subject should choose the PI schedule until the interval reaches 30 s, and then choose the FI 30-s schedule for the remainder of the session (because the PI would now be greater than 30 s if chosen). However, in "reset" conditions, each time the FI schedule was chosen, the PI schedule was reset to 0 s. It can be shown that in this situation, a subject maximizes the overall rate of reinforcement by choosing the FI 30-s schedule whenever the PI reaches 15 s (thereby resetting the PI to 0 s). Thus, in order to maximize rate of reinforcement in the long run, the subject should choose the schedule that is longer in the short run (FI 30-s instead of a progressive interval of 15 s). With points exchangeable for money as the reinforcers, Hackenberg and Axtell found behavior that was generally consistent with long-term maximization.

The widespread use of computers to control operant experiments has made it possible to implement elaborate contingencies that would have been virtually impossible to arrange in the past. Such complex contingencies can still be difficult to program, and they are often difficult to explain to nonspecialists, but in some cases they may offer the best way to distinguish between competing theories of choice.

Time Allocation in Naturalistic Settings

Bernstein and his colleagues have conducted a series of studies in which individual adults spend several weeks in an isolated room, and their behaviors are continuously monitored (Bernstein & Ebbesen, 1978; Bernstein & Michael, 1990). Contingencies are arranged in which a subject must spend a certain amount of time in one activity (e.g., sewing) to earn time for another activity (e.g., artwork). This can be considered a choice situation in which subjects must decide how to allocate their time among the limited number of activities that are available. Bernstein describes this research in Chapter 16.

CONCLUSIONS

Operant conditioning procedures have been used to study human choice in a number of different ways. Some research has examined behavior under concurrent reinforcement schedules, some has examined choice in discrete trials, and some has featured concurrent-chain procedures. This research has produced a substantial body of information about human choice, only a small part of which has been described here. There remain, however, many unanswered questions and many unexplored directions. Some important unresolved issues include the competition between schedule-controlled and rule-governed behavior, the effects of conditioning history, the different effects of primary and conditioned reinforcers, and developmental changes in choice behavior (to name just a few).

Ideally, research conducted in the operant laboratory should not only help to decide theoretical issues, it should also be relevant to behavior outside the laboratory. It remains to be seen whether operant research on human choice will have a substantial impact on how psychologists view behavior in everyday life. The value of this research will depend heavily on whether researchers are ingenious enough to design procedures that capture the important variables of everyday choice situations. Perhaps the single most important message of this chapter is that even small design features can have large effects on subjects' choices, and these details deserve the researcher's close attention. Decisions about these matters can often make the difference between an experiment that illuminates and one that confuses.

ACKNOWLEDGMENTS. Preparation of this chapter was supported by Grant MH 38357 from the U.S. National Institute of Mental Health. I thank Margaret Nygren for her technical assistance in preparing the manuscript.

REFERENCES

Autor, S. M. (1960). *The strength of conditioned reinforcers as a function of frequency and probability of reinforcement.* Unpublished doctoral dissertation, Harvard University.

Bailey, D. C., Deni, R., & Finn-O'Connor, A. (1988). Operant response requirements affect touching of visual reinforcement by infants. *Bulletin of the Psychonomic Society, 26,* 118–119.

Bangert, S., Green, L., Snyderman, M., & Turow, S. (1985). Undermatching in humans to amount of reinforcement. *Behavioural Processes, 10,* 273–283.

Baum, W. M. (1974). On two types of deviation from the matching law: Bias and undermatching. *Journal of the Experimental Analysis of Behavior, 22,* 231–242.

Baum, W. M. (1975). Time allocation in human vigilance. *Journal of the Experimental Analysis of Behavior, 23,* 45–53.

Baum, W. M. (1979). Matching, undermatching, and overmatching in studies of choice. *Journal of the Experimental Analysis of Behavior, 32,* 269–281.

Baum, W. M., & Rachlin, H. (1969). Choice as time allocation. *Journal of the Experimental Analysis of Behavior, 12,* 861–874.

Bentall, R. P., Lowe, C. F., & Beasty, A. (1985). The role of verbal behavior in human learning: II. Developmental differences. *Journal of the Experimental Analysis of Behavior, 43,* 165–181.

Berlyne, D. E. (1972). Reinforcement values of visual patterns compared through concurrent performances. *Journal of the Experimental Analysis of Behavior, 18,* 281–285.

Bernstein, D. J., & Ebbesen, E. B. (1978). Reinforcement and substitution in humans: A multiple-response analysis. *Journal of the Experimental Analysis of Behavior, 30,* 243–253.

Bernstein, D. J., & Michael, R. L. (1990). The utility of verbal and behavioral assessments of value. *Journal of the Experimental Analysis of Behavior, 54,* 173–184.

Bradshaw, C. M., Ruddle, H. V., & Szabadi, E. (1981). Studies of concurrent performances in humans. In C. M. Bradshaw, E. Szabadi, & C. F. Lowe (Eds.), *Quantification of steady-state operant behavior* (pp. 79–90). Amsterdam: Elsevier/North-Holland Biomedical Press.

Bradshaw, C. M., Szabadi, E., & Bevan, P. (1976). Behavior of humans in variable-interval schedules of reinforcement. *Journal of the Experimental Analysis of Behavior, 26,* 135–141.

Bradshaw, C. M., Szabadi, E., & Bevan, P. (1977). Effect of punishment on human variable-interval performance. *Journal of the Experimental Analysis of Behavior, 27,* 275–279.

Bradshaw, C. M., Szabadi, E., & Bevan, P. (1978). Effect of variable-interval punishment on the behavior of humans in variable-interval schedules of monetary reinforcement. *Journal of the Experimental Analysis of Behavior, 29,* 161–166.

Bradshaw, C. M., Szabadi, E., & Bevan, P. (1979). The effect of punishment on free-operant choice behavior in humans. *Journal of the Experimental Analysis of Behavior, 31,* 71–81.

Bradshaw, C. M., Szabadi, E., Bevan, P., & Ruddle, H. V. (1979). The effect of signaled reinforcement availability on concurrent performances in humans. *Journal of the Experimental Analysis of Behavior, 32,* 65–74.

Burns, D. J., & Powers, R. B. (1975). Choice and self-control in children: A test of Rachlin's model. *Bulletin of the Psychonomic Society, 5,* 156–158.

Buskist, W. F., & Miller, H. L. (1981). Concurrent operant performance in humans: Matching when food is the reinforcer. *Psychological Record, 31,* 95–100.

Catania, A. C., & Cutts, D. (1963). Experimental control of superstitious responding in humans. *Journal of the Experimental Analysis of Behavior, 6,* 203–208.

Catania, A. C., & Reynolds, G. S. (1968). A quantitative analysis of the responding maintained by interval schedules of reinforcement. *Journal of the Experimental Analysis of Behavior, 11,* 327–383.

Chait, L. D., & Zacny, J. P. (1992). Reinforcing and subjective effects of oral D-sup-9-THC and smoked marijuana in humans. *Psychopharmacology, 107,* 255–262.

Commons, M. L., Herrnstein, R. J., & Rachlin, H. (Eds.). (1982). *Quantitative analyses of behavior: Vol. 2. Matching and maximizing accounts.* Cambridge, MA: Ballinger.

Conger, R., & Killeen, P. (1974). Use of concurrent operants in small group research: A demonstration. *Pacific Sociological Review, 17,* 399–416.

Darcheville, J. C., Riviere, V., & Wearden, J. H. (1992). Fixed-interval performance and self-control in children. *Journal of the Experimental Analysis of Behavior, 57,* 187–199.

Darcheville, J. C., Riviere, V., & Wearden, J. H. (1993). Fixed-interval performance and self-control in infants. *Journal of the Experimental Analysis of Behavior, 60,* 239–254.

Davison, M., & McCarthy, D. (1988). *The matching law: A research review.* Hillsdale, NJ: Erlbaum.

de Villiers, P. A. (1977). Choice in concurrent schedules and a quantitative formulation of the law of effect. In W. K. Honig & J. E. R. Staddon (Eds.), *Handbook of operant behavior* (pp. 233–287). Englewood Cliffs, NJ: Prentice–Hall.

de Villiers, P. A., & Herrnstein, R. J. (1976). Toward a law of response strength. *Psychological Bulletin, 83,* 1131–1153.

Eisenberger, R., & Adornetto, M. (1986). Generalized self-control of delay and effort. *Journal of Personality and Social Psychology, 51,* 1020–1031.

Findley, J. D. (1958). Preference and switching under concurrent scheduling. *Journal of the Experimental Analysis of Behavior, 1,* 123–144.

Flora, S. R., & Pavlik, W. B. (1992). Human self-control and the density of reinforcement. *Journal of the Experimental Analysis of Behavior, 57,* 201–208.

Flora, S. R., Schieferecke, T. R.,& Bremenkamp, H. G. (1992). Effects of aversive noise on human self-control for positive reinforcement. *Psychological Record, 42,* 505–517.

Forzano, L. B., & Logue, A. W. (1992). Predictors of adult humans' self-control and impulsiveness for food reinforcers. *Appetite, 19,* 33–47.

Forzano, L. B., & Logue, A. W. (1995). Self-control and impulsiveness in children and adults: Effects of food preferences. *Journal of the Experimental Analysis of Behavior, 64,* 33–46.

Frazier, T. W., & Bitetto, V. E. (1969). Control of human vigilance by concurrent schedules. *Journal of the Experimental Analysis of Behavior, 12,* 591–600.

Fukui, I., & Kimura, H. (1988). Effects of reinforcement magnitude and frequency on human choice behavior. *Japanese Psychological Research, 30,* 105–113.

Hackenberg, T. D., & Axtell, S. A. M. (1993). Humans' choices in situations of time-based diminishing returns. *Journal of the Experimental Analysis of Behavior, 59,* 445–470.

Hackenberg, T. D., & Joker, V. R. (1994). Instructional versus schedule control of humans' choices in situations of diminishing returns. *Journal of the Experimental Analysis of Behavior, 62,* 367–383.

Hawkins, T. D., & Pliskoff, S. S. (1964). Brain-stimulation intensity, rate of self-stimulation, and reinforcement strength: An analysis through chaining. *Journal of the Experimental Analysis of Behavior, 7,* 285–288.

Herrnstein, R. J. (1961). Relative and absolute strength of response as a function of frequency of reinforcement. *Journal of the Experimental Analysis of Behavior, 4,* 267–272.

Herrnstein, R. J. (1970). On the law of effect. *Journal of the Experimental Analysis of Behavior, 13,* 243–266.

Herrnstein, R. J. (1991). Experiments on stable suboptimality in individual behavior. *American Economic Review, 81,* 360–364.

Herrnstein, R. J., Loewenstein, G. F., Prelec, D., & Vaughan, W. (1993). Utility maximization and melioration: Internalities in individual choice. *Journal of Behavioral Decision Making, 6,* 149–185.

Herrnstein, R. J., & Prelec, D. (1991). Melioration: A theory of distributed choice. *Journal of Economic Perspectives, 5,* 137–156.

Herrnstein, R. J., & Vaughan, W. (1980). Melioration and behavioral allocation. In J. E. R. Staddon (Ed.), *Limits to action: The allocation of individual behavior* (pp. 143–176). New York: Academic Press.

Heyman, G. M. (1979). A Markov model description of changeover probabilities on concurrent variable-interval schedules. *Journal of the Experimental Analysis of Behavior, 31,* 41–51.

Heyman, G. M., & Herrnstein, R. J. (1986). More on concurrent interval-ratio schedules: A replication and review. *Journal of the Experimental Analysis of Behavior, 46,* 331–351.

Horne, P. J., & Lowe, C. F. (1993). Determinants of human performance on concurrent schedules. *Journal of the Experimental Analysis of Behavior, 59,* 29–60.

Hyten, C., Madden, G. J., & Field, D. P. (1994). Exchange delays and impulsive choice in adult humans. *Journal of the Experimental Analysis of Behavior, 62,* 225–233.

Kelly, T. H., Fischman, M. W., Foltin, R. W., & Brady, J. V. (1991). Response patterns and cardiovascular effects during response sequence acquisition by humans. *Journal of the Experimental Analysis of Behavior, 56,* 557–574.

King, G. R., & Logue, A. W. (1987). Choice in a self-control paradigm with human subjects: Effects of changeover delay duration. *Learning and Motivation, 18,* 421–438.

King, G. R., & Logue, A. W. (1990). Humans' sensitivity to variation in reinforcer amount: Effects of the method of reinforcer delivery. *Journal of the Experimental Analysis of Behavior, 53,* 33–45.

Kohn, A., Kohn, W. K., & Staddon, J. E. (1992). Preferences for constant duration delays and constant sized rewards in human subjects. *Behavioural Processes, 26,* 125–142.

Logue, A. W., & Chavarro, A. (1992). Self-control and impulsiveness in preschool children. *The Psychological Record, 42,* 189–204.

Logue, A. W., Forzano, L. B., & Tobin, H. (1992). Independence of reinforcer amount and delay: The generalized matching law and self-control in humans. *Learning and Motivation, 23,* 326–342.

Logue, A. W., & King, G. R. (1991). Self-control and impulsiveness in adult humans when food is the reinforcer. *Appetite, 17,* 105–120.

Logue, A. W., King, G. R., Chavarro, A., & Volpe, J. S. (1990). Matching and maximizing in a self-control paradigm using human subjects. *Learning and Motivation, 21,* 340–368.

Logue, A. W., Pena-Correal, T. E., Rodriguez, M. L., & Kabela, E. (1986). Self-control in adult humans: Variation in positive reinforcer amount and delay. *Journal of the Experimental Analysis of Behavior, 46,* 159–173.

Lowe, C. F. (1979). Determinants of human operant behavior. In M. D. Zeiler & P. Harzem (Eds.), *Advances in analysis of behavior: Vol. 1. Reinforcement and the organization of behavior* (pp. 159–192). New York: Wiley.

Lowe, C. F., Beasty, A., & Bentall, R. P. (1983). The role of verbal behavior in human learning: Infant performance on fixed-interval schedules. *Journal of the Experimental Analysis of Behavior, 39,* 157–164.

Lowe, C. F., & Horne, P. J. (1985). On the generality of behavioural principles: Human choice and the matching law. In C. F. Lowe, M. Richelle, D. E. Blackman, & C. M. Bradshaw (Eds.), *Behaviour analysis and contemporary psychology* (pp. 97–115). Hillsdale, NJ: Erlbaum.

Mace, F. C., McCurdy, B., & Quigley, E. A. (1990). A collateral effect of reward predicted by matching theory. *Journal of Applied Behavior Analysis, 23,* 197–206.

Mace, F. C., Neef, N. A., Shade, D., & Mauro, B. C. (1994). Limited matching on concurrent-schedule reinforcement of academic behavior. *Journal of Applied Behavior Analysis, 27,* 585–596.

Matthews, B. A., Shimoff, E., Catania, A. C., & Sagvolden, T. (1977). Uninstructed human responding: Sensitivity to ratio and interval contingencies. *Journal of the Experimental Analysis of Behavior, 27,* 453–467.

Mazur, J. E. (1984). Tests of an equivalence rule for fixed and variable reinforcer delays. *Journal of Experimental Psychology: Animal Behavior Processes, 10,* 426–436.

Mazur, J. E. (1986). Choice between single and multiple delayed reinforcers. *Journal of the Experimental Analysis of Behavior, 46,* 67–77.

Mazur, J. E. (1987). An adjusting procedure for studying delayed reinforcement. In M. L. Commons, J. E. Mazur, J. A. Nevin, & H. Rachlin (Eds.), *Quantitative analyses of behavior: Vol. 5. The effect of delay and of intervening events on reinforcement value* (pp. 55–73). Hillsdale, NJ: Erlbaum.

Mazur, J. E. (1993). Predicting the strength of a conditioned reinforcer: Effects of delay and uncertainty. *Current Directions in Psychological Science, 2,* 70–74.

McDowell, J. J. (1988). Matching theory in natural human environments. *The Behavior Analyst, 11,* 95–109.

Millar, A., & Navarick, D. J. (1984). Self-control and choice in humans: Effects of video game playing as a positive reinforcer. *Learning and Motivation, 15,* 203–218.

Navarick, D. J. (1982). Negative reinforcement and choice in humans. *Learning and Motivation, 13,* 361–377.

Navarick, D. J. (1985). Choice in humans: Functional properties of reinforcers established by instruction. *Behavioural Processes, 11,* 269–277.

Navarick, D. J. (1986). Human impulsivity and choice: A challenge to traditional operant methodology. *Psychological Record, 36,* 343–356.

Navarick, D. J., & Chellsen, J. (1983). Matching versus undermatching in the choice behavior of humans. *Behaviour Analysis Letters, 3,* 325–335.

Neef, N. A., Mace, F. C., Shea, M. C., & Shade, D. (1992). Effects of reinforcer rate and reinforcer quality on time allocation: Extensions of matching theory to educational settings. *Journal of Applied Behavior Analysis, 25,* 691–699.

Oscar-Berman, M., Heyman, G. M., Bonner, R. T., & Ryder, J. (1980). Human neuropsychology: Some differences between Korsakoff and normal operant performance. *Psychological Research, 41,* 235–247.

Pierce, W. D., Epling, W. F., & Greer, S. M. (1981). Human communication and the matching law. In C. M. Bradshaw, E. Szabadi, & C. F. Lowe (Eds.), *Quantification of steady-state operant behavior* (pp. 345–348). Amsterdam: Elsevier/North-Holland Biomedical Press.

Poppen, R. (1972). Effects of concurrent schedules on human fixed-interval performance. *Journal of the Experimental Analysis of Behavior, 18,* 119–127.

Rachlin, H. (1978). A molar theory of reinforcement schedules. *Journal of the Experimental Analysis of Behavior, 30,* 345–360.

Rachlin, H., Battalio, R., Kagel, J., & Green, L. (1981). Maximization theory in behavioral psychology. *The Behavioral and Brain Sciences, 4,* 371–417.

Rachlin, H., Green, L., Kagel, J. H., & Battalio, R. C. (1976). Economic demand theory and psychological studies of choice. *The Psychology of Learning and Motivation, 10,* 129–154.

Rachlin, H., Green, L., & Tormey, B. (1988). Is there a decisive test between matching and maximizing? *Journal of the Experimental Analysis of Behavior, 50,* 113–123.

Ragotzy, S. P., Blakely, E., & Poling, A. (1988). Self-control in mentally retarded adolescents: Choice as a function of amount and delay of reinforcement. *Journal of the Experimental Analysis of Behavior, 49,* 191–199.

Rodriguez, M. L., & Logue, A. W. (1988). Adjusting delay to reinforcement: Comparing choice in pigeons and humans. *Journal of Experimental Psychology: Animal Behavior Processes, 14,* 105–117.

Rosenberger, P. B. (1973). Concurrent schedule control of human visual target fixations. *Journal of the Experimental Analysis of Behavior, 20,* 411–416.

Ruddle, H. V., Bradshaw, C. M., Szabadi, E., & Foster, T. M. (1982). Performance of humans in concurrent avoidance/positive-reinforcement schedules. *Journal of the Experimental Analysis of Behavior, 38,* 51–61.

Sanders, R. M. (1969). Concurrent fixed-ratio fixed-interval performances in adult human subjects. *Journal of the Experimental Analysis of Behavior, 12,* 601–604.

Schmitt, D. R. (1974). Effects of reinforcement rate and reinforcer magnitude on choice behavior of humans. *Journal of the Experimental Analysis of Behavior, 21,* 409–419.

Schoener, T. W. (1971). Theory of feeding strategies. *Annual Review of Ecology and Systematics, 2,* 27–39.

Schroeder, S. R. (1975). Perseveration in concurrent performances by the developmentally retarded. *Psychological Record, 25,* 51–64.

Schroeder, S. R., & Holland, J. G. (1969). Reinforcement of eye movement with concurrent schedules. *Journal of the Experimental Analysis of Behavior, 12,* 897–903.

Schweitzer, J. B., & Sulzer-Azaroff, B. (1988). Self-control: Teaching tolerance for delay in impulsive children. *Journal of the Experimental Analysis of Behavior, 50,* 173–186.

Shimoff, E., Catania, A. C., & Matthews, B. A. (1981). Uninstructed human responding: Sensitivity of low-rate performance to schedule contingencies. *Journal of the Experimental Analysis of Behavior, 36,* 207–220.

Shimp, C. P. (1969). Optimal behavior in free-operant experiments. *Psychological Review, 76,* 97–112.

Shull, R. L., & Spear, D. J. (1987). Detention time after reinforcement: Effects due to delay of reinforcement? In M. L. Commons, J. E. Mazur, J. A. Nevin, & H. Rachlin (Eds.), *Quantitative analyses of behavior: Vol. 5. The effect of delay and of intervening events on reinforcement value* (pp. 187–204). Hillsdale, NJ: Erlbaum.

Silberberg, A., Thomas, J. R., & Berendzen, N. (1991). Human choice on concurrent variable-interval variable-ratio schedules. *Journal of the Experimental Analysis of Behavior, 56,* 575–584.

Snyderman, M. (1983). Delay and amount of reward in a concurrent chain. *Journal of the Experimental Analysis of Behavior, 39,* 437–447.

Solnick, J. V., Kannenberg, C. H., Eckerman, D. A., & Waller, M. B. (1980). An experimental analysis of impulsivity and impulse control in humans. *Learning and Motivation, 11,* 61–77.

Sonuga-Barke, E. J. S., Lea, S. E. G., & Webley, P. (1989a). The development of adaptive choice in a self-control paradigm. *Journal of the Experimental Analysis of Behavior, 51,* 77–85.

Sonuga-Barke, E. J. S., Lea, S. E. G., & Webley, P. (1989b). An account of human "impulsivity" on self-control tasks. *Quarterly Journal of Experimental Psychology: Comparative and Physiological Psychology, 41,* 161–179.

Spiga, R., Cherek, D. R., Grabowski, J., & Bennett, R. H. (1992). Effects of inequity on human free-operant cooperative responding: A validation study. *Psychological Record, 42,* 29–40.

Stern, K. N., Chait, L. D.,& Johanson, C. E. (1989). Reinforcing and subjective effects of oral tripelennamine in normal human volunteers. *Behavioural Pharmacology, 1,* 161–167.

Takahashi, M., & Iwamoto, T. (1986). Human concurrent performances: The effects of experience, instructions, and schedule-correlated stimuli. *Journal of the Experimental Analysis of Behavior, 45,* 257–267.

Wurster, R. M., & Griffiths, R. R. (1979). Human concurrent performances: Variation of reinforcer magnitude and rate of reinforcement. *Psychological Record, 29,* 341–354.

6

Negative Reinforcement
and Punishment

John Crosbie

Although the use of negative reinforcement and punishment is sometimes controversial and unpopular, an experimental analysis of those procedures is crucial if we are to achieve our goal of predicting, controlling, and interpreting the behavior of organisms. Studying only positive consequences of behavior will reveal only half of the picture. Furthermore, negative reinforcement and punishment are particularly powerful, and constantly are present in the physical environment. Indeed, it has been argued that positive reinforcement is really only negative reinforcement in disguise, because all behavior is based on escape and avoidance (Hull, 1943). It is unfortunate that the study of negative reinforcement and punishment is in decline (Baron, 1991), because its analysis is needed to increase the data base of our discipline, and the procedures can be used therapeutically to improve the lives of many people (e.g., by reducing self-injurious behavior). One goal of the present chapter is to encourage more research on this topic with human subjects.

Given their theoretical history, and recent developments, it is appropriate that negative reinforcement and punishment should be considered together. Early punishment theories (e.g., Dinsmoor, 1954; Skinner, 1953; Thorndike, 1932) proposed that punishment reduces behavior only because organisms perform other behaviors that avoid the punisher. In other words, punishment is a secondary process based on avoidance. Later (Azrin & Holz, 1966) it was argued that punishment is a primary process that reduces behavior independently of avoidance. Currently, this is the most widely accepted theoretical position on punishment. There is, however, recent evidence that avoidance and punishment may be fundamentally related. In one study (Dunham, Mariner, & Adams, 1969), pigeons received food when they pecked a lighted key, then electric shock after each peck. Shock decreased the rate of pecking the key, and increased the rate of pecking the wall

John Crosbie • Department of Psychology, West Virginia University, Morgantown, West Virginia 26506-6040.

Handbook of Research Methods in Human Operant Behavior, edited by Lattal and Perone. Plenum Press, New York, 1998.

around the key. Off-key pecks were never followed by food or shock, and probably increased because they avoided the punisher. Another study (Arbuckle & Lattal, 1987) found that pigeons paused for long periods when pausing reduced shock frequency. In other words, pausing increased because it avoided the punisher. Punishment may indeed be a primary process, but its theoretical relation with avoidance needs to be clarified.

The relation between punishment and avoidance also is important for practical reasons. There is widespread popular and scientific resistance to the use of punishment because of a belief that it has undesirable side effects such as avoidance of the punishing agent and situation (Azrin & Holz, 1966; Newsom, Favell, & Rincover, 1983; Skinner, 1953). Although there is little evidence to support this notion, recent results described above suggest that avoidance side effects merit serious experimental consideration.

This chapter is concerned with methodological, conceptual, and ethical issues involved in conducting human studies of negative reinforcement and punishment. Within each topic, there is, wherever possible, a discussion of features common to both negative reinforcement and punishment. When that is not possible, unique features of each procedure are discussed within a parallel structure. The main goal of this chapter is to describe what has been done previously, evaluate the advantages and disadvantages of different procedures, and suggest how research in this area can be performed with greatest methodological rigor. A secondary goal is to stimulate research interest in this fascinating and important yet largely neglected topic.

DEFINITIONS

Negative Reinforcement

For present purposes, negative reinforcement is defined as the operation by which response rate increases or is maintained when the response reduces, terminates (escapes), or prevents or postpones (avoids) an aversive stimulus. Aversive stimuli are those that affect behavior in this way. If an organism responds to escape from or avoid a stimulus, then, in that situation, the stimulus is a negative reinforcer (i.e., aversive); a stimulus that does not increase responding in such a way is not.

Punishment

For present purposes, punishment is defined as the operation whereby response rate is reduced following some response-dependent stimulus change (Azrin & Holz, 1966). A punisher is a response-dependent stimulus change that reduces responding.

Aversive Control

The word *aversive* comes from the Latin "to turn away" (Mish et al., 1983). Originally (e.g., Thorndike, 1911), the technical meaning was similar to that (i.e., the ability to promote escape and avoidance; negative reinforcement). Because punishment was defined for a long time (from Thorndike, 1932, to Azrin & Holz, 1966) in terms of negative reinforcement, by association, punishment also came to be called an aversive procedure. Although, according to the definition presented above, punishment need not be based on negative reinforcement, because there is such a long tradition of calling punishment aversive, that is now done widely in the technical literature. Hence, in this chapter, the terms *aversive stimuli, aversive consequences,* and *aversive control* refer to both negative reinforcement and punishment. Furthermore, those terms refer only to negative reinforcement and punishment, and not to related procedures such as conditioned suppression (i.e., reduction in operant responding by noncontingently presenting a conditioned aversive stimulus; Estes & Skinner, 1941).

A NORMATIVE SAMPLE

Between 1958 and 1993, 56 human studies of negative reinforcement and punishment were published in the *Journal of the Experimental Analysis of Behavior* and *The Psychological Record,* the major outlets for such studies. Negative reinforcement was used in 26 of those studies, and punishment was used in 37. In this chapter, whenever I discuss how frequently a procedure has been used in human studies of negative reinforcement and punishment, those data are derived from this sample. Although human operant studies of aversive control have been published elsewhere, the present sample is convenient and representative, and all cited studies are easy to find.

ETHICAL CONCERNS

Whenever aversive stimuli are used, there is the potential for subjects to be harmed, either from physical consequences of stimuli such as electric shock and loud noise (hereafter described as *physical aversive stimuli*), or from emotional consequences of events such as monetary loss or time out from positive reinforcement (hereafter described as *nonphysical aversive stimuli;* see Aversive Stimuli section for further discussion of physical and nonphysical aversive stimuli). It is the responsibility of anybody who uses aversive stimuli to minimize that harm. Given the seriousness of that responsibility, this topic is the first discussed in this chapter. Another important concern is how to obtain Institutional Review Board approval for research on aversive procedures with human subjects. Suggestions on how that might be accomplished are offered in the following section.

Protecting Subjects

Electric Shock

Although electric shock is a useful stimulus for human operant studies of aversive control, its use carries a responsibility to ensure that subjects do not experience unnecessarily high levels of shock. A diverse assortment of shock devices, intensities, and durations have been used, and frequently, technical specifications are incomplete. It seems, however, that shock rarely, if ever, exceeded 5 mA, which is probably a reasonable upper limit to use in studies of aversive conditioning with humans. Many animal studies have used lower shock intensities effectively as negative reinforcers and punishers (Baron, 1991), and a 5-mA shock is quite strong. During pilot work it is prudent to present the proposed shock to several people to estimate its aversiveness. For example, while testing my shock device I became accustomed to strong shock, and only when my graduate students complained about the pain did I realize that the proposed intensity would have been too high for experimentally naive subjects. Furthermore, there is much individual variability in subjects' ability to take electric shock, and there is no way to predict tolerance based on subjects' physical characteristics.

In addition to using a moderate shock intensity, there are three further precautions that always should be employed whenever electric shock is used. First, shock should never be permitted to cross the subject's heart because that could be fatal (Butterfield, 1975). There are two main ways to achieve that: place electrodes on limbs rather than the thorax, and use a concentric-ring electrode so that current flows only a short distance between the rings (e.g., as is used on the SIBIS device reported by Linscheid, Iwata, Ricketts, Williams, & Griffin, 1990). Second, a fuse should be placed on the output lead so that current cannot exceed some specified safe limit. It is prudent to use a fuse that accommodates a higher intensity than the upper limit to be employed because subjects' electrical resistance, and consequently current flow, varies considerably. For example, my shock device was equipped initially with a 5-mA fuse, and 3 mA was the highest intensity I planned to use. During testing, however, the fuse blew reliably with some subjects because their electrical resistance was less than we had estimated. A 10-mA fuse was substituted, and it has never blown. Third, before and after every session, researchers should carefully inspect the body site where shock is presented to ensure that there is no damage such as reddening of the skin or burning. If there is damage, electrode jelly could be used, physical specifications of shock modified (e.g., reduce intensity or duration), or the subject excused from further participation in the study.

Loud Noise

Precautions also need to be taken whenever loud noise (see Aversive Stimuli section for further discussion of this term) is used. Indeed, loud noise has more potential problems than does electric shock. Physical problems produced by shock (e.g., skin irritation) are obvious immediately, but hearing problems produced by loud noise could take years to develop. In addition to concern for subjects' welfare, legal problems related to such damage could pose major problems for researchers and their institutions. Most studies have employed noise intensity between 68 and 110 dB, with a median of 98 dB. Given that in many countries 80 dB is the recommendation for maximum acceptable noise in the workplace, and that the decibel scale is logarithmic, the intensities used with human subjects were quite loud.

In only one study in the present sample did subjects report that the noise was more than annoying or moderately aversive (Romanczyk, 1976). The 105-dB metal-lic rasping noise used in that study had a similar intensity to noises used in other studies, so there must have been something about the rasping noise itself rather than the intensity that was aversive. If I wanted to use noise as an aversive stimu-lus, I would find aversive characteristics of the noise independent of intensity (e.g., a 3000-Hz tone is aversive even at low intensity), and use that noise with the mini-mum effective intensity established during pilot testing. Furthermore, I would en-sure that subjects received audiometric tests before and during the experiment so that any sign of hearing impairment could be detected readily.

Nonphysical Aversive Stimuli

Although aversive stimuli such as monetary loss and timeout from positive reinforcement pose no physical risks to subjects, such stimuli should be used in such a way that subjects are not unduly distressed. The most important way to do that is to minimize the intensity of aversive stimuli. Using the smallest amount of nonphysical aversive stimulation that will achieve the desired purpose (e.g., pro-ducing efficient avoidance or reducing responding below 50% of baseline) should minimize subjects' distress, and, if they are paid dependent on performance, help to ensure that they receive reasonable compensation for their participation. Al-though nonphysical aversive stimuli have no physical risks, they are powerful, and consequently must be used carefully to protect subjects' welfare.

IRB Approval

After the researcher has ensured that subjects are unlikely to be harmed with aversive stimuli, the next concern is how to obtain approval from the Institution-al Review Board for the protection of human subjects (IRB) to use them. As an ex-ample, consider the following strategy to obtain permission to use electric shock in human operant studies. First, present a detailed rationale of the clinical and the-oretical need for shock studies with humans. Second, highlight that shock is com-monly used in psychological laboratories (a recent search found approximately 100 studies that used shock in the last 5 years). Third, describe safeguards (see pre-vious section for details), and be clear that there is virtually no possibility of harm to subjects. Finally, offer to appear before the IRB to demonstrate the shock appa-ratus and address theoretical, practical, and safety issues in person. Because many people (including IRB members) have emotional rather than logical reactions to the use of aversive procedures, extra care must be taken to overcome that bias. If such care is taken, however, it is possible to obtain approval to use physical aver-sive stimuli with humans.

SUBJECT RETENTION

Human subjects present two problems for studies of aversive control that ani-mals do not. First, humans are under social control of the experimenter, and some-times need specific permission to respond. Second, they can escape from the study.

For example, consider a study by Ader and Tatum (1961). College students sat in front of a board that contained only a button. Electrodes were attached to their left calves, and electric shock intensity was adjusted so that it produced involuntary leg flexion. Subjects reported that the shock was unpleasant, uncomfortable, or bothersome (p. 275). A shock was programmed every few seconds, and every button press delayed the next shock by the same period (i.e., shock was presented on a Sidman avoidance schedule). Of the 36 subjects, 17 acquired the avoidance response, 10 removed the electrodes and terminated the experiment, and 7 did not make a response. Although they were seated at a table that contained only the button, 20% of subjects never pressed it. That is probably because they were not given permission to touch the button. Subjects were explicitly told not to stand, smoke, vocalize, or touch the electrodes; why should they assume that they could touch the button? Specific instructions concerning contingencies may not be required, but permission to touch operanda is. Alternatively, responding could be shaped (Matthews, Shimoff, Catania, & Sagvolden, 1977), but that seems an unnecessary complication.

Ader and Tatum's (1961) results highlight an additional problem with human subjects. Because humans are not physically restrained, special care must be taken when aversive stimuli are used (e.g., using large positive reinforcers or slowly increasing the intensity of aversive stimuli), or subjects may terminate the experiment. Another useful technique is to provide reinforcers and punishers for attendance and nonattendance, respectively. For example, in my lab reinforcement conditions are arranged such that subjects earn approximately 75% of their payment for their performance during sessions, and 25% for perfect attendance. In addition, if they miss a session without a good reason, they lose the perfect-attendance bonus, plus $5 for each session missed (this technique was originally proposed by Kaufman, 1964). In my experience, subjects rarely miss sessions when these contingencies are arranged (see Pilgrim, Chapter 2, for further discussion of this issue).

RESPONSES

In over 70% of studies in the present sample, the response device was a button, telegraph key, computer key, or lever that required force of less than 1 N (e.g., Baron & Surdy, 1990; Bradshaw, Szabadi, & Bevan, 1977; Crosbie, 1990; McIlvane et al., 1987; Weiner, 1962). Such responses are popular because they are easy to instrument, and their use maintains continuity with animal studies in the area. Researchers also have recorded pulling plungers (e.g., Ayllon & Azrin, 1966; Bennett & Cherek, 1990; Katz, 1973), moving a computer mouse (Crosbie, 1990, 1993), moving objects with a hand (Pilgrim & Galizio, 1990), stuttering (Flanagan, Goldiamond, & Azrin, 1958), muscle twitches (Hefferline & Keenan, 1961), heart rate (Brener, 1966), skin conductance (Grings & Carlin, 1966), and vocalization (Miller, 1968a,b). One of the hallmarks of human operant research is the creativity of experimenters in terms of responses employed.

Although low-effort operanda have been used frequently, in my view, they are not ideal for studies of aversive control with humans. Because there are no published human operant aversive control studies of the relation between response effort and sensitivity, most of the argument in this section is based on extrapolation from aversive control studies with animals or human operant studies that did not consider aversive control.

For several years, researchers (e.g., Blough, 1966; Elsmore, 1971) have suggested that more effortful responses produce greater response sensitivity (i.e., appropriate changes in response rate following changes in reinforcer frequency). For example, in one study (Azrin, 1958), human adults pressed a button that required a force of 0.15 N to illuminate a dial for 100 ms so that they could detect meter-needle deflections on a darkened screen (i.e., Holland's, 1957, vigilance task). Deflections occurred every 3 min. Even after several hours on this task, subjects still were responding at a high rate throughout each 3-min period. When a button that required a force of 3 N was substituted, subjects quickly adopted a more efficient pattern of an extended pause followed by increasingly rapid responding near the end of each interval. Increased response force also has produced greater sensitivity with animals on various preparations and schedules (Blough, 1966), and humans pressing light (1 and 11 N) plus heavy (25 and 146 N) levers on variable-interval (VI; reinforcers follow the first response after an interval that varies about the VI mean) schedules (McDowell & Wood, 1985). The relation between response force and schedule sensitivity may be particularly important with human subjects because their ratio of response requirement to body size is much smaller than for animals. Although sensitivity is not a goal unique to studies of aversive control, it is important when producing a baseline with which to compare effects of punishment.

In studies of punishment with humans, moderate- or high-effort responses are preferable because they produce lower response rates (McDowell & Wood, 1985) and consequently less intense punishers are required (Azrin & Holz, 1966; Church, 1963), and, as was discussed above, they probably are more sensitive to change in contingencies. If low-effort operanda are used in such studies, then subjects may be exposed to more intense punishers than are required to produce criterion suppression, and more punishment sessions will probably be required to produce stable response patterns. In my studies of human punishment, subjects press a lever or pull a plunger with a force of 30 N, which is sufficient to promote sensitivity, but not so effortful that it is onerous. In my view, it is unwise to use low-effort operanda in studies of punishment with humans.

BASELINE

Previous sections of this chapter considered features of negative reinforcement and punishment that were common to both procedures. This is the first section where there is no commonality. To study punishment in the human-operant paradigm, responding must previously be reinforced to ensure that it is stable and at a moderate rate (i.e., a baseline must be produced). Studies of negative reinforcement do not require a baseline. Consequently, this section considers how best to establish a baseline for studies of punishment.

Reinforcers

Most studies in the sample (55%) used money to produce a baseline maintained by positive reinforcement (e.g., Baron & Surdy, 1990; Bennett & Cherek, 1990; Bradshaw, Szabadi, & Bevan, 1977, 1978, 1979; Crosbie, 1990, 1993; Miller, 1970). Several studies (32%) provided no programmed consequences for responding (e.g., Azrin, 1958; Flanagan et al., 1958; Maltzman, Holz, & Kunze, 1965), or paid subjects an hourly rate that was independent of performance (e.g., Weiner, 1962, 1963, 1964a–c). A few studies (12%) used other positive reinforcers such as tokens exchangeable for privileges (Ayllon & Azrin, 1966), cigarettes (Herman & Azrin, 1964; Miller, 1970), and M&M's (Romanczyk, 1976).

Given that studies of punishment require a baseline condition without punishment, a punishment condition, then usually another condition without punishment, many sessions are required to achieve steady-state performance. Furthermore, subjects need to be sufficiently motivated to persist during the punishment condition. Although some studies of punishment have been conducted without programmed reinforcers, that technique is risky. Subjects need adequate compensation if they are to complete the study and produce orderly data, and, in my experience, that compensation should largely be response dependent. Using social control or points without a backup can result in high subject dropout rates, subjects not taking the study seriously, and the researcher continually trying to cut corners to shorten the study.

Although reinforcers such as food have been used with humans (e.g., Buskist, Miller, & Bennett, 1980), money has several advantages: It is a generalized reinforcer that requires no specific deprivation, most subjects usually are deprived of things obtainable with money, it can be presented quickly in precise amounts, and no experimental time is lost consuming it (although a procedural analogue of consumption can be arranged; Shull & Lawrence, Chapter 4).

Given that money is the reinforcer, how should it be presented? A convenient method is to display a message such as "Your total has increased by 20 cents." Alternatively, a running total of points exchangeable for money could be displayed continuously, and some exteroceptive stimulus (e.g., a sound or light) could accompany point increase (Bradshaw et al., 1977, 1979; Crosbie, 1990, 1993; Weiner, 1963). One potential disadvantage of using a running total is that points obtained later in training may be subjectively devalued because they increase the total by a progressively smaller proportion (Weber's law).

How large should reinforcers be? They should be as large as is feasible given the budget and IRB recommendations. It is difficult to specify an exact amount, but there are two important considerations. First, to obtain data comparable with those obtained with hungry animals, reinforcers must be sufficiently large. Using small total amounts of reinforcement may be false economy. Second, when aversive stimuli are used with human subjects, there should be no suggestion that subjects are coerced to participate. Hence, in such studies reinforcer magnitude should not be too large. In my recent studies of punishment with humans, subjects received approximately $5 per hour, which is sufficient to produce orderly data without raising concerns of subject coercion.

Money has several procedural advantages, but it also has problems not encountered in animal studies. For example, because human subjects usually are not paid until the end of an experiment, missing sessions has only minor, delayed consequences. One way to increase subjects' reliability is to reinforce perfect attendance and punish missing sessions (see Subject Retention). Such measures often are necessary in studies of negative reinforcement and punishment because they frequently require many sessions.

Schedules

In 90% of punishment studies in the sample, baseline responding was maintained by positive reinforcement arranged (in decreasing frequency) on variable-interval (e.g., Bradshaw et al., 1977, 1978, 1979), fixed-ratio (e.g., Weiner, 1964b), continuous (Baron & Surdy, 1990), fixed-interval (Azrin, 1958; Weiner, 1962, 1964c), and variable-ratio schedules (Romanczyk, 1976; Scobie & Kaufman, 1969). In the other 10% of punishment studies, responding was maintained with negative reinforcement arranged on some version of the Sidman avoidance procedure.

The most appropriate baseline schedule for a study of punishment is determined by the aims of the study. There is no one best baseline schedule for all studies. In this section, typical characteristics of common schedules are described and guidelines presented to help researchers select the most appropriate baseline for their needs.

Fixed-ratio schedules (FR; reinforcers follow a fixed number of responses) generally produce a high response rate (unless the ratio requirement is so high that the behavior is strained), and sometimes responding is so high that it cannot increase. Such a ceiling effect would pose problems for studies of punishment contrast (i.e., increased responding in unpunished components; Brethower & Reynolds, 1962; Crosbie, Williams, Lattal, Anderson, & Brown, 1997), for example. Furthermore, on FR schedules, responses often are emitted in chains such that the most potent discriminative stimulus for a response is the previous response. Consequently, changing reinforcement or punishment conditions has less effect than with other schedules (Sidman, 1960). This causes a problem with punishment because more intense punishers are required to achieve criterion suppression. In addition, on FR schedules, when response rate is reduced during punishment conditions, reinforcer rate also must decline, which could be an experimental and theoretical nuisance. Frequently the resultant response pattern is a pause followed by an increasing response rate (pause and run). Such an unsteady baseline often is problematic for assessing changes related to punishment, but it may be useful to determine whether punishment differentially affects pause duration and run rates, for example.

The continuous schedule (CRF; a reinforcer follows every response) has all of the problems faced by FR schedules except for pausing and insensitivity (provided that reinforcers must be collected). In addition, CRF also has the potential problem of satiation, though this is uncommon in human studies because money is the predominant reinforcer.

Variable-ratio schedules (VR; reinforcers follow a number of responses that varies about the ratio) have all of the disadvantages of FR schedules except pausing.

Fixed-interval schedules (FI; reinforcers follow the first response after a fixed interval) produce good punishment baselines: Resultant response rates are moderate, so responding can increase or decrease (e.g., to study punishment contrast and induction); baselines are sensitive to changes in reinforcement and punishment conditions; and reinforcement rates are held constant during punishment conditions. Scalloping is the only significant disadvantage.

VI schedules establish excellent punishment baselines. They produce moderate, steady responding that is sensitive to changes in reinforcement and punishment conditions, reinforcement rate is held constant across a range of response rates, and satiation is avoided. For these reasons, most punishment baselines are produced with VI schedules.

Pretraining

During the first sessions it is useful to reinforce responding on CRF or FR schedules to increase response rate before moving to VI schedules. In early studies in my lab, subjects received one or two sessions of FR reinforcement with the ratio requirement increasing steadily, then VI reinforcement with the interval increasing slowly to the final baseline level (VI 3-min). A few subjects, however, responded more slowly when the schedule changed from FR to VI (i.e., they seemed to discriminate the change from ratio-based to interval-based reinforcers). With subsequent subjects we used VR schedules in pretraining, and the change to VI was indiscriminable. In my experience, it is important to provide extensive careful pretraining with humans as is done routinely with animals.

Multiple Schedules

Even when the main concern is change from baseline for the punished response, it may be useful to have an unpunished component arranged on a multiple schedule for an additional assessment of change within the punishment condition. Behavior drifts during a long experiment (especially when an operation as powerful as punishment is effected), so between-phase comparisons sometimes are inadequate to provide a convincing demonstration of change. When between-phase and within-phase comparisons are used in concert, however, it usually is possible to assess change reliably.

Stability Criteria

In the sample, stability was assessed by visual inspection, a fixed number of sessions, or statistical criteria.

Visual Inspection

In Azrin's (1958) study with an avoidance baseline, phases lasted until there was no increasing or decreasing trend in response rate, and cumulative records showed steady performance for at least 30 min. Flanagan et al. (1958) and Miller (1968a) used similar criteria. Visual inference also was used to assess stability in studies of punishment (e.g., Azrin, 1958; Romanczyk, 1976; Scobie & Kaufman, 1969).

Number of Sessions

In some studies, responding was considered stable when a predetermined number of sessions had been completed. For example, Ruddle, Bradshaw, Szabadi, and Foster (1982) had three avoidance phases that lasted for either ten or fifteen 70-min sessions. Similarly, Weiner's (1963) avoidance phases lasted for four or five 1-hr sessions. Similar criteria were used in studies of punishment. For example, Bradshaw et al. (1977, 1978, 1979) conducted experimental phases for 20 to 30 sessions, and Weiner's (1962, 1963, 1964c) phases lasted between 4 and 5 sessions.

Statistical Criteria

In some studies, stability was defined according to avoidance efficiency. For example, the criterion used by Matthews and Shimoff (1974) was perfect avoidance in eighteen of twenty 10-s cycles, and Ader and Tatum (1963) defined acquisition as the first 5-min period in which subjects received fewer than six shocks. Another popular criterion is based on the mean difference between the first and last halves of an N-session block (see Baron & Perone, Chapter 3, for further details). A 4-session block was used with a maximum mean difference of 10% (Baron & Galizio, 1976; Shipley, Baron, & Kaufman, 1972) or 15% (Galizio, 1979). In a variation, for a 6-session block, the standard deviation divided by the mean had to be less than 15% (Cherek, Spiga, & Egli, 1992). Alternatively, all responses within a 3- or 5-session block were required to be within 10% (Miller, 1968a,b) or 5 responses (Kelly & Hake, 1970), respectively.

Similar statistical criteria have been used to assess stability in studies of punishment. Stability was inferred when matching performance was greater than 90% (McIlvane et al., 1987), the mean difference between the first and second 3-session blocks was less than 10% (Pilgrim & Galizio, 1990), there was less than 20% interblock variability in response rate over four successive 30-s blocks (Johnson, McGlynn, & Topping, 1973), and between-session variability of matching performance (i.e., the number of incorrect responses divided by the number of correct responses) was no greater than within-session variability for five consecutive sessions (Miller & Zimmerman, 1966). In one study of punishment (Crosbie, 1993), the following atypical statistical criteria (see Killeen, 1978, for details) were employed over the final eight sessions of baseline: mean difference between first and second 4-session blocks, coefficient of variability (standard deviation divided by the mean), and coefficient of linearity (which assessed increasing or decreasing trend).

Recommendations

Although it is impossible to specify a stability assessment strategy that will be appropriate for all studies of aversive control with humans, the following guidelines will help researchers select the best technique for their circumstances.

There are three important issues to consider when assessing stability with human avoidance behavior. First, there is considerable variability among subjects in time taken to achieve steady-state performance. Hence, conducting an avoidance phase for a predetermined number of sessions is ill-advised because stable responding may not be obtained for some subjects, and for other subjects responding will be stable before the criterion number of sessions. For the latter subjects, arbitrarily extending the phase will waste time and money. Second, in my view, the experimental analysis of human operant behavior will progress more quickly and steadily if all human operant researchers use and report stability criteria. Other researchers can better assess the methodological rigor of a study, and replicate it more easily. For those reasons, using visual criteria is not ideal. Third, because human avoidance acquisition is so fast and terminal behavior is so steady, typical stability criteria can be relaxed slightly without compromising methodological rigor. Consequently, for avoidance studies I recommend statistical criteria such as the mean difference.

For the reasons outlined in the previous paragraph, in studies of punishment with humans, it is important to specify stability criteria quantitatively, and conducting phases for a predetermined period is unwise. Punishment, however, provides a special problem for stability. Statistical stability assessments are sensitive to the magnitude of the dependent variable. For example, occasional fluctuations of 3 responses per minute will not affect stability when the base rate is 100 responses per minute. When the base rate is 5 responses per minute, however, such fluctuations will preclude the possibility of obtaining statistical stability (Baron & Perone, Chapter 3; Perone, 1991). For that reason, some researchers (e.g., Crosbie et al., 1997; Lattal & Griffin, 1972) have not demanded that the punished response be stable according to statistical criteria. Rather, the punishment phase may last for 10 to 20 consecutive sessions that satisfy some other criterion such as a response rate less than 50% of baseline (Azrin & Holz, 1966). If response rate is not so low as to be affected by this statistical problem, then statistical criteria such as mean difference are recommended. Otherwise, I recommend some criterion such as 10 consecutive sessions with response rate less than 50% of baseline plus visual inspection of no increasing or decreasing trend.

AVERSIVE STIMULI

It is common in the aversive control literature to draw a distinction between two types of aversive stimuli: events such as electric shock and loud noise, which frequently are labeled painful, unconditioned, or physical, and events such as loss of points or money and timeout from positive reinforcement, which frequently are labeled nonpainful, conditioned, or nonphysical. None of these labels, however, is entirely satisfactory.

Typically, there is little, if any, evidence of pain when electric shock or loud noise are presented, nor any evidence that money loss or timeout from positive reinforcement are not painful. Furthermore, pain has unnecessary emotional connotations, so that term probably should be avoided.

Technically, unconditioned aversive stimuli are aversive without training, and conditioned aversive stimuli are previously neutral stimuli that become aversive by frequent pairing with unconditioned aversive stimuli. There are two main problems with labeling the two types of aversive stimuli *unconditioned* and *conditioned*. First, although events such as electric shock are aversive without training, so are events such as loss of positive reinforcers and timeout from positive reinforcement. Second, money loss and timeout from positive reinforcement are almost never paired with unconditioned aversive stimuli. Consequently, the unconditioned–conditioned distinction is technically unsatisfactory.

The physical–nonphysical distinction also has problems. All stimuli are necessarily physical, so the term *nonphysical stimulus* is an oxymoron. On balance, however, the physical and nonphysical labels have fewer problems than the other two, and consequently are used throughout this chapter.

Physical Aversive Stimuli

Physical aversive stimuli such as electric shock have provided most of what is known about negative reinforcement and punishment with animals (Azrin & Holz, 1966; Baron, 1991), and punishment with humans who engage in self-injurious behavior (Harris & Ersner-Hershfield, 1978; Linscheid et al., 1990), but they have been used only occasionally in the human operant laboratory (though they are more common in other areas of psychology). There are both theoretical and practical reasons to conduct more human operant research with physical aversive stimuli. Theoretically, it is possible that organisms respond differently to biologically relevant physical aversive stimuli than to biologically irrelevant nonphysical aversive stimuli. Both are effective, but it is uncertain whether they have similar patterns of adaption and recovery, and produce similar by-products such as emotion and overgeneralization. On a practical level, we need to know more about the direct and indirect effects of physical aversive stimuli with humans in the laboratory to determine the parameters within which such procedures are effective and safe for therapeutic use.

Although only 30% of studies in the present sample used physical negative reinforcers or punishers, they will be considered first in this section to establish links with animal research, and to set the stage for discussion of nonphysical aversive stimuli.

Electric Shock

Electric shock is a useful stimulus for human studies of aversive control: Its physical characteristics such as intensity and duration can be specified and controlled precisely (Azrin & Holz, 1966; Baron, 1991; Church, 1969), it is a negative reinforcer and punisher at levels that produce no damage, it permits a close comparison with animal studies, and results with humans are similar to those with animals (i.e., avoidance is steady and suppression is immediate and sustained).

Negative Reinforcement. A few studies have used electric shock as a negative reinforcer with humans. For example, in Ader and Tatum's (1961) study, subjects pressed a button to postpone strong shock for 5, 10, or 20 s (response–shock or RS interval), depending on the group. If no response was made, shocks were scheduled every 5, 10, or 20 s (shock–shock or SS interval). In each group, subjects had identical RS and SS intervals. With a 5-s RS interval, subjects received only a few shocks, and response rate was high (approximately 25 responses per minute) and steady. With a 10-s RS period, several shocks were received initially and then no more were received, and response rate was moderate (approximately 12 responses per minute) and steady. With a 20-s RS period, only a few shocks were received, and a low, steady response rate (approximately 4 responses per minute) was obtained. Similar results are obtained with rats on similar schedules of electric-shock avoidance. For example, Sidman (1966) described a rat's performance when electric shock was presented on RS 15-s SS 15-s. Early in training, many shocks were received and response rate was low. Over time, however, fewer shocks were received and response rate became higher and more stable.

In another study with humans (Dardano, 1965), subjects pressed a button to detect meter-needle deflections that occurred every 6 min. Later, shock (described by subjects as painful but tolerable) was presented via electrodes to subjects' upper arms if no response was made during an interval that varied randomly about 6 min. Response rate doubled when shock avoidance was added to the vigilance task. Shock also was used to increase autonomic responses in two experiments. In one of these studies (Brener, 1966), subjects postponed electric shock (the type and intensity were not reported in the article) for a few seconds if their heart rate remained below a slowly decreasing criterion. Subjects avoided shock more effectively than did yoked controls. In the other study (Grings & Carlin, 1966), shock (at an intensity that subjects reported as uncomfortable) was presented via electrodes to subjects' forearms immediately after cessation of a conditioned stimulus (a small red triangle) if skin conductance did not increase during the conditioned stimulus. Skin conductance increased, and subjects avoided most shocks.

Punishment. Electric shock also has been used as a punisher in human operant studies. In one study (Kaufman, 1965), subjects pressed a button and received money on an FR-20 schedule. Later, shock (of steadily increasing intensity) was presented via electrodes to subjects' ankles after every response. Greater shock intensity produced greater response suppression. In another study (Scobie & Kaufman, 1969), shock (up to 14 mA) was presented via electrodes to subjects' index fingers while subjects pressed a button for money on VI and VR schedules. Greater shock intensity produced greater response suppression, particularly for VI schedules. Although response suppression was reliable with such strong shock, I recommend that, in studies of aversive control with humans, electric-shock intensity should not exceed 5 mA (see Ethical Concerns and Subject Retention). An inductorium also has been used to present shock at an intensity just above pain threshold to subjects' forefingers (Senter & Hummel, 1965). In that study, shock punished spontaneous increase in skin conductance. Shock also suppressed the normal increase in skin conductance following presentation of a conditioned aversive stimulus (Grings & Carlin, 1966).

Loud Noise

In the aversive control literature, *loud noise* refers to aversive stimuli based on the presentation of sound, regardless of whether the sound is a pure tone, white noise, or a nonrandom combination of tones. Intensity is the most common sound parameter that is manipulated. Typically, sound intensity is around 100 dB, but intensities as low as 68 dB have been used effectively (Kelly & Hake, 1970). Given that the risk of damage to subjects is positively correlated with sound intensity, less intense sounds in the range of 60 to 80 dB should be used wherever possible (see Protecting Subjects for further suggestions and recommendations).

Loud noise is a useful aversive stimulus: Its physical characteristics can be specified precisely, it is difficult to avoid by unauthorized means, and any computer can produce it. The ease with which noise can be produced and presented with no additional equipment makes it a particularly attractive physical aversive stimulus, provided that only moderately intense sound is used to minimize the risk of damage to subjects.

Negative Reinforcement. Loud noise has been used as a physical negative reinforcer. In Azrin's (1958) experiment, subjects pressed a button. Later, loud white noise (80 to 8000 Hz at 95 dB) was presented (via speakers 60 cm from each side of the subject's chair) until the button was pressed. Each button press postponed the noise for 5 s, and response rate increased. In another study (Kelly & Hake, 1970), high school students pressed a 7-N button to terminate or postpone loud noise (2800 Hz at 68 dB) for 60 s. Button presses remained at a high steady rate for many sessions. Flanagan et al. (1958) tried to determine whether stuttering is an operant. During baseline, loud noise (6000 Hz at 105 dB) was presented to subjects continuously via earphones. During the next phase, stuttering terminated the noise for 5 s. Stuttering increased.

Punishment. Loud noise has been used in a few studies as a physical punisher (e.g., Ayllon & Azrin, 1966; Azrin, 1958; Flanagan et al., 1958; Herman & Azrin, 1964; Katz, 1973; Romanczyk, 1976). For example, stuttering was suppressed when 2 s of loud noise (95 dB) followed each stutter (Flanagan et al., 1958). Similarly, in Azrin's (1958) experiment, when loud noise (110 dB) was presented for 5 s after each button press, response rate was suppressed throughout the punishment phase. In another study (Herman & Azrin, 1964), psychiatric patients pulled two plungers (with criterion force of 10 and 5 N) for cigarettes on a single VI 1-min schedule for both plungers. After baseline, loud noise (96-dB buzz 2 feet from subjects) was presented for 1 s after every pull on Plunger A. Sometimes the baseline schedule was maintained on Plunger B, and sometimes Plunger B was made inoperative. Loud noise suppressed responding on Plunger A, and, as has been found with animals punished with electric shock (Azrin & Holz, 1966), greatest suppression was found when there was a reinforced alternative response (i.e., pulling Plunger B).

Response Effort

Response effort has many of the advantages of electric shock and loud noise: Its physical characteristics can be specified precisely, it is effective without causing damage, and it cannot be avoided by unauthorized means. Conceptually, response effort is an interim step between physical and nonphysical aversive stimuli.

Negative Reinforcement. Increase in response effort has been used as a negative reinforcer by Miller (1968a). Subjects pulled two plungers for money or cigarettes on separate VI 60-s schedules. The left and right plungers had criterion forces of 5 N (low effort) and 250 N (high effort), respectively. After baseline, no reinforcement was programmed on the low-effort plunger, but one response on the high-effort plunger followed by a vocal response reinstated baseline conditions on the low-effort plunger for 60 s. Criterion vocal-response intensity was increased gradually during the study, until only loud vocal responses (90 to 102 dB) were effective. Although loud vocal responses were not made during baseline, they were subsequently made at a high steady rate when they produced escape from effortful plunger responses.

Punishment. Miller (1970) also used response effort as a punisher. Adults pulled a plunger 1 inch for money or cigarettes on a VI 60-s schedule arranged on a two-component chain. Component 1 required a 5-N pull for 0.25 inch, and Component 2 required a pull between 5 and 250 N (depending on the condition) for the remaining 0.75 inch. Component 1 responses decreased in rate and increased in latency when Component 2 response-force requirement increased. In other words, high response effort for Component 2 punished Component 1 responses.

One potential problem with Miller's (1970) punishment procedure (and many others in which response force is manipulated) is that the force requirement for reinforcement is confounded with the force requirement for recording a response. For example, consider the following hypothetical situation. A subject pulls a plunger with a force of 10 N once every second. During baseline, response and reinforcement requirements are both 5 N, so every pull is recorded as a response. When response and reinforcement requirements are changed to 20 N, however, no pulls are recorded as responses. The subject's behavior has not changed; reduction in response rate is a function of the change in response definition. This has been a perennial problem for studies of response force. The typical technique of tightening a spring or adding extra weight to a balance pan on the end of a lever is problematic. Notterman and Mintz (1965) overcame this problem by recording response force. They were therefore able to have a different force requirement for a response and reinforcement, and thereby maintain a constant response definition regardless of the force requirement for reinforcement. A similar procedure has been used in studies of aversive control with humans (Crosbie, 1993; Crosbie et al., 1997).

Nonphysical Aversive Stimuli

Most studies in the sample employed nonphysical aversive stimuli such as monetary loss and timeout from positive reinforcement.

Point or Money Loss

Loss of money or points may be the ideal aversive stimulus for human operant research: Its characteristics can be specified and controlled precisely, it can be

presented quickly, it does not produce skeletal reactions that impair operant behavior, it probably does not produce habituation and sensitization, it causes no tissue damage, it can be instrumented easily, and IRB approval for its use is obtained
routinely.

Negative Reinforcement. Point and money loss was used as a negative reinforcer in 42% of studies in the sample (e.g., Baron & Kaufman, 1968; Cherek, Spiga, Steinberg, & Kelly, 1990; Galizio, 1979; Matthews & Shimoff, 1974; Ruddle et
al., 1982; Weiner, 1963, 1964a, 1969). In a prototypical experiment (Baron & Kaufman, 1968), college students sat in front of a panel that could be lit with green or
red light, and that contained a 4-cm square plastic push button with a force requirement less than 1 N. The stimulus light was green throughout each session except for 1-s periods (arranged on an RS 30-s SS 10-s schedule) when it was red.
When the light was green, money was added to the subject's total independently
of responding (3.6 cents/min). When the light was red, no money was added, and
5 cents was deducted for each presentation of the red light. Button pressing was
maintained at a moderate steady rate, and few points were lost. In a similar study
(Galizio, 1979), subjects rotated a crank handle with criterion force of 23 N to postpone 5-cent losses by 10, 30, or 60 s (arranged on a multiple schedule). As has been
found with animals performing on similar schedules to avoid electric shock (e.g.,
Baron, 1991; Sidman, 1953, 1966), moderate, steady responding was obtained
quickly, few aversive stimuli were received, and response rate decreased as post-
ponement duration increased.

Weiner (1963) arranged two variations on this general procedure: Subjects
avoided losing points (which were not exchangeable for money; subjects were paid
an hourly rate), and points were lost during an extended point-loss period. Subjects pressed a key with a force of 0.2 N to postpone point loss by 10 s. If a response
was not made within 10 s, a 20-s point-loss period began. During that period, 1
point was lost approximately every 250 ms until either a response was made (escape and avoidance) or 20 s had elapsed (avoidance without escape). Avoidance
of point loss produced steady, efficient patterns of responding with minimal point
loss. The point-loss period procedure is interesting. Because the aversive stimulus
is presented for an extended period, subjects can escape and avoid it, and both
types of negative reinforcement can be studied separately, and there is a finer gra-
dation of aversive stimulation. For example, with standard Sidman avoidance,
subjects would lose either 0 or 80 points, but, with a point-loss period, subjects
could lose any number of points between 0 and 80.

Punishment. Nonphysical punishers such as point or money loss were used
in 50% of studies in the sample (e.g., Bradshaw et al., 1977, 1979; Crosbie, 1990,
1993; Weiner, 1962, 1963, 1964a–c). For example, in Weiner's (1963) study, after
avoidance responding was stable, each button press lost 1 point from the total. Response rate was suppressed immediately, and avoidance was impaired. Weiner
also studied effects of response-cost punishment on responding maintained by
positive reinforcement. For example, in his 1962 study, subjects pressed a lever
with a force of 0.2 N to detect target lights that were illuminated every 1 min (FI

schedule; Experiment 2), or every 1, 2, or 3 min on average (VI schedule; Experiment 1). Each target detection earned 100 points. After responding had stabilized, each response lost 1 point from the total (i.e., response-cost punishment). Response cost improved temporal control on FI schedules (as Azrin, 1958, found with a similar procedure and loud noise), and suppressed responding on VI schedules (as has been found when animals' responding on similar schedules was punished with electric shock; e.g., Azrin & Holz, 1966).

Crosbie (1990, Experiment 2) employed a different procedure. Four colored squares were displayed concurrently on a computer screen, and the response was pressing a mouse button while the mouse cursor was in one of the squares. Hence, four responses were concurrently available. During baseline, making Responses 1 to 4 produced 2, 4, 6, and 8 cents, respectively, on concurrently available VI 30-s schedules. In the next phase, baseline conditions continued, but 40 cents also was lost every time Response 3 was made. Response 3 was suppressed quickly, and stayed at a low level throughout the punishment phase.

In a recent series of experiments (Crosbie et al., 1997), response-cost punishment with humans was compared with electric-shock punishment with pigeons. In both preparations, reinforcement was arranged on VI schedules, baseline continued until responding was stable according to similar stability criteria, and punisher magnitude was increased slowly each session until responding was less than 50% of its baseline rate. Punishment results were virtually indistinguishable. With both punishers, there was almost no change in response rate for several sessions, then a sudden drop in responding that was maintained until the punishment condition ceased. Such a step function is characteristic of physical punishers. The only difference between the punishers was that subjects habituated to electric shock (i.e., there was suppression early in sessions followed by recovery) but not to response cost.

Occasionally, critics ask whether response cost really is aversive. The question may be recast as "what are the similarities and differences between response-dependent electric shock and response cost?" There is no doubt that shock is aversive, so significant similarities between shock and response cost would suggest that response cost also is aversive. Both shock and response cost suppress behavior on which they are made contingent, and organisms will work to escape or avoid them. Thus, both stimuli satisfy both major definitions of punishers (i.e., Azrin & Holz, 1966, and Skinner, 1953, respectively). Both stimuli produce similar patterns of response-rate reduction (i.e., they both act quickly in a step function), and overt emotional reactions (rats squeal, pigeons flap or stand immobile, and humans loudly say words often considered vulgar). Perhaps response cost is effective because small monetary losses aggregate to reduce reinforcer magnitude which is positively correlated with response rate. It also is possible that electric shock reduces response rate in a similar way: Hedonic value of food for a hungry pigeon is reduced by every shock received before food is delivered. An increase in response effort would have similar effects (Miller, 1970). In summary, response cost is similar to electric shock in many ways. They produce the same pattern of response reduction and recovery which is quite different from extinction and reduced reinforcer magnitude. Consequently, there is strong evidence that response cost has its effect via aversive control.

Timeout from Positive Reinforcement

Another way to use money and points as aversive stimuli is to remove the opportunity to obtain them (i.e., arrange timeout from positive reinforcement). Response cost involves removal of previously acquired reinforcers. Timeout from positive reinforcement involves losing the opportunity to acquire reinforcers. Those procedures are conceptually similar, and may be functionally identical. Although they are arranged differently, both conditions are presented contingent on subjects' responding, and the net effect is that subjects obtain fewer reinforcers than they did before the punishment condition was in effect.

As with point and money loss, timeout from positive reinforcement also is precisely quantifiable, is resistant to adaptation, does not elicit skeletal responses, cannot harm subjects, and produces similar results to those obtained with physical aversive stimuli such as electric shock and loud noise.

Negative Reinforcement. Avoidance of timeout from positive reinforcement has been studied extensively. In one study (Baron & Kaufman, 1966, Experiment 1), approximately 2.5 cents was added to a subject's total every minute independently of responding. Subjects earned money only while a light blinked. The light was programmed to stop blinking for 15 s (during which period no money was obtained; timeout) unless subjects pressed a low-effort button (force requirement was not reported). Each button press postponed the next timeout by 10 s, and terminated current timeout periods. Response rate was moderate, steady, and similar to those obtained with identical schedules of electric shock, noise, and point-loss avoidance.

In another study (Shipley et al., 1972), college students read novels, and were tested on their content. Lights in the laboratory were programmed to go off for 5 s (timeout from room illumination) every 5 s unless a button was pressed. When lights were on, each button press kept them on for a further 15 s. In addition, while a green console light was on, money was earned (3.6 cents/min) independently of responding. Without a response, the green light was scheduled to go off (timeout from money) for 15 s every 15 s; a response postponed timeout from money by 5 s. Timeout from both reinforcers (money and room illumination) maintained responding at a high, consistent rate.

Punishment. Timeout from positive reinforcement also has been used as a punisher (e.g., Miller & Zimmerman, 1966; Shipley et al., 1972; Streifel, 1972; Zimmerman & Baydan, 1963). In one study (Miller & Zimmerman, 1966), adults performed a match-to-sample procedure: A sample stimulus was projected on the center window; pressing the center key removed the sample and projected a stimulus on both side windows; and a correct response was pressing the key below the window that contained a stimulus that matched the sample. Twenty cents was obtained for each correct response on FR schedules that were adjusted until earnings were between $4.50 and $10.00 per 2-hr session. An incorrect response removed the possibility of obtaining money for 1 or 4 min (i.e., timeout). Timeout decreased the number of incorrect responses, and longer timeout periods produced greater decreases.

In Shipley and colleagues' (1972) study, subjects pressed a button regularly to keep a green light on; while the light was on they earned 3.6 cents/min. Later, any response that followed another response by less than 5 or 20 s (depending on the condition) turned off the light for 15 s (i.e., 15-s timeout was programmed according to a differential punishment of high rates schedule). Response rate was suppressed immediately.

Schedules

Negative Reinforcement

Although 70% of negative reinforcement studies in the sample used Sidman avoidance, some studies used a modification of that procedure. For example, in Matthews and Shimoff's (1974) study, money was lost if subjects did not press a key during the final 1 s of each 10-s period. This modification was used to obtain a scalloped pattern similar to that often produced by animals on FI schedules. In another study, preschool children pressed a bar to escape or avoid timeout from cartoons (Baer, 1960). If the bar was not pressed, after 10 s (in one condition) the picture and sound were disabled but the tape continued until a response was made. The modification to the standard Sidman avoidance procedure was that each response either reset the next stoppage 10 s from that response, or increased the next stoppage time by 10 s. Both procedures were effective. In another interesting variation (Ruddle et al., 1982), point loss was programmed after variable intervals independently of subjects' behavior (e.g., VT 10-s), but the first response in an interval canceled the point loss at the end of that interval.

Punishment

Every Response. In 79% of punishment studies in the sample, punishers were presented immediately after every response (e.g., Ayllon & Azrin, 1966; Crosbie, 1990, 1993; Herman & Azrin, 1964; Johnson et al., 1973; Kaufman, 1965; Weiner, 1962, 1963, 1964b,c). As was found when animals were punished on such a schedule (Azrin & Holz, 1966; Baron, 1991), suppression was immediate, and sustained throughout the punishment phase. When punishment was arranged on other schedules, however (e.g., Bennett & Cherek, 1990; Bradshaw et al., 1977, 1978, 1979; Romanczyk, 1976; Scobie & Kaufman, 1969), results were less predictable.

Intermittent. In the sample, punishment was arranged on only three intermittent schedules: VR (e.g., Bennett & Cherek, 1990; Bradshaw et al., 1977, 1979; Romanczyk, 1976), VI (Bradshaw et al., 1978), and differential punishment of high rates (Shipley et al., 1972).

In Bennett and Cherek's (1990) study, plunger pulls produced money on VI 20-s and then lost money on VR 30 or VR 20. Although responding was not suppressed on VR-30 money loss, it was on VR 20. Similarly, Bradshaw et al. (1977) arranged a 5-ply multiple schedule in which button pressing produced 1 point on VI schedules with means of 8, 17, 51, 171, and 720 s, then also lost 1 point on a VR-34 schedule. Responding was suppressed reliably for all five VI schedules. In contrast, Romanczyk (1976) had problems when he reinforced responding on VR 33 and then presented loud noise on VR 5, VR 10, and VR 20. For some subjects there was no change in response rate, and for others there was complete suppression.

Bradshaw and colleagues also used VI punishment. Button pressing produced money on multiple (VI 8-s, VI 17-s, VI 51-s, VI 171-s, and VI 720-s) and then also lost money on VI 170-s. Responding was suppressed only on baseline schedules leaner than the punishment schedule (i.e., VI 171-s and VI 720-s).

Shipley et al. (1972) arranged differential punishment of high response rates. Any response that followed another response by less than a specified time (e.g., 5 s) turned off the laboratory light for 15 s. Responding was suppressed while the condition was in effect.

Although no study in the sample reports the use of punishment on FI or FR schedules, given the results with animals (e.g., Azrin & Holz, 1966, pp. 397–398), those arrangements are likely to be effective with humans. With pigeons, Azrin, Holz, and Hake (1963) provided reinforcement on VI schedules, then presented electric shock on FR schedules with ratios between 1 and 1000. For a given shock intensity, smaller ratios produced greater response suppression and a steady response rate with virtually no pausing. In another study when every bar press was followed by food, then electric shock was presented on FR-10 or FR-20 schedules, both response suppression and pausing were found (Hendry & Van-Toller, 1964). Similar results were obtained when pigeons' key pecks were punished with strong electric shock on FI schedules (Azrin, 1956).

Conclusion. Virtually all basic and applied studies have found that suppression is greater, more immediate, and more permanent when a punisher follows every response (Azrin, 1956; Azrin & Holz, 1966; Baron, 1991; Harris & Ersner-Hershfield, 1978; Newsom et al., 1983). If, for theoretical or practical reasons, an intermittent schedule of punishment is desirable, then VR is probably the most reliable way to arrange it. Care must be taken to ensure that the punishment schedule is richer than the reinforcement schedule, but suppression should be obtained reliably. Punishment on VI, FR, and FI schedules is possible, but more difficult to obtain.

RECENT RESULTS FROM ADDITIONAL RESPONSE MEASURES

Not only is human operant research a strong area of behavior analysis, but it also is moving in novel directions. Here are a few recent examples of studies in my lab in which we have obtained measures in addition to response rate.

In one study, college students pressed a lever with criterion force of 30 N for 25-cent reinforcers on a VI 3-min schedule in the presence of either a red or a green rectangle. In the next condition, each lever press also lost money, and the magnitude of loss was slowly increased until response rate in the punished component was less than 50% of its baseline rate. With the combination of a large VI schedule and a slowly increasing response-cost magnitude, responding in the punished component never ceased, and consequently reinforcer rate did not change. Figure

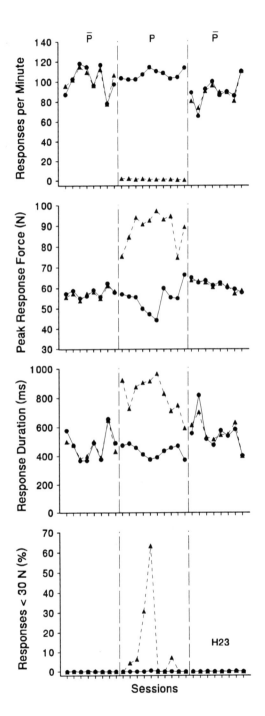

FIGURE 6.1. Rate, peak force, and duration of functional responses (i.e., peak force ≥ 30 N), and the percentage of subcriterion responses (i.e., peak force 10 to 29 N) in each component during the final 8 sessions of conditions without punishment (P̄) and the final 10 sessions of the condition with punishment (P). Circles show the component in which responding was never punished; triangles show the component in which every response was punished during P. Circle components were correlated with a green rectangle; triangle components were correlated with a red rectangle. There was a 15-s blackout between components.

6.1 shows, for one subject and the final sessions of each condition, response rate, force, and duration, and the proportion of lever presses with force below the 30-N criterion for reinforcement and punishment. The top panel shows that punishment was obtained (triangles), and that unpunished responses (circles) did not change from their baseline rate. Furthermore, lower panels show that for the punished response there was an increase in response force, response duration, and subcriterion responding.

Because punishers were presented when the lever was released, longer responses would have postponed the punisher, and therefore may have increased by negative reinforcement. To test this proposition, in a subsequent study the punisher was presented either at response termination (i.e., force less than 3 N) or when criterion force was applied (30 N), and durations of response subcomponents were recorded. If subjects were postponing the punisher, then response subcomponents prior to the punisher should have been differentially lengthened. There was no systematic difference in response subcomponent durations, which suggests that negative reinforcement was not responsible for increases in total response duration.

The increase in subcriterion responses also might be related to avoidance. Those lever presses never were reinforced, but neither were they punished, so they may have increased by negative reinforcement, as with Dunham and colleagues' (1969) off-key pecks.

CONCLUSION

The main theme of this chapter is similarity. Although many different procedures have been used in studies of aversive control with humans, the results are strikingly similar. Regardless of whether the aversive stimulus is electric shock, loud noise, increased response effort, point loss, or timeout from positive reinforcement, similar Sidman avoidance schedules produce similar patterns of responding, and when those stimuli follow a response, they all produce the rapid, step-function reduction in response rate that characterizes punishment. That similarity also extends across species. With similar schedules, humans and rats have virtually indistinguishable patterns of electric-shock avoidance and virtually indistinguishable patterns of electric-shock punishment. Such consistency of findings across procedures and species provides strong evidence of the robustness and generality of aversive-control results with humans.

One implication of such similarity is that studying aversive control with humans is a similar enterprise to studying aversive control with animals. Procedural details such as reinforcers, baseline schedules, stability criteria, and aversive stimuli also are important when such studies are conducted with humans. It is important that researchers do not change accepted laboratory practices merely because the species are different. For example, aversive-control studies with humans also require effective reinforcing and aversive stimuli, pretraining, and several sessions for responding to reach a steady state. When such experimental care is taken, however, results are as methodologically rigorous and robust as those obtained with animals.

Studies of aversive control with animals are becoming more politically sensitive, particularly following recent terrorist activity of animal rights groups. Given that political pressure, many institutions are becoming more reluctant to support research with animals, especially research that involves electric shock, the predominant aversive stimulus. It will become progressively more difficult for such research to be conducted, and for new researchers to establish such labs. Soon, working with humans may be the only feasible way to study aversive control. Given the theoretical and practical significance of aversive control, it is imperative that this fascinating topic receive much more experimental attention, and preferably with human subjects.

ACKNOWLEDGMENTS. Preparation of this chapter was supported in part by a grant from the Eberly College of Arts and Sciences, West Virginia University. I am grateful to Michelle Anderson and John Grago for assistance with obtaining articles.

REFERENCES

Ader, R., & Tatum, R. (1961). Free-operant avoidance conditioning in human subjects. *Journal of the Experimental Analysis of Behavior, 4*, 275–276.

Ader, R., & Tatum, R. (1963). Free-operant avoidance conditioning in individual and paired human subjects. *Journal of the Experimental Analysis of Behavior, 6*, 357–359.

Arbuckle, J. L., & Lattal, K. A. (1987). A role for negative reinforcement of response omission in punishment? *Journal of the Experimental Analysis of Behavior, 48*, 407–416.

Ayllon, T., & Azrin, N. H. (1966). Punishment as a discriminative stimulus and conditioned reinforcer with humans. *Journal of the Experimental Analysis of Behavior, 9*, 411–419.

Azrin, N. H. (1956). Some effects of two intermittent schedules of immediate and non-immediate punishment. *Journal of Psychology, 42*, 3–21.

Azrin, N. H. (1958). Some effects of noise on human behavior. *Journal of the Experimental Analysis of Behavior, 1*, 183–200.

Azrin, N. H., & Holz, W. C. (1966). Punishment. In W. K. Honig (Ed.), *Operant behavior: Areas of research and application* (pp. 380–447). Englewood Cliffs, NJ: Prentice–Hall.

Azrin, N. H., Holz, W. C., & Hake, D. F. (1963). Fixed-ratio punishment. *Journal of the Experimental Analysis of Behavior, 6*, 141–148.

Baer, D. M. (1960). Escape and avoidance response of pre-school children to two schedules of reinforcement withdrawal. *Journal of the Experimental Analysis of Behavior, 3*, 155–159.

Baron, A. (1991). Avoidance and punishment. In I. H. Iversen & K. A. Lattal (Eds.), *Techniques in the behavioral and neural sciences: Vol. 6. Experimental analysis of behavior: Part 1* (pp. 173–217). Amsterdam: Elsevier.

Baron, A., & Galizio, M. (1976). Clock avoidance of human performance on avoidance and fixed-interval schedules. *Journal of the Experimental Analysis of Behavior, 26*, 165–180.

Baron, A., & Kaufman, A. (1966). Human, free-operant avoidance of "time out" from monetary reinforcement. *Journal of the Experimental Analysis of Behavior, 9*, 557–565.

Baron, A., & Kaufman, A. (1968). Facilitation and suppression of human loss-avoidance by signaled, unavoidable loss. *Journal of the Experimental Analysis of Behavior, 11*, 177–185.

Baron, A., & Surdy, T. M. (1990). Recognition memory in older adults: Adjustment to changing contingencies. *Journal of the Experimental Analysis of Behavior, 54*, 201–212.

Bennett, R. H., & Cherek, D. R. (1990). Punished and nonpunished responding in a multiple schedule in humans: A brief report. *The Psychological Record, 40*, 187–196.

Blough, D. S. (1966). The study of animal sensory processes by operant methods. In W. K. Honig (Ed.), *Operant behavior: Areas of research and application* (pp. 345–379). Englewood Cliffs, NJ: Prentice–Hall.

Bradshaw, C. M., Szabadi, E., & Bevan, P. (1977). Effect of punishment on human variable-interval performance. *Journal of the Experimental Analysis of Behavior, 27,* 275–279.

Bradshaw, C. M., Szabadi, E., & Bevan, P. (1978). Effect of variable-interval punishment on the behavior of humans in variable-interval schedules of monetary reinforcement. *Journal of the Experimental Analysis of Behavior, 29,* 161–166.

Bradshaw, C. M., Szabadi, E., & Bevan, P. (1979). The effect of punishment on free-operant choice behavior in humans. *Journal of the Experimental Analysis of Behavior, 31,* 71–81.

Brener, J. (1966). Heart rate as an avoidance response. *The Psychological Record, 16,* 329–336.

Brethower, D. M., & Reynolds, G. S. (1962). A facilitative effect of punishment on unpunished behavior. *Journal of the Experimental Analysis of Behavior, 5,* 191–199.

Buskist, W. F., Miller, H. L., Jr., & Bennett, R. H. (1980). Fixed-interval performance in humans: Sensitivity to temporal parameters when food is the reinforcer. *The Psychological Record, 30,* 111–121.

Butterfield, W. H. (1975). Electric shock—Safety factors when used for the aversive conditioning of humans. *Behavior Therapy, 6,* 98–110.

Cherek, D. R., Spiga, R., & Egli, M. (1992). Effects of response requirement and alcohol on human aggressive responding. *Journal of the Experimental Analysis of Behavior, 58,* 577–587.

Cherek, D. R., Spiga, R., Steinberg, J. L., & Kelly, T. H. (1990). Human aggressive responses maintained by avoidance or escape from point loss. *Journal of the Experimental Analysis of Behavior, 53,* 293–303.

Church, R. M. (1963). The varied effects of punishment on behavior. *Psychological Review, 70,* 369–402.

Church, R. M. (1969). Response suppression. In B. A. Campbell & R. M. Church (Eds.), *Punishment and aversive behavior* (pp. 111–156). New York: Appleton–Century–Crofts.

Crosbie, J. (1990). Some effects of response cost on a free-operant multiple-response repertoire with humans. *The Psychological Record, 40,* 517–539.

Crosbie, J. (1993). The effects of response cost and response restriction on a multiple-response repertoire with humans. *Journal of the Experimental Analysis of Behavior, 59,* 173–192.

Crosbie, J., Williams, A. M., Lattal, K. A., Anderson, M. M., & Brown, S. (1997). Schedule interactions involving punishment with pigeons and humans. *Journal of the Experimental Analysis of Behavior, 68,* 161–175.

Dardano, J. F. (1965). Modification of observing behavior. *Journal of the Experimental Analysis of Behavior, 8,* 207–214.

Dinsmoore, J. A. (1954). Punishment: I. The avoidance hypothesis. *Psychological Review, 61,* 34–46.

Dunham, P. J., Mariner, A., & Adams, H. (1969). Enhancement of off-key pecking by on-key punishment. *Journal of the Experimental Analysis of Behavior, 12,* 789–797.

Elsmore, T. F. (1971). Effects of response force on discrimination performance. *Psychological Record, 21,* 17–24.

Estes, W. K., & Skinner, B. F. (1941). Some quantitative properties of anxiety. *Journal of Experimental Psychology, 29,* 390–400.

Flanagan, B., Goldiamond, I., & Azrin, N. (1958). Operant stuttering: The control of stuttering behavior through response-contingent consequences. *Journal of the Experimental Analysis of Behavior, 1,* 173–177.

Galizio, M. (1979). Contingency-shaped and rule-governed behavior: Instructional control of human loss avoidance. *Journal of the Experimental Analysis of Behavior, 31,* 53–70.

Grings, W. W., & Carlin, S. (1966). Instrumental modification of autonomic behavior. *The Psychological Record, 16,* 153–159.

Harris, S. L., & Ersner-Hershfield, R. (1978). Behavioral suppression of seriously disruptive behavior in psychotic and retarded patients: A review of punishment and its alternatives. *Psychological Bulletin, 85,* 1352–1375.

Hefferline, R. F., & Keenan, B. (1961). Amplitude-induction gradient of a small human operant in an escape-avoidance situation. *Journal of the Experimental Analysis of Behavior, 4,* 41–43.

Hendry, D. P., & Van-Toller, C. (1964). Fixed-ratio punishment with continuous reinforcement. *Journal of the Experimental Analysis of Behavior, 7,* 293–300.

Herman, R. L., & Azrin, N. H. (1964). Punishment by noise in an alternative response situation. *Journal of the Experimental Analysis of Behavior, 7,* 185–188.

Holland, J. G. (1957). Technique for the behavioral analysis of human observing. *Science, 125,* 348–350.

Hull, C. L. (1943). *Principles of behavior.* New York: Appleton–Century–Crofts.

Johnson, D. L., McGlynn, F. D., & Topping, J. S. (1973). The relative efficiency of four response-elimination techniques following variable-ratio reinforcement training. *The Psychological Record, 23,* 203–208.

Katz, R. C. (1973). Effects of punishment in an alternative response context as a function of relative reinforcement rate. *The Psychological Record, 23,* 65–74.

Kaufman, A. E. (1964). A procedure for reducing experimental drop-outs. *Journal of the Experimental Analysis of Behavior, 7,* 400.

Kaufman, A. (1965). Punishment shock intensity and basal skin resistance. *Journal of the Experimental Analysis of Behavior, 8,* 389–394.

Kelly, J. F., & Hake, D. F. (1970). An extinction-induced increase in an aggressive response with humans. *Journal of the Experimental Analysis of Behavior, 14,* 153–164.

Killeen, P. R. (1978). Stability criteria. *Journal of the Experimental Analysis of Behavior, 29,* 17–25.

Lattal, K. A., & Griffin, M. A. (1972). Punishment contrast during free-operant avoidance. *Journal of the Experimental Analysis of Behavior, 18,* 509–516.

Linscheid, T. R., Iwata, B. A., Ricketts, R. W., Williams, D. E., & Griffin, J. C. (1990). Clinical evaluation of the self-injurious behavior inhibiting system (SIBIS). *Journal of Applied Behavior Analysis, 23,* 53–78.

Maltzman, E., Holz, W. C., & Kunze, J. (1965). Supplementary knowledge of results. *Journal of the Experimental Analysis of Behavior, 8,* 385–388.

Matthews, B. A., & Shimoff, E. (1974). Human responding on a temporally defined schedule of point-loss avoidance. *The Psychological Record, 24,* 209–219.

Matthews, B. A., Shimoff, E., Catania, A. C., & Sagvolden, T. (1977). Uninstructed human responding: Sensitivity to ratio and interval contingencies. *Journal of the Experimental Analysis of Behavior, 27,* 453–467.

McDowell, J. J., & Wood, H. M. (1985). Confirmation of linear system theory prediction: Rate of change of Herrnstein's *k* as a function of response-force requirement. *Journal of the Experimental Analysis of Behavior, 43,* 61–73.

McIlvane, W. J., Kledaras, J. B., Munson, L. C., King, K. A. J., de Rose, J. C., & Stoddard, L. T. (1987). Controlling relations in conditional discrimination and matching by exclusion. *Journal of the Experimental Analysis of Behavior, 48,* 187–208.

Miller, L. K. (1968a). Escape from an effortful situation. *Journal of the Experimental Analysis of Behavior, 11,* 619–627.

Miller, L. K. (1968b). The effect of response force on avoidance rate. *Journal of the Experimental Analysis of Behavior, 11,* 809–812.

Miller, L. K. (1970). Some punishing effects of response-force. *Journal of the Experimental Analysis of Behavior, 13,* 215–220.

Miller, N. B., & Zimmerman, J. (1966). The effects of a pre-time-out stimulus on matching-to-sample of humans. *Journal of the Experimental Analysis of Behavior, 9,* 487–499.

Mish, F. C., et al. (1983). *Webster's ninth new collegiate dictionary.* Springfield, MA: Merriam-Webster.

Newsom, C., Favell, J. E., & Rincover, A. (1983). The side effects of punishment. In S. Axelrod & J. Apsche (Eds.), *The effects of punishment on human behavior* (pp. 285–315). New York: Academic Press.

Notterman, J. M., & Mintz, D. E. (1965). *Dynamics of response.* New York: Wiley.

Perone, M. (1991). Experimental design in the analysis of free-operant behavior. In I. H. Iversen & K. A. Lattal (Eds.), *Techniques in the behavioral and neural sciences: Vol. 6. Experimental analysis of behavior: Part 1* (pp. 135–171). Amsterdam: Elsevier.

Pilgrim, C., & Galizio, M. (1990). Relations between baseline contingencies and equivalence probe performance. *Journal of the Experimental Analysis of Behavior, 54,* 213–224.

Romanczyk, R. G. (1976). Intermittent punishment of key-press responding: Effectiveness during application and extinction. *The Psychological Record, 26,* 203–214.

Ruddle, H. V., Bradshaw, C. M., Szabadi, E., & Foster, T. M. (1982). Performance of humans in concurrent avoidance/positive-reinforcement schedules. *Journal of the Experimental Analysis of Behavior, 38,* 51–61.

Scobie, S. R., & Kaufman, A. (1969). Intermittent punishment of human responding maintained by intermittent reinforcement. *Journal of the Experimental Analysis of Behavior, 12,* 137–147.

Senter, R. J., & Hummel, W. F., Jr. (1965). Suppression of an autonomic response through operant conditioning. *The Psychological Record, 15,* 1–5.

Shipley, C. R., Baron, A., & Kaufman, A. (1972). Effects of timeout from one reinforcer on human behavior maintained by another reinforcer. *The Psychological Record, 22,* 201–210.

Sidman, M. (1953). Two temporal parameters of the maintenance of avoidance behavior by the white rat. *Journal of Comparative and Physiological Psychology, 46,* 253–261.

Sidman, M. (1960). *Tactics of scientific research: Evaluating experimental data in psychology.* New York: Basic Books.

Sidman, M. (1966). Avoidance behavior. In W. K. Honig (Ed.), *Operant behavior: Areas of research and application* (pp. 448–498). Englewood Cliffs, NJ: Prentice–Hall.

Skinner, B. F. (1953). *Science and human behavior.* New York: Macmillan Co.

Streifel, S. (1972). Timeout and concurrent fixed-ratio schedules with human subjects. *Journal of the Experimental Analysis of Behavior, 17,* 213–219.

Thorndike, E. L. (1911). *Animal intelligence: Experimental studies.* New York: Macmillan Co.

Thorndike, E. L. (1932). *Fundamentals of learning.* New York: Teachers College.

Weiner, H. (1962). Some effects of response cost upon human operant behavior. *Journal of the Experimental Analysis of Behavior, 5,* 201–208.

Weiner, H. (1963). Response cost and the aversive control of human operant behavior. *Journal of the Experimental Analysis of Behavior, 6,* 415–421.

Weiner, H. (1964a). Modification of escape responding in humans by increasing the magnitude of an aversive event. *Journal of the Experimental Analysis of Behavior, 7,* 277–279.

Weiner, H. (1964b). Response cost and fixed-ratio performance. *Journal of the Experimental Analysis of Behavior, 7,* 79–81.

Weiner, H. (1964c). Response cost effects during extinction following fixed-interval reinforcement in humans. *Journal of the Experimental Analysis of Behavior, 7,* 333–335.

Weiner, H. (1969). Conditioning history and the control of human avoidance and escape responding. *Journal of the Experimental Analysis of Behavior, 12,* 1039–1043.

Zimmerman, J., & Baydan, N. T. (1963). Punishment of S^Δ responding of humans in conditional matching to sample by time-out. *Journal of the Experimental Analysis of Behavior, 6,* 589–597.

III

Stimulus Control

7

Stimulus-Control Procedures

Kathryn J. Saunders and Dean C. Williams

The term *stimulus control* refers to "any difference in responding in the presence of different stimuli" (Catania, 1992, p. 372). Virtually all of the behavior in our everyday lives involves stimulus control. When a driver approaches a red light, he puts his foot on the brake pedal. When approaching a green light, he keeps his foot on the gas pedal. The driver's responses are thus under the stimulus control of the light's color. Analyzing existing stimulus control and analyzing the development and stability of stimulus-control relations are central to the understanding of normal and abnormal human behavior. Moreover, much of experimental psychology involves the study of stimulus control. Issues addressed under the rubrics of learning, concept formation, memory, and sensory processes usually involve differences in responding in the presence of different stimuli, and thus involve issues of stimulus control. In addition, stimulus-control procedures are used to generate behavioral baselines for the study of the effects of drugs or other physiological manipulations. As such, stimulus-control procedures are discussed throughout this volume.

This chapter will focus on the smallest units of stimulus control, the simple discrimination and the conditional discrimination. A simple discrimination is produced within a three-term contingency, which consists of a prior stimulus, a response, and a reinforcer. For example, a child is shown the letter a, he says "a," and is praised. A conditional discrimination is produced within a four-term contingency, which adds a conditional stimulus to the three-term contingency. For example, a child shown a red ball might say "red" if given the conditional stimulus "What color is this?" or he might say "ball" if asked "What is this?" Note that either response is part of a simple discrimination. The simple discrimination that is reinforced depends on which conditional stimulus is presented, hence the term *conditional discrimination*. Nearly every procedure discussed in this volume is either a pure example of these units of stimulus control, or a synthesis of two or more of these basic units. Thus, thorough understanding of simple and conditional discrimination procedures and the behavioral processes they produce will provide a foundation for issues discussed in this volume as well as for experimental psychology in general.

Kathryn J. Saunders and Dean C. Williams • Parsons Research Center, University of Kansas, Parsons, Kansas 67357.

Handbook of Research Methods in Human Operant Behavior, edited by Lattal and Perone. Plenum Press, New York, 1998.

Most of the procedures that we will discuss are forced-choice procedures, because these are prevalent in studies of stimulus control with human subjects. In these, a trial begins when a stimulus display is presented and ends when a single response is made. These are sometimes called *discrete-trial procedures,* but this usage is misleading because the procedures typically do not physically restrict responding between trials, as occurred with traditional discrete-trial procedures using animal subjects and apparatuses such as straight alleys, T-mazes, or the Wisconsin General Test Apparatus. In most studies, operanda not only remain available between trials, they are not disabled. Responses during the intertrial interval (ITI) are recorded, and there are programmed contingencies for responses during this period (typically, responses delay the presentation of the next trial). With this type of procedure, the focus is on the relative probability of a single response in the presence or absence of a stimulus.

In another type of procedure, contingencies associated with a particular stimulus can continue for a specified period of time or they can continue until a specified response requirement is met (usually, more than a single response is required). These procedures allow rate of responding as a dependent measure. Also, presenting trials for a specified period of time, rather than until a response is made, allows trials to end without a response, an important procedural option. Such procedures have traditionally been used in studies of stimulus generalization (discussed later), under the assumption that response rate reflects strength of stimulus control. Whether one's dependent measure is response rate or the relative probability of a single response in the presence of a stimulus depends on the experimental question. Reading literature in a particular area will illuminate reasons for the use of a particular procedure.

Our goals for this chapter are to consider: (1) the major forms that simple and conditional discrimination take in the laboratory, (2) standard and essential procedural details and their rationale, (3) methods for establishing the performances, (4) issues of importance to experimenters using discrimination baselines in the study of other independent variables, (5) issues in the measurement of discrimination, and (6) higher-order performances that are investigated within simple and conditional discrimination procedures. The present emphasis is on procedures that can be used with human subjects. Where possible, we cite primary sources that will provide a more complete description of a particular procedure and of the rationale for its use. Many stimulus-control procedures are used across species with little modification. Therefore, in cases where we did not find a procedure used with humans, we cite examples that involve animal subjects. Before beginning our discussion of specific procedures, we will discuss how choice of apparatus affects important aspects of procedure and measurement.

CHOICE OF APPARATUS

Nonautomated

Tabletop Procedures

It is possible to conduct discrimination procedures with virtually no special equipment. To establish a simple simultaneous discrimination,for example, some studies have used stimuli drawn on index cards. Subject and experimenter typically sit across the table from one another. To begin a trial, the experimenter places the stimuli in front of the subject. The subject typically responds by touching one of the stimuli. The experimenter then delivers the designated consequence and records the response.

Tabletop procedures are a good way to initiate a study rapidly. Also, procedures can be changed easily, a feature that speeds procedural development. There are, however, a number of drawbacks. First, making immediate decisions as to whether responses meet the experimental contingencies may be difficult. For example, a subject may barely touch one stimulus and then move quickly to another. Some of these difficulties can be overcome by careful response definition or by requiring a more definitive response such as sorting the cards or handing the cards to the experimenter. Without automated recording, however, some responses may be difficult to evaluate. In addition, when responses are recorded by human observers, the reliability of those observers must be assessed. This means that two observers must be present for some portion of the sessions. Procedural integrity must be assessed as well. Another problem is that it may be difficult to control or measure aspects of trial timing, such as the length of time between trials or response latency. In fact, the exact beginning of a trial may be somewhat ambiguous if care is not taken to prevent the subjects from viewing the stimuli before they are completely positioned. The most important concern is that the experimenter might inadvertently prompt or provide feedback to the subject. Even subjects with extreme developmental limitations bring to the laboratory a long history of following nonverbal prompts. Moreover, it is surprisingly difficult for many experimenters to suppress inadvertent cues, especially premature motions toward delivering the consequences. A related concern is that, because reinforcers are hand-delivered, there is variation in the amount of time between response and reinforcer delivery. Given all of these difficulties, researchers are more likely to question novel outcomes that are obtained with tabletop procedures than those obtained under more automated procedures.

The Wisconsin General Test Apparatus (WGTA)

The WGTA provides a low-technology solution to many of the problems noted above. Figure 7.1 shows a version of the WGTA that was used with human subjects in a study by Pilgrim and Galizio (1990). Subject and experimenter are separated by a door that can be raised ("guillotine"). With the door in the down position, the experimenter prepares a trial by arranging the stimuli on a tray. The trial begins when the screen is raised and the tray is pushed toward the subject. The experimenter observes the subject's response through the open space under the door. During the trial, the door shields the experimenter from the subject, greatly diminishing the likelihood of experimenter cuing. (Note that some aspects of the WGTA can be applied easily to tabletop tasks, for example, a simple curtain arrangement can separate the subject and experimenter during trial preparation.) Reinforcers are placed under the stimuli in small wells ("bait wells") in the tray, so their presentation occurs at a uniform time with respect to the response. An advantage of the WGTA is the ease with which three-dimensional stimuli can be used.

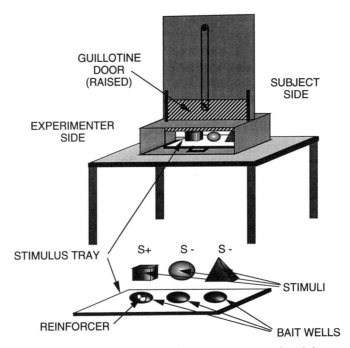

FIGURE 7.1.   An example of the Wisconsin General Test Apparatus used with human subjects, seen from the experimenter's side. The inset shows the stimulus tray containing the "bait wells." The stimulus tray is slid under the opened guillotine door to begin a trial. The experimenter observes the selection response through the opening. At the trial's end, the stimulus tray is retracted and the guillotine door closed, blocking the subject's view of stimulus and reinforcer placement for the next trial.

Automated

Automated procedures have a number of advantages over nonautomated procedures. Because session events are controlled by a microcomputer or by electromechanical equipment, trial timing is controlled precisely and responses and their latencies can be recorded automatically. Responses can be defined objectively, eliminating the need for the experimenter to make judgments about ambiguous responses, and reinforcers can be delivered immediately. Importantly, the experimenter need not be in the same room as the subject, which clearly eliminates the possibility of cuing (at least within sessions). Two methods of presenting stimuli, and the associated means of detecting and recording responses, are described below.

Keys with Projected Stimuli

In one method of transducing responses, the response area is a panel containing translucent keys onto which stimuli are projected from the rear (e.g., Sidman et al., 1982). Pressing a key displaces it slightly, operating a switch and providing tactile feedback, an advantage for some subjects. A disadvantage is that each sequence of trials (session) must be arranged by placing slides in a slide projector, a relatively inefficient endeavor compared with computer options (see below). If a small array of stimuli or simple stimuli are to be used, in-line projectors or colored lamps may be used.

Computer Monitor

Computerized image processing, storage, and display have many advantages, especially in projects involving large numbers of stimuli (see Bhatt & Wright, 1992, for a discussion). Among these are the capacity to create and store a large number of stimuli and to modify stimuli easily, a valuable feature for studies of generalization and categorization. High-resolution monitors (along with appropriate hardware and software) make it possible to display photograph-quality color pictures. Moreover, computers allow rapid randomization and counterbalancing of stimuli for daily sessions. Two methods of recording responses are used most often when stimuli are presented on computer monitors, separate operanda and touchscreens.

Separate Operanda. For normally capable adult human subjects, responses can be recorded via a standard computer keyboard or by a pointing device such as a mouse or a trackball. When the keyboard is used, subjects are instructed that particular keys correspond to stimuli that appear on the screen. For example, the subject might press the "1" key to respond to a stimulus that appears on the left side of the screen and the "2" key to respond to stimulus on the right (e.g., Markham & Dougher, 1993). The unused keys may be covered. Sometimes there is an additional requirement to press the enter key (Hayes, Kohlenberg, & Hayes, 1991), which allows the subject to change a response (prior to pressing enter). Another keyboard option is for the subject to "copy" the selected stimulus, which might be a letter or syllable, by typing it (McIlvane et al., 1987). Alternatively, stimuli can be selected by moving the cursor to the stimulus with a mouse (de Rose, McIlvane, Dube, Galpin, & Stoddard, 1988) or joystick (Gatch & Osborne, 1989) and "clicking" to record the response. More peripheral operanda such as buttons or telegraph keys can also be used, with for example, the positions of the buttons corresponding to the positions of stimuli on the screen. When reaction time is of interest, such operanda facilitate accurate measurement. In a study by Baron and Menich (1985), depressing telegraph keys to the left and right of the monitor served to initiate a trial. To respond to the stimulus that appeared on the left side of the screen, for example, the subject released the left telegraph key. Operanda such as buttons and keys may require more complex computer interfacing than mice and joysticks. Many computers are equipped with mouse and joystick ports as standard equipment, but buttons and keys may require additional circuitry to interface with the computer.

Computer Monitors with Touchscreens. Touch-sensitive computer monitors are an increasingly popular method of transducing responses. These monitors are fitted with a transparent plastic or glass covering that detects the location of physical contact. The touchscreen sensor is calibrated to match monitor locations to sensor input. The portion of the sensor area corresponding to the position of the stimulus on the monitor screen is designated as the response "key." A potential advantage of touchscreens over separate operanda is that, with a touchscreen, the response contacts the stimulus directly, rather than an operandum that is separated physically from the stimulus (see Bhatt & Wright, 1992). In addition, a touchscreen offers tremendous flexibility in the number of stimuli presented and in their arrangement. Because the entire intelligence panel (i.e., the computer monitor) is under software control, the display can be reconfigured rapidly. A potential advantage over projecting stimuli onto keys is that stimuli can be presented without a border (i.e., the key's edge). Although unlikely with normal human subjects, it is possible that the key border can become an unintended part of the stimulus. In our laboratory, a size fading program did not establish simple, simultaneous discrimination in a subject with severe mental retardation until borders outlining the stimulus presentation areas were removed from the display. We surmised that responding was controlled exclusively by the distance of the stimuli from the surrounding borders. When this difference became too small, control was lost.

A general consideration in choosing a touchscreen is that the farther the screen is from the surface of the monitor, the greater the visual parallax problem. That is, the screen's touch-sensitive zone for a stimulus may be displaced from the apparent location of the stimulus when the subject's eyes are not directly in front of the stimulus. Figure 7.2 shows that the parallax problem is greatest in inexpensive, flat touchscreens that are fitted in front of the monitor bezel, or exterior frame (bottom). Screens that are mounted behind the monitor bezel conform to the curvature of the screen, reducing the parallax problem (top).

Commercially available touchscreens use many different technologies for transducing touches; each method has characteristics that may be important to a particular project. The two most common types are the capacitance screen and the resistive screen. The capacitance screen uses changes in electrical capacitance where the conductive surface of the skin contacts the glass surface to sense the touch. Capacitance screens are sensitive regardless of the pressure of the touch. If the skin is dry or dirty, however, the screen's sensitivity can change. Moreover, if only the fingernail contacts the screen, the response will not be recorded. Another feature, likely to be a drawback, is that merely brushing the screen can activate it. This can be problematic for subjects with poor motor control. The resistive screen uses a surface composed of two thin sheets of plastic separated by a small space. A touch that has sufficient pressure to bring two plastic membranes together is detected by changes in resistance across the XY coordinates of the inner membrane. Resistive touchscreens have the advantages that the condition of the skin does not affect sensitivity and that merely brushing the screen does not activate it. In addition, any stylus (e.g., the eraser end of a pencil) can be used for subjects who have difficulty making a discrete pointing response (e.g., a quadriplegic can use a mouth stick); by comparison, conductive rods must be used with capacitance screens.

It is important to remember that different touchscreen technologies may entail different response definitions. Moreover, experience with one type of screen might affect a subject's reaction to another type. We recently changed a subject

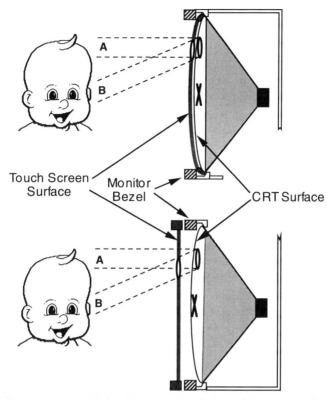

FIGURE 7.2. Touchscreens mounted behind (top panel) or in front of (bottom panel) the monitor bezel. "A" indicates the location of a stimulus on the CRT surface and "B" indicates the perceived location of the stimulus on the touchscreen. The bezel-mounted screen produces a greater shift in the perceived image location (parallax).

abruptly from a capacitance screen to a resistive screen. Initially, some of her responses did not meet the pressure requirement of the resistive screen. The problem was eliminated easily through training, and probably would not have occurred without previous experience with the capacitance screen, but it illustrates an important point.

A potential drawback is that neither type of screen provides tactile feedback analogous to that produced when a key is depressed. To compensate, one can program auditory feedback for responses that meet the response definition. Another problem is that, with the exception of the size and shape of the programmed touch zone, it can be difficult to specify precisely the response. For example, although the manufacturer may specify the minimum detectable response duration, the actual required duration will be influenced by the software and hardware with which the screen is interfaced. Some screens do allow sensing of the force of the touch as well as the location, allowing more precise response definition. Imprecise response specification could generate wide topographical variation between subjects and apparatuses.

With advances in technology come a number of other procedural changes that could affect the reproducibility of results obtained with older apparatuses. For example, questions arise concerning standardization of stimulus properties (e.g., wavelength of colors, monitor resolution). Careful description of all aspects of procedure seems especially important in times of rapid technological advance.

SIMPLE DISCRIMINATION PROCEDURES

In the prototypical simple discrimination procedure, a reinforcer is delivered after a response to one stimulus, the positive stimulus, or "S+," and not for responses to another stimulus, the negative stimulus, or "S−." A high proportion of responses in the presence of S+ indicates discriminative control by the S+ (stimulus control). There are two major variations in procedure, simultaneous discrimination, in which the S+ and S− stimuli are presented together, and successive discrimination, in which a single stimulus (either the S+ or the S−) is presented on each trial.

Simple discrimination procedures are used in a variety of experimental contexts. There is a large literature on the acquisition of simple discrimination, typically involving young children, individuals with mental retardation, or animals. Acquisition of simple discrimination is sometimes used to assess the effects of psychoactive medications on learning (Williams & Saunders, 1997). In addition, simple discrimination procedures are used in studies of perception (see Weisberg & Rovee-Collier, Chapter 11, for a discussion of signal detection procedures). Studies of sustained attention, or vigilance (Holland, 1958), often involve simple discrimination procedures. Moreover, vigilance tasks have been used to assess cognitive side effects of psychotropic and antiepileptic medications in clinical and normal populations of adults and children (see reviews by Rapport & Kelly, 1991; Wittenborn, 1978). Finally, higher-order performances studied within simple discrimination procedures include learning set, stimulus generalization, abstraction, and functional stimulus classes.

Simultaneous and Successive Discrimination

In *simultaneous* discrimination, the S+ and one or more S−'s are presented on each trial. Figure 7.3 shows an example; the subject's task is to touch the letter "b" and not the letter "d." The trial ends when a single response (touching) is made to one of the stimuli (a forced-choice procedure). Touching the S+ produces a reinforcer. Touching the S− ends the trial (other possible contingencies for errors will be noted later).

After a response is made, the consequences are presented, the stimuli are removed, and the intertrial interval (ITI) begins. The ITI is the time that elapses between the end of one trial and the presentation of the stimuli for the next trial. Typically, responses during the ITI reset the ITI, delaying the presentation of the next

FIGURE 7.3. Trial events for correct and incorrect responses under a simultaneous, simple-discrimination procedure with differential reinforcement. On each trial, both the S+ (the small letter "b") and the S− (the small letter "d") are presented. The trial continues until a selection response is made (a forced-choice procedure). Selecting "b" produces reinforcement and the intertrial interval (ITI) and selecting "d" produces extinction and the ITI.

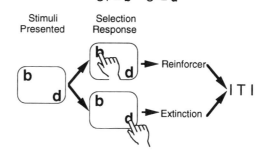

SIMULTANEOUS, SIMPLE-DISCRIMINATION PROCEDURE
S+ = **b**   S− = **d**

trial. This prevents the reinforcement of ITI responses via inadvertent, contiguous presentation of the stimuli associated with the next trial. (The onset of the next trial is likely to acquire conditioned reinforcing properties.) For human subjects, ITIs typically range from 1.5 s to 5 s and usually are held constant throughout a session. When food is used as a reinforcer, it may be beneficial to lengthen the ITI to accommodate the consumatory response. Otherwise, ITI responses might be artifactually suppressed, and response latencies for the next trial might be inflated, by the subject's eating. It is sometimes useful to have the duration of each ITI controlled by the experimenter, who initiates the next trial only after observing the completion of the consumatory response.

Procedures are designed to minimize the development of unwanted sources of stimulus control. For example, to minimize position biases, the positions of the S+ and S− change unpredictably across trials (with the constraint that the S+ is not presented in the same position on more than three consecutive trials). Also, the S+ is presented an equal number of times in each position within the session. Historically, stimuli have been displayed in only two positions (left and right). Current technology facilitates greater variation in stimulus position. For example, stimuli might be displayed anywhere within a 3 by 3 matrix on a panel of keys or a computer screen. Increasing the number of stimulus positions presumably decreases the likelihood that responding will come under the control of location rather than form, although position control may not be eliminated entirely (see Sidman, 1992).

Typically, simultaneous discrimination involves visual stimuli, whereas auditory stimulus control is studied with successive discrimination procedures. However, Harrison (1990) reported a simultaneous auditory discrimination procedure used successfully with rats that could also be used with human subjects. The procedure was directly analogous to standard simultaneous discrimination procedures with visual stimuli. Above each of two levers, mounted 25 cm apart, was a speaker. On each trial, one speaker presented the S+ and the other presented the S−, with each speaker presenting the S+ equally often across trials. Pressing the lever under the S+ produced reinforcement.

The usual dependent measure in simple discrimination procedures is accuracy—the number of trials in which the correct stimulus is selected divided by the total number of trials. Measures of latency (the time from the presentation of the stimuli to the response) are often of interest also.

Although not common in stimulus control research with human subjects, not all simultaneous discrimination procedures require only a single response per trial. Simultaneous discriminations are concurrent schedules of reinforcement (see Shull & Lawrence, Chapter 4), and as such a wide variety of scheduling and analysis options are available, some of which allow measures of relative response rate (see Baron, Myerson, & Hale, 1988, for a discussion). The measure of stimulus control is the ratio of responses to the S+ to the responses to the S+ and the S− combined.

In *successive* discrimination, only one stimulus is presented at a time. Typically, each stimulus is presented for a specified period (e.g., 5 s), rather than until a single response is made (i.e., *not* a forced choice procedure). The simplest procedure involves a single S+ (e.g., the letter "b") that alternates with an ITI. The ITI is functionally an S−, as it is associated with a period of extinction. From the subject's point of view, the contingency is "Touch the letter 'b'; Do not touch in the absence of 'b'." Note that responding must be absent during the ITI to conclude that the letter "b" controls responding.

A variation is shown in Figure 7.4: Some trials present an S+, other trials present an S−, and an ITI separates the trials. This is the successive form of the simultaneous procedure discussed previously. Note, however, that a successive discrimination may be acquired more slowly than a simultaneous discrimination involving the same two stimuli (Carter & Eckerman, 1975). The figure shows there are two types of "correct" responses—responding to the S+ (hits) and not responding to the S− (correct rejections). Also, there are two types of incorrect responses—not responding to the S+ (omission errors or misses) and responding to the S− (commission errors or false alarms). The four response possibilities may be incorporated in signal detection analyses, which go beyond simple accuracy in their evaluation of stimulus control (see Irwin & McCarthy, Chapter 10).

Procedures can also involve more than one S+ with topographically different responses reinforced in the presence of each. Figure 7.5 illustrates such a successive discrimination procedure. When the letter "b" is presented, saying "b" is reinforced. When "d" is presented, saying "d" is reinforced.

Successive discrimination procedures can also involve different reinforcement schedules (i.e., other than fixed ratio [FR] 1) that produce different patterns or rates of responding in the presence of each stimulus. For example, in the presence of the S+, 25 responses may be required for reinforcement (FR 25 schedule), and in the presence of the S−, responses are never reinforced (extinction). The rate of responding in the presence of each stimulus is the basic datum of interest. A "discrimination ratio" can be computed by dividing the number or rate of responses made in the presence of S+ by the number of responses made in the presence of the S+ and S− combined. As with the procedures shown in Figure 7.5, procedures can involve two S+ stimuli (see Saunders & Spradlin, 1989). For example, in the presence of one stimulus, responses might be reinforced on an FR

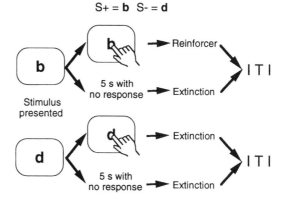

FIGURE 7.4. Trial events for correct and incorrect responses under each of two trial types in a successive, simple-discrimination procedure. On each trial, either the S+ (the letter "b") *or* the S− (the letter "d") is presented. The trial continues until a response occurs, or until a specified period (e.g., 5 s) without a response. Responses on S+ trials produce reinforcement and the ITI. Responses on S− trials produce extinction and the ITI, as do both S+ trials and S− trials without a response.

schedule, and in the presence of a second stimulus, responses that follow the previous response by more than 3 s may be reinforced (differential reinforcement of low rate). Stimulus control is indicated by differences in the pattern or rate of responding in the presence of the stimuli.

Establishing Simple Discrimination

Trial-and-Error Procedures

With many subjects, a simple discrimination can be established through differential reinforcement of the terminal performance, also called *trial-and-error training.* In such procedures, the incorrect response often merely ends the trial. The incorrect responses of human subjects sometimes produce a consequence such as a buzzer or textual error message.

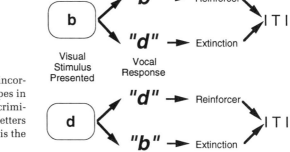

FIGURE 7.5. Trial events for correct and incorrect responses under each of two trial types in a forced-choice, successive, simple-discrimination procedure with two S+'s (the letters "b" and "d"). Vocalizing the letter name is the reinforced (correct) response.

Procedural Variations

ITI Contingencies. Current discrimination procedures seldom restrict responding during the ITI, that is, the operandum is available. Early studies of discrimination learning (e.g., using the WGTA) used discrete-trial procedures, in which the operandum was not available during the ITI. Thus, it is important not to overlook potential effects of variations in this aspect of procedure. In studies involving rats (Hachiya & Ito, 1991) and Japanese monkeys (Asano, 1976), simple, successive discriminations were acquired more rapidly when ITI responses were allowed (under extinction conditions) than when the response lever was retracted during the ITI. The effect was likely related to the extinction of responses controlled by irrelevant features of the apparatus. Studies of inexperienced discrimination learners often begin with procedures that establish discriminative control by the presence versus absence of a single stimulus (i.e., eliminate responses when no stimulus is present) before attempting to establish a discrimination between two different stimuli (e.g., Saunders & Spradlin, 1990; Serna, Dube, & McIlvane, 1997). Without the former rudimentary discrimination in place, training the latter presumably would be more difficult.

Trial-Initiation Response. Usually, discriminative stimuli are presented independently of the subject's behavior. With this procedure, variability in the subject's position with respect to the display can affect contact with the stimuli (Harrison, 1991). To help ensure that the subject is oriented toward the display, it may be desirable for the experimenter to initiate trials based on observation of the subject's readiness. Another possibility is to allow the subject to initiate the trial via an additional operandum. These procedures may be especially helpful for initial acquisition and for use with young children and individuals with mental retardation. An experiment by Dube, Callahan, and McIlvane (1993) provides an example of subject-initiated trials in a simple-discrimination procedure with animal subjects.

Correction Procedure. In its classic form, a correction procedure involves repeating a trial until a correct response is made, at which time the consequence for a correct response is delivered. Each repetition is preceded by the ITI. Calculation of accuracy is based on responses to the first presentation of a trial only. A correction procedure thus decreases the density of reinforcement for repeated presses to one position or to one stimulus, which would produce reinforcement on approximately every other trial in a two-choice, two-position task without a correction procedure.

A "within-trial" variant of the correction procedure is less often used. The "within-trial" procedure eliminates the ITI after error trials. The stimuli simply remain on the display and the trial continues until a correct response occurs. This procedure should be used with caution. The problem lies in how to consequate the corrected response. If the corrected response produces a reinforcer and the subject makes the correct response after a single error response, reinforcement density does not decrease substantially with errors (because there is no ITI). The procedure may thus establish a chain of two responses: the incorrect followed by the correct. Alternatively, if the corrected response simply ends the trial, the desired instance of stimulus control might not be strengthened.

Timeout. Errors can be followed by a period during which responses have no effect. This period often is signaled, and it occurs before and in addition to the usual ITI, such that errors increase the delay to the presentation of the next trial. For example, when a touch-sensitive computer screen is the operandum, a 5-s presentation of a black screen might be presented contingent on errors. This *timeout from positive reinforcement* is designed to punish errors. Although the procedure is often used, Mackay (1991) noted that it has received little systematic evaluation.

"Errorless" or Programmed Procedures

Most of the research on establishing simple or conditional discrimination has involved either animals, young children, or people with mental retardation. These subjects are often slow to acquire discrimination performances through differential reinforcement of the terminal performance or with verbal instruction. Such subjects provide opportunities for the analysis of discrimination performances, and for the investigation of procedures sufficient to establish them. For reviews of the literature on procedures designed to facilitate the acquisition of discriminations by individuals with mental retardation, see Lancioni and Smeets (1986) and McIlvane (1992).

A successful instructional program must face two interrelated features of stimulus control. First, although the experimenter specifies and controls the formal stimulus presentation, the stimulus–response relation cannot be observed directly. The source of stimulus control must be isolated over a number of observations (Skinner, 1935). For example, suppose we observe a subject for a single trial under a simple, simultaneous discrimination procedure. The stimuli are a circle and a square presented side by side a few inches apart on a computer screen. The subject touches the circle, which is on the left, and produces a reinforcer. What stimulus control relation has been exhibited (if any)? The circle or the left position could be controlling the response. Control by position can be maintained for many sessions because position-controlled responding produces a reinforcer on every two trials, on average. If additional trials show selection of the circle regardless of its position, stimulus control by the circle can be inferred tentatively.

A second problem is that, as with the reinforcement of a particular response topography, an instance of stimulus control must occur before it can be reinforced (Ray & Sidman, 1970). Success may be unlikely under differential reinforcement of the desired stimulus–response unit because the unit does not occur with a frequency sufficient to be strengthened by the contingencies (in fact, the unit may not occur at all). As in establishing new response topographies, stimulus control can be "shaped by changing relevant stimuli in a program which leads the organism into subtle discriminations" (Skinner, 1966, p. 18). A stimulus control shaping procedure begins by reinforcing an existing stimulus–response relation. Over trials, successive approximations to the desired form of stimulus control are reinforced (or, put differently, control of the response is transferred gradually to the desired stimulus). In essence, these procedures make the desired stimulus–response unit more likely, so that it can be reinforced. Well-designed procedures can promote acquisition of the discrimination with few "errors" (i.e., undesired stimulus–response units). Procedures such as stimulus control fading have this general characteristic.

A classic demonstration of *fading* appears in a study by Sidman and Stoddard (1967). Boys with mental retardation served as subjects. The response panel was a square matrix of nine keys; the middle key was always dark. The stimuli, a circle and seven ellipses, were projected onto the keys from behind. The circle was the S+. When differential reinforcement procedures (trial and error) were used, only one of nine control subjects acquired the discrimination.

Ten additional subjects were exposed to a fading procedure in which the intensity of the initially invisible S−'s increased, in a number of small steps, over trials. At first, trials presented the circle on a bright key, with all other keys dark. Given evidence of control by the S+ at each step (i.e., accurate performance), the blank S− keys became brighter in seven steps, until they were as bright as the S+. These steps transferred discriminative control from "bright key vs. dark keys" to "bright key with a form vs. bright keys with no form" (Sidman & Stoddard, 1967, p. 6). Seven of the ten subjects acquired the discrimination, and did so virtually without error. For these seven, faint ellipses were next presented on the S− keys. Over the next ten steps, the ellipses gradually became as distinct as the circle. All seven subjects acquired the discrimination, five with very few errors.

The procedures we have described involve increasing the intensity of the S− stimuli. There are other fading options for establishing form discriminations. One can gradually increase the size of an initially smaller S− or decrease the size of a larger S+. One can gradually change the form of the stimuli (sometimes called *stimulus shaping;* Schilmoeller, Schilmoeller, Etzel, & LeBlanc, 1979). One can superimpose a color discrimination over the form discrimination, and fade out the colors. For example, if red and green already differentially control responding, the circle/ellipse discrimination training could present the circle on a green background and the ellipses on red, and gradually change the backgrounds to white. Fading procedures can also be used for successive discrimination. In the final condition of a study by Terrace (1963), pigeons' key pecks were reinforced intermittently during a 180-s period during which the key was illuminated red (S+). Extinction was in effect during a 180-s period with the key illuminated green. Birds exposed to a three-phase fading procedure acquired this discrimination with virtually no responses during green. At first, the red key alternated with a very brief period during which the key was *not* lighted. In Phase 1, the dark key period was increased gradually until it was the same length as the red-key period. During Phase 2, the S− period was again very brief, and the intensity of the green light was increased gradually. In Phase 3, the duration of the S− was increased until it was the same length as the S+.

Implications of Using Errorless versus Trial-and-Error Procedures. The literature contains many demonstrations of the acquisition of stimulus control with errorless procedures. Less is known about whether the properties of errorlessly trained performances differ from performances established through trial-and-error training. Identical terminal discrimination performances may react differently to some manipulations depending on whether or not they were established errorlessly. For example, the sensitivity of a discrimination performance to drug effects might depend on whether or not it was established errorlessly. In a study by Terrace (1970), some pigeons were exposed to trial-and-error procedures and others to errorless training procedures. All acquired a successive discrimination between vertical (S+) and horizontal (S−), but differences were shown under subsequent drug conditions. Chlorpromazine and imipramine greatly increased S− responding (i.e., decreased accuracy) in birds that had been trained with trial-and-error procedures, but had no effect on the S− responding of birds trained with errorless procedures. Thus, the drug increased the probability of stimulus–response relations that had been demonstrated previously (i.e., errors) in the trial-and-error birds. The errorlessly trained birds had not previously demonstrated control by the S− and they did not do so under drug conditions. Experimenters using discrimination performances as baselines on which to assess the effects of other manipulations should be aware of the potential for differences resulting from methods of establishing the discrimination.

Higher-Order Simple Discrimination Performances and Procedures

Learning Set

The term *learning set* refers to the empirical observation of more rapid acquisition over successive new discriminations. Early studies were conducted with monkeys (Harlow, 1949) and, subsequently, a variety of animals (see Schrier, 1984). There is also a large literature on human subjects with mental retardation (see Kaufman & Prehm, 1966, for a review). The classic finding is that acquisition eventually occurs in one trial with trial-and-error programming. That is, if the S+ is selected on the first trial (and a reinforcer is delivered), that stimulus will control the response on all subsequent trials. If the S− is selected on the first trial (and the reinforcer is not presented), the S+ will be selected on all subsequent trials. This pattern has been described as "win–stay, lose–shift."

Knowledge of the learning set phenomenon is important to researchers planning to use simple discrimination acquisition as a baseline against which to assess the effects of other variables. Because acquisition is likely to become more rapid as a function of the number of discriminations learned, experimental manipulations should not be made until stable acquisition rates are shown. For all but the most limited of human subjects, stable acquisition rates are likely to show a ceiling effect (i.e., acquisition occurs with so few errors that improvement in performance cannot be detected). A promising procedural modification involves presenting multiple simple discriminations across trials. For example, six different simple discriminations can be presented across the first six trials, repeated in a different order across the next six trials, and so on. To adjust difficulty level, the number of discriminations can be varied. Even these procedures may rapidly generate ceiling effects in normal adults. Tests with adults with mild mental retardation suggest that stable acquisition rates can be shown that are not a function of ceiling or floor effects (Williams & Saunders, 1997).

Stimulus Generalization

Most work on stimulus generalization has been conducted with animal subjects. The present treatment can be supplemented by referring to summaries by Harrison (1991), Honig and Urcuioli (1981), and Rilling (1977). Stimulus generalization is "the spread of the effects of reinforcement . . . during one stimulus to other stimuli differing from the original along one or more dimensions" (Catania, 1992). If responding is established in the presence of a red stimulus, to what extent will an orange stimulus control the same response even though responding has not been reinforced in the presence of the orange stimulus?

A classic method of evaluating stimulus generalization begins with successive discrimination training in which responding is intermittently reinforced in the presence of a particular stimulus and extinction is in effect in the absence of the stimulus (e.g., Jenkins & Harrison, 1960). In tests, often given under extinction conditions, stimuli that vary along a dimension of the training stimulus are presented. For example, the original S+ might be light of a particular wavelength, with several stimuli of lower and higher wavelengths presented during the test. The rate, number, or percentage of total responses is plotted as a function of wavelength—a generalization gradient (but see Honig & Urcuioli, 1981, p. 409, on percentage measures). Typically, the gradient is an inverted V-shaped function that peaks at the original S+, with decreases above or below that value. Rate of responding varies continuously with the value of the stimulus. A number of training and testing variables can affect the steepness of the slope, however. When training involves an S+ and an S−, tones of two different frequencies for example, the resulting gradient is termed a *postdiscrimination gradient*. The classic outcome is a shift of the peak of the generalization gradient in the direction away from the S− (e.g., Hanson, 1959). For example, if the frequency of the S− is lower than that of the S+, the generalization gradient peaks at a value somewhat above that of the S+.

It should be noted that generalization gradients can also be obtained with procedures in which the trial ends either after a single response or after a fixed period without a response. These procedures apparently are used more often with human subjects. For example, subjects first learn to make a response to an S+. In tests, each value along the continuum is presented the same number of times, and the number of responses made in the presence of each value is plotted (see Baron, 1973; Galizio & Baron, 1976).

Relatively little work on stimulus generalization has involved human subjects. Moreover, the major reviews of stimulus generalization provide little or no discussion of issues specific to the study of humans. Baron (1973) noted that differing characteristics of postdiscrimination gradients shown in some studies with human subjects might be related to the subjects labeling the stimuli. Instead of the visual stimuli (e.g., colors) used in some studies, Baron used pure tones, which presumably are more difficult to label. Shifts in postdiscrimination gradients were inversely related to differences between the S+ and the S−, as had been shown in animal studies (see Figure 7.6). A later study explored the effects of label training (Galizio & Baron, 1976). Some groups of subjects were trained to label the pure tones involved in the generalization assessment and others did not receive label training. Relative to the label-trained subjects, the peaks of the generalization gradients of untrained subjects showed greater decreases over repeated testing. Clear-

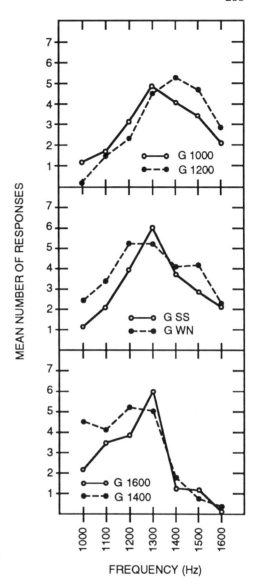

FIGURE 7.6. Postdiscrimination gradients from six groups of human subjects trained to respond to a 1300-Hz tone (S+). Five of the six groups received discrimination training; the S− is another tone at the frequency indicated after the "G" (e.g., G 1200 received training with an S− of 1200 Hz) or white noise (G WN). Group G SS was trained with the S+ only. Data are the mean number of trials in which responses were made to the tones at the frequencies indicated on the abscissa. From "Postdiscrimination Gradients of Human Subjects on a Tone Continuum" by A. Baron, 1973, *Journal of Experimental Psychology, 101,* 337–342. Copyright 1973 by the American Psychological Association. Adapted by permission of the author.

ly, studies of stimulus generalization in human subjects must consider the potential for labeling effects.

Instructions are a related aspect of procedure that might differentially affect outcome in studies with human subjects. Howard (1979) suggested that the use of instructions may have made peaked gradients like those found in animal studies more likely in human studies (e.g., Baron, 1973). He suggested that humans' propensity to label stimuli might make "categorical generalization" the likely outcome after discrimination training in the absence of instructions. In Howard's study, subjects "divided the stimuli into two categories, responding alike to stimuli classed within each category" (p. 209). Stimuli were the names of occupations that varied along the "dimension" of status, however. It seems likely that generalization along a conceptual dimension might differ from generalization along a physical dimension.

Although most studies have used a molar rate measure, because rate can vary continuously, stimulus generalization can also be analyzed at a molecular level. This alternative approach makes the strategic assumption that stimulus control is quantal in nature. When viewed molecularly, generalization outcomes may reflect a mixture of two or more stimulus–response relations. The intermediate rates reported at stimulus values between the S+ and the S− may result from averaging periods of the high rate responding (established in the presence of the S+) with periods of low rate responding (established in the presence of the S−). Thus, investigations of stimulus generalization should be designed after considering whether molar, molecular, or both levels of analysis will fulfill the study goals. For a thorough discussion of the quantal approach and supporting data, see Bickel and Etzel (1985). For a helpful introduction to the issues, see Branch (1994, pp. 56–61).

Abstraction

An abstraction is a "discrimination based on a single property of stimuli, independent of other properties" (Catania, 1992). For example, a child learns to call a variety of red objects "red," even though the objects may differ along a number of dimensions. Abstraction requires a training history in which the response "red" is reinforced in the presence of red stimuli that vary along other dimensions (an apple, a fire engine, a shirt). Training with a single stimulus will not suffice. If an apple were the only training stimulus, for example, an unintended property of the stimulus might acquire control. For example, the response "red" might subsequently occur to green apples. The term *concept* is often used to refer to abstraction involving more than a single property (although the terms *concept* and *abstraction* are often used interchangeably). Regardless of the term used, the type of reinforcement history required is the same—reinforcement of the same response in the presence of a number of stimuli that contain the element or elements to which control is being established.

Functional Stimulus Classes

For the sake of completing the present theme, we note that it is also possible to observe functional stimulus classes that are not based on common physical properties. Two or more stimuli may initially come to control the same response through direct reinforcement. When a new response is established in the presence of one of the stimuli, the others may also control that response (Goldiamond, 1962). Studies of functional stimulus classes have involved simple simultaneous and simple successive discrimination as well as conditional discrimination.

CONDITIONAL DISCRIMINATION PROCEDURES

Conditional discrimination procedures are widely used to study both human and animal behavior. In a conditional discrimination, the function of a discriminative stimulus (whether it is S+ or S−) changes based on the presence of another stimulus—the conditional stimulus. Thus, the procedures involve a four-term contingency, in which one or more three-term contingencies are under conditional control (Sidman, 1986). Conditional discrimination is involved in matching-to-sample and delayed matching-to-sample procedures. Higher-order performances studied within conditional discrimination procedures include generalized identity and oddity (or same/different), learning set, categorization, and stimulus equivalence. We will describe several variations of the conditional discrimination and illustrate their uses. For a more detailed treatment of the history of conditional discrimination procedures and a summary of empirical outcomes, we recommend a chapter by Mackay (1991).

Conditional Position Discrimination

In a conditional *position* discrimination, the discriminative stimuli are identical except for their position. For example, in a two-choice procedure, there may be a button on the left side of the response panel and a button on the right. Whether a response to the left button or to the right button produces a reinforcer depends on which of two "sample" stimuli is present. For example, if the sample is the letter "B," a response to the left button is reinforced; if the sample is the letter "D," a response to the right button is reinforced. This procedure is sometimes used to operationalize simple successive discrimination (e.g., Carter & Eckerman, 1975) because each of two or more successively presented stimuli (B or D) controls a response with a distinct topography ("Go left" or "Go right"). Because of this feature, the procedure might be considered an intermediate step between simple successive discrimination and the prototypical conditional discrimination procedure—matching to sample. Like the latter, conditional control of a simple discrimination (that of the left versus right button) is required.

Matching-to-Sample Procedures

Matching-to-sample (MTS) procedures have been used extensively to study learning, memory, and concept formation in human subjects functioning across a wide range of developmental levels. They have also been used with numerous animal species, from pigeons to primates. Differences across species in processes involved in MTS performance have long been of interest to experimental psychologists, but interest recently has been enlivened by studies of a form of stimulus equivalence that is studied within MTS procedures (Green & Saunders, Chapter 8).

Identity MTS Procedures

The prototypical simultaneous identity MTS procedure (Cumming & Berryman, 1961) involves three response keys that can be lighted different colors. A trial begins with the presentation of a sample stimulus; for example, the middle key is lighted red. A response to the sample, sometimes called an *observing response,* lights the two side keys (one red and one green). These are the comparison, or choice keys. The sample remains lighted until a response is made to one of the

SIMULTANEOUS, MATCH-TO-SAMPLE PROCEDURE

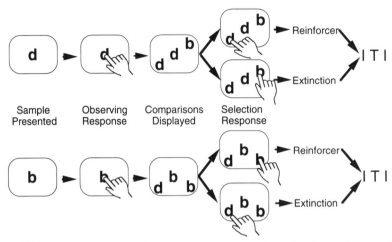

FIGURE 7.7.   Trial events for correct and incorrect responses under each of two trial types in a simultaneous, conditional, identity matching-to-sample procedure.

comparison stimuli. A response to the comparison stimulus that is identical to the sample stimulus produces a reinforcer. In an oddity-from-sample procedure, trial configurations are the same as in the identity MTS procedure. Selecting the stimulus that is different from the sample, however, produces reinforcement.

Other features of MTS—the ITI, reinforcement procedures, and controls for the development of position-based responding—are congruent with those for simple discrimination. Most often, the MTS procedures used with human subjects are virtually identical to the procedure that Cumming and Berryman (1961) used with pigeons. Usual modifications include increasing the number of comparison stimuli presented on a trial, and presenting the comparison stimuli in more than two positions (facilitated by computers and touchscreens). Figure 7.7 shows two trials of an MTS procedure with a touchscreen operandum. An important use of the identity MTS procedure is in the study of the higher-order performance of generalized identity matching, to be discussed later.

Arbitrary MTS Procedures

As the name implies, in arbitrary MTS procedures, the sample and the comparison stimuli (i.e., both the S+ and the S−) are physically different. Otherwise, trials operate exactly like those involving physically identical samples and comparisons. For example, samples could be printed words with comparisons being pictures. Each new sample–comparison relation is established through reinforcement. The procedure has been called *symbolic matching*. The symbolic nature of the performance cannot be assumed for all subjects, however, an issue that is addressed in the literature on equivalence relations (Sidman, 1986).

Training and Programming Variables

Normally capable human subjects of at least elementary school age often acquire MTS performances through trial-and-error (differential reinforcement) procedures. That is, the subject is simply exposed to the terminal form of the task. Procedures such as timeout and correction (described for simple discrimination) can facilitate acquisition. This section will discuss additional procedural considerations and variations.

Trial Sequencing. One should not use the same sequence of trials across consecutive sessions, as this may establish unwanted sources of control. For example, a subject might learn a series of position responses rather than responses to the conditional stimulus. In a study by Sidman (1971), a subject who was trained to 100% accuracy in an arbitrary MTS task using the same sequence of trials across sessions showed low accuracy with the same set of samples when they were presented in a different sequence and with different S− stimuli. The samples had not acquired control; instead, the subject had apparently learned a sequence of comparison selections.

Observing Responses. In the prototypical matching procedure, the trial begins with the presentation of the sample stimulus. A response to the sample stimulus produces the comparison stimuli. The sample response is often called an *observing response,* under the assumption that it ensures observation of the sample. Although the effects of the observing response have not been studied in humans, studies with pigeons suggest slower acquisition when the observing response is omitted (Eckerman, Lanson, & Cumming, 1968). When normal adult subjects are involved, the observing response is often omitted without deleterious effects on acquisition. Usually, the sample is presented for a second or two before the comparisons are presented; often the experimenter instructs the subject to observe the sample (e.g., Markham & Dougher, 1993).

Trial-Initiation Response. As noted for simple discrimination, it may be useful for a trial to begin (i.e., the sample to be presented) only after the subject makes a response to initiate the trial. The trial initiation response ensures that the subject is oriented toward the screen when the sample is presented. This may be especially helpful when the sample is removed after a brief display period. For example, in a study involving delayed matching by Critchfield and Perone (1993), pressing keys on the response panel produced a 1-s sample presentation.

Differential Sample Responses. Arbitrary matching performance requires the successive discrimination of the sample stimuli, and successive discrimination is acquired more slowly than simultaneous (Carter & Eckerman, 1975). Thus, arbitrary matching acquisition can sometimes be facilitated by establishing different responses in the presence of each sample, and then maintaining these responses as an element of the arbitrary matching procedure. Studies with pigeon, primate, and young and mentally retarded human subjects indicate more rapid acquisition of arbitrary matching when different observing responses are established in the presence of the two samples than when the nondifferential observing response is used (e.g., Cohen, Looney, Brady, & Aucella, 1976; Saunders & Spradlin, 1993; Sidman et al., 1982). For example, in a study of normal preschool children who had not acquired arbitrary matching when presented the terminal form of the task, an FR schedule was programmed in the presence of one sample and a differential-reinforcement-of-low-rate schedule was programmed in the presence of the other sample (Sidman et al., 1982). These produced rapid and slow rates of sample presses, respectively. Completing the schedule requirement produced the comparison stimuli. Highly similar procedures have been used with pigeons and primates. Sample naming also has been used (e.g., Saunders & Spradlin, 1993).

Instructions. Instructions are often used to facilitate the acquisition of arbitrary matching. Such instructions have ranged widely in specificity. They may consist of little more than a prompt to touch the sample followed by a nonspecific prompt to touch one of the comparison stimuli (Lynch & Green, 1991). They may involve a fairly detailed description of the nature of the task (Markham & Dougher, 1993). Or they may provide explicit prompts that include names for the stimuli of a specific matching problem (Saunders, Saunders, Kirby, & Spradlin, 1988). Unfortunately, there has been little systematic study of the effects of instructions. A study by Michael and Bernstein (1991) found modest differences in acquisition rate in preschool children across three instructional conditions. Moreover, performances changed at slightly different rates on subsequent exposure to contingency reversals. Outcomes ultimately were the same across conditions, however. On the other hand, several studies have suggested differences in subsequent tests for stimulus equivalence (Green, Sigurdardottir, & Saunders, 1991; Saunders, Saunders, Williams, & Spradlin, 1993). Sometimes it is assumed that minimal instructions provide the best insurance against unwanted instructional effects. It is currently unclear whether this assumption is warranted, or whether, especially for verbally sophisticated subjects, the provision of a standard set of instructions provides a needed correction for varying histories. Skinner (1966) pointed out that instructing performances of highly capable subjects is efficient and need not produce a confound if used judiciously—so as to facilitate, rather than circumvent, an operant analysis.

Instructional Programming. In addition to the successive discrimination between the sample stimuli, arbitrary matching performance requires two other skill components: the simultaneous discrimination of the comparison stimuli and (by definition) sample control of comparison selection (Carter & Eckerman, 1975). Thus merely establishing the successive sample discrimination may not facilitate acquisition of arbitrary matching (Saunders & Spradlin, 1989). Likewise, procedures designed to establish simple discrimination, such as fading or delayed prompting, may not be effective because they do not ensure all of the skill components of arbitrary matching. Procedures that ensure the successive discrimination of the sample stimuli and the simultaneous discrimination of the comparison stimuli along with programming for the acquisition of control by the sample stimulus, are often successful with subjects for whom trial-and-error procedures are unsuccessful.

The literature contains two procedures that accomplish this programmed acquisition, each in a different way. Saunders and Spradlin (1993) reported a procedure that first establishes the simple simultaneous discrimination between the stimuli to be used as comparisons, and its rapid reversal through standard simple-discrimination procedures. Then, differential sample responses ensure the successive discrimination between the sample stimuli. Several types of differential responses have been used: different patterns of button presses (maintained by different schedules of reinforcement; Saunders & Spradlin, 1989), sample naming (Saunders & Spradlin, 1993), and repeating an auditory sample (Glat, Gould, Stoddard, & Sidman, 1994). After training each component simple discrimination, sample control of comparison selection is established in a series of matching trials that begins by presenting the same sample for blocks of consecutive trials (while maintaining differential sample responses). Given high accuracy with one sample, a block of trials with the second sample is presented. Sample alternation continues in this manner as the size of the trial blocks is decreased gradually over trials until sample presentation is randomized. These procedures can also be used to establish the matching of physically identical stimuli in subjects who have not shown generalized identity matching (Saunders, Williams, & Spradlin, 1995). An advantage of this procedure is that it accommodates a variety of stimuli (e.g., auditory sample stimuli, or three-dimensional objects).

Another procedure, used in a study by Zygmont, Lazar, Dube, and McIlvane (1992), is efficient for establishing arbitrary matching involving visual stimuli in subjects who already match physically identical stimuli. It begins with a two-choice conditional identity-matching performance involving only the stimuli that are to be comparisons in the trained arbitrary matching problem. Over trials, the form of one sample stimulus is changed gradually into the form of the stimulus that is to be the sample in the trained arbitrary matching problem. Then the second sample stimulus is changed in the same manner. The changes occur in numerous discrete steps, with a change occurring each time selections are accurate at a given step. Figure 7.8, taken from the study by Zygmont et al., illustrates the procedure. Initially, subjects performed identity matching of delta and phi; these trials are labeled "B." In the first phase, delta was changed to sigma in 9 steps; identity matching trials with phi samples were intermixed throughout. In the next phase, phi was changed to gamma in 12 steps. Thus, this procedure begins with evidence of simultaneous discrimination and sample control (shown by the initial identity matching performance), and then gradually establishes the successive discrimination between the sample stimuli. Ideally, the change is sufficiently gradual to ensure the maintenance of accurate responding throughout the procedure. Thus, unlike the Saunders and Spradlin (1993) procedure, this procedure is potentially errorless. When errors occur, they initiate a return to a previous step.

Intermittent Reinforcement. Once a matching performance has been established, an experimenter may wish to maintain it without delivering a reinforcer on every trial. This may be important to avoid satiation when the performance must be maintained for long periods or to prepare for test trials for stimulus generalization or other forms of stimulus control transfer. There has been little systematic study of the effects of intermittent reinforcement on matching accuracy of human

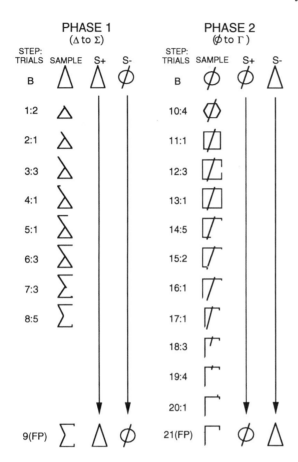

FIGURE 7.8. A stimulus control shaping program for establishing arbitrary matching to sample; used in a study by Zygmont et al. (1992). The baseline identity matching and final performance arbitrary matching trials are designated B and FP, respectively. From "Teaching arbitrary matching via sample stimulus-control shaping to young children and mentally retarded individuals: A methodological note" by D. M. Zygmont, R. M. Lazar, W. V. Dube, and W. J. McIlvane, 1992, *Journal of the Experimental Analysis of Behavior, 57,* 109–117. Copyright 1992 by the Society for the Experimental Analysis of Behavior. Reprinted by permission.

subjects. Studies using animal subjects indicate a higher likelihood of errors soon after the delivery of a reinforcer when the reinforcer is delivered after a fixed number of correct response (an FR schedule) or for the first correct response after a specified interval (fixed-interval schedule) (summarized in Mackay, 1991). A study with young, normal human subjects produced a similar outcome under a delayed identity-matching procedure (in which the sample disappears before the comparison stimuli are presented) but accuracy was generally high with simultaneous identity matching (Davidson & Osborne, 1974). When the number of required correct responses varied across reinforcer presentations (variable-ratio schedule), delayed matching accuracy was slightly lower relative to the FR schedule, but errors were uniformly distributed. The available evidence suggests that variable-ratio schedules are a good choice for the experimental needs noted above.

Procedural Variations

Varying Stimuli. Standard MTS procedures most often involve either auditory or visual samples and visual comparison stimuli. The procedure allows incorporation of a wide range of stimuli, however, including those detected by smell, touch, or even taste (Hayes, Tilley, & Hayes, 1988). The interoceptive effects of drugs can be conditional stimuli (samples) (DeGrandpre, Bickel, & Higgins, 1992). In addition, stimuli of different durations can serve as samples (McCarthy & Davison, 1980), as can aspects of the subject's own behavior, such as number of responses made to the sample stimulus (Rilling, 1968). For example, an FR discrimination procedure can be conducted with three horizontally arranged response keys. A trial begins when the middle key is lighted. On some trials, one press of the middle key lights the two side keys (FR 1), and on other trials, 10 presses light the side keys (FR 10). Pressing the left key after FR 1 and pressing the right key after FR 10 produces the reinforcer.

Single-Comparison Procedures. Variations of the prototypical procedure may be necessary to fit a particular question. In a go–no go procedure, the sample and a single comparison stimulus are presented on each trial. A response that occurs within a specified time limit (e.g., 3 s) is reinforced if the correct comparison stimulus for that sample is present. Failing to respond within 3 s constitutes an error. If the incorrect comparison is present, either extinction may be in effect (Nelson & Wasserman, 1978), or a reinforcer is delivered if no response occurs within the specified time limit (Sidman et al., 1982). Responding to the S− within 3 s constitutes an error. The effects of defining correct and incorrect responses in this manner must be carefully considered when experimental manipulations are likely to increase response latency. For example, when these procedures are used in tests for emergent performances such as stimulus equivalence, the longer latency responses that may occur on test trials (Saunders, Wachter, & Spradlin, 1988) will be recorded as errors (noted by Dube, Green, & Serna, 1993). Similar concerns may apply for pharmacological manipulations. On the other hand, an advantage of these procedures is that, because the comparison stimuli are not presented together, they can be presented in the same location. Thus, control by comparison position would not be possible (see Iversen, Sidman, & Carrigan, 1986). Another advantage of the go–no go procedure is that it can be used to present auditory comparison stimuli, providing the concerns noted above are not applicable to the planned research protocol. This avoids presenting the comparison stimuli simultaneously, which may compromise the discriminability of auditory comparisons.

Another type of single-comparison procedure has been used to evaluate the nature of the stimulus control that develops under matching procedures (McIlvane et al., 1987). It is actually a two-choice procedure, but one of the choices is a "dummy" stimulus whose function depends on the previously established function of the comparison stimulus with which it is presented. If the "dummy" stimulus is presented with a stimulus that has an S+ function, it has an S− function. If it is presented with a stimulus that has an S− function, it has an S+ function. The procedure allows an experimenter to determine, for example, whether an MTS procedure has taught the subject to avoid the S− in the presence of a particular sample (termed *S− control*), to select the S+ (*S+ control*), or whether both sources of control have been established. In addition to its usefulness in the study of stimulus control per se, the procedure may be important to researchers using MTS baselines to assess the effects of other variables. That is, it may be wise to determine the type of control that has been established before such manipulations have been made. For example, little is known about whether pharmacological manipulations affect S+ control and S− control differently.

Successive-Comparison Procedures. Dube et al. (1993) reported a technique for incorporating auditory comparison stimuli that places no constraints on response latency. Responses were made to a touch-sensitive computer screen. A trial included four successive stimulus presentations, each produced by the subject's touching a white circle that was presented in the middle of the otherwise blank screen. The circle disappeared during stimulus presentations. The first touch produced the auditory sample, the second produced the first auditory comparison and a gray square on the right side (for example) of the screen, the third touch again produced the auditory sample, and the fourth produced the second auditory comparison and a gray square on the left side of the screen. Finally, both gray squares were presented together. Touching the square that had been presented with the correct auditory comparison was reinforced. It is important to note that these procedures impose an additional burden of remembering which comparison square was associated with the correct auditory stimulus. Although they were used successfully with normally capable adolescents and adults, the procedures may be difficult for developmentally limited subjects. Moreover, even for normally capable subjects, accuracy may decrease as the number of comparisons increases. Of course, whether such accuracy decreases are an advantage or a disadvantage depends on one's experimental question.

Yes–No Procedures. Yes–no procedures are useful in that they allow a combination of identity matching and oddity matching. An example appears in a study by D'Amato and Colombo (1989). A subject-initiated trial began with the presentation of two visual stimuli that were either identical or different. If the stimuli were the same, pressing a lever on the right side of the apparatus produced reinforcement, and if the stimuli were different, pressing the left-hand lever was reinforced.

Delayed MTS

Delayed MTS procedures are heavily used in the study of memory and in behavioral pharmacology; see Wixted (Chapter 9) and Higgins and Hughes (Chapter 18), respectively, for discussion of the use of the procedures in these areas. Because of coverage in later chapters, the present treatment of delayed matching will be limited to a brief discussion of procedural options.

Figure 7.9 shows that delayed MTS trials operate like simultaneous matching trials except that the sample disappears when the observing response is made (or, in a variation, after the sample has been presented for a specified period). The comparison stimuli are then presented after a delay. The subject must select a comparison after the sample has disappeared, hence the use of the procedure to study short-term memory.

Training in delayed matching should begin (after exposure to a simultaneous matching task) with a 0-s delay procedure, in which comparison stimuli are presented immediately after the sample disappears. By varying the length of the de-

DELAYED, MATCH-TO-SAMPLE PROCEDURE

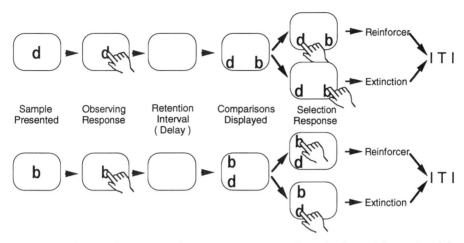

FIGURE 7.9.   Trial events for correct and incorrect responses under each of two trial types in a delayed, conditional, identity matching-to-sample procedure.

lay, a range of accuracy levels can be generated within subject. Several methods for presenting a range of delays have been used. The delay can be varied by randomly mixing various delays across trials within a session (e.g., White, 1985), by presenting several different blocks of consecutive trials, each with a single delay (e.g., Baron & Menich, 1985), or in whole sessions with a single delay. Another option is a titrating delay procedure, in which the length of the delay increases (e.g., by 0.5 s) whenever a specified number of consecutive correct responses occur (Aman, Kern, McGhee, & Arnold, 1993). In a two-choice task, at least three consecutive correct responses should be required because of the high likelihood of correct responses occurring "by chance." The delay decreases with each error. Under these procedures, delay eventually stabilizes at a particular level (e.g., the longest delay at which three consecutive correct responses are made consistently). The effects of various manipulations on the maximum delay achieved can then be assessed.

Delayed-matching accuracy may also be affected by the length of the intertrial interval. Specifically, accuracy may be higher with longer intertrial intervals because of diminished interference from the stimuli presented on the previous trial (Nelson & Wasserman, 1978).

In a useful variation of delayed matching procedures, complex samples of two or more elements are presented. The sample may be presented for a specified duration, or until an observing response is made. The choice stimuli (two or more) include one of the sample elements. Cognitive studies of memory and attention use similar procedures extensively (see Shiffrin, 1988). In a "yes–no" variation of the procedure (Scott, 1971), a single choice stimulus is presented. One response is reinforced (e.g., pressing a lever on the left) if the comparison appeared in the sample array and an alternative response (e.g., pressing a lever on the right) is reinforced if it was not. Studies that used these procedures with a 2-s sample presentation, a speed requirement for comparison selection, and normal-adult subjects, have shown decreasing accuracy as a function of the number of sample stimuli presented (Baron & Menich, 1985; Critchfield & Perone, 1993). A study by Stromer, McIlvane, Dube, and Mackay (1993) found decreased accuracy when the number of sample elements was increased from one to two in subjects with mental retardation (without the time limits used in studies of normally capable subjects). Thus, these procedures provide an alternative means of generating a range of accuracy in individual subjects (varying the number of sample elements). A study by Critchfield and Perone (1993) used this feature of the procedure to perform a signal detection analysis of self-reports of speed and accuracy on the matching task. The procedure may be valuable in other investigations that assess effects against a range of performances within subject, for example, in behavioral pharmacology (e.g., Sprague, Barnes, & Werry, 1970).

Second-Order Conditional Discriminations

Conditional discriminations can themselves be brought under conditional control. Sidman (1986) discussed five-term contingencies and their relevance to complex human behavior in detail. For example, consider a standard identity MTS problem that is modified by the presence of higher-order stimuli. When the screen is red, a reinforcer is delivered for touching the identical stimulus; when the screen is green, a reinforcer is delivered for touching the nonidentical stimulus. A similar scenario can exist for arbitrary matching. For example, when the screen background is red and stimulus "A1" is the sample, the selection of stimulus "B1" and not stimulus "B2" would be reinforced, whereas the opposite would hold true in the presence of a green background. The use of such procedures in the study of stimulus equivalence relations can be seen in Bush, Sidman, and deRose (1989).

Higher-Order Conditional Discrimination

Generalized Identity Matching

For many animal subjects, the term *identity matching to sample* may describe the procedure but not the performance. A subject may demonstrate highly accurate "matching" with a small set of stimuli after direct training. When new stimuli are presented under the matching procedure, however, accuracy may be at chance levels. That is, the physical identity of the stimuli may play no role in the subject's performance. Most human subjects, however, respond correctly to new identity matching problems on first exposure in the laboratory (or with minimal instruction as to the nature of the task). The classic finding is that individuals with developmental levels of at least 5 years demonstrate generalized identity matching (House, Brown, & Scott, 1974), although it is likely these data underestimate what is possible with optimal assessment procedures (e.g., Serna et al., 1997).

Generalized identity matching may be tested with two stimuli at a time in a standard two-choice procedure in which a stimulus serves as both S+ and S− across trials (see Figure 7.7). A "unique trials" identity task provides another option. In it, each trial presents a different sample stimulus and sample stimuli are never presented as incorrect comparisons. Because S− stimuli have no history as an S+ (and vice versa), the likelihood of the S− serving as a competing source of stimulus control is greatly diminished relative to procedures in which the same stimuli serve both S+ and S− functions across trials. See Dube, McIlvane, and Green (1992) for a conceptual analysis.

As noted, normally developing human subjects are likely to exhibit generalized identity matching under both procedures. The procedures may yield different results, however, for some subjects or under certain conditions (e.g., pharmacological manipulations). This is a largely unexplored area. It is important that researchers using identity matching procedures be aware of these distinctions, especially in comparing results across studies in which the different procedures have been used. It is worth noting that the clearest demonstration of generalized identity matching in pigeons is with a unique-trials procedure (Wright, Cook, Rivera, Sands, & Delius, 1988). (The Wright et al. procedure differed from previous studies in other potentially important ways. The most noteworthy is that subjects were exposed to a large number of different stimuli within the matching context before tests for generalized identity matching were presented.)

Generalized Conditional Responding

Learning set outcomes may occur in conditional discrimination as they do in simple discrimination. Acquisition of arbitrary matching becomes more rapid as a function of the number of conditional discriminations learned (Saunders & Spradlin, 1993). As in simple discrimination, acquisition may eventually occur in one trial. Our discussion of simple discrimination noted implications of learning set for acquisition baselines.

Further evidence of generalized conditional responding comes from demonstrations that, when a new arbitrary matching problem is presented in the absence of differential reinforcement, subjects who have experience with arbitrary matching consistently select one comparison in the presence of one sample and the other comparison in the presence of the other sample. Demonstrations have occurred within two- and three-choice procedures (Saunders, Saunders et al., 1988, and Williams, Saunders, Saunders, & Spradlin, 1995, respectively). These findings have implications for test procedures in studies of untrained stimulus control such as stimulus equivalence. If, for example, multiple presentations are given of a single type of test trial (in a two-choice procedure) and generalized conditional responding is exhibited, the probability of a positive outcome in a given single subject is .5.

A somewhat different procedure also can demonstrate generalized conditional responding. A subject might correctly select the small letter counterpart when presented either capital "A" or capital "B" as the sample (given small "a" and "b" as comparisons), but have no experience matching capital "Q" and small "q." When presented a trial with a capital "Q" sample and small "q" and "a" as comparisons, however, the subject would most likely select the small letter "q." This performance has been called *exclusion,* because the "q" presumably is selected through the rejection of "a" (Dixon, 1977; McIlvane et al., 1987).

Equivalence Relations

When human subjects exhibit arbitrary matching performances, they are usually capable of more than just rote, invariant chains. For human subjects, arbitrary matching performance has been shown to be more flexible; it can result in additional matching performances that have not been directly trained. For example, consider a subject who has learned to select a circle comparison in the presence of a triangle sample and not in the presence of a square sample. When given the opportunity, the subject is likely to select a triangle comparison (and not a square) in the presence of a circle sample (symmetry). If the subject has also learned to select green in the presence of the circle, the subject will likely select green in the presence of the triangle without explicit training. Conditional relations that allow these forms of derived stimulus control are termed *equivalence relations* (Sidman & Tailby, 1982). They are discussed by Green and Saunders (Chapter 8).

INTERPRETING DISCRIMINATION ACCURACY

Whether acquisition or maintenance of stimulus control is of interest, accuracy (the number of trials during which the correct stimulus is selected divided by the total number of trials) is often the measure of choice. Accuracy is a crude measure. It does not allow the pinpointing of stimulus control, a matter touched on in the discussion of errorless instruction. This is not to say that accuracy measures should be abandoned, just that some aspects of their interpretation must be kept in mind. One elementary issue, occasionally overlooked by students, is that any measure of stimulus control must take into account the probability of the response in the absence of the S+. For example, a subject might reliably say "b" when shown the letter "b," but he might also say "b" when shown a "d." To demonstrate discriminative control, responding in the presence of the S+ must be compared with responding in its absence.

Another interpretative pitfall: 50% accuracy in a two-choice task does not indicate that the experimenter-designated source of stimulus control is occurring on 50% of the trials. Instead, it is likely to reflect the absence of the target source of stimulus control. To give a concrete example, a complete position preference in a two-choice simple discrimination results in 50% "accuracy," although the visual S+ is not the source of control on any of the trials. As another example, consider a two-choice MTS procedure in which a subject always selects the "correct" comparison in the presence of one sample, but also selects that same comparison in the presence of the other sample, yielding a measure of 50% "correct" responding. It would be inappropriate to conclude that one of the desired sample–comparison relations had been established and the other had not. Instead, the outcome demonstrates an absence of conditional control by the sample stimuli. It follows that a change from 30% accuracy to 50% accuracy cannot be taken as progress toward acquisition of an experimenter-designated discrimination (although it does indicate some shifting of stimulus control).

A related misinterpretation can occur when training begins with the presentation of the same sample stimulus across numerous trials. When the subject learns to select the "correct" comparison stimulus, it is tempting to assume that these procedures have established a sample–comparison relation. Because the same comparison is correct across trials, the sample stimulus is irrelevant to meeting the reinforcement contingencies. Such procedures provide no evidence that sample (conditional) control has been established (see McIlvane, Dube, Kledaras, Iennaco, & Stoddard, 1990).

Intermediate accuracy also can mislead. Accuracy of 75% might be interpreted as an indication of progress toward the experimenter-specified form of stimulus control. It may be that 75% accuracy derives from the desired source of control occurring on 75% of the trials. But Sidman (1980, 1987) described another possibility. The selection of the correct comparison in the presence of one sample along with the selection of a single position in the presence of the other sample would yield accuracy of 75%.

What are some implications of these seemingly esoteric details? Consider the use of discrimination performance measures to assess the effects of variables such as drugs. If baseline accuracy is 50%, the measure will not be sensitive to decreases in the targeted form of stimulus control because the targeted form of stimulus control is likely to be completely absent already (a "floor effect"). Moreover, increases may be unlikely (without other changes in procedure), again because the targeted form of stimulus control is not occurring and performance may be under the control of alternative sources.

Another concern is that two different discrimination baselines, both of which produce the same accuracy but through different stimulus control mechanisms, might react differently to experimental manipulations of interest. Even when two subjects demonstrate 100% accuracy, their performances may involve different forms of control. One subject may learn to select the correct comparison stimulus and another may learn to reject the incorrect comparison stimulus (Sidman, 1987). Mackay (1991) cited an example of how such differences might affect interpretation when the effects of other variables are measured on conditional discrimination baselines. Phentobarbital disrupted pigeons' performance of MTS more than it disrupted their performance of oddity-from-sample (Cumming & Berryman, 1961). The literature suggests that most human subjects acquire both forms of control under standard arbitrary procedures MTS (McIlvane et al., 1987). However, the potential for differences across subjects and the unknown effects of the interaction of these differences with other variables suggest that it is important to be aware of these issues.

Signal detection analyses provide an alternative to simple accuracy as a means of quantifying performance in a discrimination task. The potential remains, however, for some of the kinds of misinterpretation described above. Signal detection analyses are fully covered by Irwin and McCarthy in Chapter 10. A paper by Sidman (1992) illustrates a signal detection analysis of an MTS performance.

SUMMARY AND CONCLUSIONS

Stimulus control procedures are fundamental tools for studying human behavior. As such, they pervade experimental psychology. Regardless of how complex the procedure, all incorporate the basic units of simple and conditional discrimination. Difficulties in establishing more complex forms of stimulus control can usually be analyzed in terms of these component units. Moreover, thorough understanding of these basic units seems critical to analyses of derived stimulus control (e.g., equivalence relations, see Green & Saunders, Chapter 8).

Despite the seeming simplicity of these fundamental units of stimulus control, researchers who use simple and conditional discrimination procedures must attend to numerous procedural details that can affect outcome. In addition, rapidly advancing technology often brings variation in procedure that may not be deliberate or recognized, so careful specification of procedure is especially important. Finally, units of stimulus control are difficult to measure precisely. Accuracy measures are useful, but it is important to be aware of their limitations.

ACKNOWLEDGMENTS. Preparation of this chapter was supported by NICHD grants 5-R29HD27314, 5-P30HD02528, and 1-PO1HD18955. We appreciate advice and assistance given by Joe Spradlin, Pat White, Mark Johnston, Jennifer O'Donnell, and Donna Dutcher.

REFERENCES

Aman, M. G., Kern, R. A., McGhee, D. E., & Arnold, L. E. (1993). Fenfluramine and methylphenidate in children with mental retardation and attention deficit hyperactivity disorder: Laboratory effects. *Journal of Autism and Developmental Disorders, 23,* 1–16.

Asano, T. (1976). Some effects of a discrete trial procedure on differentiation learning by Japanese monkeys. *Primates, 17,* 53–62.

Baron, A. (1973). Postdiscrimination gradients of human subjects on a tone continuum. *Journal of Experimental Psychology, 101,* 337–342.

Baron, A., & Menich, S. R. (1985). Reaction times of younger and older men: Effects of compound samples and a prechoice signal on delayed matching-to-sample performances. *Journal of the Experimental Analysis of Behavior, 44,* 1–14.

Baron, A., Myerson, J., & Hale, S. (1988). An integrated analysis of the structure and function of behavior: Aging and the cost of dividing attention. In G. Davey & C. Cullen (Eds.), *Human operant conditioning and behavior modification* (pp. 139–166). New York: Wiley.

Bhatt, R. S., & Wright, A. A. (1992). Concept learning by monkeys with video picture images and a touch screen. *Journal of the Experimental Analysis of Behavior, 57,* 219–225.

Bickel, W. K., & Etzel, B. C. (1985). The quantal nature of controlling stimulus–response relations as measured in tests of stimulus generalization. *Journal of the Experimental Analysis of Behavior, 44,* 245–270.

Branch, M. N. (1994). Stimulus generalization, stimulus equivalence, and response hierarchies. In S. C. Hayes, L. J. Hayes, M. Sato, & K. Ono (Eds.), *Behavior analysis of language and cognition* (pp. 51–70). Reno, NV: Context Press.

Bush, K. M., Sidman, M., & deRose, T. (1989). Contextual control of emergent equivalence relations. *Journal of the Experimental Analysis of Behavior, 51,* 29–45.

Carter, D. E., & Eckerman, D. A. (1975). Symbolic matching by pigeons: Rate of learning complex discriminations predicted from simple discriminations. *Science, 187,* 662–664.

Catania, A. C. (1992). *Learning* (3rd ed.). Englewood Cliffs, NJ: Prentice–Hall.

Cohen, L. R., Looney, T. A., Brady, J. H., & Aucella, A. F. (1976). Differential sample response schedules in the acquisition of conditional discriminations by pigeons. *Journal of the Experimental Analysis of Behavior, 26,* 301–314.

Critchfield, T. S., & Perone, M. (1993). Verbal self reports about matching to sample: Effects of the number of elements in a compound sample stimulus. *Journal of the Experimental Analysis of Behavior, 59,* 193–214.

Cumming, W. W., & Berryman, R. (1961). Some data on matching behavior in the pigeon. *Journal of the Experimental Analysis of Behavior, 4,* 281–284.

D'Amato, M. R., & Colombo, M. (1989). On the limits of the matching concept in monkeys *(Cebus apella)*. *Journal of the Experimental Analysis of Behavior, 52*, 225–236.

Davidson, N. A., & Osborne, J. G. (1974). Fixed-ratio and fixed-interval schedule control of matching-to-sample errors by children. *Journal of the Experimental Analysis of Behavior, 21*, 27–36.

DeGrandpre, R. J., Bickel, W. K., & Higgins, S. T. (1992). Emergent equivalence relations between interoceptive (drug) and exteroceptive (visual) stimuli. *Journal of the Experimental Analysis of Behavior, 58*, 9–18.

deRose, J. C., McIlvane, W. J., Dube, W. V., Galpin, V. C., & Stoddard, L. T. (1988). Emergent simple discrimination established by indirect relation to differential consequences. *Journal of the Experimental Analysis of Behavior, 50*, 1–20.

Dixon, L. S. (1977). The nature of control by spoken words over visual stimulus selection. *Journal of the Experimental Analysis of Behavior, 29*, 433–442.

Dube, W. V., Callahan, T. D., & McIlvane, W. J. (1993). Serial reversals of concurrent auditory discriminations in rats. *The Psychological Record, 43*, 429–440.

Dube, W. V., Green, G., & Serna, R. W. (1993). Auditory successive conditional discrimination and auditory stimulus equivalence classes. *Journal of the Experimental Analysis of Behavior, 59*, 103–114.

Dube, W. V., McIlvane, W. J., & Green, G. (1992). An analysis of generalized identity matching-to-sample test procedures. *The Psychological Record, 42*, 17–28.

Eckerman, D. A., Lanson, R. N., & Cumming, W. W. (1968). Acquisition and maintenance of matching without a required observing response. *Journal of the Experimental Analysis of Behavior, 11*, 435–441.

Galizio, M., & Baron, A. (1976). Label training and auditory generalization. *Learning and Motivation, 7*, 591–602.

Gatch, M. B., & Osborne, J. G. (1989). Transfer of contextual stimulus function via equivalence class development. *Journal of the Experimental Analysis of Behavior, 51*, 369–378.

Glat, R., Gould, K., Stoddard, L. T., & Sidman, M. (1994). A note on transfer of stimulus control in the delayed-cue procedure: Facilitation by an overt differential response. *Journal of Applied Behavior Analysis, 27*, 699–704.

Goldiamond, I. (1962). Perception. In A. J. Bachrach (Ed.), *Experimental foundations of clinical psychology* (pp. 280–340). New York: Basic Books.

Green, G., Sigurdardottir, Z. G., & Saunders, R. R. (1991). The role of instructions in the transfer of ordinal functions through equivalence classes. *Journal of the Experimental Analysis of Behavior, 55*, 287–304.

Hachiya, S., & Ito, M. (1991). Effects of discrete-trial and free-operant procedures on the acquisition and maintenance of successive discrimination in rats. *Journal of the Experimental Analysis of Behavior, 55*, 3–10.

Hanson, H. M. (1959). Effects of discrimination training on stimulus generalization. *Journal of Experimental Psychology, 58*, 321–334.

Harlow, H. F. (1949). The formation of learning sets. *Psychological Review, 56*, 51–65.

Harrison, J. M. (1990). Simultaneous auditory discrimination. *Journal of the Experimental Analysis of Behavior, 54*, 45–51.

Harrison, J. M. (1991). Stimulus control. In I. H. Iversen & K. A. Lattal (Eds.), *Experimental analysis of behavior: Part 1* (pp. 251–299). New York: Elsevier.

Hayes, L. J., Tilley, K. J., & Hayes, S. C. (1988). Extending equivalence class membership to gustatory stimuli. *The Psychological Record, 38*, 473–482.

Hayes, S. C., Kohlenberg, B. S., & Hayes, L. J. (1991). The transfer of specific and general consequential functions through simple and conditional equivalence relations. *Journal of the Experimental Analysis of Behavior, 56*, 119–137.

Holland, J. G. (1958). Human vigilance. *Science, 128*, 61–67.

Honig, W. K., & Urcuioli, P. J. (1981). The legacy of Guttman and Kalish (1956): 25 years of research on stimulus generalization. *Journal of the Experimental Analysis of Behavior, 35*, 405–445.

House, B. J., Brown, A. L., & Scott, M. S. (1974). Children's discrimination learning based on identity or difference. In H. W. Reese (Ed.), *Advances in child development and behavior* (Vol. 9, pp. 1–45). New York: Academic Press.

Howard, R. W. (1979). Stimulus generalization along a dimension based on a verbal concept. *Journal of the Experimental Analysis of Behavior, 32*, 199–212.

Iversen, I. H., Sidman, M., & Carrigan, P. (1986). Stimulus definition in conditional discriminations. *Journal of the Experimental Analysis of Behavior, 45,* 297–304.

Jenkins, H. M., & Harrison, R. H. (1960). Effects of discrimination training on auditory generalization. *Journal of Experimental Psychology, 59,* 246–253.

Kaufman, M. E., & Prehm, H. J. (1966). A review of research on learning sets and transfer of training in mental defectives. In N. R. Ellis (Ed.), *International review of research in mental retardation* (Vol. 2, pp. 123–149). New York: Academic Press.

Lancioni, G. E., & Smeets, P. M. (1986). Procedures and parameters of errorless discrimination training with developmentally impaired individuals. In N. R. Ellis & N. W. Bray (Eds.), *International review of research in mental retardation* (Vol. 14, pp. 135–164). New York: Academic Press.

Lynch, D. C., & Green, G. (1991). Development and crossmodal transfer of contextual control of emergent stimulus relations. *Journal of the Experimental Analysis of Behavior, 56,* 139–154.

Mackay, H. A. (1991). Conditional stimulus control. In I. H. Iversen & K. A. Lattal (Eds.), *Experimental analysis of behavior: Part 1* (pp. 301–350). New York: Elsevier.

Markham, M. R., & Dougher, M. J. (1993). Compound stimuli in emergent stimulus relations: Extending the scope of stimulus equivalence. *Journal of the Experimental Analysis of Behavior, 60,* 529–542.

McCarthy, D., & Davison, M. (1980). On the discriminability of stimulus duration. *Journal of the Experimental Analysis of Behavior, 33,* 187–211.

McIlvane, W. J. (1992). Stimulus control analysis and nonverbal instructional methods for people with intellectual disabilities. In N. W. Bray (Ed.), *International review of research in mental retardation* (Vol. 18, pp. 55–109). New York: Academic Press.

McIlvane, W. J., Dube, W. V., Kledaras, J. B., Iennaco, F. M., & Stoddard, L. T. (1990). Teaching relational discrimination to individuals with mental retardation: Some problems and possible solutions. *American Journal on Mental Retardation, 95,* 283–296.

McIlvane, W. J., Kledaras, J. B., Munson, L. C., King, K. A. J., de Rose, J. C., & Stoddard, L. T. (1987). Controlling relations in conditional discrimination and matching by exclusion. *Journal of the Experimental Analysis of Behavior, 48,* 187–208.

Michael, R. L., & Bernstein, D. J. (1991). Transient effects of acquisition history on generalization in a matching-to-sample task. *Journal of the Experimental Analysis of Behavior, 56,* 155–166.

Nelson, K. R., & Wasserman, E. A. (1978). Temporal factors influencing the pigeon's successive matching-to-sample performance: Sample duration, intertrial interval, and retention interval. *Journal of the Experimental Analysis of Behavior, 30,* 153–162.

Pilgrim, C., & Galizio, M. (1990). Relations between baseline contingencies and equivalence probe performances. *Journal of the Experimental Analysis of Behavior, 54,* 213–224.

Rapport, M. D., & Kelly K. L. (1991). Psychostimulant effects on learning and cognitive function: Findings and implications for children with attention deficit hyperactivity disorder. *Clinical Psychology Review, 11,* 61–92.

Ray, B. A., & Sidman, M. (1970). Reinforcement schedules and stimulus control. In W. N. Schoenfeld (Ed.), *The theory of reinforcement schedules* (pp. 187–214). New York: Appleton–Century–Crofts.

Rilling, M. (1968). Effects of timeout on a discrimination between fixed-ratio schedules. *Journal of the Experimental Analysis of Behavior, 11,* 129–132.

Rilling, M. (1977). Stimulus control and inhibitory processes. In W. K. Honig & J. E. R. Staddon (Eds.), *Handbook of operant behavior* (pp. 432–480). Englewood Cliffs, NJ: Prentice–Hall.

Saunders, K. J., Saunders, R. R., Williams, D. C., & Spradlin, J. E. (1993). An interaction of instructions and training design on stimulus class formation: Extending the analysis of equivalence. *The Psychological Record, 43,* 725–744.

Saunders, K. J., & Spradlin, J. E. (1989). Conditional discrimination in mentally retarded adults: The effect of training the component simple discriminations. *Journal of the Experimental Analysis of Behavior, 52,* 1–12.

Saunders, K. J., & Spradlin, J. E. (1990). Conditional discrimination in mentally retarded adults: The development of generalized skills. *Journal of the Experimental Analysis of Behavior, 54,* 239–250.

Saunders, K. J., & Spradlin, J. E. (1993). Conditional discrimination in mentally retarded subjects: Programming acquisition and learning set. *Journal of the Experimental Analysis of Behavior, 60,* 571–585.

Saunders, K. J., Williams, D. C., & Spradlin, J. E. (1995). Conditional discrimination by adults with mental retardation: Establishing relations between physically identical stimuli. *American Journal on Mental Retardation, 99,* 558–563.

Saunders, R. R., Saunders, K. J., Kirby, K. C., & Spradlin, J. E. (1988). The merger and development of equivalence classes by unreinforced conditional selection of comparison stimuli. *Journal of the Experimental Analysis of Behavior, 50,* 145–162.

Saunders, R. R., Wachter, J., & Spradlin, J. E. (1988). Establishing auditory stimulus control over an eight-member equivalence class via conditional discrimination procedures. *Journal of the Experimental Analysis of Behavior, 49,* 95–115.

Schilmoeller, G. L., Schilmoeller, K. J., Etzel, B. C., & LeBlanc, J. M. (1979). Conditional discrimination after errorless and trial-and-error training. *Journal of the Experimental Analysis of Behavior, 31,* 405–420.

Schrier, A. M. (1984). Learning how to learn: The significance and current status of learning set formation. *Primates, 25,* 95–102.

Scott, K. G. (1971). Recognition memory: A research strategy and a summary of initial findings. In N. R. Ellis (Ed.), *International review of research in mental retardation* (Vol. 5, pp. 83–111). New York: Academic Press.

Serna, R. W., Dube, W. V., & McIlvane, W. J. (1997). Assessing same/different judgments in individuals with severe intellectual disabilities: A status report. *Research in Developmental Disabilities, 18,* 343–368.

Shiffrin, R. M. (1988). Attention. In R. C. Atkinson, R. J. Herrnstein, G. Lindzey, & R. D. Luce (Eds.), *Stevens' handbook of experimental psychology: Vol. 2. Learning and cognition* (2nd ed., pp. 739–811). New York: Wiley.

Sidman, M. (1971). Reading and auditory-visual equivalences. *Journal of Speech and Hearing Research, 14,* 5–13.

Sidman, M. (1980). A note on the measurement of conditional discrimination. *Journal of the Experimental Analysis of Behavior, 33,* 285–289.

Sidman, M. (1986). Functional analysis of emergent verbal classes. In T. Thompson & M. D. Zeiler (Eds.), *Analysis and integration of behavior units* (pp. 213–245). Hillsdale, NJ: Erlbaum.

Sidman, M. (1987). Two choices are not enough. *Behavior Analysis, 22,* 11–18.

Sidman, M. (1992). Adventitious control by the location of comparison stimuli in conditional discriminations. *Journal of the Experimental Analysis of Behavior, 58,* 173–182.

Sidman, M., Rauzin, R., Lazar, R., Cunningham, S., Tailby, W., & Carrigan, P. (1982). A search for symmetry in the conditional discriminations of rhesus monkeys, baboons, and children. *Journal of the Experimental Analysis of Behavior, 37,* 23–44.

Sidman, M., & Stoddard, L. T. (1967). The effectiveness of fading in programming a simultaneous form discrimination for retarded children. *Journal of the Experimental Analysis of Behavior, 10,* 3–15.

Sidman, M., & Tailby, W. (1982). Conditional discrimination vs. matching to sample: An expansion of the testing paradigm. *Journal of the Experimental Analysis of Behavior, 37,* 45–22.

Skinner, B. F. (1935). The generic nature of the concepts of stimulus and response. *Journal of General Psychology, 12,* 40–65.

Skinner, B. F. (1966). Operant behavior. In W. K. Honig (Ed.), *Operant behavior: Areas of research and application* (pp. 12–32). Englewood Cliffs, NJ: Prentice–Hall.

Sprague, R. L., Barnes, K. R., & Werry, J. S. (1970). Methylphenidate and thioridazine: Learning, reaction time, activity, and classroom behavior in disturbed children. *American Journal of Orthopsychiatry, 40,* 615–628.

Stromer, R., McIlvane, W. J., Dube, W. V., & Mackay, H. A. (1993). Assessing control by elements of complex stimuli in delayed matching to sample. *Journal of the Experimental Analysis of Behavior, 59,* 83–102.

Terrace, H. S. (1963). Discrimination learning with and without "errors." *Journal of the Experimental Analysis of Behavior, 6,* 1–27.

Terrace, H. S. (1970). Errorless discrimination learning in the pigeon: Effects of chlorpromazine and imipramine. In T. Thompson, R. Pickens, & R. A. Meisch (Eds.), *Readings in behavioral pharmacology* (pp. 112–115). New York: Appleton–Century–Crofts.

White, K. G. (1985). Characteristics of forgetting functions in delayed matching to sample. *Journal of the Experimental Analysis of Behavior, 44,* 15–34.

Williams, D. C., & Saunders, K. J. (1997). Methodological issues in the study of drug effects on cognitive skills in mental retardation. In N. W. Bray (Ed.), *International review of research in mental re-tardation* (Vol. 21, pp. 147–185). New York: Academic Press.

Williams, D. C., Saunders, K. J., Saunders, R. R., & Spradlin, J. E. (1995). Unreinforced conditional selection within three-choice conditional discriminations. *The Psychological Record, 45,* 613–627.

Wittenborn, J. R. (1978). Behavioral toxicity in normal humans as a model for assessing behavioral toxicity in patients. In M. A. Lipton, A. DiMascio, & F. K. Killam (Eds.), *Psychopharmacology: A generation of progress* (pp. 791–796). New York: Raven Press.

Wright, A. A., Cook, R. G., Rivera, J. J., Sands, S. F., & Delius, J. D. (1988). Concept learning by pigeons: Matching-to-sample with trial-unique video picture stimuli. *Animal Learning & Behavior, 16,* 436–444.

Zygmont, D. M., Lazar, R. M., Dube, W. V., & McIlvane, W. J. (1992). Teaching arbitrary matching via sample stimulus-control shaping to young children and mentally retarded individuals: A methodological note. *Journal of the Experimental Analysis of Behavior, 57,* 109–117.

8

Stimulus Equivalence

Gina Green and Richard R. Saunders

How do organisms come to treat dissimilar events as if they are the same, particularly events that have never been related directly? This question has long fascinated philosophers and psychologists. For philosophers the events of interest were ideas, and processes by which ideas became equivalent took place inside the heads of human organisms. They conceived that ideas (A and B) that had never been associated directly but were each associated with a third idea (C) might come to be associated, such that the three ideas were interchangeable. Several psychologists who became interested in this question saw that a range of events—not just "ideas"—could potentially become equivalent to one another as a result of organism–environment interactions (Hulse, Deese, & Egeth, 1975; Jenkins, 1963; Peters, 1935). Some gave the *stimulus equivalence* construct a central place in their theories of learning (e.g., Hull, 1939; Lawrence, 1963; Miller & Dollard, 1941).

Until fairly recently, however, there were surprisingly few attempts to analyze stimulus equivalence experimentally. The first used classical conditioning methods to demonstrate that if one of two or more stimuli conditioned to the same response was conditioned to a new response, the other conditioned stimuli also evoked the new response (Shipley, 1935). Subsequently, a number of stimulus equivalence experiments were conducted by psychologists interested in verbal conditioning. This work employed paired-associates methods in attempts to determine how adult humans might learn that words that were not related in any way by explicit training were associated by virtue of their common relation with other words (e.g., Jenkins, 1963; Jenkins & Palermo, 1964; Peters, 1935). In one type of paired-associate experiment, subjects learned to pair items (such as words or letters) from list A with items from list B (A–B). Then they learned to pair items from list B with items from list C (B–C). On test trials subjects were presented with C items, to which they were asked to name items from the A list that went with them. This was considered a test for mediated associations: C and A items were not related directly in training, but could be related indirectly through their common

Gina Green • New England Center for Children, E. K. Shriver Center for Mental Retardation, and Northeastern University, Southborough, Massachusetts 01772.   **Richard R. Saunders** • Parsons Research Center, University of Kansas, Parsons, Kansas 67357.
Handbook of Research Methods in Human Operant Behavior, edited by Lattal and Perone. Plenum Press, New York, 1998.

conditioned association with B items. The B items were considered to link or mediate the C–A relations. Positive outcomes were interpreted as showing that corresponding A, B, and C items had become equivalent. This line of research ended when researchers were unable to produce consistently positive outcomes with more than two "stages," or stimuli, mediating the tested relations (Jenkins & Palermo, 1964; Sidman, 1994).

Interest in stimulus equivalence research essentially lay dormant for a number of years after the demise of the paired-associates work. It was revived in the 1970s by Murray Sidman and his colleagues (Sidman, 1971; Sidman & Cresson, 1973; Sidman, Cresson, & Willson-Morris, 1974) and Joseph Spradlin and his colleagues (Dixon & Spradlin, 1976; Spradlin, Cotter, & Baxley, 1973; Spradlin & Dixon, 1976). Since the mid-1980s stimulus equivalence has been a topic of major interest within the experimental analysis of behavior. This chapter focuses on experimental analyses of stimulus equivalence in human subjects, principally work that is conceptually consistent with the Sidman analysis introduced in 1982 (Sidman et al., 1982; Sidman & Tailby, 1982) and subsequently refined (Carrigan & Sidman, 1992; Sidman, 1986, 1990, 1992, 1994). The conceptual analysis is described first, as background for the presentation of methodological issues in stimulus equivalence research that comprises most of the chapter.

STIMULUS CLASSES AND STIMULUS EQUIVALENCE

Broadly defined, stimulus equivalence is synonymous with stimulus substitutability. When a stimulus that controls a response can be replaced with another stimulus without altering the probability that the response will occur, the inference can be made that the two stimuli are the same, in some sense, to the organism. The general term *stimulus class* has been used to describe two or more stimuli that are observed to control the same response class (e.g., Goldiamond, 1962; Skinner, 1938; Spradlin et al., 1973; Spradlin & Saunders, 1984). Stimulus classes can be inferred to result from any of several different processes; that is, there are several types of stimulus classes, discussed briefly next.

Some stimulus classes are products of primary stimulus generalization. Two or more stimuli can become discriminative for the same response because they have certain physical features in common. For example, after eating one apple is reinforced, apples with features (e.g., size, color) that are similar to the original all may evoke the response of eating them. Importantly, direct experience with every kind of apple is not required for newly encountered apples to be discriminative for eating. The substitutability of one apple for another in this context is a function of primary stimulus generalization; the resulting class of stimuli that all share some physical characteristic(s) may be described as a feature class (McIlvane, Dube, Green, & Serna, 1993) or generalized equivalence class (Adams, Fields, & Verhave, 1993). The usual test for feature class development is to present a subject with novel stimuli that have one or more physical features in common with a discriminative stimulus, and measure the probability with which the response occurs in the presence of each novel stimulus (e.g., Fields, Reeve, Adams, & Verhave, 1991).

Classes consisting of stimuli with no physical characteristics in common can also be inferred from certain behavioral observations. Primary stimulus generalization cannot account for the development of such stimulus classes; some other explanation is necessary. One possibility is that stimuli that serve a similar behavioral function (e.g., are discriminative for the same response) can become members of a stimulus class, even when they are not physically similar. For example, stoplights, upraised palms, and crosswalks full of pedestrians might constitute a stimulus class for the observant and law-abiding driver who applies a foot to the brake pedal on seeing any of them (Goldiamond, 1962). Although those signals do not resemble one another, all may become discriminative for pressing brake pedals as a result of a history of positive reinforcement (e.g., praise statements from a driving instructor), negative reinforcement (e.g., avoidance of accidents and traffic tickets), or both. Stimuli that control the same response but have no physical features in common are usually referred to as a functional class (Goldiamond, 1962; McIlvane et al., 1993; Sidman, 1994; Sidman, Wynne, Maguire, & Barnes, 1989). The usual test for functional stimulus class development is to establish a new behavioral function for one member of the putative class and observe whether the remaining members of the class also have the same new function. To follow through with our previous example, a subject could be trained directly to say the word "stop" in the presence of a stoplight, establishing a new function for that member of the previously described functional stimulus class. Tests would then evaluate whether the subject says "stop" in the presence of an upraised palm and a full crosswalk without being trained directly to do so.

The remainder of this chapter is concerned with classes of stimuli that do not have physical features in common, and do not necessarily serve identical behavioral functions (e.g., pictures, printed words, and spoken words; Sidman 1971). Normally developing humans learn with relative ease to substitute such stimuli for one another in certain contexts and not in others. For example, they learn that when the context calls for selecting one stimulus from among many ("Find apple" spoken by an adult), either a real apple, a line drawing of an apple, or the printed word APPLE may work equally well to satisfy the operative contingencies. They also learn that in a somewhat different context ("Eat apple"), the apple, line drawing, and printed word are not literally substitutable. Further, most normally developing humans relate stimuli to one another that have never been related directly. Having learned to relate a picture of an apple to the spoken word "apple," and to relate the printed word APPLE to the same spoken word, they are likely to relate the picture to the printed word on the first opportunity to do so. In other words, everyday observations of typical human behavior suggest that many untrained repertoires emerge from performances that have been taught explicitly. Stimulus equivalence research seeks to identify the variables that account for such emergent behavior.

THE SIDMAN EQUIVALENCE ANALYSIS

In the original Sidman conceptualization, stimulus equivalence was viewed as a possible product of conditional discrimination training, or experience with four-term contingencies (e.g., Sidman, 1986, 1994; Sidman et al., 1982; Sidman & Tailby, 1982). The basic unit of stimulus control is the three-term contingency, consisting of an antecedent stimulus (S), a response (R), and a consequence (C). A three-term (or simple discrimination) contingency can be described as follows: In the presence of S1 (and not S2 or S3), R1 (and not R2 or R3) is followed by reinforcer C1. Exposure to such a contingency typically establishes S1 as discriminative for reinforcement of R1, whereas S2 and S3 are not discriminative for reinforcement of R1. Analogous contingencies could establish S2 and S3 as discriminative for reinforcement of other, different responses (R2 and R3, respectively). Examples of simple discriminative control abound in everyday behavior. It would not be adaptive (or possible), however, for all discriminations in an organism's repertoire to be operative all of the time. Which of many possible discriminations is applicable from moment to moment is dependent on other antecedent stimuli. That is, three-term contingencies can be brought under stimulus control as a result of exposure to contingencies that each include a fourth term, a *conditional stimulus*. Actually, conditional stimulus control requires two or more distinct four-term contingencies: In the presence of conditional stimulus S4 (and not conditional stimulus S5 or S6), the contingency in which S1 (and not S2 or S3) is discriminative for reinforcement is in effect; in the presence of conditional stimulus S5 (and not S4 or S6), S2 (and not S1 or S3) is discriminative; and in the presence of S6 (and not S4 or S5), S3 (and not S1 or S2) is discriminative. In other words, the functions of S1, S2, and S3 as discriminative for reinforcement (S+) or not (S−) are conditional on the presence of S4, S5, and S6, respectively. When performances are observed to conform to contingencies like these, the subject is said to have learned *conditional discriminations*.

Match-to-sample (MTS) procedures are often used to arrange four-term contingencies in a series of discrete trials, with the goal of establishing conditional discriminations. On a typical MTS trial, a sample stimulus is presented first. Following a response to the sample or to an operandum associated with it (e.g., a button), two or more comparison stimuli are presented in separate locations. With each sample, one comparison is designated by the experimenter as positive, or discriminative for reinforcement (S+), whereas the other comparisons presented with it are negative (S−). Those same S− comparisons typically are designated positive, however, with other specific samples on other trials. Following the subject's response to one of the comparison stimuli on a trial, consequences scheduled by the experimenter are provided. The next trial commences after a brief intertrial interval. To meet the requirements of these contingencies consistently, the subject must discriminate among sample stimuli presented successively across trials, and among comparison stimuli presented simultaneously within trials. If samples and their designated positive comparisons have identical perceptual characteristics, the procedure is referred to as *identity* MTS. In *arbitrary* MTS, samples and comparisons have no specific, consistent perceptual similarities.

Consequences arranged for responding to S+ comparisons in stimulus equivalence experiments have included such events as the delivery of coins, points on a counter, verbal praise, and the word "Right" or "Correct" spoken or displayed on a computer screen. Responses to S− comparisons have been followed by no programmed consequences, or by specific events like a buzzer sound, or a word like

"No," "Wrong," or "Incorrect" spoken or printed on a computer screen. Usually an intertrial interval of one to several seconds separates the delivery of consequences from the onset of the next trial. Data recorded for each trial have included the latency of the subject's response to the sample, the particular comparison stimulus to which the subject responds, the position of that comparison stimulus in the array presented, the latency of the response to the comparison stimulus, and consequences delivered, where applicable.

Many variations on the typical MTS procedures described here have been reported in the literature. They are detailed in excellent discussions by other authors (e.g., Mackay, 1991; K. Saunders & Williams, Chapter 7; Sidman, 1986), but a few are reviewed briefly next. In one variation, the presentation of comparison stimuli is not contingent on a response to the sample stimulus; simultaneous presentation of the sample and comparisons begin each trial (e.g., Blough, 1959; Devany, Hayes, & Nelson, 1986). When the sample stimulus remains available to the subject throughout each trial as described above, the procedure is referred to as simultaneous MTS (e.g., Nevin, Cumming, & Berryman, 1963; Sidman, 1971). If the sample is removed following onset of the comparisons, the procedure is delayed MTS (e.g., Constantine & Sidman, 1975; Zimmerman & Ferster, 1963). The comparison stimuli can be presented either simultaneously, as described previously, or successively. In the successive procedure, the comparison stimuli are presented in the same location, one at a time, usually with responses to some other stimulus serving to change which comparison is momentarily presented (e.g., Clark & Sherman, 1970; Dube, Green, & Serna, 1993). If a correction procedure is used, following responses to S− comparisons all stimuli may remain visible until the subject responds to the S+ (e.g., Blough, 1959). Alternatively, the trial may be re-presented until the subject responds to the S+.

When the subject's behavior conforms to the contingencies, in either the identity or the arbitrary MTS case, it is typically inferred that conditional discriminations have been learned, and that a *conditional (or if . . . then) relation* has developed between each sample and its positive comparison (Carter & Werner, 1978). The term *relation* as used hereafter refers to an empirical construct, i.e., an inference based on systematically recorded observations of behavior under the control of particular contingencies of reinforcement. Just as discriminative stimulus control is inferred from observations that a particular response occurs consistently in the presence of a particular stimulus, conditional stimulus control is inferred from observations that a response to a particular discriminative stimulus (e.g., a comparison) occurs consistently if and only if a particular other stimulus is present (e.g., a sample, or conditional stimulus). The conditional stimulus and discriminative stimulus are then said to be related in a particular way; hence the term *conditional relation* (or *sample/S+ relation*, or more broadly, *stimulus–stimulus relation*). A couple of cautions about this terminology are in order, however. First, in keeping with the tenets of the experimental analysis of behavior, inferences about relations among stimuli should be made only after the relevant observations of subject behavior have been made. The term *stimulus–stimulus relation* should not be used, for example, to refer to the experimenter's behavior of arranging for two or more stimuli to occur contiguously, or to participate in a particular contingency. Second, it should be understood that the inference of a relation between a conditional stimulus and a discriminative stimulus also implies the other events involved in the contingency, i.e., the response and the consequent stimulus. In other words, terms like *stimulus–stimulus relation* or *conditional relation* are merely shorthand descriptors for the effects of particular kinds of contingencies (cf. R. Saunders & Green, 1992; Sidman 1986).

The questions that Sidman and his colleagues addressed in their early work on stimulus equivalence were provoked by the common use of the term *matching* to refer to both a set of procedures like those just outlined and a variety of performances. When *matching* was used to describe performances that appeared to be consistent with programmed MTS contingencies, it was often implied or asserted that the subject was doing something more than responding to the specific contingencies in effect on each trial; the subject was said to be demonstrating "the concept of sameness." This further implied that MTS training established more than just a set of discrete conditional relations between samples and their positive comparisons. The implication was that stimuli that were "matched" to one another were the same in some sense, or equivalent to one another (see Mackay, 1991; Sidman, 1994; Sidman et al., 1982; Sidman & Tailby, 1982).

Sidman and colleagues reasoned that the foregoing assumptions about "matching" performances might not be valid, but were sufficiently important to warrant rigorous testing. If MTS training established something more than several specific conditional relations, and also established the prerequisites for the stimuli involved to be related by equivalence, independent tests seemed necessary to make that determination. Sidman and his associates found in mathematics a set of tests for evaluating whether a relation on a set of elements had the logical properties of a relation of equivalence. Behavioral analogues of those tests were developed within the MTS procedural framework (e.g., Sidman et al., 1982; Sidman & Tailby, 1982). Briefly, the properties and behavioral (MTS) tests to determine if a conditional relation is a relation of equivalence are:

1. *Reflexivity.* Each stimulus must bear a conditional relation to itself (i.e., sample A must be related to comparison A, sample B to comparison B, and so on). Identity MTS tests with the stimuli in question evaluate this property.
2. *Symmetry.* Conditional relations must be bidirectional. When sample A has been related to comparison B in baseline training (AB), sample B must be related to comparison A (BA) without further training.
3. *Transitivity.* Evaluation of this property necessitates training conditional relations so that each relation has one stimulus in common; for example, sample A with comparison B (AB), and sample B with comparison C (BC). Transitivity tests ask if sample A is related to comparison C (AC) without explicit training.

The properties of symmetry and transitivity can be tested simultaneously. For example, if sample A is related to comparison B (AB) and sample B is related comparison C (BC) in baseline training, then testing to see if sample C will be related to comparison A (CA) without explicit training evaluates both symmetry and transitivity of AB and BC; positive outcomes are possible only if the trained relations have both of those properties. Such tests have been called *combined* (Catania,

1984; Sidman & Tailby, 1982), *global* (Sidman, 1986), and *complex* (Adams et al., 1993) tests, or simply *tests for equivalence* (e.g., Sidman, 1990; Sidman et al., 1989).

Each type of test asks if untrained conditional relations emerge after certain baseline conditional relations are trained directly. Positive results on a particular test indicate that the trained conditional relations have that particular property. Positive results on *all* tests provide the necessary proof that the trained relations are relations of equivalence, i.e., that they have all three logical properties (e.g., R. Saunders & Green, 1992; Sidman et al., 1982; Sidman & Tailby, 1982). Then the stimuli involved (e.g., A, B, and C) can be said to constitute an *equivalence class.*

Some authors have referred to reflexivity, symmetry, and transitivity as *relations* rather than as *properties* of relations (e.g., Catania, Horne, & Lowe, 1989; Fields, Adams, Verhave, & Newman, 1990; Fields, Verhave, & Fath, 1984; Wulfert & Hayes, 1988). It may seem innocuous to refer to "the symmetry relation," for example, as shorthand for "a test for the property of symmetry in a trained relation." Unfortunately, however, such usage often connotes that reflexivity, symmetry, and transitivity each represent different kinds of stimulus control, and that an equivalence class consists of stimuli that bear several different kinds of relations to one another (R. Saunders & Green, 1992). Sidman's analysis, however, defines an equivalence class as a set of stimuli that all bear the same relation to one another. That relation is equivalence if all of the tests for the properties of equivalence, derived from mathematics and logic, are satisfied. Because the mathematical model of equivalence underlies both the conceptualization and the methods used to study Sidman equivalence, it is considered in more detail next.

The Mathematics Analogy

In mathematics and logic, a common problem is determining what equivalence relation will partition a set of stimuli. A partition is the family of equivalence classes on a set of numbers, for example, wherein all of the numbers are in an equivalence class but no number is in more than one class. The number of nonoverlapping classes constitutes the family of classes—the partition. For example, a math student may be given the set of numbers 2, 3, 4, 8, 9, 16, 27, 32, 64, and 81, and asked to find a relation that partitions the set. Problems like this are solved by applying first one and then another relation to the set to test its ability to partition the set. The student might organize the problem-solving task around a matrix, such as the one shown in the left panel of Figure 8.1, in which the numbers in the set are placed across the top and along the left side in ascending order.

Next the student tests relations by placing a plus sign in any cell in which the relation holds between a number in the column and a number in the row. The relation "is divisible by the same number as" is tested in Figure 8.1. The left panel clearly shows that this relation has the property of *reflexivity* because it holds between every number and itself (e.g., "9 is divisible by the same number as 9" is true), an outcome that produces an uninterrupted diagonal of plus signs from the upper left corner of the matrix to the lower right corner. The relation also holds between other pairs of numbers, as the plentiful number of plus signs illustrates. The relation also has the property of *symmetry* because, wherever it holds between a

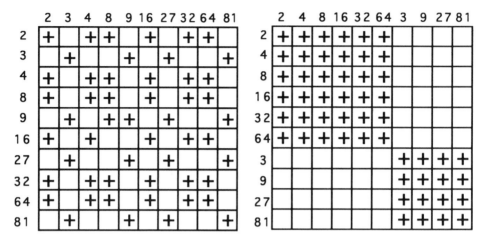

FIGURE 8.1. Two matrices showing the partition of a set of numbers by the relation "is divisible by the same number as." Plus signs in the cells indicate which numbers in the column are related to the numbers in the row by that relation. The two matrices differ only in the ordering of the numbers in the columns and rows.

number in the column and a number in a row, it also holds when we find the latter number in the column and look for the former column number in the row (e.g., that "3 is divisible by the same number as 9" and "9 is divisible by the same number as 3" are both reflected). The relation has the property of *transitivity* because whenever the relation holds for overlapping pairs of numbers (e.g., when "3 is divisible by the same number as 9" and "9 is divisible by same number as 27") it also holds between the nonoverlapping elements ("3 is divisible by the same number as 27" and vice versa because the relation also has the property of symmetry). Thus, the relation is equivalence because the three properties are represented on the matrix without exception. By rearranging the order of the numbers on the matrix in both the row and column, it becomes clear that not only is the relation an equivalence relation, it is a relation that creates a partition consisting of a family of two equivalence classes. It is important to emphasize that in this mathematical example there is but one equivalence relation for this set of numbers, but its application results in two equivalence classes.

In the mathematics example, the student is given a known relation and a particular set of numbers, and tests to determine what properties the relation has. The relation "is divisible by the same number as" might have had different properties on a different set of numbers than the one used in the example above. For example, 3 is divisible by the same number as 6 and 6 is divisible by the same number as 2, but 3 is not divisible by the same number as 2; thus, the relation would not always have been transitive if the set had contained the number 6. Further, there might be more than one equivalence relation for a given set of stimuli, presumably creating a different partition.

In the behavioral analogue, elements in the set are stimuli, often a fairly large number of "nonsense" figures, letter combinations, sounds, objects, odors, or textures. MTS training establishes several conditional relations among elements arranged in specific sample–comparison combinations by the experimenter. These relations are arbitrary (i.e., defined by reinforcement contingencies). The task of determining if the training also partitioned the original large set into two or more equivalence classes becomes analogous to the mathematics problem just described. It is as if there is a matrix in which at least two cells have plus signs in them (indicating trained conditional relations, e.g., AB and BC), but the matrix rows and columns contain arbitrary elements and the nature of the relation represented by the two plus signs is unknown. To test for the properties of equivalence, the experimenter creates new MTS trial configurations so that the subject can be observed responding to all possible untrained pairs of elements; that is, the experimenter creates a test that corresponds with each empty cell in the matrix. The experimenter hypothesizes that if the trained relations are the same relation and that relation is one of equivalence, then responding on the new (test trial) configurations will produce a pattern that can only occur when the trained baseline relations are equivalence relations for the particular set of elements. Distinct parts of the pattern each confirm one of the three properties of equivalence relations (R. Saunders & Green, 1992).

FUNDAMENTALS OF STIMULUS EQUIVALENCE METHODOLOGY

Selecting Stimuli

Basic stimulus equivalence experiments with humans typically involve sets of stimuli with which subjects are unlikely to have had previous experience—an important control if the development of equivalence relations is to be attributed to variables manipulated in the experiment rather than extraneous factors. Commonly used visual stimuli include Greek letters (e.g., Eikeseth & Smith, 1992; Sidman, Kirk, & Willson-Morris, 1984; Sidman & Tailby, 1982), Cyrillic letters (e.g., Gatch & Osborne, 1989), trigrams (e.g., Fields et al., 1990, 1991), semirepresentational forms (e.g., Devany et al., 1986; MacDonald, Dixon, & LeBlanc, 1986), and various abstract figures (e.g., Steele & Hayes, 1991; Stromer & Osborne, 1982). Auditory stimuli are usually nonsense words or syllables (e.g., Dube, Green, & Serna, 1993; R. Saunders, Wachter, & Spradlin, 1988), occasionally tones (e.g., Bush, Sidman, & de Rose, 1989). Other basic experiments have included textures (Bush, 1993), tastes (L. Hayes, Tilley, & Hayes, 1988), odors (Annett & Leslie, 1995), and haptically perceived shapes (Tierney, De Largy , & Bracken, 1995).

Applied experiments often use stimuli to which human subjects may have had a least some exposure; for example, everyday objects, pictures, or people and common English words. In such cases it is necessary to conduct pretests of subjects' entry performances with the experimental stimuli in order to document that performances demonstrated during the experiment were not preexistent, but resulted from experimental contingencies (e.g., Cowley, Green, & Braunling-McMorrow, 1992; Lynch & Cuvo, 1995; Sidman, 1971; Stromer & Mackay, 1993).

Arranging Trial Types and Sequences

The experimenter designates sample and comparison stimuli to participate in experimental contingencies, groups of stimuli to constitute prospective equivalence classes, sample and comparison combinations to be presented on each trial (referred to as *trial types*), and combinations of trials to constitute training and testing sessions. Many researchers adopt the convention of designating stimuli by alphanumeric codes, with letters identifying unique stimuli and numbers indicating prospective equivalence class membership. For example, stimuli in set A might be label A1, A2, and A3. Initial MTS training contingencies might be designed to relate each of those stimuli as samples to set B comparison stimuli labeled B1, B2, and B3. Three distinct trial types are necessary to accomplish this training, one with each of the three sample stimuli. The same three comparisons are used for each trial type; a different comparison is designated S+ with each sample, indicated by asterisks below:

	Sample	Comparisons
Trial Type 1:	A1	B1* B2 B3
Trial Type 2:	A2	B1 B2* B3
Trial Type 3:	A3	B1 B2 B3*

Each trial type is presented multiple times and the various trial types are presented equally often within a session or series of sessions. For example, a session might consist of 12 trials each of Trial Types 1, 2, and 3, in unsystematic order. A common provision is that consecutive presentations of the same trial type are limited to two or three (e.g., Sidman & Tailby, 1982). Each comparison is the designated S+ on an equal number of trials within a session. The physical positions of the comparisons are varied unsystematically from trial to trial, usually with controls that limit the number of consecutive trials with the correct comparison in the same position (e.g., Sidman & Tailby, 1982). These procedural controls are necessary to ensure the development of true conditional stimulus control by samples rather than simple discriminative control by comparison stimuli (e.g., as a function of differential correlations with reinforcement) or control by comparison position (Mackay, 1991; Sidman, 1986). Consequences that are presumed or confirmed to function as reinforcers (e.g., tokens, money, points, brief praise, musical chimes or jingles) are presented to the subject following responses to the designated correct comparisons during initial training. Responses to comparisons designated by the experimenter as incorrect are often followed by other consequences that are presumed or shown not to function as reinforcers (e.g., a brief timeout period, removal of previously earned tokens or points, brief reprimands, buzzers). Training usually continues until the subject responds to the comparison designated as the S+ in the presence of each sample with high accuracy across trial types and across sessions (e.g., at least 90% accuracy on each trial type for each of three consecutive sessions, or 100% accuracy for one session).

Accuracy criteria for concluding training on any or all sets of baseline conditional relations, for assessing whether baseline relations are maintained during testing, and for determining if test performances are consistent with stimulus equivalence should be established before the experiment begins. Stringent criteria are generally recommended, particularly when apparently high (or low) performances may arise as a function of procedural artifacts. A notable case in point is the use of two-choice MTS procedures, which often generate performance levels that appear reasonably accurate (e.g., 75%), but may not reflect stimulus control appropriate to the experimental questions (Sidman, 1980, 1987; Sidman et al, 1985). The fundamental problem with two-choice MTS procedures is that the probability of "correct" responding is .50, which means that relatively high accuracy scores can be attained spuriously, reflecting control of responding by something other than relations between samples and their designated correct comparisons (e.g., position, stimulus preference, or mixed types). It is possible to conduct internally valid stimulus equivalence experiments using two-choice MTS procedures by (1) applying stringent criteria for determining if each and every trained and untrained conditional relation is demonstrated; (2) conducting independent tests to evaluate whether training established relations between samples and positive comparisons (sample/S+ relations) or samples and negative comparisons (sample/S− relations) before conducting tests for the properties of equivalence, and retraining as needed; or (3) designing the experiment to develop relatively large equivalence classes (i.e., four or more members per class) *and* using stringent accuracy criteria. The latter strategy decreases the probability that a few spuriously high accuracy scores will lead to the erroneous inference that training established the intended sample/S+ relations. A simpler, more methodologically sound strategy is to use three or more comparisons (and corresponding samples) throughout training and testing (Carrigan & Sidman, 1992; Johnson & Sidman, 1993; Sidman, 1987).

A group of trial types like those shown above with the corresponding contingencies applied can be considered a conditional discrimination problem, because the subject must learn which of three comparison stimuli that always appear together across trials (e.g., B1, B2, or B3) is discriminative for reinforcement in the presence of the particular sample (e.g., A1, A2, or A3) that appears on each trial. If training is successful, the subject might learn three AB conditional relations: A1B1, A2B2, and A3B3. To conduct a stimulus equivalence experiment using MTS procedures, it is necessary to establish at least three additional conditional relations, each with a stimulus in common with the first relations trained. A second conditional discrimination problem might present the Set B stimuli as samples with another set of stimuli (C1, C2 and C3) as comparisons. Contingencies in that phase would be arranged to establish the BC conditional relations: B1C1, B2C2, and B3C3. Tests would then present all possible combinations of samples and comparisons that were not trained directly, to evaluate if training also established relations of equivalence among stimuli A1, B1, and C1; A2, B2,and C2; and A3, B3, and C3.

As we discuss later, contingencies like those just described constitute the minimal conditions for the development of three, three-member equivalence classes using MTS procedures. To develop larger classes, or to enlarge existing classes, additional conditional discrimination problems would be trained and potential emergent (untrained) relations tested. Usually the second conditional discrimination problem is trained in isolation from the first. After responding on the second discrimination problem meets the experimenter-established accuracy criteria, the two discrimination problems (e.g., all six trial types from the AB and BC training described above) are intermixed in the same sessions. If other conditional discrimination problems are to be taught prior to testing for stimulus equivalence, they too are usually taught one at a time, first in isolation and then intermixed with the others (but for cautions regarding a type of order confound that can arise when problems are presented in distinct sequences, see Stikeleather & Sidman, 1990). Usually, the same criteria for accuracy and consistency that are applied to conditional discrimination problems taught in isolation are applied when all problems are mixed within sessions.

The length of training and testing sessions and the number of trials or sessions to which a subject is exposed in one sitting are usually a function of the method of creating and presenting trials (e.g., paper and pencil, computer or other automation) and subject tolerances or preferences. The number of sessions on which subjects are required to demonstrate reliably accurate performances to advance from one conditional discrimination problem or experimental phase to another is usually higher when sessions include only two comparison stimuli per trial and small numbers of trials (e.g., 12) than for sessions with three or more comparison stimuli per trial and larger numbers of trials (e.g., 36).

The Basic Experiment

Table 8.1 shows all trial types for a prototypic experiment to train and test for the development of three equivalence classes including three stimuli each. Trial types for training AB and BC conditional relations are shown here, followed by trial types for tests to evaluate if training established equivalence relations. Three-member classes could also arise from conditional relations trained in sequences other than those shown in Table 8.1, as long as stimuli in two sets were related directly with one another and had stimuli from another set in common (e.g., AB and BC, BA and CA, AC and AB; see the section Training Structures). Table 8.1 does not reflect multiple presentations of each trial type with the procedural controls (e.g., unsystematic trial order, equal number of each trial type per session or across sessions, counterbalancing comparison positions across trials) that are necessary to minimize the potential development of extraneous types of stimulus control.

ESTABLISHING THE PREREQUISITES FOR STIMULUS EQUIVALENCE

Minimizing the Development of Extraneous Stimulus Control in MTS

Many published studies of stimulus equivalence used MTS procedures with just two comparisons available on every trial (e.g., Spradlin & Saunders, 1986). Un-

TABLE 8.1
Minimal Training and Test Trial Types for a Prototypic
Stimulus Equivalence Experiment

| | *Intended equivalence classes: A1B1C1, A2B2C2, A3B3C3* | |
Sample	Comparisons	Intended conditional relations
Training (baseline) trials		
A1	B1* B2 B3	A1B1
A2	B1 B2* B3	A2B2
A3	B1 B2 B3*	A3B3
B1	C1* C2 C3	B1C1
B2	C1 C2* C3	B2C2
B3	C1 C2 C3*	B3C3
Mixed AB and BC trial types		
Test trials		
Reflexivity		
A1	A1* A2 A3	A1A1
A2	A1 A2* A3	A2A2
A3	A1 A2 A3*	A3A3
B1	B1* B2 B3	B1B1
B2	B1 B2* B3	B2B2
B3	B1 B2 B3*	B3B3
C1	C1* C2 C3	C1C1
C2	C1 C2* C3	C2C2
C3	C1 C2 C3*	C3C3
Symmetry		
B1	A1* A2 A3	B1A1
B2	A1 A2* A3	B2A2
B3	A1 A2 A3*	B3A3
C1	B1* B2 B3	C1B1
C2	B1 B2* B3	C2B2
C3	B1 B2 B3*	C3B3
Transitivity		
A1	C1* C2 C3	A1C1
A2	C1 C2* C3	A2C2
A3	C1 C2 C3*	A3C3
Equivalence (combined symmetry and transitivity)		
C1	A1* A2 A3	C1A1
C2	A1 A2* A3	C2A2
C3	A1 A2 A3*	C3A3

Note. Asterisk denotes the comparison designated by the experimenter as S+ in the presence of the sample on that trial type.

fortunately, two-choice MTS procedures are likely to establish types of stimulus control that can confound tests for some of the properties of stimulus equivalence. Use of three-choice MTS procedures can greatly minimize these confounds, but they are discussed here in some detail because they are important for interpreting much published work.

Sample/S− Control

The intended outcome of MTS baseline training in stimulus equivalence experiments is the development of conditional relations between every sample and its experimenter-designated correct comparison. These kinds of relations are referred to as sample/S+ or "select" relations, because the subject may learn to select one and only one comparison in the presence of each sample (Carrigan & Sidman, 1992). MTS contingencies do not, however, guarantee the development of sample/S+ relations; sample/S− relations may develop instead or in addition. That is, in the course of training on any conditional discrimination problem, subjects might just as readily learn to respond *away from* one or more comparisons in the presence of each sample, establishing what Carrigan and Sidman (1992) termed "reject" relations. Merely observing and recording the subject's behavior during training cannot reveal what kind of stimulus control is operative, however, because in either case the response is the same: The subject responds (usually by pointing) to the S+.

Explicit tests are necessary to determine whether MTS training established sample/S+ relations, sample/S− relations, or both. For example, one type of test involves substituting novel stimuli for comparisons that were presented with each sample during training. On test trials where novel stimuli replace former negative comparison (S−), continued responding to the S+ for each sample (instead of the novel comparison) is thought to indicate that training established sample/S+ relations. Other test trials substitute novel stimuli for former positive comparisons (S+). If training established sample/S− relations, then on these test trials the subject's recorded responses should be to the novel comparison, presumably because he learned in training to respond away from S− stimuli (e.g., Stromer & Osborne, 1982). Results of tests with novel stimuli are difficult to interpret, however, because the very novelty of the stimuli may control subjects' responding in various ways. An alternative type of test that does not confound novelty with sample/S+ or sample/S− control requires pretraining subjects to respond on trials where a blank screen replaces one comparison on a trial with a particular sample, either the previously trained S+ or the previously trained S−. Essentially, subjects learn that if the comparison that is visible was an S+ with the sample in the previous training, they are to respond to it; if the visible comparison was an S− with that sample, they are to respond to the blank screen. Once subjects have learned them, these procedures can be used to test for the development of sample/S+ and sample/S− relations, respectively, following subsequent MTS training (e.g., McIlvane, Withstandley, & Stoddard, 1984).

If all tests for the properties of equivalence produce performances consistent with the development of experimenter-designated equivalence classes, explicit tests for sample/S+ or sample/S− control are not necessary. Further, the need for explicit tests can be diminished by arranging training contingencies to establish more than two equivalence classes, using more than two comparison stimuli per trial, from the outset. On the other hand, if the results of tests for stimulus equivalence are not consistently positive, and explicit tests to determine what kind of sample–comparison relations developed in training are not conducted, the experimenter might conclude incorrectly that training failed to establish stimulus equivalence. Instead, results of tests for equivalence that fall into certain patterns probably indicate that equivalence classes did develop from training, but they were based on sample/S− relations rather than the sample/S+ relations intended by the experimenter (Carrigan & Sidman, 1992; Dube, Green, & Serna, 1993; Johnson & Sidman, 1993; R. Saunders & Green, 1992). This possibility is discussed in more detail in the section on Analyzing Test Results: Mixed Outcomes.

Several procedural variables have been shown to influence the type of stimulus control that develops during MTS training. One is the relative frequency with which each comparison functions as S+ and S− in the presence of each sample. As explained previously, in true conditional discriminations, the functions of discriminative stimuli (comparisons in MTS) are determined by, or conditional on, particular other stimuli (samples in MTS). This kind of stimulus control can only develop if each comparison is discriminative for reinforcement in the presence of only one sample, and is not discriminative for reinforcement in the presence of at least one other sample. Configurations of sample–comparison combinations must be balanced across trials within training sessions such that each appears equally often, which also ensures that each comparison will function equally often as S+ and S−. Training trial types like those shown in Table 8.1 arrange this kind of balance. Any variation is likely to decrease the probability that sample/S+ relations will develop, simultaneously increasing the likelihood that tests for stimulus equivalence will be confounded because training introduced extraneous sources of stimulus control (but see Johnson & Sidman, 1993, and Harrison & Green, 1990, for trial and session arrangements that can increase the probability that sample/S+ or sample/S− relations will develop in training).

Variations of Baseline Training

Unbalanced Trial Types

One variation used in several studies presented initial training trials consisting only of one sample and one comparison, the S+; no negative comparisons were presented (e.g., Augustson & Dougher, 1992; Barnes, McCullagh, & Keenan, 1990; Devany et al., 1986). Representative trial types are sample stimulus A1 with comparison B1 only, sample A2 with comparison B2 only, and so on. These trial types may be alternated, but on each trial there is only one nominal comparison stimulus. Responses to comparisons are reinforced. The stimulus control likely to be generated by such contingencies is simple, not conditional, discrimination. The subject merely has to respond to the only stimulus that is eligible for reinforcement on each trial. Such contingencies are not likely to establish conditional stimulus control by sample stimuli, even when subjects are instructed to look at or touch the sample before touching the comparison, because responding to the samples (even simple observing) is not necessary to satisfy the contingency requirements. Eventually both comparisons (e.g., B1 and B2) are presented on every trial, and the sample (e.g., A1 or A2) differs from trial to trial. At this point the procedures have the potential for establishing conditional rather than simple discriminations; for the first time the subject must attend to the samples to satisfy the reinforcement contingencies consistently across trials. The responding of most humans will conform to these new contingencies rather quickly. For some, however, the recent training history (with only one comparison on each trial) may be difficult to overcome, because it may have trained the subjects to ignore the sample stimuli, which were irrelevant on the initial training trials. In other words, some subjects may have difficulty learning conditional discriminations involving stimuli with which they have immediate histories of simple discrimination training in the experimental context without training that is programmed explicitly to transform simple discrimination performances into conditional discrimination performances (e.g., Dube, Iennaco, & McIlvane, 1993; Dube, Iennaco, Rocco, Kledaras, & McIlvane, 1992). This may be particularly problematic for subjects who are developmentally young or those who have severe learning difficulties (e.g., Devany et al., 1986).

Another variation on MTS procedures appears to have less potential for creating confounds than single-comparison procedures. Termed a *blocked-trial procedure,* it involves presenting blocks of trial types on which two or more comparisons are always available, but the sample is the same on every trial. Comparison positions vary unsystematically from trial to trial; responses to the comparison designated as the S+ for the sample presented in a particular block of trials are reinforced. For instance, the first block of trials might have stimulus A1 as the sample, with comparisons B1 and B2 available on every trial. When the subject responds consistently to the S+ on this trial type (in this example, B1) regardless of its position, a block of trials is presented with the other sample (in this example, A2) and both comparisons available on every trial. Responses to the designated S+ for that sample (B2) are reinforced. Blocks of these two trial types are alternated repeatedly, and the number of trials per block is systematically reduced (e.g., from blocks of 16 trials with sample A1 and 16 trials with sample A2 to alternating blocks of 8, 4, and 2 trials of each type) until the trial types alternate unsystematically as in typical balanced conditional discrimination procedures. Blocked-trial, two-choice MTS procedures like those just described have proven effective for teaching conditional discriminations to subjects with mental retardation (K. Saunders & Spradlin, 1989). When they are used to train baseline conditional discriminations for potential equivalence class development, however, experimenters should be aware that such procedures can engender sample/S− rather than sample/S+ relations that can confound results of tests for equivalence, as discussed previously.

Other methods of establishing baseline arbitrary conditional discrimination performances include gradual introduction of incorrect comparisons, delayed-cue and other potentially errorless teaching techniques, sample shaping, imitation, and oral or written instructions (e.g., MacDonald, et al., 1986; Michael & Bernstein, 1991; Spradlin & Saunders, 1986; Zygmont, Lazar, Dube, & McIlvane, 1992; but for cautions regarding instructions see Sidman, 1994).

Training Structures

Training structure refers to the pattern of conditional relations that may result from MTS training designed to establish baselines for stimulus equivalence classes. Various terms have been introduced to describe components or characteristics of training structures. Some authors adopted terminology used by paired-associates researchers in describing a structure in which two stimuli are mutually related to a third (e.g., AB, BC) as a "three-stage" arrangement; adding a fourth stimulus (e.g., CD) created a "four-stage" arrangement (e.g., Sidman et al., 1985; see also Sidman, 1994). Other terminology that has been widely adopted refers to a stimulus that is related conditionally to just one other stimulus as a "single," whereas a stimulus that is related conditionally to more than one other stimulus is called a "node" (Fields & Verhave, 1987).

One common training structure presents subjects with a linear series of conditional relations in which each stimulus except the first and last stimulus in the series is a node. For example, when AB, BC, CD, and DE relations are trained (see Figure 8.2, upper panel), the B, C, and D stimuli are nodes and each node in the series links only two stimuli. A number of investigators have used this training structure (e.g., Dube, McIlvane, Maguire, Mackay, & Stoddard, 1989; Fields, Newman, Adams, & Verhave, 1992; Lazar, Davis-Lang, & Sanchez, 1984; Lynch & Green, 1991).

It is important to note that following linear-series training, the nodal stimuli (B, C, and D) will have served as both comparisons and as samples, although with different sets of stimuli (e.g., the B stimuli will have been comparisons with A sam-

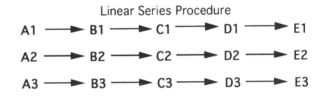

Figure 8.2. Illustrations of three basic training structures used in stimulus equivalence experiments. Each alphanumeric designation represents a different stimulus. Arrows point from sample stimuli to comparison stimuli. The arrows represent conditional relations that are trained (preferably with three-choice match-to-sample procedures) to potentially establish three equivalence classes of five stimuli each. The numeral in each alphanumeric designation indicates the equivalence class to which each stimulus is expected to belong (e.g., A1, B1, C1, D1, and E1 should constitute one equivalence class). Stimuli designated by common letters (e.g., A1, A2, A3, B1, B2, B3) appear together in each conditional discrimination trained, either as successively presented samples or as concurrently presented comparisons.

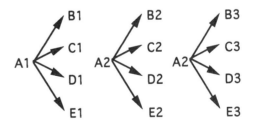

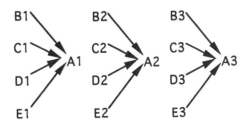

ples and samples with C comparisons). The single stimuli (A and E), however, will have served only as samples or comparisons, respectively. Some tests that involve the single stimuli (BA and ED symmetry tests; CA, DA, EA, EB, and EC combined tests), therefore, present those stimuli in entirely new roles relative to baseline training. The remaining tests (CB and DC symmetry tests; AC, AD, AE, BD, BE, and CE transitivity tests; and DB combined tests) do not have this feature.

In another common training structure, two or more comparison stimuli are related to a single sample stimulus per class, as shown in the middle panel of Figure 8.2 (e.g., Dube, McIlvane, Mackay, & Stoddard, 1987; Harrison & Green, 1990; Pilgrim & Galizio, 1990; Sidman & Tailby, 1982). Because the sample stimulus is the node that links all other members of each intended class, this training structure has been referred to as the "single-sample, multiple comparison" (R. Saunders, Wachter, et al., 1988), "sample-as-node" (K. Saunders, Saunders, Williams, & Spradlin, 1993), or "one-to-many" procedure (Urcuioli & Zentall, 1993). All tests for the property of symmetry following training with this structure (BA, CA, DA, EA) present former samples as comparisons and former comparisons as samples. All other tests (BC, CB, BD, DB, BE, EB, CD, DC, CE, EC, DE, ED) evaluate symmetry and transitivity simultaneously and present stimuli that functioned only as comparisons during baseline training as samples.

The lower panel of Figure 8.2 shows still another training structure in which one comparison is related to two or more different samples within each prospective equivalence class (e.g., Green, Sigurdardottir, & Saunders, 1991; R. Saunders, Saunders, Kirby, & Spradlin, 1988; Spradlin et al., 1973). This has been called the "multiple-sample, single-comparison" (R. Saunders, Wachter et al., 1988), "comparison-as-node" (K. Saunders et al., 1993), or "many-to-one" procedure (Urcuioli, Zentall, Jackson-Smith, & Steirn, 1989). Following training with this baseline structure, all tests for the property of symmetry (EA, EB, EC, ED) place stimuli in sample–comparison roles that are reversed relative to baseline. All other tests evaluate the properties of symmetry and transitivity, and present stimuli that functioned only as samples during training as comparisons on some tests.

Other training structures have been used, but they are all variations on the three structures just described (see Fields, Adams, & Verhave, 1993). Three variations shown in the top panel of Figure 8.3 were explored in one study (Wetherby, Karlan, & Spradlin, 1983). In each variation, two conditional discrimination problems were trained first, one with comparison as node, one with sample as node, and third with no node (unrelated pairs), represented by solid arrows in the figure. A third discrimination problem was then trained in each variation, followed by tests for the emergent relations indicated by broken arrows in the figure, which can be considered combined tests for the properties of symmetry and transitivity. The leftmost variation shown in Figure 8.3 replicated procedures used by Spradlin et al. (1973), and the middle variation overlapped considerably with Sidman and Tailby (1982). The bottom panel of Figure 8.3 shows an interlocking sample-as-node structure (Fields et al., 1993; Kennedy, 1991). Of course, training structures for experiments that employ auditory stimuli are restricted generally, because auditory stimuli are difficult to present as comparisons (but see Dube et al, 1993). When auditory samples are used in baseline training, the comparison-as-node structure is preferred because a nearly complete set of tests for the properties of equivalence can then be constructed with nonauditory comparisons.

1 & 2 = comparison as node   1 & 2 = sample as node   1 & 2 are unrelated

Based on Wetherby, Karlan & Spradlin, 1983

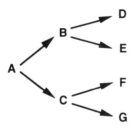

Based on Kennedy, 1991

FIGURE 8.3.   Schematic representations of training structures used in some stimulus equivalence experiments. Subject performances in the experiments on which these schematics are based showed the development of two equivalence classes (e.g., A1B1C1D1 and A2B2C2D2; top panel), but only the generic paradigms are illustrated here. Arrows point from sample stimuli to comparison stimuli. Solid lines indicate trained conditional relations; dashed lines indicate tested (emergent) relations. In the top panel, the small numerals above the solid lines indicate the order in which relations were trained, and the type of training structure is indicated beneath each schematic.

The Relevance of Training Structures: Differential Outcomes

Some investigators have maintained that test performances consistent with stimulus equivalence vary as a function of the number of nodes that linked the test stimuli during baseline training ("nodal distance"). They have suggested that performance on tests involving stimuli that were related by smaller numbers of nodes in training are consistent with equivalence class development more quickly (i.e., will be more accurate on initial tests) than performances involving stimuli that were related by larger numbers of nodes in training (e.g., Fields et al., 1990, 1993; Kennedy, 1991).

The Sidman analysis of stimulus equivalence, however, does not predict differences related to nodal distance. Regardless of training structure or other variables, if baseline training establishes the prerequisites for equivalence relations to emerge (and does not allow for the development of extraneous stimulus control), responding on all tests should be consistent with equivalence. When it is not, it is likely because some other source of stimulus control blocks control by equivalence (e.g., Sidman, 1990, 1994; Sidman et al., 1982; Sidman & Tailby, 1982). Equivalence-consistent performances that emerge only gradually with repeated testing, as reported for some subjects in several studies (e.g., Lazar et al., 1984; Sidman et al., 1985; Spradlin et al., 1973), are thought to indicate that those other types of stimulus control drop out as testing goes on because equivalence is the only basis for responding that is consistent across the various types of test trials (Sidman, 1990, 1994). In other words, the nodal distance model suggests that some untrained conditional relations within equivalence classes are stronger than others by virtue of the smaller number of stimuli mediating their indirect relation to one another. The Sidman analysis suggests that such an assertion is illogical, because it implies that some stimuli within an equivalence class are more equivalent than others.

Results of some studies suggested that differential outcomes on equivalence tests following baseline training with different structures may have been a function of subjects' language skills. Comparison-as-node and sample-as-node training structures produced differential outcomes with subjects with mental retardation who had limited language repertoires. With such subjects, the comparison-as-node ("many to one") training structure seemed to produce stimulus equivalence more readily than the sample-as-node paradigm (K. Saunders et al., 1993; R. Saunders, Wachter et al., 1988; Spradlin & Saunders, 1986), though other investigators reported ready development of equivalence classes in persons with mild or moderate retardation when the sample-as-node procedure was used (e.g., Devany et al., 1986; Green, 1990; Sidman, 1971; Sidman, Willson-Morris, & Kirk, 1986). There were some potentially important procedural differences among these studies, however. The latter group of investigators trained only two conditional discrimination problems (as opposed to the three or four described above) prior to testing for development of two, three-member equivalence classes. Sidman (1971) used auditory samples rather than visual samples. In two studies, some prospective equivalence classes were established using auditory samples and visual comparisons, and some involved only visual stimuli. All subjects were exposed to both types of training. Although most subjects' test performances eventually showed development of all intended equivalence classes, performances consistent with equivalence emerged more slowly in the all-visual classes than in classes containing auditory stimuli as training nodes (Green, 1990; Sidman et al., 1986). In one study involving preschool children with mental retardation, those who were "language able" were reported to develop all-visual equivalence classes following sample-as-node training, whereas those who were "language disabled" did not. These subjects, however, apparently were instructed to "Touch the one that goes with this one" on every training trial (and may have been similarly instructed on every test trial). This instruction could have exerted differential control of subjects' performances as a function of their language skills (Devany et al., 1986).

These and other studies also suggested that outcomes of equivalence experiments may be influenced substantially by instructions, stimulus naming, or other verbal mediation (e.g., Eikeseth & Smith, 1992; Green et al., 1991; Sigurdardottir, Green, & Saunders, 1990). This conceptualization of stimulus equivalence differs somewhat from Sidman's view that equivalence may be an "unanalyzable primitive," like reinforcement and discrimination (Sidman, 1990, 1994). In the alternative view, equivalence-consistent performances on tests indicate that stimuli have become substitutable for one another within the context of MTS procedures (e.g., Dixon & Spradlin, 1976; K. Suanders et al., 1993; R. Saunders & Green, 1992; Spradlin & Dixon, 1976; Spradlin & Saunders, 1984). Task-related variables in baseline training, however, may affect the probability with which stimuli will be substituted for one another on untrained test trials, even when care has been taken to minimize extraneous sources of stimulus control As suggested above and elsewhere, different training structures (comparison-as-node versus sample-as-node, for example) establish different functions for stimuli during training, which may in turn influence test outcomes differentially (K. Saunders et al., 1993; Spradlin & Saunders, 1986). Training structure differences also play a role in other conceptualizations of stimulus equivalence, which are too complex to discuss here (e.g., Barnes, 1994; L. Hayes, 1992).

Other Procedures

Procedures other than MTS that may establish the prerequisites for stimulus equivalence are reviewed briefly here. It appears that, regardless of establishing procedures, testing for the emergence of untrained relations that might indicate the development of equivalence classes is best done with MTS procedures (Sidman, 1994).

Simple Discrimination Reversals

Several investigators asked whether nonidentical stimuli that served the same simple discriminative functions in baseline training would be related conditionally to one another on unreinforced MTS test trials (e.g., Cohen-Almeida, 1993; Cohen-Almeida & Sidman, 1991; Galvao, Sidman, & Cohen-Almeida, 1992, all cited in Sidman, 1994). Subjects are typically presented with a series of simultaneous or successive (go/no go) discrimination trials on which arbitrary visual stimuli from one set (labeled, for example A1, B1, and C1) are discriminative for reinforcement, whereas stimuli from one or more other sets (e.g., A2, B2, C2; A3, B3, C3) are not. One simultaneous discrimination trial type, for example, might present A1, A2, and A3 to the subject with A1 the designated S+; another trial type would be B1, B2, and B3, with B1 serving as the S+; and so on. After subjects respond consistently to the designated S+ stimuli on all trial types, the contingency shifts so that Set 2 stimuli are discriminative for reinforcement and Set 1 are not. Contingency shifts, which are usually unsignaled, are repeated until responding shifts quickly to conform to the new contingency, i.e., from the second trial after each contingency shift. Then subjects are presented with opportunities to match all stimuli from each set (e.g., A1, B1, and C1) to one another without explicit training on MTS trials. If they do so, it may suggest that stimuli that serve common discriminative functions in three-term contingencies are related by equivalence (but for possible limitations see Sidman, 1994).

Sequence Training

A few experiments have shown that sequence training may establish the prerequisites for equivalence relations. Subjects were trained to sequence visual stimuli (e.g., arbitrary figures) in discrete sets. For example, they learned first to touch a set of stimuli in a specific order (e.g., A1→A2→A3). Then sequences of other stimuli were trained directly (e.g., B1→B2→B3; C1→C2→C3). MTS tests then evaluated whether stimuli that were in the same ordinal positions in the sequences, but were never related to one another directly in training. (e.g., A1, B1, and C1; A2, B2, and

C2; and so on), would be related conditionally to one another. Results were affirmative for most normally capable adults (e.g., Lazar, 1977; Sigurdardottir et al., 1990; Wulfert & Hayes, 1988), but not for two subjects with mental retardation (Maydak, Stromer, Mackay, & Stoddard, 1995).

EXPANDING EQUIVALENCE CLASSES

Once equivalence classes have been established, they can be expanded by training new relations. For each new stimulus to be added to a class, a conditional relation can be trained between that stimulus and a stimulus in the existing class. Following such training, tests can be conducted to evaluate whether the newly trained relation has the properties of an equivalence relation (i.e., whether the new stimulus has become equivalent to all members of the existing class by virtue of its trained relation with one member of the class).

Class Expansion

In an early demonstration, Dixon and Spradlin (1976) established two visual stimulus classes by using each stimulus in each prospective class as both sample and comparison in reinforced MTS trials. Then responses to one (or more) stimulus from each class were reinforced in the presence of novel auditory samples. On subsequent probe trials, subjects responded to the remaining members of each visual stimulus class in the presence of the respective auditory samples, demonstrating that the classes had expanded to include the auditory stimuli (see also R. Saunders, Wachter et al., 1988). Three-member equivalence classes have been expanded to five-member classes by training one set of new conditional relations at a time, with intervening tests for emergent relations among new stimuli and members of the established equivalence classes (e.g., Lazar et al., 1984; Sidman et al., 1985). In another demonstration, college students first demonstrated two equivalence classes, then were trained to make differential responses to each of two novel stimuli. Transfer of stimulus control of those responses to a member of each of the equivalence classes was effected with fading procedures. Subsequent tests showed that the novel stimuli were included in the equivalence classes (Fields et al., 1992). Experiments with subjects with mental retardation demonstrated that when responding on baseline arbitrary MTS trials resulted in reinforcers that were specific to each intended equivalence class, the reinforcers were included in equivalence classes with the sample and comparison stimuli that were related in training. Novel stimuli presented in identity MTS trials on which correct responses produced the same specific reinforcers as in the original baseline training then became members of the respective equivalence classes (Dube et al., 1987, 1989).

Class Merger

Equivalence classes have also been enlarged rapidly by merging two classes into one. For example, subjects in one study demonstrated three equivalence classes with three sets of stimuli (A, B, and C). They also demonstrated equivalence classes with three other sets of stimuli (D, E, and F). After conditional relations among the C and E stimuli were trained directly, five of eight subjects demonstrated that the original three-member classes merged into six-member classes, i.e., all of the remaining stimuli from the original classes were related to one another without further training (Sidman et al, 1985).

Subjects with mild mental retardation who had lengthy histories of conditional discrimination training and testing for equivalence classes tended to relate samples from each of two established equivalence classes conditionally to comparisons from each of two other classes when no differential consequences were provided for responding on such trials. Tests then revealed that the classes related by those unreinforced conditional selections merged into larger equivalence classes. Some subjects then responded conditionally on three new discrimination problems with entirely novel stimuli and, on subsequent tests, showed that those stimuli were related by equivalence, i.e., new equivalence classes developed entirely without reinforced training (R. Saunders, Saunders, et al., 1988; see also Harrison & Green, 1990). These results were replicated recently with typically developing children in experiments that employed two-choice (Drake, 1993) and three-choice (Williams, Saunders, Saunders, & Spradlin, 1995) MTS procedures.

Finally, an experiment with college students demonstrated merger of arbitrary equivalence classes and primary stimulus generalization classes. Subjects who demonstrated two equivalence classes consisting of three stimuli, one of which was a "short" or "long" line, generally maintained class-consistent performances on CA equivalence tests when novel but similar line lengths were substituted for the lines used in training (Fields et al., 1991).

TESTING PROCEDURES

Testing with or without Reinforcement

The decision to reinforce or not reinforce performances on tests is always difficult (Sidman, 1981). In equivalence research, the decision is compounded by consideration of whether to reinforce responses on baseline trials with which test trials are often intermixed. Experimenters in many early equivalence studies provided no differential consequences for responses on test trials to ensure that those responses reflected emergent by-products of the preceding baseline training, rather than products of current contingencies. Unreinforced test trials were typically interspersed, however, among reinforced training trials (e.g., R. Saunders, Wachter et al., 1988; Sidman et al., 1985; Spradlin et al., 1973). In preparation for testing, the probability of programmed consequences for responses on trained (baseline) trials was often reduced systematically until test trials could be substituted for some baseline trials without altering overall session length or reinforcement probability. In many experiments, tests for the properties of equivalence were administered without trial-by-trial consequences for responding on either baseline or test trials (e.g., Bush et al., 1989; Gatch & Osborne, 1989; Lazar & Kotlarchyk, 1986). Before testing began, some investigators reduced the probability of reinforcement for correct responses on training trials gradually (e.g., Green, 1993; Sigurdardottir et al., 1990), whereas others did so rather abruptly (e.g., Green, 1990). Other investigators instructed subjects that there would be no trial-by-trial consequences on some or all trials, but that consequences would be provided at the end of the session based on their performance (e.g., R. Saunders, Saunders et al., 1988). Following such preparations, test trials were embedded as unreinforced probes interspersed with unreinforced training trials, or administered in blocks or sessions consisting entirely of unreinforced test trials.

Probes versus Massed Test Trials

Massed testing refers to presenting the subject with blocks or sessions consisting only of test trials, with no baseline (trained) trials presented concurrently. A potential problem with massed testing is that it does not provide concurrent confirmation that the trained conditional relations are maintained. The tests evaluate properties of the trained relations; if those relations are not maintained during testing, the tests are invalidated. Some apparent failures of equivalence class development may actually represent failures to establish or maintain the prerequisites for equivalence (e.g., see commentaries about the much-cited Devany et al., 1986, experiment by McIlvane & Dube, 1996; K. Saunders & Spradlin, 1996; and R. Saunders & Green, 1996). Interspersing test trials as probes among trained trials permits continuous monitoring of the status of the relations being evaluated by the tests. Alternating blocks of test trials with blocks of training trials may accomplish the same thing. Still another alternative is to begin test sessions with reinforced reviews of baseline training, followed immediately by blocks of unreinforced test trials (e.g., Kennedy, Itkonen, & Lindquist, 1994).

There is relatively little empirical evidence about the differential effects of conducting tests for the properties of equivalence in interspersed (probe) versus massed fashion, or interspersing unreinforced test trials with baseline trials that are or are not eligible for reinforcement. One set of investigators reported a case in which accurate baseline performances were maintained without reinforcement just prior to testing, but unreinforced test performances were not consistent with expected outcomes. After the mentally retarded subject was instructed to "do as well as you can" and offered "bonus points" for highly accurate responding (delivered at the end of the test session, not trial-by-trial), test performances were consistent with predicted emergent relations (Galvao et al., 1992). In another study, one subject's responses on unreinforced test trials were not consistent with equivalence when those trials were interspersed with reinforced training trials. When similar sessions were administered with no differential consequences for responding on either baseline or test trials, responses on test trials were consistent with equivalence class development (R. Saunders, Wachter et al., 1988).

Test Order

Outcomes on tests for the properties of equivalence might be influenced by the order in which properties are tested or the order in which subjects encounter test trial types. For example, if tests for the property of symmetry in certain conditional relations were alternated with trials of those trained relations, the symmetry test outcomes might be more likely to be positive than if the tests were given in a massed test trial format or alternated with trials of other trained conditional relations. Similarly, tests for transitivity of trained relations AB and BC might be influenced positively if the test trials were preceded immediately by the training trials. Additionally, symmetry tests reverse the roles of stimuli relative to training (e.g., from comparison to sample; from discriminative stimulus to conditional stimulus). Exposure to this change within the comparative simplicity of symmetry tests may foster positive performances on subsequent tests; alternatively, "incorrect" responding on symmetry tests may establish error patterns that influence performances on subsequent tests. These are speculations, however; to our knowledge, no research has examined these possibilities directly.

The Sidman analysis of equivalence suggests that if training established equivalence relations, test performances should be consistent with equivalence regardless of where test trials occur relative to other trials. Strategic placement of test trials, however, could change the nature of the trained relations over the course of testing (R. Saunders & Green, 1992). That is, gradual emergence of equivalence during testing (e.g., Sidman et al., 1985, 1986) might be influenced by test trial order. One study appeared to confirm that possibility. College students who failed simultaneous tests for symmetry and transitivity were given tests for symmetry alone. When those outcomes were positive, they completed tests for transitivity. Those results, and outcomes on the readministration of the simultaneous tests, were also positive (Fields et al., 1992). Unfortunately, this study employed two-choice MTS procedures to develop just two equivalence classes. Each test was administered repeatedly in massed blocks until the subject's performance showed the desired pattern on all of the test trials in a block. In other words, when performances did not conform to the experimenters' expectations, test trials were repeated; when they did conform, the subject immediately moved to a new condition. Such procedures seem likely to instruct subjects to alter their response patterns, which could be construed as training rather than testing (R. Saunders & Green, 1992).

It is also important to consider what test order may convey to subjects, particularly if they are likely to discriminate subtle aspects of the experimental situation. Sidman (1992) suggested that subjects in typical equivalence experiments might learn that for each MTS trial there is one and only one correct choice. Such learning is probably an important prerequisite to consistent performances on test trials. Subjects could learn other "rules" as well, however, that would not be consistent with the expected test performances. Suppose a subject is exposed to training on several conditional discrimination problems that establish a fairly long series of relations such as AB, BC, CD, DE for each of three potential classes. The subject may learn that each new set of conditional discrimination problems involves adding a new stimulus to each series, and that each new set links former comparison stimuli, now employed as samples, with the new stimulus. If the next set of problems presented massed trials of simultaneous tests for symmetry and transitivity (EA relations), responding consistently in accordance with those "rules" might lead a subject to respond to an A stimulus in the presence of each E sample that is different from the A stimulus that was positive with that E stimulus at the beginning of the series (e.g., the subject might select A2 rather than A1 in the presence of E1 to add a new element and extend the series; R. Saunders &

Green, 1992). In summary, test order should be evaluated carefully with respect to how it may interact with other variables in equivalence experiments (e.g., class size, number of classes, types of stimuli, training structure).

In testing for the property of reflexivity, several considerations are warranted. Investigators in some early studies administered tests for reflexivity as pretests, i.e., tests administered prior to baseline training (e.g., R. Saunders, Wachter et al., 1988; Sidman & Tailby, 1982). These tests usually consisted of consecutive trials of identity MTS with the visual stimuli to be used in training. In some cases, identity matching responses on these trials were followed by reinforcement; in other cases, the tests were administered with no programmed consequences for responding except advancement to the next trial. Results were usually positive, and were taken as proof of the property of reflexivity. There is a logical problem, however, in treating pretest performances as indicative of properties of trained relations, because the relations of interest have not yet been established. The fact that identity matching pretest results were usually positive from the outset further suggests that tests for reflexivity, no matter when they are administered, likely reflect preexperimental histories of reinforcement for identity matching rather than the effects of experimental contingencies. Further, identity matching pretests might prompt subjects to look for identical or similar physical features among stimuli involved in subsequent arbitrary MTS training, which could disrupt equivalence test results. Thus, if reflexivity tests are administered, they should be conducted after arbitrary conditional relations have been trained and after the tests for the other properties of equivalence have been completed successfully. For similar reasons, tests for reflexivity probably should be conducted in sessions containing only reflexivity test trials, without trial-by-trial consequences (R. Saunders & Green, 1992;Sidman, 1994).

Whether tests for properties other than reflexivity are administered within the same session or in different sessions is at this time a matter of investigator preference. Some investigators have suggested that giving tests in a "simple-to-complex" order (i.e., symmetry, then transitivity, then combined tests for symmetry and transitivity) may increase the likelihood of positive results (Fields et al., 1992). Other investigators have raised the possibility that discriminations between stimuli in prospective classes may be incomplete when the sample stimuli are nodes (K. Saunders et al., 1993; Spradlin & Saunders, 1986). Symmetry testing may improve discriminations among stimuli in each prospective class and between classes; therefore, conducting symmetry tests prior to tests for combined properties might be desirable. It should also be noted that following single-node training with either the sample-as-node or comparison-as-node structure (e.g., AC and BC relations), the only possible tests for transitivity (AB, BA) also necessarily test for symmetry in the trained relations. In other words, no test of transitivity alone is possible following single-node training; logically, tests for that property also test for symmetry.

Designing a Test Protocol

Given all of the issues about testing reviewed above, it can be difficult to decide how to design a test protocol for a particular equivalence experiment. To date, the literature does not include explicit decision rules, but some general guidelines are suggested. The most important is that the testing protocol should support the aims of the experiment in a logical way. For example, if the purpose of an experiment is to determine whether the development of equivalence classes fosters reading or some other socially important repertoire, then testing from simple to complex with test trials interspersed among related training trials might be advisable. In fact, anything short of explicitly reinforcing responses on test trials might be acceptable if the goal is to develop useful equivalence classes relatively quickly. Alternatively, suppose the purpose of an experiment is to test proposition that "if trained relations are equivalence relations, then the trained relations have all of the properties of equivalence." If the proposition is true, then testing from complex to simple, with test trials interspersed among training trial types unrelated to the tested relations, should have no adverse effect on test outcomes. This testing protocol should minimize the likelihood that equivalence will develop as a function of testing rather than as an emergent product of training contingencies.

Other recommendations are made with the caveat that they should not supersede the primary consideration just discussed. We favor testing with probes interspersed among baseline training trials to monitor maintenance of the trained relations. Probe trials should not occur consecutively, but should be separated by varying numbers of baseline trials, with a minimum of two baseline trials between probes. Test sessions should be constructed so that each probe trial type is presented several times. If performances on any probe trial type (e.g., tests for symmetry in the originally trained relations) are variable within or across test sessions, the sessions should be repeated until probe performances stabilize (assuming that baseline performances are also maintained consistently). Alternatively, if performances on particular probe trial types meet the experimenter's criteria within the first few test sessions, it is probably best to discontinue those probes while other probes are administered, or if they are continued, to reinforce correct responses on those trial types. These procedures offer the advantage of sampling unreinforced probe performances enough to see the initial pattern, but not so often as to produce changes in probe performances related to extinction.

Analyzing Test Results

Positive Outcomes on All Tests

Assume that a subject has been trained in a well-designed protocol that minimized the probability that something other than the intended sample/S+ relations would develop. The subject now completes tests for symmetry and transitivity, either separately or simultaneously. If responding on these test trials is consistent with the experimenter-defined equivalence classes, it suggests that the trained relations had the properties of symmetry and transitivity, the trained relations are all instances of the same relation, and, thus, the stimuli in each experimenter-defined class are related by equivalence within the context of the preceding training and testing. It should be reiterated that in two-choice MTS experiments using one-node comparison-as-node or sample-as-node training structures, positive results on tests for symmetry and combined tests for symmetry and transitivity may reflect the establishment of either select (sample/S+) or reject (sample/S−) relations during baseline training, either or both of which may be equivalence relations. Additional tests and careful analyses of results are necessary to determine which type of control developed in training (for more detailed discussions, see Carrigan & Sidman, 1992; R. Saunders & Green, 1992).

Apparent Failures

Responding on test trials in accordance with experimenter-designated equivalence classes—or equivalence classes other than those intended by the experimenter—is only one possible outcome. Several other patterns have been observed. For one, responses on tests can be highly unsystematic. If each test trial were presented more than once and the subject responded to a different comparison stimulus each time, little could be inferred about the nature of the trained relations. Completely unsystematic responding is unusual, however; more often particular types of competing stimulus control are evident. For example, if a subject responds to a particular comparison position on all trials regardless of samples, or in the presence of a particular sample, the inference is that training produced simple discriminative control by location or relations between samples and particular comparison positions. Similarly, if a subject responds to particular comparison stimuli regardless of the samples and other comparisons with which they appear, some form of bias toward particular stimuli is evident. These examples reflect some of the more obvious sources of extraneous stimulus control. Other response patterns are more difficult to interpret.

Retesting

When testing produces performances indicative of control by something other than stimulus equivalence, further training and/or testing may alter responding on test trials until it is consistent with the development of the intended equivalence classes. In several studies, when performances on initial tests were not as predicted, subjects were reexposed to aspects of baseline training deemed critical to the stimulus control desired, and then tests for the properties of equivalence were repeated (e.g., Sigurdardottir et al., 1990). In others, subjects were reexposed to particular tests (e.g., symmetry) that might be expected to foster the emergence of equivalence-consistent performances on other tests (e.g., combined symmetry and transitivity; R. Saunders, Wachter et al., 1988; Sidman et al., 1985).

Mixed Outcomes

Sometimes performances by a particular subject are consistent with the development of predicted equivalence classes on some tests whereas responses on other tests are not consistent with predictions. Such mixed outcomes may indicate that training and testing partitioned the stimuli into equivalence classes of different composition than the experimenter planned. For example, as mentioned above, if EA combined tests for symmetry and transitivity are given first following AB, BC, CD, DE training, responding to A1 in the presence of E3, A2 in the presence of E1, and A3 in the presence of E2 could effectively link all of the stimuli into one class. If so, performances on all subsequent tests for symmetry should be as predicted, but results of transitivity and combined tests could be equivocal because every stimulus is related by equivalence to every other stimulus. Thus the partition that occurs could be a family of one large class rather than three distinct classes. This outcome is more likely when two-choice MTS procedures are used than when three or more comparisons are available on every trial, with trials balanced within and across sessions as described previously (see R. Saunders & Green, 1992; Sidman, 1994).

Mixed outcomes can also arise when training establishes sample/S− control, or what Carrigan and Sidman (1992) referred to as "reject" relations. As their analysis indicated, following linear series training in which responses to the designated correct comparison stimuli were based on rejection of the other comparison stimuli, tests for transitivity will be consistent with equivalence when the number of nodes spanned by the tests is even. Conversely, reject-based responding should lead to performances on transitivity tests with odd numbers of nodes that are not consistent with equivalence. Symmetry tests should produce performances consistent with experimenter-designated equivalence classes. Thus, only tests involving odd numbers of nodes will produce results that appear to be inconsistent with equivalence (Carrigan & Sidman, 1992). This same pattern of responding occurs if, in training, the subject responds on the basis of arbitrary oddity rather than arbitrary matching (R. Saunders & Green, 1992).

Another type of mixed outcome occurs when performances appear to show that some of the stimuli in an experimenter-designated class are related by equivalence, but other stimuli are not. For example, R. Saunders, Wachter et al. (1988, Phase 1) reported that Subject LE had class-consistent responses on 89% of trials testing for combined transitivity and symmetry with three stimuli in each of two prospective classes. On test trials involving another stimulus in each prospective class, however, responses were only 64% consistent with equivalence.

CONCLUSION

Stimulus equivalence has been the subject of an enormous number of experimental and conceptual behavioral analyses in recent years. One of the reasons the Sidman paradigm has generated so much excitement and research activity is that it provides the conceptual and methodological means to analyze and produce a variety of generative performances—responses that are not trained directly—within an operant framework. Complex repertoires that have long been considered by many to be outside the explanatory scope of operant principles, in particular those that are often labeled language and cognition, now seem to be amenable to behavioral analyses. The seminal experiments by Sidman, Spradlin, and their colleagues in the 1970s and the conceptual and experimental analyses published by Sidman and colleagues in the early 1980s inspired a flurry of basic and applied experiments showing that rather complex performances could be generated without direct training, even in individuals with severe learning difficulties. Naturally, those findings suggested extensions of the original logical and mathematical analogy of equivalence relations to a broad range of repertoires involving complex relations among stimuli (for some examples, see Barnes, 1994; Donahoe & Palmer, 1994; Green, Stromer, & Mackay, 1993; L. Hayes, 1992; S. Hayes,1991, 1994; Sidman, 1994). Also understandably, considerable controversy and debate have arisen around such issues as the relation between equivalence and verbal behavior, whether stimulus equivalence is a uniquely human phenomenon, the "goodness of fit" between mathematical and behavioral models of equivalence, and the suggestion that stimulus equivalence may be, like reinforcement, an "unanalyzable primitive" (e.g., see Horne & Lowe, 1996,and related commentaries; S. Hayes, 1994; R. Saunders & Green, 1992; Sidman, 1994).

In this chapter we have endeavored to present only the fundamentals of stimulus equivalence research methods. There are countless methodological variations and permutations in the literature, corresponding with the conceptual extensions and elaborations of the original Sidman analysis just mentioned. Our objective has been to emphasize methods that maximize experimental control through application of principles derived from experimental analyses of stimulus control in both humans and nonhumans. As interest in stimulus equivalence and related processes continues to grow, and ever more complex human repertoires are explored in laboratory analogues, the importance of sound experimental methodology looms ever larger.

ACKNOWLEDGMENTS. Development of this chapter was supported in part by National Institute of Child Health and Human Development Grants HD25995-06 to the E. K. Shriver Center and HD18955 and HD02528 to the Schiefelbusch Institute for Life Span Studies, University of Kansas, and by the New England Center for Children.

REFERENCES

Adams, B. J., Fields, L., & Verhave, T. (1993). Formation of generalized equivalence classes. *The Psychological Record, 43*, 553–566.

Annett, J. M., & Leslie, J. C. (1995). Stimulus equivalence classes involving olfactory stimuli. *The Psychological Record, 45*, 439–450.

Augustson, K. G., & Dougher, M. J. (1992). Teaching conditional discrimination to young children: Some methodological successes and failures. *Experimental Analysis of Human Behavior Bulletin, 9*, 21–24.

Barnes, D. (1994). Stimulus equivalence and relational frame theory. *The Psychological Record, 44*, 91–124.

Barnes, D., McCullagh, P. D., & Keenan, M. (1990). Equivalence class formation in nonhearing impaired children and hearing impaired children. *The Analysis of Verbal Behavior, 8*, 19–30.

Blough, D. S. (1959). Delayed matching in the pigeon. *Journal of the Experimental Analysis of Behavior, 2*, 151–160.

Bush, K. M. (1993). Stimulus equivalence and cross-modal transfer. *The Psychological Record, 43*, 567–584.

Bush, K. M., Sidman, M., & de Rose, T. (1989). Contextual control of emergent equivalence relations. *Journal of the Experimental Analysis of Behavior, 51*, 29–45.

Carrigan, P. F., & Sidman, M. (1992). Conditional discrimination and equivalence relations: A theoretical analysis of control by negative stimuli. *Journal of the Experimental Analysis of Behavior, 58*, 183–204.

Carter, D. E., & Werner, T. J. (1978). Complex learning and information processing by pigeons: A critical analysis. *Journal of the Experimental Analysis of Behavior, 29,* 565–601.

Catania, A. C. (1984). *Learning* (2nd ed.). Englewood Cliffs, NJ: Prentice–Hall.

Catania, A. C., Horne, P., & Lowe, C. F. (1989). Transfer of function across members of an equivalence class. *The Analysis of Verbal Behavior, 7,* 99–110.

Clark, H. B., & Sherman, J. A. (1970). Effects of a conditioned reinforcer upon accuracy of match-to-sample behavior in pigeons. *Journal of the Experimental Analysis of Behavior, 13,* 375–384.

Cohen-Almeida, D. (1993). *Simple discrimination tests for the merger of functional classes.* Unpublished master's thesis, Northeastern University, Boston.

Cohen-Almeida, D., & Sidman, M. (1991, May). *Simple discrimination tests for transfer of functional class membership.* Poster presented at the annual conference of the Association for Behavior Analysis, Atlanta.

Constantine, B., & Sidman, M. (1975). The role of naming in delayed matching to sample. *American Journal of Mental Deficiency, 79,*680–689.

Cowley, B. J., Green, G., & Braunling-McMorrow, D. (1992). Using stimulus equivalence procedures to teach name–face matching to adults with brain injuries. *Journal of Applied Behavior Analysis, 25,* 461–475.

Devany, J. M., Hayes, S. C., & Nelson, R. O. (1986). Equivalence class formation in language-able and language-disabled children. *Journal of the Experimental Analysis of Behavior, 46,* 243–257.

Dixon, M. H., & Spradlin, J. E. (1976). Establishing stimulus equivalence among retarded adolescents. *Journal of Experimental Child Psychology, 21,* 144–164.

Donahoe, J. W., & Palmer, D. C. (1994). *Learning and complex behavior.* Boston: Allyn & Bacon.

Drake, K. M. (1993). *Stimulus classes: The result of differential response and delayed conditional discrimination training.* Unpublished doctoral dissertation, University of Kansas, Lawrence.

Dube, W. V., Green, G., & Serna, R. W. (1993). Auditory successive conditional discrimination and auditory stimulus equivalence classes. *Journal of the Experimental Analysis of Behavior, 59,* 103–114.

Dube, W. V., Iennaco, F. M., & McIlvane, W. J. (1993). Generalized identity matching to sample of two-dimensional forms in individuals with intellectual disabilities. *Research in Developmental Disabilities, 14,* 457–477.

Dube, W. V., Iennaco, F. M., Rocco, F. J., Kledaras, J. B., & McIlvane, W. J. (1992). Microcomputer-based programmed instruction in generalized identity matching for persons with severe disabilities. *Journal of Behavioral Education, 2,* 29–51.

Dube, W. V., McIlvane, W. J., Mackay, H. A., & Stoddard, L. T. (1987). Stimulus class membership established via stimulus–reinforcer relations. *Journal of the Experimental Analysis of Behavior, 47,* 159–174.

Dube, W. V., McIlvane, W. J., Maguire, R. W., Mackay, H. A., & Stoddard, L. T. (1989). Stimulus class formation and stimulus–reinforcer relations. *Journal of the Experimental Analysis of Behavior, 51,* 65–76.

Eikeseth, S., & Smith, T. (1992). The development of functional and equivalence classes in high-functioning autistic children: The role of naming. *Journal of the Experimental Analysis of Behavior, 58,* 123–133.

Fields, L., Adams, B. J., & Verhave, T. (1993). The effects of equivalence class structure on test performances. *The Psychological Record, 43,* 697–712.

Fields, L., Adams, B. J., Verhave, T., & Newman, S. (1990). The effects of nodality on the formation of equivalence classes. *Journal of the Experimental Analysis of Behavior, 3,* 345–358.

Fields, L., Newman, S., Adams, B. J., & Verhave, T. (1992). The expansion of equivalence classes through simple discrimination training and fading. *The Psychological Record, 42,*3–15.

Fields,L., Reeve, K. F., Adams, B. J., & Verhave, T. (1991). Stimulus generalization and equivalence classes: A model for natural categories. *Journal of the Experimental Analysis of Behavior, 55,* 305–312.

Fields, L., & Verhave, T. (1987). The structure of equivalence classes. *Journal of the Experimental Analysis of Behavior, 48,* 317–332

Fields, L., Verhave, T., & Fath, S. (1984). Stimulus equivalence and transitive associations: A methodological analysis. *Journal of the Experimental Analysis of Behavior, 42,* 143–158.

Galvao, O. D., Calcagno, S., & Sidman, M. (1992). Testing for emergent performances in extinction. *Experimental Analysis of Human Behavior Bulletin, 10,* 18–20.

Galvao, O. D., Sidman, M., & Cohen-Almeida, D. (1992, May). *Does the repeated-reversals procedure establish functional classes?* Poster presented at the annual conference of the Association for Behavior Analysis, San Francisco.

Gatch, M. B., & Osborne, J. G. (1989). Transfer of contextual stimulus function via equivalence class development. *Journal of the Experimental Analysis of Behavior, 51,* 369–378.

Goldiamond, I. (1962). Perception. In A. J. Bachrach (Ed.), *Experimental foundations of clinical psychology* (pp. 280–340). New York: Basic Books.

Green, G. (1990). Differences in development of visual and auditory-visual equivalence relations. *American Journal on Mental Retardation, 95,* 260–270.

Green, G. (1993). Stimulus control technology for teaching number/quantity equivalences. *Proceedings of the 1992 National Autism Conference (Australia).* Melbourne: Victorian Autistic Children's and Adults' Association.

Green, G., Sigurdardottir, A. G., & Saunders, R. R. (1991). The role of instructions in the transfer of ordinal functions through equivalence classes. *Journal of the Experimental Analysis of Behavior, 55,* 287–304.

Green, G., Stromer, R., & Mackay, H.A. (1993). Relational learning in stimulus sequences. *The Psychological Record, 43,* 599–616.

Harrison, R. J., & Green G. (1990). Development of conditional and equivalence relations without differential consequences. *Journal of the Experimental Analysis of Behavior, 54,* 225–237.

Hayes, L. J. (1992). Equivalence as process. In S. C. Hayes & L. J. Hayes (Eds.), *Understanding verbal relations* (pp. 97–108). Reno, NV: Context Press.

Hayes L. J., Tilley, K. L. & Hayes, S. C. (1988). Extending equivalence class membership to gustatory stimuli. *The Psychological Record, 38,* 473–482.

Hayes, S. C. (1991). A relational control theory of stimulus equivalence. In L. J. Hayes & P. N. Chase (Eds.), *Dialogues on verbal behavior* (pp. 19–40). Reno, NV: Context Press.

Hayes, S. C. (1994). Relational frame theory: A functional approach to verbal events. In S. C. Hayes, L. J. Hayes, M. Sato, & K. Ono (Eds.), *Behavior analysis of language and cognition* (pp. 9–30). Reno, NV: Context Press.

Horne, P. J., & Lowe, C. F. (1996). On the origins of naming and other symbolic behavior. *Journal of the Experimental Analysis of Behavior, 65,* 185–241.

Hull, C. L. (1939). The problem of stimulus equivalence in behavior theory. *Psychological Review, 46,* 9–30.

Hulse, S. H., Deese, J., & Egeth, H. (1975). *The psychology of learning* (4th ed.). New York: McGraw–Hill.

Jenkins, J. J. (1963). Mediated associations: Paradigms and situations. In C. N. Cofer & B. S. Musgrave (Eds.), *Verbal behavior and learning: Problems and processes* (pp. 210–245). New York: McGraw–Hill.

Jenkins, J. J., & Palermo, D. S. (1964). Mediation processes and the acquisition of linguistic structure. *Monographs of the Society for Research in Child Development, 29,* 141–175.

Johnson, C., & Sidman, M. (1993). Conditional discrimination and equivalence relations: Control by negative stimuli. *Journal of the Experimental Analysis of Behavior, 59,* 333–347.

Kennedy, C. H. (1991). Equivalence class formation influenced by the number of nodes separating stimuli. *Behavioural Processes, 24,* 219–245.

Kennedy, C. H., Itkonen, T., & Lindquist, K. (1994). Nodality effects during equivalence class formation: An extension to sight-word reading and concept development. *Journal of Applied Behavior Analysis, 27,* 673–683.

Lawrence, D. H. (1963). The nature of a stimulus: Some relationships between learning and perception. In S. Koch (Ed.), *Psychology: A study of science* (Vol. 5, pp. 179–212). New York: McGraw–Hill.

Lazar, R. M. (1977). Extending sequence-class membership with matching to sample. *Journal of the Experimental Analysis of Behavior, 27,* 381–392.

Lazar, R. M., Davis-Lang, D., & Sanchez, L. (1984). The formation of visual stimulus equivalences in children. *Journal of the Experimental Analysis of Behavior, 41,* 241–266.

Lazar, R. M., & Kotlarchyk, B. J. (1986). Second-order control of sequence-class membership. *Behavioural Processes, 13,* 205–215.

Lynch, D. C., & Cuvo, A. J. (1995). Stimulus equivalence instruction of fraction–decimal relations. *Journal of Applied Behavior Analysis, 28,* 115–126.

Lynch, D. C., & Green, G. (1991). Development and crossmodal transfer of contextual control of emergent stimulus relations. *Journal of the Experimental Analysis of Behavior, 56,* 139–154.

MacDonald, R. P. F., Dixon, L. S., & LeBlanc, J. M. (1986). Stimulus class formation following observational learning. *Analysis and Intervention in Developmental Disabilities, 6,* 73–87.

Mackay, H. A. (1991). Conditional stimulus control. In I. Iversen & K. A. Lattal (Eds.), *Experimental analysis of behavior, Part I* (pp. 301–350). London: Elsevier Science Publishers.

Maydak, M., Stromer, R., Mackay, H. A., & Stoddard, L. T. (1995). Stimulus classes in matching to sample and sequence production: The emergence of numeric relations. *Research in Devlepmental Disabilities, 16,* 179–204.

McIlvane, W. J., & Dube, W. V. (1996). Naming as a facilitator of discrimination. *Journal of the Experimental Analysis of Behavior, 65,* 267–272.

McIlvane, W. J., Dube, W. V., Green, G., & Serna, R. W. (1993). Programming conceptual and communication skill development: A methodological stimulus-class analysis. In A. P. Kaiser & D. B. Gray (Eds.), *Enhancing children's communication: Research foundations for intervention* (pp. 243–285). Baltimore: Brookes.

McIlvane, W. J., Withstandley, J. K., & Stoddard, L. T. (1984). Positive and negative stimulus relations in severely retarded individuals' conditional discrimination. *Analysis and Intervention in Developmental Disabilities, 4,* 235–251.

Michael, R. L., & Bernstein, D. J. (1991). Transient effects of acquisition history on generalization in a matching-to-sample task. *Journal of the Experimental Analysis of Behavior, 56,* 155–166.

Miller, N. E., & Dollard, J. (1941). *Social learning and imitation.* New Haven, CT: Yale University Press.

Nevin J. A., Cumming, W. W., & Berryman, R. (1963). Ratio reinforcement of matching to sample. *Journal of the Experimental Analysis of Behavior, 6,* 149–154.

Peters, H. N. (1934). Mediate association. *Journal of Experimental Psychology, 18,* 20–48.

Pilgrim, C., & Galizio, M. (1990). Relations between baseline contingencies and equivalence probe performances. *Journal of the Experimental Analysis of Behavior, 54,* 213–224.

Saunders, K. J., Saunders, R. R., Williams, D. C., & Spradlin, J. E. (1993). An interaction of instructions and training design on stimulus class formation: Extending the analysis of equivalence. *The Psychological Record, 43,* 725–744.

Saunders, K. J., & Spradlin, J. E. (1989). Conditional discrimination in mentally retarded adults: The effect of training the component simple discriminations. *Journal of the Experimental Analysis of Behavior, 52,* 1–12.

Saunders, K. J., & Spradlin, J. E. (1996). Naming and equivalence relations. *Journal of the Experimental Analysis of Behavior, 56,* 304–308.

Saunders, R. R., & Green, G. (1992). The nonequivalence of behavioral and mathematical equivalence. *Journal of the Experimental Analysis of Behavior, 57,* 227–241.

Saunders, R. R., & Green, G. (1996). Naming is not (necessary for) stimulus equivalence. *Journal of the Experimental Analysis of Behavior, 56,* 312–314.

Saunders, R. R., Saunders, K. J., Kirby, K. C., & Spradlin, J. E. (1988). The merger of equivalence classes by unreinforced condtional selection of comparison stimuli. *Journal of the Experimental Analysis of Behavior, 50,* 145–162.

Saunders, R. R., Wachter, J. A., & Spradlin, J. E. (1988). Establishing auditory stimulus control over an eight-member equivalence class via conditional discrimination procedures. *Journal of the Experimental Analysis of Behavior, 49,* 95–115.

Shipley, W. C. (1935). Indirect conditioning. *Journal of General Psychology, 12,* 337–357.

Sidman, M. (1971). Reading and auditory-visual equivalences. *Journal of Speech and Hearing Research, 14,* 5–13.

Sidman, M. (1980). A note on the measurement of conditional discrimination. *Journal of the Experimental Analysis of Behavior, 33,* 285–289.

Sidman, M. (1981). Remarks. *Behaviorism, 9,* 127–129.

Sidman, M. (1986). Functional analysis of emergent verbal classes. In T. Thompson & M. D. Zeiler (Eds.), *Analysis and integration of behavioral units* (pp. 213–245). Hillsdale, NJ: Erlbaum.

Sidman, M. (1987). Two choices are not enough. *Behavior Analysis, 22,* 11–18.

Sidman, M. (1990). Equivalence relations: Where do they come from? In D. E. Blackman & H. Lejeune (Eds.), *Behaviour analysis in theory and practice: Contributions and controversies* (pp. 93–114). Hillsdale, NJ: Earlbaum.

Sidman, M. (1992). Equivalence relations: Some basic considerations. In S. C. Hayes & L. J. Hayes (Eds.), *Understanding verbal relations* (pp. 15–27). Reno, NV: Context Press.

Sidman, M. (1994). *Equivalence relations and behavior: A research story.* Boston: Authors Cooperative.

Sidman, M., & Cresson, O., Jr. (1973). Reading and crossmodal transfer of stimulus equivalences in severe retardation. *American Journal of Mental Deficiency, 77,* 515–523.

Sidman, M., Cresson, O., Jr., & Willson-Morris, M. (1974). Acquisition of matching-to-sample via mediated transfer. *Journal of the Experimental Analysis of Behavior, 22,* 261–273.

Sidman, M., Kirk, B., & Willson-Morris, M. (1985). Six-member stimulus classes generated by conditional-discrimination procedures. *Journal of the Experimental Analysis of Behavior, 43,* 21–42.

Sidman, M., Rauzin, R., Lazar, R., Cunningham, S., Tailby, W., & Carrigan, P. (1982). A search for symmetry in the conditional discrimination of rhesus monkeys, baboons, and children. *Journal of the Experimental Analysis of Behavior, 37,* 23–44.

Sidman, M., & Tailby, W. (1982). Conditional discriminations vs. matching-to-sample: An expansion of the testing paradigm. *Journal of the Experimental Analysis of Behavior, 37,* 5–22.

Sidman, M., Willson-Morris, M., & Kirk, B. (1986). Matching-to-sample procedures and the development of equivalence relations: The role of naming. *Analysis and Intervention of Developmental Disabilities, 6,* 1–20.

Sidman, M., Wynne, C. K., Maquire, R. W., & Barnes, T. (1989). Functional classes and equivalence relations. *Journal of the Experimental Analysis of Behavior, 52,* 261–274.

Sigurdardottir, Z. G., Green, G., & Saunders, R. R. (1990). Equivalence classes generated by sequence training. *Journal of the Experimental Analysis of Behavior, 53,* 47–63.

Skinner, B. F. (1938). *The behavior of organisms.* New York: Appleton–Century–Crofts.

Spradlin, J. E., Cotter, V. W., & Baxley, N. (1973). Establishing a conditional discrimination without direct training: A study of transfer with retarded adolescents. *American Journal of Mental Deficiency, 77,* 556–566.

Spradlin, J. E., & Dixon, M. H. (1976). Establishing conditional discriminations without direct training: Stimulus classes and labels. *American Journal of Mental Deficiency, 80,* 555–561.

Spradlin, J. E., & Saunders, R. R. (1984). Behaving appropriately in new situations: A stimulus class analysis. *American Journal of Mental Deficiency, 88,* 574–579.

Spradlin, J. E., & Saunders, R. (1986). The development of stimulus classes using match-to-sample procedures: Sample classification versus comparison classification. *Analysis and Intervention in Developmental Disabilities, 6,* 41–58.

Steele, D., & Hayes, S. C. (1991). Stimulus equivalence and arbitrarily applicable relational responding. *Journal of the Experimental Analysis of Behavior, 56,* 519–555.

Stikeleather, G., & Sidman, M. (1990). An instance of spurious equivalence relations. *The Analysis of Verbal Behavior, 8,* 1–11.

Stromer, R., & Mackay, H. A. (1993). Delayed identity matching to complex samples: Teaching students with mental retardation spelling and the prerequisites for equivalence classes. *Research in Developmental Disabilities, 14,* 19–38.

Stromer, R., & Osborne, J. G. (1982). Control of adolescents' arbitrary matching-to-sample by positive and negative stimulus relations. *Journal of the Experimental Analysis of Behavior, 37,* 329–348.

Tierney, K. J., De Largy, P., & Bracken, M. (1995). Formation of an equivalence class incorporating haptic stimuli. *The Psychological Record, 45,* 431–437.

Urcuioli, P. J. & Zentall, T. R. (1993). A test of comparison–stimulus substitutability following one-to-many matching by pigeons. *The Psychological Record, 43,* 745–759.

Urcuioli, P. J., Zentall, T. R., Jackson-Smith, P., & Steirn, J. N. (1989). Evidence for common coding in many-to-one matching: Retention, intertrial interference, and transfer. *Journal of Experimental Psychology: Animal Behavior Processes, 15,* 264–273.

Wetherby, B., Karlan, G. R., & Spradlin, J. E. (1983). The development of derived stimulus relations through training in arbitrary-matching sequences. *Journal of the Experimental Analysis of Behavior, 40,* 69–78.

Williams, D. C., Saunders, K. J., Saunders, R. R., & Spradlin, J. E. (1995). Unreinforced conditional selection within three-choice conditional discriminations. *The Psychological Record, 45,* 613–627.

Wulfert, E., & Hayes, S. C. (1988). Transfer of a conditional ordering response through conditional equivalence classes. *Journal of the Experimental Analysis of Behavior, 44,* 411–439.

Zimmerman, J., & Ferster, C. B. (1963). Intermittent punishment of S– responding in matching-to-sample. *Journal of the Experimental Analysis of Behavior, 6,* 349–356.

Zygmont, D. M., Lazar, R. M., Dube, W. V., & McIlvane, W. J. (1992). Teaching arbitrary matching via sample stimulus-control shaping to young children and mentally retarded individuals: A methodological note. *Journal of the Experimental Analysis of Behavior, 57,* 109–117.

9

Remembering and Forgetting

John T. Wixted

In its most common usage, the word *memory* refers to an assemblage of mental representations of past experience. To study memory from this point of view is to study the structures and processes that have evolved to store and manipulate these representations. In its behavior-analytic sense, by contrast, memory refers not to static mental entities but to the potential to manifest in behavior the effects of past experience. To study memory from this point of view is to study behavior that reflects a previously presented stimulus (i.e., remembering) or the loss of that kind of stimulus control (i.e., forgetting). The vast majority of memory research with humans has been performed with the former interpretation in mind, but many of the techniques developed in that literature are well-suited to the behavioral analysis of remembering and forgetting as well.

Why would anyone be interested in studying memory from a behavior-analytic point of view? One compelling answer to this question was given by Watkins (1990). This article was recently reprinted in *The Behavior Analyst* because of its obvious appeal to behaviorally oriented psychologists. In essence, Watkins argued that the experimental analysis of memory has reached a dead end because of the field's heavy reliance on *mediationism,* according to which the act of remembering is best explained by the existence of a mental representation (or trace) that bridges the gap between the occurrence of an event and the remembering of that event. This practice, according to Watkins, has shifted attention away from behavior and toward an ever-growing and increasingly complicated collection of hypothetical constructs and processes that are impervious to empirical disconfirmation. As an alternative, Watkins suggests focusing on empirical laws relating the stimulus conditions that prevail during learning to the behavior we call remembering. This chapter reviews some of the techniques and procedures that might be used to advance such an endeavor. Before describing what those methods are, a brief review of traditional memory terminology is in order. Although some of these terms are associated with theoretical constructs and hypothetical mental pro-

John T. Wixted • Department of Psychology, University of California at San Diego, La Jolla, California 92093-0109.

Handbook of Research Methods in Human Operant Behavior, edited by Lattal and Perone. Plenum Press, New York, 1998.

cesses, their importance from a behavior-analytic point of view lies in the procedural and conceptual distinctions to which they refer (Wixted, 1989).

THE LANGUAGE OF MEMORY

All learned behavior, including classically conditioned eye blinks and simple
operants such as a keypeck, can be construed as involving memory. Several comprehensive memory classification schemes have been proposed in recent years that
attempt to organize all learned behavior according to the different types of memory they reflect (e.g., Squire, Knowlton, & Musen, 1993). Rather than focus on the
entire gamut of learned behavior, however, the present chapter will focus on the
analysis of behavior that (most would agree) qualifies as remembering. This section outlines some of the language used by researchers involved in the study of remembering in humans. Behavior analysts might prefer a different terminology, but
it is important for anyone planning to conduct research in this area to be aware of
some of the conceptual distinctions that have guided research in this area for most
of the twentieth century.

Short-Term versus Long-Term Memory

Perhaps the most fundamental and well-known distinction is that between
short-term and long-term memory. In their simplest usage, these terms refer to
nothing more than the approximate time interval since the discriminative stimulus was last presented. Tests of short-term memory typically involve delay intervals that range up to 30 seconds or so, with tests of long-term memory involving
delays of days, weeks, or even years.

A distinction based only on temporal parameters is not really very helpful because it is easy to imagine situations in which the time since stimulus presentation is irrelevant. For example, if the stimulus in question is a phone number, a
simple and effective mnemonic strategy is to repeat the phone number continuously until the call is made. Under these conditions, it does not matter if the delay interval is less than 10 or greater than 60 seconds. No forgetting is likely to occur because the effective delay interval is continuously reset to zero by means of
behavioral strategy (rehearsal). Thus, an alternative and more useful interpretation
of the difference between short-term and long-term memory is that the former involves the continuous, uninterrupted control of responding by a stimulus whereas the latter involves the noncontinuous, delayed control by a stimulus. Although
both cases constitute valid examples of remembering, they are quite distinct. Indeed, the well-known amnesic H. M. can easily remember the name of a new acquaintance for an indefinite period of time so long as the name is continuously repeated. By contrast, if H. M.'s behavior is momentarily controlled by another
stimulus (e.g., if he engages in a brief conversation with another person), the name
is lost forever. Unlike normal subjects, H. M. cannot learn a new name (Ogden &
Corkin, 1991).

Note that this chapter will be primarily concerned with delayed stimulus control, which is what others would refer to as long-term memory (even though the
amount of time between stimulus presentation and the behavior it controls may be

quite small). The critical feature of an experiment concerned with delayed stimulus control is an intervening period of time during which behavior is brought under the control of another stimulus. In experiments concerned with the study of long-term memory, this is usually accomplished by means of a distractor task. That is, while subjects may be given a list of pictures or a story to memorize, a short irrelevant task intervenes between study and test. A common distractor task used in verbal learning studies is counting backwards by 3s, but many other tasks may be used.

Semantic versus Episodic Memory

A second dichotomy, advanced most recently by Endel Tulving (1972), distinguishes between responding based on cumulative learning across time and situations (semantic memory) versus responding based on a discrete prior learning experience (episodic memory). Asking a subject to name as many U.S. cities as possible is an example of a semantic memory task because the subject need not (and usually cannot) describe the situations under which each piece of information was acquired. Instead, the information was learned over time under many different conditions. In an episodic memory task, by contrast, the subject is required to identify a situationally specific stimulus. Thus, for example, asking a subject what he or she ate for breakfast that morning or to name the words on a recently presented list would represent tests of episodic memory.

As with the short-term/long-term memory distinction, cognitive psychologists regard episodic and semantic memory as different memory systems (perhaps subserved by different areas of the brain). Whether or not that is the case, the distinction also serves a useful purpose at the level of procedure, which is why it is considered here. Most of the studies discussed below would be classified as episodic (because the experimenter supplies the to-be-remembered material), but a few semantic memory studies will be considered as well.

Implicit versus Explicit Memory

A relatively recent distinction that currently commands a great deal of attention is that between explicit and implicit memory. Explicit memory tasks are those in which the subject is explicitly asked to remember a previously presented stimulus (whether presented during the course of the experiment or not), which is what is done in most human memory experiments. Implicit memory tasks, on the other hand, are indirect tests of memory because the subject is asked to perform some task that does not require, but may nevertheless reveal, the influence of a previous episode. Interest in this distinction is high, in part because amnesic subjects who are severely impaired on explicit memory tasks (be definition) are often unimpaired on implicit tasks (e.g., Warrington & Weiskrantz, 1970). An example of an implicit memory task is "mirror reading." At first, reading textual information in a mirror is a slow and difficult process because the image is reversed. With practice, however, the task becomes much easier. Amnesic subjects often show improvement on this task that rivals that of normal subjects even though the amnesic subjects have no recollection of having performed the task before.

Although the study of implicit memory is currently in high gear, the present chapter will mainly be concerned with tests of explicit memory. Only explicit memory tests set the occasion for what can properly be described as an act of remembering. The most commonly used tests in this regard involve either *recall or recognition.* In a recall test, the subject is asked to reproduce some facsimile of the stimulus in question. For example, the subject might be asked to say aloud or write down all of the words that were presented on a list 10 minutes ago, or to draw as accurately as possible a series of geometric forms that were presented earlier in a session, or to describe a crime enacted on a video that he or she watched the day before. In each case, a reproduction (in one form or another) of the original stimulus is required.

Unlike recall tests, recognition tests do not require the subject to generate previously presented stimuli. Instead, the experimenter presents those stimuli again and asks the subject to decide whether or not the item was seen before. Thus, for example, after studying a list of words, subjects may be presented with those words again and asked to decide whether or not they appeared on the list. Typically, half of the items are old (i.e., they did appear on the list) and half are new (i.e., they did not appear on the list), but other arrangements are certainly possible. In a lineup study, for example, the subject must decide whether or not a "criminal" seen earlier in a video clip is included in a set of six photographs. Alternatively, in a *continuous recognition* procedure, study and test are intermingled. In this procedure, subjects are asked to decide whether or not each item in a long list of items is being presented for the first time or whether it was presented earlier in the list.

The following sections review specific procedures used to investigate remembering in humans. Although the discussion to follow necessarily makes use of the terms presented above, the main emphasis is placed on how one might investigate remembering and forgetting from a behavior-analytic perspective. The first section considers a variety of procedures used to study the effect of reinforcement on recall and recognition. Subsequent sections consider procedures designed to investigate the rate and pattern of remembering and the role of interference in forgetting.

REINFORCEMENT AND HUMAN MEMORY

The last comprehensive review of the effects of reinforcement on human memory was provided by Nelson (1976), and anyone interested in this subject would be well-advised to consult that source. This section reviews some of the methods discussed by Nelson as well as a variety of additional methods a behavior analyst may wish to employ.

Reinforcement Manipulations during Study

A number of studies conducted in the early 1970s were concerned with the effect of reinforcement on learning that was later explicitly tested by means of recall or recognition. Loftus (1972), for example, used a recognition memory procedure in which subjects were presented with pairs of pictures to memorize. During study, subjects were informed that one picture of each pair would be worth nine points for being correctly recognized on a later test whereas the other would be worth only one point. As might be expected, the number of eye fixations to the high-value pictures was greater than to the low-value pictures during list presentation (although that behavior was not itself reinforced). On the subsequent recognition test, subjects were also more likely to correctly recognize high-value pictures than low-value pictures. However, when the data were plotted according to the number of eye fixations a picture received, no effect of reinforcer magnitude was observed. That is, regardless of its assigned value, if a picture happened to receive few fixations during study it was unlikely to be recognized on a later test, but if it happened to receive many fixations during study the probability of correct recognition was high. Thus, the reinforcement manipulation influenced study time, which in turn influenced the accuracy of recognition.

Nelson (1976) reported an interesting study along the same lines that varied reinforcement magnitude either between-subjects or within-subjects. In the between-subject design, subjects studied a list of 40 words and were later asked to recall the words in any order they wished. Half of the subjects (the low-value group) were told they would receive 1 cent for each word correctly recalled. The other half (the high-value group) were told they would receive 10 cents for each correctly recalled word. In agreement with many other studies of this kind, the manipulation was essentially ineffective (probably because subjects were already sufficiently motivated to attend to the task even without a financial incentive). In the within-subject design, by contrast, some of the words on the list were designated as low-value words (1 cent for each one correctly recalled) and others were designated a high-value words (10 cents for each one correctly recalled). When reinforcement magnitude was manipulated in this manner, the effect on subsequent performance was quite large, with the advantage going to the high-value words. Note that his within-subject manipulation is like the one reported by Loftus (1972) for pictures, and the result was basically the same. Thus, although adult subjects are generally sufficiently motivated to perform to the best of their ability (which is why the between-subject manipulation was ineffective), it is possible to differentially manipulate attention within a list by varying reinforcer magnitude associated with the remembering response.

Cuvo (1974) reported findings in direct support of the idea that monetary incentive can be used to influence which words subjects study and rehearse (and, therefore, which words they are most likely to subsequently recall). This study also illustrates a procedural detail that will be of particular interest to behavioral psychologists involved in the study of remembering and forgetting. As in the within-subject condition of Nelson's study, subjects were asked to learn a list of words, some of which would earn the subject 10 cents if correctly recalled (and these words were designated as such) and some of which earn 1 cent. While learning the list, subjects were instructed to repeat aloud any words they happened to be thinking about. This overt rehearsal procedure renders behavior that is ordinarily covert observable (cf. Fischler, Rundus, & Atkinson, 1970; Rundus, 1971). Cuvo found that the effect of reinforcer magnitude on later recall was mediated by differential rehearsal. That is, high-value words were rehearsed to a greater extent and were more likely to be recalled than low-value words. When rehearsal was prevented by means of a distractor task during list presentation, on the other hand, the effect of monetary incentive was not significant. Similar findings have been reported by a number of research groups (Eysenck & Eysenck, 1982; Kuzinger & Witryol, 1984).

Note that the results discussed above suggest that, under certain conditions, reinforcement manipulations can affect the *amount* of rehearsal applied to different items in a list (i.e., a higher reinforcer magnitude induces subjects to selectively rehearse the high-value words). Although the issue has not yet been extensively investigated, it seems likely that reinforcement manipulations could also be used to affect the *kind* of rehearsal an item receives. Wixted and McDowell (1989), for example, showed that when the amount of overt rehearsal was held constant for different thirds of a 15-item list, the effects on delayed recall varied considerably. In this study, subjects were instructed to overtly rehearse 5 items from the list for 15 seconds. The remaining 10 items were presented very rapidly and therefore received very little rehearsal. Sometimes the 5 rehearsed items were the first 5 items of the list, sometimes the second 5, and sometimes the last 5. Each list was followed by free recall. At the end of the session an unexpected delayed recall test was administered for all of the previously studied lists (cf. Craik, 1970). Even though the original amount of overt rehearsal was the same for different thirds of the list, the effect of rehearsal on the 5 items at the beginning of each list was much more pronounced than the effect of rehearsal on the last 5 items of each list. Indeed, the latter items were no more likely to be recalled than items receiving no rehearsal.

Effects like these are usually explained by differing kinds of rehearsal. The general conclusion is that elaborative rehearsal (e.g., forming associations, creating mental images) facilitates later recall whereas maintenance rehearsal (rote repetition) does not. In the study discussed above, subjects presumably relied on elaborative rehearsal for items at the beginning of each list (because they knew more items were on the way) and maintenance rehearsal for items at the end of each list (because they knew those items could be rehearsed right up to the point of recall). In one of the few studies of its kind, Bauer and Peller-Porth (1990) found evidence that reinforcement manipulations can influence the kind of rehearsal an item receives. More specifically, they found that the use of monetary reinforcement for correct recall increased the number of items recalled from early list positions in children (including some learning-disabled children) but had no effect on recall for words occupying later positions in the list. They interpreted their findings in terms of incentive-induced elaborative rehearsal applied to the initial items of a list.

Research on differing types of rehearsal may seem foreign to many behavior analysts. However, it is important to keep in mind that "rehearsal" is nothing more than behavior governed by prevailing reinforcement contingencies (whether those contingencies are specified by the experimenter or not). The fact that this behavior is ordinarily covert creates special complications but does not impose an insurmountable obstacle. Moreover, the fact that elaborative rehearsal affects later recall, whereas rote repetition does not, is a simple principle of behavior, not a theory. Cognitive theories of the kind Watkins (1990) criticized seek to explain *why* elaborative rehearsal has the effects it does (e.g., elaborative rehearsal creates multiple retrieval routes to the memory trace), but, thus far, those theories add little to the principle of behavior they seek to explain. Although cognitive theories of that kind certainly fall outside the domain of behavior analysis, the investigation of be-havior–behavior relationships (e.g., the effect of elaborative rehearsal on later re-call) should not.

Reinforcement Manipulations during a Recall Test

Can reinforcement be used to influence the likelihood that something will be correctly recalled after the study phase is completed? To investigate this issue, re-searchers do not explain the reinforcement contingencies to the subject until they are about to be tested. Thus, for example, subjects might be asked to study a list of words for later recall. Following a distractor task, one group of subjects might be informed that each correctly recalled word will be reinforced with a relatively large amount of money and another group would be informed that each correctly recalled word will be reinforced with a relatively small amount of money. Typi-cally, this manipulation has little or no effect on performance (e.g., Heinrich, 1968), although an interesting exception is discussed below.

Loftus and Wickens (1970) showed that, under certain conditions, reinforce-ment contingencies manipulated at test can affect the accuracy of recall. In this study, subjects studied nonsense syllables paired with letters (e.g., DAX-P). On a later test, the nonsense syllable was presented as a cue and the subject was asked to supply the letter with which it has been paired. The critical feature of this ex-periment was that the trials were self-paced. That is, subjects were free to spend as much time as they wished trying to recall the associated letter before moving on to the next item. Note that this is unlike the typical study in which recall time is fixed. Loftus and Wickens found that recall performance was enhanced at test when the stimulus (e.g., DAX-) was designated as a high-value item (such that cor-rect recall would yield a relatively large reinforcer) compared with when the stim-ulus was designated as a low-value item. Reaction-time data suggested that this ef-fect occurred because subjects spent more time in the presence of a high-value stimulus (before moving on to the next item) relative to a low-value stimulus. Be-cause recall is not an instantaneous process (a point considered in much more de-tail later), the more time spent in the presence of the stimulus, the more likely the subject was to eventually produce the correct response. Thus, whenever time to recall is allowed to freely vary, reinforcement is likely to influence performance.

Note that in free recall (in which subjects are asked to recall all previously pre-sented items in any order), it is not possible to vary reinforcement magnitude on an item-by-item basis. In cued recall, however, it is possible. The study reported by Loftus and Wickens represents one example of how this can be done, but many other possibilities exist. For example, imagine that subjects were given a long list of words (say, 60) to study, followed by a free recall test. A subject who could suc-cessfully recall 20 words from the list would probably require about 15 minutes or more to do so. Unfortunately for the experimenter, recalling words is only one of several activities the subject might engage in for those 15 minutes. That is to say, the rate of reinforcement for extraneous activity (r_e) unrelated to recall may not be zero even in a bleak running room equipped with nothing more than a computer. Thus, if the payoff for correct recall is low, other stimuli in the environment may begin to control the subject's behavior after just a few minutes (such that the recall total would never reach 20 words). If the payoff is high relative to r_e, on the other hand, time devoted to remembering would probably increase considerably (and correspondingly more words would be recalled). Students of the matching law will recognize this argument as a variant of Herrnstein's (1970) interpretation of behavior (for additional information, see Mazur, Chapter 5). According to this account, the effect of a given rate of reinforcement on an operant response (e.g., a pigeon pecking a key) will vary inversely with the amount of extraneous reinforcement (r_e). A similar idea may apply in the case of free recall. The details of how one might quantify the flow of remembering in a free recall task (and thereby more precisely measure the effects of a reinforcement manipulation, for example) is covered in more detail in a later section concerned with the rate and pattern of remembering.

The examples discussed above illustrate the effect of reinforcement on recall. The results essentially show that reinforcement manipulations can affect performance by influencing time on task. If time to recall is fixed by the experimenter, reinforcement manipulations have little or no effect. The next section considers the effects of reinforcement manipulations on recognition.

Reinforcement Manipulations during a Recognition Test

In a yes/no recognition experiment, test items are presented one at a time during the test phase and the subject must indicate whether or not the item appeared on the list. One cannot study the effect of reinforcement on recognition performance without first considering the dependent measure used to assess performance. At first glance, the most natural dependent measure to use in a situation such as this is the same one used for recall, namely, the percentage of correct responses. However, the use of percent correct as the dependent measure can easily lead to incorrect conclusions about the role of a reinforcement manipulation (or any other manipulation for that matter).

The subject's responses on a yes/no recognition test can be classified according to a 2-by-2 matrix formed by the combination of the response (yes or no) and the item's status (old or new). If the item is old (i.e., if it did appear on the list), a yes response is termed a *hit* whereas a no response is termed a *miss*. If the item is new (i.e., if it did not appear on the list), a yes response is termed a *false alarm* whereas a no response is termed a *correct rejection*. Thus, the hit *rate* is the proportion of old test trials in which the subject correctly reported yes and the false alarm *rate* is the proportion of new test trials in which the subject incorrectly reported yes. The hit and false alarm rates provide the information needed to assess a subject's performance.

Note that if a subject is asked to respond in a liberal manner, the percentage of yes responses will increase (thereby increasing both the hit and the false alarm rate). If that same subject is then asked to respond in a conservative manner, the percentage of yes responses will decrease (thereby decreasing both hit and false alarm rates). Although the percentage of correct responses will usually change considerably as a result of this manipulation (because the change in hits will not exactly offset the change in false alarms), other measures designed to capture discriminability independent of the biasing manipulation will (ideally, at least) remain essentially constant.

Signal Detection Theory

As discussed by Irwin and McCarthy (Chapter 10), the most commonly used dependent measure on a task such as this is d' of signal detection theory (which also yields a measure of bias, β). Figure 9.1 illustrates the signal detection analysis of yes/no recognition data. The abscissa represents strength of evidence (a subjective variable) that an individual test item was seen before. The analysis assumes that the evidence variable associated with new test items (i.e., lures) varies from trial to trial according to a Gaussian distribution. The evidence variable associated with old items (i.e., targets) is also normally distributed and is, on average, stronger than that associated with new items. The vertical line c represents the subject's decision criterion. On trials in which evidence exceeds c, the subject responds positively, otherwise the response is negative.

The placement of the criterion c and the distance between the two distributions (d') determine the pattern of hits, misses, correct rejections, and false alarms. Whereas d' is determined by trial-specific factors (e.g., study time), the position of c is determined by the biasing condition. In the liberal biasing condition, the criterion would be placed more to the left, whereas in the conservative biasing condition, it would be placed more to the right. The hit rate and false alarm rate from an experimental condition can be taken to a reference table and used to determine d' and β (e.g., McNicol, 1972). Similar measures can be derived from a less theoretical detection account described by Davison and Tustin (1978).

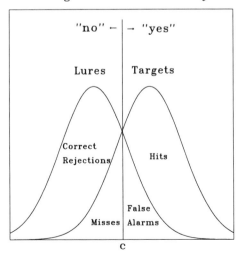

FIGURE 9.1. A graphical illustration of signal detection theory. The target and lure distributions correspond to previously seen and previously unseen test items, respectively. The decision criterion is represented by c. When strength of evidence exceeds c, the subject responds "yes," otherwise the response is "no."

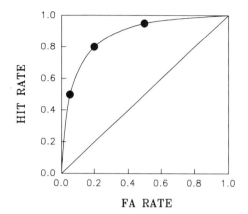

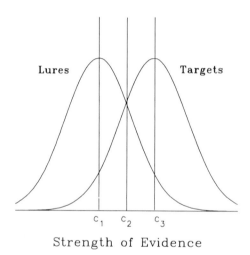

FIGURE 9.2. (Top) Hypothetical ROC plot for three biasing conditions. (Bottom) Signal detection representation of the ROC data (c_1, c_2, and c_3 represent three different criterion placements that might result from a reinforcement manipulation).

ROC Analysis. One advantage of using the yes/no recognition procedure is that a receiver operating characteristic (ROC) analysis can be performed on the data to answer interesting theoretical questions. An ROC plot depicts the hit rate versus false alarm rate obtained from several (at least three) biasing conditions in which memory variables like study time and delay interval are held constant. Figure 9.2 depicts a hypothetical ROC curve (top panel) and corresponding signal detection interpretation (bottom panel). The point higher and to the right in the ROC reflects a liberal criterion for giving a "yes" response (corresponding to c_1 in the bottom panel). The point lower and to the left reflects a conservative criterion for giving a "yes" response (corresponding to c_3). Some older and intuitively appealing theories predict that the form of this function will be linear. Indeed, "high threshold theory," which once prevailed as an account of recognition memory, predicts a linear relationship between the hit rate and false alarm rate (Green & Swets, 1966). The Gaussian distributions of signal detection theory are consistent with the curvilinear shape shown in the figure. The shape of this function also serves as a test of the assumption that the new and old distributions have equal variances. If so, the curve will be symmetrical about the diagonal, otherwise a more serpentine path will be traced out by the data points.

ROC plots are best analyzed using data from individual subjects rather than using hit rates and false alarm rates averaged over subjects. This generally means that subjects should be run for multiple sessions during which they learn and attempt to recognize multiple lists of words. Ratcliff, Sheu, and Gronlund (1992), for example, tested four subjects for 20 recognition sessions during which they learned 10 lists per session. Bias was manipulated by varying the probability that a test item was a target or a lure. For example, when 80% of the test items were lures (and subjects were informed of that fact), response bias was tilted in favor of a "no" response. When 80% of the test items were targets, bias was tilted in favor of a "yes" response. Over the 20 sessions, a sufficient amount of data was collected to permit an ROC analysis for each subject. The ROC data were not perfectly symmetrical, suggesting that the most accurate detection representation would involve a target distribution with slightly greater variance than the lure distribution.

Effect of Reinforcement on Bias in Recognition. Instead of varying the mix of target and lures on the recognition test to influence bias, reinforcement contingencies can be manipulated. Thus, for example, when a correct "yes" response yields a much larger reinforcer (or a higher probability of reinforcement) than a correct "no" response, subjects will be much more inclined to give "yes" responses (and give "no" responses only when they are certain the test item did not appear on the list). Although such effects have not been thoroughly investigated, the general assumption is that monetary incentives affect criterion placement (i.e., bias) without affecting d' (e.g., Zimmerman & Kimble, 1973). However, this is an issue that probably needs to be examined in greater detail. In the animal literature, for example, reinforcement manipulations in discrimination tasks can affect both bias (the general inclination to choose one alternative) and discriminability (the ability to distinguish between two previously presented sample stimuli). The literature on the differential outcomes effect in animals shows this quite clearly (e.g., Santi & Roberts, 1985). That may be true in humans as well, in which case signal detection theory would not unambiguously disentangle these two measures of performance.

Baron and Surdy (1990), in one of the few human memory studies reported in the *Journal of the Experimental Analysis of Behavior,* used a continuous recognition procedure to study the effect of reinforcement on bias and discriminability (i.e., remembering) in older and younger adults. As indicated earlier, a continuous recognition procedure intermingles the study and test phases of the experiment. During a session, a long string of items is presented and some of the items are occasionally repeated and for every item, the subject must decide (yes or no) whether or not it was presented earlier in the series. Baron and Surdy manipulated the type of stimuli used (alphanumeric strings, words, or sentence) and manipulated the payoff matrix to influence bias as well. Their results showed that accuracy (measured by A', which is conceptually similar to d') was lower for older subjects, and the reinforcement manipulation affected bias to a greater extent in younger subjects. This latter result suggested that older subjects tended to adopt a more rigid response style than younger subjects. That is, when reinforcement contingencies change in a recognition procedure, older subjects do not adapt to the changed contingencies as readily as younger subjects. This result may or may not be restricted to the domain of remembering, but this study nevertheless illustrates the potential value of a behavioral analysis of human recognition.

Detection Theory and Behavior Analysis. Classical detection theory obviously entails slightly more theoretical assumptions than most accounts in behavior analysis. However, it is worth noting that the classical model has stood the test of time in a way that other theoretical accounts have not. Indeed, its developmental history is quite unlike that associated with the personalized cognitive theories described by Watkins (1990). Unlike most models, signal detection theory has not been relentlessly embellished with a collection of trace features, time tags, mental conveyor belts, and the like. Instead, as applied to a simple yes/no recognition task, it is exactly the same theory that was introduced to psychology more than 30 years ago. The theory avoids gratuitous embellishment because it is mathematically precise and self-contained (constrained as it is by the shape of an ROC). Indeed, the theory can be viewed as merely one way to represent behavioral data (as much a tool as a theory). Unlike unconstrained cognitive models that become increasingly divorced from the empirical world over time, important components of signal detection theory (e.g., the location of the decision criterion) are directly translatable into behavior. The next section considers some issues concerning criterion placement that may be of particular interest to behavior analysts.

Reinforcement and Confidence in Recognition Decisions

Yes/no recognition decisions are sometimes made with little or no confidence and sometimes made with great confidence. Asking a subject to supply a confidence rating for each response introduces a new and interesting angle to consider. How are those ratings to be interpreted and why would anyone, especially a behavior analyst, be interested in them? On the surface, the analysis of subjective ratings may seem to be better suited to cognitive psychology than behavior analysis. However, despite appearances to the contrary, this is one area of research where the information processing perspective encounters an uncomfortable dilemma that is rather easily explained in terms of a subject's reinforcement history.

The Confidence-Based ROC Analysis

The signal detection framework discussed above can be readily extended to the analysis of confidence judgments. As a first step, ROC plots can be produced by computing hit and false alarm rates separately for each confidence rating (instead of for different biasing conditions). Consider, for example, an experiment in which each yes or no judgment is accompanied by a confidence rating on a 1 to 3 scale (ranging from guessing to absolute certainty). With this scheme, the possible responses to any test item are *no-3, no-2, no-1, yes-1, yes-2, or yes-3* in increasing order of confidence that the test item appeared on the list. Note that this provides a richer set of data to analyze than is provided by simple yes or no responses.

For the target items (i.e., those that were on the list), a hit rate can be determined separately for each confidence rating by simply computing the proportion of targets that receive a rating at least as high as the confidence rating in question. Every target receives a rating of at least no-3 (because no-3 is the lowest possible rating), so a meaningful hit rate for this confidence rating cannot be computed (i.e., the hit rate is always 1.0 for the no-3 rating). However, a smaller proportion of targets (perhaps .95) receives a confidence rating of at least no-2 (i.e., no-2, no-1, yes-1, yes-2, or yes-3). That proportion is the "hit" rate associated with the no-2 confidence criterion even though, technically, any targets receiving a response of no-2 or no-1 represent incorrect responses. In a similar way, one can compute the hit rate associated with the no-1 criterion by calculating the proportion of target responses that receive a rating of at least no-1. Continuing in this manner yields five meaningful hit rates, one each for no-2, no-1, yes-1, yes-2, and yes-3. False alarm rates for each of these five confidence criteria can be computed in exactly the same way. The false alarm rate for the no-2 confidence criterion, for example, is the proportion of *lures* receiving a rating of at least no-2, and the false alarm rate for the no-1 confidence criterion is the proportion of lures receiving a rating of at least no-1. The five hit and false alarm rates produced in this manner can be used to construct an ROC (which, again, is simply a plot of hit rate versus false alarm rate). Almost invariably, the procedure yields an orderly (and quite typical) ROC plot (MacMillan & Creelman, 1991).

Figure 9.3 shows the signal detection interpretation of the confidence-based ROC. The locations of the five confidence criteria are nothing more than direct translations of the five false alarm rates. The criteria are placed such that the proportion of the lure distribution exceeding each criterion corresponds to the false alarm rate associated with that criterion. For example, if 2.5% of the lures receive

FIGURE 9.3. A graphical illustration of the signal detection interpretation of confidence judgments. Each vertical line represents a different confidence criterion. When strength of evidence exceeds y_3, a high-confident yes response is given. When it exceeds y_2 but no y_3, a less confident yes response is given (i.e., yes-2). Similarly, if strength of evidence falls above n_2 but below n_1, a response of no-2 if given. Note that if evidence falls below n_2, a high-confident no response is given (i.e., no-3).

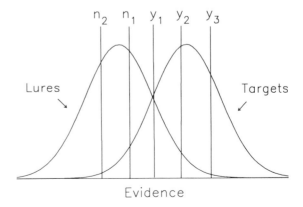

a high-confident yes response (i.e., if the false alarm rate for yes-3 is 2.5%), then the yes-3 criterion is assumed to be located 2 standard deviations above the mean of the lure distribution (such that only 2.5% of the lure distribution falls to the right of yes-3). If 50% of the lures receive a response of no-1 or greater, then the no-1 criterion is located at the mean of the lure distribution (such that half of that distribution falls to the right of no-1). Similarly, the target distribution is positioned in such a way that the proportion of the signal distribution to the right of each confidence criterion is equal to the hit rate associated with the level of confidence. For the sake of simplicity, equal variance distributions are assumed in this example (although that assumption need not be made). The smooth curve drawn through the ROC data represents the locus of points that would be produced by an infinite number of confidence criteria.

One question of interest is how the ROC plots (and corresponding signal detection representations) change as a function of discriminability (i.e., d'). To answer this question, one merely manipulates discriminability (e.g., by manipulating study time) and plots the confidence-based ROCs for each condition. To avoid carry-over effects in the use of the confidence scale, the two discriminability conditions should probably be run in separate sessions. Figure 9.4 shows a representative finding from my laboratory. In this study, 14 subjects studied two lists of 48 words in each of two sessions. Each of the four lists (two in each session) was followed by a yes/no recognition test involving the 48 targets randomly intermixed with 48 lures. During the recognition tests, subjects were asked to decide whether or not the item appeared on the previous list (yes of no) and to supply a confidence rating (1 to 5). In one session (the weak condition), the words comprising each list were presented at a rate of one per second. In another session (the strong condition), the words were presented three times each during list presentation. The left panel of Figure 9.4 shows the confidence-based ROCs using group data, and the right panel shows the signal detection interpretation of these results (the identical analysis performed on individual subject data showed these findings to be representative of individual subjects). The finding of interest here is that the confidence criteria fan out as d' decrease (which is tantamount to saying that the points in behavioral ROC data spread out).

This fan effect is just what one venerable information-processing theory of discriminability predicts. That theory states that subjects place their criteria in such a way as to maintain constant likelihood ratios (e.g., Glanzer, Adams, Iverson, & Kim, 1993). Thus, for example, the yes-3 criterion might always be placed at the point where (say) the odds are 10 to 1 in favor of a yes response being correct (regardless of what d' is). That is, no matter what d' might be, the yes-3 criterion will be placed at the point where the height of the target distribution is 10 times that of the noise distribution. Although not intuitively obvious, this theory requires the fan effect shown in Figure 9.4.

This theory makes the right prediction, but even many cognitively oriented psychologists are dubious of the likelihood ratio account because of the extensive knowledge and considerable computational ability the theory assumes that subjects have in their possession. Specifically, in order to maintain a constant likelihood ratio of 10 to 1 for yes-3, subjects would need to know the mathematical forms of the target and lure distributions (Gaussian) and be able to compute the ratio of

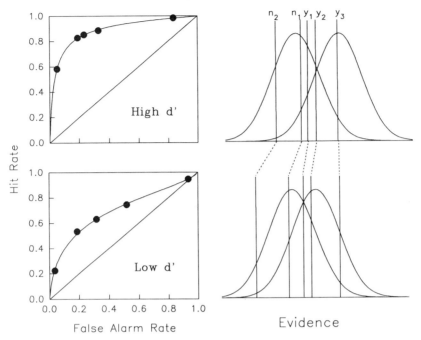

FIGURE 9.4. (Left) Two confidence-based ROC plots corresponding to two conditions in which discriminability was manipulated. (Right) Signal detection representation of the ROC plots.

the heights of those two distributions at a given point on the evidence axis. Assuming such abilities, subjects could, no matter what d' is, locate the point on the evidence axis where the height of the target distribution is 10 times that of the lure distribution and place the yes-3 criterion at that point. Doing so would ensure that the odds that a high-confident yes response is correct is always better than 10 to 1 (and the fan effect shown in Figure 9.4 would be observed).

The problem with this account is that it seems to throw the concept of parsimony to the winds. Even if subjects are aware of the Gaussian shapes of the target and lure distributions (which seems like a rather strong assumption), the further assumption that subjects can compute the ratio of two Gaussian distributions at a given point on the evidence axis stretches the imagination to the breaking point. Nevertheless, it is hard to imagine an information-processing explanation for the results shown in Figure 9.4 without appealing to this computationally intensive idea.

On the other hand, the result shown in Figure 9.4 is almost obvious when the subject's probable reinforcement history is taken into account. Indeed, when considered from this point of view, the likelihood ratio computation required by an information-processing account is readily seen as a surrogate for the subject's reinforcement history. Subjects do not step out of a vacuum into the experimental situation, but instead arrive after long training in the use of the English language. As part of that training, subjects have presumably encountered extensive feedback concerning expressions of confidence in their recognition decisions. Sometimes, perhaps, they have expressed a great deal of confidence in decisions that turned out to be wrong (and in those cases there may have been considerable consequences to pay). Other times, the subject may have expressed low confidence in recognition decisions that turned out to be correct, in which case the subject may have missed out on rewards that the verbal community may otherwise have offered (given that confidence is a highly regarded trait).

What would the effect of that kind of training be? Unless they are immune to the consequences of their behavior, subjects would learn that when conditions are unfavorable (e.g., when learning time was brief), one should be very conservative before giving a high-confident yes or not response. In terms of signal detection theory, this translates into a more conservative placement of the extreme no-2 and yes-3 criteria when d' is low. If a more conservative strategy were not adopted when conditions were unfavorable (e.g., if the criteria did not fan out), subjects would soon find themselves making many high-confident errors under those conditions.

The effect of consequences on confidence ratings has not been extensively investigated, but the area seems ripe for behavior analysis. Some general strategies that have been used in this regard are reviewed next. Note that, as evidenced by the discussion presented below, one need not adopt the signal detection model to investigate this issue in a productive way. Nevertheless, interpreting the results in terms of that relatively simple model offers a way to connect to the cognitive literature and directly contrast the interpretation of findings from a behavioral point of view versus an information-processing point of view.

The Experimental Analysis of the Effects of Feedback on Confidence

The developmental literature shows that, on a variety of tasks, young children exhibit confidence judgments that are poorly calibrated to accuracy compared with those of older children. In fact, young children have been referred to as "eternal optimists" because of their tendency to express high confidence in all of their decisions (Newman & Wick, 1987). With feedback, however, the calibration exhibited by both younger and older children improves. An example of the effect of feedback on confidence in a nonmemory task is provided by Newman and Wick (1987). They exposed children to a task in which they were required to estimate the number of random dots in a display and to report their confidence in each response. Some displays were relatively easy (involving relatively few dots) and some were hard (involving many dots). In the absence of feedback about whether or not the response was correct, subjects' confidence ratings were poorly calibrated to accuracy (i.e., confidence did not decrease as difficulty increased and performance worsened). Following feedback, however, the calibration exhibited by older children improved significantly (as it did for higher skilled younger children as well). That is, as accuracy decreased with increasing task difficulty, confidence decreased as well.

Dot counting is not the same as remembering, but this experiment serves to underscore the point that feedback can affect the validity of confidence judgments. Using a continuous recognition procedure, Berch and Evans (1973) found that even children in kindergarten were capable, to some extent, of monitoring the accuracy of their own performance. In this experiment, subjects were given a series of digits and asked to recognize each one as being new (i.e., as being presented for the first time) or old (i.e., as having appeared before in the series). Confidence judgments were obtained by having the child point to one of two pictures representing differing degrees of confidence. One picture showed a child with a puzzled expression (low confidence) and another showed a child with a self-satisfied smile (high confidence). Thus, a two-point confidence rating scale was used. The older children exhibited a clear awareness of their own abilities. That is, when accuracy was low, confidence was low as well (as it should be). The younger children show the same effect, but it was much less pronounced. Presumably, the younger children exhibited lower calibration because they had not yet experienced sufficient training in expressions of confidence. In terms of signal detection theory, the younger children would probably be less likely to exhibit the fan effect shown in Figure 9.4.

Very little research using adults has been directed at the effects of feedback on confidence in remembering, but a study by Stock, Kulhavy, Pridemore, and Krug (1992) is consistent with the ideas presented earlier. Subjects in this experiment completed self-paced general-knowledge multiple-choice questions (i.e., this was a semantic memory task) and provided a confidence rating for each response. The experimenter-supplied feedback (correct versus incorrect) after every response. The finding of interest was that subjects spent more time studying the feedback (before moving on to the next question) for high-confident errors than for low-confident errors. Similarly, they spent less time studying feedback for high-confident correct responses than for low-confident correct responses. The authors interpreted their findings in the following way: "These results were explained by the proposition that people try to reduce discrepancies between what they think they know and what feedback indicates they know" (p. 654). One can reasonably assume that the same happens in everyday life and that this, perhaps, accounts for what looks to be rather extraordinary likelihood ratio computation when a subject's learning history is ignored.

The limited amount of work reviewed above on the relationship between confidence and accuracy on the one hand and corrective feedback on the other shows that this area of research is wide open. The behavior-analytic community seems particularly well-suited to investigate these issues because it is unlikely to follow the information-processing path that ends with the necessary assumption that subjects are capable of extraordinary computational feats.

RATE OF AND PATTERN OF REMEMBERING

One of the defining features of early behavior analysis was a detailed inquiry into the rate and pattern of a continuous stream of behavior. That same approach applied to remembering may eventually prove to be equally fruitful. The act of remembering, at least by means of free recall, is generally not an instantaneous process, but instead occurs over an extended period of time. When a subject is asked to list as many foreign capitals as possible (a semantic memory task), or to recall a recently presented list of words (an episodic memory task), the result is almost always the same: a rapid burst of responding followed by a gradual decline to zero. Performance in this situation is perhaps best thought of as being under the control of multiple temporally remote stimuli, each competing for the control of behavior in a given instant (which is the behavioral interpretation of what a cognitive psychologist would call a *search set*). Almost all of the previous research on free recall has been concerned with the number or proportion of items correctly recalled. More interesting behavioral properties, such as the rate and pattern of free recall, have received scant attention. These are properties that seem to be of natural interest to the behavioral community, which has long been concerned with the rate of pattern of behavior maintained by schedules of reinforcement.

As indicated above, the time course of free recall can be studied using either semantic or episodic memory procedures. In a semantic memory procedure, the subject is simply asked to list as many items in a category as possible (e.g., "Name as many cities as you can think of"). The responses are timed, literally producing a cumulative record. Originally, timing methods were quite crude, but adequate. Subjects were asked to write down their responses (instead of saying them aloud) and to draw a line under the most recently recalled word every minute. In that way, the experimenter could later reconstruct cumulative progress (i.e., the number of words recalled up to each minute of the recall period).

Another timing method that more closely approximates the operations of a cumulative recorder was first used by Bousfield and Sedgewick (1944) and, apparently, next used by Wixted and Rohrer (1993). In this method, subjects are asked to recall items aloud and the *experimenter* taps a lever attached to a recording device. That device might be a rolling drum that traces out a record (Bousfield & Sedgewick, 1944) or a computer, which records the time of each response and permits the later plotting of progress in either cumulative or noncumulative form (Wixted & Rohrer, 1993). A voice-activated relay attached to a computer provides an even more accurate way to time recall. Figure 9.5 shows one recall record produced by a single subject studied by Bousfield and Sedgewick (1944). The subject was asked to name as many U.S. cities as possible and the resulting "kymographic" record is shown in the figure (estimated from their Figure 4). This figure clearly shows the negatively accelerated time course that typifies free recall.

The record presented in Figure 9.5 does not include repetitions. Thus, for example, if the subject said "Tucson" 10 seconds into the recall period and repeated that city 5 minutes later, only the first response would be included. Also, if the subject mistakenly said "Arkansas," the response key would not be depressed. Fortunately, such errors occur very rarely and do not significantly affect the cumulative record whether they are included or not.

Exactly the same procedures can be followed to study free recall performance on an episodic memory procedure. In this case, the subject is first exposed to a list of words and is then asked to remember as many of the words as possible (with each response timed as before). In a typical case, a subject might be asked to read 10 words presented one at a time for 1 second each on a computer screen. Following a short distractor task designed to prevent rehearsal, the signal to begin recalling the words is given. The duration of the recall period should be long enough to allow performance to approach asymptotic levels. For lists involving 5 or fewer words, 30 seconds is probably sufficient. However, for lists as long as 60 words,

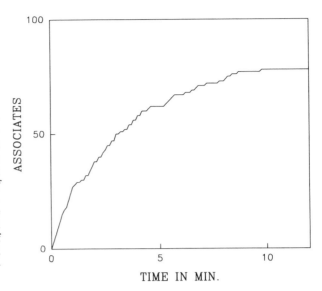

FIGURE 9.5. The cumulative number of U.S. cities (labeled "associates") generated by a single subject over a 12-min period. The data were estimated from Figure 4 of Bousfield and Sedgewick (1944), *Journal of General Psychology,* Vol. 30, p. 159. Reprinted with permission of the Helen Dwight Reid Educational Foundation. Published by Heldref Publications, 1319 18th St. NW, Washington, DC 20036-1802. Copyright 1944.

a recall period of 15 to 20 *minutes* may be needed. This fact suggests an interesting point about how contingencies of reinforcement might affect free recall. Specifically, reinforcement for correct responding may not improve memory per se, but, as indicated earlier, it may nevertheless improve performance by motivating subjects to continue on task long after they mistakenly believe they have exhausted the supply of recallable words (Nelson, 1976).

Generally, too few words are recalled on a single trial to produce a smooth record. Therefore, recall totals over multiple trials (and over subjects) are often summed together. Bousfield and Sedgewick (1944) observed that their individual and group cumulative recall functions were reasonably well described by an exponential of the form

$$F(t) = N(1 - e^{-t/\tau}) \tag{1}$$

where *F(t)* represents the cumulative number of items recalled by time *t*, *N* represents the number of items recalled given unlimited time (i.e., asymptotic recall), and τ represents the average latency to recall associated with the *N* items that are ultimately recalled. The smaller τ is, the faster the rate of approach to asymptote and vice versa.

Figure 9.6 presents a group cumulative free recall function taken from one of the conditions reported by Bousfield and Sedgewick (pleasant activities) along with the best-fitting exponential. This figure, which shows the cumulative number of items recalled up to each point in the recall period, clearly illustrates the two properties that characterize the time course of free recall: asymptotic recall (indicated by the dashed line) and rate of approach to asymptote, which in this case is rather gradual. Experimental manipulations that affect one property of recall may or may not affect the other. Most free recall experiments report the num-

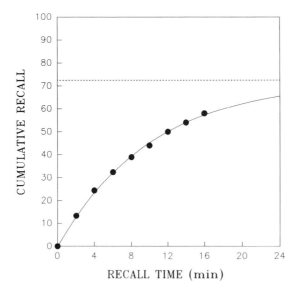

FIGURE 9.6   The cumulative number of pleasant activities generated as a function of time. The data were taken from Table 1 of Bousfield and Sedgewick (1944), *Journal of General Psychology*, Vol. 30, p. 151. The points represent the average values of 18 subjects and the smooth curve represents the best fit of Equation 1. The estimated asymptotic level of recall is indicated by the dashed line. Reprinted with permission of the Helen Dwight Reid Educational Foundation. Published by Heldref Publications, 1319 18th St. NW, Washington, DC 20036-1802. Copyright 1944.

ber of items recalled by the end of an arbitrarily defined recall period (which represents a single point on the cumulative recall curve). This measure fails to indicate whether or not subjects were still making progress when the recall period ended and, if not, whether the final level of performance was achieved rapidly or slowly. A much better alternative is to track the entire time course of recall and analyze the data by fitting a two-parameter growth function (or, equivalently, by analyzing the noncumulative recall latency distributions).

What variables affect the pattern of behavior shown in Figure 9.6? The first question that might occur to an operant psychologist in this regard is how reinforcement for correct responses affects N and τ. The answer is unknown because the experiment has never been performed. Based on the review presented earlier, one might surmise that a simple schedule of reinforcement (e.g., 25 cents for each correct response) would induce subjects to remain engaged in the task for a longer period of time. If so, asymptotic recall (N) might increase. The effect on τ is harder to predict. Rohrer and Wixted (1994) and Wixted and Rohrer (1993) showed that some procedural variables (e.g., list length) affect τ and some (e.g., study time) do not, but much more work is needed to elucidate the principles governing this basic property of remembering.

The considerations discussed above do not apply to situations in which accurate recall consists of a single response (e.g., "Who was the lead actor in *Taxi Driver?*"). However, much remembering in the real world consists of a stream of behavior, as when a witness is asked to describe a crime scene, or a student is asked to recall the details of a lecture. Under these conditions, questions about the factors that govern the rate and pattern of responding become relevant. With some notable exceptions (e.g., Roediger & Thorpe, 1978), such questions have been all but ignored by cognitive researchers and, it seems fair to say, by behavior analysts as well.

INTERFERENCE AND FORGETTING

The ability of a stimulus to exert delayed control over behavior is not independent of the stimuli that precede or follow it. Thus, for example, it is relatively easy to remember the name of one new student introduced to a class. Remembering that student's name after hearing 20 more students introduced is quite a bit more difficult. This example illustrates the obvious point that much forgetting is related to the learning of other material (i.e., interference). This section reviews some of the procedures that can be used to study this phenomenon. Research conducted along these lines may be of particular interest to behavior analysts because, as we shall see, the contrast between cognitive theories advanced to explain interference effects and an empirical law proposed by Watkins (1990) is stark indeed.

Paired-Associates

In this procedure, subjects learn one list of item pairs, which can be represented as the A-B list, and then learn a second list of item pairs in which the first item remains the same but the second is changed. This list can be represented as the A-C list. The individual items may consist of digits, nonsense syllables, words, or any combination of these. During the recall test, subjects are presented with the A items and asked to recall either the corresponding B items or the corresponding C items. An impairment in the ability to recall the targeted items relative to a control group that learns only one list can be attributed to interference caused by the learning of the other list.

Retroactive Interference

To study retroactive interference (i.e., interference by subsequent learning), investigators typically used the A-B, A-C, A-[B] paradigm, in which subjects study one list of A-B item pairs, followed by a list of A-C item pairs, followed by a cued recall test in which the A terms are supplied and subjects are asked to supply the B terms. A control group might receive no A-C list or be given a list consisting of all new items. A decrement in recall performance for the experimental group relative to the control group (the typical finding) can be attributed to interference of A-B associations caused by the subsequent learning of A-C associations. The typical finding with this procedure is that performance is quite impaired immediately after the A-C list is learned, but the degree of impairment relative to the control group lessens as the retention interval increases (see Crowder, 1976, for a review).

Although the analysis discussed above relied on lists of words, many other conceptually similar procedures can be used. Prominent among these are studies of event memory (Loftus, Feldman, & Dashiell, 1995). In a typical experiment of this kind, subjects view an event (such as a videotaped robbery or car accident) and later answer questions about it. One prominent issue in this literature concerns the effect that misleading postevent information has on what a subject reports as having occurred. For example, if the event involved a car accident at an intersection controlled by stoplights, the subject might be asked the following misleading question: "Did the red car or the blue car run the stop sign?" Later, when asked to describe the accident scene, subjects will often report having seen a stop sign. Note that this can be construed as a retroactive interference design because the interfering material is presented after the to-be-remembered even is observed.

Proactive Interference

To study proactive interference (i.e., interference by prior learning), investigators often used a similar procedure represented by A-B, A-C, A[C]. In this case, recall is cued by the A terms (as before) but subjects are asked to supply the C terms. A control group either receives no A-B list or studies a list of word pairs that share no items with the subsequent A-C list. A decrement in recall performance here can be attributed to interference of A-C associations caused by the *prior* learning of A-B associations. The typical finding with this procedure is that performance is relatively unimpaired immediately after the A-C list is learned but drops off rapidly as the retention interval increases.

Variations of this basic procedure were developed to answer interesting questions about the status of associations that appeared to be lost via interference. Did those associations fully extinguish or were they merely overshadowed by the interfering associations? For example, in the modified free recall (MFR) procedure, subjects were asked to supply the first item that the A stimulus brought to mind (rather than instructing them to recall the B term or the C term) to determine which association still exists. This technique, however, still does not reveal whether both associations (A-B and A-C) are simultaneously intact. Thus, in the modified modified free recall (MMFR) procedure, subjects were asked to supply both the B and C terms in response to A. In the proactive interference procedure, this technique helps to reveal if a subject's inability to recall a particular C item is related to the continued survival (or perhaps spontaneous recovery) of the B item previously associated with A. Curiously, results from studies like this often reveal that the especially rapid forgetting of C items as a function of time occurs despite the fact that B items cannot be remembered either (Crowder, 1976).

The Brown–Peterson Task

Another popular procedure designed to study interference and forgetting is the Brown–Peterson task. In this procedure, subjects are presented with a to-be-remembered item (such as a word or a nonsense syllable), followed by a distractor task of varying duration (e.g., requiring the subject to count backwards by 3s), followed by a free recall test (i.e., the subject is asked to supply the word). The typical finding is that performance declines in curvilinear fashion as a function of the duration of the retention interval (i.e., the duration of the distractor task). Note that if no distractor task were used, performance would almost surely remain close to 100% correct (because the subject would simply rehearse the item continuously).

Retroactive Interference

As with the paired-associates procedure, variants of the Brown–Peterson task can be used to study the effects of retroactive and proactive interference. For example, the similarity of the distractor task material to the to-be-remembered item can be varied to study retroactive interference. Such effects are most easily observed when the to-be-remembered item consists of items such as digits or nonsense syllables rather than words. For example, if the to-be-remembered item is "hkj," recall performance will be worse if subjects are asked to shadow (i.e., repeat) consonants during the retention interval than if they are asked to shadow digits.

As an aside, it might be noted here that the standard Brown–Peterson procedure described above can be used to study the time course of forgetting over the short term. Wixted and Ebbesen (1991), for example, presented subjects with lists of six words to study. Each list was followed by a demanding distractor task (repeating additional words) for varying lengths of time ranging from 2.5 to 40 s. If subjects are run for several sessions, forgetting functions (i.e., performance plotted as a function of delay) can be plotted for each subject individually. The advantage of this procedure is that it allows for a rather precise quantification of the behavior of interest. Wixted and Ebbesen (1991) found that the time course of forgetting was well-described by a power function and poorly described by the exponential. The quantification of behavior has not been a main focus of cognitively oriented memory researchers, but it seems to be a natural focus for behavior analysts. As yet, little or no work has investigated what variables affect the parameters of the power function.

Proactive Interference

The Brown–Peterson procedure turned out to be an especially useful way to study the powerful effects of proactive interference as well. Initially, it was observed that the rate of forgetting on the first trial of a session was much less than that on later trials. More specifically, Keppel and Underwood (1962) found that whereas performance following a 3-s retention interval was relatively unaffected by the number of previous trials, performance following an 18-s retention interval was profoundly (and negatively) affected with each passing trial.

Wickens (1972) developed an illuminating procedure that showed rather convincingly that the proactive interference effects described above stemmed from the similarity of the to-be-remembered item and previously learned items. In this procedure, the to-be-remembered items were drawn from a single category for several trials in succession. For example, the items for Trials 1 through 4 might be *ruby, diamond, emerald,* and *sapphire.* On the first trial, the probability of recalling *ruby* after a 15-s retention interval might be quite high. With each ensuing trial, however, the probability of recalling the precious stone presented on that list would decline. Wickens showed that the original level of performance could be restored by switching to a new category. For example, if the to-be-remembered item on the fifth trial were *Spain,* the probability of recall would increase to a level close to that observed on Trial 1 (but would decline with subsequent trials involving countries). This phenomenon is known as *release from proactive interference.* That phenomena such as this might be of interest to behavior analysts is perhaps best illustrated by considering the radically different ways such data can be explained.

Cognitive versus Behavioral Accounts of Interference

Most accounts of the interference phenomena discussed above are (not surprisingly) cognitive in nature. However, one notable exception can be found in the literature. Watkins (1990) forcefully argued that such mediationist accounts of remembering tend to remove attention from basic principles of behavior that accommodate the data in a more direct and much simpler way. Specifically, all of the interference phenomena discussed above are consistent with the *cue overload principle* (a principle that involves no hypothetical constructs). This principle simply states that the more items associated with a cue, the less effective that cue will be. The power of this principle is easy to underestimate because of its sheer simplicity.

The cue overload principle easily accounts for both retroactive and proactive interference effects. In both cases, associating more items with a cue results in the loss of that cue's effectiveness. The main difference between the two procedures concerns when the interfering items are associated with the cue. In the retroactive interference procedure described above, the interfering item is associated with the cue after the to-be-remembered item is associated with the cue. In the proactive interference procedure (both the paired-associates and release from PI paradigms), the interfering items are associated with the cue before the to-be-remembered item is.

This principle can also accommodate a number of other robust findings. Prominent among these is the list-length effect. This simply refers to the fact that the longer a list is, the worse performance tends to be (and this is true whether recall or recognition is used). A number of cognitive models designed to explain this result (for recognition) assume that, when faced with a test item on a yes/no recognition test, subjects mentally compare the test item to each memorized item from the list. Each comparison yields at least some feeling of familiarity (even it the test item does not match the memorized item). The closer the match between the memorized item and the test item, the higher the familiarity is. Thus, for targets, the comparison process yields a series of low familiarity values and one high familiarity value (which occurs when the target is compared with the matching item from the list stored in memory). For lures, the comparison process yields a series of low familiarity values only (because the lure does not match any of the memorized items). Finally, the familiarity values from all such comparisons are summed to yield the actual familiarity associated with the test item. If that value exceeds a decision criterion, a yes response is given, otherwise the response is no. This kind of model is known as a global matching model (e.g., Clark & Gronlund, 1996). It can accommodate list length and interference because each new item in the list (or each interfering item) contributes noise to the process, thereby decreasing discriminability.

Although global matching models can explain the list-length effect, its theoretical intricacies are plain to see. By contrast, the cue overload principle accounts for the effect in a much more efficient way. The more items on the list, the more burdened the cue becomes (the cue in this case being nothing more than the experimental context). The claim by Watkins (1990) that his is a simpler and more empirically testable approach is especially evident when the cue overload principle is compared with a global matching model.

CONCLUSION

Some of the procedures devised to investigate remembering and forgetting in humans have a cognitive flavor to them, but that should not necessarily be taken to imply that the interesting phenomena they generate are immune to a behavioral analysis. Indeed, the selective review presented here suggests that many important topics in this field are more profitably studied from a behavioral perspective than from a purely information-processing point of view. Although it is perhaps true that the behavioral analysis of human memory to date does not have an especially Skinnerian look and feel, it is nevertheless clear that much can be gained by pursuing the subject according to principles most closely identified with the field of behavior analysis.

One important aspect of remembering that is conspicuously missing from nearly all cognitive models of memory is the effect of the subject's reinforcement history. By excluding any consideration of the consequences of remembering, purely cognitive theories are sometimes forced to rely on seemingly implausible assumptions about a subject's computational abilities. This was especially true of theories concerned with the confidence a subject expresses in his or her recognition decisions. Because subjects appear to behave in a more-or-less optimal way, the implication appears to be that they are capable of computing likelihood ratios on a moments' notice. How else could it be that subjects know when to appropriately express high confidence in a recognition decision and when to appropriately concede that they are merely guessing? It is a question a behavior analyst is likely to ask, and the answer, undoubtedly, involves some consideration of the subject's learning history. The details of this learning process are mostly unknown, but only because behavior analysts have not yet taken a close look at this interesting issue.

Another important issue that may be of particular interest to behavior analysts concerns the search for empirical laws of remembering. Over the last few decades, the search for empirical laws has given way to the construction of comprehensive theories about the inner working of memory. Watkins (1990) bemoaned that disturbing trend and offered a concrete example of what simple empirical laws have to offer. His cue overload principle is surprisingly powerful, but it is surely not the only one of its kind. Other, equally powerful laws are presumably waiting to be discovered by those who are willing to search for them. Behavior analysts have always been adept at finding general empirical laws of behavior, and it is hard to imagine why they would not be equally successful within the domain of remembering and forgetting.

REFERENCES

Baron, A. Surdy, T. M. (1990). Recognition memory in older adults: Adjustment to changing contingencies. *Journal of the Experimental Analysis of Behavior, 54,* 201–212.

Bauer, R. H., & Peller-Porth, V. (1990). The effect of increased incentive on free recall by learning-disabled and nondisabled children. *Journal of General Psychology, 117,* 447–461.

Berch, D. B., & Evans, R. C. (1973). Decision processes in children's recognition memory. *Journal of Experimental Child Psychology, 16,* 148–164.

Bousfield, W. A., & Sedgewick, C. H. W. (1944). An analysis of restricted associative responses. *Journal of General Psychology, 30*, 149–165.

Clark, S. E., & Gronlund, S. D. (1996). Global matching models of recognition memory: How the models match the data. *Psychonomic Bulletin & Review, 3*, 37–60.

Craik, F. I. (1970). The fate of primary memory items in free recall. *Journal of Verbal Learning & Verbal Behavior, 9*, 143–148.

Crowder, R. G. (1976). *Principles of learning and memory.* Hillsdale, NJ: J Wiley.

Cuvo, A. J. (1974). Incentive level influence on overt rehearsal and free recall as a function of age. *Journal of Experimental Child Psychology, 18*, 167–181.

Davison, M. C., & Tustin, R. D. (1978). The relation between the generalized matching law and signal-detection theory. *Journal of the Experimental Analysis of Behavior, 29*, 331–336.

Eysenck, M. W., & Eysenck, M. C. (1982). Effects of incentive on cued recall. *Quarterly Journal of Experimental Psychology: Human Experimental Psychology, 34A*, 489–498.

Fischler, I., Rundus, D., & Atkinson, R. C. (1970). Effects of overt rehearsal procedures on free recall. *Psychonomic Science, 19*, 249–250.

Glanzer, M., Adams, J. K., Iverson, G. J., & Kim, K. (1993). The regularities of recognition memory. *Psychological Review, 100*, 546–567.

Green, D. M., & Swets, J. A. (1966). *Signal detection theory and psychophysics.* New York: Wiley. Reprinted 1974 by Krieger, Huntington, NY.

Heinrich, B. A. (1968). Motivation and long-term memory. *Psychonomic Science, 12*, 149–150.

Herrnstein, R. (1970). On the law of effect. *Journal of the Experimental Analysis of Behavior, 13*, 243–266.

Keppel, G., & Underwood, B. J. (1962). Proactive inhibition in short-term retention of single items. *Journal of Verbal Learning and Verbal Behavior, 1*, 153–161.

Kunzinger, E. L., & Witryol, S. L. (1984). The effects of differential incentives on second-grade rehearsal and free recall. *Journal of Genetic Psychology, 144*, 19–30.

Loftus, E. F., Feldman, J., & Dashiell, R. (1995). The reality of illusory memories. In D. L. Schacter (Ed.), *Memory distortion: How minds, brains, and societies reconstruct the past.* Cambridge, MA: Harvard University Press.

Loftus, G. R. (1972). Eye fixations and recognition memory for pictures. *Cognitive Psychology, 3*, 525–551.

Loftus, G. R., & Wickens, T. D. (1970). Effect of incentive on storage and retrieval processes. *Journal of Experimental Psychology, 85*, 141–147.

MacMillan, N. A., & Creelman, C. D. (1991). *Detection theory: A user's guide.* London: Cambridge University Press.

McNicol, D. (1972). *A primer of signal detection theory.* London: Allen & Unwin.

Nelson, T. O. (1976). Reinforcement and human memory. In W. K. Estes (Ed.), *Handbook of learning and cognitive processes* (Vol. 3, pp. 207–246). Hillsdale, NJ: Erlbaum.

Newman, R. S., & Wick, P. L. (1987). Effect of age, skill, and performance feedback on children's judgments of confidence. *Journal of Educational Psychology, 79*, 115–119.

Ogden, J. A., & Corkin, S. (1991). Memories of H. M. In W. C. Abraham, M. C. Corballis, & K. G. White (Eds.), *Memory mechanisms: A tribute to G. V. Goddard* (pp. 195–215). Hillsdale, NJ: Erlbaum.

Ratcliff, R., Sheu, C., & Gronlund, S. D. (1992). Testing global memory models using ROC curves. *Psychological Review, 99*, 518–535.

Roediger, H. L., & Thorpe, L. A. (1978). The role of recall time in producing hypermnesia. *Memory & Cognition, 6*, 296–305.

Rohrer, D., & Wixted, J. T. (1994). An analysis of latency and interresponse time in free recall. *Memory & cognition, 22*, 511–524.

Rundus, D. (1971). Analysis of rehearsal processes in free recall. *Journal of Experimental Psychology, 89*, 63–77.

Santi, A., & Roberts, W. A. (1985). Reinforcement expectancy and trial spacing effects in delayed matching-to-sample by pigeons. *Animal Learning & Behavior, 13*, 274–284.

Squire, L., Knowlton, B., & Musen, G. (1993). The structure and organization of memory. *Annual Review of Psychology, 44*, 453–495.

Stock, W. A., Kulhavy, R. W., Pridemore, D. R., & Krug, D. (1992). Responding to feedback after multiple-choice answers: The influence of response confidence. *Quarterly Journal of Experimental Psychology: Human Experimental Psychology, 45A,* 649–667.

Tulving, E. (1972). Episodic and semantic memory. In E. Tulving & W. Donaldson (Ed.), *Organization of memory* (pp. 381–403). New York: Academic Press.

Warrington, E. K., & Weiskrantz, L. (1970). Amnesic syndrome: Consolidation or retrieval? *Nature, 228,* 628–630.

Watkins, M. J. (1990). Mediationism and the obfuscation of memory. *American Psychologist, 45,* 328–335.

Wickens, D. D. (1972). Characteristics of word encoding. In A. W. Melton & E. Martin (Eds.), *Coding processes in human memory* (pp. 195–215). Washington, DC: Winston.

Wixted, J. T. (1989). The vocabulary of remembering: A review of Kendrick, Rilling, and Denny's theories of animal memory. *Journal of the Experimental Analysis of Behavior, 52,* 441–450.

Wixted, J. T., & Ebbesen, E. (1991). On the form of forgetting. *Psychological Science, 2,* 409–415.

Wixted, J. T., & McDowell, J. J. (1989). Contributions to the functional analysis of single-trial free recall. *Journal of Experimental Psychology: Learning, Memory, & Cognition, 15,* 685–697.

Wixted, J. T., & Rohrer, D. (1993). Proactive interference and the dynamics of free recall. *Journal of Experimental Psychology: Learning, Memory, and Cognition, 19,* 1024–1039.

Zimmerman, J., & Kimble, G. A. (1973). Effects of incentive on false recognition. *Journal of Experimental Psychology, 97,* 264–266.

10

Psychophysics
Methods and Analyses of Signal Detection

R. John Irwin and Dianne McCarthy

Psychophysics is the branch of psychology concerned with the relation between the physical properties of events and the sensations they give rise to. The subject has two major fields of inquiry: global psychophysics, which studies readily discriminable stimuli that differ by large amounts, and local psychophysics, which studies the fine differences between barely discriminable stimuli (Luce & Krumhansl, 1988). Global psychophysics is concerned with psychological scaling, whereas local psychophysics is concerned with detection and discrimination. Because this chapter is concerned with signal detection theory, it outlines some of the basic methods of local psychophysics and will exclude from consideration the methods of global psychophysics. It will discuss how to study and measure the limits of human sensory systems.

The relation between methods for investigating human operant behavior and methods for measuring the limits of the human senses may not seem obvious. In fact, however, modern psychophysical procedures allow an objective analysis of human sensory systems; those methods do not invite a consideration of the private accompaniments of detection or discrimination. In this analysis, an experimenter presents one or more events and records whether the observer, after appropriate instruction, responds differentially to those events. In studying, for example, whether a person discriminates between two aurally presented sinusoidal waveforms that differ in frequency, the psychophysicist does not need to ask whether the observer perceived different pitches associated with each waveform. The pitch of a sinusoid is a private experience that may or may not accompany the presentation of the waveform. The question of interest to the psychophysicist is the discrimination of waveforms by an observer: The experimenter knows the difference, and the psychophysicist wishes to find out, through proper procedures, whether the observer "knows" the difference too. Like much research

R. John Irwin • Department of Psychology, University of Auckland, Auckland, New Zealand.
Dianne McCarthy • Department of Physiology, University of Auckland, Auckland, New Zealand.

Handbook of Research Methods in Human Operant Behavior, edited by Lattal and Perone. Plenum Press, New York, 1998.

on operant behavior, what is usually of interest in psychophysics is steady-state or asymptotic behavior rather than the acquisition of that behavior.

What, then, are the proper procedures for investigating human psychophysical responses? We assert that they are the methods of signal detection theory. In this chapter, however, we shall not emphasize the theories that give rise to these methods: The conventional theory is well known, and there are standard texts that present it fully (Green & Swets, 1966/1989; McNicol, 1972). A second, and more recent, approach, known as *behavioral detection theory* (Davison & Tustin, 1978; Nevin, Jenkins, Whittaker, & Yarensky, 1977, 1982), is based on a well-documented empirical description of choice derived in the operant laboratory. Its theoretical underpinnings have been summarized by Davison and McCarthy (1988). Rather, the purpose of this chapter is to offer practical advice on how to implement and analyze some of the psychophysical methods of both conventional and behavioral detection theory. Nonetheless, we shall have to allude to aspects of the theories when we introduce concepts or indices of performance that can be understood only by reference to those theories. For example, we shall emphasize the use of detection-theoretic indices of performance such as d' and d'_e; to appreciate the benefits of these indices requires an understanding of the shape of the receiver operating characteristic (ROC) that these various indices imply (Swets, 1986a), and the shape of the ROC in turn involves theoretical analysis. We also shall illustrate how the effects of reinforcer, or biasing, variables can be measured; such an illustration requires a brief description of the quantitative formulations of behavioral detection theory.

THE SINGLE-INTERVAL EXPERIMENT

The psychophysical methods that we shall review all require the presentation of a number of discrete trials. Although free-operant procedures were standard in the early development of the study of operant behavior, many operant experiments use discrete trial procedures (e.g., see Nevin, 1967, 1969). In a psychophysical experiment, a trial comprises a sequence of temporal intervals of which the two essential elements are an observation interval and a response interval. In the fundamental detection problem, there is but one observation interval and during that interval the event to be detected may, or may not, occur. The observer's task is to indicate whether the event was presented during the observation interval. If the observer is allowed only two responses—"yes, the event occurred" or "no, the event did not occur"—then the procedure is usually called the *yes–no* method (in the animal literature, the procedure is sometimes called the *go/no-go* method). If more than two responses are allowed, so that the observer can report various shades of confidence about the occurrence of the event, then the procedure is called the *rating method.* Analyses of the yes–no and rating methods are sufficiently distinct that they deserve separate treatment.

The event to be detected is often called the *signal,* and the absence of the signal is often called *noise.* The use of this terminology is instructive. *Signal* and *noise* are terms from communication engineering, but they can be aptly applied to the measurement of the human senses. As is well known, the senses are never quiescent, even in the absence of stimulation, and their activity in this state can appropriately be called *noisy*. Use of the term *signal,* on the other hand, allows us to draw a distinction between the general nature of the event to be detected (e.g., the presentation of a light of a given luminance) and the particular realization of that event as a stimulus presented on a given trial. Although the signal may, for example, have a fixed luminance, its input to the receptor will vary from trial to trial, perhaps because of imperfections in the apparatus that produces it, or perhaps because of inherent uncertainties stemming from the quantal nature of light itself, or perhaps because it is added to the "dark light" (as Fechner called it) of the visual system. We say that the signal gives rise to a *stimulus,* which can be defined as a particular realization of an event, a realization that will vary from trial to trial.

Therefore, we draw a distinction between the events to be discriminated and the stimuli they give rise to on a trial. The task of the observer can then be formulated as one of indicating, on the basis of the evidence presented by the *stimulus,* whether the *signal* plus noise occurred or whether *noise* alone occurred during the observation interval. At a more general level, Egan and Clarke (1966) used the term *event* to refer to the things to be detected or discriminated. The events might be signal plus noise or noise alone, sinusoidal frequency A or sinusoidal frequency B, distilled water with added sucrose or distilled water alone, an X-ray photograph of a diseased lung or a photograph of a healthy lung. Psychophysical methods allow the investigator to determine whether an observer can discriminate between these events on the basis of the stimuli they give rise to.

THE YES–NO EXPERIMENT

Because there are two possible events, A and B, and two possible responses, Yes and No, the outcome of a trial in the yes–no experiment can be represented by one of four possibilities. The outcome of the complete set of trials in the experiment is represented by the frequency with which each of the four possibilities occurred. The frequencies can be entered in the familiar 2×2 contingency table of the yes–no experiment. In Table 10.1, we represent these frequencies by the letters $w, x, y,$ and z. The clerical task of keeping track of these frequencies as the experiment progresses is usually performed by a computer. The frequencies in Table 10.1 can be converted into proportions conditional on the occurrence of each event. Thus, the proportion $w/(w + x)$ is the proportion of trials on which an observer responded "Yes" when Event A occurred, and the proportion $y/(y + z)$ is the proportion of trials on which the observer responded "Yes" when Event B occurred. Suppose Event A was the signal plus noise, and Event B was the noise alone. Then the proportion $w/(w + x)$ is known as the *hit rate,* and the proportion $y/(y + z)$ as the *false-alarm rate.* These proportions can be considered "rates" because they estimate the observers' rate of responding in each of these ways. As is well known, these two rates summarize all of the information in the table because the miss rate, $x/(w + x)$, is the complement of the hit rate, and the correct-rejection rate, $z/(y + z)$, is the complement of the false-alarm rate.

Because only two conditional proportions are free to vary in this representation of a yes–no experiment, the outcome of the experiment can be represented as

TABLE 10.1
A 2 × 2 Response Matrix
of a Yes–No Experiment

	Response		
Event	Yes	No	Sum
A	w	x	$w + x$
B	y	z	$y + z$
Sum	$w + y$	$x + z$	$w + x + y + z$

Note. The symbols w, x, y, and z represent the frequency with which each response was made to each event.

a point in a two-dimensional graph of hit rate versus false-alarm rate. Such a graph is known as a *receiver operating characteristic* (ROC) and an example of a point in the ROC square is shown in Figure 10.1. What determines the location of that point? The location of the point is determined by three factors according to the theory of signal detectability: (1) the likelihood that the observation stemmed from signal plus noise in relation to the likelihood that the observation stemmed from noise alone, (2) the prior probability of presenting the signal on a trial, and (3) the values and costs—the rewards and punishments—contingent on the response. Of course, whether these same factors influence the behavior of a human observer is an empirical question. The theory of signal detectability is a theory about the *detectability* (not necessarily the *detection*) of events. The *detectability* of a signal can be determined for a theoretically ideal observer. But the *detection* achieved by a human or animal observer will fall short of the ideal for various reasons. One reason is that human observers do not always take advantage of the information avail-

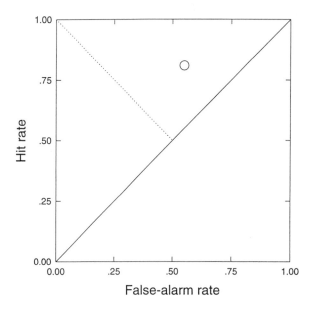

FIGURE 10.1. A point in the receiver operating characteristic (ROC) square corresponding to $d' = 1$ and $\beta = 0.71$ for the dual-Gaussian equal-variance model. The dotted line is the minor diagonal of the square and represents unbiased responding according to this model. Because there is only one point in the square, an infinite number of other models, each with their own estimate of accuracy and bias, could be fitted to it.

able concerning the likelihood that the observation stemmed from each event (e.g., see Hautus, Irwin, & Sutherland, 1994), and it has been known since Neyman and Pearson presented their lemma in 1933 that basing decisions on the ratio of these likelihoods will maximize performance.

After obtaining a data point like that in Figure 10.1, the result can be summarized by two parameters of detection theory: a *discriminability*, or *accuracy* parameter, d', and a *bias*, or *criterion* parameter, β (among several other possibilities). (In conventional detection theory, d' is normally referred to as a *sensitivity* parameter. Given that we use the term *sensitivity* in a different context later in this chapter, to avoid confusion we henceforth refer to d', and related measures, as indices of discriminability or accuracy.) The discriminability parameter, d', assumes that each event gives rise to stimuli that are normally distributed and of common standard deviation; hence, this model is known as the *normal–normal equal-variance model,* or the *dual-Gaussian equal-variance model.* For the point in Figure 10.1, standard tables show that $d' = 1$ and $\beta = 0.71$ (the point represents a hit rate of .81 and a false-alarm rate of .55). Many investigators stop at this stage, but this can be a hazardous practice. The problem is that *any* detection-theory model with its associated ROC can pass through this point. There is only one free parameter (d') of the ROC for the standard equal-variance model, and that is all that is needed to describe the point. The goodness of fit of the model therefore cannot be assessed with one experimental point. However, if there is a body of experimental work that has assessed the goodness of fit of the model to data of the kind being summarized by a single point in ROC space, then use of the model without further assessment may well be justified.

To test the fit of a particular model to experimental data requires increasing the number of degrees of freedom in the data: For the yes–no experiment one can obtain further points of the ROC. One way to do that is to manipulate the observer's bias (more on this later) while keeping the detectability of the signal constant. The experimental points should then lie on a single ROC that represents a single level of accuracy. Many of the early yes–no experiments of detection theory were designed for just that purpose. In order to review aspects of this procedure, and to emphasize the experimental labor that it entails, we present here some additional data from Kennedy (1990). These data are more fully described and analyzed in a later section.

In one of Kennedy's (1990) experiments, human observers were asked to discriminate between two separate noises that differed in their root-mean-square amplitude. The *events* to be discriminated were two broadband noises that differed only in intensity, but because of the random nature of noise, the *stimuli* those events gave rise to varied from trial to trial. In this experiment, the lower-intensity noise can be regarded as the "noise" of the experiment, whereas the higher-intensity noise can be regarded as having the "signal" added to it. Every trial began with a 500-ms warning light. After a 500-ms pause, a single observation interval, also marked by a light, occurred; the duration of the observation interval was 100 ms—the same duration as the stimulus. After each observation interval the observer pressed a key to indicate which event occurred; the observer was then informed which event had in fact occurred.

Kennedy (1990) varied the prior probability of presenting each event on dif-

TABLE 10.2
Data from an Experiment of Kennedy (1990) with Five Signal Probabilities

Parameter	Probability of signal presentation				
	.1	.3	.5	.7	.9
sn $(w + x)$	24	86	152	204	272
Hits (w)	9	60	114	175	250
Hit rate, $H = (w/(w + x))$	0.375	0.698	0.750	0.858	0.919
$z(H)$	−0.319	0.518	0.674	1.071	1.399
n $(y + z)$	276	214	148	96	28
False alarms (y)	27	41	59	45	21
False-alarm rate, $F = (y/(y + z))$	0.098	0.192	0.399	0.469	0.750
$z(F)$	−1.294	−0.872	−0.257	−0.078	0.674
Criteria, z	−1.330	−0.814	−0.315	−0.003	0.542

Note. sn refers to the signal-plus-noise event, and $w + x$ is the number of trials on which the signal was presented; w is the number of those trials the subject decided the signal was presented; the hit rate, H, is $w/(w + x)$; and $z(H)$ is the inverse normal transform of the hit rate. The other rows in the table are the corresponding values for the noise alone, except for the last row, which gives the criterion placement in z-units for each signal probability.

ferent experimental sessions from a probability of .1 to a probability of .9. After some 4500 trials of practice, each observer made 300 judgments for each of five different prior probabilities. The results for one observer for one signal-to-noise ratio (−5 dB) are shown in Table 10.2. Thus, when the signal probability was .1, the hit rate was .38 and the corresponding false-alarm rate was .10. These are therefore the coordinates of one point on the ROC for this set of data. Instead of showing this point on the coordinates of hit rate and false-alarm rate of Figure 10.1, we illustrate it—as is commonly done—for the inverse normal transform of the point. These are shown as z-values in Table 10.2. (Note that this transformation is not the usual z-score of psychological statistics; that score has the opposite sign to those in Table 10.2.) Figure 10.2 shows the five data points, transformed to the new coordinates, for this observer. Each point represents a transform of the hit rate and the corresponding false-alarm rate for one signal probability. The bottom point, for example, shows the z-transform of a hit rate of .38, which equals −0.32, and the z-transform of a false-alarm rate of .10, which equals −1.29. This is the outcome for the experiment when the signal was presented with a prior probability of .1. The other four points in Figure 10.2 correspond to the results for the other four signal probabilities (see Table 10.2).

The reason for the popularity of the z-transform representation of ROC data is that an ROC stemming from two underlying Gaussian distributions is then represented as a straight line. Fitting a straight line to a set of points is easier than fitting a curve, hence the appeal of this representation. However, fitting the *best* straight line to data of this kind is not straightforward. Least squares is not acceptable because there is experimental error in each of the dimensions. One solution is to find a maximum-likelihood fit (further described in the section on the

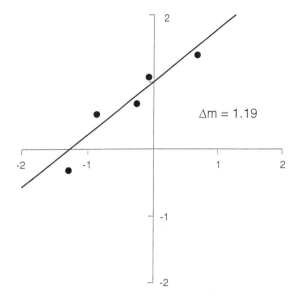

FIGURE 10.2. Plot of the z-transforms of the hit rate and the false-alarm rate of the yes–no data of the observer whose data are shown in Table 10.2. The straight line is a maximum-likelihood fit of the dual-Gaussian unequal-variance model to the transforms. Δm is an index of accuracy for this model.

rating method), and that solution has been applied here. Dorfman and Alf (1968) described how to implement this procedure for yes–no ROCs. Their procedure fits the dual-Gaussian *unequal*-variance model, which has a parameter additional to the single parameter of the equal-variance model. The two parameters reported by the model are the intercept, b, and the slope, s, of the fit. For the data in Table 10.2, these estimates and their standard errors are: $b = 1.01 \pm 0.09$ and $s = 0.79 \pm 0.15$. The parameters have the following meanings. The intercept, b, is the difference between the means of the underlying distributions $(\mu_{sn} - \mu_n)$ divided by the standard deviation of the signal-plus-noise distribution, σ_{sn}. The slope is equal to the ratio of the standard deviation of the noise distribution to that of the signal-plus-noise distribution, σ_n/σ_{sn}. By definition, $\sigma_n = 1$, so for these data $\sigma_{sn} = 1.27$. As inferred from the fitted ROC, the variance of the signal-plus-noise distribution is therefore larger than that of the noise alone. The intercept, b, is not a commonly reported index of discriminability, because it is defined in units of the signal-plus-noise distribution. An index recommended by Green and Swets (1966) is Δm, the distance between the means of the distributions in units of the noise distribution. $\Delta m = b/s$, and for the data shown in Figure 10.2, $\Delta m = 1.19$. On its own, Δm (or b) does not define the path of the ROC, so a complete specification of the path for this model requires that two parameters be stated, for example, Δm and s. This specification of accuracy is usually called $D(\Delta m,s)$. Several other indices of discriminability or accuracy are available, but we defer a discussion of them until we review the more efficient rating method in the next section.

Two other results that Dorfman and Alf's (1968) program can provide deserve mention. One is the criterion associated with each experimental point. There are several ways of specifying the placement of a criterion for this model, and a common one is to express it in z-units relative to the mean of the noise distribution. These criterion placements are shown in the last row of Table 10.2. Another result that the program reports is the goodness of fit of the model to the data. The value of chi-square returned for the fit in Figure 10.2 is 4.71. This chi-square has three degrees of freedom: There are five independent points, and a degree of freedom is lost for each parameter estimated. Because the probability of χ^2 (3) $\geq$ 4.71 = .19, we can conclude that the data do not depart significantly from the model at, say, the .05 level.

Much labor is expended in obtaining an ROC like that in Figure 10.2 from the yes–no method, and such ROCs are rarely reported. It has also been suggested (Laming, 1986) that yes–no ROCs obtained from varying signal probability are of limited theoretical value. The reason advanced is that an observer may come to know more about the properties of a signal presented frequently than the properties of a signal presented infrequently. Thus, it is argued, experimental points obtained from experiments with different signal probabilities will lie on different ROCs rather than the assumed single ROC. For Kennedy's (1990) experiments, this argument loses some of its force, because the signal was a sample of the noise, and it is hard to envisage how its properties become better known in that case.

Whatever the merits of that argument, there is a much more practical reason for eschewing experiments on yes–no ROCs: The single-interval rating method affords all of the benefits of ROC analysis without the experimental labor of the yes–no method. We describe this method next, and deal more fully with ROC analysis as it applies to this single-interval procedure.

THE RATING METHOD

Consider an experiment in which an observer was asked to discriminate between two narrow-band noises that differed in amplitude. The noises were presented by earphones, and it was the observers' task to rate their confidence that the waveform presented during the observation interval contained a signal. The signal was a band of noise of the same duration and same spectrum as the noise to which it might be added. In effect, observers were asked to rate their confidence about which of two noise sources of different amplitude had been presented during the observation interval.

Every trial began with a warning light of 250-ms duration, and then, after a 500-ms pause, the observation interval was presented for 10 ms. The duration of the observation interval was marked by a light, so that there was no ambiguity about when the stimulus was presented. After the observation interval, the observers entered judgments of their confidence that the signal had been added to the noise on that trial. This response ended the trial and a new trial began after a 300-ms pause.

In this experiment, observers rated their confidence on a 10-point rating scale; they made their judgments by pressing a numeric key on a computer keyboard. Observers responded "1" if they were very confident the signal had not been added to the noise and "10" if they were very confident the signal had been added to the noise. Intermediate numbers were given intermediate meanings. (The meanings were displayed on a computer screen beside the observer.) This 10-point scale is more fine-grained than usual: a 6-point scale is often recommended, and observers may find fewer categories easier to use. One of the objectives of this experiment, however, was to test the shape of the obtained ROC against certain theoretical models, and it was thought that a 10-point scale might provide a more detailed picture of the shape of the ROC, and therefore a stronger test of the appropriate model. Moreover, the observers who took part in the experiment were highly practiced (over 2000 trials) and had been given instructions to use all of the points on the scale. It is doubtful, however, whether a 10-point scale provides much more information than a 6-point one because there has been considerable evidence, at least since Pollack's (1952) study on discriminating between sound frequencies, that observers are unable to distinguish among more than a few categories of unidimensional stimuli. Miller (1956) stated that the number was seven (plus or minus two).

The duration of the answer interval was not prescribed in this experiment, and so the observers had as long as they wanted to respond. However, the decision time for these practiced observers was always quite brief. With less experienced observers it might be desirable to define the duration during which a response must be made. (No feedback was offered after each response, but a summary of performance could be viewed at the conclusion of a 200-trial block of responses.) Altogether, each observer undertook 800 ratings. There was an a priori probability of .5 that the signal would be added to the noise on any trial. In this experiment, the probability that the signal would occur was determined at random by a computer (see Press, Flannery, Teukolsky, & Vetterling, 1986, for a useful discussion of how to obtain random events from deterministic computers) with the constraint that there would be an equal number of trials (400) in which each kind of event occurred.

Table 10.3 shows the frequency with which one observer made each of the 10 ratings after the presentation of the signal plus noise (sn) and after the presentation of the noise alone (n). In Table 10.4, the frequencies in each row of Table 10.3 have been converted into proportions. The row immediately beneath each set of proportions shows the cumulated proportions (cumulated from right to left) based on these ratings. These cumulated proportions correspond to hit rates (the cumulated proportions corresponding to the presentation of the signal plus noise) and false-alarm rates (the cumulated proportions corresponding to the presentation of the noise alone). Figure 10.3 illustrates the nine points that can be obtained from these cumulated proportions; the figure shows an empirical ROC (the points) as well as a best-fitting theoretical ROC (the curve). Although there were 10 ratings, only nine points can be obtained because one point always corresponds to the coordinates (1, 1) and therefore contains no information.

TABLE 10.3
Frequency with Which Each Rating Was Used for Each Event by One Observer Detecting Whether an Increment Had Been Added to a Narrow-Band Noise

Event	Rating									
	1	2	3	4	5	6	7	8	9	10
sn	11	21	23	22	37	19	49	73	68	77
n	62	54	51	48	45	25	59	32	18	6

TABLE 10.4
Proportion of Times Each Rating Was Used by One Observer, and the Cumulated
Proportions for Each Event, Derived from the Frequencies in Table 10.2

Event	Rating									
	1	2	3	4	5	6	7	8	9	10
sn	0.03	0.05	0.06	0.06	0.09	0.05	0.12	0.18	0.17	0.19
	1.00	0.97	0.92	0.86	0.81	0.72	0.67	0.55	0.36	0.19
n	0.16	0.14	0.13	0.12	0.11	0.06	0.15	0.08	0.05	0.02
	1.00	0.85	0.71	0.58	0.46	0.35	0.29	0.14	0.06	0.02

This way of constructing the rating ROC exposes the logic of the method. The bottom point on the graph with the coordinates (0.02, 0.19) is based on the ratings labeled "10" in Tables 10.3 and 10.4. These are the trials for which the observer was very confident that the signal had been added to the noise. The next higher point with the coordinates (0.06, 0.36) includes the ratings labeled "9." These are the trials for which the observer was still confident, but not as confident as on those trials given a rating of "10," that the signal had been added to the noise. The proportions that this second point represents are based on ratings of both "9" and "10" (see Table 10.4). In other words, if the observer made a judgment of "9" *or* "10," the judgment will contribute to the position of this point. The justification for cumulating the proportions to obtain the separate points of the ROC is therefore based on the assumption that if the observer could have decided with confidence that the signal had been added to the noise, that observer would have come to the same conclusion if the decision were made with a lesser degree of confidence (rating "9" instead of "10"). The remaining points in the figure can be understood in the same way.

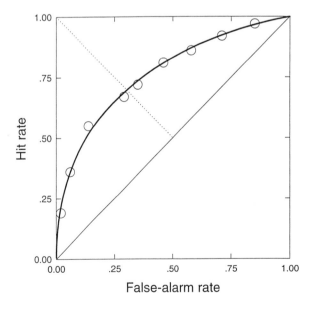

FIGURE 10.3. Best-fitting ROC of the dual-Gaussian unequal-variance model to the cumulated proportions of Table 10.4 (omitting the uninformative point corresponding to (1,1)). The ROC for this model can be asymmetric about the negative diagonal of the square, as here. The maximum likelihood of the parameters of the fit are shown in Table 10.5.

Analysis of the Rating ROC

Fortunately, there are several computer programs available for the analysis of rating experiments (Dixon, 1992; Dorfman, 1982; Stenson, 1988), and so what would otherwise be a difficult operation is now a routine matter. We have analyzed the data in Table 10.3 with Dorfman's program. This program computes maximum-likelihood estimates of parameters of the dual-Gaussian unequal-variance model of detection theory. This model, which is one of the earliest models developed for signal detection, has been found to provide a satisfactory fit to nearly all empirical ROCs (Swets, 1986b). It can accommodate ROCs, like that illustrated in Figure 10.3, that are asymmetrical about the negative diagonal of the ROC space. In this respect, the unequal-variance model encompasses a wider range of results than the standard equal-variance Gaussian model of detection theory, or the logistic model of choice theory, both of which assume symmetrical ROCs. The dual-Gaussian unequal-variance model has, however, some theoretical limitations: One problem is that the strength of the evidence for this model is no longer monotonic with likelihood ratio, and so decisions based on this evidence variable cannot be optimal (Swets, 1973).

Table 10.5 shows the parameters estimated by Dorfman's program for the data in Table 10.3 and the ROC in Figure 10.3. Because there is error variance associated with both the hit rate and the false-alarm rate, least-squares estimation of the model's parameters is not appropriate. Instead, the program finds the value of the parameters that maximize the likelihood that the data stemmed from the model. (See Dorfman and Alf, 1969, for the theoretical basis of this technique for fitting the dual-Gaussian model to rating data. Ogilvie and Creelman, 1968, present the theory for fitting the logistic distribution of choice theory. Pollard, 1977, provides a more general introduction to maximum-likelihood methods.) We next define each of these parameters in turn. Three of them (d_e', d_a, and A_z) are indices of accuracy, and the other two (s and b) are parameters of the linearized ROC on z-coordinates—parameters we encountered in the analysis of the yes–no ROC.

Indices of Accuracy

The accuracy index, d_e', is analogous to the more familiar detection-theory index, d', but is reserved for asymmetric ROCs where d' is inappropriate. The subscript e is a reminder that this index was first proposed by James P. Egan, one of

TABLE 10.5
Parameters of the Best-Fitting Dual-Gaussian Unequal-Variance Model
for the Data in Table 10.3

Parameter	Estimate	Standard error of estimate	95% confidence interval
d_e'	1.040	0.0768	0.890–1.191
d_a	1.036	0.0766	0.886–1.186
Az	0.768	0.0165	0.736–0.800
Slope, s	0.847	0.0030	0.841–0.853
Intercept, b	0.960	0.0059	0.948–0.972

the pioneers of the theory of signal detection. The idea behind this index is that when the variance of the two Gaussian distributions are not equal, the best estimate of the standard deviation of the postulated distribution will be the average of the two different estimates, one from the signal-plus-noise distribution, and one from the noise alone. The unit in which the distance between the means of these distributions, $\mu_{sn} - \mu_n$, is measured is therefore $\frac{1}{2}(\sigma_{sn} + \sigma_n)$, and so $d_e' = (\mu_{sn} - \mu_n)/\frac{1}{2}(\sigma_{sn} + \sigma_n)$. Alternatively, d_e' can be defined in terms of the slope and intercept parameters (see below) as $d_e' = 2b/(s + 1)$.

The accuracy index, d_a, is similar in spirit to d_e', but for this index the unit is the root mean square of the two estimates of the standard deviation. Because variances are additive, an acceptable estimate of an average of two standard deviations is obtained from the square root of the average of the two variance, that is, $[\frac{1}{2}(\sigma_{sn}^2 + \sigma_n^2)]^{1/2}$. Hence, $d_a = \sqrt{2}(\mu_{sn} - \mu_n)/(\sigma_{sn}^2 + \sigma_n^2)^{1/2}$. In terms of the slope and intercept parameters, $d_a = \sqrt{2}b/(s^2 + 1)^{1/2}$.

The accuracy index, A_z, is the proportion of the area of the ROC square that lies under the fitted dual-Gaussian unequal-variance ROC curve. Use of this index has been advocated by Swets and his co-workers (e.g., Swets, 1986a; Swets & Pickett, 1982) on the grounds that many empirical ROCs are asymmetrical and therefore not adequately described by the more familiar index d' and its relatives. A_z is uniquely related to d_a by the relation, $A_z = \Phi(d_a/\sqrt{2})$, where $\Phi(\ )$ is the normal distribution function. This equation is analogous to the one that relates the area, A, under the standard detection-theory curve to d', for which $A = \Phi(d'/\sqrt{2})$.

Another area index, not shown in Table 10.5, we designate $p(A)$. This is the area under the ROC when the empirical points are connected by straight lines. This index is not computed by Dorfman's program, but O'Mahony (1992) provides a formula for its calculation. For the points in Figure 10.3, $p(A) = 0.76$—very similar to A_z. The two area measures are virtually identical in this case because (1) the theoretical curve provides an excellent fit to the data and (2) there are many data points that are evenly spaced, so that straight lines drawn between them do not underestimate the theoretical curve by much. One virtue of $p(A)$ over A_z is that $p(A)$ makes no assumptions about the nature of the distributions underlying performance: The index is therefore said to be nonparametric. On the other hand, for some empirical ROCs, $p(A)$ may seriously underestimate performance. This will arise for ROCs (unlike that illustrated in Figure 10.3) for which the empirical points are sparse or not well spaced. The position of the points of an ROC reflects the criterion for that point, and so to this extent $p(A)$ is not entirely criterion free. A_z, by contrast, is independent of the particular criteria that an observer adopts in the experiment. It must be conceded, though, that the theoretical path of an ROC may be harder to estimate if the points are not well spaced, and this will give rise to a larger standard error of estimate of its accompanying area measure, A_z.

The meaning of the accuracy index, A_z, can be understood by considering Green's area theorem (Green, 1964; Green & Swets, 1966; see also Hautus, 1994). This theorem states that the area under the yes–no or rating ROC is equal to the proportion correct of an unbiased observer in a two-alternative forced-choice experiment. This gives an intuitive meaning to the area measure that makes it an especially appealing one. It is important to appreciate that the equivalent proportion correct is for an *unbiased* observer, and that the validity of proportion correct as a measure of accuracy depends on this assumption.

The intercept and slope parameters, b and s, are parameters of the linearized ROC. As we noted when discussing yes–no ROCs, ROCs stemming from Gaussian processes are linear when plotted on z-transformations of hit rate and false-alarm rate. Indeed, this linearization was useful in the early analysis of ROCs because it allowed the investigator to judge the fit of the data to the model. With the development of computer programs to undertake maximum-likelihood fits, viewing ROCs in this way is now perhaps less important. Nevertheless the slope parameter provides useful information on the ratio of the standard deviations of the noise distribution and the signal-plus-noise distribution, that is, $s = \sigma_n/\sigma_{sn}$. For the dual-Gaussian equal-variance model, this ratio is unity, and so the test of whether the data conform to that model is provided by examining the 95% confidence limits of the estimated value. For the example in Tale 10.4, the ratio of 1 does not fall within the 95% confidence limits of the estimated s, and so that model can be rejected. (We discuss another goodness-of-fit test below.) The intercept parameter is rarely reported on its own because its significance depends on s. When $s = 1$, so that the equal-variance model holds, then $b = d'$. Otherwise, $b = (\mu_{sn} - \mu_n)/\sigma_{sn}$.

Criterion Measures

Dorfman's program reports the criteria adopted in a rating experiment. These criteria are boundaries that separate the rating categories, and so there is always one less criterion boundary than there are categories. For the data in Table 10.3, the nine criteria, $z(k)$, are: -1.04, -0.54, -0.19, 0.10, 0.42, 0.58, 1.03, 1.55, and 2.16. The program reports these boundaries in z-units; they are expressed as deviations from the mean of the noise distribution, μ_n, which by definition is zero. Various other conventions are possible for specifying criterion placement, several of which are simple transformations of the one provided by Dorfman's program. An alternative specification is in terms of likelihood ratio, that is, the ratio of the likelihood that an observation at the boundary stemmed from signal plus noise to the likelihood that it stemmed from noise alone. The importance of this specification resides in the fact that it is an optimal decision variable for achieving a wide variety of goals. There is some evidence, however—at least from animal observers—that the z specification remains constant when the signal-to-noise ratio is varied whereas the likelihood ratio changes (McCarthy & Davison, 1984).

Because the rating method yields a full ROC, the position of the criterion boundaries is usually not critical. The theoretical ROC fitted to the empirical points provides a criterion-free summary of performance, independent of any particular criterion. The position of the criteria assumes importance only if the criteria are not well placed so that the path of the ROC is not well determined. Hence, the criteria are not usually reported for a rating experiment. We shall return to a discussion of the measurement of criterion, or response bias, later.

Goodness of Fit

We have already seen how the slope parameter, s, can provide some information on the goodness of fit of the Gaussian equal-variance model. A more useful measure is the chi-square goodness of fit statistic that Dorfman's program returns. For the rating data being analyzed here, chi-square is 5.81. The degrees of freedom associated with this statistic is in this case 7: There were 10 rating categories, and one degree of freedom is lost because the total number of trials is known, and therefore the ratings of only 9 categories are free to vary; two other degrees of freedom are lost for the two parameters of the model—b and s, or their transformations. In general, the number of degrees of freedom for testing the chi-square from the dual-Gaussian unequal-variance model is $n - 3$, where n is the number of rating categories. For this example, the probability of $\chi^2_{(7)} \geq 5.81 = .56$. This means that, given that the model is correct, the probability of the data departing from the model to the extent obtained is .56. One can then adopt a conventional level of significance, say .05, and conclude that the model cannot be rejected at the .05 level of significance. A good model is therefore one for which the probability is *not* significant. Of course, such a result does not mean that the tested model is the correct one. For one thing, other models might fit the data too. Indeed, the data in Table 10.3 were reported by Hautus and Irwin (1992) who did *not* fit the dual-Gaussian unequal-variance model. For theoretical reasons, they fitted a chi-square model, which also turned out to provide a satisfactory account of the data. So the final choice of the correct model has to be made not solely on the basis of the probability of the chi-square that the program reports. Indeed, the dual-Gaussian unequal-variance model can accommodate most experimental ROCs, and the data in Table 10.3 are no exception.

Meaning of the Response in the Rating Method

The response in the rating method may seem surrounded by a vague aura of subjectivity. How can subjective ratings fall within the compass of the analysis of operant behavior? What needs to be borne in mind here, we think, is that it is not the *meaning* of the response that ROC analysis makes use of, but the *frequency* with which such a response is emitted. If an observer can reliably provide a set of ratings for one event with different frequencies from another event, then the observer can be said to discriminate between the two events. So the rating method of detection theory has a very different status, we believe, from the ratings of global psychophysics. In experiments on psychological scaling, for example, the ratings of a stimulus given by an observer have often been interpreted literally, as though the observer were reporting on private measurements. This distinction between the interpretation of the rating response in signal detection and in psychophysical scaling is developed further by Irwin, Hautus, and Stillman (1992).

Virtues of ROC Analysis

Obtaining a complete ROC salvages any psychophysical method prone to response bias. Usually it is the single-interval methods that are thought to be most susceptible to such bias, but some two-interval experiments, such as the same–different experiment, are also prone to response bias. They can therefore benefit from ROC analysis as much as their single-interval cousins (e.g., see Irwin, Stillman, Hautus, & Huddleston, 1993). Many practical problems are of the single-interval kind and do not lend themselves to forced-choice designs (e.g., deciding whether an X-ray photograph shows evidence of disease, or forecasting the weather) and therefore evaluation of the accuracy with which such tasks can be performed invites an ROC analysis.

In addition, we emphasize the virtue of obtaining a full ROC—not just a single point on the presumed ROC curve. Estimating accuracy from a single point of an ROC depends on assuming that the path of the ROC is known. As Swets (1986a) showed, every index of discriminability implies an ROC. This is just as true for the index proportion correct as it is, for example, for d', so proportion correct is as theory-laden as d'. Hence, we would assert that, unless there is a body of previous work to rely on, it can be hazardous to extrapolate an entire ROC from one point by estimating an index from that single point. For this reason we hope that the rating method will assume greater prominence in the implementation of detection theory.

Handling Extreme Proportions

A problem arises in any detection-theoretic analysis of experimental data when proportions near zero or unity are encountered. The problem is at its most acute when a proportion is exactly zero or unity. This is because the z-transformation, for example, of such proportions is not useful (the z-transform for 0 is $-\infty$, and the z-transform for 1 is $+\infty$). Unfortunately, proportions of zero or unity do arise in single-interval experiments because of sampling errors. If too few trials are administered, then the true proportion of hits or false alarms will not be estimated with sufficient precision to distinguish a very low or very high proportion from zero or unity. The larger the difference in discriminability of the events, the larger is the number of trials needed to estimate these extreme proportions precisely.

Our analysis supposes that proportions of zero or unity are never the *true* proportions in a detection or discrimination task, and this indeed is the implication of most detection-theoretic models. Swets (1986b) expressed this idea by stating that all ROCs are *regular*. By a regular ROC, Swets meant that the ROC always lies interior to the ROC square, and never intersects the axes of the square except at the coordinates (0,0) and (1,1). This is another way of saying that an observer can never achieve a zero false-alarm rate except with a zero hit rate, and never achieve a perfect hit rate except with a 100% false-alarm rate. Counterintuitive as it may seem, such a statement implies that noise is all pervasive in sensory systems.

Two methods for handling extreme proportions in single-interval experiments have been evaluated by Hautus (1995). One method (implemented in Dorfman's 1982 program, for example) replaces proportions of zero with proportions equal to $1/(2N)$, where N is the number of trials, and replaces proportions of unity with $1-1/(2N)$. A second method adds 0.5 to every cell of the frequency matrix. Hautus showed that each type of correction introduces biases into the estimation of d' or of log d. In general, the biases are most pronounced when N is small or when response bias is extreme, that is, for points in the ROC space near the bottom-left or top-right corners of the square. Hautus recommended the second correction because the bias it introduces is usually smaller than that introduced by the first method, and because the bias is such that the obtained index always underestimates the true value of the index. The $1/(2N)$ rule sometimes overestimates the true index and sometimes underestimates it.

These corrections are more likely to be needed for the single-interval yes–no method than for the rating method. This is especially so if the observer in a rating experiment is given firm instructions to use all of the rating categories available (though not necessarily equally often, or course), and given sufficient practice with the method. But another solution is available for zero entries in the rating matrix: The cell frequencies of adjacent categories can be combined. Collapsing categories in this way reduces the number of ROC points, but it averts the biases that the other corrections introduce. By this means, estimated indices are still based on obtained proportions, not corrected ones. In our view, this is still another advantage of the rating method over the yes–no method.

MORE THAN ONE OBSERVATION INTERVAL

We have confined our discussion so far to the single-interval design. We have done this because this design represents a fundamental and important case. As we have stated, many practical problems are of this kind. However, detection theory also speaks to designs that involve more than one observation interval. The best-known example is the forced-choice design, of which the two-alternative forced-choice task is the most common variant. In this design, the signal always occurs in one of the observation intervals, and the noise alone fills the other interval(s). The detection-theoretic analysis of the two-alternative forced-choice experiment closely resembles Thurstone's analysis of the paired-comparison task, and the Law of Comparative Judgment, which he developed for that task, can readily be accommodated by detection theory. These designs are popular because, *for an unbiased observer,* a suitable index of accuracy is provided by the proportion of correct responses. It is important to bear this proviso in mind, however, when adopting proportion correct as a measure of performance.

Forced-choice designs are fully discussed in standard texts on detection theory. There are several other multiple-interval designs for which a detection-theoretic analysis has been provided by Macmillan and his colleagues (e.g., Macmillan, Kaplan, & Creelman, 1977), and the recent text of Macmillan and Creelman (1991) provides an extensive account of these designs. Multiple-interval designs include the same–different task, which, like the two-alternative forced-choice experiment, contains two observation intervals, but which requires a very different analysis of its performance; and the triangle or oddity task, which is popular in the food industry, but which is not the same as the three-alternative forced-choice experiment.

MATCHING-TO-SAMPLE

Another multiple-interval design, often used in the study of operant behavior, is that of matching-to-sample. Because of its popularity in this field, we briefly review it here from the point of view of detection theory. We owe this application of detection theory (as well as several others) to Macmillan et al. (1977). In a matching-to-sample experiment, an observer is presented with two stimuli that are samples of two different events, and then asked to decide which of the two samples a third stimulus matches. For example, in the first two observation intervals of a trial, an observer might be presented with two tones, one of 1000 Hz and one of 1005 Hz (in this example, the stimuli are presented successively and their order or presentation varies randomly from trial to trial). In the third observation interval, a tone of either 1000 or 1005 Hz is presented, and the observer decides which of the two sample tones it matches, the first or the second. The order of the trials can be reversed without affecting the logic of the design: A stimulus can be presented followed by two samples, one of which must be selected as matching the first stimulus.

The analysis of accuracy in the matching-to-sample experiment might seem straightforward, but there are pitfalls to avoid. First, consider the index d'. A hit rate can be computed from the number of times the observer correctly identified the third stimulus with the first, and a false-alarm rate from the number of times the observer mistakenly identified the third stimulus with the first. (The miss rate is based on the number of times the third stimulus was mistakenly identified with the second, and the correct-rejection rate on the number of times the third stimulus was correctly identified with the second.) However, such a hit rate and false-alarm rate cannot be used to compute d' by looking up tabulated values for the single-interval experiment: Matching-to-sample contains three observation intervals, not one. As Macmillan et al. showed, the design can be decomposed into two parts. One component is a two-alternative forced-choice task (the first two observation intervals), and the other component is a yes–no task (the last observation interval). By taking into account these two components of the complete task, they provided tables for measuring accuracy with this design (Kaplan, Macmillan, & Creelman, 1978; Macmillan & Creelman, 1991) and these tables should be consulted if the investigator wants to estimate the distance between the means of the two distributions of signal plus noise and noise alone in units of their common standard deviation; that is, if the investigator wants to estimate d' so that it has the same meaning as it does in other designs, such as yes–no.

Second, consider the index proportion correct as a measure of accuracy for this design. As always, proportion correct is a proper index of accuracy only for an unbiased observer, and the yes–no component of the matching-to-sample design may make it prone to response biases. Furthermore, a given proportion correct in a matching-to-sample experiment cannot be equated with the same value in some other design: This is a general weakness of proportion correct as an index of accuracy. Consider an obvious example: A proportion correct of .75 in a two-alternative forced-choice experiment is not as impressive as it is in a four-alternative forced-choice experiment. One of the appealing properties of detection-theory indices of accuracy, like d', is that they are theoretically independent of the psychophysical task by which they are measured. Proportion correct is not.

Several multiple-interval designs have a special place in psychophysics, and the interested reader will find Macmillan and Creelman's (1991) text a valuable guide to them as well as to the single-interval designs that we have described.

ADVICE ABOUT THE CONDUCT OF A PSYCHOPHYSICAL EXPERIMENT

Useful advice about the conduct of psychophysical experiments can be found in Appendix III of Green and Swets (1966) and in Robinson and Watson (1972). Here we summarize some of the main points.

Instructions. One of the attractive features of psychophysical investigations with human observers is that it is good practice to tell observers as much as possible about the nature of the task and the experiment. Rarely is it necessary to deceive the observer about the purpose of the experiment. Of course, the experimenter would not normally inform the observer about the particular hypothesis under study for fear that it might influence the observer's behavior. Even so, a hypothesis about, for example, the shape of the ROC is so removed from trial-by-trial decisions that it is doubtful whether even knowing the exact hypothesis under test in that case would influence an observer's behavior. It would normally be wise to inform the observer about the prior probability with which each event will be presented. If it is known to the experimenter, the observer could also be told about the probability distributions of the events under study. As a result of practice at the task, observers will come to know about these features of the experiment, but explicit instructions are also advisable.

Session length. In our experience, observers prefer several short sessions (of about a half-hour's duration) rather than fewer longer sessions. It is arduous to maintain performance on a difficult discrimination for long periods and the resulting fatigue is likely to impair performance. It is customary to divide a session into several *blocks* of trials, of say 100 trials per block. In this way observers can take frequent rests during a session, and view their results after a block. The number of trials in a block depends on the duration of each trial; in many psychophysical investigations, a trial lasts only a few seconds, so that 100 trials can be performed in a few minutes.

Practice. Unless the purpose of the experiment is to investigate the acquisition of performance, most psychophysical tasks require that each observer undertake many trials—sometimes thousands of trials—before data on asymptotic performance are collected. To expedite learning it is customary to provide feedback—knowledge of results—during the practice sessions. No hard-and-fast rule can be offered for what constitutes sufficient practice for an observer. For the detection of a simple auditory signal, Gundy (1961) found that asymptotic performance was reached after 250 trials when observers were provided with trial-by-trial feedback. More complex tasks may require more trials. Whatever the task, the investigator needs to monitor how accuracy changes with practice over blocks of, say, 100 trials by using a standard index, such as d' of log d: however, these indices can have large standard errors when based on few trials, and so the standard error of each estimate of accuracy needs to be borne in mind when assessing whether asymptotic performance has been reached.

Feedback. During practice sessions, feedback can be provided on a trial-by-trial basis. For human observers, feedback normally amounts to providing information to the observer about what happened on a trial. After a response, a light may be momentarily presented to inform the observer whether or not a signal was presented in the observation interval, or, in a forced-choice experiment, a light may indicate in which interval the signal in fact occurred. In the experimental sessions, feedback is useful to sustain performance. Feedback can be given on a trial-by-trial basis, or on a block-by-block basis. Sometimes, however, trial-by-trial feedback can disrupt performance. Recall that the observer responds on the basis of the stimulus presented during the observation interval, and a sensible decision (the decision more likely to be correct) may be that the stimulus stemmed from one event, when in fact it stemmed from another. To be informed that one has made a mistake after such a trial may upset performance. On the other hand, allowing the observer to view a summary of performance after each block of trials circumvents that problem while helping to motivate performance.

BEHAVIORAL DETECTION THEORY AND THE EFFECTS OF PAYOFF VARIABLES

To this point, we have focused almost exclusively on antecedent events and how their effect on performance can be measured. In this section, we consider payoff a reinforcer variables and describe how their effects on performance may be quantified.

According to conventional detection theory, when making decisions on the basis of uncertain sensory information, observers are assumed to set a decision criterion, or standard, of how certain they must be that a signal had occurred before they will report it. Consider the decision processes facing a physician who must decide whether or not a particular disease is present. The consequences of the diagnostic decision clearly will affect the doctor's decision criterion (Swets, 1992). On the one hand, most physicians will not require much evidence of a bacterial infection to prescribe a course of antibiotics, as they and the patient have little to lose and much to gain if an infection is present and can be cured. On the other hand, doctors will be reluctant to make diagnoses that result in more radical interventions such as surgery unless they have compelling evidence to support the diagnosis because the consequences of an incorrect decision would be too costly to them and to the patient. The consequences of a decision affect an observer's preference, or bias, for reporting whether or not a particular stimulus gave rise to a signal.

Although the conventional theory of signal detection affords several measures of bias, or criterion (see above), we shall not discuss them further here. Rather, we shall introduce the reader to behavioral detection theory, and illustrate its description of human data obtained using yes–no tasks in which payoff, or reinforcer, variables have been explicitly manipulated.

Relative Reinforcer Magnitude

As a first example, consider data collected by Green and Luce (1973), as published by Luce (1986), in which humans were asked to detect a 1000-Hz tone in noise that was presented at near-threshold intensity. The subjects reported the presence or absence of the tone before a specified time had elapsed. In one procedure, the response deadline (i.e., time to respond) was set at 600 ms on both signal and nonsignal trials; in another procedure, it was 500 ms applicable on signal trials only. In both procedures, the number of points earned for correct reports (hits and correct rejections) was varied across experimental conditions. That is, Green and Luce varied the *magnitude* of the payoff obtained for correctly reporting the presence of the tone relative to that obtained for correctly reporting its absence. Such a manipulation should bias performance in such a way that the observer

TABLE 10.6
The Matrix of Events in Green
and Luce (1973)

EVENT	RESPONSE	
	Yes	No
Tone + noise	w	x
Noise alone	y	z

would be more likely to report the presence of the tone rather than its absence when more points could be earned for such a response. How might this bias be measured?

Table 10.6 displays the matrix of events in Green and Luce's (1973) experiment, with the frequencies of responses and payoffs denoted, for convenience, by w, x, y, and z as before. In contrast to the conventional theory discussed above, behavioral detection theory does not refer to any theoretical distributions. Rather, it treats the detection task as two concurrent schedules of reinforcement (Davison & Tustin, 1978). That is, in the presence of each event (tone plus noise, noise alone), two choices (respond "yes" or respond "no") are concurrently available to the subject. In Green and Luce's study, correctly responding "yes" in the presence of the tone, and "no" in the absence of the tone, produced different amounts, or magnitudes, of reinforcement across experimental conditions. A substantial literature attests to the fact that behavior on such concurrently available schedules may be adequately described by the generalized matching law (Baum, 1974, 1979):

$$\frac{B_y}{B_n} = c \left(\frac{M_y}{M_n} \right)^a$$

that is, the ratio of "yes" to "no" responses (B_y to B_n) is a power function of the ratios of the magnitudes of the reinforcers (M_y to M_n). The exponent of the power function, a, is a measure of how sensitive behavior is to changes in reinforcer magnitude, and c is a measure of inherent bias—the degree to which a subject favors a "yes" or "no" response independent of variations in reinforcer magnitude. Logarithmic transformation produces an equation of the form

$$\log \left(\frac{B_y}{B_n} \right) = a \log \left(\frac{M_y}{M_n} \right) + \log c$$

which is a straight line relating the dependent variable (log B_y to B_n; the behavior ratio) to the independent variable (log M_y/M_n; the reinforcer magnitude ratio) with slope a and an intercept of log c.

Translated to the detection situation in Table 10.6, this law states that the ratio of yes/no responses in the presence of each event is a power function of the ratio of the reinforcer magnitudes obtained for accurately reporting the events, and a function of the extent to which the tone is distinguishable from noise alone. Thus, (in logarithmic terms) in the presence of the tone.

$$\log \left(\frac{B_w}{B_x}\right) = a \log \left(\frac{M_w}{M_z}\right) + \log c + \log d \qquad (1)$$

and, in the presence of the noise alone:

$$\log \left(\frac{B_y}{B_z}\right) = a \log \left(\frac{M_w}{M_z}\right) + \log c - \log d \qquad (2)$$

In these equations, the subscripts w, x, y, and z refer to the cells of the matrix in Table 10.6, and B and M denote behavior and reinforcer magnitude, respectively. For example, B_w tallies the number of "yes" responses in the presence of the tone, and M_z is the magnitude of the reinforcer obtained for correctly responding "no" in the absence of the tone. The parameter $\log d$ (analogous to d') is a measure of the *discriminability* of the stimuli; the better the subject can discriminate tone plus noise from noise alone, the larger will be the ratio B_w/B_x and the smaller will be the ratio B_y/B_z. As the numerators in both equations are "yes" responses, $\log d$ is positive in Equation 1 and negative in Equation 2. The parameter $\log c$ measures *inherent bias,* a constant preference toward responding "yes" or "no" which remains invariant when stimulus difference or the reinforcer-magnitude ratio are changed. The parameter a measures the *sensitivity* with which the behavior ratio changes with changes in the obtained reinforcer-magnitude ratio. (As noted earlier, this sensitivity parameter is not to be confused with that of conventional detection theory.) If a equals unity, changes in the behavior ratio match changes in the reinforcer-magnitude ratio. Typically, however, in animal detection studies, behavior ratios substantially undermatch ($a < 1.0$) reinforcer-magnitude ratios (Boldero, Davison, & McCarthy, 1985; Davison & McCarthy, 1988). Although variations in the size of the payoffs for correct responses have often been reported to produce some degree of bias in human studies (e.g., Dusoir, 1983), we know of no human detection studies in which measures of the *sensitivity* of performance to variations in payoff magnitude have been reported. A reanalysis of Green and Luce's (1973) data in terms of behavioral detection theory allows us to do just that.

Figure 10.4 shows Equations 1 and 2 fitted to the auditory-detection data obtained by Green and Luce (1973). Here, straight lines of the form $Y = aX + I$ (where a, the slope, measures sensitivity, and I, the intercept, equals $\log c \pm \log d$) were fitted using least-squares linear regression with the logarithm of the response ratios on tone-plus-noise (S_1) and noise-alone (S_2) trials as the dependent variables and the logarithm of the obtained reinforcer-magnitude ratio as the independent variable. These data are group data, averaged across the individual-subject data reported by Luce (1986, Appendix C6), for both the 600- and 500-ms deadlines. The equations of the best-fitting straight lines are shown for each stimulus for both conditions.

As noted above, the slopes of Equations 1 and 2 are measures of the sensitiv-

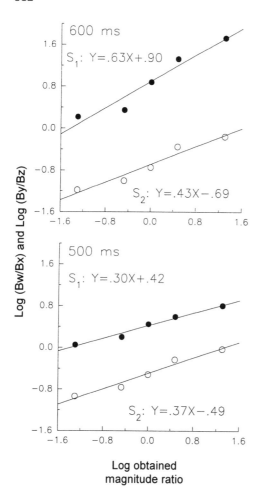

FIGURE 10.4. The logarithm of the response ratios on S_1 (tone plus noise) and S_2 (noise alone) trials as a function of the logarithm of the obtained reinforcer-magnitude ratio for the 600-ms (upper panel) and 500-ms (lower panel) response-deadline procedures reported by Green and Luce (1973). The best-fitting straight lines by the method of least squares, together with their equations, are shown for each stimulus in each procedure.

ity of performance to changes in the reinforcer-magnitude ratio. Under the 600-ms response deadline, the slopes were 0.63 (SD = 0.09) and 0.43 (SD = 0.06) for the tone plus noise and noise alone, respectively. Under the 500-ms deadline, they were 0.30 (SD = 0.03) and 0.37 (SD = 0.04). There are three important points to note about these slopes. First, they were all positive, implying that variation in relative reinforcer magnitude did indeed bias performance in the predicted manner. That is, when correct "yes" responses produced a larger reward than correct "no" responses, the subjects emitted more "yes" than "no" responses. Second, behavior ratios in the presence of each event substantially undermatched reinforcer-magnitude ratios. In other words, changes in the reinforcer-magnitude allocation did not produce as great a change in the behavior allocation. Third, behavior ratios were generally equally sensitive to changes in relative reinforcer magnitude in the presence of each event.

The intercepts of the fitted equations (log $c \pm$ log d) provide estimates both of the observers' ability to discriminate between the tone-plus-noise and noise-alone events (log d) and of inherent bias (log c). When the intercept of Equation 2 is subtracted from the intercept of Equation 1, the result is 2log d. An estimate of how well the subjects could detect the tone (discriminability, log d) is given by one-half the difference between the intercepts, a value that here was 0.80 for the 600-ms condition and 0.46 for the 500-ms condition. Thus, the subjects were less accurate in detecting the tone for the shorter response deadline. Furthermore, as the two lines were approximately parallel in both conditions, discriminability did not change in any systematic way with changes in relative reinforcer magnitude, thus validating log d as a bias-free measure of accuracy (but see Alsop & Davison, 1991, for evidence of an interdependence between log d and bias in some animal detection paradigms).

In a similar manner, an estimate of inherent bias, log c, may be obtained by computing one-half the sum of the intercepts of Equations 1 and 2. Such a computation shows that in both conditions, inherent bias was negligible (log $c = 0.11$ and -0.04 for the 600- and 500-ms conditions, respectively). That is, the observers showed no constant preference toward reporting the presence or the absence of the tone across different reinforcer-magnitude ratios.

Relative Reinforcer Frequency

Research in the animal operant laboratory has shown that the relative frequency with which alternative behaviors are reinforced is a potent determinant of the way in which a subject will choose between those behaviors (e.g., de Villiers, 1977; Herrnstein, 1961). Kennedy (1990) varied relative reinforcer frequency in a human auditory detection experiment by varying the prior probability of signal presentation and allowing the numbers of reinforcers obtained for correct "yes" and "no" detections to covary. As McCarthy and Davison (1979, 1984) empirically demonstrated, it is this covariation of reinforcer-frequency ratios, rather than changes in a priori probabilities per se, that determines the oft-reported change in response criterion with variations in a priori probabilities (e.g., Clopton, 1972; Elsmore, 1972; Galanter & Holman, 1967; Hume & Irwin, 1974; Markowitz & Swets, 1967; Schulman & Greenberg, 1970; Terman & Terman, 1972). The covariation arises because, in detection procedures, it is common to reinforce (or provide payoff for) every correct response (e.g., Dusoir, 1983; Hume, 1974a,b; Hume & Irwin, 1974), or to reinforce correct responses intermittently on probabilistic or variable-ratio schedules (e.g., Elsmore, 1972; Hobson, 1975, 1978). These procedures are called *uncontrolled reinforcer-ratio* procedures (McCarthy & Davison, 1980, 1984) because the relative numbers of reinforcers obtained for correct detections can vary widely with the subject's behavior and with variations in a priori probabilities. Suppose, for example, that a tone is presented on 80% of trials and noise alone on only 20% of the trials. Conventional theorists would argue that the more frequently a signal occurs the more likely a subject is to report the stimulus as a signal. However, if (as is usual) every correct "yes" response is reinforced, 80% of the sessional reinforcers will be obtained for "yes" responses and only 20% for "no" responses. Variations in signal probability have, therefore, typically been confounded with variations in the obtained reinforcer-frequency ratio. When relative reinforcer frequency was held constant and equal between the two response alternatives and signal probability alone was varied, McCarthy and Davison (1979) found *no* change in response bias. Thus, McCarthy and Davison (1979, 1984) argued that it was the variation in reinforcer-frequency ratios, produced by changes in a priori probabilities, that controlled the resultant change in criterion.

We now present a reanalysis of data reported by Kennedy (1990), some of which we have already discussed. Two single-interval experiments were conducted. In the first (an increment-detection task), four observers were required to detect increments in the intensity of a continuous Gaussian noise background of 60 dB SPL. These increments were set at one of three signal-to-noise (S/N) ratios, -4, -8, and -13 dB, and for each, the probability of an increment (signal) being presented was varied over the values .1, .3, .5, .7, and .9. Recall that each trial began with a 500-ms delay, after which a green warning light was presented for 500 ms. A pause of 500 ms followed the warning signal and then the observation interval of 100-ms duration occurred. Feedback was provided to the observers by a pair of red lights, one of which would light for 300 ms after each trial signaling which response had been correct. Before the commencement of the experiment proper, each observer was presented with at least 2500 practice trials employing many combinations of S/N ratios and a priori signal probabilities. A further 4500 trials were then required from each observer in order to obtain three ROCs, one for each S/N ratio. Each ROC was constructed from five points, representing the five a priori probabilities, and the estimation of each point was based on 300 trials. In the second experiment (a difference-discrimination task that we discussed earlier), the base noise was presented only during the observation interval and the observers were required to indicate whether or not the base noise had a signal added to it. The three S/N ratios used in this second experiment were -1, -5, and -10 dB.

To illustrate an alternate analysis from that performed on Green and Luce's (1973) data, Equations 1 and 2 were combined in two ways. First, Equation 2 was subtracted from Equation 1 to yield a bias-free point estimate of discriminability. With some rearrangement, this subtraction yields:

$$0.5 \log \left(\frac{B_w \times B_z}{B_x \times B_y} \right) = \log d$$

Equation 3 may be called a *stimulus function* (McCarthy & Davison, 1980) because it relates behavior to the stimuli independent of any biaser. Discriminability (as measured by Equation 3) is identical to accuracy indices used by some detection theorists (e.g., η; Luce, 1963) and analogous to those used by others (e.g., d'; Green & Swets, 1966). Log d can range from 0 to infinity, with zero denoting no discriminability, and infinity perfect discriminability. Figure 10.5 shows point estimates of discriminability for two of Kennedy's (1990) observers, computed using the expression on the left of Equation 3, and plotted as a function of the logarithm of the obtained reinforcer-frequency ratio. These estimates are shown for both tasks and for each of the three S/N ratios. Two main points can be made. First, discriminability was systematically related to the S/N ratio, with high S/N ratios yielding the highest levels of accuracy, and low S/N ratios resulting in very poor accuracy. Second, accuracy, as measured by Equation 3, did not change in any systematic way with variations in the reinforcer-frequency ratio. This last point is particularly important because it is in accordance with one of the basic premises of any the-

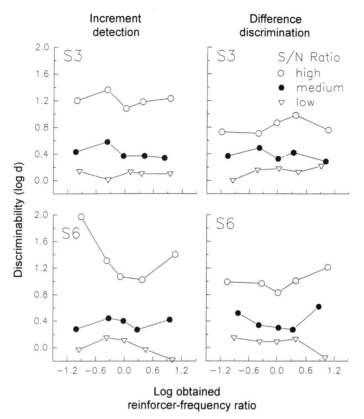

FIGURE 10.5.   Point estimates of discriminability (log d, Equation 3) as a function of the logarithm of the obtained reinforcer-frequency ratio for two subjects (S3 and S6) on increment-detection (left panels) and difference-discrimination (right panels) tasks reported by Kennedy (1990). The three signal-to-noise (S/N) ratios are denoted by open circles (high), filled circles (medium), and inverted triangles (low).

ory of signal detection, that measures of discriminability be independent of changes in criterion or bias.

It should be noted at this point that instead of estimating log d from each separate data point as we have done above, it is possible to fit a yes–no ROC to estimate performance from the whole data set, as we illustrated. Figure 10.6 shows these ROCs, together with the values of d_e', for each S/N ratio.

When Equations 1 and 2 are added together, the discriminability parameter, log d, is removed and a *bias function* (McCarthy & Davison, 1980) results. With some rearrangement, this addition yields:

$$0.5 \left(\frac{B_w \times B_y}{B_x \times B_z} \right) = a \log \left(\frac{R_w}{R_z} \right) + \log c \qquad (4)$$

The measure on the left side of Equation 4 is called *response bias* (or *criterion*) and the right side specifies the environmental conditions that produce that bias. [Note

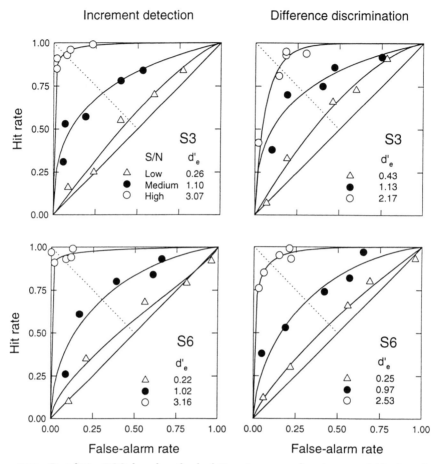

FIGURE 10.6.   Best-fitting ROCs based on the dual-Gaussian unequal-variance model for two observers in Kennedy (1990).

here that the reinforcer-bias term is written as R_w/R_z to distinguish it from the re-inforcer-magnitude term M_w/M_z used in Equations 1 and 2—animal research has suggested other independent variables that may also be expected to bias detection performance, and hence substitute for this term in Equation 4. These include re-inforcer delay (Williams & Fantino, 1978), reinforcer quality (Hollard & Davison, 1971), and response requirements (Hunter & Davison, 1982).] As in Equations 1 and 2, the parameter a measures the *sensitivity* of behavior to changes in the spec-ified biaser. Thus, unlike conventional theories of signal detection, behavioral de-tection theory separates response bias into a *variable* component—that arising from variations in reinforcer or response parameters (the variables as specified on the right side of Equation 4 and generically called *reinforcer bias*—and a *constant* component—that arising from constant differences between reinforcer or response parameters (inherent bias, log c). The sensitivity of detection performance to vari-ations in reinforcer bias (the a parameter) and a measure of the constant compo-nent (log c) are given by the slope and intercept, respectively, of a least-squares lin-ear regression fit to Equation 4.

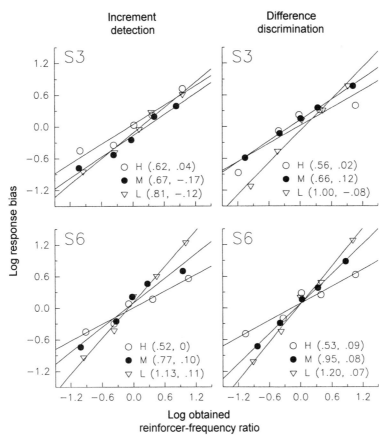

FIGURE 10.7.   Point estimates of response bias (measured by Equation 4) as a function of the logarithm of the obtained reinforcer-frequency ratio for two subjects (S3 and S6) on the increment-detection (left panels) and difference-discrimination (right panels) tasks reported by Kennedy (1990). The three signal-to-noise (S/N) ratios are denoted by open circles (high), filled circles (medium), and inverted triangles (low). The best-fitting straight lines by the method of least squares, together with their slope and intercept, respectively, in parentheses, are shown for each S/N ratio.

Figure 10.7 shows Equation 4 fitted to Kennedy's (1990) data. Here, point estimates of the logarithm of response bias (computed using the expression on the left side of Equation 4) are plotted as a function of the logarithm of the obtained reinforcer-frequency ratio. These data are shown for both observers on both tasks. The best-fitting straight lines by the method of least squares are shown, together with their slopes and intercepts, respectively, in parentheses for each S/N ratio. All slopes are positive showing that the variation in relative reinforcer frequency did indeed bias performance. Further, a comparison of the sensitivities (i.e., slopes) shown here with those shown in Figure 10.4 suggests that, consistent with animal-detection studies (e.g., Boldero et al., 1985), humans are more sensitive to variations in the frequency of payoffs than they are to variations in the magnitude of the payoffs. Second, at each S/N ratio, similar sensitivities were obtained on both tasks. Third, and most interestingly, as S/N ratios became smaller (and discriminability decreased, Figure 10.5), both observers became more sensitive to variations in the relative frequency with which reinforcers were obtained. Sensitivities ranged from a mean of 0.56 (high S/N ratio) to 1.04 (low S/N ratio). In other words, as discriminability decreased, and hence control by the stimuli decreased, the observers' performance was more strongly controlled by the reinforcers.

CONCLUSIONS

This chapter has outlined some of the basic methods of signal detection that we believe are the most appropriate for studying and measuring the limits of human perception. We have offered practical advice on how to implement and analyze these methods when the relation between the physical properties of events and the sensations they give rise to is under empirical study. Additionally, we have illustrated how the consequences of decision making can be manipulated in order to alter an observer's preference, or bias, for reporting those events, and we have described the manner in which such response biases can be measured and understood.

Although conventional detection theory emphasizes the role of antecedent events, and behavioral detection theory emphasizes the consequences of responses, this difference in emphasis does not, however, survive more than a superficial analysis, for conventional detection theory does not neglect the values and costs contingent on a response, and behavioral detection theory does not ignore the stimulus function (Equation 3). Nevertheless, these two approaches to detection theory rest on different foundations: The origin of conventional detection theory resides in the behavior of an ideal observer detecting signals in noise, and for this problem knowledge of the statistics of the signal and noise is crucial. Behavioral detection theory, by contrast, stems from an analysis of the factors affecting the choice between events, an analysis based on reinforcement theory (see Mazur, chapter 5). The usual presentation of conventional detection theory starts with a consideration of theoretical distributions of noise and signal plus noise, whereas the usual presentation of behavioral detection theory starts with a consideration of the relation between response ratios and reinforcement ratios, a relation summarized by the matching law.

Although these approaches have different starting points, they may converge at a deeper level. The original development of behavioral detection theory eschewed consideration of any underlying distributions of the events to be discriminated, but it later became evident that its index of accuracy, $\log d$, could be derived from a pair of logistic distributions in the same way that d' could be derived from a pair of Gaussian distributions. Furthermore, a pair of logistic distributions implies an ROC, just as a pair of Gaussian distributions does. And because the logistic resembles the Gaussian distribution, so does the logistic ROC resemble its Gaussian counterpart. The resemblance is sufficiently close that it is unlikely that the two ROCs could be distinguished empirically. From this perspective, the two approaches presented in this chapter to the measurement of detection, though very different in spirit, can be seen to be related both in theory and in practice. The reader will find applications of these approaches, and some of the measures they give rise to, in the discussions by Wixted (Chapter 9) and Critchfield, Tucker, and Vuchinich (Chapter 14).

ACKNOWLEDGMENTS. We gratefully acknowledge the constructive commentary provided by Michael Hautus on an earlier draft of this chapter.

REFERENCES

Alsop, B., & Davison, M. (1991). Effects of varying stimulus disparity and the reinforcer ratio in concurrent-schedule and signal-detection procedures. *Journal of the Experimental Analysis of Behavior, 56,* 67–80.

Baum, W. M. (1974). On two types of deviation from the matching law: Bias and undermatching. *Journal of the Experimental Analysis of Behavior, 22,* 231–242.

Baum, W. M. (1979). Matching, undermatching and overmatching in studies of choice. *Journal of the Experimental Analysis of Behavior, 32,* 269–281.

Boldero, J., Davison, M., & McCarthy, D. (1985). Reinforcer frequency and reinforcer magnitude as biasers of signal detection. *Behavioral Processes, 10,* 131–143.

Clopton, B. M. (1972). Detection of increments in noise by monkeys. *Journal of the Experimental Analysis of Behavior, 17,* 473–481.

Davison, M., & McCarthy, D. (1988). *The matching law: A research review.* Hillsdale, NJ: Erlbaum.

Davison, M. C., & Tustin, R. D. (1978). The relation between the generalized matching law and signal-detection theory. *Journal of the Experimental Analysis of Behavior, 29,* 331–336.

de Villiers, P. A. (1977). Choice in concurrent schedules and a quantitative formulation of the law of effect. In W. K. Honig & J. E. R. Staddon (Eds.), *Handbook of operant behavior* (pp. 233–287). Englewood Cliffs, NJ: Prentice–Hall.

Dixon, W. J. (Ed.). (1992). *BMDP statistical software manual, Vol. 2.* Los Angeles: University of California Press.

Dorfman, D. D. (1982). RSCORE II. In J. A. Swets & R. M. Pickett, *Evaluation of diagnostic systems: Methods from signal detection theory* (pp. 212–232). New York: Academic Press.

Dorfman, D. D., & Alf, E., Jr. (1968). Maximum-likelihood estimation of parameters of signal detection theory—a direct solution. *Psychometrika, 33,* 117–124.

Dorfman, D. D., & Alf, E., Jr. (1969). Maximum-likelihood estimation of parameters of signal-detection theory and determination of confidence intervals—Rating method data. *Journal of Mathematical Psychology, 6,* 487–496.

Dusoir, T. (1983). Isobias curves in some detection tasks. *Perception and Psychophysics, 33,* 403–412.

Egan, J. P., & Clarke, F. R. (1966). Psychophysics and signal detection. In J. B. Sidowski (Ed.), *Experimental methods and instrumentation in psychology* (pp. 211–246). New York: McGraw–Hill.

Elsmore, T. F. (1972). Duration discrimination: Effects of probability of stimulus presentation. *Journal of the Experimental Analysis of Behavior, 18,* 465–469.

Galanter, E., & Holman, G. L. (1967). Some invariances of the isosensitivity function and their implications for the utility function of money. *Journal of Experimental Psychology, 73,* 333–339.

Green, D. M. (1964). General predictions relating yes-no and forced-choice results. *Journal of the Acoustical Society of America, 36,* 1024 (A).

Green, D. M., & Luce, R. D. (1973). Speed–accuracy trade off in auditory detection. In S. Kornblum (Ed.), *Attention and performance IV* (pp. 547–569). New York: Academic Press.

Green, D. M., & Swets, J. A. (1966). *Signal detection theory and psychophysics.* New York: Wiley. Republished (1989). Los Altos, CA: Peninsula.

Gundy, R. F. (1961). Auditory detection of an unspecified signal. *Journal of the Acoustical Society of America, 33,* 1008–1012.

Hautus, M. J. (1994). Expressions for the area under the chi-square receiver operating characteristic. *Journal of the Acoustical Society of America, 95,* 1674–1676.

Hautus, M. J. (1995). Corrections for extreme proportions and their biasing effects on estimated values of d'. *Behavior Research Methods Instrumentation and Computers, 27,* 46–51.

Hautus, M. J., & Irwin, R. J. (1992). Amplitude discrimination of sinusoids and narrow-band noise with Rayleigh properties. *Perception and Psychophysics, 52,* 53–62.

Hautus, M. J., Irwin, R. J., & Sutherland, S. (1994). Relativity of judgments about sound amplitude and the asymmetry of the same–different receiver operating characteristic. *Quarterly Journal of Experimental Psychology, 47A,* 1035–1045.

Herrnstein, R. J. (1961). Relative and absolute strength of response as a function of frequency of reinforcement. *Journal of the Experimental Analysis of Behavior, 4,* 267–272.

Hobson, S. L. (1975). Discriminability of fixed-ratio schedules for pigeons: Effects of absolute ratio size. *Journal of the Experimental Analysis of Behavior, 23,* 25–35.

Hobson, S. L. (1978). Discriminability of fixed-ratio schedules for pigeons: Effects of payoff value. *Journal of the Experimental Analysis of Behavior, 30,* 69–81.

Hollard, V., & Davison, M. C. (1971). Preference for qualitatively different reinforcers. *Journal of the Experimental Analysis of Behavior, 16,* 375–380.

Hume, A. L. (1974a). Auditory detection and optimal response biases. *Perception and Psychophysics, 15,* 425–433.

Hume, A. L. (1974b). Optimal response biases and the slope of ROC curves as a function of signal intensity, signal probability, and relative payoff. *Perception and Psychophysics, 16,* 377–384.

Hume, A. L. & Irwin, R. J. (1974). Bias functions and operating characteristics of rats discriminating auditory stimuli. *Journal of the Experimental Analysis of Behavior, 21,* 285–295.

Hunter, I., & Davison, M. (1982). Independence of response force and reinforcement rate on concurrent variable-interval schedule performance. *Journal of the Experimental Analysis of Behavior, 37,* 183–197.

Irwin, R. J., Hautus, M. J., & Stillman, J. A. (1992). Use of the receiver operating characteristic in the study of taste perception. *Journal of Sensory Studies, 7,* 291–334.

Irwin, R. J., Stillman, J. A., Hautus, M. J., & Huddleston, L. M. (1993). The measurement of taste discrimination with the same–different task: A detection-theory analysis. *Journal of Sensory Studies, 8,* 229–239.

Kaplan, H. L., Macmillan, N. A., & Creelman, C. D. (1978). Tables of *d'* for variable-standard discrimination paradigms. *Behavior Research Methods and Instrumentation, 10,* 796–813.

Kennedy, J. A. (1990). *Response bias parameters in an auditory detection and discrimination task: An experimental analysis.* Unpublished MSc thesis, University of Auckland.

Laming, D. (1986). *Sensory analysis.* New York: Academic Press.

Luce, R. D. (1963). Detection and recognition. In R. D. Luce, R. R. Bush, & E. Galanter (Eds.), *Handbook of mathematical psychology* (pp. 105–189). New York: Wiley.

Luce, R. D. (1986). *Response times: Their role in inferring elementary mental organization.* London: Oxford University Press.

Luce, R. D., & Krumhansl, C. L. (1988). Measurement, scaling, and psychophysics. In R. C. Atkinson, R. J. Herrnstein, G. Lindzey, & R. D. Luce (Eds.), *Stevens' handbook of experimental psychology* (Vol. 1, 2nd ed., pp. 3–74). New York: Wiley.

Macmillan, N. A., & Creelman, C. D. (1991). *Detection theory: A user's guide.* Cambridge: Cambridge University Press.

Macmillan, N. A., Kaplan, H. L., & Creelman, C. D. (1977). The psychophysics of categorical perception. *Psychological Review, 84,* 452–471.

Markowitz, J., & Swets, J. A. (1967). Factors affecting the slope of empirical ROC curves: Comparison of binary and rating responses. *Perception and Psychophysics, 2,* 91–100.

McCarthy, D., & Davison, M. (1979). Signal probability, reinforcement, and signal detection. *Journal of the Experimental Analysis of Behavior, 32,* 373–386.

McCarthy, D., & Davison, M. (1980). On the discriminability of stimulus duration. *Journal of the Experimental Analysis of Behavior, 33,* 187–211.

McCarthy, D., & Davison, M. (1981). Towards a behavioral theory of bias in signal detection. *Perception and Psychophysics, 29,* 371–382.

McCarthy, D., & Davison, M. (1984). Isobias and alloisobias functions in animal psychophysics. *Journal of Experimental Psychology: Animal Behavior Processes, 10,* 390–409.

McNicol, D. (1972). *A primer of signal detection theory.* London: Allen & Unwin.

Miller, G. A. (1956). The magical number seven, plus or minus two: Some limits on our capacity for processing information. *Psychological Review, 63,* 81–97.

Nevin, J. A. (1967). Effects of reinforcement scheduling on simultaneous discrimination performance. *Journal of the Experimental Analysis of Behavior, 10,* 251–260.

Nevin, J. A. (1969). Interval reinforcement of choice behavior in discrete trials. *Journal of the Experimental Analysis of Behavior, 12,* 875–885.

Nevin, J. A., Jenkins, P., Whittaker, S., & Yarensky, P. (1977). *Signal detection and matching.* Paper presented at the November meeting of the Psychonomic Society, Washington, DC.

Nevin, J. A., Jenkins, P., Whittaker, S., & Yarensky, P. (1982). Reinforcement contingencies and signal detection. *Journal of the Experimental Analysis of Behavior, 37,* 65–79.

Neyman, J., & Pearson, E. S. (1933). On the problem of the most efficient tests of statistical hypotheses. *Philosophical Transactions of the Royal Society of London Series A, 231,* 289–337.

Ogilvie, J. C., & Creelman, C. D. (1968). Maximum-likelihood estimation of receiver operating characteristic curve parameters. *Journal of Mathematical Psychology, 5,* 377–391.

O'Mahony, M. (1992). Understanding discrimination tests. A user-friendly treatment of response bias, rating and ranking R-index tests and their relationship to signal detection. *Journal of Sensory Studies, 7,* 1–47.

Pollack, I. (1952). The information of elementary auditory displays. *Journal of the Acoustical Society of America, 24,* 745–749.

Pollard, J. H. (1977). *A handbook of numerical and statistical techniques.* Cambridge: Cambridge University Press.

Press, W. H., Flannery, B. P., Teukolsky, S. A., & Vetterling, W. T. (1986). *Numerical recipes: The art of scientific computing.* Cambridge: Cambridge University Press.

Robinson, D. E., & Watson, C. E. (1972). Psychophysical methods in modern psychoacoustics. In J. V. Tobias (Ed.), *Foundations of modern auditory theory* (Vol. 2, pp. 101–131). New York: Academic Press.

Schulman, A. I., & Greenberg, G. Z. (1970). Operating characteristics and a priori probability of the signal. *Perception and Psychophysics, 8,* 317–320.

Stenson, H. (1988). *SIGNAL: A supplementary module for SYSTAT and SYGRAPH.* Evanston, IL: SYSTAT Inc.

Swets, J. A. (1973). The receiver operating characteristic in psychology. *Science, 182,* 990–1000.

Swets, J. A. (1986a). Indices of discrimination or diagnostic accuracy: Their ROCs and implied models. *Psychological Bulletin, 99,* 100–117.

Swets, J. A. (1986b). Form of empirical ROCs in discrimination and diagnostic tasks: Implications for theory and measurement of performance. *Psychological Bulletin, 99,* 181–198.

Swets, J. A. (1992). The science of choosing the right decision threshold in high-stakes diagnostics. *American Psychologist, 47,* 522–532.

Swets, J. A., & Pickett, R. M. (1982). *Evaluation of diagnostic systems: Methods from signal detection theory.* New York: Academic Press.

Terman, M., & Terman, J. S. (1972). Concurrent variation of response bias and sensitivity in an operant-psychophysical test. *Perception and Psychophysics, 7,* 428–432.

Williams, B. A., & Fantino, E. (1978). Effects on choice of reinforcer delay and conditioned reinforcement. *Journal of the Experimental Analysis of Behavior, 29,* 77–86.

IV

Verbal and Social Behavior

11

Behavioral Processes of Infants and Young Children

Paul Weisberg and Carolyn Rovee-Collier

When behavior analysts began to study children intensively in the mid-1950s, they drew their experimental problems and paradigms from studies of animals. The variables manipulated were those that were influential in the existing models of Skinner and Hull—magnitude of reinforcement, delay of reinforcement, deprivation, and so forth. Not surprisingly, children yielded data resembling those of animals. For ethical and other reasons, however, it was not possible to merely manipulate those conditions and variables successfully used with animals and apply them directly to children. Instead, similar operations were employed so that deprivation was instituted in terms of social deprivation, magnitude of reinforcement was studied in terms of the number of tokens, and punishment was enacted by withdrawing visual access to cartoons.

When experimental attention turned to infants a decade later, new problems surfaced. The sensory capacities of infants were unknown, their response capabilities were limited, and their attention to the relevant stimuli was a fluctuating commodity. Moreover, it was difficult to determine what events would function as reinforcers or for how long they would do so. Although classical conditioning was viewed as the most primitive form of associative learning, the Russians had concluded that before 6 months of age, the infant's brain was too immature to support the cortical connections thought to mediate classically conditioned responses, and early data from laboratories in this country and abroad seemed to support this conclusion. Likewise, although Piaget's diaries of his own infants' development contained numerous examples of shaping and operant conditioning, he described these as merely "elicited joy reactions" or "secondary circular reactions" and asserted that infants were incapable of acquiring behavior to alter their environment until late in their first year (Piaget, 1952). Against this theoretical backdrop, it is

Paul Weisberg • Department of Psychology, University of Alabama, Tuscaloosa, Alabama 35487-0348. Carolyn Rovee-Collier • Department of Psychology, Rutgers University, New Brunswick, New Jersey 08903.

Handbook of Research Methods in Human Operant Behavior, edited by Lattal and Perone. Plenum Press, New York, 1998.

hardly surprising that many developmental psychologists were unconvinced when researchers documented operant conditioning in infants only 2½ to 4 months old (Brackbill, 1958; Rheingold, 1956; Rheingold, Gewirtz, & Ross, 1959; Rheingold, Stanley, & Cooley, 1962; Rovee & Rovee, 1969; Sheppard, 1969; Weisberg, 1963).

The free-operant method was a major technological advance in psychological research (Skinner, 1956). By permitting an organism to distribute its responses freely over time, the method offered a means by which the "value" to the organism of its own response consequences could be measured directly. The effect of systematically manipulating aspects of the experimental context could then be assessed in terms of changes in the frequency and distribution of responses. The free-operant method offered several advantages to the discrete-trials procedures that had dominated research under Thorndike and Hull. First, it provided a continuous record of behavior over the course of an entire experimental session (behavior occurring between discrete trials was otherwise missed). Second, it revealed the power of reinforcement contingencies and stimulus-correlated events for the creation and maintenance of a variety of different rates and patterns of behavior. And, third, the free-operant procedure eliminated potential confusion associated with the onset and termination of a trial as well as the effects of special handing procedures during the intertrial interval.

In this chapter, we review considerations associated with conducting operant conditioning research during the first 4 years of life, but by concentrating on the first two years, we suggest solutions to some of the problems that such research engenders, and we also provide examples of how such research has been implemented. When giving experimental details, exact ages expressed in terms of weeks, months, or years and months will be reported for individual subjects and means and age ranges for groups. More generic subject descriptions, which signify protracted age periods—such as infants (first year of life), toddlers (12–18 months), and young children (2–5 years)—will be employed to summarize developmental descriptions and findings or to make general statements about a particular aspect of the life span. In the case of qualifying terms such as younger or older infants, infants in their second year, or preschool children, the reader is asked to consider the context in which they are used.

RESEARCH STRATEGIES FOR INFANTS AND YOUNG CHILDREN

Creating Favorable Experimental Conditions

Infants and young children bring to an experiment a backlog of experiences that may either facilitate or disrupt their performance in the ensuing task (Bijou, 1993). An inactive infant who has experienced a relatively barren or unchanging environment or one lacking effective reinforcement contingencies might be a successful learner in an experimental setting that offers a variety of consequences for active and sustained responding. Conversely, if awakened suddenly from a nap, an otherwise excellent subject might either resist experimental participation, only partially complete a session, or produce unusable data.

Conducting research in familiar settings can reduce the unwanted effects of distracting but extraneous stimuli. Thus, for example, infants and toddlers might be tested in their homes or day-care centers or in other places where they spend considerable periods of time. Familiar settings also minimize the unwanted state changes that are often induced by changes in the daily routine or by travel to a university-based laboratory site. To counteract unpredictable occurrences on the test day (e.g., oversleeping) that necessitate treating the infant differently (e.g., rousing the infant) in order to adhere to a prescheduled appointment time, a home-located researcher can simply wait until the infant normally achieves an alert, playful state—usually after waking, diaper-changing, and feeding. When possible, the mother can phone the researcher if her infant is still sleeping or when the infant finally awakens, thus reducing the waiting time. In one study, the mother agreed to interact minimally with her infant before the researcher's arrival in order to improve the subsequent potency of the researcher-delivered social consequences for infant smiling (Brackbill, 1958). As another variant of maternal participation, Leuba and Friedlander (1968) demonstrated to the mother the use of an automated crib-mounted toy (to be described later) during an initial home-based training session. In subsequent sessions the mother became the "experimenter." Told that her baby could be placed in an experimental playpen whenever it was suitable, the mother had to preset a timer and remove her baby when it rang. Setting the timer to a prearranged, hopefully realistic value obviously can prevent otherwise prolonged experimental sessions that can result in rapid satiation of the programmed consequences and in a refusal of further infant participation. Prescheduling session length can also guard against the practice of removing the infant only after performance conformed to preexisting expectations of the mother. Worth noting in this study is that the mother was left to ensure that other family members remained still and silent during a session. Nowadays, an added measure of control would include videotapings of a sample or all of the parent-directed sessions.

Because home-based sessions require a shorter initial period of behavioral adaptation and involve less disruption of the infant's normal routine, they often can last longer than sessions conducted in the laboratory, which rarely exceed 10 to 20 min during the first year of life. The researcher's fundamental concern is to allow sufficient time for the infant to acquire the task and to attain a stable level of final performance. Although scheduling multiple sessions for infant research may compensate for a single briefer session, multiple sessions can reduce the number of participants and dramatically increase the opportunity for attrition.

When non-laboratory-based research is precluded by either space restrictions, technical requirements, or cumbersome apparatus, steps must be taken to ensure a pleasant and smooth laboratory experience for both mother and child. Because travel-induced fluctuations in the infant's state are particularly disruptive, laboratory sessions should be scheduled whenever possible at times when the mother normally takes her infant on errands. Also, the experimenter should provide a napping area, and the mother should be encouraged to feed and diaper her infant prior to testing. Clear-cut travel directions and accessible parking spaces must be provided. When possible, an assistant should meet the mother in the parking lot and accompany her to the laboratory so as to minimize difficulties and confusion associated with transporting the infant from the car to the laboratory.

Laboratory procedures that restrict or alter the infant's normal interactions with its caretaker or environmental surround may produce unintended troublesome behaviors. Denying visual access to, or contact with, the mother, for example, may induce fussiness and impair performance in older infants, who typically sit on their mothers' lap while reacting to novel displays. The typical practice of placing infants in a sling seat inside of a three-sided enclosure to remove visual access to all but the experimental stimuli (Rovee-Collier & Gekoski, 1979), for example, is likely to be effective only with infants younger than 8 to 10 months. Eliminating normal conversation between the experimenter and the mother or asking the mother to remain silent may also distract or upset the infant.

The availability of a nearby familiar person, although appropriate for purposes of facilitating experimental adaptation and of lessening disruptive behaviors, can nonetheless create its own problems. Most prominent are the unintended actions of the "neutral" adaptive agent at critical times in the experiment. Does this person inadvertently provide response-dependent (mainly social) consequences for the infant's behavior in addition to the experimentally arranged consequences that are possibly under investigation? Does this person provide subtle cues at the time of the infant's response, as in nudging or angling the infant to move toward or away from an important stimulus? Clarification of these unwanted intrusions and procedures to overcome them are discussed later in the section on Familiarization Procedures. Suffice it to say that preexperimental proactive measures need to be employed whereby a supportive adult is told, shown, and perhaps practiced in the kinds of permissible infant interactions so as to prevent the generation of data that are not usable because of inadvertent adult interference.

In addition, before beginning a study, a set of behavioral criteria for retaining subjects in the final sample must be established, and the number and reason for nonparticipation must be reported in a final write-up. Such criteria might include crying or inattention to the stimulus array for a given number of consecutive minutes, a baseline rate higher or lower than a specified value, failure to maintain the requisite seating posture, scheduling problems, missed appointments, illness, experimenter error, or apparatus failure (e.g., Hill, Borovsky, & Rovee-Collier, 1988; Rheingold et al., 1962). A reasonable learning criterion in operant studies with young infants is the attainment of an individual response rate at least 1.5 times the baseline rate for two of any three consecutive minutes during an acquisition phase (Hill et al., 1988). Researchers must include nonreinforcement phases or response-independent reinforcement phases in their designs to ensure operant control and to distinguish between behavioral arousal and a learned increase in responding over a session. Failure to control properly for behavioral arousal will make the resulting data uninterpretable, hence of no scientific value. Finally, the parent's right to terminate participation at any time must be conveyed and respected. If the infant becomes emotionally upset at any point, efforts must be taken to alleviate the distress and create a positive postexperimental experience.

Response Selection

Prior to the 1960s, researchers frequently assumed that the relatively limited response repertoire of very young infants placed severe constraints on experimental attempts to study learning. However, a large number of the possible responses originally described by Dennis (1934) have now been studied with remarkable success, suggesting that the ingenuity of the investigator rather than response limitations of the infant was the rate-limiting step. Still, sensitivity to developmental constraints and advancements must be exercised in the selection of an appropriate response in certain contexts. Infants younger than 2½ months are unlikely to emit prehension responses (as in cord pulling) or coordinated and directed finger or hand movements (as in lever or panel pressing) because of the characteristic clenched-fist topography associated with this age range. Moreover, actions that, when executed, block observation of visual consequences are similarly to be avoided. Instead, attaching a cord to the infant's wrist or ankle and measuring hand or leg pulls is a more reasonable approach with infants unable to operate manipulanda requiring grasping or prehension skills. Requiring leg movements or kicks against a panel enables a supine-positioned infant to see overhead sensory consequences without the visual obstruction likely with arm pulls (Rovee & Rovee, 1969). On the other hand, requiring 1-year-olds to remain seated or on their knees in an unrestricted playpen so they can readily manipulate response devices placed at midbody is apt to compete with naturally occurring and frequent attempts to pull up to an erect posture and stand with support. Such competing activities led Leuba and Friedlander (1968) to select younger infants not engaged in such practices.

A cursory overview of the responses used to index infant learning is presented next. We have cited only the first report of learning involving each response. The earliest operant-learning experiments with infants followed variations of procedures used successfully with animals and involved changes in *specific reflexes.* Pavlov's research on feeding and defensive reflexes, for example, formed the basis for converting reflexive actions into operants (for review, see Rovee-Collier, 1987). Thus, the rooting reflex acquired operant properties if reinforced with milk when infants turned their heads to the left or right at the sound of a buzzer or tone, respectively (Papousek, 1961). Among the defensive reflexes studied in infants was the instrumental escape behavior of Little Albert (J. B. Watson & Rayner, 1920).

A second class of responses, described by Peiper (1963) as *general reactions,* are not elicited by the stimulation of a specific organ by a specific stimulus, although they may reflect stimulus intensity. Thus, activity changes (most often, stabilimeter activity), increases or decreases in distress (e.g., crying, calming), and psychophysiological responses (e.g., heart rate, respiration, galvanic skin responses, EEG evoked potentials; for review, see Berg & Berg, 1987) were used either singly or in combination to index learning. Interest in heart-rate measures was spurred by Graham and Clifton's (1966) hypothesis that cardiac deceleration and acceleration were physiological reflections of orienting reflexes ("information processing") and defensive reflexes ("stimulus rejection"), respectively. From the observation that the form of the heart-rate response changes from acceleratory to deceleratory during the third month of life (Lipton, Steinschneider, & Richmond, 1966), it was a small step to the conclusion that infants younger than 3 months are limited in their ability to process information. This appealing analysis of the meaning of directional heart-rate changes has gained widespread acceptance and influences current interpretations of research with preverbal organisms (Campbell & Ampuero, 1985).

The preceding responses have been used more often in studies of classical conditioning than of operant conditioning with infants. Operant learning of preverbal infants has usually been indexed by changes in relatively simple *recursive motoric acts* such as kicks (Rovee & Rovee, 1969), arm pulls (Friedlander, 1961), nonnutritive sucks (Siqueland, 1968a,b), smiles (Brackbill, 1958), vocalizations (Rheingold et al., 1959), visual fixations (J. S. Watson, 1966), panel presses (Simmons & Lipsitt, 1961), pillow presses (J. S. Watson & Ramey, 1972), head turns (Caron, 1967), and sphere touches (Rheingold et al., 1962).

Response patterns that require greater degree of coordination have been exploited in tasks with infants between 10 and 18 months of age. These include selective reaching to objects in discrete-trial discrimination paradigms (Fagen, 1977; Weisberg, 1970a; Weisberg & Simmons, 1966), and head-poking into a looking chamber (Weisberg & Fink, 1968). Responses used with preschoolers and older children include pressing levers or telegraph keys and manipulating panels (Bijou, 1957; Hively, 1962; Long, 1959).

Naturally occurring behaviors that have become "problem behaviors" have attracted the interest of applied behavior analysts, who have sought to modify them. The number of modifiable classes of dysfunctional behaviors is large and beyond the scope of this chapter. We emphasize, however, that each form of problem behavior need not require a unique treatment or explanatory mechanism (one for excessive thumbsucking, another for self-destructive behaviors, and so on). Rather, behavior analysts have attempted to apply a unified and consistent set of principles, based on well-established functional relations between changes in observable behavior and the controlling environmental variables, to a variety of natural response forms of individuals of all ages. In contrast, use of operant procedures in the traditional areas of developmental psychology has been relatively limited. Representative behavioral phenomena that have been investigated are infant perception (Rovee-Collier, Hankins, & Bhatt, 1992) and memory (Sullivan, Rovee-Collier, & Tynes, 1979), categorization (Hayne, Rovee-Collier, & Perris, 1987), maternal attachment and separation (Gewirtz & Palaez-Nogueras, 1992), creativity (Holman, Goetz, & Baer, 1977), and conservation of mass, weight, and volume (Parsonson & Naughton, 1988). Scores of other developmental phenomena beg for similar systematic investigation (Novak, 1995).

Reinforcer Selection

In operant studies with infants and young children, appetitive consequences (positive reinforcers) have been used more frequently than aversive consequences (punishers) to modify and maintain responding. Because experimenters using nutritive reinforcers usually have access to infants only between feedings, their manipulations are generally restricted to the administration of sugar water or milk in small amounts that will not influence subsequent intake. The use of nonnutritive consequences for infants sidesteps such a problem. Nonnutritive reinforcement most often involves the presentation or termination of an auditory or visual stimulus, although the opportunity to engage in nonnutritive sucking is also an effective reinforcer. Brown (1972), for example, observed that newborns sucked most on a standard Davol nipple, next most on a blunt Davol nipple, and least on a piece of rubber tubing. Applying Premack's (1965) response-probability theory of reinforcement, she then increased the rate of tube-sucking by making sucking on a standard nipple dependent on tube-sucking. Although blunt-nipple sucking did not increase when followed by the opportunity to suck on the standard nipple, it was significantly *slowed* when followed by the lower-probability response opportunity—tube-sucking. Infants achieved these rate changes by decreasing or increasing the interval of pausing between successive sucking bursts (Brassell & Kaye, 1974). Finally, many researchers have used "social" reinforcers, that is, auditory or visual stimulation provided by other humans. Paradoxically, although social reinforcers appear to be particularly effective, infants satiate to them rapidly when they are presented in a standardized format. Of added concern, social reinforcers often *elicit* reciprocal social or affective behaviors that can compete with or mimic conditioning (Bloom, 1979; Bloom & Esposito, 1975).

There is no essential biological relation between the type of reinforcer and the operant response it influences. Infants increase the rate of sucking, for example, as readily when their sucks are followed by their mother's voice (DeCasper & Fifer, 1980; Mills & Melhuish, 1974), a computer-generated speech sound (Eimas, Siqueland, Jusczyk, & Vigorito, 1971; Trehub & Rabinovitch, 1972), music (Butterfield & Siperstein, 1972), a movie (Bower, 1967; Kalnins & Bruner, 1973), colored slides of geometric shapes (Franks & Berg, 1975; Milewski & Siqueland, 1975), the movement of a crib mobile (Little, 1973; Rovee & Rovee, 1969), or termination of white noise (Butterfield & Siperstein, 1972), as when their sucks are followed by a squirt of sugar water (Kobre & Lipsitt, 1972) or milk (Hillman & Bruner, 1972; Sameroff, 1968)! Head-turning is similarly reinforced by a variety of biologically unrelated consequences—a visual pattern (Levinson & Levinson, 1967) or a novel toy (Koch, 1968), a human jack-in-the-box (Bower, 1964), visual access to the mother or a stranger (Koch, 1968), a squirt of milk (Papousek, 1961) or sugar water (Clifton, Siqueland, & Lipsitt, 1972), a nonnutritive nipple (Siqueland, 1968a), or simply by "being correct" (Papousek, 1967). Vocalizations have been reinforced by both auditory (Hulsebus, 1973; Todd & Palmer, 1968) and visual stimulation (J. S. Watson & Ramey, 1972), as have visual behavior (J. S. Watson, 1969), foot-kicking (McKirdy & Rovee, 1978), and panel-pressing (Lipsitt, Pederson, & DeLucia, 1966).

The major commonality among these reinforcers perhaps is that the infant's behavior changes the environment. A number of researchers have reported that infants may have continued to perform an old response and even acquired a new one while concurrently rejecting the presentation of the nominal reinforcer (Papousek, 1969). In the absence of an explicit primary or nominal reinforcer, Skinner (1953) points to the possibility of a baby's repetitive acts being maintained by the consequences received simply by "making the world behave." Such a mechanism could have developed during the course of evolution so that "any organism which is reinforced by its success in manipulating nature, regardless of the momentary consequences, will be in a favored position when important consequences follow" (Skinner, 1953, p. 78). Rovee-Collier (1983) surmised that on many of these occasions the infant engages in *problem solving* as a means to produce novel and sometimes functional changes in the physical environment.

The rapidity with which infants satiate to a reinforcer is a major constraint on session length. Siqueland (1968b) found that slides to which infants had been pre-exposed for 2 min were less efficacious in reinforcing high-amplitude sucks in the succeeding 8 min than slides that were novel. Similarly, when looking was reinforced with a series of different pictures, 20-month-olds persisted longer in looking than when their responding produced the same picture on each occasion (Weisberg & Fink, 1968). If reinforcers are too simple or their range of variation is too restricted, satiation may be rapid. Conversely, complex reinforcers that are "relatively novel" (Berlyne, 1960) can remain effective for very long periods. Rovee and Rovee (1969), for example, exploited the reinforcing efficacy of the countless number and variety of visual rearrangements of a highly detailed five-component mobile with 10-week-olds in a single session lasting more than 45 min, and Smith (reported in Lipsitt, 1969) used this same reinforcer in long daily sessions with an infant between 2 and 5 months of age.

A wide assortment of response-dependent consequences have been used to establish and sustain operant responses of preschoolers and older children. As with infants, these accomplishments occur more often by presenting positive consequences rather than by withdrawing negative events contingent on responding. In a few cases, behavior (thumbsucking) that terminated positive consequences (uninterrupted movie cartoons) became less probable (Baer, 1960, 1962a). Bijou and Sturges (1959) advocated using "consumables" (e.g., snacks; see Weisberg, 1970b) and "manipulatables" (e.g., trinkets, charms; see Long, 1962) as reinforcers. Reinforcement devices also have been loaded with either trinkets (Long, 1959; Long, Hammack, May, & Campbell, 1958) or generalized conditioned reinforcers such as pennies (Long, 1963) and tokens that subjects can exchange for other items (Bijou & Baer, 1966).

Zeiler and Kelley (1969) found that cartoons could maintain preschooler's responding (see also Baer, 1960), but they could not identify whether presentation of the cartoons or curtailment of periods without cartoons was the reinforcement. The duration of cartoon-viewing, however, was important: Short (10 s) viewing periods were less effective than long (30 s) ones. A reinforcer effective in building classes of imitative and nonimitative behavior was the attention and verbal approval of a mechanized (talking and animated) puppet (Baer & Sherman, 1964). The advantages of a talking puppet instead of a talking adult as the source of reinforcement include the ability to standardize and control the variety and subtlety of social stimuli (e.g., nods, smiles, raised eyebrows, winces) and the greater likelihood that children will adapt more readily to (and be more accepting of) the social gestures of a puppet than of an unfamiliar experimenter (Baer, 1962b).

To enhance the effectiveness of reinforcers and make them longer lasting, child researchers often must resort to special procedures. These include varying a single reinforcer type (e.g., trinkets) within and across sessions (Long, 1959), mixing different types of reinforcers (e.g., edibles and manipulatables) in known proportions (Bijou & Baer, 1966), replacing old reinforcers with new ones (Long et al., 1958), or gradually reducing the presentation rate of a target reinforcer (e.g., a trinket) while at the same time increasing the delivery rate of potential conditioned reinforcers (e.g., visual or auditory events) that had previously accompanied the target reinforcer (Bijou, 1958).

RESEARCH METHODS FOR INFANTS

Three reinforcement schedules that have been used successfully with very young infants are *conjugate reinforcement, synchronous reinforcement* and *threshold tasks.* In these schedules, the intensity or duration of reinforcement as well as its availability are programmed to vary with these corresponding dimensions of responding: increases or decreases in frequency, amplitude, speed, or rate of responding as well as response occurrence. Because these three schedules can produce long-lasting, multiple stimulus consequences, instead of a single discrete event such as food, which is either consumed or removed for a specified period, there is a greater possibility of the response-reinforcement dependency being discriminable to the infant.

Conjugate Reinforcement

In a conjugate reinforcement schedule, each response that meets a minimum effort requirement changes the environment in several ways, most notably by modifying some intensive aspect. It differs from a traditional fixed-ratio 1 schedule, however, in that the rate or amplitude of a response directly determines the nature of its consequences. Lindsley (1963) used the conjugate schedule with a 5-month-old who was placed in a bassinet beneath an overhead projection screen with her feet resting against a vertical panel. Discrete kicks that produced a 2.54-cm displacement of the panel increased the intensity of the projection lamp for a brief period. With increases in response rate, the intensity of the lamp grew brighter, with the intensity falling exponentially during interresponse pauses. The reinforcer was a silent movie of a smiling female, so that each kick effectively constituted an observing response. This procedure engendered rapid learning with high and sustained response rates.

Lindsley (1962, 1963), who introduced the conjugate schedule, regarded the "striptease" effect achieved by the gradual presentation and withdrawal of a reinforcer to be more effective than the abrupt presentation and termination of a reinforcer at full strength. Thus, the response consequences are not a series of discrete changes but vary continuously along an intensity dimension that ranges from 0 to 100% in proportion to response changes from zero to some maximum value, the latter being limited only by the experimenter's manipulations or the organism's physiology. As infants are found to learn the characteristics of the conjugate schedule, they are perhaps more able to detect the relation between the properties of their responses and the properties of the consequences. Eventually, as some have claimed (e.g., Rovee-Collier & Fagen, 1981), *control* of the consequences becomes the major factor.

The advantages of a conjugate schedule are threefold. First, because every response produces a known change on some stimulus dimension, the reinforcing value of these changes to the organism can be indexed by the time or energy expended to produce it. This aspect of the schedule eliminates the arbitrary decision of the experimenter about which single value of a reinforcer to use. Instead, each subject can "shop" from a vast array of intensity-based consequences for the value that proves optimal relative to the response cost of obtaining and retaining it. This value will differ from age to age, from individual to individual, and even from moment to moment for a given individual. Second, because each infant determines the momentary value of his or her own reward, the problem of equating reinforcers for infants of different ages is eliminated. The third advantage pertains to the possibility of infants directly and independently determining their own parameters of reinforcement for each and every stimulus feature along relatively complex dimensions that include intensity, movement, variety, and other modalities. Such a possibility circumvents Brackbill and Koltsova's (1967) caution associated with an experimenter preselecting a "representative" set of stimulus dimensions and assuming that each member in the set reflects some optimal value.

The HAS Procedure

The development of the high-amplitude sucking (HAS) procedure (Siqueland, 1968b, 1969a,b; Siqueland & DeLucia, 1969) was a direct outgrowth of Lindsley's (1962, 1963) early work. In the HAS conjugate reinforcement procedure, infants sit in a cradle chair or on an assistant's lap and view a series of projected visual images that are contingent on their nonnutritive sucking behavior. Each suck that exceeds a predetermined amplitude threshold value activates a cumulative recorder and is simultaneously fed into a conjugate programmer, which triggers the brief and immediate delivery of the visual reinforcer whose intensity is proportional to the rate of all suprathreshold (i.e., high-amplitude) responses. The changing frequency and quality of the visual display results from the conjugate activation of a 500-W lamp within a standard 35-mm slide projector. Increasing rates of HAS gradually increase the intensity of illumination from zero to maximum brightness, and an HAS rate of 2/s maintains maximum intensity without interruption. Infants too young to remain upright are tested in a cradle, and projected images are reflected through an overhead mirror arrangement.

Siqueland and DeLucia (1969) documented that the HAS of 4-month-olds is sensitive to changes in conjugately presented visual reinforcers. Infants received either a presentation (reinforcement group) or a 5-s interruption (withdrawal group) of colored slides (geometric forms, cartoon figures, human faces) contingent on the rate of HAS (sucks with a positive pressure amplitude equaling or exceeding 18 mm Hg). The slide tray was advanced every 30 s, and a complete series of eight slides was available for viewing within each acquisition phase. Experimental phases consisted of baseline (2 min), acquisition (4 min), extinction (2 min), reacquisition (4 min), and reextinction (3 min). A control group that sucked nonnutritively for 10 min in the presence of a dimly illuminated screen without changing the visual display produced a reference curve showing a typical downward shift in HAS baseline rate.

Although the withdrawal and the control groups did not differ, infants in the reinforcement group exhibited reliable changes in HAS responses during each test phase. The proportion of HAS in relation to total number of sucks indicated that their behavior reflected true changes in the amplitude of sucking rather than merely an increase in total sucking activity. The effect of contingent stimulation on the response differentiation was rapid: By min 4 of acquisition, the proportion of HAS had almost doubled and was more than twice that of the other groups.

A variant of the HAS technique was described by Kalnins and Bruner (1973), who investigated the capacity of infants to exhibit "voluntary control" over their visual environments. Specifically, the clarity of a silent motion picture was made dependent on the nonnutritive sucking rate of infants tested twice weekly for 12 sessions beginning at 5 weeks of age. Infants who were initially exposed to a blurred picture produced increasing clarity by sucking, whereas others, initially exposed to a clear picture, produced increasing blur by sucking. These groups were analogous to Siqueland's (1968b) stimulus presentation and stimulus withdrawal groups, respectively. In addition, for some infants in each focus condition, the response consequences were reversed in later sessions. A maturational control group, tested only during the baseline and extinction phases, provided an index of normal rates of response followed by random consequences (varying degrees of clarity). Any suck that exceeded 0.37 mm Hg altered the focus; maximum clarity or blur was achieved within 2.3 s by a normal suck rate of 2/s and was maintained by a rate of at least 1.5/s.

Infants in the suck-for-clear condition rapidly increased suck rates during acquisition and rapidly decreased suck rates following the reversal, but infants in the suck-for-blur condition did not deviate from their baseline rates either initially or following the reversal. An analysis of looking behavior suggests that infants in the latter condition may not have been sensitive to the contingency shift. Looking behavior of all infants always was greatest during sucking pauses and looked away during sucking bursts, whereas infants in the suck-for-clear condition looked and sucked simultaneously. This observation underscores the importance of recording looking behavior when visual reinforcers are used in order to ensure that the specified reinforcer is actually received when the infant produces a criterion response. The experimenter may even choose to limit response counts to "fixated operants."

The HAS-Recovery Procedure

The rapidity with which 4-month-olds satiate to specific visual stimuli led to the melding of the conjugate HAS procedure and the habituation-discrimination paradigm used in infant visual-attention research (for review, see Clifton & Nelson, 1976; Cohen & Gelber, 1975). In the resulting *HAS-recovery procedure,* HAS is initially increased by the conjugate presentation of a novel visual reinforcer. When responding subsequently declines with continued exposure to the same reinforcer (typically to 50% of the initial response rate), another visual reinforcer is substituted for the original one, and HAS is reinstated. The magnitude of HAS recovery can thus provide an index of the relative effectiveness between the original and the substituted reinforcers.

Bruner (1973) argued that sucking is incompatible with simultaneous visual information processing, raising questions about using the HAS technique with visual reinforcers. However, the success of HAS experiments casts doubts on the generality of his thesis. Likewise, Atkinson and Braddick (1976) complained that the HAS-recovery procedure is "laborious" relative to a visual-preference procedure, which is also more flexible in accommodating to state changes. However, the HAS-recovery procedure is immune to position (side) biases that interfere with the visual-preference technique. Given the difficulty in maintaining the alertness of very young infants when they are not sucking (MacFarlane, Harris, & Barnes, 1976), the laboriousness of the HAS-recovery technique appears to be a reasonable price to pay for data that otherwise might not be obtained.

Conjugately Reinforced Panel Pressing

Lipsitt et al. (1966) adapted the conjugate procedure for use with 12-month-olds. The operant was panel-pressing—a response highly compatible with the active manipulative and exploratory behavior of infants this age. Subjects sat in front of a darkened viewing box and gained visual access to a rotating picture of a colorful clown by pressing (banging) a panel mounted on the box, briefly activating a light source inside it. Increases or decreases in response rate produced gradual and proportional increases or decreases, respectively, in the frequency and intensity of the illumination; two to three presses per second produced continuous illumination at maximum intensity. As before, the target response was readily acquired under these response-reinforcement dependencies.

Mobile Conjugate Reinforcement

The mobile conjugate reinforcement procedure stemmed from Hunt and Uzgiris's (1964) observation that infants in flexible cribs not only learned to shake themselves to produce movements in mobiles that hung from stands affixed to their cribs, but also "appeared to take delight from their ability to activate them" (p. 9). The mobile technique differs from the previous conjugate techniques in that the intensity of the conjugate reinforcer (mobile movement) is determined by two parameters of response—rate and amplitude. Depending on response rate, the inertial properties of the mobile permit recurrent kicks to drive the intensity of mobile movement up to some maximum (unmeasured) point of activation. A response initiated before the mobile components have ceased swaying produces a consequence of greater intensity than the same response produces in a completely still mobile. In addition, the greater the kick amplitude, the greater is the amplitude with which the mobile suspension bar is drawn and released, and the greater is the extent to which the components jerk or bounce. Because infants' kicks are conditioned so rapidly in this procedure, the need for an extended series of multiple sessions in order to establish the response is eliminated—a critical factor in research with infants, to whom access is limited.

Rovee and Rovee (1969) demonstrated that 2½-month-olds could be operantly conditioned within 3 to 6 min in the mobile conjugate reinforcement procedure. Infants were tested in their own cribs at a time of day when they were likely to be alert and playful. The mobile was hung over the infant's chest from a suspension stand clamped to one crib rail. For 3 min at the outset of the session (*baseline*), a

 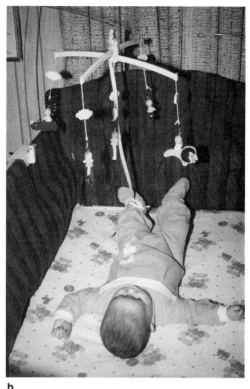

a   b

FIGURE 11.1.   The experimental arrangement for mobile conjugate reinforcement used with 2- and 3-
month-olds. (a) A nonreinforcement phase (baseline, extinction); (b) a reinforcement phase (acquisition).

narrow ribbon was connected without slack from one of the infant's ankles to an
"empty" suspension stand that was clamped to the opposite crib rail (see Figure
11.1a). In this arrangement, the infant could view the mobile, but kicks could not
activate it. Next, the experimenter hooked the ribbon to the same stand as the
mobile for 15 min (*acquisition*) (see Figure 11.1b). In this arrangement, each kick
conjugately activated the mobile causing its hanging wooden figures to make a variety of movements and, at high kicking rates, the figures collided, affording auditory feedback. Finally, the session ended with a 5-min nonreinforcement period
(*extinction*) that was procedurally identical to the baseline phase, when the mobile was visible but stationary. Yoked control groups received either response-
independent visual or visual plus somesthetic stimulation from the moving mobile during the acquisition phase.

The experimental group showed a rapid and sustained increase in kick rate
during acquisition and a return to the baseline rate during extinction, whereas both
control groups maintained their baseline rates and response topography throughout the session (see Figure 11.2). The performance of two infants who received a
10-min reacquisition phase and a 5-min reextinction phase on 2 successive days
is shown in Figure 11.3. The conjugate reinforcer clearly controlled responding

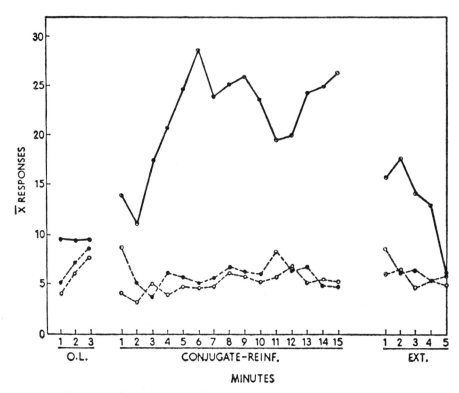

FIGURE 11.2. Mean rate of response as a function of reinforcement condition. Each x-axis point represents a successive minute of observation; approximately 2 min separates phases. The solid line represents the experimental group (conjugate reinforcement); dashed lines represent noncontingent-reinforcement control groups (●, visual plus somesthetic stimulation; ○, visual stimulation only). From Rovee and Rovee, 1969, *Journal of Experimental Child Psychology.* Reproduced by permission of Academic Press.

throughout all phases, despite the fact that the latter sessions lasted 46 min! This study was notable for the length of the session (at least triple that of sessions previously used with infants), the young age of the infants, and the arousal control groups, which demonstrated that a moving mobile—even when attached to the ankle by a tugging ribbon—does not elicit kicking as implied by Piaget's description of elicited "joy" reactions (1952, p. 160).

The mobile conjugate reinforcement procedure now has been standardized so that 2- and 3-month-olds receive a 15-min session on 2 successive days and a procedurally identical test session after a specified delay. Three or four daily sessions are used for discrimination studies (Rovee-Collier & Fagen, 1981). Each daily acquisition phase lasts 9 min and is preceded and followed by a 3-min nonreinforcement period. Although 5 min is typically required to achieve extinction at this age, the mean response rate during the final 3-min nonreinforcement phase usually reflects the mean response rate during the final 3 min of acquisition, thereby providing an index of the final level of conditioning and of immediate retention (performance after zero delay). These measures serve as reference points for

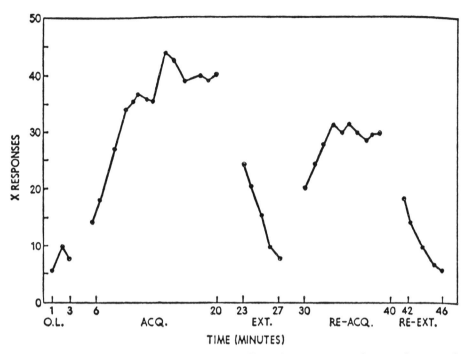

FIGURE 11.3. Mean rate of response of two infants collapsed over 2 training days as a function of session phase over 46 min of continuous testing. Note that the reinforcer continued to control behavior at min 40, when the response rate was still approximately 2.5 times operant level. From Rovee and Rovee, 1969, *Journal of Experimental Child Psychology.* Reproduced by permission of Academic Press.

individual performance in subsequent manipulations. The response rate in the 3-min nonreinforcement phase at the outset of each succeeding session, for example, veridically reflects the response rate in the final 3-min nonreinforcement phase of the prior session (Rovee & Fagen, 1976).

Rovee-Collier and Capatides (1979) placed 3-month-olds on a multiple conjugate reinforcement schedule that, when in effect, had one stimulus (S+) correlated with a conjugate reinforcement schedule component and a different stimulus (S−) correlated with an extinction component. The S+ and S− consisted of distinctive colors and patterns (green bulls' eyes and stripes on yellow; blue squares and dots on white) displayed on all sides of the mobile blocks (see Figure 11.4). Reinforcement was the conjugate movement of the blocks that was produced by kicking. The stimulus associated with the fewest kicks during baseline was designated as the S+ for a given infant. In Experiment 1, infants received a 1-min baseline phase with each stimulus followed by a 9-min reinforcement phase with S+ and a 3-min extinction phase with S−. On Day 2, infants were placed on a multiple conjugate reinforcement (3 min) extinction (1 min) schedule for 8 min and then on a multiple conjugate reinforcement (2 min) extinction (2 min) schedule for 36 min. In Experiment 2, infants received a 2-min baseline period with each stimulus, after which responding to both stimuli was reinforced during successive, al-

FIGURE 11.4.   Mobile blocks displaying one of the two sets of discriminative stimuli used by Rovee-Collier and Capatides (1979) with 3-month-olds.

ternating 2-min periods for 16 min prior to the introduction of the multiple con-jugate reinforcement (2 min) extinction (2 min) schedule at the outset of Session 2. During the final 12 min of the study (i.e., Session 4), responding in both com-ponents again was reinforced during alternating 2-min stimulus presentations.

After the multiple schedule was introduced in Session 2, kicks in both ex-periments increased during S+ and decreased during S− and remained high for the remaining sessions. In Experiment 1, 9 of 10 infants responded significantly more during S+ than during S− on every presentation after only 10 min on the multiple schedule; after 28 min, no reversals occurred (see Figure 11.5). The per-sistence of their increased responding to S+ is highly characteristic of behavioral contrast (Mackintosh, 1974).

Hill et al. (1988) modified the mobile procedure to make it suitable for 6-month-olds, who cannot be tested supine. These infants are placed in a sling seat

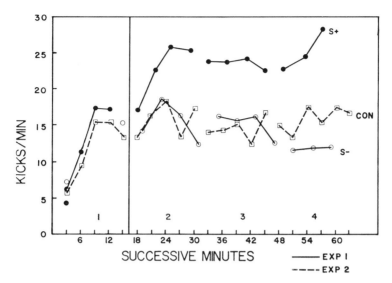

FIGURE 11.5.   Changes in mean response rate over successive minutes of four sessions during which kicks to S+ (●–●) were reinforced and kicks to S– (○–○) were not. Session 1 was a training session; the two mobiles were successively alternated beginning in Session 2. The control group (dashed lines) received reinforcement from the original mobile throughout all sessions. From Rovee-Collier and Capatides, 1979, Experiment 1. *Journal of the Experimental Analysis of Behavior, 32,* 15–27. Copyright 1979 by permission of the Society for the Experimental Analysis of Behavior, Inc.

inside their home playpens, and the mobile is suspended in front of them from a horizontal rod attached to a floor microphone stand (see Figure 11.6). The ankle ribbon is simply detached from the mobile hook during periods of nonreinforcement. In addition, sessions are one-third shorter, and the mobile reinforcer contains more components (seven objects instead of five plus jingle bells on each suspension line). Six-month-olds learn faster (within 1 to 2 min) than younger infants, but response-independent reinforcement controls still do not increase responding during reinforcement phases (see Figure 11.7).

Although the mobile procedure is not effective with infants older than 6 months, a panel-pressing procedure that mimics it was developed for 9- to 12-month-olds (Campos-de-Carvalho, Bhatt, Wondoloski, Klein, & Rovee-Collier, 1993), and has also been used effectively with 6-month-olds (Hartshorn, Rovee-Collier, Bhatt, & Wondoloski, 1994). In this procedure, infants receive two training sessions 24 hr apart and a procedurally identical test session at a later time, but sessions are shorter for 9- and 12-month-olds (1.5-min baseline, 4-min acquisition, 0.5-min extinction) than for 6-month-olds (2-min baseline, 6-min acquisition, 1-min extinction). Infants sit on their mother's lap or in a Sassy Seat (infant chair) in front of a large viewing box; pressing a wide Plexiglas lever affixed to the front of the box moves a miniature train inside the box around a circular track, turns on flashing lights, and activates a toy car containing Sesame Street characters for 1 s (2 s at 6 months) (see Figure 11.8). As in the mobile procedure, the stimulus array is complex and completely visible to the infant during the initial nonreinforcement period; when the reinforcement period subsequently is introduced,

FIGURE 11.6.   The experimental arrangement used with 6-month-olds in the mobile conjugate reinforcement procedure.

lever-pressing moves the train just as kicking had moved the mobile, but the movement is not conjugate. Each lever press, while the train is moving, is recorded but has no effect on reinforcement; the lever must be released after each response in order to deliver the next reinforcer. Also, as in the mobile procedure, presentation of the reinforcer independently of responding does not increase responding during acquisition phases. The conditioning functions of infants in the mobile and train tasks are indistinguishable, as are the acquisition functions of infants of different ages in the train task.

Synchronous Reinforcement

Presentation of a reinforcer can be made contingent on dimensions of responses other than their rate or amplitude. When the onset and offset of the reinforcer are perfectly synchronized with the onset and offset of response, respectively, the duration of the response directly controls the duration of the reinforcer. This is called *synchronous reinforcement*. Because synchronous reinforcement schedules produce responses that are increasingly extended over time, and increasing response duration implies decreasing response frequency within a given period, measures of response frequency are not appropriate indices of reinforcing efficacy. In fact, increases in frequency might indicate that responses are reinforced by stimulus change or discontinuity rather than by continuity of access to the stimulus.

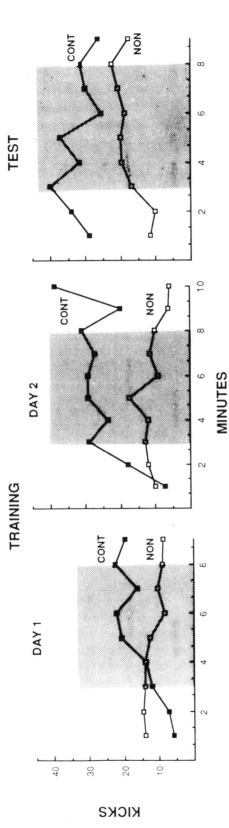

FIGURE 11.7. Mean kicks per minute of an experimental group receiving response-contingent reinforcement (CONT) and an arousal control group receiving matched noncontingent reinforcement (NON) during acquisition phases (min 3–8), indicated by stippling. During nonreinforcement phases (baseline, extinction), indicated by no stippling, the mobile was in view but could not be moved by kicking. Infants were trained for two sessions 24 hr apart and were tested for retention in a procedurally identical test session 1 day after the end of training. Note the extent of response carry-over during the nonreinforcement phase at the outset of the test session. From Hill, Borovsky, and Rovee-Collier, Experiment 1. *Developmental Psychobiology, 21*, 43–62.

FIGURE 11.8.   The experimental apparatus used to study lever-pressing with 6- to 12-month-olds. Each lever press moves the train around a circular track for 1 s, turns on flashing lights, and shakes the toy car.

Siqueland (1969b) synchronously reinforced premature infants' eye-opening responses in excess of 5 s with 5-s presentations of contingent or noncontingent auditory (female voice) or intraoral (nonnutritive nipple) stimulation. This schedule is analogous to natural situations in which eye opening produces visual stimulation for the duration of the response. In Siqueland's procedure, however, the consequences shared no apparent biological relation with the response that produced them. Over 10 daily, 11-min conditioning sessions, infants receiving response-dependent stimulation exhibited significantly longer durations of eye opening than control groups receiving either response-independent or no reinforcement, irrespective of reinforcer modality.

Using a different synchronous reinforcement procedure with older infants, Smith and Smith (1962; Smith, Zwerg, & Smith, 1963) placed 10- to 38-month-olds in a circular playpen that moved continuously at a rate of 1 revolution/26 s. An adjacent television monitor provided an image of either the infant's own mother or a female stranger either displaying a standard series of animated movements (e.g., playing with a ball, dancing and clapping) or reading a nursery story while remaining relatively motionless. Infants received alternating exposures to the experimental conditions for 1 min and a blank monitor screen for 3 s. To continuously view the monitor, the infant had to make compensatory body movements by either crawling or turning as the playpen revolved. In this way, the duration of the visual reinforcer was synchronized with response duration. Although older infants were more skilled in producing the requisite bodily adjustments, all infants were at least partially successful in increasing total fixation time, irrespective of the particular image on the monitor.

Ramey, Hieger, and Klisz (1972) used synchronous reinforcement to increase the vocal output of two failure-to-thrive infants (7 and 14 months old) who exhibited growth retardation, listlessness, and apathy. For 10 min/day until discharge, each suprathreshold vocalization triggered a voice-activated relay and illuminated a brightly colored translucent geometric form situated behind a white panel for the duration of each vocalization and for 50 ms following response cessation. From baseline to terminal acquisition, infants showed significant increases in both mean vocalization rate (from 3.8/min to 17.5/min) and duration (from 0.2 s to 0.4 s). Also, infants attained peak response levels after only 4 to 5 min of acquisition. Age-matched controls who were hospitalized for other medical reasons learned in half the time but otherwise performed equivalently.

Finally, synchronous reinforcement can be used in discrimination learning procedures. Leuba and Friedlander (1968), for example, tested 10 infants 7 to 11 months old in playpens with an automated toy mounted on one side. The toy consisted of two large, cylindrical, translucent plastic knobs that protruded into the playpen from a flat panel attached to one side of the enclosure. Knobs were separated so that an infant could not respond on both simultaneously. Any force exceeding 2-oz pressure on one of the knobs (the high-feedback knob) closed a circuit, which activated door chimes pulsing at 2 beats/s and illuminated a string of seven multicolored lights within the knob for as long as the circuit remained closed (synchronous reinforcement). Pressure on the other knob (the low-feedback knob) produced only tactile and proprioceptive feedback and a quiet click. The position of the high-feedback knob was alternated from infant to infant. Red lights on the tips of the knobs flashed to attract the infant's attention at the outset of the first session; after responding began, these were turned off. The apparatus remained in an infant's home for 2 to 3 days. Prior to a session, a mother judged the state of her infant, then preset a timer (usually for 5 min) that determined session duration and finally placed her infant in the experimental playpen. Infants typically accumulated total play times ranging from 10 to 53 min over six to seven sessions.

Every infant responded significantly more and significantly longer on the high-feedback knob. Whereas the values for response frequency and response duration were fairly close on the low-feedback knob, response duration was 1.5 times greater than response frequency on the high-feedback knob. In general, however, infants increased response duration as they increased response frequency on the high-feedback knob. This was the first study of infant discriminative responding in which infants had unrestricted access to the operanda.

Threshold Tasks

Recall that in the HAS procedure, a minimum amplitude of nonnutritive sucking had to be exceeded for a suck to be defined as "high amplitude." This criterion was usually set at 18 mm Hg, ensuring that approximately 35% of all spontaneous nonnutritive sucks fell within the HAS category. During the ensuing reinforcement phase, the intensity of the reinforcer (e.g., the brightness of a visual target) was increased in proportion to the rate of sucks that exceeded that 18 mm Hg threshold value. A *threshold task* is a variant of the HAS procedure except that the conjugate aspect of reinforcers delivered for above-threshold responses is elim-inated. As a result, each suprathreshold response produces a consequence of the same intensity as the preceding consequence, irrespective of the rate of respond-ing or the extent to which the minimal threshold value for defining a response is exceeded.

Trehub (1973; Trehub & Rabinovitch, 1972), for example, used this variant of the HAS-recovery procedure to study the speech perception of 1- to 4-month-olds. A 500-ms auditory stimulus of fixed intensity (24, 56, or 64 dB) followed each HAS, as defined by the amplitude of each infant's "stronger" sucks during an ini-tial 30-s observation period. Infants received a 1-min baseline of nonreinforced HAS, a habituation phase that was carried out until infants exhibited a response decrement of 33% for 2 consecutive min, and a 5-min HAS-recovery phase. Infants in a baseline control condition received the same stimulation throughout. Reliable recovery of HAS occurred to changed speech sounds in the consonant pairs b/p and d/t, in the vowel consonant pairs pa/pi and ta/ti, and in singly presented vow-els a, i, and i, u.

PROBLEMS IN OPERANT RESEARCH WITH INFANTS

Although there is now abundant evidence of the rapidity and efficiency with which even very young infants are responsive to operant contingencies, re-searchers must be sensitive to several factors that might confound findings from studies with immature organisms.

Eliciting versus Reinforcing Effects of Stimuli

Distinguishing between the eliciting and the reinforcing effects of a putative reinforcer is particularly critical in operant studies involving social reinforcement. Adults, for example, respond to infants in predictable ways (e.g., eye contact and eye-widening, raised brows, smiling, infant-directed high-pitched speech), and in-fants often exhibit distress when they do not. Our phylogenetic histories also may have left a social legacy that includes the triggering of infant social responses by specific adult-produced "releasing" stimuli (e.g., raised brows, smiling, vocaliz-ing). To ensure that a social reinforcer does not activate or elicit the behavior that is being measured, but that the increase observed in responding during reinforce-ment phases is solely attributable to the response–reinforcer relation, experi-menters must include appropriate controls.

Consider two often-cited experiments, both of which contained a "condition-ing" phase requiring an adult to deliver social stimuli, on either a continuous or an intermittent basis, as soon as a 3- to 4-month-old displayed a designated re-sponse. In the Brackbill (1958) study, the target infant response was smiling, and in Rheingold et al. (1959), it was vocalizing. In both experiments, conditioning or acquisition sessions were preceded and followed by sessions consisting of the non-presentation of adult interaction, procedurally identified as baseline and extinc-tion, respectively. Brackbill found higher acquisition and extinction rates by in-fants receiving response-dependent consequences on an intermittent schedule (eventually after every fourth smile) compared with those always receiving them for every smile. She claimed that the former presentation reflected the more powerful response-maintenance functions of intermittent operant reinforcement. Equally likely, however, is that the stronger resistance to extinction by the intermittently stimulated children could have resulted from them having experienced lower levels of stimulus satiation (or alternatively less habituation) than the levels produced by the continuously stimulated children. In the Rheingold et al. study, infant vocalizing increased reliably above baseline during the first acquisition session and even further during the second, but it declined to baseline levels after the second of two extinction sessions. Here the increases in vocalizing could be related to an arousal effect caused by an escalation in adult interaction in reaction to the growing rate of infant vocalizations during acquisition.

Three procedures have been invoked to determine if response increments evident during acquisition are a function of the environmental changes contingent on its occurrence or the result of some other process. The first procedure compares the behavioral outcomes generated by response-dependent (or contingent) events expected of operant reinforcement versus response-independent (or noncontingent) events expected of the eliciting or arousal-inducing effects of stimulation. For purposes of control, the frequency or rate of stimulus presentations should be equal (or yoked to each other) in both kinds of arrangements. Using these procedures, Weisberg repeated the Rheingold et al. (1959) experiment. The same methods employing baseline–acquisition–extinction sessions (each condition for two sessions) were used, as was the same form of adult interaction (smiling, emitting three "tsk" sounds, and lightly touching the infant's abdomen for 1 to 2 s). Because infants provided contingent social interaction for vocalizing increased their rate to a significantly higher extent than those provided noncontingent social interaction, the case was made that operant control of behavior had been established. The effect of behavioral control by nonsocial events also was evaluated with two groups: a door chime was presented either dependent or independent of vocalizing. Although no group differences emerged, and hence no evidence for operant conditioning, the failure could be related to the lack of variation in this stimulus; variations in nonsocial events (chimes and lights) as consequences have modified a number of infant manipulative responses (Rheingold et al., 1962; Simmons, 1964; Simmons & Lipsitt, 1961) as well as vocal behaviors (Ramey et al., 1972).

A second procedure has kept the contingent relation between behavior and environmental consequences intact, but has varied the interval between these two entities. Intervals approaching immediate delivery of consequences should elevate the probability of behavior more so than delayed consequences. Ramey and Ourth (1971) delayed adult social reinforcement for the vocalizing of 6- and 9-month-olds by either 0, 3, or 6 s. Increases in behavior occurred only for subjects in the 0-s group. The same number of consequent events received by the two other delay groups effectively controlled for elicitation effects.

The third procedure uses a within-subjects design and arranges for the delivery of social consequences contingent on the occurrence of a target response on one occasion and on another occasion on its nonoccurrence. If the consequences had a stimulus-eliciting function, equal rates of responding should obtain under both arrangements. In contrast, if the consequences strengthened behavior, differential effects should favor the reinforced behavior. Applying this shifting contingency tactic to infant vocalizations, Poulson (1983) found the response rates always highest when vocalizing was explicitly reinforced and when nonvocalizing was reinforced. Poulson's study is an excellent demonstration of the development of different forms of behavior through the specification of response classes.

Infant State

The degree of an infant's "arousal" on a sleep–wakefulness continuum is a critical determinant of what the infant will detect, and of the manner in which the infant will respond (for reviews, see Ashton, 1973; Korner, 1972; Prechtl, 1974). The relative effectiveness of stimulation in different modalities changes from waking states to sleep (Brackbill & Fitzgerald, 1969), as does the actual form of many reflexes that are elicited by the same physical stimulus (Lenard, von Bernuth, & Prechtl, 1968). This relation is not simple, however, because stimulus detection is impaired when infants are highly aroused and crying as well as when they are sleeping.

The changing state of the infant varies widely between and within infants (Aylward, 1981; Brown, 1964) and these distinctions present a number of problems for an experimental analysis of infant behavior. First, because an infant's state can change throughout an experiment, so can the perceived intensity of a constantly presented stimulus. Second, large individual differences inevitably result in subjectively different stimulus intensities for different subjects, irrespective of the specified level. Third, some state changes may result directly from the learning process per se, whereas others may follow from difficulties with the learning task, and yet others may reflect state changes in response to stimulation that have no relation to learning. Three-month-olds, for example, exhibit less fussing (Rovee-Collier, Morrongiello, Aron, & Kupersmidt, 1978); Sullivan, Lewis, & Alessandri, 1992) and heightened alertness (Siqueland, 1969a,b) during contingent than during noncontingent reinforcement, and fussing and inattentiveness often increase during periods in which reinforcement has been withdrawn (Rovee-Collier & Capatides, 1979; Sullivan et al., 1992). Papousek (1977) reported that newborns and older infants who were confronted with either learning problems they could not solve or an extinction procedure occasionally reverted to sleeplike inhibitory states. This is reminiscent of Pavlov's description of "paradoxical sleep" in dogs during extinction (Pavlov, 1927). Fourth, behavior at state extremes (sleeping or extreme crying) is the major source of attrition in infant studies. Cairns and Butterfield (1975) had to test 125 infants in order to obtain usable data from 40 subjects. Because the probability of exclusion varied as a function of postmeal interval, they eventually maximized the likelihood of a completed session by testing infants only at specific hours in relation to a feed.

RESEARCH METHODS FOR TODDLERS AND YOUNG CHILDREN

Schedules of Reinforcement: Background Considerations

Generally speaking, the age of the subject seemingly has been a decisive factor in determining the kind of operant phenomena sought as well as how to attain them. With infants younger than 3 months, and especially with neonates, focus has been on the documentation of operant conditioning as a robust and relatively enduring process in early life. In the main, the performances of groups receiving response-dependent versus response-independent consequences were observed usually during a single session of brief duration with evidence of operant learning taken as statistically superior acquisition by the response-dependent groups (see the review by Hulsebus, 1973). Similar research tactics have provided the framework with older infants roughly between 3 and 12 months, with the aim to generate rapid operant acquisition in different contexts for a variety of responses, consequences, and contingencies. Although sessions were longer and sometimes of greater frequency (Leuba & Friedlander, 1968; Smith et al., 1963), basic operant pursuits readily obtainable with animals, as steady-state behavior under various schedules of reinforcement as well as a search for the controlling variables, were not avidly researched both with this age range and with younger infants. That the achievement of stable schedule performance is not necessarily limited by age considerations is evident in the research of Sheppard (1969) with a 1-month-old and of Lowe, Beasty, and Bentall (1983) with two 9- to 10-month-olds, wherein characteristic fixed-ratio and fixed-interval performances were, respectively, established and examined across 25 to 60 training sessions.

Researchers were drawn to undertake an analysis of schedules of reinforcement with children and special populations (Bijou, 1958; Bijou & Orlando, 1961; Ferster & DeMeyer, 1961; Long et al., 1958) for many of the same reasons that animal researchers were attracted to schedules a decade or two earlier. Reflecting on the historical importance of schedules, Zeiler (1984) disclosed that they provided an effective means to control behavior with precision and to produce orderly patterns of behavior that were, to some schedule enthusiasts, "things of beauty." Schedules also produced an almost endless flow of steady-state behavior or stable baseline patterns, against which the effects of schedule-related and other variables could be modulated and assessed. Selected schedules could be studied separately or in combination with each other, affording the researcher a firsthand opportunity to determine the effects of special reinforcement histories. In the event that noncharacteristic schedule performances turned up, there was further opportunity to identify the controlling variables and to devise procedures to modify those performances.

These research considerations initially occupied investigators of operant behavior in children. Only later was the proposition that schedule-controlled behavior is regular and fits all species members applied to children and adults and, in some aspects, found wanting (Lowe, 1979; Weiner, 1969). Before getting into the procedural matters that pertain to the development of reinforcement schedule and stimulus control in infants and children, there are two fundamental questions that require some consideration: how to promote favorable adaptation to and continued participation in an experimental setting and how to establish responding that will withstand the effects of nonreinforcement and possible satiation of the reinforcers. The types and combinations of reinforcers used with children have already been discussed.

Familiarization Procedures

What transpires prior to an experimental session can serve as a setting operation to modify known classes of environment–behavior relations, most notably the effectiveness of the programmed reinforcers (Bijou, 1993). A favorable operation is likely when a preschooler's snack period has long preceded a session employing edible reinforcers, whereas a limiting operation is possible when homeroom movies have immediately preceded the experimental presentation of cartoon consequences. Setting operations can also lead to the child's refusal to participate. Such circumstances can occur at any time, beginning with the separation of a child from one's group and accompanied by a stranger to laboratory settings containing unusual furnishings or being confronted suddenly with novel and possibly aversive events associated with strange apparatuses and loud recording equipment (Bijou & Baer, 1966; Weisberg & Fink, 1966). To mollify the effects of an aversive event, one could repeatedly present it alone to facilitate habituation as well as in the presence of response-independent positive consequences, presentations that will also provide the researcher with information about their future reinforcing effectiveness (Bijou & Baer, 1966).

One procedure for creating a favorable experimental condition for preschool children could include having a supportive person spend sufficient time interacting with children in their homeroom and take note of the potential interfering effects of ongoing activities prior to the removal of the child for a session (Bijou, 1958). If a child is very shy or has limited expressive language, asking a series of open-ended questions can become overwhelming and serve to reduce the child's interest in participating (Blank, 1973). Sometimes "coaxing" behaviors offered by a well-meaning teacher to reassure an unsure participant can have effects opposite to those intended, as when a teacher continually holds onto a child and makes no provisions to encourage separation. Maternal separation research has shown that excessive maternal coaxing can increase rather than decrease subsequent childhood distress (Adams & Passman, 1981). For toddlers and young children, a favorite cuddly object has been shown to accelerate adaptation to a strange environment (Passman & Weisberg, 1975).

The nature and frequency of social interaction occurring as a child is being escorted to the experimental room are known to influence the effectiveness of subsequent social consequences. Gewirtz and Baer (1958) found that minimal and high levels of preexperimental child-escort social interactions served, respectively, as deprivation and satiation operations that were functionally related to the effectiveness of programmed social consequences. Weisberg (1975) showed that different forms of preexperimental activities, specifically either tickling or cuddling, can determine a child's choice of these same activities as differential consequences. A statistically significant age by type of contact interaction was found in that the youngest children ($M = 3.4$ years) favored cuddling over tickling whereas 4- to 6-year-olds preferred tickling. The gender of the experimenter also was a factor in that the youngest girls avoided male adult experimenters, independently of whether they furnished cuddling or tickling stimulation. An examination of tickling interactions suggested that brief, intermittent tickling episodes were preferred over more intense sustained efforts at tickling, which some children avoided. Additionally, it appeared that the higher the ratio of adult verbal teasing ("I'm going to tickle you!") to actual tickles, the more likely was the child to remain close to that person.

As noted earlier, attempts to adapt and prepare preverbal infants for multisession operant research have succeeded by observing them in the familiar confines of their homes with their mothers either nearby (Leuba & Friedlander, 1968; Smith et al., 1963) or holding them on their laps (Lowe et al., 1983). It is likely that the mothers participated extensively in the familiarization process by providing physical and verbal support, although the exact nature of the support contingencies are not specified. There is nothing inherently wrong with these efforts and they should be encouraged as long as they are implemented during the beginning research phases. A potential problem, however, can surface if the mother continues her participation during the repeated scheduling of programmed consequences. Then the question becomes whether the development of steady-state behavior is related to the scheduled reinforcer or to the surplus reinforcers furnished by the mothers. For example, snack reinforcers, multisensory feedback, and keeping sight of an animated person on TV were, respectively, arranged to follow the infant's target responses in the studies by Leuba and Friedlander (1968), Lowe et al. (1983), and Smith et al. (1963). Any finding that the mother expressed continuous or intermittent acclaim or approval whenever her infant earned any of these scheduled consequences would make it difficult to pinpoint the source and extent of reinforcement control. In this regard, Sheppard (1969) noted that because certain behaviors such as infant vocalizing can be evoked by several conditions, it is important to remove as many antecedents of responding as possible, including maternal interaction. For this reason, the infant studied was continually observed by a noninteracting experimenter behind a concealed vantage point.

A similar confounding is possible when a mother inadvertently cues the infant as to the moment of response execution, especially when temporal-based schedules are in effect. Again, left unanswered is whether a record of stable responding reflects sensitivity to the contingencies underscored by the actions of the mother, of her infant, or of some combination. The types of unwanted adult forms of surplus reinforcement and unintended instructional cues elaborated by Bijou and Baer (1966) and which they applied to preschool children need to be matched by a similar set that apply to infants in order to bring home the point of experimental caution.

To minimize the influence of adult participation and guidance, Weisberg (1969, 1970b; Weisberg & Fink, 1966; Weisberg & Tragakis, 1967) employed familiarization and response-shaping procedures modeled after those commonly implemented in animal research. The children were between 1½ and 2½ years old. They either resided at a shelter home awaiting placement or attended a day-care center. Administrators and staff were told the research project involved the role of rewards on learning. Permission was granted to switch the serving of their afternoon snacks (bite-sized pieces of cookies and cereal) normally given in their homeroom to their presentation in a small interview room converted into an experimental setting.

Once the child accepted and ate approximately 15 pieces from the experimenter's hand during snack time, that child was taken to the experimental room and offered the remaining snack portion. The snacks were dropped one at a time into a Plexiglas collecting tray mounted to the base of a large wooden cabinet that housed a 70-bucket Universal Feeder. When the child's apprehension had lessened, he or she was strapped into a highchair in front of the feeder, and the experimenter continued to drop snacks into the tray until each was quickly retrieved and consumed. This preliminary familiarization process required from two to three sessions.

Food–magazine training was begun next. The preloaded feeder was activated via a hand-held microswitch to deliver snacks at variable intervals until the average interval between successive reinforcers approached 30 s. In general, a new snack was not delivered until the previous one was eaten. Care was also taken to avoid reinforcing recurring behavioral sequences that might lead to "superstitious" behavior. Once the child looked toward the food tray whenever the feeder motor was activated, which produced an audible hum and snack delivery, the experimenter gradually edged away from the child and reduced the amount of social interaction. Eventually, the experimenter was able to dispense snacks from behind an equipment cart, out of the child's view. Wall-mounted mirrors to the left and right of the child enabled the experimenter to monitor the child's behaviors. Magazine training usually took one session for older children and two to three sessions for younger ones.

Efforts by Long et al. (1958) to train children younger than 3 years proved unsuccessful because they refused to remain alone in the experimental setting for more than a few minutes. On the other hand, older children given limited familiarization to the settings, with response training initiated immediately during the first session, apparently displayed little or no emotional upset once the experimenter left. If the younger children had received similar familiarization and response training of short duration, the distress they displayed could be blamed in part on the experimenter's rather sudden withdrawal from the setting. In contrast, less than 10% of these same-aged children evidenced distress, requiring their removal and nonparticipation in Weisberg's research (e.g., Weisberg, 1970b; Weisberg & Fink, 1966). Less attrition was likely for a combination of factors: spending more time familiarizing the toddlers and children to the research settings; delaying response training (no response device present during magazine training) until the snacks were eaten without hesitation and without intervening signs of distress; having the experimenter remain near the child as snacks were dispensed, and during the gradual distancing process, each backward step came after an absence of subject intolerance. The child could thus witness the slow disappearance of the experimenter who had never left the room, but remained behind the equipment cart; when the session ended, he simply reappeared from his concealment.

Establishing Behavior

In Long's response-training procedures (Long, 1962, 1963; Long et al., 1858), children 4 to 7 years old initially were shown and told to operate the response device. The first response always produced a reinforcer (e.g., a trinket). To demonstrate that reinforcement would not occasion every response, the next requested response did not result in a reinforcer. The child was told that operation of the device would sometimes result in a "prize" and sometimes it would not, but to win it, the device had to be operated. Following these instructions, the experimenter left the room and training began.

Response strengthening with infants and children younger than 3 has relied more on the response consequences received directly from the programmed contingencies and less on adult demonstration and instructions acting to mediate control (Lowe, 1979; Sheppard, 1969; Weisberg, 1969; Weisberg & Fink, 1966). Here, each response is typically reinforced on a continuous reinforcement (CRF) schedule to initiate and keep responding going until a high enough rate is developed. A drawback of CRF training is that it establishes sustained rapid responding reinforced by trinkets and snacks and, as a result, reinforcer oversupply can induce early satiation and a quick deceleration of the overall rate within a session. This high-rate pattern occurred with Long and colleagues' (1958) children who very soon came to possess all of the different kinds of trinkets available, resulting in a diminution of their reinforcing influence. Instead of the CRF as the entry schedule, the session started with a small fixed ratio (FR 15), after which the size of the ratio was increased to values as high as FR 50. Both the entry and subsequent ratio schedules produced strong control.

To prevent a large accumulation of snack reinforcers as an outgrowth of CRF response bursts, Weisberg and Tragakis (1967) substituted an entry schedule that required 2 s of nonresponding before the next response was reinforced. Aside from delaying satiation effects and enabling extra time for training, the pausing requirement served to teach the young child to mediate time by eating the just-earned snack before executing another response. Learning to eat one snack at a time is a much safer activity than attempting to swallow and possibly choke on the many quickly obtained snacks via high-rate CRF responding.

Single Schedule Control

Aside from the already reviewed conjugate schedules of reinforcement, the analysis of the behavior of infants and children also has been investigated with several well-known basic schedules, examples of which are included below.

Fixed Ratio (FR) Performance

The manner by which the number of required responses for reinforcement is successively advanced until a terminal FR value is reached has varied as a function of the subject's age. With preverbal infants, the FR progression has been to start with low values, usually FR 1, and to increase the size of the ratio in a gradual fashion. The final values achieved for a 1-month-old have been FR 3 for vocalizing and FR 5 for leg kicking, both of which necessitated five or six 30-min FR sessions (Sheppard, 1969). The terminal FR values for lever-pressing by children in their second year of life have been FR 10 or FR 15, attainable within four to nine FR sessions (Weisberg & Fink, 1966). As previously mentioned, the means to initiate lever-pressing in 4- to 7-year-olds has relied on instructional control (Long et al., 1958). FR-progression procedures preserving the potency of the trinket reinforcers have proved more effective in generating ratiolike performance than those fostering a loss of trinket control. Thus, the common procedure of starting and continuing a session with small FR values followed by gradual increments in subsequent sessions, a practice that led to early satiation, was not as effective as starting with small FRs and, within the same session, increasing the ratio to values as high as FR 60, which served to postpone satiation. The strong ratio control of the latter procedure consisted of a uniform high rate of responding (frequently two or more lever presses per second) that was free of postreinforcement pauses (PRP), except under high ratios (FR 100), and a "grainless" cumulative record that revealed an absence of negative curvature. In contrast, with gradual FR advancement the record resembled the FR performance of pigeons maintained at their inactive weight. That is, a decline in the overall rate associated with increases in the PRP, split and intermediates running rates, instances of negative curvature, and a sporadic grainy picture.

The FR performance of preverbal infants, though not as characteristic as that of food-deprived animals receiving extensive FR training, is nevertheless ratiolike, marked by an all-or-none pattern of responding with the response rate positively related to ratio size and to length of training. The rates generated are also much higher and longer-lasting than are those produced by CRF schedules (Sheppard, 1969; Weisberg, 1969; Weisberg & Fink, 1966). The terminal FR rates for the five infants given from four to nine 25-min sessions of FR 10 or FR 15 in Weisberg and Fink (1966) were 25, 34, 45, 54, and 61 responses per minute. Nonpresentation of the reinforcers used for the infants both in Sheppard's and in Weisberg and Fink's research produced an early extinction record of fairly high sustained levels of responding, noted also by an increase in vigor, followed by increasingly longer periods of nonresponding. Moreover, FR extinction performance was related to the infant's rate and response output seen during training. A single FR reconditioning session provided to Sheppard's infant rapidly restored the preextinction FR 5 performance pattern.

Raising the ratio size abruptly to higher than workable values is known to "strain" ratio performance causing FR irregularities largely in the form of longer PRPs. Such occasions occurred with some children in the research of Long et al. (1958) and of Weisberg and Fink (1966). Once FR deterioration was discovered, the ratio size was shifted downwards and successfully returned to higher values through a ratio-shaping process.

Fixed Interval (FI) Performance

The FI schedule always programs a reinforcer following a set period of time that starts after every reinforced response. Responding between adjacent reinforcements in well-trained animals often takes on a scalloped appearance: pausing after reinforcement followed by a rate of responding that accelerates positively up until the delivery of the next reinforcer. The gradually increasing rate of responding occurs even though only one response is required for reinforcement after the interval has expired.

Although FI scalloping is commonplace in animals given extensive FI training, it occurs infrequently in humans. Lowe (1979) claimed that only animals and preverbal human infants display the characteristic scalloped pattern whereas verbally adept children and adults ordinarily do not. There is some truth to Lowe's (1979) assertions. Lowe et al. (1983) obtained strong FI control with two infants younger than 1 year. After two sessions of CRF training with food or music consequences, FI schedules were programmed with FI durations ranging from 10 to 50

s. The FI values were changed once responding (touching a metal cylinder) stabilized over three consecutive sessions. Responding during the initial intervals was negatively accelerated, but it gradually turned into a scalloped pattern with further training, and this pattern became the final form for all schedule values. Aside from the presence of scallop-shaped cumulative records, three other evaluative measures validated the presence of typical FI performance. As a function of FI durations of 10, 20, and 30 s, (1) response rate, excluding the PRP, decreased; (2) the length of the PRP increased; and (3) the relative PRP, whereby the pause is expressed as a proportion of the FI duration, decreased.

In contrast, the FI 1-min record produced by verbally competent children between 4 and 7 years of age has been scallop-free, yielding instead one of two response patterns: a continuously high (inefficient) rate of responding between reinforcers or a steady, very low (efficient) rate. When intermediate rates occur, the record is usually devoid of scalloping. The absence of interval-like performance is found regardless of whether the FI schedule is evaluated as the only component (Bijou, 1958; Long et al., 1958) or as one of two schedule components (DeCasper & Zeiler, 1972; Long, 1959, 1962, 1963). Adults on FI schedules also show the bivalued rate pattern (Lowe, 1979; Pierce & Epling, 1995; Weiner, 1969).

The failure to find animal-like FI behavior in older children does not imply that FI performances are insensitive to schedule parameters and other conditions. The following schedule-related variables have been shown to affect FI performance, either by lengthening the PRP, by producing a nonscalloped, but nevertheless a moderate or abrupt shift in response rate between reinforcers, or by inducing both changes: (1) increasing the duration of an interval, from an FI 1 to an FI 2 (Long et al., 1958); (2) preceding or temporarily replacing the FI with certain schedules that, by generating low rates, prevented high-rate FI performance, or by generating high rates prevented very low-rate FI performance (DeCasper & Zeiler, 1972; Long, 1962; Long et al., 1958); and (3) increasing the size of the FR in a multiple FI FR schedule (Long, 1962). Nonschedule variables affecting FI performance have included: (1) improving the value of the trinket reinforcers by doubling the number given (Long et al., 1958); (2) replacing a colorful picture present during each interval with a new picture at the moment of reinforcement (Long et al., 1958); (3) increasing the intersession interval (Long et al., 1958); and (4) providing external support as a basis for a temporal discrimination, created by increasing the brightness of a colored screen throughout the interval (Long, 1963).

Differential Reinforcement of Low Rates (DRL)

Weisberg and Tragakis (1967) used the DRL schedule to generate stable, low response rates with pausing between adjacent responses. A timer was preset to some value and, on "timing out," it programmed the delivery of a reinforcer for the next response that occurred. Each nonreinforced response before the interval expired reset the timer, as did each reinforced response. Each of five children, 15 to 41 months of age, were initially reinforced for responding for two sessions according to a DRL 2-s schedule, after which the schedule was changed without forewarning to a DRL 10-s for six to nine sessions and then, for three children, to a DRL 18-s for another 8 to 10 sessions.

Throughout the DRL 10-s sessions, response rates were low (between 6 and 10 responses per minute) and in marked contrast to the terminal FR rates (between 19 and 54) obtained by Weisberg and Fink (1966). In addition, both the relative frequency of very short (less than 2 s) interresponse times (IRTs) and the proportion of IRTs shorter than the reinforced interval declined, while IRTs in the middle range of the distribution (between 10 and 14 s) progressively increased. Two other indices, the number of reinforcements earned per response and the observed reinforcement rate relative to the optimal reinforcement rate, were computed in the final DRL 10-s session. The first measure indicated that 40 to 50% of all responses emitted by a given child resulted in a reinforcer. The second measure indicated that the actual rate of reinforcement was within 34 to 45% of matching the optimal rate. Both sets of values are well within the limits reported in studies with animals (Staddon, 1965) and children (Stoddard, 1962).

Five minutes of nonreinforcement then was interpolated between two 10-min blocks of (reinforced) DRL 10-s responding for three children. The extinction period yielded a very low level of lever-pressing that matched the DRL 10-s reinforcement blocks that preceded and followed it. That the extinction operation did not disrupt DRL 10-s conditioning performance by increasing response rate argues against a view of extinction as always leading to high-rate frustrative acts caused by reinforcer removal. Nor did any of the children become petulant during DRL extinction. Rather, it seems more appropriate to view the low-rate DRL extinction performance as a specific outcome of control by the prior DRL reinforcement schedule, just as the initially high-rate FR extinction performance observed by Weisberg and Fink (1966) reflected a history of FR control. Finally, reinstatement of a DRL 18-s schedule for three children reduced their previous DRL 10-s response rates still further and, as with the DRL 10-s schedule, yielded a profile of efficient temporal responding.

Complex Schedules: Development and Assessment of Stimulus Control

Having specified procedures for conditioning unique behavioral patterns with single schedules, it is instructive to consider the means by which separate schedules have been sequentially combined to generate multiple schedules of reinforcement and whether schedule-based control over responding is evident under these complex contingencies. Because distinctive stimuli are correlated with each schedule's programmed occurrence, an examination of stimulus control procedures is also in order. Weisberg's (1969) use of multiple schedules with eight 15- to 20-month-olds will be highlighted. This research is relevant because the procedures used encompassed much of what was done with older children, replicating both the initial difficulties and eventual attainment of schedule control.

Response Strengthening

Rate strengthening consisted of shaping the toddlers' lever-pressing according to one of two terminal schedules, either a VR 15 (ratio values ranged from 5 to 40 responses) or a VI 25-s (reinforcers delivered on the average every 25 s with an interreinforcement interval ranging from 5 to 40 s). When at least 20 responses/min were emitted in two consecutive rate-strengthening sessions, in the next session a green indicator light, mounted approximately 4.45 cm above the lever, was turned on and lever-pressing in its presence was reinforced according to one of the two prevailing schedules. For half of the children, the S+ was a 1 cycle/s flashing green light; for the remaining half, the S+ was a steady green light. In the next session, discrimination training began and a second component was added whereby responding was not reinforced. The other light source served as S− and occasioned nonreinforcement. The merging of two basic schedules arranged sequentially with each schedule signaled by different stimuli constitutes a multiple schedule of reinforcement (Pierce & Epling, 1995).

Discrimination Training

One purpose for using the multiple schedule was to develop differential responding such that substantially higher rates would occur in the S+ component relative to the S− component. Such a finding might indicate that the children had selectively attended to or discriminated between the steady and 1 cycle/s flashing light. In every discrimination session, either the VI 25-s or the VR 15 schedule was programmed in all S+ components, while the following schedule conditions were associated with S− components: extinction (EXT), the differential-reinforcement-of-other-behavior (DRO), or a combination of the two programmed sequentially (EXT DRO). A problem using EXT as the sole S− component is that lever presses made near the end of an S− period are met by the onset of S+, which, because of its consistent correlation with snack reinforcers, could establish the S+ as a conditioned reinforcer for unwanted S− responding. Programming the DRO schedule in S− avoided this possibility. Here, a clock set for a prearranged time (from 4 to 20 s) was continually reset whenever lever-pressing occurred in S−; thus, S+ always came on after a sustained absence of lever-pressing. Worth emphasizing is that food reinforcers were not given for the absence of responding in S−. Instead, the DRO contingency served a protective function: to prevent responses in S− from being reinforced by S+ onset. Although the DRO condition occasionally was the sole S− component, more often it was preceded by a 20- to 30-s period of extinction (EXT DRO).

Early in discrimination training, the durations of S+ were usually three times longer than those of S−. This discrepancy was reduced gradually over training sessions until S+ durations were either equal to S− or no more than twice its length. The final S+ durations varied from 30 to 60 s and the final S− components varied from 30 to 50 s. During the final stages of training, sessions were 25 to 30 min long, during which time S+ and S− components were presented sequentially approximately 20 times each. From 30 to 50 reinforcements were delivered per session.

Efficacy of differential responding was assessed by computing a discrimination index (Pierce & Epling, 1995). The index is the ratio of total S+ responses divided by the sum of total S+ responses and total S− responses. (To correct for the smaller amount of time usually devoted to S− durations, the index was weighted by the multiplication of the proportion of S+/S− durations.) A discrimination index of .50 represents equal response probability in S+ and S− and thus lack of discriminative control, whereas an index of 1.00 indicates perfect control. The goal

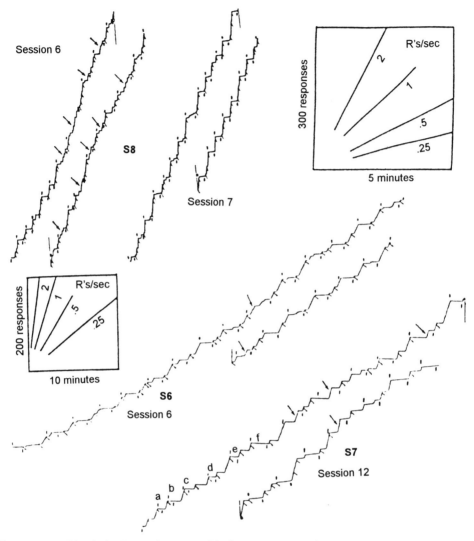

FIGURE 11.9. Discrimination performance of the last two pregeneralization sessions for S8 (20 months old) and the last session for S6 and S7 (both 16 months old). The cumulative recorder ran at a slower speed for S8 than for S6 and S7. From Weisberg, 1969, *Journal of Experimental Child Psychology*. Reproduced by permission of Academic Press.

was to establish overall session indices above .75, with higher values expected for the second half as compared with the first half of a training session. All children satisfied this criterion (median index = .80 and .88, respectively, for the first and second halves). Counting nonsuccessful training sessions (particularly with the multiple VI 25 EXT schedule), from 7 to 16 training sessions were required to achieve criterion performance.

Figure 11.9 shows the terminal discrimination performance of three toddlers—S6, S7, and S8. For each child, the S+ component consisted of the VR 15 schedule, and the S− component consisted of EXT DRO (except during intervals *a* through *f* in S7's Session 12, when EXT was omitted). As the cumulative records indicate, the rate of lever-pressing in S+ for S6 and S7 was maintained fairly well throughout a session, whereas responding in S− was virtually nil except for a few places (see arrows) where the response rate in S− was moderate. The discrimination indices of S6 and S7 for the last half of their session were .87 and .84, respectively. The last two session records of S8 document a case of sudden transition in differential responding. As is evident, the uniformly high S− rates (at arrows) in Session 6 are sharply attenuated, and S8's performance became "errorless" in Session 7; here, the first- and second-half session discrimination indices were .91 and 1.00, respectively.

Difficulties in creating differential responding using EXT as the sole S− component were also experienced in research with older children and, in each case, the problem was rectified by adding or substituting a DRO or DRL (pause-requirement) schedule (Bijou & Orlando, 1961; Long, 1962). Beginning discrimination training with multiple DRO FR or multiple DRL FR schedules further facilitated schedule control (Long, 1962). Noncontrol with multiple FI FR schedules has already been mentioned (DeCasper & Zeiler, 1972; Long, 1959), as have several descriptions of successful remediational procedures (Bijou & Orlando, 1961; Long, 1959, 1962, 1963). Sheppard (1969) reported a terminal discrimination index of .72 by a 1-month-old after nine sessions in which one of two permissible responses, either vocalizing or kicking, was reinforced on an FR 3 during alternating 5-min periods, while the other response was subject to extinction.

Evaluation of Stimulus Control

When two schedules are alternated, the possibility of control by the stimuli correlated with the schedules must be dissociated from schedule order. Long (1962) assessed the influence of external stimulus control in 4- to 7-year-olds by two procedures. In the first, schedule order was maintained while the discriminative function of schedule-correlated cues were reversed. Hence, in a multiple FI FR schedule the cue that occasioned the FI component now occasioned the FR component and the former FR-correlated cue now signaled the FI component. Had the former discriminative stimuli exerted control, a breakdown in performance would be expected. In the second procedure, schedule order was altered, but the stimuli signifying the prevailing schedule were not changed. Thus, the FR component in a multiple FI FR was repeated from four to six times in succession, but the FI- and FR-correlated stimuli were not changed. Control by the prior stimuli would be evidenced by no change in FI and FR performance. Unfortunately, clearcut cases of discriminative stimulus control did not emerge with both evaluation procedures.

Another procedure, identified as stimulus generalization testing, entails the presentation of a series of different stimuli, the original schedule-associated stimuli and several new stimuli, the entire set of which belong to the same stimulus dimension. All of these test stimuli usually are presented during nonreinforcement periods. The resulting generalization gradient should reflect the same level of differential responding to the original stimuli as that established during discrimination training. Generalized responding to the new stimuli should be ordered so that the levels to stimuli closer to the former S+ should be higher than those more distant or closer to S−. Weisberg (1969) conducted generalization test trials using stimuli on the dimension of flicker frequency. In addition to the steady and 1 cycle/s lights, six lights that flickered at rates ranging from 2 to 10 cycles/s were presented during nonreinforced generalization test trials, each of which lasted 30 s. Altogether, 48 test trials were provided per session, with the eight lights appearing randomly within each of six blocks. A 3-s "blackout" period, during which the light source was darkened, separated the trials. Two sessions were devoted to generalization testing. A 10-min period of discrimination training preceded each generalization test, and an entire session of discrimination training was interpolated between the two tests. Throughout these discrimination-training periods, the same stimulus-schedule conditions prevailed as those presented prior to the generalization test sessions.

The percentage of responses to each of the eight stimuli, ordered by flicker frequency, appears in Figure 11.10. For four children, the former S+ and S− were the steady and 1 cycle/s lights (left side), and for the other four, the former S+ and S− functions were opposite in nature (right side). The generalization gradients for both sessions were parallel, with the percentage of responses always greatest to the previous S+, and even more so in the second than in the first generalization test session. Computation of discrimination indices based on responses to the former S+ (steady light) and to the former S− (1 cycle/s light) (Figure 11.10, left side) yielded median values of .90 and .92, respectively, for the first and second generalization tests. These values were within the range of discrimination indices based on S+ and S− responding both during 10-min pregeneralization discrimination periods and during the entire intervening discrimination session. Computation of indices based on responding to the 1 cycle/s as the former S+ and to the steady light as S− (Figure 11.10, right side) came to .75 and .90, respectively, for the first and second tests.

The left side of Figure 11.10 shows a substantially higher percentage of responses to the steady light, as distinguished from the lower and equal percentage to all flickering lights. The gradient suggests that the children responded exclusively on a go/no go basis, that is, respond to the steady light and not to lights that flicker. On the other hand, the gradients on the right side reflect a systematic decrement in responding, suggesting that these young children attended to certain flicker values. For example, S8's performance in the second generalization test indicates an accurate ordering of the first three flicker values. The generalization gradient not only provides information about the toddlers' sensitivity to different flicker values, but also indicates whether any of the higher flicker values approached the point of critical fusion frequency, that is, whether the lights that flickered at either 8 or 10 cycles/s were perceived as single, steady lights of uniform brightness.

The present generalization test trials reflect the concurrent operation of two opposing processes—one in which the former S+ (and stimuli similar to it) functions to *maintain* behavior across time and one in which the operation of extinction functions to *discourage* the support of behavior across time. Trying to demonstrate continued stimulus control while the behavior supporting that control is

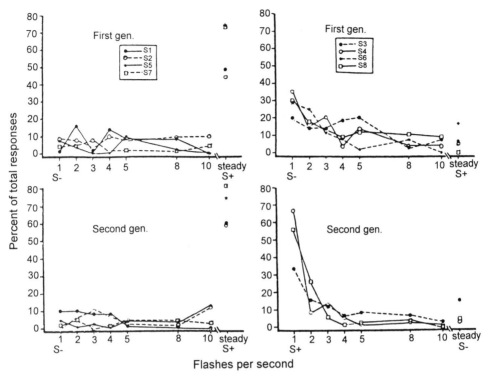

Figure 11.10. Relative generalization gradients for the first and second test sessions. From Weisberg, 1969, *Journal of Experimental Child Psychology.* Reproduced by permission of Academic Press.

disappearing is a major limitation of lengthy generalization tests conducted during extinction. Future studies with children should consider the use of maintained-generalization procedures (see Koegel & Wilhelm, 1973), which can take the form of: (1) providing occasional reinforcement of responses during several preselected S+ periods and (2) programming a large number of S+/S− discrimination segments that are intermittently followed by shorter and less intrusive blocks of nonreinforced generalization test trials.

EFFECTS OF REINFORCEMENT HISTORY

In the Laboratory

What transpires behaviorally after a schedule has been effected is qualified both by the parameters of the schedule and by the preexperimental repertoires established prior to implementing the schedule (Lattal & Neef, 1996). The contribution of previous experience to some ongoing behavior is most profitably realized when subjects, initially conditioned to display unique behavioral patterns because of different histories with a schedule, are subsequently placed on a common schedule, and the process of adjustment to these contingencies examined. To this end, Weisberg (1970b) determined the extent to which the special repertoires created by different schedules would affect spaced responding of children on a DRL 18-s schedule. Children (2–3 years old) were taught to lever press on a DRL 2-s schedule for two sessions followed by six sessions of either DRL 10-s, FI 18-s, or VR 10 training ($N = 3$ per schedule condition) before all of them spent six sessions on the DRL 18-s schedule. A fourth group called Limited Experience ($N = 3$) received only two DRL 2-s sessions before being placed on the six DRL 18-s sessions.

Children trained on the DRL 10-s schedule, when initially placed on the DRL 18-s schedule, had the highest rate of reinforcement and emitted the lowest number of responses per reinforcement. Not surprisingly, children trained on the VR 10 schedule had the greatest difficulty in adjusting to the DRL 18-s requirement: Their rate of reinforcement was one-half that of the experienced DRL 10-s group and, for each reinforcement earned, they responded 85 more times than necessary. The Limited Experience and FI 18-s groups were next in terms of the two indices of behavior adaptation to the DRL 18-s schedule.

Across the six DRL 18-s sessions, the most significant change was the dramatic decline of the response rates of the VR 10-trained children, which by their sixth session was one-fifth of their Session 1 rate. Nevertheless, the VR 10-trained children continued to emit a high proportion of relatively short IRTs (80% less than 5.9 s), whereas the FI 18-s-trained children exhibited the most variability on measures of DRL 18-s proficiency. Ultimately, the Limited Experience group (only two prior sessions of DRL 2-s training) matched the DRL 10-s-trained group on almost every measure of temporal responding during the last DRL 18-s session. The rather short time required for this accomplishment supports a claim that 2- to 3-year-olds can withhold responses if known interfering repertoires like those induced by VR 10 or FI 18-s histories are minimized.

In accounting for the relatively efficient performance on the DRL 18-s schedule by the DRL 10-s-trained children, Weisberg (1970b) suggested two possibilities, both based on a response-differentiation hypothesis that young children can learn to discriminate subtle aspects of their own behavior. The first emphasized the learning of a distinctive response pattern: Reinforcement for DRL 10-s responding occasions waiting and then making a single response—a routine that could be subsequently deployed with the DRL 18-s regimen. The second stressed the immediate and functional effects of unreinforced lever-pressing during training. On the DRL 10-s schedule, a response with an IRT less than 10 s is not only unreinforced, it also delays the next available reinforcer. Accordingly, unreinforced responding should become discriminative for prolonged pausing behavior, and such a tendency could facilitate DRL 18-s performance. In this regard, the DRL 10-s-trained children acquired repertoires in which 40% of their IRTs were longer than 10 s and, most importantly, nearly 25% were longer than 18 s. Similarly long IRTs were not evident in the training repertoires of the other groups.

The return to the DRL 18-s schedule for three children after a 3-week period of experimental inactivity rapidly reinstated and maintained spaced responding comparable to that seen in their last DRL 18-s session. The immediate recovery of spaced responding indicates that a particular property of an operant can be restored quickly when one of its controlling conditions (e.g., nonreinforced lever-pressing or delivery of a reinforcer) returns. Following DRL 18-s retesting, attempts to shape *high-rate* responding through a schedule sequence of CRF, small FR values, VR 10, and VR 15 proved successful for a child who had a VR 10 history. Children who had an earlier history of low-rate responding (DRL 10 s and FI 18 s) never developed behavioral patterns appropriate to ratio schedules in the four or five sessions allotted for this purpose.

Taken together, these findings support Weiner's (1965) contention that both recent and remote behavioral histories determine behavioral adaptation to a given schedule. Using Weiner's measure of schedule adjustment as the rate of delivered reinforcers, it may be said that it was the recent DRL 10-s history that furnished children with the necessary performances to attain high and substantial rates of reinforcement under the DRL 18-s schedule, whereas for other children it was their recent VR 10 history that proved to be most "maladaptive." On the other hand, the combined histories of DRL 10-s and DRL 18-s performances, which generated low-rate, temporally spaced responding, were maladaptive for building high-rate, closely spaced responding of the kind necessary for a high density of VR 15 reinforcement. For these latter performances, it was the remote history of the VR 10-trained children that led to higher payoffs.

It is possible that the DRL 10-s trained children adjusted more effectively to the DRL 18-s contingencies because these time-based schedules are in accord with the scheduling arrangements they experience in their everyday settings. Pierce and Epling (1995) proposed that because infants receive nourishment and other means of support from caregivers largely when they have the time to do so, the dominant contingencies in early life will be time-dependent. However, as the developing organism learns to control the environment through its own efforts (gaining control in self-feeding, ambulatory, and language skills), ratio-based schedules take over. Evaluating such a proposal would entail both a descriptive and an experimental analysis of the prevailing schedules in force in a variety of different surroundings taken at different age periods.

In Natural Settings

That reinforcement schedules can be incorporated into the daily routine of 4- to 5-year-olds without difficulty is indicated by DeCasper and Zeiler's (1972) innovative research. Access to a preschool locker (for storing clothing and materials) served as the reinforcing event. The locker opened (and ended a session) only after responding on a device had turned on all of 10 lights, with the onset of each light dependent on the completion of one of two schedules, usually an FI 1-min or FR 20. After just one session, the children went to their lockers immediately on arriving at school without the need for any experimenter direction. Considering Long's (Long, 1962; Long et al., 1958) observations that many same-aged children also exposed to FI 1-min schedules, but in laboratory settings, found the FI so aversive that they often left the room and/or failed to return for another session, the children's continued participation in the naturalistic research settings of DeCasper and Zeiler's (1972) is remarkable. None of the children, having engaged in from 18 to 32 sessions, expressed a desire to terminate participation despite the fact that the task was framed neither as a game nor an occasion for winning prizes.

Basic schedules of reinforcement have been employed directly or at least implied in basic and applied research with infants (Lancioni, 1980) and even more so with children (Davey & Cullen, 1988). For example, in Experiment III of Weisberg and Clements (1977), a complex schedule was arranged in order to sustain the unison answering of concept-related questions by a group of 12 disadvantaged preschoolers (mean age 2½ years) seated at one of three tables having lunch. A teacher's aide asked the questions and provided intermittent social approval that was delivered more often for the answers by the least-responsive child at a preselected table and less often, but still attainable, by the moderate- and most-responsive children at that table. The child's ranking, which was based on the previous day's rate of responding (conforming to an adjusting schedule), was never announced to the group. As it turned out, the average weekly rates of reinforcement across 10 weeks became evenly distributed among the children at each table, as did their attempts to answer questions.

There are a host of daily situations that lend themselves to a moment-by-moment analysis of the development of naturally occurring operants in infants and children. Often the scheduling of behavioral consequences requires only a small and readily achievable change in an existing routine. One possibility involves the development of infant locomotor behavior, for which Gustafson (1984) has provided a non-operant-based interpretation of the perpetuation of these forms of behaviors in the laboratory, but which can be studied equally well in many daily routines. Gustafson's study suggests that brief adult interaction for locomoting can serve as an effective reinforcer and other studies (e.g., Rheingold & Eckerman, 1969) point to the use of novel toys in free-field settings.

Investigations of the ease and the effects of different kinds of scheduling arrangements for locomotoring would have relevance for Pierce and Epling's (1995) formulations about the dominant schedule in force during the course of development. Is early ambulatory behavior under the control of interval rather than ratio schedules? Can locomotor responding under one context be placed under ratio reinforcement requirements and under another context on an interval schedule? An operant analysis of the controlling variables involved in maternal separation, as Gewirtz and Palaez-Nogueras (1992) conducted in the laboratory, also seems workable in the real-life settings of infants and their caretakers. The implication here is that operant reinforcement is a major contributor to the establishment of precise and long-lasting repertoires in the young. Careful experimental examination of the role of recent and remote reinforcement histories on the emergence of behavior, if carried out in real-life settings, would be helpful in highlighting the significance of an operant approach of development.

CONCLUDING REMARKS

Prior to the 1960s, only a few scattered studies of operant conditioning with infants and young children had been reported. Today, the experimental analysis of behavior of these populations is gaining a fairly prominent position in some areas of developmental psychology. This advance has not always occurred, however, as a result of simply applying to young subjects the experimental techniques that were originally developed for adults or animals. Rather, research with infants and young children presents a number of unique and unanticipated problems, and considerable ingenuity in translating or modifying traditional procedures for use with immature subjects is necessary. In the present chapter, we have considered many of these problems and have suggested solutions to them. In addition, we have provided explicit examples of how operant conditioning procedures with infants and young children have been implemented in both the laboratory and other settings. Also furnished is an extended list of references to research details for those who wish to pursue a particular experimental technique in greater depth. Hopefully, this chapter will alleviate some of the mystique that surrounds research with these populations and encourage further research into the fundamental processes of learning during early development.

REFERENCES

Adams, R. E., & Passman, R. H. (1981). The effects of preparing two-year-olds for brief separation from their mothers. *Child Development, 51,* 1068–1071.

Ashton, R. (1973). The state variable in neonatal research. *Merrill-Palmer Quarterly, 19,* 3–20.

Atkinson, J., & Braddick, O. (1976). Stereoscopic discrimination in infants. *Perception, 5,* 29–38.

Aylward, G. P. (1981). The developmental course of behavioral state in preterm infants: A descriptive study. *Child Development, 52,* 564–568.

Baer, D. M. (1960). Escape and avoidance response of preschool children to two schedules of reinforcement withdrawal. *Journal of the Experimental Analysis of Behavior, 3,* 155–159.

Baer, D. M. (1962a). Laboratory control of thumbsucking through the withdrawal and re-presentation of positive reinforcement. *Journal of the Experimental Analysis of Behavior, 5,* 525–528.

Baer, D. M. (1962b). A technique for the study of social reinforcement in young children: Behavior avoiding reinforcement withdrawal. *Child Development, 33,* 847–858.

Baer, D. M., & Sherman, J. A. (1964). Reinforcement control of generalized imitation. *Journal of Experimental Child Psychology, 1,* 37–49.

Berg, W. K., & Berg, K. M. (1987). Psychophysiological development in infancy: State, startle, and attention. In J. D. Osofsky (Ed.), *Handbook of infant development* (2nd ed., pp. 238–317). New York: Wiley.

Berlyne, D. E. (1960). *Conflict, arousal, and curiosity.* New York: McGraw–Hill.

Bijou, S. W. (1957). Methodology for an experimental analysis of child behavior. *Psychological Reports, 3,* 243–250.

Bijou, S. W. (1958). Operant extinction after fixed interval schedules in young children. *Journal of the Experimental Analysis of Behavior, 1,* 25–29.

Bijou, S. W. (1993). *Behavior analysis of development.* Reno, NV: Context Press.

Bijou, S. W., & Baer, D. M. (1966). Operant child behavior and development. In W. K. Honig (Ed.), *Operant behavior: Areas of research and application* (pp. 718–789). New York: Meredith.

Bijou, S. W., & Orlando, R. (1961). Rapid development of multiple schedule performance with retarded children. *Journal of the Experimental Analysis of Behavior, 4,* 7–16.

Bijou, S. W., & Sturges, P. T. (1959). Positive reinforcers for experimental studies with children—Consumables and manipulables. *Child Development, 30,* 151–170.

Blank, M. (1973). *Teaching learning in the preschool: A dialogue approach.* Columbus, OH: Merrill.

Bloom, K. (1979). Evaluation of infant vocal conditioning. *Journal of Experimental Child Psychology, 27,* 60–70.

Bloom, K., & Esposito, A. (1975). Social conditioning and its proper control procedures. *Journal of Experimental Child Psychology, 19,* 209–222.

Bower, T. G. R. (1964). Discrimination of depth in premature infants. *Psychonomic Science, 1,* 368.

Bower, T. G. R. (1967). Phenomenal identity and form perception in an infant. *Perception and Psychophysics, 2,* 74–76.

Brackbill, Y. (1958). Extinction of the smiling response in infants as a function of reinforcement schedule. *Child Development, 29,* 115–124.

Brackbill, Y., & Fitzgerald, H. E. (1969). Development of sensory analyzers during infancy. In L. P. Lipsitt & H. W. Reese (Eds.), *Advances in child development and behavior* (Vol. 4, pp. 173–208). New York: Academic Press.

Brackbill, Y., & Koltsova, M. M. (1967). Conditioning and learning. In Y. Brackbill (Ed.), *Infancy and early childhood* (pp. 207–386). New York: Free Press.

Brassell, W. R., & Kaye, H. (1974). Reinforcement from the sucking environment and subsequent modification of sucking behavior in the human neonate. *Journal of Experimental Child Psychology, 18,* 448–463.

Brown, J. (1964). States in newborn infants. *Merrill-Palmer Quarterly, 10,* 313–327.

Brown, J. L. (1972). Instrumental control of the sucking response in human newborns. *Journal of Experimental Child Psychology, 14,* 66–80.

Bruner, J. S. (1973). Pacifier-produced visual buffering in human infants. *Developmental Psychobiology, 6,* 45–51.

Butterfield, E. C., & Siperstein, G. N. (1972). Influence of contingent auditory stimulation upon nonnutritional suckle. In J. Bosma (Ed.), *Third symposium on oral sensation and perception: The mouth of the infant* (pp. 313–334). Springfield, IL: Thomas.

Cairns, G. F., & Butterfield, E. C. (1975). Assessing infants' auditory functioning. In B. Z. Friedlander (Ed.), *Exceptional infant: Vol. 3. Assessment and intervention* (pp. 84–108). New York: Brunner/Mazel.

Campbell, B. A., & Ampuero, M. X. (1985). Conditioned orienting and defensive responses in the developing rat. *Infant Behavior and Development, 8,* 425–434.

Campos-de-Carvalho, M., Bhatt, R., Wondoloski, T., Klein, P., & Rovee-Collier, C. (1993, July). *Learning and memory at nine months.* Paper presented at the meeting of the International Society for the Study of Behavioural Development, Recife, Brazil.

Caron, R. F. (1967). Visual reinforcement of head-turning in young infants. *Journal of Experimental Child Psychology, 5,* 489–511.

Clifton, R. K., & Nelson, M. N. (1976). Developmental study of habituation in infants: The importance of paradigm, response system, and state. In T. J. Tighe & R. N. Leaton (Eds.), *Habituation* (pp. 159–205). Hillsdale, NJ: Erlbaum.

Clifton, R. K., Siqueland, E. R., & Lipsitt, L. P. (1972). Conditioned headturning in human newborns as a function of conditioned response requirements and states of wakefulness. *Journal of Experimental Child Psychology, 13,* 43–57.

Cohen, L. B., & Gelber, E. R. (1975). Infant visual memory. In L. B. Cohen & P. Salapatek (Eds.), *Infant perception: From sensation to cognition: Vol. 1. Basic visual processes* (pp. 347–403). New York: Academic Press.

Davey, G., & Cullen, C. (1988). *Human operant conditioning and behavior modification.* New York: Wiley.

DeCasper, A. J., & Fifer, W. P. (1980). Of human bonding: Newborns prefer their mothers voices. *Science, 208,* 1174–1176.

DeCasper, A. J., & Zeiler, M. D. (1972). Steady-state behavior in children: A method and some data. *Journal of Experimental Child Psychology, 13,* 231–239.

Dennis, W. A. (1934). A description and classification of the response of the newborn infant. *Psychological Bulletin, 31,* 5–22.

Eimas, P. D., Siqueland, E. R., Jusczyk, P., & Vigorito, J. (1971). Speech perception in infants. *Science, 171,* 303–306.

Fagen, J. W. (1977). Interproblem learning in ten-month-old infants. *Child Development, 48,* 786–796.

Ferster, C. B., & DeMeyer, M. K. (1961). The development of performances in autistic children in an automatically controlled environment. *Journal of Chronic Disorders, 13,* 312–345.

Franks, A., & Berg, W. K. (1975). Effects of visual complexity and sex of infant in the conjugate reinforcement paradigm. *Developmental Psychology, 11,* 388–389.

Friedlander, B. Z. (1961). Automated measurement of differential operant performance. *American Psychologist, 16,* 350.

Gewirtz, J. L., & Baer, D. M. (1958). Deprivation and satiation of social reinforcers as drive condition-ers. *Journal of Abnormal and Social Psychology, 57,* 165–172.

Gewirtz, J. L., & Palaez-Nogueras, M. (1992). B. F. Skinner's legacy to human infant behavior and de-velopment. *American Psychologist, 47,* 1411–1422.

Graham, F. K., & Clifton, R. K. (1966). Heart-rate change as a component of the orienting response. *Psy-chological Bulletin, 65,* 305–320.

Gustafson, G. E. (1984). Effects of the ability to locomote on infants' social and exploratory behaviors: An experimental study. *Developmental Psychology, 20,* 397–405.

Hartshorn, K., Rovee-Collier, C., Bhatt, R. S., & Wondoloski, T. (1994, November). *Operant learning and retention of 6-month-olds: A confirming analysis.* Paper presented at the meeting of the Interna-tional Society for Developmental Psychobiology, Islamorada, FL.

Hayne, H., Rovee-Collier, C., & Perris, E. E. (1987). Categorization and memory retrieval in 3-month-olds. *Child Development, 58,* 750–767.

Hill, W. H., Borovsky, D., & Rovee-Collier, C. (1988). Continuities in infant memory development over the first half-year. *Developmental Psychobiology, 21,* 43–62.

Hillman, D., & Bruner, J. S. (1972). Infant sucking in response to variations in schedules of feeding re-inforcement. *Journal of Experimental Child Psychology, 13,* 240–247.

Hively, W. (1962). Programming stimuli in matching to sample. *Journal of the Experimental Analysis of Behavior, 5,* 279–298.

Holman, J., Goetz, E. M., & Baer, D. M. (1977). The training of creativity as an operant and examination of its generalization characteristics. In B. Etzel, J. M. LeBlanc, & D. M. Baer (Eds.), *New develop-ments in behavioral research: Theory method and application* (pp. 441–471). Hillsdale, NJ: Erl-baum.

Hulsebus, R. C. (1973). Operant conditioning of infant behavior: A review. In H. W. Reese (Ed.), *Ad-vances in child development and behavior* (Vol. 8, pp. 111–158). New York: Academic Press.

Hunt, J. M., & Uzgiris, I. C. (1964, September). *Cathexis from recognitive familiarity.* Paper presented at the meeting of the American Psychological Association, Los Angeles.

Kalnins, I. V., & Bruner, J. S. (1973). The coordination of visual observation and instrumental behavior in early infancy. *Perception, 2,* 307–314.

Kobre, K. R., & Lipsitt, L. P. (1972). A negative contrast effect in newborns. *Journal of Experimental Child Psychology, 14,* 81–91.

Koch, J. (1968). Conditioned orienting reactions to persons and things in 2–5-month-old infants. *Hu-man Development, 11,* 81–91.

Koegel, R. L., & Wilhelm, H. (1973). Selective responding to the components of multiple visual cues by autistic children. *Journal of Experimental Child Psychology, 15,* 442–453.

Korner, A. F. (1972). State as variable, as obstacle, and as mediator of stimulation in infant research. *Merrill-Palmer Quarterly, 18,* 77–94.

Lancioni, G. E. (1980). Infant operant conditioning and its implications for early intervention. *Psycho-logical Review, 88,* 516–530.

Lattal, K. A., & Neef, N. A. (1996). Recent reinforcement-schedule research and applied behavior analy-sis. *Journal of Applied Behavior Analysis, 29,* 213–230.

Lenard, H. G., von Bernuth, H., & Prechtl, H. F. R. (1968). Reflexes and their relationship to behavioral state in the newborn. *Acta Paediatrica Scandinavica, 57,* 177–185.

Leuba, C., & Friedlander, B. Z. (1968). Effects of controlled audio-visual reinforcement on infant's ma-nipulative play in the home. *Journal of Experimental Child Psychology, 6,* 87–99.

Levinson, C. A., & Levinson, P. K. (1967). Operant conditioning of headturning for visual reinforcement in three-month-old infants. *Psychonomic Science, 8,* 529–530.

Lindsley, O. R. (1962). A behavioral measure of television viewing. *Journal of Advertising Research, 2,* 2–12.

Lindsley, O. R. (1963). Experimental analysis of social reinforcement: Terms and methods. *American Journal of Orthopsychiatry, 33,* 624–633.

Lipsitt, L. P. (1969). Learning capacities of the human infant. In R. J. Robinson (Ed.), *Brain and early behaviour* (pp. 227–249). New York: Academic Press.

Lipsitt, L. P., Pederson, L. J., & DeLucia, C. A. (1966). Conjugate reinforcement of operant responding in infants. *Psychonomic Science, 4,* 67–68.

Lipton, E. L., Steinschneider, A., & Richmond, J. B. (1966). Autonomic function in the neonate: VII. Maturational changes in cardiac control. *Child Development, 37*, 1–16.

Little, A. H. (1973). *A comparative study of trace and delay conditioning in the human infant.* Unpublished doctoral dissertation, Brown University, Providence, RI.

Long, E. R. (1959). The use of operant conditioning techniques in children. In S. Fisher (Ed.), *Child research in psychopharmacology* (pp. 111–136). Springfield, IL: Thomas.

Long, E. R. (1962). Additional techniques for producing multiple-schedule control in children. *Journal of the Experimental Analysis of Behavior, 5*, 443–455.

Long, E. R. (1963). Chained and tandem scheduling with children. *Journal of the Experimental Analysis of Behavior, 6*, 459–472.

Long, E. R., Hammack, J. T., May, F., & Campbell, B. J. (1958). Intermittent reinforcement of operant behavior in children. *Journal of the Experimental Analysis of Behavior, 1*, 315–339.

Lowe, C. F. (1979). Determinants of human operant behavior. In M. D. Zeiler & D. Harzen (Eds.), *Advances in analysis of behavior: Reinforcement and the organization of behaviors* (pp. 159–172). New York: Wiley.

Lowe, C. F., Beasty, A., & Bentall, R. P. (1983). The role of verbal behavior in human learning: Infant performance on fixed-interval schedules. *Journal of the Experimental Analysis of Behavior, 39*, 157–164.

MacFarlane, A., Harris, P., & Barnes, I. (1976). Central and peripheral vision in early infancy. *Journal of Experimental Child Psychology, 21*, 532–538.

Mackintosh, N. J. (1974). *The psychology of animal learning.* New York: Academic Press.

McKirdy, L. S., & Rovee, C. K. (1978). The efficacy of auditory and visual conjugate reinforcers in infant conditioning. *Journal of Experimental Child Psychology, 25*, 80–89.

Milewski, A. E., & Siqueland, E. R. (1975). Discrimination of color and pattern novelty in one-month human infants. *Journal of Experimental Child Psychology, 19*, 122–136.

Mills, M., & Melhuish, E. (1974). Recognition of mother's voice in early infancy. *Nature, 252*, 123–124.

Novak, G. (1995). *Developmental psychology: Dynamical systems and behavior analysis.* Reno, NV: Context Press.

Papousek, H. (1961). Conditioned head rotation reflexes in infants in the first months of life. *Acta Pediatrica, 50*, 565–576.

Papousek, H. (1967). Experimental studies of appetitional behavior in human newborns and infants. In H. W. Stevenson, E. H. Hess, & H. L. Rheingold (Eds.), *Early behavior: Comparative and developmental approaches* (pp. 249–278). New York: Wiley.

Papousek, H. (1969). Individual variability in learned responses in human infants. In R. J. Robinson (Ed.), *Brain and early behaviour* (pp. 251–266). New York: Academic Press.

Papousek, H. (1977). The development of learning ability in infancy. In G. Nissen (Ed.), *Intelligence, learning, and learning disturbances* (pp. 75–93). Berlin: Springer-Verlag.

Parsonson, B. S., & Naughton, K. H. (1988). Training generalized conservation in 5-year-old children. *Journal of Experimental Child Psychology, 46*, 375–390.

Passman, R. H., & Weisberg, P. (1975). Mothers and blankets as agents for promoting play in young children in a novel environment: The effects of social and non-social attachment objects. *Developmental Psychology, 11*, 170–177.

Pavlov, I. P. (1927). *Conditioned reflexes* (G. V. Anrep, Trans.). London: Oxford University Press.

Peiper, A. (1963). *Cerebral function in infancy and childhood.* New York: Consultants Bureau.

Piaget, J. (1952). *The origins of intelligence in children.* New York: International Universities Press.

Pierce, W. D., & Epling, W. F. (1995). *Behavior analysis and learning.* Englewood Cliffs, NJ: Prentice–Hall.

Poulson, C. L. (1983). Differential reinforcement of other-than-vocalization as a control procedure in the conditioning of infant vocalization rate. *Journal of Experimental Child Psychology, 36*, 471–489.

Prechtl, H. F. R. (1974). The behavioral states of the newborn infant (a review). *Brain Research, 76*, 185–212.

Premack, D. (1965). Reinforcement theory. In D. Levine (Ed.), *Nebraska symposium on motivation* (pp. 123–188). Lincoln: University of Nebraska Press.

Ramey, C. T., Hieger, L., & Klisz, D. (1972). Synchronous reinforcement of vocal responses in failure-to-thrive infants. *Child Development, 43*, 1449–1455.

Ramey, C. T., & Ourth, L. L. (1971). Delayed reinforcement and vocalization rates of infants. *Child Development, 42,* 291–297.

Rheingold, H. L. (1956). The modification of social responsiveness in institutional babies. *Monographs of the Society for Research in Child Development, 21* (2, Serial No. 63).

Rheingold, H. L., & Eckerman, C. O. (1969). The infant's free entry into a new environment. *Journal of Experimental Child Psychology, 8,* 271–283.

Rheingold, H. L., Gewirtz, J. L., & Ross, H. W. (1959). Social conditioning of vocalizations in the infant. *Journal of Comparative and Physiological Psychology, 52,* 68–73.

Rheingold, H. L., Stanley, W. C., & Cooley, J. A. (1962). Method for studying exploratory behavior in infants. *Science, 136,* 1054–1055.

Rovee, C. K., & Fagen, J. W. (1976). Extended conditioning and 24-hour retention in infants. *Journal of Experimental Child Psychology, 21,* 1–11.

Rovee, C. K., & Rovee, D. T. (1969). Conjugate reinforcement of infant exploratory behavior. *Journal of Experimental Child Psychology, 8,* 33–39.

Rovee-Collier, C. (1983). Infants as problem-solvers: A psychobiological perspective. In M. D. Zeiler & P. Harzem (Eds.), *Advances in analysis of behaviour: Vol. 3. Biological factors in learning* (pp. 63–101). Chichester, England: Wiley.

Rovee-Collier, C. (1987). Learning and memory. In J. D. Osofsky (Ed.), *Handbook of infant development* (2nd ed., pp. 98–148). New York: Wiley.

Rovee-Collier, C., & Capatides, J. B. (1979). Positive behavioral contrast in 3-month-old infants on multiple conjugate reinforcement schedules. *Journal of the Experimental Analysis of Behavior, 32,* 15–27.

Rovee-Collier, C., & Fagen, J. W. (1981). The retrieval of memory in early infancy. In L. P. Lipsitt (Ed.), *Advances in infancy research* (Vol. 1, pp. 225–254). Norwood, NJ: Ablex.

Rovee-Collier, C., & Gekoski, M. J. (1979). The economics of infancy: A review of conjugate reinforcement. In H. W. Reese & L. P. Lipsitt (Eds.), *Advances in child development and behavior* (Vol. 1, pp. 195–255). New York: Academic Press.

Rovee-Collier, C., Hankins, E., & Bhatt, R. S. (1992). Textons, visual pop-out effects, and object recognition in infancy. *Journal of Experimental Psychology: General, 121,* 435–445.

Rovee-Collier, C., Morrongiello, B. A., Aron, M., & Kupersmidt, J. (1978). Topographical response differentiation and reversal in 3-month-old infants. *Infant Behavior and Development, 1,* 323–333.

Sameroff, A. J. (1968). The components of sucking in the human newborn. *Journal of Experimental Child Psychology, 6,* 607–623.

Sheppard, W. C. (1969). Operant control of infant vocal and motor behavior. *Journal of Experimental Child Psychology, 7,* 36–51.

Simmons, M. W. (1964). Operant discrimination learning in human infants. *Child Development, 35,* 737–748.

Simmons, M. W., & Lipsitt, L. P. (1961). An operant-discrimination apparatus for infants. *Journal of the Experimental Analysis of Behavior, 4,* 233–235.

Siqueland, E. R. (1968a). Reinforcement patterns and extinction in human newborns. *Journal of Experimental Child Psychology, 6,* 431–442.

Siqueland, E. R. (1968b, April). *Visual reinforcement and exploratory behavior in infants.* Paper presented at the meeting of the Society for Research in Child Development, Worcester, MA.

Siqueland, E. R. (1969a, March). *The development of instrumental exploratory behavior during the first year of human life.* Paper presented at the meeting of the Society for Research in Child Development, Santa Monica, CA.

Siqueland, E. R. (1969b, July). *Further developments in infant learning.* Paper presented at the meeting of the XIXth International Congress of Psychology, London.

Siqueland, E. R., & DeLucia, C. A. (1969). Visual reinforcement of nonnutritive sucking in human infants. *Science, 165,* 1144–1146.

Skinner, B. F. (1953). *Science and human behavior.* New York: Macmillan Co.

Skinner, B. F. (1956). A case history in the scientific method. *American Psychologist, 11,* 221–233.

Smith, K. U., & Smith, W. M. (1962). *Perception and motion.* Philadelphia: Saunders.

Smith, K. U., Zwerg, C., & Smith, N. J. (1963). Sensory-feedback analysis of infant control of the behavioral environment. *Perceptual and Motor Skills, 16,* 725–732.

Staddon, J. E. R. (1965). Some properties of spaced responding in pigeons. *Journal of the Experimental Analysis of Behavior, 8,* 19–27.

Stoddard, L. T. (1962). *Operant conditioning of timing behavior in children.* Unpublished doctoral dissertation, Columbia University, New York.

Sullivan, M. W., Lewis, M., & Alessandri, S. M. (1992). Cross-age stability in emotional expressions during learning and extinction. *Developmental Psychology, 28,* 58–63.

Sullivan, M. W., Rovee-Collier, C., & Tynes, D. M. (1979). A conditioning analysis of infant long-term memory. *Child Development, 50,* 152–162.

Todd, G. A., & Palmer, B. (1968). Social reinforcement of infant babbling. *Child Development, 39,* 591–596.

Trehub, S. E. (1973). Infants' sensitivity to vowel and tonal contrasts. *Developmental Psychology, 9,* 91–96.

Trehub, S. E., & Rabinovitch, M. S. (1972). Auditory-linguistic sensitivity in early infancy. *Developmental Psychology, 6,* 74–77.

Watson, J. B., & Rayner, R. (1920). Conditioned emotional reactions. *Journal of Experimental Psychology, 3,* 1–14.

Watson, J. S. (1966). The development and generalization of "contingency awareness" in early infancy: Some hypotheses. *Merrill-Palmer Quarterly, 12,* 123–135.

Watson, J. S. (1969). Operant conditioning of visual fixation in infants under visual and auditory reinforcement. *Developmental Psychology, 1,* 508–516.

Watson, J. S., & Ramey, C. T. (1972). Reactions to response-contingent stimulation in early infancy. *Merrill-Palmer Quarterly, 18,* 219–227.

Weiner, H. (1965). Conditioning history and maladaptive human operant behavior. *Psychological Reports, 17,* 935–942.

Weiner, H. (1969). Controlling human fixed-interval performance. *Journal of the Experimental Analyses of Behavior, 12,* 349–373.

Weisberg, P. (1963). Social and non-social conditioning of infant vocalizations. *Child Development, 34,* 377–388.

Weisberg, P. (1969). Operant procedures for the establishment of stimulus control in two-year-old infants. *Journal of Experimental Child Psychology, 7,* 81–95.

Weisberg, P. (1970a). Delayed response learning in two-year-old children: Gradual versus sudden changes in the delay interval. *Psychonomic Science, 19,* 85–86.

Weisberg, P. (1970b). Effect of reinforcement history on DRL performance in young children. *Journal of Experimental Child Psychology, 9,* 348–362.

Weisberg, P. (1975). Developmental differences in children's preferences for high- and low-arousing forms of contact stimulation. *Child Development, 46,* 957–979.

Weisberg, P., & Clements, P. (1977). Effects of direct, intermittent, and vicarious reinforcement procedures on the development and maintenance of instruction-following behaviors in a group of young children. *Journal of Applied Behavior Analysis, 11,* 314.

Weisberg, P., & Fink, E. (1966). Fixed ratio and extinction performance of infants in the second year of life. *Journal of the Experimental Analysis of Behavior, 9,* 105–109.

Weisberg, P., & Fink, E. (1968). Effect of varying and nonvarying stimulus consequences on visual persistence in twenty-month-old infants. *Perceptual and Motor Skills, 26,* 883–887.

Weisberg, P., & Simmons, M. W. (1966). A modified WGTA for infants in their second year of life. *Journal of Psychology, 63,* 99–104.

Weisberg, P., & Tragakis, C. J. (1967). Analysis of DRL behavior in young children. *Psychological Reports, 21,* 709–715.

Zeiler, M. D. (1984). The sleeping giant: Reinforcement schedules. *Journal of the Experimental Analysis of Behavior, 42,* 485–493.

Zeiler, M. D., & Kelley, C. A. (1969). Fixed-ratio and fixed-internal schedules of cartoon presentation. *Journal of Experimental Child Psychology, 8,* 306–313.

12

The Verbal Governance of Behavior

Eliot Shimoff and A. Charles Catania

> If we are interested in perpetuating the practices responsible for the present
> corpus of scientific knowledge, we must keep in mind that some very
> important parts of the scientific process do not now lend themselves to
> mathematical, logical, or any other formal treatment.
> —SKINNER (1956, p. 221)

The above quotation can be interpreted to mean that some research practices are verbally governed and others are not. The topic of verbal governance is mainly concerned with how human behavior depends on its verbal antecedents. The language in which the topic of verbal governance has usually been framed is fraught with difficulties and inconsistencies (see Catania, Chapter 13). For example, verbal governance has often been discussed under the rubric of rule-governed behavior (e.g., Skinner, 1969). Yet in many disciplines outside of behavior analysis, rules are not regarded as instances of verbal behavior, and issues of verbal governance are often couched in terms of awareness or of distinctions between implicit and explicit learning (e.g., Reber, 1976).

Even with rules strictly treated as instances of verbal behavior, their status has been controversial, with some arguing that only verbal constructions that specify contingencies qualify as rules and others that any verbal antecedent is sufficient, without regard to whether it specifies contingencies. Another problem is that verbal antecedents enter into three-term contingencies but do not necessarily function as discriminative stimuli (Schlinger & Blakely, 1987): The effects of verbal antecedents are often extended over time, but one need not be continuously in the presence of an instruction to follow it.

We have chosen to speak in terms of *verbally governed behavior* because such locutions do not implicitly constrain the kinds of verbal antecedents that qualify.

Eliot Shimoff and A. Charles Catania • Department of Psychology, University of Maryland Baltimore County, Baltimore, Maryland 21250.
Handbook of Research Methods in Human Operant Behavior, edited by Lattal and Perone. Plenum Press, New York, 1998.

The distinction between nonverbally and verbally governed behavior captures the instructional function of verbal behavior. To the extent that definitions or statements of fact generate relevant verbal or nonverbal behavior, they function as verbal antecedents as effectively as commands or instructions. For example, giving definitions and stating facts are instructions with respect to the listener's future verbal behavior (see Skinner, 1957). Where prior accounts have typically applied the terminology of rule-governed versus contingency-shaped behavior, we will speak instead of verbally governed and nonverbally governed behavior.

Much human behavior is jointly determined by both verbal and nonverbal contingencies, and the task of an experimental analysis is to tease apart these joint contributions. The success of a chemical analysis depends on both a proper classification of the elements that make up compounds and a proper understanding of the various ways in which those elements can combine; similarly, the effectiveness with which a behavior analysis is accomplished depends on both the adequacy of our taxonomy of behavioral processes and our skill in determining how those processes can combine to produce complex cases. Our taxonomy of behavioral processes is validated by the success of our analyses.

TOPOGRAPHY, FUNCTION, AND BEHAVIOR CLASSES

One significant strength of verbal governance is that it establishes behavior that closely resembles nonverbally governed behavior; one significant weakness is that such behavior is rarely if ever precisely identical to the corresponding nonverbally governed behavior. For example, the storytelling of a skilled raconteur, shaped by extensive exposure to the natural contingencies of telling stories, is marked by finely honed timing and intonation; with appropriate instructions, a novice might learn to tell the story in much the same way. Similarly, the diagnosis by an intern fresh from medical training may be the same as one by an experienced specialist, and the bookcase built by an apprentice who has followed a skilled carpenter's instructions may share features with one built by the carpenter. In each example, effective instructions are those that produce the same outcomes as those generated by contingencies (the aptly told story, the accurate diagnosis, the well-built bookcase); indeed, the effectiveness of the instructions is defined by the closeness of the match between the verbally and the nonverbally governed behavior.

This match is topographical rather than functional; the two classes seem similar but are members of distinctly different operant classes. Consider a student pressing a button that occasionally produces points exchangeable for money. The button pressing may be maintained solely by the contingent relation between presses and point deliveries; in this case, the points are reinforcers and button pressing is the operant class. Or the student may be following instructions; in this case, the performance depends on a history of reinforced compliance with instructions; and instruction following rather than button pressing is the operant class. Sometimes button pressing may depend on both contingencies and instructions; in this case, performance is jointly governed by both nonverbal contingencies and verbal antecedents.

To the extent that button pressing is nonverbally governed by the contingent relation between presses and point deliveries, it will be independent of instructions; to the extent that it is verbally governed, it will be insensitive to changes in nonverbal contingencies. Skinner (1969) suggested that verbally governed behavior is established by verbal communities precisely because it is insensitive to contingencies. We often resort to instructions when natural consequences are weak (as when we tell children to study) or remote (as when we tell drivers to wear seatbelts) or likely to maintain undesirable behavior (as when we warn against drug abuse).

The contingencies that establish verbally governed behavior make consequences depend on relations between verbal antecedents and the behavior that follows. Thus, they establish and maintain verbal governance as a higher-order class of behavior (Estes, 1971). The consequences involved in maintaining such a class differ from those that operate on specific instances. For example, when a child is told to put on boots before going out to play in the snow, we must distinguish the social consequences of disobeying the parents from the natural consequences of unshod feet. Verbally governed behavior as a higher-order class is initially shaped by social contingencies, but effective instruction demands also that the governing verbal behavior must be correlated reasonably well with the contingencies that would operate if behavior were not verbally governed.

PREREQUISITES FOR AND CONSEQUENCES OF VERBAL GOVERNANCE

Verbally governed behavior is well-established in humans by an early age. For example, in tasks in which responses such as button presses produce simple consequences like snacks or opportunities to hear music according to various schedules (Bentall & Lowe, 1987; Bentall, Lowe, & Beasty, 1985; Lowe, Beasty, & Bentall, 1983), performances of children under 2 years old do not differ substantially from those of other nonverbal organisms such as pigeons or rats. Between the ages of about 2 and 4 or 5, most children show transitional performances with variable properties characteristic of both nonverbally and verbally governed behavior. By the age of 5, the performances of most children become verbally governed almost exclusively, with the insensitivity to contingencies that characterizes adult performance in these sorts of tasks (see Lovaas, 1961, 1964a,b).

Sensitivity to nonverbal contingencies must be judged from how performance changes with changes in contingencies and not from topography. Verbal antecedents, however, are often less accessible than changes in contingencies. The ease with which we can identify verbal behavior as an effective part of an environment depends on who generated it, whether it is overt or covert, and which properties of behavior it specifies. For example, a minimal instruction that only mentions a button on a console may be functionally equivalent to an instruction to press, and a verbal antecedent overtly provided by an experimenter in a set of instructions will be easier to identify than one covertly generated by the subject (and the most potent verbal antecedents may be those that are self-generated; see Rosenfarb, Newland, Brannon, & Howey, 1992).

We cannot give an exhaustive list of ways to modify verbal behavior. In experimental settings, contributions of verbal responding to the maintenance of other behavior have been examined by manipulating instructions (e.g., Hayes, Brownstein, Haas, & Greenway, 1986; Kaufman, Baron, & Kopp, 1966), by sampling verbal behavior following different conditions (e.g., Ericsson & Simon, 1984), or by requiring some verbal behavior that is incompatible with other verbal behavior, as when a subject must shadow or repeat aloud continuously presented verbal material (e.g., Lowe, 1979). The shaping of verbal behavior (Greenspoon, 1955; Rosenfeld & Baer, 1970), once controversial, is now a standard experimental procedure. For example, verbal responding can be modified by requiring subjects to respond to questions in writing after periods of nonverbal responding and then shaping that verbal behavior by differentially awarding points exchangeable for money.

In any of these cases, analysis can be complicated by the interaction of variables. For example, instructions interact with nonverbal contingencies when they affect the contact of behavior with those contingencies, and the sampling of verbal behavior via questionnaires or other verbal antecedents interacts with verbal governance when existing verbal behavior is altered just by the sampling of it (e.g., Hayes, Brownstein, Zettle, Rosenfarb, & Korn, 1986; Joyce & Chase, 1990; Svartdal, 1989, 1992).

We can only be sure whether behavior is governed by verbal antecedents or nonverbal contingencies when the verbal antecedents and the contingencies are pitted against each other. If we studied verbal antecedents and contingencies that produced comparable performances, we would have no way to decide whether the verbal antecedents or the contingencies were effective. Consider again the student whose button presses produce points. If we provided instructions specifying high-rate pressing while contingencies operated that would otherwise generate low-rate pressing, we could then distinguish between verbally governed and nonverbally governed performances on the basis of the different rates. Another strategy would be to determine whether performances changed with changes in the verbal antecedents or changes in the contingencies. Regardless of which experimental strategy we adopted, the conclusion that a performance was verbally governed would be based on its insensitivity to nonverbal contingencies and its sensitivity to verbal interventions.

The point of such examples is that they call for experimental analyses. In such analyses, we cannot expect all subjects to do the same thing. The experimental analysis of human verbally governed behavior is concerned with the behavior of individual organisms and usually leads to procedures that are incompatible with group designs (e.g., Catania, Lowe, & Horne, 1990; Shimoff, Matthews, & Catania, 1986). Such procedures are defining features of behavior analysis as a discipline (Baron & Perone, Chapter 3).

VERBALLY GOVERNED AND CONTINGENCY-GOVERNED RESEARCH

There is an irony in our describing methodologies for the experimental analysis of verbal antecedents. To describe experimental procedures is to risk creating verbal antecedents that may interfere with some research skills at the same time that they facilitate others. With some presumption, therefore, we follow some precedents of Skinner's (1956) case history in scientific method. By doing so in the context of two experimental case studies, we can acknowledge the ways in which our subjects' behavior shaped our behavior as experimenters.

Skinner's case history provided a list of five informal research principles. The first is probably the best known: "when you run into something interesting, drop everything else and study it" (p. 223). It is the only one that takes the form of an instruction. The others are: "some ways of doing research are easier than others"; "some people are lucky"; "apparatus sometimes breaks down"; and, finally, a nod to serendipity or "the art of finding one thing while looking for something else" (pp. 224–227). We would add to these the dictum, drawn from Sidman (1960), that variability is to be analyzed, not averaged.

All of these principles came into play, some more explicitly than others, as we took advantage of opportunities and accidents during the research we describe here in our two case studies. Some grew out of our research on nonverbal behavior, but we offer the case studies because they illustrate detailed strategic and tactical points as they apply specifically to analyses of verbal behavior. We have listed all of our points as imperatives. So as to provide easier access to them and so as not to break up the continuity of our presentations of the case studies, we list our three tactical and five strategic points here and occasionally refer to them in passing later (we use Arabic numerals for the tactical points and Roman numerals for the strategic ones for convenience of reference).

Three Tactical Points

Our three tactical points bear on each of the terms of the three-term contingency. The first, on antecedents, is about instructions; the second, on verbal responses, is about their shaping and measurement; the third, on consequences, is about assessing their functions as reinforcers.

1. Make Instructions Replicable, Comprehensive, and Comprehensible

When we present instructions in writing, we make it easier for other researchers to replicate procedures. But we also avoid the variability inherent in vocally presented instructions. Having the written instructions continuously available throughout sessions may limit some of the variability that comes about because subjects differ in their understanding of and memory for instructions. (It cannot eliminate all; for example, subjects may stop attending to instructions that are always present.) Instructions should be complete, simple, and understandable, and it is appropriate to test to be sure that they have been understood.

2. Remember that Shaping Is an Art and Verbal Shaping Is Especially So

A problem with verbal shaping is that it is difficult to quantify the semantic and other properties of verbal responses. We should choose quantifiable variables whenever we can, but we must also use judgment when necessary, as in shaping.

One major bit of advice on verbal shaping is that we should not make it a crucial part of an experiment without practicing it first.

3. Check Whether Reinforcers Are Functional or Just Nominal Ones

There are many ways in which consequences can appear to function as reinforcers, and to the extent that verbally governed behavior can come to correspond to contingency-governed behavior, even the changes that seem to be attributable to reinforcers can sometimes be verbally governed instead. The detailed analysis of reinforcer function may call for comparisons not only across experimental procedures but also across the performances of verbal and nonverbal organisms (note that the latter can include preverbal children or developmentally disabled human adults as well as nonhuman organisms). But even when a reinforcer appears to be only nominal, it may be worthwhile to consider whether the response class on which it operates has been properly identified (as when an otherwise functional reinforcer appears not to have an effect on a subclass of a higher-order class of behavior).

Five Strategic Points

1. Treat Verbal Behavior as Behavior

We should treat it with respect but not with awe (in other words, we should not assign magical properties to it). To study it, we should not stop at just observing it; we should manipulate it. When we do sample it, we should sample it often and in close proximity to other behavior to which we think it may be related. Multiple samples are also useful when experimental prospects include the option of moving on to shape verbal behavior, because they show the range of verbal responses on which the shaping may operate.

2. Pit Variables against Each Other

Many examples of multiple causation in human verbal behavior imply that the multiple variables work in the same direction, but when that happens we cannot tell what their respective contributions are. Whenever possible, we should pit the variables against each other, so that the primacy of one will produce an outcome different from the primacy of the other. We can also accomplish this by looking at more than one dimension of behavior, so that each variable operates primarily on a different dimension (e.g., in shaping of verbal content, the consequence used to shape content should not also share the function of keeping the subject talking).

3. Assume that Different Subjects Will Follow Different Paths

Experimental analyses of the behavior of individuals imply branching, and the branching should be made explicit. For example, if an experimental procedure might show verbally governed behavior with some subjects and contingency-governed behavior with others, we should plan for the different experimental tracks each will follow. We must also allow for different histories as one source of variability (e.g., students in an experiment on verbal governance may talk to each other outside of the experiment, or may enter with prior coursework on reinforcement schedules). Such histories should be controlled when possible, and assessed when control is impossible.

4. Distinguish Verbal Topographies from Verbal Functions

We have already made the point that it is critical to remember that different verbal topographies can have similar functions, and similar topographies can have different functions. Our own participation in verbal behavior makes it easy for us to be fooled by verbal topographies. One way to distinguish functions experimentally is to study topographically similar repertoires created by different procedures, as when we compare the properties of instructed versus shaped verbal behavior. We should also distinguish necessary from sufficient conditions, and contingencies that maintain behavior from those that differentiate it.

5. Compare Verbal Behavior with Nonverbal Behavior

To appreciate the properties of human behavior, we must compare it with the behavior of other organisms; analogously, to appreciate the properties of verbal behavior, we must compare it with nonverbal behavior. We must also look at directions of effect. Verbal behavior can modify nonverbal behavior, as when we change what subjects do by shaping what they say, but nonverbal behavior can modify verbal behavior, as when subjects' reports of their own behavior change depending on what they are doing. The best way to determine directions of effect is to modify one or the other response class, but whenever we examine such directions of effect, we must also examine our assumptions about the symmetry of the relations we study.

Summary

Our three tactical points concern (1) instructions, (2) verbal shaping, and (3) nominal reinforcers. Our five strategic points concern (I) verbal behavior as behavior, (II) pitting variables against each other, (III) different experimental paths, (IV) function versus topography, and (V) verbal versus nonverbal behavior. In what follows, we examine various properties of verbally governed behavior in the context of two case studies in experimental analysis that illustrate our tactical and strategic points. The procedures of the first case study used the shaping and instruction of verbal behavior to determine the prerequisites for creating verbally governed behavior that is consistent with nonverbal contingencies. The procedures of the second one used a nonverbal task that involved both latency and direction of movement to illustrate the differential sensitivity of different dimensions of responding to verbal antecedents and to nonverbal contingencies. (Undergraduates were recruited for our procedures from Introductory Psychology courses in which laboratory participation was an option in satisfying course requirements and protocols were approved by appropriate Human Subject committees.)

CASE STUDY A: THE ANALYSIS OF VERBAL ANTECEDENTS

In our studies of the relation between nonverbal behavior and shaped verbal behavior (Catania, Matthews, & Shimoff, 1982), students' button presses earned points worth money according to random-ratio (RR) and random-interval (RI) schedules. In nonverbal organisms, RR schedules, which arrange consequences for a response after varying numbers of responses, consistently produce higher response rates than RI schedules, which arrange consequences for a response at the end of varying time intervals. Sensitivity of human behavior to these schedule contingencies can therefore be assessed on the basis of whether RR and RI rate differences emerge and, if they do, whether they change appropriately when the schedules assigned to the two buttons are reversed.

Previous studies of the role of verbal behavior typically sampled verbal repertoires ("hypotheses about the experiment") relatively infrequently, usually at the end of experimental sessions. These verbalizations had no specific consequences, but special status was sometimes attributed to them, with an implicit assumption that they were in some sense causally involved in the nonverbal performance. Instead, we assumed that these verbalizations were as amenable to experimental analysis as the nonverbal button presses; we sampled them more often and arranged consequences for them (see I: Treat Verbal Behavior as Behavior).

Between periods of responding, students filled in sentence completions such as "The way to earn points with the left button is to . . . ," and points were also used to shape the student's verbal behavior, that is, they were awarded for successively closer approximations to target statements about performance. The shaping of verbal behavior is necessarily harder to describe than the shaping of nonverbal behavior, because it is difficult to specify the quantitative dimensions along which verbal behavior may change (compare the verbal shaping simulation in Catania, Matthews, & Shimoff, 1989). As we discovered, our shaping itself had to be shaped, as students entered with verbal repertoires available for selection that differed in range, content, variability, and other properties.

The nonverbal performance, button pressing, was determined not by the contingencies arranged for pressing but rather by the shaped verbal behavior (see II: Pit Variables against Each Other). For example, statements that points depended on slow left pressing and fast right pressing reliably produced corresponding pressing rates, slow left and fast right, even though these schedules respectively produce high and low rates when responding is not verbally governed. Thus, the shaping of performance descriptions had created nonverbal behavior insensitive to the RR and RI contingencies. But verbal responses may describe contingencies as well as performances. People who tell others about contingencies probably assume that descriptions of contingencies will somehow produce appropriate behavior. Descriptions of contingencies with implications for performance, however, are not equivalent to explicit descriptions of that performance.

Our concern with differences between descriptions of performance and of contingencies began when, in attempting to shape a performance description, we inadvertently shaped a contingency description and found no differences in corresponding button pressing rates. We discovered that pressing rates, typically consistent with shaped performance descriptions, are often inconsistent with shaped contingency descriptions (Matthews, Catania, & Shimoff, 1985). We obtained three different kinds of outcomes: rates appropriate to contingencies specified in verbal reports, regardless of whether those reported contingencies corresponded to those actually arranged for pressing; undifferentiated response rates unrelated to contingency descriptions; and rates sensitive to contingencies but independent of contingency descriptions (see III: Assume that Different Subjects Will Follow Different Paths).

These findings set the stage for experiments that first attempted to account for the inconsistent effects of contingency descriptions on rates by examining the verbal repertoires brought into the setting by different students, and then became concerned with specifying necessary and sufficient conditions for synthesizing human behavior that is sensitive to contingencies. The prerequisites for human behavior that is sensitive to contingencies include discrimination of the contingencies along with verbal behavior that describes both contingencies and appropriate performances. In other words, subjects must know both what to do and when to do it. We summarize here the experimental procedures occasioned by our findings (for a more complete account, see Catania, Shimoff, & Matthews, 1989).

Technical Details

Each of our three tactical points is implicit in our experimental procedures. Students sat facing a console with a point counter between two small green lamps and above a small black button. When the green lamps were lit, a press on the black button turned them off and added a point (the nominal reinforcer) to the counter. The lower portion of the console contained two red buttons, each beneath a blue lamp. When the blue lamp above either red button was lit, a press on that button briefly interrupted a masking noise. All instructions were provided in writing (usually posted on the wall behind the console throughout each session). They included general information about procedures, as in the following excerpt:

> At the lower center of the console are two red push buttons. At any time, only one of the two red buttons will work (the blue lights above the buttons will tell you which one is working).
>
> If you press in the right way: (1) The GREEN LIGHTS next to the counter will light up, and (2) when the green lights come on, you can add 1 point to your total by pressing the small BLACK BUTTON next to the counter. Each point you earn is worth 1 cent.
>
> Do not remove your headphones once the experiment is under way.

Presses on one red button (usually the left) produced points according to an RR schedule that selected responses with a fixed probability (usually .05 or RR 20). Presses on the other produced points according to an RI determined by selecting with constant probability pulses generated at the rate of one per second (usually $p = .1$, or RI 10-s). The two lamps lit alternately for 1.5 min each, and presses on the button beneath an unlit lamp had no scheduled consequences. Technically, the presses produced points according to multiple RR RI schedules; one RR and one RI component constituted a cycle (in multiple schedules, two component schedules alternate, each during a different stimulus). Sessions lasted about 50 min. Verbal procedures included verbal shaping, instructions (lessons), and the sampling of verbal behavior. The written instructions on the wall were supplemented with instructions about these verbal procedures as appropriate.

Verbal Shaping

In sessions of verbal shaping, "guess sheets" with three left- and three right-button sentences to be completed were available beside the console. We provided three opportunities for "guesses" to allow more opportunity for variable responding, which usually facilitates shaping. In the shaping of contingency descriptions, sentences were of the form "The computer will let your press turn on the green lights depending on. . . ." In the shaping of performance descriptions, they were of the form "The way to turn the green lights on with the left [right] button is to. . . ." Students passed each completed sheet through a curtained hole in the wall near the console.

To shape guesses, we assigned each guess 0 to 3 points, writing point values next to it and passing the sheet back through the hole. Guess periods occurred after each schedule cycle and ended with the return of the graded sheet. We did not distinguish between technical and colloquial vocabularies. For example, we typically awarded the 3-point maximum to both "variable ratios" and "a changing number of presses" in shaping descriptions of ratio contingencies. After the session students were given a card showing total session earnings (points on the counter and points on the guess sheets); they were paid at the end of their final sessions.

Lessons

Schedule instructions were provided in written form at a table in a separate room, usually before a session. For example, in some performance lessons students were asked to imagine they could earn points by pressing a button and they then read statements about ratio and interval contingencies: "The computer lets your press earn a point after a random number of presses. The more presses you make, the more points you earn. The best thing to do is to press fast" and "The computer lets your press earn a point after a random time interval. The number of presses does not matter, so there is no reason to press fast. The best thing to do is to press at a moderate rate."

To ensure that students had mastered the lesson, we gave them quizzes with sentence completions such as "If the button works only after a random number of presses, you should press. . . ." In some instances, we presented lessons inconsistent with appropriate schedule performance: "The computer lets your press earn a point after random time intervals. There is no way to know when the time intervals are up. To earn every point as soon as it becomes available (and thus to earn as many points as possible), the best thing to do is press fast." Lesson presentations and quizzes were repeated until the student reliably answered all questions consistently with the lesson.

Sampling Verbal Behavior

Students were seated at a table in a separate room and were given a written passage that asked them to imagine that they could earn points by pressing a button. The passage was followed by sentences to be completed. For example, performance hypotheses were sampled with sentence completions such as "If the button works only after a random number of presses, you should . . . ," or "If the button works only at random time intervals, you should. . . ." No feedback was provided for this verbal behavior.

Contingency Descriptions and Performance Hypotheses

We guessed that the variability in button pressing rates after the shaping of contingency descriptions might be a consequence of uncontrolled and unexamined verbal repertoires. One student, correctly identifying the contingencies, might respond faster on the RR on saying to herself "The more I press this one, the more points I earn"; another, also identifying contingencies appropriately, might show no rate difference, saying to himself "Points are random, so I might as well press both buttons the same way." Both performances would be verbally governed, but only the first student would show rate differences appropriate to the schedules.

In one experiment, therefore, we shaped contingency descriptions and then sampled performance hypotheses about the "way to earn the most points." Eight of ten students specified higher rates for RR than RI contingencies, and their RR and RI response rates diverged correspondingly. Results from the other two are represented by data from one (Student 1A) in Figure 12.1. Before the first session, this student's performance hypotheses for RR and RI schedules were "press it a lot of times" and "press it constantly"; after the first session, the student wrote "press it a lot of times" for both schedules. We completed our shaping of contingency descriptions by the guess period following the fifth schedule cycle, after which the student consistently identified the RR contingency as depending on "# of presses" and the RI contingency as depending on "time intervals." But although we had shaped guesses that accurately described schedule contingencies, RR and RI rates remained about equal.

We began shaping performance descriptions in the second session (dashed vertical line); response rates diverged at about the same time as the student began describing appropriate performance as "fast" for the RR and "slow" for the RI button. In performance hypotheses obtained after that session, the student wrote "press it fast" for the RR and "slowly" for the RI schedule. In other words, shaped contingency descriptions governed different rates only for students who also reported that different rates were appropriate to those contingencies. The RR RI rate difference emerges quickly and reliably in the behavior of nonverbal organisms, but it seems to emerge in human behavior only if it is incorporated into a verbal repertoire.

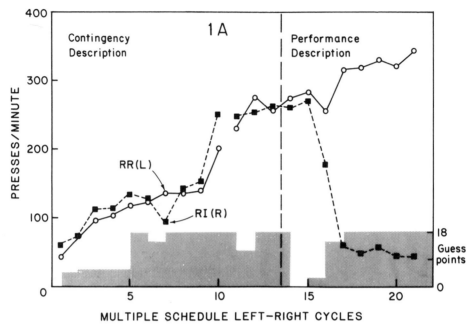

FIGURE 12.1.   Left (L) and right (R) response rates over cycles of multiple random-interval (RR) random-ratio (RI) schedules of point delivery for the button presses of Student 1A. Shaded areas show
points awarded for verbal behavior (guesses) during shaping of contingency and performance descriptions (right y-axis). Connected data were obtained within a single session; unconnected data indicate
the break between sessions.

   Given the implication that performances appropriate to schedules can be created by first establishing accurate hypotheses about how best to respond on RR and
RI schedules and then shaping descriptions of those contingencies, we continued
the analysis by providing lessons that described RR and RI contingencies and also
specified rates appropriate for each. All seven students introduced to this procedure produced substantially higher RR than RI rates, and for four of them our later reversal of contingency descriptions through further verbal shaping was accompanied by corresponding reversals of response rates; in other words, rates
conformed to contingency descriptions rather than to actual contingencies between presses and points. For most of the others, however, rate reversals were produced by contingency reversals rather than by reversals of the shaped contingency
descriptions; in these cases, rates conformed to and appeared to be governed by
the contingencies rather than by verbal antecedents. One remaining instance
seemed to involve competing verbal and contingency governance (see III: Assume
that Different Subjects Will Follow Different Paths).
   We established appropriate rate differences by instructing appropriate performance hypotheses. What would happen if we instructed inappropriate performance hypotheses? In this procedure, the presession lesson specified high-rate
pressing as appropriate for both schedules. When we shaped accurate contingency

descriptions after this misleading lesson with six students, three responded at high rates on both buttons, consistent with the performance hypotheses in the lesson. In other words, instructing a high-rate performance hypothesis for RI contingencies produced high-rate responding inappropriate to this schedule; rates maintained by an RI schedule correctly identified as RI were about equal to those maintained by the RR schedule.

The remaining students produced appropriate RR and RI rate differences. Despite our best efforts to mislead them, some students formulated more accurate hypotheses on how best to respond given RI contingencies, and these in turn produced lower rates on the schedule their shaped verbal reports had identified as RI. As illustrated in Figure 12.2 (Student 3B), however, this performance was not necessarily sensitive to the RR and RI contingencies; when we reversed contingencies, rates on the left button (shifted from RR to RI) remained high. The performance was verbally governed after all.

Verbal behavior that identified contingencies seemed to govern behavior appropriate to those contingencies reliably if it was accompanied by verbal behavior that specified performances appropriate to those contingencies. Nevertheless, variability remained, because rates were in some cases governed by contingency descriptions, in others by schedule contingencies independent of contingency de-

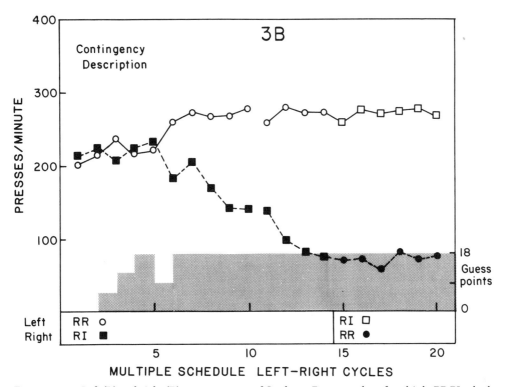

FIGURE 12.2. Left (L) and right (R) response rates of Student 3B over cycles of multiple RR RI schedules, during shaping of contingency descriptions and later reversal of schedule contingencies. Details as in Figure 12.1.

scriptions, and in occasional others even by both contingency descriptions and schedule contingencies in unstable competition. The experimental analysis was not complete. Despite substantial differences across students, however, we saw our task not as one of deriving population estimates of how often rate differences appear given specific instructions but rather as one of isolating the determinants of this behavioral variability.

Contingency Sensitivity and the Discrimination of Contingencies

Our next procedures attempted to establish behavior that was sensitive to contingencies by providing instructions about how to tell the difference between RR and RI schedules and explored the limitations of instructed sensitivity to contingencies by observing performances when the RR component was replaced by other schedules. In these procedures, we did not shape or sample descriptions of contingencies; they might otherwise have constituted a competing source of governance. Also, our original schedules usually generated similar RR and RI rates of point delivery, so we changed schedule parameters to make the average rates of point delivery produced by typical response rates substantially lower in RR than in RI components, on the assumption that this would make the difference between schedule components more discriminable. Finally, we provided a schedule discrimination lesson that described a method for discriminating RR from RI schedules.

If RR and RI schedule components did not maintain different response rates partway into the first session, we interrupted the session and gave the following lesson about discriminating RR from RI contingencies: "To tell which rule the computer is using, you should WAIT FOR A WHILE WITHOUT PRESSING. If your next press makes the green lights come on, the button is probably working after RANDOM TIME INTERVALS, and there is no reason to press fast. If your next press does not make the green lights come on, the button is probably working after RANDOM NUMBERS OF PRESSES, and the faster you press the more you will earn." Then we gave a schedule discrimination quiz. We repeated the lesson and quiz until the student was able to describe the "wait and press" strategy; the session then continued.

If RR and RI rate differences appeared, we reversed schedule contingencies to test for contingency sensitivity. We had to drop four students who still did not show different RR and RI pressing rates from the experiment at this point, because they were available for only a limited time (we would rather have adhered to Strategy III and studied their verbal repertoires further).

The performances of six other students were insensitive to contingencies after initial lessons describing schedules and appropriate performance; both RR and RI schedules maintained high and approximately equal rates. But after the lesson performances on the multiple RR RI schedule became sensitive to contingencies; rates changed quickly and appropriately when contingencies were reversed and rereversed between the two buttons. Figure 12.3 presents data from Student 4A. A large rate difference emerged immediately after the schedule discrimination lesson (at the dashed vertical line), and later reversals of rates with reversals of contingencies occurred rapidly. In fact, the sensitivity in most cases appeared greater

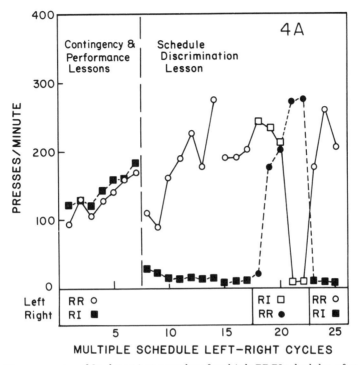

FIGURE 12.3.   Response rates of Student 4A over cycles of multiple RR RI schedules, after contingency, performance, and schedule lessons and during later left–right reversals of schedule contingencies, as indicated along the bottom frame. Details as in Figure 12.1.

than that seen with nonverbal organisms (the behavior of a pigeon does not reverse so quickly: e.g., Catania, Matthews, Silverman, & Yohalem, 1977).

This procedure involved instructing all of the verbal repertoire necessary to produce sensitivity to the difference between RR and RI contingencies: descriptions of the contingencies themselves, descriptions of performances appropriate to those contingencies, and a method for determining which contingencies were in effect. The lessons, minimal as they were, reliably generated performances that were highly sensitive to the difference between RR and RI contingencies for most students; contingency reversals quickly produced corresponding changes in performance.

But the similarity between these performances and nonverbally governed performances was primarily topographical. We still did not know if the behavior was nonverbally governed and therefore sensitive to all contingencies or verbally governed and therefore sensitive only to those contingencies that had been instructed (we have occasionally referred to such verbally governed sensitivity, evident only within some limited domain, as pseudosensitivity; see IV: Distinguish Verbal Topographies from Verbal Functions).

Our remaining procedures therefore introduced tests for the generality of contingency sensitivity. We offer only two examples here. In one case, after sensitivity to the difference between RR and RI contingencies had been taught through lessons describing contingencies, appropriate performances, and a way to determine which schedule was in effect, we noted that the student always waited several seconds before pressing in the first schedule component. If the first press after the wait produced a point, rates were low in that component and high in the other, which never included a wait; the rates were reversed if the press did not produce a point. We replaced the RR contingency with a low-rate contingency (a response otherwise eligible to produce a point does so only if some minimum time has elapsed since the last response). Rates on that button quickly decreased, but rates on the other, which continued to produce points according to the RI schedule, increased to the level previously maintained by the RR schedule. Changing the contingencies revealed the limitations of the student's verbally governed sensitivity to them.

In another case in which performance seemed sensitive to the RR and RI contingencies, we noted that the student waited a few seconds before the first press in each component. If the press produced a point, the student pressed slowly for the rest of that component; if not, the student pressed fast. When we changed the schedule from multiple RR RI to multiple RI RI components that produced about the same rates of point delivery and added a contingency that made the first few responses of some components ineligible for producing points, response rates were high throughout any component in which the first five or six responses did not produce a point and were otherwise low. The student's schedule performance consisted of only two response rates, fast and slow. Those rates were determined solely by the consequences of the first few responses of a component. Performance had again been only superficially sensitive to schedule contingencies.

Of course, questions remain. For example, we did not demonstrate a correlation between verbal and nonverbal behavior in the last two examples. Had these and other students been available for additional sessions, it would have been appropriate to sample their verbal behavior; presumably it would have included appropriate verbal antecedents (see III: Assume that Different Subjects Will Follow Different Paths). We have concluded that verbally governed sensitivity to contingencies is unlike the corresponding schedule sensitivity observed with nonverbal organisms, because it is governed by verbal antecedents rather than by relations between responding and consequences. Despite substantial differences across students, this conclusion was supported in every case where we were able to complete the analysis; our variable results were totally consistent in this respect. It is our conviction that future analyses of these and related phenomena of human behavior must turn increasing attention not to schedule parameters and other variables involved in nonverbal contingencies, but rather to the variables that establish verbal repertoires and that determine the relations among those repertoires and between those repertoires and nonverbal performances.

CASE STUDY B: DIFFERENTIAL CONTINGENCIES
ALONG TWO RESPONSE DIMENSIONS

The experimental strategies in Case Study A concentrated on a single dimension of nonverbal responding, rate of a simple button press. Case Study B used a nonverbal task involving both latency and direction of movement to illustrate the differential sensitivity of different dimensions of responding to verbal antecedents and to nonverbal contingencies. We often safely ignore unmeasured response properties but it is often important to examine more than one dimension. Consider an American traveling in France who, on asking about the location of the nearest restroom, finds that the French-speaking listeners fail to respond appropriately. Our speaker has learned to repeat requests when listeners fail to comply and is soon repeating the request more loudly. The listeners, of course, remain uncomprehending. Under such circumstances, a French-speaking traveler would repeat the request in French rather than repeating it more loudly in English. The two speakers differ in the specific response dimensions that vary with the listeners' noncompliance: vocal intensity for the first and alternative languages for the second.

At various points, this research is relevant to all five of our strategic points (but especially II, III, and V). In our studies, undergraduates performed on a task in which trials were initiated by pressing a button and terminated by moving a joystick. We measured two independent response dimensions: latency, defined by the time from pressing the button to completing joystick movement, and the angle to which the joystick was moved. An automated shaping procedure, in which points worth money were arranged as consequences, operated on one of the two dimensions, while instructions in one experiment or verbal feedback in another specified either that dimension or the irrelevant other dimension.

Verbal behavior with respect to the response dimensions was a more important determinant of performance than the dimension on which consequences depended. For example, a student given instructions about the latency but not the angle of the joystick response repeated latencies but not angles on trials after those that earned points, even if points depended systematically on angles rather than latencies (and vice versa). Similarly, if the student was consistently given the angle but not the latency of the last response as feedback, the student was likely to repeat angles rather than latencies on trials after those earning points, even if points depended systematically on latency rather than angle (and vice versa).

Technical Details

Our three tactical points involved instructions as antecedents, the shaping of verbal responses, and the status of consequences as reinforcers. In its attention to what functions as an instruction, this case study is most relevant to our first tactical point. It concerns itself explicitly with shaping but not along verbal dimensions, and only implicitly with the nominal or functional status of its reinforcers.

Undergraduates sat in a sound-attenuated cubicle at a table on which rested a 9-inch video monitor and a joystick assembly (A2D Company Model 2001). White masking noise was presented through headphones during sessions. The joystick assembly consisted of a plastic case with a button on one side and a rod protruding 3.5 cm above its top. A metal plate with a 13-mm hole concentric to the rod limited its movement from the vertical resting position. Responding occurred in trials and consisted of pressing the button and then moving the rod from its center position until it touched the metal plate, when the time from the button press to contact with the metal plate and the angle of movement (with 3° resolution) were calculated and recorded by a computer in the adjacent room; the rod was spring-loaded so that it returned to its vertical position on release. The following written instructions were taped across the top portion of the screen of the computer monitor:

> Your task is to earn as many points as possible. You can earn points by using the joystick. When the "READY" signal appears on the screen, start the trial by pressing the button on the joystick box; this will make the "READY" signal go off. Next, move the joystick until it touches the metal cover of the joystick box. The screen will then show either a white bar or the flashing message "COR-RECT" along with your total point earnings. YOU WILL BE PAID 1 CENT FOR EVERY POINT YOU EARN.

The ready signal appeared at the bottom center of the screen and remained until the button was pressed. The trial ended when the rod touched the metal plate or after 10 s. Whether a response earned a point depended on either its angle or its latency. Correct responses produced the word "CORRECT" and total points earned on the right half of the bottom line of the screen during a 5-s intertrial interval; if a response was incorrect, that part of the screen remained blank. Two groups of students in one procedure differed only in a line added to the end of the instructions taped to the monitor: for latency instructions, it was "The points you earn will depend on how long you wait between pressing the button and moving the joystick"; for angle instructions, it was "The points you earn will depend on the direction in which you move the joystick." For two groups in another procedure, time or angle instructions were omitted and one of two forms of feedback was presented on the bottom left of the screen after each response. For latency feedback, the screen showed "TIME" with latency to the nearest 0.05 s. For angle feedback, it showed "ANGLE" with the angle in degrees. In some sessions, angle was shaped, and in others, latency was shaped; shaping was carried out by the computer.

Angle shaping began with any angle from 0 to 60° eligible to produce a point, regardless of latency. The 60° range was constant but its minimum increased as a function of performance: it was set at the mean of the last 10 correct angles, with two constraints. First, if a current angle equaled the minimum, the minimum was raised 3° regardless of the last mean. Second, any three consecutive identical correct responses raised the minimum to that angle. These constraints prevented students from earning points by repeating the same value on all trials. The minimum correct angle could not decrease. Sessions usually ended when the minimum exceeded 300° or after 400 trials, whichever came first (a few ended early because of time constraints, and one session was extended beyond 400 trials). Thus, angle shaping gradually moved the shaping criterion clockwise from 0 to 300°. This automated procedure differed from standard manual shaping in that the criterion was never relaxed and angles more than 60° above the minimum never produced points.

Latency shaping was similar, except that the latency range that produced points was constant at 1 s and began with a minimum of 0 s; the minimum was raised by increments of 0.05 s. Thus, the session started with latencies from 0 to 1 s eligible to produce points. The minimum was set to the mean of the last 10 correct latencies, with two constraints: a latency equal to the minimum increased it by 0.05 s, and three consecutive identical correct latencies raised the minimum to that latency, regardless of the previous mean. Sessions usually ended when the minimum latency was 4 s or 400 trials, whichever came first (again, a few ended early because of time constraints, and one session was extended beyond 400 trials). As in angle shaping, this differed from standard manual shaping in that the criterion was never relaxed and latencies more than 1 s longer than the minimum never produced points.

The lower boundary of the latency continuum was nominally 0 s but in practice was the minimum latency that a student could produce. The upper boundary was arbitrary, in that latencies between 5 and 10 s were treated as 5 s (trials longer than 10 s were automatically terminated, but this contingency was rarely if ever contacted). The angle continuum, of course, had no boundaries, closing on itself at $0° = 360°$.

Two sessions separated by a 5-min break were generally arranged for each student. In procedures using response-dimension instructions, with three students angle was shaped with angle instructions in Session 1 and latency with angle instructions in Session 2; with another three, latency was shaped with latency instructions in Session 1 and angle with latency instructions in Session 2. In both cases instructions accurately specified the response dimension on which points were contingent in Session 1 but not Session 2.

The procedures using response-dimension feedback also examined sequences of sessions in which the verbal variable was consistent or inconsistent with contingencies, each usually with three or four students. The main variations were: angle shaping with angle feedback (Session 1) and then latency shaping with angle feedback (Session 2); latency shaping with latency feedback and then angle shaping with latency feedback; angle shaping with latency feedback and then angle shaping with angle feedback; and latency shaping with angle feedback and then latency shaping with latency feedback.

Contingency Sensitivity Restricted to One of the Two Dimensions

Data from Student AA1's Session 1, angle shaping with angle instructions, are shown in Figure 12.4. Latency in 0.05-s increments (top graph) and angle in 3° increments (bottom graph) are plotted over successive trials; trials in which a response produced a point are shown as heavy data points. Latencies remained relatively short and angles gradually increased in conformity with the shaping procedure, except for some blocks of trials without points during which the student searched a range of angles. Shaping took 104 trials.

Figure 12.5 shows Session 2 after a short break for the same student. Angle instructions were unchanged but shaping operated for latency rather than angle. Latencies on early trials were short and produced points; as the criterion increased, they remained relatively short and few points were earned. In most cases when latency was long enough to meet shaping criteria and therefore a point was earned, latency decreased substantially and angle was repeated on the next trial. Angle search patterns were evident through most of Session 2, and shaping was unsuccessful within its 400 trials.

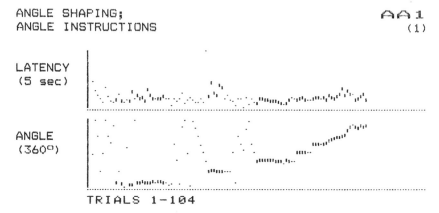

FIGURE 12.4.   Angle shaping with angle instructions for Student AA1 in Session 1. Latencies over trials are plotted in 0.05-s increments in the top graph and angles in 3° increments in the bottom one. In both graphs, heavy data entries represent trials in which responding produced a point, but all points depended on angle. Latencies remained relatively short across trials whereas angles gradually increased in conformity with the shaping procedure.

Students AA2 and AA3 were similar to Student AA1, except that in AA3's Session 1 (angle shaping, angle instructions) angles were at first restricted to the cardinal points (0, 90, 180, and 270°), so that no points were delivered over roughly the first 100 trials. After the first point deliveries, angle shaping progressed to completion in 214 trials; for AA2, angle shaping took 70 trials. Latency shaping in Session 2 was unsuccessful for both AA2 and AA3.

Figure 12.6 presents the data from Figures 12.4 and 12.5 as scatterplots with response values on trial $N + 1$ plotted against those on trial N. These plots show how responding on trial $N + 1$ varied with responding on trial N depending on whether or not the trial N response produced a point. The top four graphs show data from Session 1 (angle shaping, angle instructions); the bottom four show data from Session 2 (latency shaping, angle instructions). Within each block of four graphs, the top row presents angle data and the bottom row latency data; the left column presents data only from trials in which the response did not produce a point on trial N and the right column only from those in which the response did produce a point on trial N.

The scatterplots conveniently show that in both sessions trial N and trial $N +$ 1 responses were strongly correlated only for angle, and for angle mainly when a point was earned on trial N (upper right). In other words, angles but not latencies were likely to be repeated over successive trials, and angles that produced points were much more likely to be repeated than those that did not produce points. This presentation depends on the shaping procedure, which moved responding along the response continuum; without shaping, the different trial N to $N + 1$ dependencies would not have been visible, because responding would have bunched up in a small range and attenuated the correlations.

The scatterplots for Session 2 include many more trials but show similar patterns. Trial N and trial $N + 1$ angles were highly correlated, with angles again much

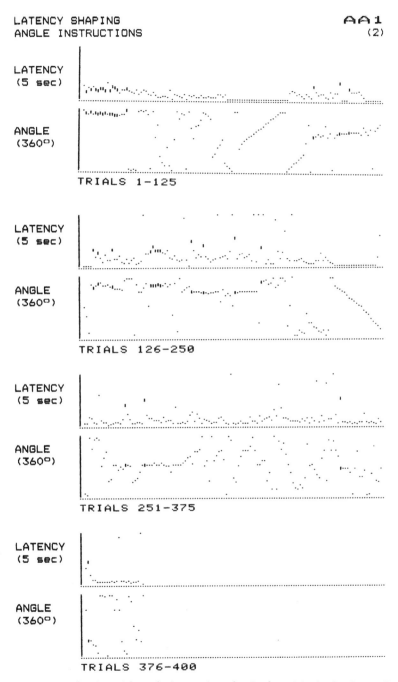

FIGURE 12.5.   Latency shaping with angle instructions for Student AA1 in Session 2. Details as in Figure 12.4, except that all points depended on latency. Shaping was unsuccessful, and the graphs show several instances in which trials after those with points included repetitions of angle but marked decreases in latency even though points depended on latency.

ANGLE SHAPING;　　　　　　　　　　　　·　　　　　　　　AA1
ANGLE INSTRUCTIONS

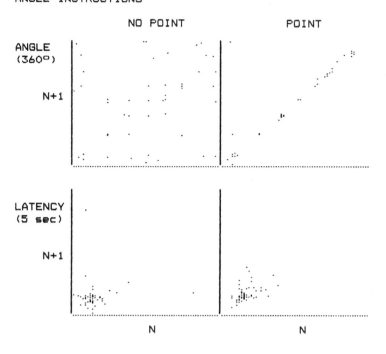

LATENCY SHAPING;
ANGLE INSTRUCTIONS

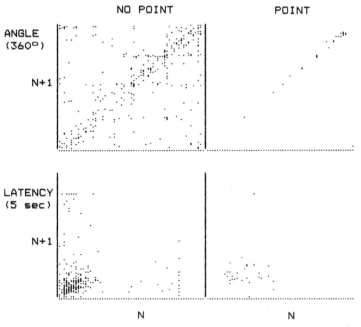

FIGURE 12.6.　Scatterplots of response values on trial $N + 1$ given those on trial N for the sessions for AA1 in Figures 12.4 and 12.5. The top block of graphs shows data from angle shaping with angle instructions (Session 1); the bottom block shows data from latency shaping with angle instructions (Session 2). Within each block, the top row presents angle data and the bottom row latency data; the left column presents data from trials in which the response did not produce a point on trial N and the right column data from those in which the response did produce a point on trial N. In both sessions angles but not latencies were more likely to be repeated on trials following those that included a point than on trials following those that did not.

more likely to be repeated after trials with points than after those without points. As in Session 1, however, the latency scatterplots show no substantial effects of point deliveries even though latency was now the dimension on which points depended. Based on these data, we can say here that latencies were insensitive to or insulated from their consequences; the data provide no evidence that latencies were reinforced by points. The conclusion is stronger given the comparison between the two dimensions than it could have been on the basis of either alone; the simultaneous observation of at least two response dimensions is crucial to the analysis.

In the parallel procedure with latency instructions, latency was shaped in Session 1 but points were contingent on angle in Session 2. As shown in Figure 12.7 (Student LL3), latency shaping took 110 trials while angles remained fairly stereotyped in Session 1; early in the session they were concentrated in the range from 270 to 360° and by its end they were fairly constant at 90°, as shown by the successive responses plotted in the top portion of the figure.

The scatterplots at the bottom of Figure 12.7, in the same format as for AA1 in Figure 12.6, show higher trial N to trial $N + 1$ correlations for latencies after trials with points than after trials without points; the correlations for latencies after points are somewhat weaker than the comparable ones for angles in Figure 12.6 (upper right), probably because it is easier to reproduce angles measured in 3° increments than latencies measured in 0.05-s increments. Trial N to $N + 1$ correlations for angle were high whether or not a point was delivered in trial N. But this was a product of response stereotypy along the angle dimension. In estimating the effect of the shaping contingency on response probability, it is not enough to observe high correlations; the effect is given by the difference between the correlations with points and with no points on trial N and not by their absolute magnitudes.

Student LL3's Session 2 (angle shaping, latency instructions), shown in Figure 12.8, included extensive latency search patterns and intermittent angle search patterns. Angles were mostly stereotyped from the start, so that angles that produced points occurred only after about 170 trials without points. Trials with latencies but not angles repeated after trials with points were overshadowed by the stereotypy of angle responding. After about 225 trials, latencies became more consistently short, points became more frequent, and angles increased, though slowly. Shaping took 452 trials.

In Session 1 for LL1 and LL2, latency shaping with latency instructions was slower than but similar to that for LL3, taking 217 and 159 trials for completion, respectively; for both, angles were stereotyped throughout the session. The variability of latencies later during latency shaping suggested that shaping became progressively more difficult as eligible latencies became longer while their eligible range remained constant at 1 s. In Session 2 for LL1 (angle shaping, latency instructions), systematic latency search patterns dominated the first 75 or so trials, with angles primarily at 270 and 360°, and few points were delivered. After about 100 trials, latencies began to decrease systematically and angles increased rapidly, with angle shaping complete in 165 trials. Session 2 for LL2 was similar, except that latencies were longer than 5 s in most trials, including those later in the session when angles began to change with angle shaping. Angle shaping took 143 tri-

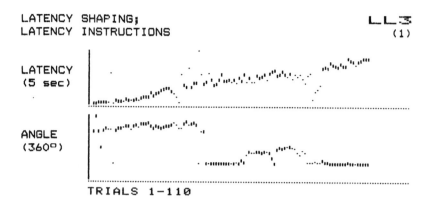

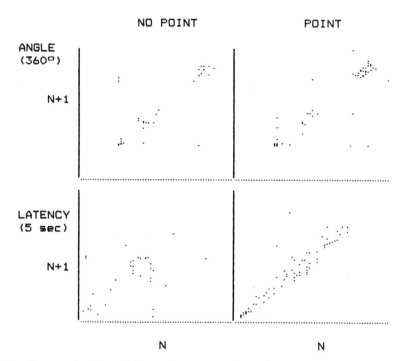

FIGURE 12.7. Latency shaping with latency instructions for Student LL3 (Session 1). The top portion of the figure shows latencies and angles over trials, with details as in Figures 12.4 and 12.5; the bottom portion shows corresponding scatterplots of response values on trial $N + 1$ given those on trial N, with details as in Figure 12.6. Stereotyped angle responding over the course of latency shaping produced scatterplots with high trial N to trial $N + 1$ angle correlations after trials without as well as those with a point.

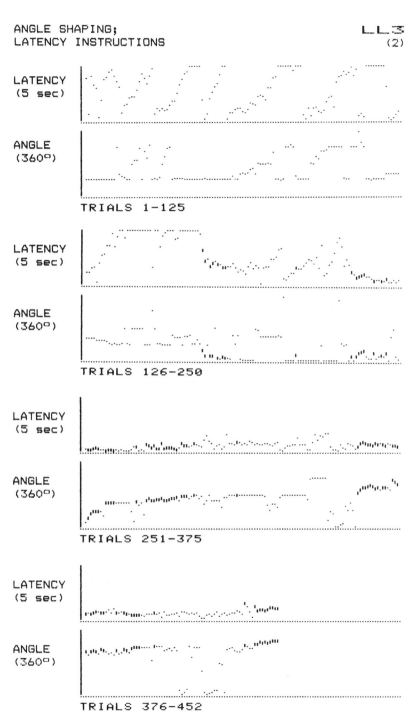

FIGURE 12.8. Angle shaping with latency instructions for Student LL3 in Session 2. Details as in Figures 12.4, 12.5, and 12.7. The session was extended beyond the usual 400-trial limit and angle shaping was complete after 452 trials.

als. Thus, in these cases latency instructions slowed the onset of effective angle shaping but did not prevent its completion within the limits of the session.

Compared across procedures, angle was more likely to be shaped even given verbal behavior with respect to latency than vice versa, presumably because students were more likely to formulate hypotheses about the direction than the latency of moving a joystick. Without instructions or other verbal interventions, angle shaping in these procedures is almost always successful whereas latency shaping is unreliable; also, in the absence of contingencies angles tend to move to cardinal points and latencies tend to shorten. Fortunately, the effects of these asymmetries of the two dimensions are small compared with those of instructions.

In summary, when angle was shaped with angle instructions, angles gradually increased whereas latencies were not systematically affected; later shaping of latency with angle instructions was unsuccessful. Similarly, when latency was shaped with latency instructions, latencies gradually increased whereas angles were not systematically affected; later shaping of angle with latency instructions was retarded though not blocked. Thus, shaping was consistently successful with instructions that were consistent with the shaping dimension but not with instructions that were inconsistent with it.

These procedures, however, confound instructions with experimental history, in that sessions with inconsistent relations between instructions and shaping always followed successful shaping along the other dimension. Our next procedures therefore arranged different sequences of conditions with consistent or inconsistent relations between verbal antecedents and contingencies, and instead of instructions they provided angle or latency feedback after each response, on the assumption that with such feedback students would be more likely to generate their own verbal behavior with respect to a dimension (we ruled out verbal shaping as an alternative because it would have reduced time available for trials and would also have entailed their frequent interruption).

Correlations and Contingencies

Data in scatterplots such as those of Figures 12.6 and 12.7 can be used to compute correlations between trial N and trial $N + 1$ responses (essentially, autocorrelations with lag 1). They may be underestimates when behavior is inhomogeneous over different blocks of time in extended sessions and when similar trial N and $N + 1$ angles are at opposite ends of the angle continuum (e.g., 3 and 357° are separated by only 6°). For example, correlations derived from just the early or later trials of Figure 12.5 would differ from each other and from those derived from the session as a whole, and the correlation for the top right graph of Figure 12.6 is attenuated by the single point at the upper left though its angular separation from the points at the lower left is small (its correlation of $r = .89$ would be .99 if the upper left point were treated instead as a small negative angle). Nevertheless, such correlations conveniently summarize our findings with angle and latency feedback and are presented in Table 12.1.

Students are identified by Session 1 conditions, with the first letter indicating shaping dimension and the second dimensional feedback (e.g., LA corresponds to latency shaping with angle feedback); conditions in Session 2 are coded by the let-

TABLE 12.1

Trials, Total Points, and Correlations of Trial N to Trial $N + 1$ Responses
with Angle or Latency Shaping and Angle or Latency Feedback

| | | | First session | | | | Second session | | | |
| | | | Angle | | Latency | | Angle | | Latency | |
Student	Trials	Total points	NP[a]	P[b]	NP	P	NP	P	NP	P
AA101 /LA	154/265	79/77	.09	.66	.23	.24	−.06	.33	.59	.81
AA102 /LA	147/400+	114/34	.88	.99	.82	.41	.43	.79	.22	−.20
AA103 /LA	144/400+	64/42	.27	.83	.25	.24	.00	.99	.26	.42
LL101 /AL	116/400+	70/76	.61	.84	.85	.97	.37	.92	.06	.78
LL102 /AL	202/275+	67/36	.12	.00	.97	.97	.33	.94	.61	.78
LL103 /AL	146/300+	88/32	.43	.85	.83	.94	.25	.88	.25	.86
AL101 /AA	400+/109	30/73	.34	−.46	.60	.96	.71	.89	.59	.47
AL103 /AA	400+/115	1/77	—	—	—	—	.89	.99	−.07	.38
AL104 /AA	400+/165	19/91	.73	−.37	.10	−.01	.13	.96	.08	.04
LA101 /LL	400+/96	21/75	.22	.47	.23	.26	−.28	.18	.82	.96
LA102 /AA	310/272	89/66	.45	.85	.82	.91	.31	.94	.60	.78
LA103 /LL	400+/130	43/75	.34	.27	.01	.13	.76	.99	.63	.90

Note. Students are identified by abbreviations for the conditions in Session 1, where the first letter indicates the shaping dimension and the second the feedback dimension (e.g., AL corresponds to angle shaping with latency feedback); conditions in Session 2 are shown after the slash. The table excludes one student, AL102, given only a single session because angle shaping with latency feedback was complete in 184 trials (we had reason to suspect that this student had talked with earlier participants in the study), and another, LA104, with an overall performance similar to that of LA102 but for whom correlations could not be computed because of problems with the data set.
[a]NP = no point on trial N. [b]P = point on trial N.

ters after the slash, and data from the two sessions in the next two columns are separated by slashes. In the second column (trials in each session), a plus sign indicates that the session ended before shaping was complete. The third column shows total points earned in each condition. The remaining columns show correlations (r) between trial N and trial $N + 1$ response values; those eight columns correspond to the illustrative scatterplots in Figure 12.6 (Student AL103 produced only one point in Session 1, so correlations were not computed for that session).

Dimensional feedback had effects similar to those of instructions. When feedback specified angle, angles were more likely to be repeated after trials with points than otherwise, and latencies usually were less likely than angles to be repeated. Conversely, when feedback specified latency, latencies were more likely to be repeated after trials with points than otherwise, and angles were usually less likely than latencies to be repeated. The feedback dimension was a more powerful determinant of performance than whether the shaping contingencies were arranged for angles or for latencies.

Shaping was successful whenever feedback was consistent with the dimension along which responding was shaped (all AA and LL conditions in Table 12.1), regardless of whether it was arranged in Session 1 or Session 2. When feedback was inconsistent with the dimension along which responding was shaped, shaping was ordinarily unsuccessful, regardless of whether it was arranged in Session 1 or Session 2. Shaping was successful in only two of six cases of latency shaping with angle feedback, and both successful cases (AA101, Session 2, and LA102, Session 1) involved a relatively large number of trials. Shaping was unsuccessful in all six cases of angle shaping with latency feedback (Session 2 is ambiguous for LL102 and LL103 because their sessions had to be terminated before 400 trials; nevertheless, total trials had by then already exceeded those in almost all cases of successful shaping with consistent shaping and feedback dimensions).

In general, even when successful the shaping of angle with latency feedback or latency with angle feedback took three to four times as many trials as shaping of either with corresponding feedback (angle–angle or latency–latency), and the effects did not depend on which dimension was shaped first; they were as likely to appear in Session 1, without a prior history in which points depended on the other response dimension, as in Session 2, after such a history. In the one case where feedback inconsistent with the shaping dimension was introduced in Session 1 and feedback was successful (LA102), feedback consistent with the other dimension was introduced during shaping along that dimension in Session 2, and that shaping was relatively slow (272 trials); determining whether the slow shaping depended on the prior history or on some verbal consequences of successful shaping in the context of an inconsistent relation between the feedback and shaping dimensions was a matter of more thorough experimental analysis than was possible in the available time (see III: Assume that Different Subjects Will Follow Different Paths).

In Table 12.1, correlations given a point on trial N that are higher than those with no point on trial N show that responses along the feedback dimension were more likely to be repeated after trials with points than those without points and responses along the other dimension were not. In Session 1 for Student AA101, for example, the trial N to trial $N + 1$ correlations for angle were .09 with no point in trial N and .66 with a point in trial N; the corresponding latency correlations were respectively .23 and .24. Similarly, in Session 1 for AL101 the correlation for angle was .34 with no point in trial N and −.46 with a point in trial N; the corresponding latency correlations were respectively .60 and .96. In both cases, the feedback dimension and not the shaping dimension was the one that mattered. The differences in Table 12.1 between correlations given points and no points on trial N were variable overall, but were more consistently determined by the feedback dimension than by the shaping dimension. Verbal antecedents, either in instructions or in verbal feedback, were more important determinants of which dimensions of responding were sensitive to the shaping contingencies than the shaping contingencies themselves.

It is reasonable to assume that the feedback contributed to these results by way of its effect on self-generated verbal behavior with respect to the contingencies. Feedback with respect to response dimensions presumably generates talk about those dimensions, even if only covertly. Other ways of manipulating verbal behavior (e.g., by instructions or by shaping of verbal behavior) presumably have functionally equivalent effects, though all such procedures have an intrinsic source of variability in the different sorts of verbal behavior with which subjects enter such experiments and which they produce in the course of them.

Our findings are paradoxical. The property of responding that was likely to be affected by point deliveries depended on verbal behavior. But if points are reinforcers, they should affect the likelihood of whatever they follow and not just the dimension for which verbal behavior has been established. When reinforcers select some responses and not others, they ordinarily reduce variability (e.g., Silva & Pear, 1995), but it is not clear why they should affect some response properties and not others or, in other words, why some properties should be insulated from their consequences by verbal antecedents. The point versus no point graphs for angle at the top of Figure 12.6 would appear to define what reinforcers should do, in that they show repetitions of responding mainly after responding has produced a consequence. But the primary dependence of that responding on verbal variables (instructions or feedback) rather than on the dimension for which shaping was arranged suggests that it was not governed by the nonverbal contingencies. If so, it may even be inappropriate to refer to our procedures as angle shaping and latency shaping. In this return to the issue of the insensitivity of verbally governed behavior to nonverbal contingencies, we may recall our tactic of distinguishing nominal from functional reinforcers and note that we would have been unable to do so here if we had measured just one response dimension.

A Pigeon Analogue

Our fifth strategic point is to compare verbal with nonverbal behavior. In judging the sensitivity of human behavior to contingencies, research has sometimes turned to comparisons with the behavior of other species (e.g., in the search for performances characteristic of reinforcement schedules: see Weiner, 1969; see also Shull & Lawrence, Chapter 4). But comparisons across species, and even across individuals entering an experiment with different repertoires (e.g., nonverbal and verbally able children), are inevitably confounded. Differences attributed to verbal versus nonverbal governance may instead depend on differences in other variables, such as reinforcers or histories or sensory and motor capacities (see Baron & Leinenweber, 1995; Wanchisen, Tatham, & Mooney, 1989). Even so, pigeon analogues of human performance reveal what behavior is like in the absence of verbal behavior and may help us to make explicit our assumptions about the variables that contribute to complex behavior.

In an attempt to parallel the preceding arrangement of shaping procedures for one of two response dimensions, we introduced three pigeons to sessions in a two-key chamber in which the keys irregularly alternated between green and red conditions. In trials during one condition, the left key was lit green and the first peck on that key also lit the other key green; a peck on the right key was reinforced after at least N pecks on the left key, without regard to the time from the last left peck to the right peck (a right peck after fewer than N left pecks produced a brief intertrial interval). In trials during a second condition, the left key was lit red and the first peck also lit the other key red; a peck on the right key was reinforced if at least T s had elapsed since the last peck on the left key (a right peck after fewer than T s produced a brief intertrial interval). In each session, a shaping procedure similar to the ones for the human joystick responding was arranged for each condition;

during green it automatically produced increments in the required number of left pecks, and during red in the required time from the last left peck to a right peck.

Table 12.2 shows, for each pigeon, trial N to trial $N + 1$ correlations with or without reinforcers on trial N and, analogous to those in Table 12.1, for each of the two response dimensions in each condition. The table includes three sessions: (A) the first in which sufficient responses occurred for the correlations to be calculated, (B) the one that included trial 1000, and (C) the one that included trial 2000.

In contrast to the effects of point deliveries shown in Table 12.1, Table 12.2 provides only a little evidence that pigeons' responses on trial $N + 1$ tend to repeat what was followed by a reinforcer on trial N. In some cases correlations are higher given a reinforcer than given no reinforcer on trial N, but in many others those correlations are reversed. Most correlations are low relative to those of Table 12.1 and roughly a third are negative. Presumably the pigeon's responding is determined not just by the response reinforced most recently but by the population of responses reinforced over some extended period of time (perhaps effects of the most recent reinforcer on current responding remain easily visible only over the first few instances of reinforcement in a given setting, when that population is still very small).

For our purposes, however, this pigeon analogue illustrates another way in which the sensitivity of human verbally governed behavior to contingencies differs from that of nonverbal organisms. Verbally governed behavior may sometimes be insensitive to contingencies, but when verbal antecedents are highly consistent with contingencies it is sometimes executed with a precision that might not be achievable in other ways (see the high correlations obtained with angle shaping and angle latency in Figure 12.6). The selection of verbally governed behavior in

TABLE 12.2

Correlations of Trial N to Trial $N + 1$ Response Values with Shaping of Number of Left Pecks before a Reinforced Right Peck (Green) or Time from Last Left Peck to the Reinforced Right Peck (Red), for Three Pigeons

| | | | Green | | | | Red | | | |
| | | | Number | | Time | | Number | | Time | |
	Session	Trials	NR[a]	R[b]	NR	R	NR	R	NR	R
Pigeon 37	A	30	.00	−.22	.44	.36	−.15	.00	−.16	.00
	B	177	.26	.37	−.15	.56	.25	.07	.13	−.14
	C	188	.41	.92	−.02	.26	.18	.43	.28	.22
Pigeon 72	A	91	−.04	.18	−.04	−.03	−.06	.59	.21	−.16
	B	139	−.14	−.45	.00	.28	.00	−.01	−.06	.21
	C	271	.21	.36	.47	.55	−.13	−.32	.03	−.33
Pigeon 98	A	84	−.02	−.43	.70	.28	.04	−.05	−.09	−.41
	B	250	.42	.07	.08	−.03	−.19	.33	.11	.23
	C	146	.70	.83	.16	−.23	.09	.00	.01	−.08

Note. Correlations are analogous to those in Table 12.1. Sessions are (A) the first session in which enough responses occurred for the correlations to be calculated, (B) the session that included trial 1000, and (C) the session that included trial 2000.
[a]NR = no reinforcer on trial N. [b]R = reinforcer on trial N.

the evolution of human language (Catania, 1994) implies that it has substantial advantages that compensate for the disadvantages entailed by its insensitivity to nonverbal contingencies.

It is time to return to human verbal behavior. As with Case Study A, had the students who participated in the joystick procedures been available for additional sessions, it would have been appropriate to sample their verbal behavior; presumably it would have included appropriate verbal antecedents. The manipulations of verbal behavior arranged here have been modest and the experimental analysis has been of limited scope. In demonstrating ways to assess effects of contingencies on different response dimensions, the joystick research may provide an experimental tool but it is still primarily concerned with existing relations between verbal behavior and nonverbal contingencies. We therefore repeat our conviction that future analyses of these and related phenomena of human behavior must give increasing attention to the variables that establish verbal repertoires and verbal governance.

SOME IMPLICATIONS

Our case studies illustrate our tactical and strategic points in so many ways that it seems redundant to recapitulate them here. It is perhaps as important that they illustrate the potency of the verbal governance of behavior. Nevertheless, human behavior must sometimes make direct contact with contingencies. It is difficult to see how some skilled motor performances could depend on verbal mediation (consider gymnastics or the tying of shoelaces), and some behavior that is initially verbally governed seems eventually to occur without verbal accompaniment. For example, student drivers are instructed about the use of a stick shift but experienced drivers probably rarely talk to themselves about what they are doing (their performance is sometimes called automatic; in such cases, abrupt changes in contingencies may trigger the reappearance of relevant verbal behavior). Such behavior probably is not sensitive to contingencies in the same way as nonverbally governed behavior that has never been verbally governed (see Dreyfus & Dreyfus, 1986).

Our distinction between verbal governance based on shaped or instructed verbal behavior has practical implications. For example, formal procedures based on explicit instructions are often described as cookbook, but the mark of a great chef is being able to deviate from the recipe when appropriate (e.g., as when some ingredients are unavailable). But we have been making the same point with respect to a scientist's deviation from recipes for experimental design. Scientific training can emphasize formal statistical designs or the interaction of the experimenter's behavior with natural contingencies in the laboratory. Either form of instruction may lead to verbally governed experimenting, but the experimental behavior generated by the latter is more likely to be consistent with the contingencies of the research environment (and with experimental analysis).

We have made the case that modifying human nonverbal behavior indirectly, by shaping relevant verbal behavior, is more likely to be successful than doing so directly, by shaping the nonverbal behavior itself. To the extent that human behavior is verbally governed, contingencies affect performance by altering relevant verbal behavior. In that case, the sensitivity of human nonverbal performance to contingencies depends on the sensitivity of the governing verbal behavior to those contingencies. Much nonverbal behavior is verbally governed, but it may be that verbal behavior itself is ordinarily nonverbally governed. If so, contingencies may act on verbal behavior in the long run so that it becomes more likely to produce nonverbal behavior consistent with natural contingencies.

This observation may be clinically relevant, because verbal manipulations are common in therapeutic treatments. (Cognitive behavior modification does not change cognitions; it changes verbal behavior: see Catania, 1995.) Perhaps some pathologies of human behavior (e.g., delusions or compulsions) may be interpreted as verbally governed behavior gone awry (Chadwick, Lowe, Horne, & Higson, 1994). Or consider the implicit shaping of client talk in Rogerian therapy (Truax, 1966). If human behavior is dominated by verbally rather than by nonverbally governed behavior, it makes sense to work on a client's verbal rather than nonverbal behavior. Behavior change established within the therapeutic setting in this way may transfer to environments outside that setting. But one hope of clinical intervention is that behavior established in therapy will be maintained outside the therapeutic setting when taken over by the natural contingencies operating there. The problem is that behavior established through verbal antecedents necessarily makes that behavior verbally governed and therefore relatively insensitive to natural contingencies, thereby interfering with transfer to new settings.

The experimental analysis of verbal antecedents may fruitfully be applied to various other areas of psychology. Judgments of probability offer an example (e.g., Tversky & Kahneman, 1983). Studies of such judgments often show systematic discrepancies between those judgments and nonverbal (usually quantitative) contingencies. They stop where behavior analyses might well begin. For instance, given the unknown self-instructions with which subjects enter experiments, it may be of more interest to explore ways to establish relevant verbal behavior before subjects enter a probability matching study (e.g., by shaping accurate probability estimations) than to pool results statistically so as to estimate likelihoods of different verbal antecedents in a population. Precisely the sorts of experimental analyses that were used here as illustrations could be applied to such substantive domains of psychology. Experimental analyses of verbal antecedents in such contexts may lead to a technology of verbal governance (it is a badly needed one; other names for it are education and teaching).

ACKNOWLEDGMENTS. Many colleagues and students deserve thanks for their contributions to the research described in this chapter. We must give particular mention to Byron A. Matthews for his extensive participation in the human studies, to Daniel Cerutti for the construction of the joystick apparatus, and to David Carlson and Margaret Wilhelm for their work on the pigeon analogue of the joystick experiment. Some of the research was supported by Grant BNS86-07517 from the National Science Foundation and by a research grant from the Cambridge Center for Behavioral Studies. The authors are at the Department of Psychology, University of Maryland Baltimore County, 1000 Hilltop Circle, Baltimore, MD 21250 (email:SHIMOFF@UMBC.EDU and CATANIA@UMBC.EDU).

REFERENCES

Baron, A., & Leinenweber, A. (1995). Effects of a variable-ratio conditioning history on sensitivity to fixed-interval contingencies in rats. *Journal of the Experimental Analysis of Behavior, 63,* 97–110.

Bentall, R. P., & Lowe, C. F. (1987). The role of verbal behavior in human learning: III. Instructional effects in children. *Journal of the Experimental Analysis of Behavior, 47,* 177–190.

Bentall, R. P., Lowe, C. F., & Beasty, A. (1985). The role of verbal behavior in human learning: II. Developmental differences. *Journal of the Experimental Analysis of Behavior, 43,* 165–181.

Catania, A. C. (1994). The natural and artificial selection of verbal behavior. In S. C. Hayes, L. Hayes, M. Sato, & K. Ono (Eds.), *Behavior analysis of language and cognition* (pp. 31–49). Reno, NV: Context Press.

Catania, A. C. (1995). Higher-order behavior classes: Contingencies, beliefs, and verbal behavior. *Journal of Behavior Therapy and Experimental Psychiatry, 26,* 191–200.

Catania, A. C., Lowe, C. F., & Horne, P. (1990). Nonverbal behavior correlated with the shaped verbal behavior of children. *Analysis of Verbal Behavior, 8,* 43–55.

Catania, A. C., Matthews, B. A., & Shimoff, E. (1982). Instructed versus shaped human verbal behavior: Interactions with nonverbal responding. *Journal of the Experimental Analysis of Behavior, 38,* 233–248.

Catania, A. C., Matthews, B. A., & Shimoff, E. (1989). *Behavior on a disk.* Columbia, MD: CMS Software.

Catania, A. C., Shimoff, E. H., & Matthews, B. A. (1989). An experimental analysis of rule-governed behavior. In S. C. Hayes (Ed.), *Rule-governed behavior* (pp. 119–150). New York: Plenum Press.

Catania, A. C., Matthews, T. J., Silverman, P. J., & Yohalem, R. (1977). Yoked variable-interval and variable-ratio responding in pigeons. *Journal of the Experimental Analysis of Behavior, 28,* 155–161.

Chadwick, P. D. J., Lowe, C. F., Horne, P. J., & Higson, P. J. (1994). Modifying delusions: The role of empirical testing. *Behavior Therapy, 25,* 35–49.

Dreyfus, H. L., & Dreyfus, S. E. (1986). *Mind over machine.* New York: Free Press.

Ericsson, A. K., & Simon, H. A. (1984). *Protocol analysis: Verbal reports as data.* Cambridge, MA: MIT Press.

Estes, W. K. (1971). Reward in human learning: Theoretical issues and strategic choice points. In R. Glaser (Ed.), *The nature of reinforcement* (pp. 16–36). New York: Academic Press.

Greenspoon, J. (1955). The reinforcing effect of two spoken sounds on the frequency of two responses. *American Journal of Psychology, 68,* 409–416.

Hayes, S. C., Brownstein, A. J., Haas, J. R., & Greenway, D. E. (1986). Instructions, multiple schedules, and extinction: Distinguishing rule-governed from schedule-controlled behavior. *Journal of the Experimental Analysis of Behavior, 46,* 137–147.

Hayes, S. C., Brownstein, A. J., Zettle, R. D., Rosenfarb, I., & Korn, Z. (1986). Rule-governed behavior and sensitivity to changing consequences of responding. *Journal of the Experimental Analysis of Behavior, 45,* 237–256.

Joyce, J. H., & Chase, P. N. (1990). Effects of response variability on the sensitivity of rule-governed behavior. *Journal of the Experimental Analysis of Behavior, 54,* 251–262.

Kaufman, A., Baron, A., & Kopp, R. E. (1966). Some effects of instructions on human operant behavior. *Psychonomic Monograph Supplements, 1*(11), 243–250.

Lovaas, O. I. (1961). The interaction between verbal and nonverbal behavior. *Child Development, 32,* 329–336.

Lovaas, O. I. (1964a). Cue properties of words: The control of operant responding by rate and content of verbal operants. *Child Development, 35,* 245–256.

Lovaas, O. I. (1964b). Control of food intake in children by reinforcement of relevant verbal behavior. *Journal of Abnormal and Social Psychology, 68,* 672–678.

Lowe, C. F. (1979). Determinants of human operant behaviour. In M. D. Zeiler & P. Harzem (Eds.), *Advances in analysis of behaviour: Vol. 1. Reinforcement and the organization of behaviour* (pp. 159–192). New York: Wiley.

Lowe, C. F., Beasty, A., & Bentall, R. P. (1983). The role of verbal behavior in human learning: Infant performance on fixed-interval schedules. *Journal of the Experimental Analysis of Behavior, 39,* 157–164.

Matthews, B. A., Catania, A. C., & Shimoff, E. (1985). Effects of uninstructed verbal behavior on nonverbal responding: Contingency descriptions versus performance descriptions. *Journal of the Experimental Analysis of Behavior, 43,* 155–164.

Reber, A. S. (1976). Implicit learning of synthetic languages: The role of instructional set. *Journal of Experimental Psychology: Human Learning and Memory, 2,* 88–94.

Rosenfarb, I. S., Newland, M. C., Brannon, S. E., & Howey, D. S. (1992). Effects of self-generated rules on the development of schedule-controlled behavior. *Journal of the Experimental Analysis of Behavior, 58,* 107–121.

Rosenfeld, H. M., & Baer, D. M. (1970). Unbiased and unnoticed verbal conditioning: The double agent robot procedure. *Journal of the Experimental Analysis of Behavior, 14,* 99–107.

Schlinger, H., & Blakely, E. (1987). Function-altering effects of contingency-specifying stimuli. *Behavior Analyst, 10,* 41–45.

Shimoff, E., Matthews, B. A., & Catania, A. C. (1986). Human operant performance: Sensitivity and pseudosensitivity to contingencies. *Journal of the Experimental Analysis of Behavior, 46,* 149–157.

Sidman, M. (1960). *Tactics of scientific research.* New York: Basic Books.

Silva, F. J., & Pear, J. J. (1995). Stereotypy of spatial movements during noncontingent and contingent reinforcement. *Animal Learning and Behavior, 23,* 245–255.

Skinner, B. F. (1956). A case history in scientific method. *American Psychologist, 11,* 221–233.

Skinner, B. F. (1957). *Verbal behavior.* New York: Appleton–Century–Crofts.

Skinner, B. F. (1969). An operant analysis of problem solving. In B. F. Skinner, *Contingencies of reinforcement* (pp. 133–171). New York: Appleton–Century–Crofts.

Svartdal, F. (1989). Shaping of rule-governed behavior. *Scandinavian Journal of Psychology, 30,* 304–314.

Svartdal, F. (1992). Sensitivity to nonverbal operant contingencies: Do limited processing resources affect operant conditioning in humans? *Learning and Motivation, 23,* 383–405.

Truax, C. B. (1966). Reinforcement and nonreinforcement in Rogerian therapy. *Journal of Abnormal Psychology, 71,* 1–9.

Tversky, A., & Kahneman, D. (1983). Extensional versus intuitive reasoning: The conjunction fallacy in probability judgment. *Psychological Review, 90,* 293–315.

Wanchisen, B. A., Tatham, T. A., & Mooney, S. E. (1989). Variable-ratio conditioning history produces high- and low-rate fixed-interval performance in rats. *Journal of the Experimental Analysis of Behavior, 52,* 167–179.

Weiner, H. (1969). Controlling human fixed-interval performance. *Journal of the Experimental Analysis of Behavior, 12,* 349–373.

13

The Taxonomy of Verbal Behavior

A. Charles Catania

The vocabulary of behavior analysis was established in the context of research with nonverbal organisms (Skinner, 1938). That vocabulary is based on a taxonomy of function rather than one of structure. For example, it identifies operant classes by their environmental effects rather than by their topographies. No major additions were made to this vocabulary when it was applied to the general properties of human behavior (Skinner, 1953), but the extension to specific features of verbal behavior was accompanied by a substantial expansion of technical terms (Skinner, 1957). Some of those terms categorize verbal responses in terms of the basic processes that contribute to their emission; for example, the term *tact* captures the role of discriminative stimuli in the control of a verbal response. Others take topographical features into account; for example, echoic and textual behavior are distinguished by whether relevant stimuli are auditory or visual. The taxonomy of verbal behavior did not originate in the laboratory. Instead, it was based on observations of verbal behavior in natural environments:

> The emphasis is upon an orderly arrangement of well-known facts, in accordance with a formulation of behavior derived from an experimental analysis of a more rigorous sort. The present extension to verbal behavior is thus an exercise in interpretation rather than a quantitative extrapolation of rigorous experimental results. (Skinner, 1957, p. 11)

Nonetheless, the taxonomy of verbal behavior identifies units into which complex verbal behavior can be decomposed in an experimental analysis, and the continuing expansion of experimental analysis of verbal behavior is likely to add to that taxonomy.

A ubiquitous property of verbal behavior is its multiple causation. A particular verbal utterance is likely to be determined jointly by discriminative stimuli, prior verbal responses, possible reinforcing or aversive consequences, the condi-

A. Charles Catania • Department of Psychology, University of Maryland Baltimore County, Baltimore, Maryland 21250.

Handbook of Research Methods in Human Operant Behavior, edited by Lattal and Perone. Plenum Press, New York, 1998.

tion of the speaker, and the nature of the listener. In the technical vocabulary of verbal behavior, the effects of these variables might be treated as interactions of tacts, intraverbals, mands, autoclitics, and audiences. The fluid relations that exist among the several processes that enter into verbal behavior pose problems for its experimental analysis, because most methods of recording verbal behavior preserve topographies rather than controlling variables. For example,

> . . .we cannot tell from form alone into which class a response falls. *Fire* may be (1) a mand to a firing squad, (2) a tact to a conflagration, (3) an intraverbal response to the stimulus *Ready, aim. . .,* or (4) an echoic or (5) textual response to appropriate verbal stimuli. It is possible that formal properties of the vocal response, especially its intonation, may suggest one type of controlling variable, but an analysis cannot be achieved from such internal evidence alone. In order to classify behavior effectively, we must know the circumstances under which it is emitted. (Skinner, 1957, p. 186)

The most crucial methodological implication of these considerations is that records of verbal behavior must include not only the behavior itself but also the details of its antecedents and consequences. The point is illustrated by a standard linguistic example: Little can be said about the functions of *They are eating apples* without relevant context (e.g., whether the speaker's environment includes both cooking and eating apples or just people eating fruit).

The varied topographies of verbal behavior preclude recording in standard formats such as cumulative records. Written verbal behavior, unlike vocal verbal behavior, at least has the advantage that it produces its own record. Different research objectives may call for different measures (e.g., word frequencies, sequential dependencies), but the most formidable challenge is to record verbal behavior in such a way as to show clearly its relations to antecedents and consequences (cf. Moerk, 1992). There are various precedents (e.g., see experimental papers in the journal *Analysis of Verbal Behavior*), but none has become standard.

The technical vocabulary of verbal behavior can be entered at any of a number of different points, and therefore the material in this chapter is organized as a glossary with cross-references and commentary. The reader can begin with the terms most relevant to a particular application and can explore relations among terms to whatever depth seems appropriate. Technical vocabularies evolve, so the extent to which any glossary can resolve terminological or conceptual issues is limited; a glossary provides a starting place but the final authority is provided by actual usages within appropriate verbal communities.

This glossary assumes a familiarity with the basic vocabulary of behavior analysis (see especially Catania, 1991a). Most entries have been drawn with revision from Catania (1992, pp. 363–402; for a discussion of dictionaries and glossaries in psychology, see Catania, 1989). A primary source for much of the terminology and the indispensable reference on this topic is Skinner's *Verbal Behavior* (1957); the treatment of rule-governed behavior in Skinner (1969) is also invaluable. The glossary includes a few cognitive terms often applied to important classes of human behavior (e.g., remembering) and some terms applicable to stimulus and response classes that may have special relevance for verbal behavior (e.g., equivalence classes, higher-order classes). The source literature is extensive, so the references provided in the commentaries should be regarded only as pointers into that literature. The glossary format provides terms in boldface followed by entries in italics with cross-references capitalized; when commentary accompanies an entry, it appears in standard Roman type.

GLOSSARY

Abstraction • *discrimination based on a single property of stimuli, independent of other properties; thus, generalization among all stimuli with that property (e.g., all red stimuli as opposed to specific red objects).*

Many tacts are controlled by stimulus properties rather than by particular stimuli. The property of color, for example, determines the verbal response *red* whether occasioned by red noses, traffic lights, or sails in the sunset. The property is defined by the practices of the verbal community and not by independent physical measurement. For example, no range or distribution of wavelengths exists such that all visual stimuli within that range are called red whereas all those outside are not.

Natural environments do not ordinarily include contingencies that arrange consequences on the basis of single properties. For example, certain colors may be correlated with certain edible foods but in other contexts they will also be correlated with inedible objects. "Abstraction is a peculiarly verbal process because a nonverbal environment cannot provide the necessary restricted contingency" (Skinner, 1957, p. 109).

Adduction • *the production of novel behavior when new combinations of stimulus properties that separately control different classes or properties of behavior engender new combinations of those classes or properties (as when a child appropriately combines a color name and an animal name on seeing a horse of a different color for the first time); the novel coming together of different repertoires.*

Although adduction is most obvious in verbal behavior, in which novel utterances may come about as a result of novel combinations of stimulus properties that occasion different tacts, it can also occur with nonverbal behavior. For example, if color controls rate of responding and form controls location, novel combinations of color and form may produce novel combinations of rates and locations (cf. Andronis, 1983; Catania & Cerutti, 1986; Epstein, 1981).

Audience • *the discriminative stimuli that set the occasion on which verbal behavior may have consequences. Different audiences may set the occasion for different classes of verbal behavior.*

Audience stimuli are typically social (as when a speaker is influenced by the cues provided by an attentive human listener), but they are not exclusively so (as when someone interacts verbally with a computer terminal). "An effective audience is hard to identify. The presence or absence of a person is not enough" (Skinner, 1957, p. 176).

Augmenting stimulus • *see INCENTIVE.*

Autoclitic • *a unit of verbal behavior that depends on other verbal behavior for its occurrence and that modifies the effects of that other verbal behavior on the lis-*

tener. Relational autoclitics *involve verbal units coordinated with other units in such a way that they cannot stand alone, as when grammatical tenses depend on temporal features of events.* Descriptive autoclitics *involve discriminations of one's own behavior, as when the word* not *depends on a mismatch between what one is inclined to say and the appropriateness of saying it.*

"An important fact about verbal behavior is that speaker and listener may reside within the same skin" (Skinner, 1957, p. 163). "Part of the behavior of an organism becomes in turn one of the variables controlling another part" (Skinner, 1957, p. 313). The complexities created when verbal behavior is built on other verbal behavior need special comment. Note that intraverbals also depend on other verbal behavior but are distinguished from autoclitics because they do not require discriminations of one's own behavior; for example, one can respond intraverbally to someone else's verbal behavior rather than to one's own.

Relational Autoclitics. Some verbal responses specify events only through their relations to other verbal responses. For example, *above* and *before* occur in combination with other verbal responses and depend on these other verbal responses for their effects. A given set of events may occasion the words of a sentence in a particular grammatical order, and incidental features of responding may vary consistently with particular combinations of properties, as when stress patterns vary consistently across different grammatical forms. Under some circumstances, responding appropriate to novel combinations of stimulus properties may emerge (cf. Esper, 1973, and see ADDUCTION). When environmental properties occasion verbal responses that are invariant across different combinations with other verbal behavior, we may treat such classes as verbal units (e.g., as when present-tense sentence structure remains invariant across a variety of different tacted events). But note that "as verbal behavior develops in the individual speaker, larger and larger responses acquire functional unity, and we need not always speculate about autoclitic action when a response appears to include an autoclitic form" (Skinner, 1957, p. 336). "Many instances of verbal behavior which contain grammatical or syntactical autoclitics may not represent true autoclitic activity" (Skinner, 1957, p. 343).

The new arrangements that relational autoclitic processes can generate are important because verbal behavior may occasion later verbal or nonverbal behavior. For example, the structure of numerical verbal responding corresponds to environmental structure in such a way that new verbal responses generated arithmetically may then function effectively as tacts (e.g., *twelve* tacts the number of eggs in a full dozen box; the eggs need not be counted every time). Also, some verbal behavior permits responding to properties of the world that cannot be responded to in other ways. For example, noon or Saturday cannot be tacted; these exist only by virtue of clocks and calendars and cannot stand independently of verbal behavior.

Descriptive Autoclitics. Many verbal responses tact the conditions under which other verbal behavior is emitted and thereby modify responses of the listener. The phrase *I doubt* in "I doubt the coffee is ready" modifies how the listener may act on the statement that the coffee is ready. For the listener, *I doubt* is a conditional stimulus; with or without the phrase, the listener has heard *the coffee is ready,* but the listener is less likely to pour the coffee in the former case than in the latter.

With regard to the speaker, *I doubt* cannot be just a tact of the coffee's readiness. It must depend on the relation between the speaker's tendency to say "The coffee is ready" and the state of the coffee, and therefore on discrimination of the speaker's own behavior; the speaker must be able to tell whether it is appropriate to say "The coffee is ready." We sometimes respond as though tacting when the stimulus is absent. The qualifying autoclitic accompanying such verbal behavior is often some form of the verbal response *no,* and may occur when circumstances set the occasion for saying "The coffee is ready" even though that response would be inappropriate. "Negative autoclitics qualify or cancel the response which they accompany but imply that the response is strong for some reason" (Skinner, 1957, p. 317).

Assertion is also autoclitic, but the verb *is* serves many functions. Sometimes it specifies that it accompanies a tact ("This is a book"), sometimes that it prescribes equivalences between verbal responses ("A human is a featherless biped"), and sometimes that it specifies temporal properties ("It is cold now"). Autoclitics can have quantitative as well as qualitative effects; examples are *few, some,* and *many.* Other descriptive autoclitics tact the speaker's reaction to current verbal behavior, as in "I am sorry to say that I don't understand." Saying "This is so" or "That is probable" or "It cannot be" is also verbal behavior that depends on the strength of other verbal behavior.

Autology • *the scientific study of the self. Cf. PRIVATE EVENTS.*

This little-known term characterizes a field to which the analysis of verbal behavior has made a special contribution: "The speaker is . . . a locus—a place in which a number of variables come together in a unique confluence to yield an equally unique achievement" (Skinner, 1957, p. 313). "The contingencies which generate a response to one's own verbal behavior are unlikely in the absence of social reinforcement. It is because our behavior is important to others that it eventually becomes important to us" (Skinner, 1957, p. 314). The seminal work on this topic can be found in Skinner (1945).

Chaining • *the emission of a sequence of discriminated operants such that responses during one stimulus are followed by other stimuli that reinforce those responses and set the occasion for subsequent ones. Not all temporally integrated sequences are maintained through chaining; those that are must be distinguished from those that are not.*

Behavior sequences can consist of successions of different operants, each defined by the reinforcing consequence of producing an opportunity to engage in the next. Any segment of a sequence serves the dual function of reinforcing the last response and occasioning the next one (a discriminative stimulus that serves such a reinforcing function is sometimes called a *conditioned reinforcer*). Some behavior sequences are reducible to smaller units in this way, and an experimental analysis simply examines how independent the components are from each other. But this is not the only way behavior sequences can hang together. Historically, some had held that sequential behavior could always be interpreted in terms of such concatenations of components, whereas others had held that sequential behavior could not be interpreted adequately in such terms.

In answer to the argument that each movement may serve as a unique stimulus for the next, Lashley (1951) considered sequential patterns of responding that cannot be reduced to successions of chained units. When a skilled typist rapidly types *the,* these letters cannot be discriminative stimuli for the next stroke, first because the typist will execute that stroke even before the typed letters can have stimulus effects, and second because the letters cannot be unique discriminative stimuli if they can be followed by any of a variety of other keys depending on which word the typist is typing.

No choice is forced between assuming that sequential behavior depends on chained sequences or assuming that it depends on temporally extended units of behavior not reducible to such sequences. The issue instead is that of deciding which type a sequence is: Some are put together so that each response produces stimulus conditions setting the occasion for the next, whereas others are integrated so that responses appear in the proper order without each depending on consequences of the last.

Coding, coding response • *an inferred variety of mediating behavior, as when visually presented letters are remembered on the basis of sound rather than geometric properties, perhaps as a result of saying or subvocally rehearsing them. Errors based on acoustic rather than visual similarity support the inference. Tacting is one kind of coding. Cf. REMEMBERING, REPRESENTATION.*

Cognition, cognitive processes • *knowing, and the ways in which it takes place. Processes said to be cognitive are usually varieties of behavior that need not be manifested as movements and therefore must be measured indirectly (e.g., doing mental arithmetic, shifting attention, imagining).*

Concept • *a class of stimuli such that an organism generalizes among all stimuli within the class but discriminates them from those in other classes.*

Concepts play much the same role in analyses of discriminative stimuli as operants do in analyses of response classes (Keller & Schoenfeld, 1950).

Context • *the constant features of a situation (e.g., the setting of an experimental session). Experimental contexts acquire behavioral function because they are embedded in the still larger context that includes them.*

Contingency • *in operant behavior, the conditions under which responses produce consequences; the conditional probabilities that relate some events (e.g., responses) to others (e.g., stimuli). An organism is said to* come into contact with a contingency *when its behavior produces some consequences of the contingency.*

Contingency-governed behavior *or* **contingency-shaped behavior** • *operant behavior.*

This terminology is ordinarily used to contrast responding not occasioned by verbal behavior with *verbally governed* or *rule-governed behavior,* behavior controlled by verbal antecedents such as instructions. The former term, *contingency-governed,* emphasizes the current conditions maintaining the behavior, whereas the latter, *contingency-shaped,* emphasizes its origins (the latter is therefore typically also redundant, because shaping necessarily involves the application of contingencies).

Correspondence (between saying and doing) • *see VERBALLY GOVERNED BEHAVIOR.*

Covert behavior • *behavior that is unobserved or unobservable and therefore only inferred; alternatively, behavior on such a small scale that it is unrecordable or recordable only with special equipment (e.g., counting to oneself, inferred from a verbal report).*

"There is no point at which it is profitable to draw a line distinguishing thinking from acting on this continuum. So far as we know, the events at the covert end have no special properties, observe no special laws, and can be credited with no special achievements" (Skinner, 1957, p. 438). Cf. PRIVATE EVENTS.

Cultural selection • *the selection of behavior as it is passed on from one organism to another (examples include imitation and verbal behavior).*

Deictic verbal behavior, deixis • *verbal behavior in which the function of a term is based on its relation to the speaker (e.g.,* here *versus* there*).*

In its dependence on discriminations of the speaker's own behavior in relation to the listener rather than of intrinsic properties of events or objects, deixis (e.g., Wales, 1986) shares properties with autoclitic behavior. In *this* versus *that*, for example, the appropriate term depends on where one is located. In combination with pronouns, the functions of deictic terms in language are analogous to those of variables in algebra; things can be spoken of even if they cannot be named. A special case of the deictic vocabulary is that of the personal pronoun.

Dictation-taking • *a formal verbal class in which a vocal verbal stimulus occasions a corresponding written response. The correspondence is defined by the one-to-one relation of verbal units (e.g., letters or words).*

The units of dictation-taking are typically entire words or phrases, but individual letters may also serve (e.g., as when an unusual name is spelled out for a stenographer). Some special properties of dictation-taking follow from the relatively permanent record produced in the written text. Occasions for dictation-taking are limited relative to textual behavior, because, unlike the vocal apparatus, writing implements are not parts of the human anatomy. Perhaps for this reason, there is less temptation to pursue its possible covert manifestations; we are less likely to speak of submanual writing or typing than of subvocal reading (cf. ECHOIC BEHAVIOR, TEXTUAL BEHAVIOR, TRANSCRIPTION).

Discriminated operant • *an operant defined in terms of the stimuli during which it occurs as well as its environmental effect. This operant depends on the relations among three events (the three-term contingency): an antecedent stimulus in the presence of which a response may be followed by consequences. In one sense, the stimulus sets the occasion on which the response may have consequences; in another, it defines a property of the operant class and so sets the occasion for the response.*

Echoic behavior • *a formal verbal class in which a vocal verbal stimulus occasions a corresponding vocal verbal response. The correspondence is defined by the one-to-one relation of verbal units (e.g., phonemes or words) and not by acoustic similarity.*

When a child repeats a parent's "mama," the child's response is echoic to the extent that it is occasioned by the parent's utterance and to the extent that the phonemes of the child's utterance have a one-to-one correspondence to those of the parent's. As with other formal classes, echoic behavior does not imply that the speaker has understood what has been echoed (cf. TEXTUAL BEHAVIOR). Echoic units can vary from individual speech sounds to extended phrases or sentences. For adult speakers, the units of echoic behavior are often whole words or phrases (e.g., as in repeating a phone number).

The relation between stimulus and response in echoic behavior is not simple. The stimulus is a complex sound pattern and the response consists of coordinated movements of lungs, vocal cords, tongue, lips, and so on. The significant dimensions of phonemes, the units of speech, are more easily defined by articulation (e.g., tongue position) than by acoustic properties. Echoic behavior is defined by correspondences of phonetic units rather than by acoustics. For example, an adult's voice is deeper than a child's, a woman's voice differs from a man's, and people speak with varying regional dialects, but differences in vocal quality and regional dialect are irrelevant to whether verbal behavior is echoic. Thus, the duplication of human sound patterns by parrots does not qualify as echoic behavior because their duplications are acoustic rather than phonetic. For example, a parrot's response would reproduce the *th* sound if a child lisps an *s*, but the echoic response of a nonlisping adult would ordinarily include the unlisped phoneme instead.

Echoic behavior depends at least in part on the shaping of articulations by their vocal consequences. Even before their own vocalizations begin to be differentiated, infants have learned some discriminations among aspects of the speech of others (such discriminations of speech sounds may be more difficult to learn later; e.g., Werker, 1989). Their initial babbling includes a range of human speech sounds, but native sounds are ordinarily retained in their spontaneous vocalizations whereas nonnative sounds gradually disappear as the babbling evolves to echolalic self-repetition and then to repetition of the speech of others (echoic speech).

The vocalizations of infants are engendered and maintained by what the infants hear themselves saying; without these auditory consequences (as in cases of hearing impairment), the behavior does not develop. Perhaps native speech sounds become reinforcing relative to nonnative sounds simply because they often accompany the activities of important caregivers in an infant's environment. Consistent with the demonstration of generalized vocal imitation in infants (Poulson, Kymissis, Reeve, Andreatos, & Reeve, 1991), articulations that produce something that sounds more or less like what the parents say may be reinforced automatically by this correspondence between the infant's and the parents' utterances. "The young child alone in the nursery may automatically reinforce his own exploratory vocal behavior when he produces sounds which he has heard in the speech of others" (Skinner, 1957, p. 58; see also Risley, 1977).

Emergent relation • *a new behavioral relation (especially conditional stimulus control) that emerges as a by-product of other relations rather than through differential reinforcement. For example, if arbitrary matching has been arranged only for pairs AB and BC (where the first letter of each pair corresponds to the sample and the second to the matching comparison) and a test for transitivity demonstrates matching with the new pair, AC, this new matching relation is said to be emergent. See also ADDUCTION.*

Equivalence class   •   *a stimulus class with at least three members, usually pro-*
duced through conditional discriminations in matching-to-sample, in which the
relations among members are characterized by the properties of reflexivity, sym-
metry, and transitivity, especially when at least some of the relations are emergent
rather than directly trained (if all relations are already directly trained, emergent
relations can be tested by adding a new member to the class).

Studies of equivalence classes must involve at least two stimulus classes. For
example, consider one stimulus class consisting of members ABCDE and another
consisting of members LMNOP. In a matching task with A as a sample stimulus
and B and M as comparison stimuli, a response to B is reinforced, because A and
B are members of the same class; with L as a sample and B and M as comparisons,
however, a response to M is reinforced, this time because L and M are members of
the same class. For convenience, the examples below list samples and comparisons from the first class but omit nonmatching comparisons from the other class.

The relations among the members of an equivalence class have the properties
of reflexivity, symmetry, and transitivity. Reflexivity refers to the matching of a
sample to itself, sometimes called identity matching: A → A, B → B, C → C (in these
examples, each letter pair represents a sample and its matching comparison; the
arrow, →, can be read as "is matched to"). Symmetry refers to the reversibility of a
matching relation: if A → B, then B → A. Transitivity refers to transfer of the relation to new combinations through shared membership (if A → B and B → C, then
A → C). If the relations among the members of a stimulus class have these properties, then training A → B and B → C should produce A → C, B → A, C → A, and C →
B as emergent relations. Given A → B and B → C, for example, the combination of
symmetry and transitivity implies the C → A relation. The emergence of all possible matching relations after the training of only a subset (usually A → B and B →
C) is the criterion for calling the stimuli members of an equivalence class. The class
can also be extended to new stimuli (e.g., if C → D is learned, then A → D, D → A,
B → D, D → B, and D → C may be created as emergent matching relations). Stimuli
that are members of an equivalence class may also be functionally equivalent, but
it remains to be seen whether the behavioral properties of these classes are fully
consistent with their logical ones.

At various times, equivalence classes have been treated as fundamental properties of behavior (Sidman, 1994), as derivatives of other processes such as naming (Horne & Lowe, 1996), and as subclasses of more general relational frames established by verbal communities (e.g., consider the relation *greater than*, with the
property of transivity but not symmetry; Hayes, 1994). The transfer from individual matches to equivalences can also be regarded as the product of establishing a
higher-order class of behavior with respect to these relations. For example, equivalence classes could be regarded as members of a higher-order class if, after each
of several different A → B and B → C stimulus sets has been followed by tests of the
C → A relation, an organism responds correctly on the first presentation of the C →
A test for a new stimulus set.

Establishing operation   •   *any operation that changes the status of a stimulus as*
a reinforcer or punisher: deprivation, satiation, procedures that establish former-
ly neutral stimuli as conditioned reinforcers or as conditioned aversive stimuli,

and stimulus presentations that change the reinforcing or punishing status of oth-er stimuli (as when an already available screwdriver becomes a reinforcer in the presence of a screw that needs tightening). Cf. MAND.

More than most other technical terms in this glossary, forms of *establish* are also likely to occur in standard discourse in their dictionary sense (as in "the stan-dards of usage established by a verbal community"). The technical and colloquial usages will usually be easily distinguished by their contexts, but teachers should be alert to pedagogical problems that may be created by the dual usages. The ter-minology is well established (sic), in the sense that it has been in use for some time, and no alternative that is likely to supersede it is in current use.

Evocation • *the production of a response, usually by an establishing operation (as when food deprivation is said to evoke behavior that has led to food in the past). Sometimes responding is said to be evoked if it is unclear whether it was emitted or elicited.*

Extrinsic reinforcer • *a reinforcer that has an arbitrary relation to the responses that produce it (as when a musician plays for money rather than because the play-ing produces music).*

This term has also been applied to stimuli presumed to function as reinforcers because their function has been instructed (as when children are told that it is im-portant to earn good grades); despite their label, such stimuli are often ineffective as reinforcers. Cf. INTRINSIC REINFORCER, NOMINAL REINFORCER.

Fluency • *accurate performance that occurs at a high rate and/or with short la-tency, and that is well retained after substantial periods without practice.*

Skills that become fluent, such as student mastery of verbal mathematical skills (cf. Johnson & Layng, 1992), are also more likely to combine with other be-havior in novel ways (cf. ADDUCTION, EMERGENT BEHAVIOR, PRODUCTIVI-TY), perhaps because training to the point of fluency causes verbal mediation to drop out. If so, such behavior may be more effective because it is less susceptible to the insensitivities to contingencies often characteristic of verbally governed be-havior.

Formal verbal classes • *see DICTATION-TAKING, ECHOIC BEHAVIOR, TEX-TUAL BEHAVIOR, TRANSCRIPTION.*

Correspondences between verbal stimuli and verbal responses in the formal verbal relations are implicit in our saying that words are the same whether heard, spoken, seen, or written. The formal terms are distinguished from colloquial vo-cabularies in their restriction solely to the reproduction of verbal units. For ex-ample, textual behavior does not imply understanding and therefore cannot be equated with reading. The reproduction of verbal behavior is an essential verbal function, and the account of these classes here, limited to vocal and written stim-uli and responses, could have been extended to other language modes (e.g., send-ing and receiving Morse code).

The formal classes illustrate the importance of distinguishing verbal stimuli from verbal responses. The distinction presents little difficulty in the analysis of nonverbal behavior. For example, if a rat presses a lever only when a light is pre-sent, the light is called a *stimulus* and the lever press a *response;* there is no temp-tation to reverse the terms. In verbal behavior, however, a speaker's response is a listener's stimulus and a writer's response is a reader's stimulus; furthermore, a speaker or writer at one time becomes a listener or reader at another.

Functional class • *a class the members of which have common behavioral functions, either produced by similar histories or acquired through emergent relations. If two stimuli are members of a functional class, then the behavior occasioned by one will also be occasioned by the other; such stimuli are sometimes said to be functionally* equivalent.

In an experiment by Vaughan (1988), photographic slides were divided into two arbitrary sets of 20 slides each. Pigeons' pecks were reinforced given slides from one set but not the other. Occasionally the correlation between the slide sets and reinforcement was reversed. After several reversals, pigeons began to switch responding from one slide set to the other after only a few slides. In other words, the common contingencies arranged for the 20 slides in a set made them functionally equivalent, in that changes of contingencies for just a few slides in a set changed behavior appropriately for all of them. This functional equivalence must be distinguished from the emergence of equivalence relations in arbitrary matching (cf. Sidman, Wynne, Maguire, & Barnes, 1989).

By definition, functional equivalence implies transfer of function, in the sense that behavior established with respect to some class members should transfer to other class members. The practical significance can be illustrated by an example. A child has learned to obey a parent's words, *go* and *stop,* while crossing at traffic intersections. Separately, the child has been taught that *go* and green traffic lights are equivalent and that *stop* and red traffic lights are equivalent. If the discriminative functions of the words *stop* and *go* transfer to the respective traffic lights, the child will obey the traffic lights without additional instruction.

Functional equivalence is a defining property of the members of an operant class (as when a rat's lever presses, regardless of topography, become members of an operant class by virtue of common contingencies). Most examples in this glossary involve stimulus classes, but the main points about function are relevant to response classes also. All members of an operant class are by virtue of that membership functionally equivalent. Common contingencies can create the sometimes arbitrary functional classes called *operants,* but they may also be relevant to nonarbitrary classes. When class members share physical properties, for example, nonarbitrary functional classes may be created not because of some direct effect of those shared properties but rather because, by virtue of those shared properties, all of the class members are necessarily involved in common contingencies. Common consequences are not equivalent to common contingencies (i.e., response classes are differentiable even if they produce the same reinforcer, as long as they do so according to different contingencies).

Hierarchical organization • *the nesting of some classes of behavior within others. Cf. HIGHER-ORDER CLASS OF BEHAVIOR.*

The analysis of hierarchical structure is a general problem in behavior. In verbal behavior especially, different units enter into different levels of analysis. For example, letters and phonemes combine in morphemes and words, which in turn form phrases and sentences, which in turn make up paragraphs and texts, and so on.

Higher-order class of behavior • *a class that includes within it other classes that can themselves function as operant classes (as when generalized imitation includes all component imitations that could be separately reinforced as subclasses). A higher-order class is sometimes called a* generalized *class, in the sense that contingencies arranged for some subclasses within it generalize to all the others. Generalized matching and verbally governed behavior are examples of higher-order classes.*

Higher-order classes may be a source of novel behavior (e.g., as in generalized imitation of behavior the imitator had not seen before). They also have the property that contingencies may operate differently on the higher-order class than on its component subclasses. For example, if all instances of imitation are reinforced except those within one subclass (e.g., jumping whenever the model jumps), that subclass may not become differentiated from the higher-order class and so may change with the higher-order class rather than with the contingencies arranged for it (i.e., the imitation of jumping may not extinguish even though it is no longer reinforced). Control by the contingencies arranged for the higher-order class rather than by those arranged for the subclasses defines these classes; the subclasses may then be said to be *insensitive* to the contingencies arranged for them.

Higher-order classes of behavior are held together by the common contingencies shared by their members, just as the various topographies of a rat's food-reinforced lever-pressing (e.g., left paw, right paw, both paws) are held together by the common contingencies according to which they produce food. Common contingencies are the glue that holds higher-order classes of behavior together. Furthermore, when a class of responses seems insensitive to its consequences, the possibility must be entertained that the class is a subclass of a larger class the other members of which continue to have consequences according to former contingencies (cf. FUNCTIONAL CLASS).

Imitation • *behavior that duplicates some properties of the behavior of a model. Imitation need not involve the matching of stimulus features (e.g., when one child imitates the raised hand of another, the felt position of the child's own limb has different stimulus dimensions than the seen position of the other's). Cf. HIGHER-ORDER CLASS OF BEHAVIOR, OBSERVATIONAL LEARNING.*

Imitation may be limited to the duplication of explicitly taught instances, or it may include correspondences between the behavior of model and observer even in novel instances, when it is called *generalized imitation*. In the latter case, imitative responding is a higher-order class of behavior (Baer, Peterson, & Sherman, 1967; Gewirtz & Stingle, 1968).

Imitation does not imply that the imitating organism has learned something about contingencies, and not all imitations are advantageous (e.g., a coyote that sees another coyote step into a trap would do well not to imitate that behavior but might learn from what it had seen).

Incentive • *discriminative effects of reinforcing stimuli (as when the smell of food makes responses reinforced by food more likely); occasionally, a stimulus that changes the reinforcing or punishing status of other stimuli. A verbal response that has such effects is sometimes called an* augmenting *stimulus. Cf. ESTABLISHING OPERATION.*

Information • *strictly, the reduction in uncertainly provided by a stimulus, as quantified in bits, the number of binary decisions needed to specify the stimulus. One bit specifies 2 alternatives, two bits 4, three bits 8, and so on in increasing powers of 2. The term more often appears in its nontechnical sense, as when applied to* information processing. *Cf. INFORMATIVE STIMULUS.*

Informative stimulus • *a discriminative stimulus, though not necessarily a conditioned reinforcer.*

A stimulus predicts an event if the probability of the event given the stimulus differs from that without the stimulus. As shown by research on observing behavior (Dinsmoor, 1983), organisms do not work to produce informative stimuli per se; instead, they work to produce informative stimuli correlated with reinforcers. For example, a stimulus correlated with differential punishment and superimposed on ongoing reinforced behavior is informative, but its onset does not ordinarily reinforce observing responses. If reinforcement alternates with extinction, observing responses that produce correlated stimuli are maintained by the reinforcement stimulus and not by the extinction stimulus, even though the two stimuli are equally informative. The finding undercuts the appeal to information processing as a primary cognitive process and, perhaps more important, implies that the effectiveness of a message depends more on whether its content is reinforcing or aversive than on whether it is correct or complete (e.g., it is consistent with this finding that people often hesitate to have medical symptoms diagnosed and that the bearer of good news is welcome but not the bearer of bad).

Instructional stimulus, instruction • *in nonverbal settings, usually a conditional discriminative stimulus; in verbal settings, a verbal antecedent of either verbal or nonverbal behavior. See VERBALLY GOVERNED BEHAVIOR.*

Intraverbal • *a verbal response occasioned by a verbal stimulus, where the relation between stimulus and response is an arbitrary one established by the verbal community. Intraverbal behavior is chaining as it occurs in verbal behavior. Either the speaker or someone else may provide verbal stimuli (thus, intraverbals do not require discrimination of one's own behavior; they are not autoclitic).*

Intraverbal behavior is involved only in cases in which successive parts of an utterance serve as discriminative stimuli for later parts (cf. CHAINING). When extended utterances function as independent verbal units (e.g., *He who hesitates is lost* or *Look before you leap*), it is inappropriate to say that the relations among their parts are intraverbal.

Learning to recite the alphabet is an example of the establishment of intraverbal behavior. The alphabet is arbitrary but is taught because so much is ordered according to it. We are less able to recite the order of letters on computer keyboards because we do not have to behave with respect to keyboards the way we do with respect to alphabetized lists. Similar points apply to chronologies, geographies, and much else of our everyday knowledge. We do not ordinarily learn historical details by experiencing them. Instead, given names or dates, we learn to say when or in what order events occurred. "[T]he verbal behavior of the modern historian is still mostly intraverbal. If we exclude pictures, statues, impersonations, and so on, *Caesar* cannot be a tact in the behavior of a contemporary speaker" (Skinner, 1957, p. 129).

Intraverbal behavior has been the focus of much research on human verbal learning, perhaps because of the relative ease with which verbal materials can be manipulated as stimuli. Paired-associates learning (learning word pairs) and serial learning (learning ordered lists, as in learning to count) represent relatively pure cases of intraverbal behavior.

Much intraverbal behavior is weakly determined. A current verbal stimulus may alter the probability of what follows without completely determining it. "The intraverbal relations in any adult repertoire are the result of hundreds of thousands of reinforcements under a great variety of inconsistent and often conflicting contingencies. Many different responses are brought under the control of a given stimulus word, and many different stimulus words are placed in control of a single response" (Skinner, 1957, p. 74).

Intrinsic reinforcer • *a reinforcer that is naturally related to the responses that produce it (as when a musician plays not for money but because the playing produces music).*

Some reinforcers are intrinsically effective whereas the effectiveness of others has to be established (Ferster, 1967; cf. EXTRINSIC REINFORCER). Experiments involving so-called extrinsic reinforcers have been used to argue against their use (e.g., Lepper, Greene, & Nisbett, 1973). For example, one group of children received gold stars for artwork; after the gold stars were discontinued, the children engaged in less artwork than those in another group who never received gold stars. The gold stars, extrinsic reinforcers, were said to have undermined the intrinsic reinforcers, the natural consequences of drawing. But the children were told to earn the gold stars, and their effectiveness as reinforcers was not tested. If the gold stars were reinforcers at all, they were reinforcers established by instructions. Thus, the results probably had nothing to do with a difference between intrinsic and extrinsic reinforcers; instead, they probably demonstrated the insensitivity of instructed behavior to contingencies.

Language • *the practices shared by the members of a verbal community, including consistencies of vocabulary and grammar.*

Language differs from verbal behavior. "The 'languages' studied by the linguist are the reinforcing practices of verbal communities. When we say that *also* means *in addition* or *besides* 'in English,' we are not referring to the verbal behavior of any one speaker of English or the average performance of many speakers. . . . In studying the practices of the community rather than the behavior of the speaker, the linguist has not been concerned with verbal behavior in the present sense" (Skinner, 1957, p. 461).

Language development • *the emergence of language in the individual.*

Among the controversial issues in accounts of language development is the extent to which consequences play a role in the child's acquisition of language. In appeals to the *poverty of the stimulus,* some have argued that the verbal environment is not rich enough to support language acquisition and therefore that many structural features of language must be "prewired," in the sense that they will emerge in the absence of relevant contingencies (e.g., Chomsky, 1959; Crain, 1991). On the basis of examining exchanges between parents and children, others have argued that contingencies play a crucial role (e.g., Moerk, 1992).

At issue is the kind of verbal behavior available in the child's environment, not its quantity. The case for the poverty of the stimulus argues that verbal environments do not include the negative or ungrammatical instances that should be there in support of claims that a child's grammatical behavior is shaped through natural contingencies (in the sense that such instances do not occur in the speech that children hear, or in the sense that such instances are not corrected when the child makes them, or in both senses.) But negative instances are not necessary for all kinds of learning (e.g., as in the combination of behavior classes in adduction).

Now consider a child who sleeps, eats, and performs other functions for 16 hours of the day, leaving only 8 hours for the acquisition of verbal behavior. Let accidental contingencies work slowly, in the everyday verbal interactions between parent and child, so that an hour or so must be allowed for each new word. That is still eight words a day, or several thousand words in a year or two, a figure not too far from the vocabulary of a 5-year-old. Even under the most extreme assumptions about phylogenic constraints on the syntax of natural human languages, a substantial role is demanded for ontogeny by the many specific features that must be mastered in the child's acquisition of a language.

One issue is whether contingencies of selection that can be arranged artificially also can operate naturally in children's environments to shape properties of their verbal behavior (the arguments parallel those marshaled in defense of Darwin's natural selection; the reality of artificial selection in horticulture and animal husbandry was never in dispute). The consequences of verbal behavior are subtle and probably do not have to be explicitly arranged (cf. ECHOIC BEHAVIOR). Contrived reinforcers such as praise or candies may be less effective than such natural consequences of verbal behavior as hearing oneself say something similar to what others have said, or hearing someone say something relevant to something one has just said, and so on. "The behavior of the alert, mature speaker is usually closely related to particular effects. Generalized reinforcement is most obvious and most useful in the original conditioning of verbal behavior" (Skinner, 1957, p. 151). With regard to whether language is innate or learned, a reasonable assumption is that both phylogeny and ontogeny contribute.

Suppose for the sake of argument that a case had been made for grammatical universals by demonstrations that children learn certain types of sentence structures much more easily than others. Those universals would still involve structural rather than functional features of verbal behavior. Even if it were proved that children do not have to learn all the details of grammar because some aspects are built in, that would not account for the many other things about verbal behavior that they would still have to learn. In fact, there is plenty of evidence that rich verbal environments in which parents spend lots of time interacting verbally with their children can make vast and lasting differences in their verbal competence (Hart & Risley, 1995).

Linguistics • *the study of language, usually divided into the topics of* syntax *or* grammatical structure, semantics *or meaning, and* pragmatics *or the functions of language.*

Mand • *a verbal response that specifies its reinforcer. In human verbal behavior, manding is usually a higher-order class, in the sense that newly acquired verbal responses can be incorporated into novel mands.*

Because it is defined by its relation to its reinforcer, one feature of a mand is that its occurrence should depend on relevant establishing operations (i.e., conditions of deprivation or aversive stimulation). Some consequences that may reinforce human verbal behavior are nonverbal (e.g., someone comes when called); others are verbal (someone answers a question). If a child says "milk" and receives a glass of milk, we may say that the child has manded the milk. Unlike the tact, this response may occur in either the presence or the absence of the milk, but when it occurs in the presence of the milk its status as mand or tact is ambiguous. "A mand is a type of verbal operant singled out by its controlling variables. It is not a formal unit of analysis. No response can be said to be a mand from its form alone" (Skinner, 1957, p. 36).

Imagine a child who sees a new toy, learns its name, and then asks for it even though asking for it could never have been reinforced in the past. As a category of verbal behavior, the mand cannot consist of many separate response classes corresponding to each of the many consequences that could be manded; rather it must be a single class of responses in which a reinforcer is specified by the verbal responses that in other circumstances tact it. "The speaker appears to create new mands on the analogy of old ones. Having effectively manded bread and butter, he goes on to mand the jam, even though he has never obtained jam before in this way" (Skinner, 1957, p. 48; cf. HIGHER-ORDER CLASS OF BEHAVIOR).

Mands may be classified according to a variety of features: for example, as *prompts* when the appropriate verbal response is already known to the speaker (e.g., giving a hint to a child who is unable to solve a riddle) and as *probes* when it is not known (e.g., in a police interrogation). In everyday discourse, mands are often distinguished by the consequences that may follow for the listener (pleas, requests, orders, and so on); for instance, a demand usually specifies aversive consequences for noncompliance.

Meaning • *in verbal behavior, a response to verbal stimuli; or the defining properties of a class, usually including some verbal components, in which the members can serve either as stimuli or as responses.*

When a speaker's verbal behavior provides discriminative stimuli for a listener, the listener's behavior is simply what is occasioned by these verbal stimuli. Whether the critical stimulus is a red light, a traffic officer's outstretched hand, the word *stop,* or a tree fallen across the road, the driver's stepping on the brakes illustrates stimulus control. Thus, the problem of meaning must reside at least in part in properties of the listener's responses to verbal stimuli. "It is easy to demonstrate that the listener often says or can say what the speaker is saying, and at approximately the same time" (Skinner, 1957, p. 269).

Whatever else is involved in the listener's behavior, the response to a tact must share some properties with the response to what is tacted (as with nonverbal stimuli, not all responses to verbal stimuli are operant; for example, if a stimulus elicits autonomic responses, the name of the stimulus may come to elicit these responses).

Definitions are not meanings: ". . .dictionaries do not give meanings; at best they give words having the same meaning" (Skinner, 1957, p. 9). "Technically, meanings are to be found among the independent variables in a functional account, rather than as properties of the dependent variable" (Skinner, 1957, p. 14). We say that someone understands something that has been said when the individual repeats what has been said not because the other person said it but for the same reasons that the other person said it (cf. Skinner, 1968, p. 139).

Mediation • *the contribution of intervening behavior (mediating behavior) to the relation between other events (as when coding mediates between the presentation of an item and its recall).*

Metacognition • *the differentiation and discrimination of one's own cognitive processes (as in shifting attention among tasks, or distinguishing between seeing something and just imagining it). One variety is* metamemory, *the differentiation and discrimination of one's own remembering (as in keeping track of a constantly changing list of items, or judging whether some material just studied will be remembered).*

Metaphor • *the extension of concrete terms to complex and/or abstract events or relations for which relevant verbal responses are otherwise unavailable (as when pain is described by the properties of objects that can produce it: e.g., sharp or dull).*

Metaphor is a pervasive property of language. Children learn it readily and adults cannot ignore it. It is not just the stuff of poetry; it is a fundamental aspect of verbal behavior. Much of our technical and nontechnical language of behavior evolved metaphorically from concrete everyday sources (cf. Skinner, 1989).

Language itself provides an example when spoken of in the metaphor of communicating ideas. According to this metaphor, ideas and meanings are objects placed into words and then delivered to someone else (Lakoff & Johnson, 1980). We put ideas into words and get them across to others; words carry meaning; ideas can be grasped; and so on. The metaphor is so well established that it is difficult to speak of language in other ways (but if anything is transmitted in language, it is verbal behavior itself).

Metaphor tempts talk about shared abstract properties captured by words, but its most important feature may be that it allows us to deal concretely with the abstract. For example, through metaphor the abstract dimension of time becomes a spatial one (e.g., the future is ahead of us and the past behind us). Metaphor makes the abstract concrete.

Modeling • *providing behavior to be imitated. Cf. IMITATION.*

Naming • *a higher-order class that involves arbitrary stimulus classes (things or events with particular names) and corresponding arbitrary verbal topographies (the words that serve as their names) in a bidirectional relationship.*

Prerequisites for naming include at least three components: listener behavior, in looking for things and pointing based on what has been said; echoic behavior, in repeating names when they are spoken; and tacting, in saying the names given the objects. Naming relations, unlike those of tacting, are bidirectional rather than unidirectional. For example, one can point to an object when given its name or name the object when it is pointed to; and one can name the object in its absence given an appropriate description or describe the object given its name. These are not relations of symmetry, however. A seen object cannot be exchanged with a point at it, and a heard word cannot be exchanged with a spoken one: "the relation between a name and that which it names is fundamentally asymmetrical" (Horne & Lowe, 1996, p. 234).

Like other cases of sophisticated human behavior, naming is an example of a higher-order behavior class. Horne and Lowe (1996) provide an account of the ways in which the ordinary interactions of caregivers with children can establish speaker and listener behavior the fusion of which comes about through the common terms of each (e.g., the same word both heard and spoken: cf. ECHOIC BEHAVIOR): "naming is a higher-order bidirectional behavioral relation that combines conventional speaker and listener functions so that the presence of either one presupposes the other" (Horne & Lowe, 1996, p. 207). Once established as a higher-order class, naming allows for expansions of vocabulary in which the introduction of new words in particular functional relations (e.g., as tacts) involves those words in a range of other emergent functions (e.g., manding, pointing to named objects).

Natural reinforcer • *see INTRINSIC REINFORCER.*

Nominal reinforcer • *an event presumed to be a reinforcer but the reinforcing function of which has not yet been determined. Cf. EXTRINSIC REINFORCER, INTRINSIC REINFORCER.*

Novel behavior • *see PRODUCTIVITY.*

Observational learning • *learning based on observing the responding of another organism (and/or its consequences). Observational learning need not involve imitation (e.g., organisms may come to avoid aversive stimuli on seeing what happens when other organisms produce them).*

Observing response • *a response that produces or clarifies a discriminative stimulus and that may be maintained by the effectiveness of that stimulus as a conditioned reinforcer. See INFORMATIVE STIMULUS.*

Operant • *See FUNCTIONAL CLASS.*

Overt behavior • *behavior that is observed or observable, or that affects the organism's environment. Cf. COVERT BEHAVIOR.*

Pliance • *See VERBALLY GOVERNED BEHAVIOR.*

Predictive stimulus • *See INFORMATIVE STIMULUS.*

Private events • *in verbal behavior, events accessible only to the speaker (usually, events inside the skin). Private events have the same physical status as public events, but it is more difficult for the verbal community to shape tacts of private events.*

Tacted stimuli are sometimes accessible only to the speaker, as in the report of a headache. Such tacts depend on the verbal community for their origin and maintenance. The problem is how the verbal community can create and maintain these responses without access to the stimuli. "In setting up the kind of verbal operant called the tact, the verbal community characteristically reinforces a given response in the presence of a given stimulus. This can be done only if the stimulus acts upon both speaker and reinforcing community. A private stimulus cannot satisfy these conditions" (Skinner, 1957, pp. 130–131).

The vocabulary of private events can be taught only through extension from tacts based on events to which the verbal community has access. Skinner (1945, pp. 131–133) suggests "at least four ways in which a reinforcing community with no access to a private stimulus may generate verbal behavior with respect to it." The verbal community may differentially respond to reports of private events based on (1) common public accompaniments, (2) collateral behavior, (3) shared properties of public and private events, as in metaphorical extension, and (4) generalization from public to private behavior along the dimension of response magnitude. For example, a child's report of pain (1) may follow a public event that produced it (e.g., a cut); (2) it may also be accompanied by behavior (e.g., crying). Furthermore, (3) the vocabulary of pain derives from properties of public objects that produce particular kinds of pain (e.g., sharp edges produce sharp pains). Finally, (4) a report of talking to oneself can generalize from cases in which the talking is overt to those in which it is no longer of public magnitude.

The public origin of the language of expectancies is illustrated by student reports of a pigeon's behavior on a classroom demonstration: "They were describing what *they* would have expected, felt, and hoped for under similar circumstances. But . . . whatever the students knew about themselves which permitted them to infer comparable events in the pigeon must have been learned from a verbal community which saw no more of their behavior than they had seen of the pigeon's" (Skinner, 1963, p. 955; cf. Wellman, 1990).

A toothache is a discriminable event, but the person with the toothache has different access to it than the dentist called on to treat it. Both respond to the unsound tooth, but one does so by feeling the tooth and the other by looking at it and probing it with dental instruments. Their contacts with the tooth might be compared with the different ways a seeing and a sightless person make contact with a geometric solid if one tries to teach its name to the other; the seeing person does so by sight and the sightless person by touch. One kind of contact is not necessarily more reliable than the other. For example, in the phenomenon of referred pain, a bad tooth in the lower jaw may be reported as a toothache in the upper jaw. In this case, the dentist is a better judge than the patient of where the pain really is.

"It is only through the gradual growth of a verbal community that the individual becomes 'conscious'" (Skinner, 1957, p. 140). Many tacts of private events involve the discrimination of properties of one's own behavior. The significance of the capacity to discriminate such properties must not be underestimated. For example, the student who cannot tell the difference between superficial and thorough readings of a text may stop studying too soon, and drinkers who are good judges of blood alcohol levels should know when to hand the car keys over to someone else.

A problem with the language of private events is that control of these tacts is weak, because the verbal community has inconsistent access to their public correlates. For example, when someone reports a headache and leaves a social gathering, it is not clear whether the verbal response tacted a private stimulus or simply allowed the speaker to escape unwanted company. But verbal behavior does not ordinarily require that stimuli be simultaneously available to both speaker and listener. In fact, some of the important consequences of verbal behavior occur when the speaker tacts some event unavailable to the listener.

The existence of the language of private events implies its selection by natural contingencies, but even artificial selection seems to present a problem here because the inaccessibility of private events makes it difficult to discover and arrange appropriate contingencies. The solution is that any feasible account of the acquisition of the language of private events must appeal to their public accompaniments. For example, consider the vocabulary of remembering, forgetting, and never having known (cf. Wellman, 1990). We can often report whether we have forgotten something or never knew it. The distinction is not usually taught explicitly and yet natural contingencies are good enough for most children to learn it.

The artificial contingencies that follow suggest what to look for in natural contingencies (cf. Catania, 1991b). Assume that one day a child is given the task of learning names for a novel set of objects. The next day the child is asked to name those objects and a few new ones. Appropriate differential reinforcement can now be arranged for three different verbal responses: "I remembered" given successful naming; "I forgot" given one of the original objects and unsuccessful naming; and "I don't know" given one of the new objects and, necessarily, unsuccessful naming.

It would be misleading to seek the controlling variables of such reports inside the organism, because they are established on the basis of the public events available to the verbal community. Private correlates presumably exist, but studies of such correlates would not make them appropriate substitutes for the public correlates on which the relevant verbal behavior is based (similarly, studies of events in visual areas of the brain are not appropriate substitutes for studies of how contingencies establish the discriminative functions of visual stimuli).

Probabilistic stimulus class • *a stimulus class in which each member contains some subset of features but none is common to all members. Such classes do not have well-defined boundaries, though class members may have family resemblances. Examples include* natural concepts *and classes defined by reference to a* prototype.

"If the world could be divided into many separate things or events and if we could set up a separate form of verbal response for each, the problem would be relatively simple. But the world is not so easily analyzed, or at least has not been so analyzed by those whose verbal behavior we must study. In any large verbal repertoire we find a confusing mixture of relations between forms of response and forms of stimuli" (Skinner, 1957, p. 116).

When pigeons have been taught to discriminate between pictures that contain trees and those that do not (e.g., Herrnstein, Loveland, & Cable, 1976), no single feature of the stimuli determines which class a given picture falls into. Leaves, for example, are not a property of a tree that is bare in winter. Discriminations among such classes are sometimes called *natural concepts.* Such classes, sometimes also called *fuzzy sets,* do not have well-defined boundaries and class membership is sometimes ambiguous (Rosch, 1973). Class members may have family resemblances and membership may be defined by reference to a prototype, a typical member of the class defined in terms of a weighted average of all of the features of all of the class members. For example, more birds have feathers than have webbed feet; thus, a robin is more prototypical than a duck because it shares more features with other birds.

Problem solving • *constructing discriminative stimuli, either overtly or covertly, in situations involving novel contingencies; these stimuli may set the occasion*

for effective behavior (as when a verbal problem is converted into a familiar math-
ematical formula or a listing of options clarifies complex contingencies).

Productivity • *the generation of novel behavior through the recombination*
and/or reorganization of existing response classes.

Shaping, emergent behavior engendered by higher-order classes, and the recombination of existing classes (see ADDUCTION) are some of the ways in which
novel behavior can be generated. An exhaustive taxonomy of sources of novel behavior is probably not feasible.

Novel performances of porpoises have been shaped by reinforcing in each session some class of responses not reinforced in any previous session (Pryor, Haag,
& O'Reilly, 1969). Eventually porpoises began to emit responses in each new session that the experimenters had never seen before. But reinforcers are produced
by individual responses whereas properties such as novelty cannot be properties
of individual responses. A given response might be novel in the context of one sequence of past responses and stereotyped in the context of another. Thus, the differential reinforcement of novelty implies that contingencies can operate on properties of behavior manifested only over successive instances of responding
extended in time.

Reconstruction • *memory interpreted as a way of constructing rather than repli-*
cating what is remembered. Current accounts of remembering favor reconstruction
over reproduction (memory interpreted as the production of copies of past events).

Relational frame • *See EQUIVALENCE CLASS.*

Remembering • *responding occasioned by a stimulus no longer present. Re-*
membering is often discussed in terms of a metaphor of storage and retrieval, in
which storage *occurs when the stimulus is presented and* retrieval *when it is re-*
called. What is stored or retrieved, however, must be behavior with respect to the
stimulus rather than the stimulus itself. See also STORAGE and RETRIEVAL.

Short-term memory is remembering based on a single presentation of items
and without coding and/or rehearsal; it is of short duration (e.g., 10 to 20 s) and
limited to roughly five to nine items (historically, the span of immediate memory).
Long-term memory occurs after coding or rehearsal and/or multiple presentations
of items, and is therefore of unlimited duration and capacity. Remembering is also
classified in terms of what is remembered. Examples include *procedural memory*
(remembering operations or ways of doing things), often contrasted with declara-
tive memory (remembering facts); *autobiographical* or *episodic memory* (remembering specific events in one's life); *semantic memory* (remembering aspects of
one's language); and *spatial memory* (remembering paths and things located on
them).

A crucial feature of remembering is that what is remembered is behavior with
regard to events rather than the events themselves. For example, errors in remembering visually presented letters are typically based on acoustic rather than visual similarity, implying that the learner remembered their subvocalization rather
than their appearance (cf. CODING). Direct responses to events differ functionally from responses mediated by other behavior. This is why verbal classes distinguish between current and past stimuli: "A distinction must also be drawn between echoic behavior and the later reproduction of overheard speech. The answer

to the question *What did so-and-so say to you yesterday?* is not echoic behavior" (Skinner, 1957, p. 59; cf. TACT).

Representation • *a transformation of stimuli occurring either when an organism responds to the stimuli or later.*

It is important to note that in some accounts representations are copies, whereas in others they have arbitrary relations to stimuli (as when a visually presented letter is represented by its sound; cf. CODING and REMEMBERING). A representation in the latter sense can have behavioral dimensions.

Reproduction • *See RECONSTRUCTION.*

Retrieval • *in the memory metaphor of storage and retrieval, what the learner does at the time something is remembered. Retrieval is typically occasioned by a discriminative stimulus that sets the occasion for it (e.g., a recall instruction).*

Rule-governed behavior • *see VERBALLY GOVERNED BEHAVIOR and cf. CONTINGENCY-GOVERNED BEHAVIOR.*

Self-control • *a term derived from the colloquial vocabulary that applies to cases in which a relatively immediate small reinforcer is deferred in favor of a later large reinforcer or in favor of avoiding a later large aversive event, or in which a relatively immediate small aversive event is accepted when the acceptance leads to a later large reinforcer or avoids a later large aversive event. The opposite of self-control is called* impulsiveness.

Self-reinforcement • *a misnomer for the delivery of a reinforcer to oneself based on one's own behavior.*

In so-called self-reinforcement, the contingencies and establishing operations that affect the behavior that is purportedly reinforced are confounded with those that affect the delivery of the reinforcer to oneself. The organism that appears to self-reinforce must be able to discriminate behavior that qualifies for the reinforcer from behavior that does not; this behavior is more appropriately described in terms of the discrimination of properties of one's own behavior.

Signal detection analysis • *an analysis of stimulus detectability in terms of conditional probabilities of a response given a signal in noise or noise alone.*

A response given a signal in noise is a *correct detection* or *hit* and one to noise alone is a *false alarm;* no response given a signal in noise is a *miss* and given noise alone is a *correct rejection.* A measure of *sensitivity* to the signal derived from these measures is called d' (d-prime); another measure based on whether false alarms or misses are favored is called *bias.*

Specification • *the correspondence between a verbal response and what it tacts, when the verbal response occurs outside of the tact relation (as when a mand is said to specify its reinforcer even though the reinforcer is absent).*

The term is typically used in reference to effects on a listener, as when the listener's response to a word is said to share properties with responses to what the word ordinarily tacts. "A mand is characterized by the unique relationship between the form of the response and the reinforcement characteristically received in a given verbal community. It is sometimes convenient to refer to this relation by saying that a mand 'specifies' its reinforcement" (Skinner, 1957, p. 36).

Storage • *in the memory metaphor of storage and retrieval, what the learner does when something to be remembered is presented. Some of the behavior relevant to the stimulus that occurs at or after storage has been called* rehearsal.

Tact • *a verbal discriminative response (as when the verbal response* apple *in the presence of an apple is said to* tact *the apple). The tact captures stimulus control as it enters into verbal behavior. The tact relation includes only responding in the presence of or shortly after the tacted stimulus and therefore is not equivalent to naming or reference.*

In tacting, verbal behavior makes contact with events in the environment. Tacting is distinguished from naming by the presence of the tacted stimulus. An absent object can be named but not tacted. The major reason for the distinction is that responses to past events are only indirectly controlled by those events; they instead depend on our prior behavior with respect to those events (cf. REMEMBERING). "The tact is a relation, not merely a response, and in the absence of a controlling stimulus no relation can be established' (Skinner, 1957, p. 105). A difficulty with the terminology of tacting is that its usages are similar to those of referring and naming, so that it is all too easy to inappropriately substitute one of these terms for another (cf. NAMING, SPECIFICATION).

We tact inanimate objects, living things, activities, relations among stimuli, and innumerable other features of the environment. The wealth of available tacts may be taken as a remarkable feature of human language but should not obscure the simple relation that defines an instance of tacting. Sometimes the properties controlling a tact can be identified more with the speaker's own behavior than with any particular stimulus feature. For example, if a painting or musical composition occasions the word *marvelous,* this tact must depend on response generated in the speaker in addition to or (more likely) rather than physical properties common to these stimuli.

As with other verbal relations, tacting can combine with other verbal classes. Impure or distorted tacting may occur when stimulus control is affected by other variables such as conditions of deprivation (cf. MAND). Tacts can also be extended to new classes of events, as in metaphor or in word combination (e.g., the creation of *dishwasher* from *dish* and *wash*). It is not feasible to provide a detailed account here of the ways in which tacts can be modified and extended.

Tacting is not defined by parts of speech or other linguistic categories, so what of words that superficially seem to be tacts but cannot occur in the presence of what they name? Political units like states or nations and subject matters like biology or economics are not stimuli, and verbal contingencies can shape vocabularies of unicorns and elves as well as those of mice and men. Such entities must enter into verbal behavior in other ways; they do not exist in a form that can be tacted.

Textual behavior • *a formal verbal class in which a written stimulus occasions a corresponding vocal verbal response. The correspondence is defined by the one-to-one relation of verbal units (e.g., letters or words).*

In textual behavior, the arbitrary correspondence between verbal stimuli and responses is more obvious than in either echoic behavior or transcription, because the stimuli and the responses are in different modes. As visual stimuli, letters have no sound; as auditory stimuli, phonemes have no shape. These correspondences are so well established that their arbitrary nature is rarely noticed. As with transcription, textual behavior is usually taught explicitly, and some controversies in teaching are based on assumptions about the behavioral unit (letters, syllables, or entire words) appropriate to various stages of instruction.

As with other formal classes, textual behavior must be distinguished from other kinds of responses to written verbal stimuli. For example, if a sign says *STOP*, reading the word aloud is textual but stopping is not. In mature readers, textual responses become less important than other kinds of responses to written verbal stimuli. Vocal responses diminish in magnitude, become subvocal and perhaps disappear completely in proficient readers. Textual responses are at best only one part of reading: "Since the term 'reading' usually refers to many processes at the same time, the narrower term 'textual behavior' will be used" (Skinner, 1957, pp. 65–66). In fact, "pure" textual behavior implies reading without understanding, as in finding oneself in the middle of a page unable to say what has just been read. Reading for understanding must include other behavior along with or instead of vocal or subvocal speech.

Thinking • *behavior, especially covert and/or verbal behavior.*

The crucial point is that thinking is behavior and not some other sort of thing that produces behavior. "The speaker's own verbal behavior automatically supplies stimuli for echoic, textual, or intraverbal behavior, and these in turn generate stimuli for further responses . . . [but] thinking is more productive when verbal responses lead to specific consequences *and are reinforced because they do so*" (Skinner, 1957, p. 439). "The simplest and most satisfactory view is that thought is simply *behavior*—verbal or nonverbal, covert or overt. It is not some mysterious process responsible for behavior but the very behavior itself in all the complexity of its controlling relations" (Skinner, 1957, p. 449).

Tracking • *see VERBALLY GOVERNED BEHAVIOR.*

Transcription • *a formal verbal class in which a written stimulus occasions a corresponding written response. The correspondence is defined by the one-to-one relation of verbal units (e.g., letters or words) and not by similarity of visual features (e.g., a typed original may be transcribed in longhand, or vice versa).*

Just as vocal articulations are distinguished from the sounds they produce in echoic behavior, the movements involved in producing words are distinguished from the looks of the words in transcription. Echoic behavior depends on correspondences of verbal rather than acoustic properties, and transcription depends on correspondences of verbal rather than visual properties. A handwritten sentence may look very different from the print sentence from which it was transcribed, but its writing qualifies as transcription if the two sentences match in spelling, word order, and punctuation (transcription has also included written responses occasioned by vocal stimuli in some usages; cf. Skinner, 1957, and DICTATION-TAKING).

Units of transcription can vary from individual characters to extended passages. A child learns to copy single letters before whole words. In doing so, the child learns correspondences between arbitrary visual forms, such as printed and script or upper- and lowercase letters. There may be no visual property common to all forms of some letters.

Transcription must be distinguished from copying in the pictorial sense. A skilled Asian calligrapher may produce an accurate copy of a printed alphabetic text even though unfamiliar with the European language in which the text is written, but such copying would not be verbal. The distinction is based on the behavioral units in the two kinds of copying. The critical features of the calligrapher's copying are geometrical properties of the text letters and the marks produced by the calligrapher's strokes, whereas the critical features of transcription are the verbal units such as letters, words, and phrases in the source text and its copy. Visually the calligrapher's copy might resemble the original more closely than a handwritten copy by a speaker of the language, but only the latter counts as transcription.

Pure transcription, in the sense of transcription unaccompanied by other verbal behavior, probably occurs only rarely. A skilled typist, for example, may sometimes transcribe a text while not responding verbally to it in other ways, as when listening to a conversation elsewhere in the office; in such circumstances, the typist may be unable to report the text content even though it was accurately transcribed (cf. ECHOIC BEHAVIOR, TEXTUAL BEHAVIOR).

Verbal behavior • *any behavior involving words, without regard to modality (e.g., spoken, written, gestural). The units that function as words are determined by the practices of verbal communities. Cf. VOCAL BEHAVIOR.*
Verbal behavior involves both speaker behavior shaped by its effects on listener behavior and listener behavior shaped by its effects on speaker behavior. The field of verbal behavior is concerned with the behavior of individuals, and the functional units of their verbal behavior are determined by the practices of a verbal community (cf. LANGUAGE). Defining verbal behavior by its function distinguishes it from language, which is defined by structure. For example, the definitions, spellings, and pronunciations in dictionaries and the rules in a grammar book describe the standard structures of various verbal units in a language; thus, they summarize some structural properties of the practices of a verbal community. The verbal behavior of a speaker occurs in the context of those practices, but those maintaining practices, language, must not be confused with what they maintain, which is verbal behavior.

In a speech episode such as a simple two-person conversation, each person provides an audience for the other. It requires no laboratory experiment to demonstrate that a listener's response can maintain a speaker's talk. To this extent, we may say that the listener's responses reinforce the speaker's verbal behavior (cf. Greenspoon, 1955). One of the most general consequences of verbal behavior is that through it speakers change the behavior of listeners. Verbal behavior is a way of getting people to do things; it is "effective only through the mediation of other persons" (Skinner, 1957, p. 2).

But that is true for all social behavior. "If we make the further provision that the 'listener' must be responding in ways which have been conditioned *precisely in order to reinforce the behavior of the speaker,* we narrow our subject to what is traditionally recognized as the verbal field" (Skinner, 1957, p. 225). Some nonhuman behavior qualifies in a minimal way, as when a horse is taught to turn in a given direction in response to a touch of the reins to its neck (the appropriate turn then reinforces the trainer's behavior). But the crucial difference between the horse

and its trainer and a child as a language learner and an adult as a teacher is that
the latter relation soon becomes reciprocal: the child learns how to ask as well as
to answer and to say "thank you" as well as "you're welcome." Verbal behavior allows such reciprocal contingencies. In other words, to some extent all verbal cultures are mutual reinforcement societies (cf. Skinner, 1957, pp. 224–226).

Verbally governed behavior • *behavior, either verbal or nonverbal, under the
control of verbal antecedents. It has also been called rule-governed behavior or instruction-following. Cf. CONTINGENCY-GOVERNED BEHAVIOR.*

Contingencies operate for the following of instructions. To the extent that instruction-following is characterized by the correspondence between an instruction
and the listener's behavior and is therefore more than the following of a particular
instruction, it is a higher-order class of behavior (cf. Risley & Hart, 1968; see also
Baer, Detrich, & Weninger, 1988). Verbal antecedents may alter the functions of other stimuli (as when something neutral becomes a reinforcer after one is told it is
worth having). They may also produce instruction-following, but they do not qualify as discriminative stimuli if they do so even when they are no longer present.

Sometimes the contingencies that maintain instruction-following are social,
as when someone follows orders because of the socially imposed aversive consequences of not doing so. Sometimes they depend on the relation between verbal
formulations and nonverbal contingencies, as when someone successfully makes
a repair by following a service manual. The term *pliance* has been suggested for
instruction-following based on social contingencies and *tracking* for instruction-
following based on correspondences between verbal behavior and environmental
events (Zettle & Hayes, 1982).

The verbal behavior of one individual may provide verbal antecedents for another, but verbal antecedents may also be shaped or self-generated. Once verbal
contingencies have created correspondences between saying and doing so that saying is often accompanied by doing, other behavior may be modified by such shaped
or self-generated verbal behavior. In fact, it may be easier to change human behavior by shaping what someone says than by shaping what someone does (cf. Lovaas, 1964; Catania, Matthews, & Shimoff, 1990). One reason may be that human
nonverbal behavior is often verbally governed whereas human verbal behavior is
usually contingency-shaped (presumably because we do not often talk about the
variables that determine our own verbal behavior).

Because of the practical advantages of instruction, the verbal community
shapes instruction-following across a substantial range of activities throughout a
substantial portion of each individual's lifetime. This can happen only if the contingencies that maintain instruction-following are more potent than the natural
contingencies against which they are pitted (we need not ask people to do things
they do on their own). Thus, instructions may begin to override natural contingencies and people may do things when told to do them that they would never do
if only the natural contingencies operated.

A problem with verbally governed behavior is that we usually do not want
others to do what we say simply because we say it. A teacher who gives instructions to a child might prefer but cannot be confident that the natural contingencies
will eventually control the relevant behavior and make instructions unnecessary.
If the child always obeys instructions, the natural contingencies will never act on

the child's behavior; if the child disobeys, the natural consequences may enhance control by instructions on future occasions. Thus, if we try to teach by telling others what to do, we may reduce the likelihood that they will learn from the consequences of their own behavior. There is no easy solution. The immediacy and convenience of verbal instructions will sometimes but not always compensate for their longer-term effects on the listener's sensitivity to the consequences of behavior.

In many usages, verbally governed behavior has been called *rule-governed behavior.* In some of these usages, any verbal antecedent qualifies as a rule (as when one is told to do or say something). In others, rules are only those verbal antecedents that specify contingencies (as when one is told what will happen if one does or says something); such rules may alter the functions of other stimuli. Some rules are self-produced (the most effective verbal antecedents may be those one generates oneself). Whether rule-following occurs in the presence of a rule is often ambiguous (one may or may not repeat a rule to oneself at the time of following it); for that reason, rules do not necessarily qualify as discriminative stimuli even though they function as verbal antecedents (Schlinger & Blakely, 1987).

It is important to recognize that verbally governed behavior differs functionally from contingency-shaped behavior. "Rule and contingency are different kinds of things; they are not general and specific statements of the same thing" (Skinner, 1969, p. 144). More specifically,

> Rule-governed behavior is in any case never exactly like the behavior shaped by contingencies. . . . [Even] when topographies of response are very similar, different controlling variables are necessarily involved, and the behavior will have different properties. When operant experiments with human subjects are simplified by instructing the subjects in the operation of the equipment . . . , the resulting behavior may resemble that which follows exposure to the contingencies and may be studied in its stead for certain purposes, but the controlling variables are different, and the behaviors will not necessarily change in the same way in response to other variables. (Skinner, 1969, pp. 150–151)

Because of the varied definitions of "rule" both inside and outside the discipline, "rule-governed behavior" is one of the most problematic expressions in behavior-analytic terminology (cf. Horne & Lowe, 1996). In many cognitive usages, for example, rules are regarded not as instances of verbal behavior but rather as the internal codification of central processes or concepts; they therefore have no verbal status. Other locutions (e.g., "verbally governed behavior," as in this entry) do not pose the problems that arise from the varied definitions of "rule" and for that reason may be less prone to ambiguity and/or misinterpretation, but none has yet become well enough established to displace it.

Vocal behavior • *behavior of lips, tongue, and other structures, that modulates air flow and produces sound. Vocal behavior is not necessarily verbal. Cf. VERBAL BEHAVIOR.*

REFERENCES

Andronis, P. T. (1983). *Symbolic aggression by pigeons: Contingency coadduction.* Ph.D. dissertation, University of Chicago.

Baer, D. M., Peterson, R. F., & Sherman, J. A. (1967). The development of imitation by reinforcing behavioral similarity to a model. *Journal of the Experimental Analysis of Behavior, 10,* 405–416.

Baer, R. A. Detrich, R., & Weninger, J. M. (1988). On the functional role of the verbalization in correspondence training procedures. *Journal of Applied Behavior Analysis, 21,* 345–356.

Catania, A. C. (1989). Speaking of behavior. *Journal of the Experimental Analysis of Behavior, 52,* 193–196.

Catania, A. C. (1991a). Glossary. In I. H. Iversen & K. A. Lattal (Eds.), *Experimental analysis of behavior. Part 2* (pp. G1–G44). Amsterdam: Elsevier/North Holland.

Catania, A. C. (1991b). The phylogeny and ontogeny of language function. In N. A. Krasnegor, D. M. Rumbaugh, R. L. Schiefelbusch, & M. Studdert-Kennedy (Eds.), *Biological and behavioral determinants of language development* (pp. 263–285). Hillsdale, NJ: Erlbaum.

Catania, A. C. (1992). *Learning* (3rd ed.). Englewood Cliffs, NJ: Prentice–Hall.

Catania, A. C., & Cerutti, D. (1986). Some nonverbal properties of verbal behavior. In T. Thompson & M. D. Zeiler (Eds.), *Analysis and integration of behavioral units* (pp. 185–211). Hillsdale, NJ: Erlbaum.

Catania, A. C., Matthews, B. A., & Shimoff, E. H. (1990). Properties of rule-governed behaviour and their implications. In D. E. Blackman & H. Lejeune (Eds.), *Behavior analysis in theory and practice* (pp. 215–230). Hillsdale, NJ: Erlbaum.

Chomsky, N. (1959). A review of B. F. Skinner's *Verbal Behavior. Language, 35,* 26–58.

Crain, S. (1991). Language acquisition in the absence of experience. *Behavioral and Brain Sciences, 14,* 597–650.

Dinsmoor, J. A. (1983). Observing and conditioned reinforcement. *Behavioral and Brain Sciences, 6,* 693–728.

Epstein, R. (1981). On pigeons and people: A preliminary look at the Columban Simulation Project. *Behavior Analyst, 4,* 43–55.

Esper, E. A. (1973). *Analogy and association in linguistics and psychology.* Athens: University of Georgia Press.

Ferster, C. B. (1967). Arbitrary and natural reinforcement. *Psychological Record, 17,* 341–347.

Gewirtz, J. L., & Stingle, K. G. (1968). Learning of generalized imitation as the basis for identification. *Psychological Review, 75,* 374–397.

Greenspoon, J. (1955). The reinforcing effect of two spoken sounds on the frequency of two responses. *American Journal of Psychology, 68,* 409–416.

Hart, B., & Risley, T. R. (1955). *Meaningful differences in the everyday experience of young American children.* Baltimore: Brookes.

Hayes, S. C. (1994). Relational frame theory: A functional approach to verbal events. In: S. C. Hayes, L. J. Hayes, M. Sato, & K. Ono (Eds.), *Behavior analysis of language and cognition* (pp. 9–30). Reno, NV: Context Press.

Herrnstein, R. J., Loveland, D. H., & Cable, C. (1976). Natural concepts in pigeons. *Journal of Experimental Psychology: Animal Behavior Processes, 2,* 285–311.

Horne, P. J., & Lowe, C. F. (1996). On the origins of naming and other symbolic behavior. *Journal of the Experimental Analysis of Behavior, 65,* 185–241.

Johnson, K. R., & Layng, T. V. J. (1992). Breaking the structuralist barrier: Literacy and numeracy with fluency. *American Psychologist, 47,* 1475–1490.

Keller, F. S., & Schoenfeld, W. N. (1950). *Principles of psychology.* New York: Appleton–Century–Crofts.

Lakoff, G., & Johnson, M. (1980). *Metaphors we live by.* Chicago: University of Chicago Press.

Lashley, K. S. (1951). The problem of serial order in behavior. In L. A. Jeffress (Ed.), *Cerebral mechanisms in behavior: The Hixon Symposium* (pp. 112–146). New York: Wiley.

Lepper, M. R., Greene, D., & Nisbett, R. E. (1973). Undermining children's intrinsic interest with extrinsic reward: A test of the "overjustification" hypothesis. *Journal of Personality and Social Psychology, 28,* 129–137.

Lovaas, O. I. (1964). Cue properties of words: The control of operant responding by rate and content of verbal operants. *Child Development, 35,* 245–256.

Moerk, E. L. (1992). *A first language taught and learned.* Baltimore: Brookes.

Poulson, C. L., Kymissis, E., Reeve, K. F., Andreatos, M., & Reeve, L. (1991). Generalized vocal imitation in infants. *Journal of Experimental Child Psychology, 51,* 267–279.

Pryor, K. W., Haag, R., & O'Reilly, J. (1969). The creative porpoise: Training for novel behavior. *Journal of the Experimental Analysis of Behavior, 12,* 653–661.

Risley, T. R. (1977). The development and maintenance of language: An operant model. In B. C. Etzel, J. M. LeBlanc, & D. M. Baer (Eds.), *New developments in behavioral research* (pp. 81–101). Hillsdale, NJ: Erlbaum.

Risley, T. R., & Hart, B. (1968). Developing correspondence between the nonverbal and verbal behavior of preschool children. *Journal of Applied Behavior Analysis, 1,* 267–281.

Rosch, E. H. (1973). Natural categories. *Cognitive Psychology, 4,* 328–350.

Schlinger, H., & Blakely, E. (1987). Function-altering effects of contingency-specifying stimuli. *Behavior Analyst, 10,* 41–45.

Sidman, M. (1994). *Equivalence relations and behavior: A research story.* Boston: Authors Cooperative.

Sidman, M., Wynne, C. K., Maguire, R. W., & Barnes, T. (1989). Functional classes and equivalence relations. *Journal of the Experimental Analysis of Behavior, 52,* 261–274.

Skinner, B. F. (1938). *The behavior or organisms.* New York: Appleton Century.

Skinner, B. F. (1945). The operational analysis of psychological terms. *Psychological Review, 52,* 270–277.

Skinner, B. F. (1953). *Science and human behavior.* New York: Free Press.

Skinner, B. F. (1957). *Verbal behavior.* New York: Appleton–Century–Crofts.

Skinner, B. F. (1963). Behaviorism at fifty. *Science, 140,* 951–958.

Skinner, B. F. (1968). *The technology of teaching.* New York: Macmillan Co.

Skinner, B. F. (1969). An operant analysis of problem solving. In B. F. Skinner, *Contingencies of reinforcement* (pp. 133–157). New York: Appleton–Century–Crofts.

Skinner, B. F. (1989). The origins of cognitive thought. *American Psychologist, 44,* 13–18.

Vaughan, W., Jr. (1988). Formation of equivalence sets in pigeons. *Journal of Experimental Psychology: Animal Behavior Processes, 14,* 36–42.

Wales, R. (1986). Deixis. In P. Fletcher & M. Garman (Eds.), *Language acquisition* (2nd ed., pp. 401–428). London: Cambridge University Press.

Wellman, H. M. (1990). *The child's theory of mind.* Cambridge, MA: MIT Press.

Werker, J. F. (1989). Becoming a native listener. *American Scientist, 77,* 54–59.

Zettle, R. D., & Hayes, S. C. (1982). Rule-governed behavior: A potential theoretical framework for cognitive-behavioral therapy. In P. C. Kendall (Ed.), *Advances in cognitive-behavioral research and therapy* (Vol. 1, pp. 73–118). New York: Academic Press.

14

Self-Report Methods

Thomas S. Critchfield, Jalie A. Tucker, and Rudy E. Vuchinich

Human communication is unique among behavioral phenomena. No other type of behavior so readily serves both as a focus of study and as a measurement tool in the study of other behavior. Put simply, when we study human behavior, we have the luxury of asking our subjects what they know about it, and in many areas of psychology, this has been regarded as an offer too good to refuse. Unlike most areas of psychology, however, the experimental analysis of behavior matured primarily in the animal laboratory (Iversen & Lattal, 1991a,b; Skinner, 1996). This historical context may help to explain the trepidation with which operant researchers have faced the fact that humans regularly talk, write, and otherwise exchange information. Verbal capabilities have not been a central focus in the extension of the experimental analysis of behavior to human behavior (e.g., Oah & Dickinson, 1989), and consistent with this pattern, researchers have shown relatively little interest in data generated through verbal self-reports. In a recent 5-year survey of the *Journal of the Experimental Analysis of Behavior,* for example, self-report data provided a dependent measure in only about one-third of the studies conducted with human subjects.[1] In about 70% of these cases, self-reports served as a collateral measure rather than the primary dependent variable.

We hold that the experimental analysis of behavior can gain much from self-report data, and we acknowledge that the trustworthiness of such data remains a point of contention. Indeed, the history of disagreement about self-report methods is as long as the history of empirical psychology (e.g., Boring, 1953; Lieberman, 1975). On the one hand, self-report methods have been valued, despite possible

---

[1]This percentage excludes studies of infants and persons with developmental disabilities, who presumably are incapable of providing the same quality of information as normal adults, and omits the use of self-report data in subject screening, an application addressed briefly later in the chapter.

Thomas S. Critchfield, Jalie A. Tucker, and Rudy E. Vuchinich • Department of Psychology, Auburn University, Auburn, Alabama 36849.

Handbook of Research Methods in Human Operant Behavior, edited by Lattal and Perone. Plenum Press, New York, 1998.

limitations, because they may provide information where none is otherwise available, and some issues are deemed to be too important not to investigate. On the other hand, self-report methods have been distrusted in part because they are so often employed in situations where corroboration is unlikely.

Proponents and critics alike have tended to oversimplify the issues that should guide an investigator's choice and design of self-report methods. The present chapter defines some dimensions along which decisions must be made, but often stops short of making firm recommendations under the assumption that the optimal characteristics of self-report methods vary with the research problem (e.g., Babor, Brown, & Del Boca, 1990). Importantly, there currently exist no standards for self-report methods specific to the experimental analysis of behavior. Each human operant researcher therefore must decide whether to use self-report methods after considering the research environment, the nature of the phenomenon under study, and the methodological standards of the audience to which research results will be communicated, among other factors. When self-report methods are employed, they may require special justification, which could include empirical steps to establish the "operating characteristics" of the methods.

A unifying theme of this chapter is that any data collection method that is applied too casually will yield problematic data, and human operant researchers often have applied self-report methods too casually to yield readily interpretable results. Yet concerns regarding self-report data, although considerable, do not necessarily render them less informative than data collected in other ways. Much can be accomplished by combining self-report methods and the traditional methodological rigor that human operant researchers traditionally have applied to the study of nonverbal behavior.

We begin by illustrating the appeal of self-report methods. In the section below, we describe some of the many data collection opportunities that they provide. Subsequent sections discuss the basis of some concerns raised by self-report data, explore some factors that influence the plausibility of inferences based on self-report data, and outline some important steps in planning and utilizing self-report methods.

SOME ROLES OF SELF-REPORTS IN HUMAN OPERANT RESEARCH

Self-reports can provide information about a vast array of behavioral phenomena, many of which would be difficult to measure in other ways. Throughout this chapter, we discuss self-reports primarily as a form of behavioral assessment (Cone, 1978), providing data analogous to what might otherwise be obtained through mechanical measurement devices or external human raters. Psychometric instruments based on self-report (e.g., Cronbach, 1984) traditionally have not played an important role in human operant research and thus are not considered here. The present section describes a few of the uses of self-report methods in human operant studies.

Evaluating Verbal Mediation of Operant Performance

One of the more popular applications of self-report methods is to address the question of whether performance is guided by a subject's awareness of, or covert hypothesis about, experimental contingencies (Hineline & Wanchisen, 1989). The extent to which human operant performance is mediated verbally remains an important theoretical question (e.g., see Horne & Lowe, 1996, including peer commentary; Shimoff & Catania, Chapter 12; Wearden, 1988). Given that operant performance by nonverbal animals is unlikely to depend on the same type of mediation, some have regarded this as *the* essential question in evaluating the generality of operant principles to human behavior (e.g., Brewer, 1974; Speilberger & DeNike, 1966).

In some studies, self-report methods are employed in an attempt to create a real-time public record of "correlated hypothesizing" (Hineline & Wanchisen, 1989) or other covert verbal episodes. Typically, subjects are asked to speak aloud their thoughts, as they occur, during the course of an experiment (e.g., Wulfert, Dougher, & Greenway, 1991). In other studies, subjects participate in interviews, or answer written questions, on completion of a session, an experimental condition, or the entire experiment. In most cases, mediational variables have been regarded as freely occurring (Hineline & Wanchisen, 1989), but attempts have been made to bring them under experimental control, for example, by shaping overt verbal rule statements during the course of an experiment (e.g., Catania, Matthews, & Shimoff, 1982).

Detecting Unexpected Events within the Experiment

Some self-report data have less theoretical relevance but nevertheless are useful in good experimentation. Subjects often make spontaneous comments on entering or exiting the laboratory, and these can alert the investigator to equipment malfunctions, computer programming errors, or environmental variables likely to detract from performance, such as poor temperature control in the subject's room (e.g., Perone, 1988). In the early stages of a recent conditional discrimination study, for example, casual comments alerted investigators to the fact that subjects, who were charged with choosing among three comparison stimuli presented on a computer screen, sometimes selected a blank screen location that was supposed to have been inactivated (Innis, Lane, Miller, & Critchfield, in press).

Subject comments also can guide the development of experiments in positive ways. For example, in a master's thesis conducted at Auburn University, Aley[2] initially had difficulty maintaining orderly operant performance using commonly employed consequences such as points, money, and lottery chances. Noting that subjects routinely complained that the experimental task was boring and frequently asked how soon their participation would end, Aley revised the procedure

---

[2]Aley, K. R. (1996). *The efficacy of stimuli traditionally used as reinforcers in adult human operant research.* Unpublished master's thesis, Auburn University.

to make session-time reduction a main consequence of responding. Orderly data followed. Thus, subject comments promoted speculation about reinforcer efficacy, which in turn influenced the evolution of the research project.

Monitoring Extraexperimental Variables

Human operant studies often reveal greater intersubject and intrasubject variability than comparable animal research, and this variability is a major obstacle in attempts to establish general behavioral principles based on the data of only a few subjects (e.g., Baron, Perone, & Galizio, 1991; Bernstein, 1988; Branch, 1991; Kollins, Newland, & Critchfield, 1997). Variability sometimes is attributed to variations in subject learning histories or to their contemporary experiences outside the experiment (e.g., Branch, 1991), but neither of these factors is routinely evaluated in human operant research (e.g., Wanchisen & Tatham, 1991). For practical reasons, it is difficult to involve human subjects in the kind of extended experimentation that Sidman (1960) and others have recommended to resolve unexplained variability. And even when repeated observations of individual human subjects are possible, investigators normally observe only a small portion of each subject's day, and thus have limited information regarding extraexperimental variables that might influence experimental performance (Bernstein, 1988). What cannot be controlled, however, potentially can be measured, including through self-reports.

A recent laboratory study of caffeine reinforcement (Evans, Critchfield, & Griffiths, 1994) illustrates how self-reported subject information can shed light on seemingly disorderly data. The left panel of Figure 14.1 provides no insight into the reasons why blind preference for caffeine over placebo capsules ranged from 38 to 100% in 11 moderate caffeine users. The right panel, however, shows that (with the exception of Subject K) preference was a negatively accelerating function of self-reported dietary (i.e., extraexperimental) caffeine intake, as measured through a detailed survey completed daily for 1 week prior to the study. The self-reports do not explain individual differences in extraexperimental caffeine consumption, but they do provide information about the relation between caffeine reinforcement and prior caffeine exposure. Previous studies had shown reliable caffeine reinforcement only in heavy caffeine users, but the Evans et al. self-report data suggest graded prior exposure effects that could place heavy and moderate caffeine users on the same continuum of measurement.

Variables worth monitoring in studies of basic behavioral processes include those likely to have global effects on performance (e.g., sleep patterns, alcohol and drug consumption, and interpersonal, academic, or job-related stressors) and those likely to influence specific aspects of the study (e.g., a subject's financial situation, which could influence the reinforcing properties of point consequences exchangeable for money). The stability or variability of these factors during a prestudy period may suggest grounds for selecting individuals for further study. Variability encountered during the study might help to explain within-session or between-subject variability, and thus suggest a course for subsequent investigation.

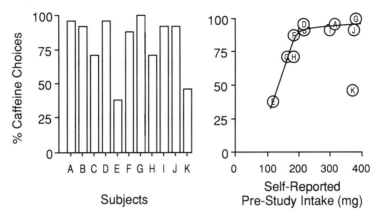

FIGURE 14.1. Percent caffeine (versus placebo) choices by 11 moderate caffeine consumers in blind tests. The left panel shows only the choice data. The right panel shows choice percentages as a function of self-reported dietary caffeine intake during the week preceding the study. Data replotted from Evans et al. (1994), Tables 1 and 2.

Measuring Behavior in Field Settings

As behavior principles are established with increasing precision in the laboratory, external validation efforts will gain in importance, particularly in the form of studies aimed at evaluating fundamental processes in natural settings. Some extensions already have occurred in moderately constrained environments where experimental manipulation is possible. For example, one study found that the performance of students on variable-interval schedules of reinforcement in a classroom setting (Mace et al., 1988) conformed to predictions based on the laboratory-derived concept of behavioral momentum (Nevin, 1992). Other studies have used naturalistic observation to evaluate the role of basic reinforcement processes in less controlled situations such as college basketball games (Mace, Lalli, Shea, & Nevin, 1992) and naturally occurring mother–infant verbal interactions (Moerk, 1990).

Unfortunately, investigators may have limited access to many of the everyday behaviors on which laboratory-based principles presumably operate, leaving self-reports as an obvious alternative source of information. For example, drug-taking, which can be conceptualized within the frameworks of behavioral choice and behavioral economics (L. Green & Kagel, 1996; Vuchinich, 1995; Vuchinich & Tucker, 1988), often is impractical to observe in natural environments. Because self-report methods relevant to naturalistic alcohol consumption are relatively well developed (e.g., Sobell & Sobell, 1990a,b), they can be employed to evaluate the generality of choice and economic models, at least at a qualitative level. Although self-report error cannot be ruled out when results based on self-report data diverge from laboratory-based predictions, another possibility is that field extensions will suggest new variables worthy of investigation and thus allow laboratory researchers to expand their models of behavior (Mace, 1994).

Analyzing Verbal Behavior as a Primary Subject Matter

In each of the previous examples, self-reports are suggested as a means of measurement, but self-reports also can be viewed as the behavior under investigation. For example, self-reports can be a convenient medium in which to study the effects of punishment or drugs on verbal behavior (Critchfield, 1993b, 1996b). Additionally, a few studies have made self-reports explicitly the response class of interest, examining the correspondence between self-reports and public behavior, both past (e.g., Critchfield, 1993a, 1994; de Freitas Ribeiro, 1989) and future (e.g., R. Baer & Detrich, 1990). Other studies have examined how well self-reports predict the effects of putative reinforcers (e.g., Bernstein & Michael, 1990), or describe correlations between responses and external events (e.g., Neunaber & Wasserman, 1986). Still others have considered what self-reports, in the form of hypothetical judgments about choice situations, may tell us about the effects of delay and probability on reinforcer efficacy (e.g., Myerson & Green, 1995; Rachlin, Raineri, & Cross, 1991). Because much remains to be learned about the behavior of self-reporting, each of these research avenues may contribute to the development of self-report measurement, and thus further the understanding of basic behavioral processes.

THE BASIS OF CONCERNS ABOUT SELF-REPORT DATA

Although self-report methods can have many applications in human operant research, there are legitimate concerns about the quality of data they produce. Certainly some information is most easily obtained through self-reports, but no method can be defended solely in terms of the limitations of its alternatives. The planning, execution, and justification of self-report methods all require cognizance of factors likely to influence the degree of measurement error (e.g., Babor, Stephens, & Marlatt, 1987). Sources of error become easier to anticipate when self-reports are regarded both as one type of observational method and as one type of behavior. The present section discusses these two perspectives, and concludes with some special considerations that accompany self-reports about private events.

Self-Reports in Methodological Context

Direct observation methods based on machines or trained observers typically are viewed as a relatively direct and objective approach to measurement, whereas self-report methods often are characterized as producing indirect and subjective data (e.g., Cone, 1978). This view obscures the fact that all forms of observation are indirect in the sense that they require an intermediate step between the occurrence of a target event and the production of data records. In "direct" observation, machines or external observers transduce the events of interest, whereas in self-report methods, the individual who emits target responses also transduces them. At issue, therefore, is not the extent to which different forms of observation are direct or objective, but rather the extent to which the transduction process is understood and accepted by the experimenter.

The operating characteristics of any transducer reflect an interaction between prior conditions and current circumstances. Machines are deemed trustworthy for data collection purposes because of faith in the prior conditions (e.g., manufacturing standards) that allow them to serve as transducers. Researchers do not routinely corroborate the readings of their measurement devices (e.g., devote several mechanical counters to measuring the same behavior) because the likelihood of correspondence with measured events is established in the design and manufacturing of the devices. The training of external observers serves roughly the same purpose as the controlled manufacturing of recording devices, although human observers are more sensitive to vagaries of a local environment and thus require more frequent calibration than do machines (e.g., Reid, 1982).

Investigators who distinguish between "objective" and "subjective" observations appear to refer to different levels of certainty about the prior conditions and local variables that affect a transducer's operating characteristics. In this sense, self-reports may differ from other forms of observation in degree, but not in kind. Dichotomies such as "objective" versus "subjective" therefore add nothing to our understanding of self-report methods. Placing all recording methods on a single continuum reminds us that when the conditions are wrong, any form of observation, no matter how venerable or "objective," can fail. For example, most experienced investigators have encountered systematic error in a trusted apparatus or external observer, and even the most reliable equipment operates properly only within certain tolerances of temperature, electrical current, and so forth.

Importantly, under optimal conditions, any form of observation can produce scientifically useful data. There is no a priori reason, based strictly on criteria of directness or objectivity, to exclude self-report methods from the arsenal of observational methods. Self-reports *can* be accurate (Sobell & Sobell, 1990b; Vuchinich, Tucker, & Harlee, 1988). Just as in the case of mechanical or external human observers, at issue is how well factors likely to influence the quality of self-reported information are known and have been controlled.

Self-Reports in Behavioral Context

Self-reports form the basis for one type of observational method, but at a more fundamental level they are also a type of behavior, consisting of two primary components, a referent event (e.g., a response or the relation between responses and contingencies) and the act of reporting.[3] Viewing the report–referent relation as an interaction between two response classes underscores an important source of uncertainty about self-report data. When responses are recorded by specialized apparatus, the events to be observed and explained operate primarily in one domain (behavior), whereas the transducer of these events operates primarily in others (e.g.,

[3]Some theoretical perspectives view the self-report as consisting of three components: the referent, a private act of detecting the referent event, and a public act of making the self-report. Theoretical arguments aside, the approach of considering self-observation and self-reporting separately may have heuristic value to the extent that it reminds us that different variables can influence the stimulus control and response strength of self-reports. The distinction can even be expressed quantitatively, as in the case of signal-detection analyses that estimate the discriminability and bias of self-reports (e.g., Critchfield, 1993a; Hosseini & Ferrell, 1982).

physics). Interpreting the output of devices that transduce behavior is relatively straightforward because the scientific and technical domains in which they operate are fairly well understood. By contrast, self-observers (and external human observers) operate in the same scientific and technical domain as the referents they are used to measure. Both referents and reports are behavior, and attempts to use one response pattern to transduce another represent a bootstrapping operation that is feasible only when the investigator's understanding and control of the "transducing response" (in this case, the self-report) exceeds that of the referent response. Other sciences have employed this bootstrapping process successfully, and there are notable precedents in psychology for using one well-understood response pattern as an assay for the study of another (e.g., Estes & Skinner, 1941; Overton, 1987). It is arguable whether current understanding of the behavior of making a self-report is sufficiently advanced to support the widespread application of self-report methods, but the requisite bootstrapping is, in principle, possible.

When self-reports and the referents important to human operant research both are viewed as behavior, there is no a priori reason to expect a naturally close correspondence between them. Although both report and referent presumably are governed by the same fundamental behavioral principles, the variables controlling them at any given moment may not be identical (e.g., Skinner, 1945, 1957). As a result, referent responses can occur without occasioning self-reports, and self-reports may not be influenced by their putative referents. Correspondence between the two should emerge as a product of circumstance and experience (Skinner, 1957; see also D. Baer, 1982), meaning that self-reports are intrinsically neither accurate nor inaccurate. Rather, a variety of factors can place self-reports anywhere along a continuum whose endpoints reflect perfect positive and negative covariation with the putative referent and whose midpoint reflects an absence of covariation.

Because the relation between referent and report is structurally—and probably functionally—similar to that of discriminative stimulus and operant response (Bem, 1967; Skinner, 1957), the literature on discriminated operants and stimulus control may suggest classes of factors likely to influence report–referent correspondence. The first two columns of Table 14.1 illustrate some factors that can influence stimulus control, including: features of the discriminative stimulus, competing sources of stimulus control, consequences for emitting the discriminated operant, learning histories, and drugs and other physiological variables. If these examples portray a coherent theme, it is that stimulus control is multiply determined and therefore, in some sense, always complex (e.g., Harrison, 1991; Mackay, 1991; Rilling, 1977).

Self-reports have not been studied systematically as discriminated operants (e.g., Critchfield & Perone, 1990), but the right column of Table 14.1 suggests that they may be subject to some of the same influences as other behavior under discriminative control. Whether specific effects in the basic stimulus control literature map perfectly onto human verbal self-reports is less important than the general implication that it would be unwise to underestimate the complexity of control over even "simple" self-reports. Thus, the operating characteristics of self-observers may be difficult to delineate without empirical investigation of report–referent correspondence.

TABLE 14.1
Some Sources of Variance in Stimulus Control

Source of variance in stimulus control	Examples from the stimulus control literature	Possible examples from the self-report literature
Characteristics of discriminative stimulus	Pigeons detecting long versus short time intervals overreport short intervals (Spetch & Wilkie, 1983).	Pigeons detecting their own long versus short response sequences overreport short sequences (Fetterman & McEwan, 1989).
	Bias in psychophysical judgments varies with frequency of stimulus presentation (Craig, 1976).	Bias in self-reports varies with frequency of referent-response occurrence (Critchfield, 1994).
Competing stimulus control	Pigeons' responding reinforced in presence of a compound (color plus shape) stimulus sometimes is controlled by color, sometimes by shape (Reynolds, 1961).	Humans' self-reports about the success of choices under time pressure sometimes are more influenced by response accuracy, sometimes more influenced by response speed (Critchfield, 1993a).
Consequences for making "reporting" response	Differential reinforcement promotes bias in psychophysical judgments (McCarthy & Davison, 1981).	"Socially desirable" referents tend to be overreported, and "socially undesirable" referents tend to be underreported (Nelson, 1977).
Learning history	Stimulus control varies as a function of presence of, and type of exposure to, differential contingencies involving negative stimuli during training (Rilling, 1977).	Japanese students tend to underestimate, and American students tend to overestimate, their relatively modest academic performance (Stevenson, Chen, & Lee, 1993), possibly as a result of differential child-rearing practices with respect to individual achievement (Tobin, Wu, & Davidson, 1989).
Physiological variables	Alcohol decreases discriminability in visual signal-detection (Jansen, de Gier, & Slangen, 1985).	Diazepam may decrease the discriminability of self-reports about match-to-sample performance (Critchfield, 1993b).

Self-Reports about Private Events

A special kind of uncertainty arises in the case of self-reports about private events that are, in principle, observable only by a single individual. If one assumes that the operating characteristics of any self-observer are the product of experience, then one must ask how these characteristics became established with respect to private events. Skinner (1957) discussed this problem at some length, noting as a point of departure that accurate descriptions of public events are easy to establish and maintain in everyday social interactions because "teacher" and "pupil" share equal access to the same events.[4] The resulting social contingencies have such robust and reliable effects, in fact, that researchers and laypersons alike rarely bother to verify certain kinds of easily corroborated self-reports, such as those of

[4]Skinner (1957) can be viewed more broadly as proposing that the development of self-knowledge depends on the involvement of aspects of the self in three-term operant contingencies. In this respect, Skinner's view is consistent with that of a variety of theorists who assume that self-observation emerges in part because of environmental demands (e.g., Gibson, 1993; Povinelli, 1994; Tomasello, 1993). We acknowledge, however, that all discussions of private events impinge on complex epistemological issues that cannot be adequately addressed here. In the present context, sources that include a critique of Skinner's approach to private events provide a useful point of departure for the interested reader (e.g., Kvale & Griness, 1967; Natsoulas, 1978, 1988; Rachlin, 1985; Zuriff, 1985).

age, educational status, or gender. By contrast, establishing accurate self-reports of inner events is a conundrum for the social community, which lacks access to the relevant events and thus must rely on likely public correlates as a basis for teaching. For example, a father may state, "That hurts," and accept thematically related self-reports, when a child shows tissue damage or falls in a manner that the parent knows has been painful for him in the past. A peer may say, "You must feel sad," and accept similar self-reports, when a child has just experienced events like those that have made the peer feel sad. Importantly, though, these public correlates are imperfect guides to the occurrence and characteristics of inner events. As a result, naturally occurring human introspective abilities have a somewhat uncertain genesis compared with the performance of precisely manufactured measurement devices or well-trained human raters of public behavior. Put another way, their operating characteristics are more difficult to estimate.

THE VALUE OF SELF-REPORTS AS DATA

The value of a data set depends on the quality of inferences that it supports about events the data are believed to represent. Knowledge of operating characteristics therefore is an essential ingredient in judgments about whether data correspond to target events. In the case of self-report data, strength of inference will reflect the degree of correspondence that can be assumed to exist between self-report and reference (e.g., Ericsson & Simon, 1984; Lieberman, 1975). This process of inference, as applied to basic behavioral research, differs in at least three ways from approaches often employed elsewhere in psychology. First, the goal of some clinical studies may be the prediction of a broad syndrome, consisting of many types of behavior, rather than quantification of behavior in a single functional response class. In such cases, it matters less whether the events implicated by self-reports actually occurred as described than whether a particular type of self-report reliably predicts clinically important outcomes. Second, in some studies an important variable, and thus the "referent" of self-reports, may be an abstract construct rather than a behavioral episode (e.g., Cronbach, 1984). In such cases, the self-report is viewed as valuable when it "agrees with diverse manifestations of the construct, and does so in a way consistent with the investigator's model of the construct" (Baker & Brandon, 1990, p. 38). Third, in some clinical research, individual self-reports bear no obvious relationship to a particular target variable until transformed in some way (e.g., via a scale summing a collection of responses, as in the scoring of the MMPI). In such cases, it is difficult to assume a specific referent at all (Baker & Brandon, 1990).

If self-reports bear similarity to discriminated nonverbal operants (Table 14.1), then it is safe to assume that the degree of correspondence between self-reports and their referents will vary across situations. Common sense suggests that this general rule holds even for seemingly straightforward self-reports. For example, self-reports of age, educational status, and gender—normally uncontroversial in the context of human operant research—may require corroboration if one is, respectively, a bartender, employer, or patron of an establishment frequented by transvestites. Researchers considering the use and interpretation of self-report data must discriminate situations in which correspondence is likely to be high from those in which it is not. The present section examines some potential sources of guidance in this process.

Although the term *validation* has many connotations, it is used here in the relatively straightforward sense of establishing the degree of correspondence between self-reports and their referents that can be expected under a given set of circumstances. The clearest way to evaluate the operating characteristics of any transducer is to measure them (for elaboration, see the concluding section of this chapter) in a process of *empirical validation*. But investigators often employ self-report methods when the referent cannot be readily corroborated, as in the measurement of private events or overt behavior not readily accessible to the investigator. When report–referent correspondence cannot be empirically established during the main study, it is sometimes estimated through a process that we will call *theoretical validation*.

Theoretical Validation

Theoretical validation is an interpretative process that begins with assumptions about the intrinsic characteristics of self-awareness, referents, and report–referent correspondence. These assumptions often suggest similarities between self-observation and other better-understood processes. For example, the broad assumption that the reporting of an event depends on memory processes (e.g., Ericsson & Simon, 1984; Nisbett & Wilson, 1977; Wearden, 1988) brings to bear on self-reports the vast empirical memory literature. One implication would be that, because many factors can render memory less complete with the passage of time, self-reports should be collected as soon as possible after the occurrence of the referent event, or generated with queries associating the referent event in time with other readily remembered events (e.g., Nurco, 1985; Sudman & Bradburn, 1982; Vuchinich et al., 1988).

Part of the uncertainty surrounding theoretical validation efforts is that core assumptions can vary widely, and at times there may be no dependable means of distinguishing among them. Conflicting assumptions create problems for theoretical validation efforts of all types, but the difficulties are magnified when self-reports describe private events. Depending on the theorist, for example, private events are held to be generally accessible to self-observation (e.g., Pekala, 1991), accessible to self-observation only under selected conditions (e.g., Ericsson & Simon, 1984; Skinner, 1957), or generally inaccessible to self-observation (e.g., Nisbett & Wilson, 1977).

When corroboration is impossible in principle, accepting of logical premises regarding private events becomes a matter of personal preference, or at least a matter open to debate (White, 1988). As a result, theoretical approaches to validation can admit two special forms of uncertainty. The first arises when the validity of self-reports presumably is determined by variables that, like private referents themselves, cannot be observed by an experimenter. For example, Ericsson and Simon (1984) proposed that self-reports can accurately describe only events that are represented verbally in short-term memory. Events that are not verbally represented in short-term memory can be described, but only through well-intended, and fallible, speculation and reconstruction rather than "direct" self-observation (see also Nisbett & Wilson, 1977). Unfortunately, cognitive scientists do not always agree on what events reside in short-term memory, are verbally represented, or are inherently accessible to awareness (e.g., Intons-Peterson, 1993). Moreover, a substantial amount of research on self-awareness and apparently nonconscious cognitive processes has accumulated in the past decade (e.g., Fox, 1995; Nelson, 1992; Roediger, 1997), and it remains to be seen whether these findings require a reappraisal of Ericsson and Simon's basic position.

A second source of uncertainty occurs when theoretical proposals about self-observation invoke principles believed to apply only to self-observation or to certain kinds of private referents (e.g., Nisbett & Wilson, 1977; D. Rosenthal, 1986). These phenomenon-specific principles would appear to preclude the application of more general principles to the development and interpretation of self-report methods. For example, if at least some of the processes involved in observing and recalling one's thoughts and actions are idiosyncratic (e.g., Nisbett & Wilson, 1977), then it would seem risky to design self-report procedures based on the findings of memory experiments not involving self-observation.

Empirical Validation

It makes sense to adopt a theoretically coherent approach to self-report methods (e.g., the earlier section on Self-Reports in Behavioral Context involves a speculative extension of operant principle to the analysis of self-reports). But because theoretical validation efforts require substantial faith in underlying assumptions, it should be productive to seek empirical validation whenever possible. All efforts at empirical validation involve comparing self-reports with other measures believed to provide similar information. Yet self-report data are collected most often when other data sources appear to be lacking. The challenge of empirical validation, therefore, lies in identifying meaningful standards with which to compare self-reports. At least four useful strategies can be identified.

Comparing Self-Reports with Different Measures of the Same Referent Behavior

This approach bears similarity to the "concurrent validity" stage of developing psychometric instruments, in which the results obtained from one standardized questionnaire are defended in terms of their correspondence to the results of another commonly used questionnaire that presumably measures the same construct. For purposes of fundamental behavioral research, self-reports can be compared to relatively concrete measures, not involving self-reports, that are believed to covary with the referent event. Self-reports about whether dreams have occurred, for example, usually are assumed to be trustworthy because they correlate strongly with rapid eye movement sleep, another phenomenon that is plausibly related to dreaming (Dement & Kleitman, 1957). Similarly, in several field investigations of alcohol consumption in the elderly, good correspondence has been found between subject self-reports and the reports of persons who know them well, over recall periods of up to 3 months (e.g., Samo, Tucker, & Vuchinich, 1989; Tucker, Vuchinich, Harris, Gavornik, & Rudd, 1991). In related research with inpatient alcoholics (described in Vuchinich et al., 1988), subject recall of daily alcohol consumption during the year prior to hospitalization was significantly correlated with collateral reports of subject drinking over the same interval, and with biochemical indices of heavy drinking assessed at the time of hospital admission. These studies helped to identify conditions under which self-report measures could be applied, with relative confidence, in research on drinking practices over extended periods in natural environments.

The value of comparing self-reports with other types of measures depends in part on how clearly the comparison measures are related to referent events of interest. For example, measures of energy balance have proven useful in evaluating the self-reports of food consumption by obese persons because energy balance is unambiguously related to caloric intake (Bandini, Schoeller, Cyr, & Dietz, 1990). By contrast, response latency, which has been used to evaluate self-reports of the amount of cognitive effort expended (Ericsson & Simon, 1984), could be influenced by factors other than the expenditure of cognitive effort, including response strength, motivation, and stimulus control (e.g., Baron & Menich, 1985; Baron, Menich, & Perone, 1983).

Seeking Converging Evidence from Several Types of Self-Reports

One way to minimize reliance on the properties of any single comparison measure is to incorporate a variety of thematically related measures into the same investigation. One appealing approach employed in some human behavioral pharmacology studies, particularly those designed to estimate the reinforcing properties of drugs (e.g., Evans, Critchfield, & Griffiths, 1991; Roache & Griffiths, 1989; see also Higgins & Hughes, Chapter 18), involves gathering information from the same subjects using several different measures in at last three categories. First, standardized questionnaires produce factor analytically derived scales that purport to measure internal states. Some, such as the Profile of Mood States (POMS; McNair, Lorr, & Droppelman, 1971), include scales that may suggest global pleasant or unpleasant effects of drugs (e.g., depression-dejection and vigor). Others, such as the Addiction Research Center Inventory (ARCI; Haertzen, 1966), include scales that have been demonstrated to distinguish the effects of specific drug classes, some of which (e.g., the "euphoria" scale) are considered to be closely related to reinforcing properties. Second, custom-designed symptom checklists allow subjects to endorse statements or adjectives created to fit the specific needs of the study. Some items (such as ratings of liking) have obvious face validity in research related to reinforcing effects, whereas others are intended to assess more specific pleasant and unpleasant sensations specific to the study drugs (e.g., relaxed, lightheaded, dizzy, energetic). Third, when the subjects are experienced drug users, pharmacological identification questionnaires allow them to characterize a drug effect as similar to effects produced by other drugs that they have taken, many of which will have known reinforcing properties.

Knowledge of the operating characteristics of any single self-report measure becomes relatively unimportant when several measures provide analogous results. For example, it seems safe to predict that a drug will be used recreationally when a variety of self-reports indicate that it elevates reinforcement-related scales on standardized instruments like the POMS and ARCI; when it is well-liked; and when it produces many presumably pleasant internal effects, especially sensations like those created by other drugs known to be commonly abused (Evans et al., 1991). Confidence in this conclusion would be strengthened further if the self-reports agreed with data obtained in other ways. For example, in choice procedures, the same subjects might prefer the target drug over placebo or other drugs of known reinforcing properties (e.g., Troisi, Critchfield, & Griffiths, 1993), and epidemiological data might indicate that the target drug is commonly stolen from pharmacies or involved in hospital admissions for drug overdose.

Calibrating Self-Reports at Times Other Than the Main Study

Sometimes, as in field research, the research goals may include studying behavior that is public in principle but difficult to measure for practical reasons (like naturalistic drug use). In such cases, it may be possible to first study self-reporting under controlled conditions in which corroboration is possible. This preliminary experimentation, involving the same reference events as in the main experiment, can provide empirical guidance about the circumstances under which self-reports are likely to be accurate. Moreover, if the subjects are the same ones to be used in the main investigation, this effort could include training self-observers in much the same way that external human observers are trained.

Calibrating Self-Reports with Well-Understood Alternative Referent Behaviors

Even when self-reports of the referent behavior cannot be directly corroborated, it may be possible to establish the operating characteristics of presumably related classes of self-reports. Consider the approach used in a study designed to explore whether self-reports could provide a means of distinguishing among untrained arbitrary stimulus relations that all emerged, equally accurately, following conditional discrimination training in a stimulus equivalence paradigm (Lane & Critchfield, 1996). Self-reports about the emergent relations could not be directly corroborated because these emergent relations, by definition, involve novel stimulus combinations that subjects have never encountered prior to tests for stimulus equivalence. Thus, there was no way to establish in advance what an accurate self-report of an emergent relation should look like (this was, in fact, the research question). Instead, during a preliminary training phase, subjects learned to make accurate, unbiased self-reports about responses on typical conditional discrimination trials and on "catch" trials, in which no correct response option was available. Then, in a phase that included no self-reports, subjects acquired the conditional discriminations that were prerequisite to the formation of equivalence classes. Finally, the self-report procedure was reinstated during tests for the expected emergent relations, in which subjects received no response-contingent feedback or reinforcement. Importantly, these tests also included some catch trials and some involving previously trained conditional relations. Thus, both in a preliminary phase and during the equivalence test, self-reports about trained relations and catch trials provided a standard of comparison against which to evaluate the self-reports of emergent relations. As a result, it could be readily determined whether subjects described emergent relations more like trained performances, which were virtually always correct, or more like catch trial performances, which could produce only incorrect responses.

The strategy just described is essentially that employed in drug discrimination research (e.g., Overton, 1987), which can be loosely thought of as a means for generating self-reports about the internal sensations produced by drugs. In the typical procedure, one type of response is reinforced following administration of a dose of a training drug, and another is reinforced following administration of a pharmacologically inactive placebo (or in some studies, a different drug). Subsequent generalization tests expose subjects to new drugs (e.g., Preston, Bigelow, Bickel, & Liebson, 1989) or different doses of the training drug (e.g., Rush, Critchfield, Troisi, & Griffiths, 1995). Of interest is whether these other compounds and doses will reliably occasion responding similar to what is occasioned by the drug stimuli used in training. Importantly, investigators may know nothing directly of the specific internal stimuli associated with any of the drugs. They can evaluate performance in the generalization tests only against the standard of comparison provided by responding occasioned by the training compounds.

Benefits and Risks of Empirical Validation

The strength of the empirical validation steps just described is that circumstances promoting good correspondence are empirically determined rather than assumed. An additional advantage is that, if the same subjects participate in both the validation process and the main portion of the experiment, the validation process can also serve to reduce reactive effects of the self-report procedure during the main experiment. Two obvious risks of empirical validation effort bear mention here as well. First, no two measurements are conducted under precisely the same conditions, and any differences between the validation process and the main study in terms of setting, procedure, or subjects could influence self-reports. Second, assumptions about the validity of self-report data in an uncorroborated main experiment are only as strong as patterns in the validation data. If self-reports during the validation process prove to be less than perfectly accurate, then some degree of uncertainty is introduced into the measurement of the main experiment.

Generalizing from Other Research Programs

Empirical validation efforts are likely to be laborious and time-consuming. As a result, researchers may look instead to other research programs for insights into self-report accuracy, under the assumption that effects identified in one research context will generalize to others. Available resources include vast literatures on interview and questionnaire methods in social psychology, forensic psychology, behavioral assessment, sociology, clinical psychology, marketing, medicine, and other fields. These literatures suggest general patterns of influence on self-reports by

TABLE 14.2
Some Variables Found to Influence Self-Reports in Two Large-Scale Reviews
of Survey and Questionnaire Literature

Type of variable	Examples of possible effects on self-reports
Individual differences	• Different individuals may show different patterns of accuracy across several types of related self-reports. • Elderly subjects may provide less detailed self-reports than younger subjects.
Type of referent behavior	• Socially desirable and undesirable responses tend to be over- and underreported, respectively. • Salient (personally important) referent responses may be more accurately reported.
Frequency of referent behavior	• Very frequent or infrequent referent responses may be over- or underreported, respectively.
Time since referent behavior occurred	• More recent responses may be reported more accurately. • Memory may be improved by specifying salient boundary events between which targeted referent responses may have occurred.
Contingencies on accuracy	• Accuracy may be higher when respondents believe reports will be corroborated.
Method used to generate self-reports	• Interviews may introduce a higher probability of experimenter effects than questionnaires. • Unstructured interviewer probing may bias self-reports or prompt "reconstructed" reports of forgotten or unobserved events. • Less information may be obtained when more than one interviewer or observer is present. • Questions requiring binary responses may produce higher accuracy than those requiring nonbinary responses. • Closed-ended questions may produce more omission errors than open-ended questions. • "Threatening" questions and interview situations may reduce accuracy, especially for personally sensitive information.
Interactions	• Many of the factors listed above are known to interact.

Note. Adapted from Sudman and Bradburn (1974) and Wentland and Smith (1993).

situational, subject, and referent–event variables, some of which are illustrated in Table 14.2.

It makes sense to consider the available wisdom, but generalities like those in Table 14.2 should not be accepted uncritically. The primary literature on which these generalities are based will show, for example, that self-reports have rarely been validated under conditions exactly like those that human operant researchers hope to establish in their research, which increases the probability of unknowingly manipulating factors that affect self-reports. Human operant researchers also may find, on close inspection, reason to doubt the means by which some generalities were derived. In particular, self-report validity is not always measured in the sense described here, that of correspondence between self-reports and referents. More commonly, researchers have evaluated the effects of variables on thoroughly uncorroborated self-reports (Wentland & Smith, 1993). It can be shown, for instance, that different question formats produce self-reports of relatively higher or lower personal incomes (e.g., Locander & Burton, 1976), but without otherwise measuring income, it is impossible to determine which features of the wording contribute to accurate self-reporting. Thus, existing discussions of the factors that influence self-reports may not clearly distinguish between effects on report–referent correspondence and effects on the topography of uncorroborated self-reports.

More directly relevant to the needs of human operant researchers is the data base on clinical self-monitoring procedures as described in the behavioral assessment literature (e.g., Babor et al., 1987; Barlow, Hayes, & Nelson, 1984, Chapter 4; Nelson, 1977). The primary studies comprising this literature typically address public behavioral referents, often in analogue or laboratory settings, allowing questions of report accuracy to be addressed more explicitly than may be possible in studies employing survey methods.

Corroboration and Tolerance for Uncertainty

To summarize, uncertainty creeps into the interpretation of self-report data when operating characteristics of the self-observer remain a matter of assumption. Uncertainty is not unique to self-report data, but substantially more is known about the boundary conditions under which other forms of observation produce useful data. Uncertainty about self-reports will be minimized when multiple sources of validation promote the same inferences. Even when direct empirical corroboration can be undertaken, for example, it seems advisable to design self-report procedures with the general body of knowledge regarding interview and questionnaire methods in mind, to select several types of concurrent self-report measures, and to employ them with the benefit of hindsight that pilot investigation permits.

Should the inability to conduct empirical corroboration preclude the use of self-report methods? A common approach has been to acknowledge that self-reports can provide imperfect information and yet use them uncritically when no other source of information is readily available (e.g., Lieberman, 1975; Pekala, 1991). Unfortunately, no clear guidelines exist for weighing the need for data against the uncertainties of uncorroborated self-reports. How much uncertainty can be tolerated with respect to self-report data depends in part on the precision of the research question (Babor et al., 1990; Sobell & Sobell, 1990b). Precise questions, like those asked by laboratory researchers studying fundamental processes, demand precise data, but other kinds of questions may be addressed adequately by data admitting a greater possibility of measurement error. This may be another way of saying that tolerance for uncertainty hinges on the extent to which self-report data are capable of generating agreement among scientists about the phenomenon under study. Historical examples suggest that when uncorroborated self-reports are used as primary data, emphasis can shift rapidly from a consideration of the fundamental nature of behavioral phenomena to unresolvable arguments over the nature of the self-reports used to measure them. This describes, in part, the fate of early introspection research (Adair, 1973; Boring, 1953), but examples more relevant to human operant research can be identified.

Consider, for example, the literature on "conditioning without awareness," which gained some prominence with the publication of Greenspoon's (1955) study showing that listener agreement reinforced subject verbal responses, even when postexperiment interviews suggested that subjects were not aware of the reinforcement contingency or its effects on their behavior. Many replications followed, and some elegant procedures were devised (e.g., Hefferline & Perera, 1963). Unfortunately, in historical perspective, conceptual arguments about the measurement of awareness loom larger than the empirical legacy of this line of inquiry. Critics of conditioning without awareness have argued that brief or casual postexperiment interviews, as employed by Greenspoon, are unlikely to detect subject awareness, and that semistructured, interactive discussions permitting probes by the interviewer provide a much more sensitive assay (e.g., Speilberger & DeNike, 1966). Proponents of conditioning without awareness have responded that interactive interviews, or even simple requests for self-reports during the conditioning process, have the potential for generating awareness where none would otherwise exist (e.g., Rosenfeld & Baer, 1969). There remains little consensus over whether conditioning can occur without awareness (e.g., Brewer, 1974; Ericsson & Simon, 1984; Hineline & Wanchisen, 1989; Rosenfarb, Newland, Brannon, & Howey, 1992; White, 1988), in part because it is impossible to separate the research question, involving a referent that is difficult (at best) to corroborate, from more general methodological problems involving the interpretation of self-reports (Krasner & Ullman, 1963). With the emphasis on a referent (awareness) that can only be validated theoretically, scientific conclusions can be guided as much by theoretical bias as by data (Erikson, 1960; White, 1988).

DESIGNING AND DESCRIBING SELF-REPORT METHODS

Behavioral researchers go to great lengths to evaluate and describe the operating characteristics of their automated measurement devices. New mechanical tools and computer programs are subjected to demanding tests, the results of which often are published in technical articles. Similarly, the training and calibration of human observers is routinely described in Methods sections of published reports. These practices allow consumers of behavioral research to evaluate independently whether operating characteristics are adequate to the measurement task, and to replicate the measurement if desired. To date, human operant investigators employing self-report methods rarely have extended the same courtesy to consumers of their research. In a recent 5-year sample of human operant studies in the *Journal of the Experimental Analysis of Behavior,* self-report methods were almost never described completely enough to permit replication. Many articles mentioned, as an afterthought in the Discussion section, that subject comments of some sort were collected. Only a few listed, verbatim, the questions that subjects were asked or described the setting in which the self-reports were generated. Some published reports did not specify the procedure through which self-reports were generated (questionnaire or interview) or, in the case of interview methods, the interviewer's training, characteristics, or knowledge of the goals and details of the study.

If self-report data are important enough to present publicly, then self-report methods are important enough to select and describe with the same care as other methods. In fact, given the ambiguities that can surround uncorroborated self-reports, the methods used to obtain them probably require *exceptional* levels of experimenter care. Moreover, interview (and even questionnaire) situations often require more contact between experimenter and subject than traditional operant methods, in which subjects typically work alone in a distraction-free room. The collection of self-report data thus can increase the risk of experimenter effects, which are most prevalent in relatively unstructured social situations (e.g., Adair, 1973; R. Rosenthal, 1966).

In the absence of a well-developed literature on self-report methods specific to human operant research, individual investigators may be forced to develop their own self-report methods. A few considerations important to that process can be mentioned here, most of which have been addressed in detail outside of the experimental analysis of behavior.

Obtaining Background Information

We have already noted that events outside the experiment can have an impact on human operant performance, and where possible it makes sense to include these events among those to be measured through self-reports. Planned measurement of subject characteristics and other background information reduces the need to rely on unreliable alternative sources of information such as spontaneous subject comments ("I was up all last night cramming for a chemistry exam") or impromptu post-hoc interviews with atypical subjects. The more systematically subject information is obtained, the richer the source of hypotheses regarding variability in the study's main data, and the lower the likelihood that special inquiries will produce reactivity in either the self-reports or their referents. To obtain systematic subject information, it may be useful to ask subjects to maintain a daily diary of events and activities that could affect experimental performance (e.g., see Barlow et al., 1984, Chapter 4; see also the earlier section Monitoring Extraexperimental Variables). Self-recording might start a week or more before data collection begins, in part to facilitate subject selection, and then continue throughout the study. In the study of caffeine reinforcement that produced Figure 14.1, self-reports of food and beverage consumption were used both to identify moderate caffeine users as potential participants and to monitor the stability of extraexperimental caffeine intake across the 24 weeks of the study (Evans et al., 1994).

Developing Queries

Questions that prompt self-reports should be carefully selected and worded to maximize clarity and to minimize demand characteristics and social-desirability effects (e.g., Babor et al., 1987; Sudman & Bradburn, 1982). The type of query used to prompt self-reports will dictate the form of the response, which can range from a simple categorical response (e.g., "Yes" or "No") to a complex narrative utterance. The form of the raw self-report data in turn influences the types of analyses that can be conducted (see Quantifying Self-Report Data). Of course, the form of the query should match the needs of the research. For example, very specific queries are most appropriate when much is known about the dimensions along which referents can vary, and the environmental variables that are likely to influence them. Broader, more open-ended, queries may better fit the needs of pilot research, because they allow for a greater range of responses and therefore may help to shape the development of more specific approaches to be applied later in the research program.

Selecting and Training Interviewers

Although self-reports may not always be influenced by the setting in which they are obtained or the personal characteristics of the person obtaining them (Sudman & Bradburn, 1974), these variables should be monitored and examined for possible effects. Interviewers, when used, may need to be blind to the purposes of the experiment to minimize experimenter bias (e.g., R. Rosenthal, 1966) and should be rigorously trained to use standardized procedures. Interviewer standardization should be empirically evaluated using objective observations of the interview process, both during training and during the experiment proper (e.g., Billingsley, White, & Munson, 1980; Bradburn, Sudman, & Associates, 1979; Johnston & Pennypacker, 1980).

Reducing Reactivity

Behavior change, in either the referent or reporting response, apparently can result from the act of making a self-report. Self-monitoring, or the creation of records of one's own behavior, is sometimes employed as a clinical tool precisely because it engenders transient referent–response reactivity (Nelson, 1977). If reactive effects occur, the general pattern is for socially desirable responses to increase in frequency, and for socially undesirable responses to decrease in frequency, when self-monitored (Nelson & Hayes, 1981). The responses measured in human operant laboratory studies, such as button presses, may be relatively free of social valence, and thus presumably free of some types of reactive effects, but it would be a mistake to assume that referent–response reactivity never occurs with arbitrarily chosen responses. For example, when subjects in one study made self-reports about their responses in a delayed matching-to-sample task, the latencies of the match-to-sample responses increased for unknown reasons (Critchfield & Perone, 1990).

Because the mechanisms underlying referent–response reactivity to self-observation are poorly understood (Nelson & Hayes, 1981), few absolute guidelines exist for how to minimize it. At a general level, common sense suggests that behavior that is strongly controlled by experimental contingencies is unlikely to be perturbed by other variables (e.g., Cerutti, 1989; Nevin, 1992), including by the process of self-observation. At a more specific level, reviews of the literature on clinical self-monitoring suggest that reactivity is less likely when the referent response is verbal rather than nonverbal, when individuals make self-reports about

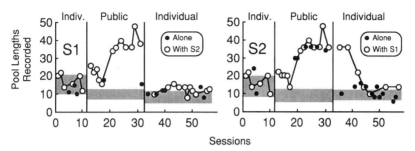

FIGURE 14.2.   Amount of swimming self-reported by two young competitive swimmers. In the Individual conditions self-reports were written on a personal recording form. In the Public condition, these reports were also posted to a publicly visible graph. The two swimmers shown here were present together for some workouts (open circles) but not others (closed circles). Shaded areas summarize actual performance (condition means ±1 standard deviation). Unpublished data combined with data replotted from Critchfield and Vargas (1991), Figure 1.

multiple behaviors rather than a single one, and when self-reports occur intermittently rather than after every response (e.g., Nelson, 1977). The relevance of these observations to self-reports in human operant investigations, however, remains to be established. Some authors have drawn parallels between self-observation and observation by external observers as sources of reactivity (Nelson, 1977; Nelson, Lipinski, & Black, 1976). If the analogy holds, then precautions used to reduce reactivity to external observers (e.g., Harris & Lahey, 1982a) should apply to self-report methods as well. For example, reactivity to external observers often attenuates with exposure, and there is evidence that reactivity to self-observation does as well (e.g., Critchfield & Vargas, 1991).

A second type of reactivity occurs when reporting responses, but not the responses they supposedly describe, are influenced by social variables. Figure 14.2 shows data from two 8-year-old girls who, like other members of a competitive swim team, were asked to record the number of pool lengths swum during a segment of daily workouts (Critchfield & Vargas, 1991). The shaded areas summarize actual swimming (condition means ±1 standard deviation). Note that the correspondence of self-reports to swimming was good when reports were written down individually, and poor when the reports were also posted in public graphs. Because not all swimmers attended all workouts, a second possible social effect was evident for these two swimmers, who knew each other well. For S2, public posting inflated self-reports generally. For S1, this effect apparently was specific to workouts completed with S2.

Reactivity can alter both the quantitative and qualitative content of self-reports, but in general socially desirable responses are overestimated and socially undesirable responses are underestimated (e.g., Nelson, 1977; Sudman & Bradburn, 1974). Suggestions for reducing these effects include: asking "nonthreatening" questions, taking visible precautions to ensure the confidentiality of the data, increasing anonymity through questionnaires rather than interviews, establishing "rapport" with subjects, asking longer questions, asking open-ended questions, informing subjects that their self-reports will be checked against some independent measure of the referent event (either the "bogus pipeline" technique or an actual assessment), and asking for self-reports about multiple referents (Babor et al., 1990; Nurco, 1985; Sudman & Bradburn, 1982; Vuchinich et al., 1988).

Steps can be taken to minimize the likelihood of reactivity, but it is important to know when precautions have failed. This is especially problematic in the case of self-reports about private events or other referents that cannot be corroborated. For example, when the interest is in retrospectively estimating subject awareness or in understanding events that occurred during an experiment, it is important to ensure that queries do not prompt subjects to analyze and integrate events differently than they would have without being questioned (Rosenfeld & Baer, 1969). One intractable problem in the "learning without awareness" literature mentioned earlier has been the impossibility of determining whether self-reported awareness, overt performance, or both change as a function of investigator queries.

Deciding How Often, and in What Form, to Collect Data

Self-report data can be collected frequently, after very small samples of behavior, or as infrequently as once per subject per experiment, as in the case of postexperimental interviews or questionnaires. For some purposes a single, summary self-report may provide essentially the same information as event-by-event self-monitoring (e.g,. Midanik, Klatsky, & Armstrong, 1989), but other experimental questions may call for additional detail in the data. Studies exploring the moment-by-moment correspondence between verbal rules and nonverbal performance, for example, would appear to demand the collection of self-report data on a regular basis (e.g., Hackenberg & Axtel, 1993; Wanchisen, Tatham, & Hineline, 1992; Wearden, 1988).

An additional consideration is the impact that data collection procedures can have on analytical strategies. The use of global measurement strategies often commits the investigator, before data are collected and inspected, to a limited number of approaches to quantifying report–referent correspondence, some of which (e.g., percent accuracy) can be relatively uninformative about the behavior of individual subjects or the variables controlling individual self-reports (e.g., Critchfield, 1993a). By contrast, event-by-event records, or other highly detailed forms of data, permit a variety of analyses and thus provide greater freedom to match analyses to research questions and to the natural lines of fracture in the data.

Thought should be given to the means by which permanent records of self-reports are created. Categorical self-reports can be recorded automatically (e.g., through button presses or computer input devices such as a mouse or joystick). Written questionnaires allow subjects to create their own permanent records, but when the interest is in open-ended self-reports, the effort of writing can lead to shorter and less complete responses than may be obtained vocally (Bradburn et al., 1979; Ericsson & Simon, 1984). Vocal responses can be coded by observers (see Quantifying Self-Report Data) at the time of emission, or recorded verbatim for later coding. On-the-spot coding creates a transformed record that permanently commits the experimenter to the original behavior code and thus constrains recoding if the focus of the research should shift at a later date. Taped responses can be reevaluated at any time, allowing modification of behavior codes as circumstances require (e.g., Walbott, 1982). Nevertheless, information also can be lost when self-reports are taped for later analysis. For example, audiotape does not preserve gestures and facial expressions that might help define verbal response categories. Similarly, lip movements aid in an observer's interpretation of speech, but subjects may not always face toward a videocamera. Moreover, there is evidence that in some cases human raters actually may perform more poorly when watching videotapes rather than live behavioral episodes (Fagot & Hagan, 1988).

Behavior (especially verbal behavior) can occur rapidly, and as a convenience to observers, taped verbal responses often are transcribed before coding. Transcription reduces the time pressure on the individuals who will categorize self-reports, but also eliminates evidence of pausing, inflection, and other possible clues to coding. Transcription should be undertaken with the same care as other forms of data manipulation. For example, the records of independent transcribers can be compared to estimate the reliability of transcription (e.g., Barnes & Keenan, 1993).

Thoroughly Describing Self-Report Methods

Given the variety of decisions that must be made when constructing self-report methods, perhaps the most important consideration for a human operant investigator is the most general one: All aspects of the procedures used to generate self-reports should be fully described and justified in the Methods section of a published research report. The more extended an investigator's inferences about the operating characteristics of the self-observer, the greater is the potential for conflicting interpretations of the self-report data. Thus, it will be important to provide the reader with maximum opportunity to judge independently whether the methods employed were appropriate, and to replicate the procedures if desired. Two especially good examples of thorough disclosure can be found in reports by Barnes and Keenan (1993) and Wanchisen et al. (1992).

QUANTIFYING SELF-REPORT DATA

A good Methods section describes an investigator's influence, intended or otherwise, on research outcomes. But that influence does not cease when the last subject is discharged from the laboratory. Raw data must be reduced in some fashion, organized for presentation to the research community, and subjected to other forms of analysis such as curve-fitting or inferential statistical tests. A good Results section both displays finished data products and describes the steps taken in data reduction and analysis. The trend in human operant research, however, has been to describe self-report data selectively and casually. Typical practices are illustrated by the following example from an otherwise well-conducted study of nonverbal choice in concurrent schedules of reinforcement (Savastano & Fantino, 1994). The Methods section describing the experiment included one brief sentence indicating that "after all sessions were complete, subjects were given questionnaires from which verbal reports of their performance were taken" (p. 457). Self-report data were not presented in the Results section, but instead were mentioned in the Discussion section as evidence supporting the authors' interpretations of the nonverbal data. For instance, after suggesting that the data may have been influenced by a decrease in reinforcer efficacy across the study, the authors noted that

> This possible factor is consistent with subjects' verbal reports between sessions and following the experiment. Subjects also reported increasing boredom with the task as sessions progressed, adding that they "did not care about getting points" and "just wanted to finish" by the end of the 31 sessions. (p. 459)

Patterns in the self-report data thus were described qualitatively, in terms of the (apparent) modal categories of response, and verbatim quotes were used to illustrate these patterns. Many questions were left unanswered, including (1) how between-session verbal report data became available (the Methods section referred only to the collection of postexperiment reports); (2) what aspects of the verbal reports, other than those quoted, are consistent with a motivational interpretation; (3) from whom the selected quotes were drawn; and (4) how representative the quoted passages were of the responses of other subjects.

The study just described typifies practices in human operant studies that include self-report measures, and illustrates two common, and largely uninformative, approaches to describing self-report data. First, authors sometimes attempt to capture the essence of self-report data by providing verbatim comments from "typical" subjects in lieu of a quantitative summary. Second, authors sometimes mention patterns in self-report data without specifying the means by which the patterns were identified or without providing quantitative verification of the pattern. Unfortunately, isolated quotations omit much of the data set, and qualitative summaries obscure the process by which generalities were derived from the data.

Self-report data can carry a greater explanatory burden when they are analyzed and presented using the same heuristics applied to the study's nonverbal data. The present section addresses some considerations to be applied in the process of reducing and analyzing both categorical and open-ended self-report data. The section concludes by revisiting the possible contributions of verbatim quotation.

Summarizing Categorical Self-Reports

Quantifying self-report data is relatively straightforward when the procedures used to generate them place constraints on the forms that self-reports can take. When self-reports are generated only infrequently during a study, as in the case of postexperiment questionnaires, it may be appropriate to present a simple descriptive summary of binary (e.g., yes–no) or categorical data. For example, in an abuse-liability assessment of the anxiolytics lorazepam and buspirone, recreational polydrug users were given unidentified doses of two study drugs and asked to indicate which class of drugs (e.g., opiates, benzodiazepines, hallucinogens) the study compounds felt most like. The results were readily summarized as the percentage of subjects identifying endorsing each drug class at each dose of the study compounds (Troisi et al., 1993).

More detailed self-reports permit more sophisticated analyses, especially when the reports provide an event-by-event description of a referent that can be corroborated. One promising approach is to adapt the conventions of signal-detection analysis (D. Green & Swets, 1966); see also Irwin & McCarthy, Chapter 10), which can be conducted most easily with binary (e.g., yes–no) data and some Likert-type ratings. A signal-detection analysis describes report–referent correspondence with greater resolution than more global measures such as percent correct (Critchfield, 1993a, 1994, 1996a; Critchfield & Perone, 1993; Hosseini & Ferrell, 1982), in part by distinguishing between false detections (errors of commission) and false rejections (or errors of omission) in self-reports. Calculations involving false-detection and false-rejection rates allow the formal disentanglement of discriminability (control by the referent) and bias (predispositions to make certain kinds of self-reports independent of the status of the referent), two factors that are confounded in more global measures such as accuracy scores.

Figure 14.3 shows data from a representative subject in an experiment in which, after each response in a match-to-sample procedure, the subject made a self-report indicating whether the response met a reinforcement contingency with which the experimental protocol provided substantial prior experience (Critchfield, 1993a). The top, right panel shows how self-reports were categorized for the purposes of a signal-detection analysis. Although varying the difficulty of the match-to-sample task produced no systematic changes in the global measure of self-report accuracy (top left), clear changes occurred in rates of the two types of self-report errors implicated in the signal-detection analysis (bottom left). As match-to-sample success decreased, false reports of success became less frequent and false reports of failure became more frequent. The conjunction of these patterns produced, in part, systematic changes in self-report bias (bottom right).

Signal-detection analyses have been productively applied to the analysis of many types of self-reports (e.g., Critchfield, 1993a,b, 1994, 1996a; Hosseini & Ferrell, 1982). Nevertheless, two cautions are in order regarding their use. First, al-

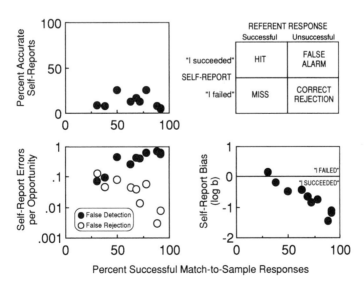

FIGURE 14.3.   One subject's self-reports about delayed match-to-sample success as a function of actual success. Here accuracy scores (top, left) are relatively uninformative compared with analyses in the bottom row based on the response categories of a signal-detection analysis. Data replotted from Critchfield (1993a), Figures 3, 4, and 5.

though discriminability and bias can be calculated in a number of different ways, they are not statistically independent in all approaches or at all magnitudes of false-detection and false-rejection rates (e.g., MacMillan & Creelman, 1990). The log d and log b indices of discriminability and bias, respectively, have proven to be relatively independent across a variety of conditions and are recommended for this reason (McCarthy & Davison, 1981). Second, false-detection and false-rejection rates are proportions, and the indices based on them can become volatile when only a small number of observations are available. Thus, a signal-detection approach requires that self-reports be collected repeatedly rather than on a single occasion, such as at the conclusion of each subject's participation.

Coding Open-Ended Self-Reports

For open-ended comments to be quantified, they must first be placed into response categories. Although elaborate taxonomies of verbal responses have been described (e.g., MacWhinney, 1991; Stiles, 1992), few are likely to be specific to the purposes of human operant investigations. Thus, response categories may have to be created for each research program (for an example, see Wanchisen et al., 1992). Deriving response categories is not always a simple matter (e.g, Begelman, 1976; Fassnacht, 1982; Hawkins, 1982; Johnston & Pennypacker, 1980, Chapters 6 and 7). Some guidance on how to create and refine response categories is available from researchers who have studied communication in other contexts (e.g., see Als, Tronick, & Brazelton, 1979; Crutcher, Ericsson, & Wichora, 1994; Feldstein & Welkowitz, 1987; Moerk, 1990; Sherer & Ekman, 1982). In general, a good set of response categories will: (1) account for all or most subject comments; (2) include functional response classes that clearly reflect the research question of the experiment; (3) describe self-reports, where possible, using the dimensional characteristics along which other forms of behavior typically are categorized; and (4) lend itself easily to the training of raters who will apply the categories to the self-reports (Hawkins, 1982; Johnston & Pennypacker, 1980).

A related concern is whether the coding scheme is designed to categorize specific self-report responses, or categorize individual subjects based on the modal characteristics of their self-reports. The latter strategy has often been employed in studies that addressed whether awareness of contingencies or covert mediation influenced overt performance. For example, following a study of human concurrent schedule performance, Horne and Lowe (1993) asked subjects to describe "the scheduled contingencies and to give an account of the factors they considered determined their responding" (p. 33). Based on the resulting open-ended comments, subjects then were categorized as having employed one of five performance rules to mediate behavior–consequence relations during the experiment (matching, undermatching, overmatching, indifference, and exclusive preference). The difficulty with using self-reports to classify subjects is that self-reports are treated as stable personal characteristics rather than as instances of behavior subject to variation. Complex utterances probably reflect multiple influences (Skinner, 1957), and treating self-reports as behavior would be more likely to prompt a consideration of whether subjects' self-reports reflected multiple sources of control, contained multiple response types, or varied from moment to moment during the experiment.

Once response categories have been developed, they must be applied to the raw self-report data. Human raters nearly always are employed for this purpose, bringing to bear the concerns that normally apply to the use of human observers in research. Observers can be major source of variance in behavioral data (Harris & Lahey, 1982a,b), so they should be selected carefully and trained rigorously. Training procedures have been detailed elsewhere, most often reflecting the following steps adapted from Reid (1982). Training begins with creation of an observation manual or other standardized instructions that operationally define the response categories and provide examples and nonexamples of each. Note, however, that neither the manual nor subsequent instructions to subjects should explain the purposes of the experiment, because blind observers are less likely to exhibit recording biases than observers who are aware of the study's purposes. Once observers have memorized the manual and received instruction in the use of any special coding forms or equipment, they can begin applying the code to verbal-report episodes selected initially to fit easily into the categories. As observers gain fluency with the code, they can begin rating more ambiguous examples. Feedback should be provided throughout the training, and sources of confusion should be addressed on an instance-by-instance basis. Observers can be considered well trained when they exhibit near-perfect agreement with each other and with criterion data sets with known characteristics.

Because the effects of observer training can diminish rapidly once a study begins, it may be useful to: select observers who have demonstrated meticulous attention to detail in previous scientific projects; overtrain observers prior to the start of the experiment; periodically retrain observers during the experiment; regularly monitor and calibrate observer reliability and accuracy; and provide incentives for reliable recording, such as requiring laborious retraining sessions when reliability or accuracy fall below a criterion level (Reid, 1982).

It has become customary to evaluate the quality of observational data partly by using multiple observers and calculating interobserver agreement scores. Interobserver agreement scores cannot indicate whether a coding system has been well-designed or flawlessly employed, but they do indicate whether response categories have been employed consistently across raters. For these scores to be informative, raters must employ the coding system independently during both training and the main study. Raters who can view one another during scoring or talk about the coding procedure between scoring sessions can influence each other's observations, potentially introducing bias or creating artificially inflated agreement levels. Even with independent raters, the calculation of interobserver agreement scores is a subject matter unto itself, and the reader is referred to more detailed discussions of the relevant issues (e.g., Hawkins & Dotson, 1975; Siegel & Castellan, 1988).

To summarize, the analysis of open-ended self-report data begins with definition of response categories, selection and training of raters, and evidence that the raters performed reliably. Each step merits thorough description in a published report of the research, especially when the coding strategy has not been employed previously in published research. Once these considerations have been addressed, attention can turn to the search for patterns in the self-report data, using graphic and statistical methods appropriate to other forms of behavioral data. Wanchisen et al. (1992) provide an especially thorough example of describing a novel behavior code and the data reduction procedures used in conjunction with it.

Quoting Verbatim

In rare cases, it may be useful to reproduce self-reports verbatim. An advantage of this approach is that it eliminates any risk of distortion through coding procedures, but a primary disadvantage is the appearance of subjectivity in selecting comments to reproduce, unless all comments made by all subjects can be presented. Thus, verbatim comments may be most useful in cases where only a limited number of self-reports have been collected. Because only limited data can be presented, they should bear on limited aspects of the study.

Consider the aforementioned abuse-liability assessment of lorazepam and buspirone (Troisi et al., 1993). Self-report data from early phases of the study (Critchfield & Griffiths, 1991) suggested that lorazepam was more likely to be used recreationally by habitual sedative abusers, in that lorazepam appeared to produce pleasant effects, and buspirone appeared to produce dysphoric mood effects. In a portion of the main study, subjects received forced administrations of a moderate dose of each drug and then were asked, in a rough analogue of drug self-administration procedures, to choose between them for a final drug administration. At the time of choice, subjects also were asked to describe, in writing, their reasons for choosing one drug and rejecting the other. Eight of nine subjects chose lorazepam, and Table 14.3 shows how subject comments, presented verbatim and in their entirety, helped to strengthen the inference that buspirone produced unpleasant effects for most subjects. The table also shows, however, that even verbatim quotation may not eliminate ambiguity in self-report data. Two of nine subjects failed to record any comment regarding buspirone. At least two of the comments are difficult to interpret in the context of drug reinforcement (Subject 5's statement that buspirone "made it hard to see" and Subject 6's comment regarding lorazepam that "I don't know why I want the drug"). Importantly, more direct procedures exist for assessing the reinforcing and aversive properties of drugs. For example, aversive properties would be demonstrated if subjects proved willing to expend effort or forego other reinforcers to avoid scheduled administrations of the drug (Griffiths, Bigelow, & Liebson, 1989; Griffiths, Troisi, Silverman, & Mumford, 1993).

Is it ever appropriate to quote *selectively* from subject verbal self-reports? It is easy to understand how such a practice could arise. First, good investigators explore every avenue in accounting for unexplained variability, but the need for self-report data (e.g., postexperiment interviews) may not become clear until an aberrant subject is identified. Thus, when self-report methods are not planned as part of the original research protocol, investigators may seek self-report data only from aberrant subjects. Second, even when self-reports have been obtained systematically from all subjects, only those of aberrant subjects may appear to be informative (that is, only atypical subjects have substantial variability left to explain).

TABLE 14.3

Verbatim Comments Written by Recreation Drug Users on Choosing between Lorazepam and Buspirone

Subject	Lorazepam	Buspirone
1	*It didn't make me feel bad like the other	I was miserable and depressed
2	*Mellowness of mood	Feeling of anxiety and muscle twitching
3	*Has better effect than other	Not intense enough. Left with a headache
4	*No bad after effect	Bad after effect
5	*The Hi!	It made it hard to see
6	*I don't know why I want the drug	[Subject recorded no comment]
7	*Made me feel relaxed and at peace	Made me feel sick, nasty attitude, nauseous
8	Made me feel sleepy, more difficult to do tasks	*Didn't make me feel sleepy like the other
9	*Effects of the drug were mild, and I didn't get an upset stomach from the drug	[Subject recorded no comment]

Note. Based on Table IV of Troisi, J. R., II, Critchfield, T. S., & Griffiths, R. R. (1993). Buspirone and lorazepam abuse liability in humans: Behavioral effects, subjective effects, and choice. *Behavioral Pharmacology, 4,* 217–230.
Note. Subjects first received blind administrations of both drugs (4 mg/70 kg lorazepam and 60 mg/70 kg buspirone) in identical capsules labeled with a letter code. In the choice procedure, they indicated their drug of choice via the letter code. The form on which subjects registered their choices asked why subjects selected the drug they chose, and why they did not select the alternative.
*Drug actually chosen by each subject.

Subject comments may be worth heeding, and the variables they suggest may be worth investigating in future studies, but if subject comments correlate with response patterns, then the comments of "typical" subjects will be just as informative as those of atypical subjects. In fact, one cannot be interpreted without reference to the other. For the same reason that investigators present data for both experimental and control conditions—to facilitate independent comparisons by other scientists—they should present self-report data for both typical and atypical subjects. If equivalent data are not available for both typical and atypical subjects, then it is not appropriate to present verbatim comments (or, indeed, any other form of data) in a published report.

CONCLUSIONS

Within the experimental analysis of behavior, the absence of standardized approaches to designing self-report methods places a special burden on investigators who seek to collect and interpret self-report data. There is a role for self-reports in the arsenal of human operant methods, but self-report procedures require both strong justification and systematic application that may include empirical validation efforts. Part of being systematic, however, means not reinventing the wheel, and human operant researchers can accelerate their development of self-report methods by drawing on the expertise of researchers in other areas who have more explicitly addressed the quandaries inherent in self-report data.

It is sometimes asserted that the primary contribution of operant psychology is neither its empirical legacy nor its conceptual framework, but rather its general emphasis on methodological rigor (e.g., Adair, 1973). In this regard, human operant researchers are long overdue in developing their own methodological standards specific to the collection and interpretation of self-report data (Perone, 1988). The empirical work necessary to establish new standards can have broad impact, because the widespread reliance on self-report methods in psychological science, clinical practice, and everyday discourse belies an ironic state of affairs. Empirically speaking, surprisingly little is known about the behavior of making a self-report and the ways in which laboratory-based behavioral principles interact with it (Critchfield & Perone, 1990, 1993).

It would be difficult to underestimate the potential impact of research aimed at exploring regularities in report–referent correspondence. To cite only a few examples, a systematic experimental analysis of report-referent correspondence could produce benefits for researchers seeking dependable measures of otherwise unobservable referents; for theorists attempting to delineate the role of self-observation and self-evaluation in other types of functioning; for clinicians attempting to monitor client behavior patterns outside the therapeutic session; for health care professionals attempting to monitor compliance with medical regimens; and for individuals such as jurors and physicians making socially important decisions based on self-reported information.

A few characteristics of the initial phases of an experimental analysis of verbal self-reports can be imagined. The analysis would treat report–referent correspondence as its primary dependent variable, placing a premium on the measurement of both report and referent through means likely to generate agreement among scientists. Because characteristics of the referent are one important source of control over self-reports, it would be advantageous in many cases to experimentally control these characteristics, much as one would control the characteristics of a light or tone intended to serve as a discriminative stimulus (Critchfield & Perone, 1993). The correspondence between referent and self-reports would require quantification at the level of individual subjects. Consistent with traditions in the experimental analysis of behavior, such studies would include enough observations of individual subjects to permit the description of both molar and molecular patterns of correspondence, both at steady state and, ideally, during periods of transition between steady states. In addition, environmental variables such as contingencies of reinforcement and punishment would be viewed as an important source of variance in correspondence.

The research approach just outlined would be far from typical in the history of self-report methods. For example, one large-scale review of survey literature (Wentland & Smith, 1993) located only 37 studies published between 1944 and 1988 that met a few simple methodological criteria, including that self-reports (1) could in principle be corroborated (e.g., excluding those about attitudes or private events) and (2) were actually corroborated at the individual level (rather than through comparison of aggregate measures such as group mean income and group mean self-estimate of income). There is every reason to expect that human operant research can help address this gap in the self-report literature and, in the process, reveal as much about the behavior of making a self-report as it has about other behavioral phenomena.

REFERENCES

Adair, J. G. (1973). *The human subject: The social psychology of the psychology experiment.* Boston: Little, Brown.

Als, H., Tronick, E., & Brazelton, T. B. (1979). Analysis of face-to-face interaction in infant–adult dyads. In M. E. Lamb, S. J. Suomi, & G. R. Stephenson (Eds.), *Social interaction analysis: Methodological issues* (pp. 33–77). Madison: University of Wisconsin Press.

Babor, T. F., Brown, J., & Del Boca, F. K. (1990). Validity of self-reports in applied research on addictive behaviors: Fact or fiction? *Behavioral Assessment, 12,* 5–31.

Babor, T. F., Stephens, R. S., & Marlatt, G. A. (1987). Verbal report methods in clinical research on alcoholism: Response bias and its minimization. *Journal of Studies on Alcohol, 45,* 410–424.

Baer, D. M. (1982). The imposition of structure on behavior and the demolition of behavioral structures. In D. J. Bernstein (Ed.), *Response structure and organization* (pp. 217–254). Lincoln: University of Nebraska Press.

Baer, R. A., & Detrich, R. (1990). Tacting and manding in correspondence training: Effects of child selection of verbalization. *Journal of the Experimental Analysis of Behavior, 54,* 23–30.

Baker, T. R., & Brandon, T. H. (1990). Validity of self-reports in basic research. *Behavioral Assessment, 12,* 33–51.

Bandini, L. G. Schoeller, D. A., Cyr, H. N., & Dietz, W. H. (1990). Validity of reported energy intake in obese and nonobese adolescents. *American Journal of Clinical Nutrition, 52,* 421–425.

Barlow, D. H., Hayes, S. C., & Nelson, R. O. (1984). *The scientist practitioner: Research and accountability in clinical and educational settings.* New York: Pergamon Press.

Barnes, D., & Keenan, M. (1993). Concurrent activities and instructed human fixed-interval performance. *Journal of the Experimental Analysis of Behavior, 59,* 501–520.

Baron, A., & Menich, S. R. (1985). Reaction times of older and younger men: Effects of compound samples and a prechoice signal on delayed matching-to-sample performances. *Journal of the Experimental Analysis of Behavior, 44,* 1–14.

Baron, A., Menich, S. R., & Perone, M. (1983). Reaction times of younger and older men and temporal contingencies of reinforcement. *Journal of the Experimental Analysis of Behavior, 40,* 275–287.

Baron, A., Perone, M., & Galizio, M. (1991). Analyzing the reinforcement process at the human level: Can application and behavioristic interpretation replace human research? *The Behavior Analyst, 14,* 95–106.

Begelman, D. A. (1976). Behavioral classification. In M. Hersen & A. S. Bellack (Eds.), *Behavioral assessment: A practical handbook* (pp. 23–48). New York: Pergamon Press.

Bem, D. J. (1967). Self-perception: An alternative interpretation of cognitive dissonance phenomena. *Psychological Review, 74,* 183–200.

Bernstein, D. J. (1988). Laboratory lore and research practices in the experimental analysis of human behavior: Designing session logistics—How long, how often, how many? *The Behavior Analyst, 11,* 51–58.

Bernstein, D. J., & Michael, R. L. (1990). The utility of verbal and behavioral assessments of value. *Journal of the Experimental Analysis of Behavior, 54,* 173–184.

Billingsley, F., White, O. R., & Munson, R. (1980). Procedural reliability: A rationale and example. *Behavioral Assessment, 2,* 229–241.

Boring, E. G. (1953). A history of introspection. *Psychological Bulletin, 50,* 169–189.

Bradburn, N. M., Sudman, S., and Associates. (1979). *Improving interview methods and questionnaire design.* San Francisco: Jossey–Bass.

Branch, M. N. (1991). On the difficulty of studying "basic" behavioral processes in humans. *The Behavior Analyst, 14,* 107–110.

Brewer, W. F. (1974). There is no convincing evidence for operant or classical conditioning in adult humans. In W. B. Weimer & D. S. Palermo (Eds.), *Cognition and the symbolic processes* (pp. 1–33). Hillsdale, NJ: Erlbaum.

Catania, A. C., Matthews, B. A., & Shimoff, E. (1982). Instructed versus shaped human verbal behavior: Interactions with nonverbal responding. *Journal of the Experimental Analysis of Behavior, 38,* 233–248.

Cerutti, D. T. (1989). Discrimination theory of rule-governed behavior. *Journal of the Experimental Analysis of Behavior, 51,* 259–276.

Cone, J. D. (1978). The Behavioral Assessment Grid (BAG): A conceptual framework and a taxonomy. *Behavioral Therapy, 9,* 882–888.

Craig, A. (1976). Signal-recognition and the probability-matching decision rule. *Perception and Psychophysics, 20,* 157–162.

Critchfield, T. S. (1993a). Signal-detection properties of verbal self-reports. *Journal of the Experimental Analysis of Behavior, 60,* 495–514.

Critchfield, T. S. (1993b). Behavioral pharmacology and verbal behavior: Diazepam effects on verbal self-reports. *Analysis of Verbal Behavior, 11,* 43–54.

Critchfield, T. S. (1994). Bias in self-evaluation: Signal-probability effects. *Journal of the Experimental Analysis of Behavior, 62,* 235–250.

Critchfield, T. S. (1996a). Self-reports about performance under time pressure: Bias and discriminability. *The Psychological Record, 46,* 333–350.

Critchfield, T. S. (1996b). Differential latency and selective nondisclosure in verbal self-reports. *The Analysis of Verbal Behavior, 13,* 49–63.

Critchfield, T. S., & Griffiths, R. R. (1991). Behavioral and subjective effects of buspirone and lorazepam in sedative abusers: Supratherapeutic doses. *NIDA Research Monograph, 105,* 318.

Critchfield, T. S., & Perone, M. (1990). Verbal self-reports of delayed matching to sample by humans. *Journal of the Experimental Analysis of Behavior, 53,* 321–344.

Critchfield, T. S., & Perone, M. (1993). Verbal self-reports about matching to sample: Effects of the number of elements in a compound sample stimulus. *Journal of the Experimental Analysis of Behavior, 59,* 193–214.

Critchfield, T. S., & Vargas, E. A. (1991). Self-recording, instructions, and public self-graphing: Effects on swimming in the absence of coach verbal interaction. *Behavior Modification, 15,* 95–112.

Cronbach, L. J. (1984). *Essentials of psychological testing.* New York: Harper & Row.

Crutcher, R. J., Ericsson, K. A., & Wichora, C. A. (1994). Improving the encoding of verbal reports by using MPAS: A computer-aided encoding system. *Behavior Research Methods, Instruments, and Computers, 26,* 167–171.

de Freitas Ribeiro, A. (1989). Correspondence in children's self-report: Tacting and manding aspects. *Journal of the Experimental Analysis of Behavior, 51,* 361–367.

Dement, W., & Kleitman, N. (1957). The relation of eye movements during sleep to dream activity. *Journal of Experimental Psychology, 53,* 339–346.

Ericsson, K. A., & Simon, H. A. (1984). *Protocol analysis: Verbal reports as data.* Cambridge, MA: MIT Press.

Erikson, C. W. (1960). Discrimination and learning without awareness: A methodological survey and evaluation. *Psychological Review, 67,* 279–300.

Estes, W. K., & Skinner, B. F. (1941). Some quantitative properties of anxiety. *Journal of Experimental Psychology, 29,* 390–400.

Evans, S. M., Critchfield, T. S., & Griffiths, R. R. (1991). Abuse liability assessment of anxiolytic/hypnotics: Rationale and laboratory lore. *British Journal of Addiction, 86,* 1625–1632.

Evans, S. M., Critchfield, T. S., & Griffiths, R. R. (1994). Caffeine reinforcement demonstrated in a majority of moderate caffeine users. *Behavioural Pharmacology, 5,* 231–238.

Fagot, B., & Hagan, R. (1988). Is what we see what we get? Comparisons of taped and live observations. *Behavioral Assessment, 10,* 367–374.

Fassnacht, G. (1982). *Theory and practice of observing behaviour.* New York: Academic Press.

Feldstein, S., & Welkowitz, J. (1987). A chronography of conversation: In defense of an objective approach. In A. W. Siegman & A. Feldstein (Eds.), *Nonverbal behavior and communication* (pp. 435–499). Hillsdale, NJ: Erlbaum.

Fetterman, J. G., & McEwan, D. (1989). Short-term memory for responses: The "choose-small" effect. *Journal of the Experimental Analysis of Behavior, 52,* 311–324.

Fox, E. (1995). Negative priming from ignored distractors in visual selection: A review. *Psychonomic Bulletin & Review, 2,* 145–173.

Gibson, E. J. (1993). Ontogenesis of the perceived self. In U. Neisser (Ed.), *The perceived self: Ecological and interpersonal sources of self-knowledge* (pp. 25–42). London: Cambridge University Press.

Green, D. M., & Swets, J. A. (1966). *Signal detection theory and psychophysics.* New York: Wiley.

Green, L., & Kagel, J. H. (Eds.). (1996). *Advances in behavioral economics: Vol. 3. Substance use and abuse.* Norwood, NJ: Ablex.

Greenspoon, J. (1955). The reinforcing effect of two spoken sounds on the frequency of two responses. *American Journal of Psychology, 68,* 409–416.

Griffiths, R. R., Bigelow, G. E., & Liebson, I. A. (1989). Reinforcing effects of caffeine in coffee and capsules. *Journal of the Experimental Analysis of Behavior, 52,* 127–140.

Griffiths, R. R., Troisi, J. R., II, Silverman, K., & Mumford, G. K. (1993). Multiple-choice procedures: An efficient approach for investigating drug reinforcement in humans. *Behavioral Pharmacology, 4,* 3–13.

Hackenberg, T. D., & Axtell, S. A. M. (1993). Choice in situations of diminishing returns. *Journal of the Experimental Analysis of Behavior, 59,* 445–470.

Haertzen, C. A. (1966). Development of scales based on patterns of drug effects, using the Addiction Research Inventory (ARCI). *Psychological Reports, 18,* 163–194.

Harris, F. C., & Lahey, B. B. (1982a). Subject reactivity in direct observational assessment: A review and critical assessment. *Clinical Psychology Review, 2,* 523–538.

Harris, F. C. ,& Lahey, B. B. (1982b). Recording system bias in direct observational methodology. *Clinical Psychology Review, 2,* 539–556.

Harrison, J. M. (1991). Stimulus control. In I. H. Iversen & K. A. Lattal (Eds.), *Experimental analysis of behavior, Part 1* (pp. 351–399). Amsterdam: Elsevier.

Hawkins, R. P. (1982). Developing a behavior code. In D. P. Hartmann (Ed.), *Using observers to study behavior* (pp. 21–35). San Francisco: Jossey–Bass.

Hawkins, R. P., & Dotson, V. A. (1975). Reliability scores that delude: An Alice in Wonderland trip through the misleading characteristics of interobserver agreement scores in interval recording. In E. Ramp & G. Semb (Eds.), *Behavior analysis: Areas of research and application* (pp. 359–376). Englewood Cliffs, NJ: Prentice–Hall.

Hayes, S. C. (1986). The case of the silent dog—Verbal reports and the analysis of rules: A review of Ericsson and Simon's *Protocol analysis: Verbal reports as data. Journal of the Experimental Analysis of Behavior, 45,* 351–363.

Hefferline, R. F., & Perera, T. B. (1963). Proprioceptive discrimination of a covert operant without its observation by the subject. *Science, 139,* 834–835.

Hineline, P. N., & Wanchisen, B. A. (1989). Correlated hypothesizing and the distinction between contingency-shaped and rule-governed behavior. In S. C. Hayes (Ed.), *Rule-governed behavior: Cognition, contingencies, and instructional control* (pp. 221–268). New York: Plenum Press.

Horne, P. J., & Lowe, C. F. (1993). Determinants of human performance on concurrent schedules. *Journal of the Experimental Analysis of Behavior, 59,* 29–60.

Horne, P. J., & Lowe, C. F. (1996). On the origins of naming and other symbolic behavior. *Journal of the Experimental Analysis of Behavior, 65,* 185–353 (includes peer commentary).

Hosseini, J., & Ferrell, W. R. (1982). Detectability of correctness: A measure of knowing that one knows. *Instructional Science, 11,* 113–127.

Innis, A., Lane, S. D., Miller, E. R., & Critchfield, T. S. (in press). Stimulus equivalence: Effects of a default-response option on emergence of untrained stimulus relations. *Journal of the Experimental Analysis of Behavior.*

Intons-Peterson, M. J., ed. (1993). Short-term memory (special section). *Memory and Cognition, 21,* 141–197.

Iversen, I. H., & Lattal, K. A. (Eds.). (1991a). *Experimental analysis of behavior, Part 1.* Amsterdam: Elsevier.

Iversen, I. H., & Lattal, K. A. (Eds.). (1991b). *Experimental analysis of behavior, Part 2.* Amsterdam: Elsevier.

Jansen, A. A. I., de Gier, J. J., & Slangen, J. L. (1985). Alcohol effects on signal detection performance. *Neuropsychobiology, 14,* 83–87.

Johnston, J. M., & Pennypacker, H. S. (1980). *Strategies and tactics of human behavioral research.* Hillsdale, NJ: Erlbaum.

Kollins, S. H., Newland, M. C., & Critchfield, T. S. (1997). Human sensitivity to reinforcement in operant choice: How much do consequences matter? *Psychonomic Bulletin & Review, 4,* 208–220.

Krasner, L., & Ullman, L. P. (1963). Variables affecting report of awareness in verbal conditioning. *Journal of Psychology, 56,* 193–202.

Kvale, S., & Griness, C. E. (1967). Skinner and Sartre: Towards a radical phenomenology of behavior. *Review of Existential Psychology and Psychiatry, 7,* 128–148.

Lane, S. D. & Critchfield, T. S. (1996). Verbal self-reports of emergent relations in a stimulus equivalence procedure. *Journal of the Experimental Analysis of Behavior, 65,* 355–374.

Lieberman, D. A. (1975). Behaviorism and the mind: A (limited) call for a return to introspection. *American Psychologist, 34,* 319–333.

Locander, W. B., & Burton, J. P. (1976). The effect of question form on gathering income data by telephone. *Journal of Marketing Research, 13,* 189–192.

Mace, F. C. (1994). Basic research needed for stimulating the development of behavioral technologies. *Journal of the Experimental Analysis of Behavior, 61,* 529–550.

Mace, F. C., Hock, M. L., Lalli, J. S., Shea, M. C., West, B. J., Belfiore, P., Pinter, E., & Brown, D. K. (1988). Behavioral momentum in the treatment of noncompliance. *Journal of Applied Behavior Analysis, 21,* 123–141.

Mace, F. C., Lalli, J. S., Shea, M. C., & Nevin, J. A. (1992). Behavioral momentum in college basketball. *Journal of Applied Behavior Analysis, 25,* 657–663.

Mackay, H. A. (1991). Conditional stimulus control. In I. H. Iversen & K. A. Lattal (Eds.), *Experimental analysis of behavior, Part 1* (pp. 301–350). Amsterdam: Elsevier.

MacMillan, N. A., & Creelman, C. D. (1990). Response bias: Characteristics of detection theory, threshold theory, and "nonparametric" indices. *Psychological Bulletin, 107,* 401–413.

MacWhinney, B. (1991). *The CHILDES Project: Tools for analyzing talk.* Hillsdale, NJ: Erlbaum.

McCarthy, D., & Davison, M. (1981). Towards a behavioral theory of bias in signal detection. *Perception and Psychophysics, 29,* 371–382.

McNair, D., Lorr, M., & Droppelman, L. (1971). *Profile of Mood States manual.* San Diego: Educational and Industrial Testing Service.

Midanik, L. T., Klatsky, A. L., & Armstrong, M. A. (1989). A comparison of 7-day recall with two summary measures of alcohol use. *Drug and Alcohol Dependence, 24,* 127–134.

Moerk, E. L. (1990). Three-term contingency patterns in mother–child verbal interactions during first-language interaction. *Journal of the Experimental Analysis of Behavior, 54,* 293–305.

Myerson, J., & Green, L. (1995). Discounting of delayed rewards: Models of individual choice. *Journal of the Experimental Analysis of Behavior, 64,* 263–276.

Natsoulas, T. (1978). Toward a model for consciousness in the light of B. F. Skinner's contribution. *Behaviorism, 6,* 139–175.

Natsoulas, T. (1988). On the radical behaviorist conception of pain experience. *Journal of Mind and Behavior, 9,* 29–56.

Nelson, R. O. (1977). Assessment and therapeutic functions of self-monitoring. In M. Hersen, R. M. Eisler, & P. M. Miller (Eds.), *Progress in Behavior Modification* (Vol. 5, pp. 263–308). New York: Academic Press.

Nelson, R. O., & Hayes, S. C. (1981). Theoretical explanations for reactivity in self-monitoring. *Behavior Modification, 5,* 3–14.

Nelson, R. O., Lipinski, D. P., & Black, J. L. (1976). The relative reactivity of external observations and self-monitoring. *Behavior Therapy, 7,* 314–321.

Nelson, T. O. (1992). *Metacognition: Core readings.* Boston: Allyn & Bacon.

Neunaber, D. J., & Wasserman, E. A. (1986). The effects of unidirectional versus bidirectional rating procedures on college students' judgments of response-outcome contingency. *Learning and Motivation, 17,* 162–179.

Nevin, J. A. (1992). An integrative model for the study of behavioral momentum. *Journal of the Experimental Analysis of Behavior, 57,* 301–316.

Nisbett, R. E., & Wilson, T. D. (1977). Telling more than we can know: Verbal reports on mental processes. *Psychological Review, 84,* 231–259.

Nurco, D. N. (1985). A discussion of validity. In B. A. Rouse, N. J. Kozel, & L. G. Richards (Eds.), *Self-report methods of estimating drug use: Meeting current challenges to validity* (pp. 4–11). Rockville, MD: National Institute on Drug Abuse.

Oah, S., & Dickinson, A. M. (1989). A review of empirical studies of verbal behavior. *The Analysis of Verbal Behavior, 7,* 53–68.

Overton, D. A. (1987). Applications and limitations of the drug discrimination method for the study of drug abuse. In M. A. Bozarth (Ed.), *Methods of assessing the reinforcing properties of abused drugs* (pp. 291–340). Berlin: Springer-Verlag.

Pekala, R. J. (1991). *Quantifying consciousness: An empirical approach.* New York: Plenum Press.

Perone, M. (1988). Laboratory lore and research practices in the experimental analysis of human behavior: Use and abuse of subjects' verbal reports. *The Behavior Analyst, 11,* 71–75.

Povinelli, D. J. (1994). How to create self-recognizing gorillas (but don't try it on macaques). In S. T. Parker, R. W. Mitchell, & M. L. Boccia (Eds.), *Self-awareness in animals and humans* (pp. 291–301). London: Cambridge University Press.

Preston, K. L., Bigelow, G. E., Bickel, W. K., & Liebson, I. A. (1989). Drug discrimination in human postaddicts: Agonist–antagonist opioids. *Journal of Pharmacology and Experimental Therapeutics, 250,* 184–196.

Rachlin, H. (1985). Pain and behavior. *Behavioral and Brain Sciences, 8,* 43–83 (includes peer commentary).

Rachlin, H., Raineri, A., & Cross, D. (1991). Subjective probability and delay. *Journal of the Experimental Analysis of Behavior, 55,* 233–244.

Reid, J. B. (1982). Observer training in naturalistic research. In D. P. Hartman (Ed.), *Using observers to study behavior* (pp. 37–50). San Francisco: Jossey–Bass.

Reynolds, G. S. (1961). Attention in the pigeon. *Journal of the Experimental Analysis of Behavior, 4,* 203–208.

Rilling, M. (1977). Stimulus control and inhibitory processes. In W. K. Honig & J. E. R. Staddon (Eds.), *Handbook of operant behavior* (pp. 432–480). Englewood Cliffs, NJ: Prentice–Hall.

Roache, J. D., & Griffiths, R. R. (1989). Abuse liability of anxiolytics and sedative/hypnotics: Methods assessing the likelihood of abuse. In M. W. Fischman & N. K. Mello (Eds.), *Testing for the abuse liability of drugs* (pp. 123–146). National Institute on Drug Abuse Research Monograph No. 92. Washington, DC: National Institute on Drug Abuse.

Roediger, H. L., ed. (1997). Implicit learning: A symposium. *Psychonomic Bulletin & Review, 4,* 1–78.

Rosenfarb, I. S., Newland, M. C., Brannon, S. E., & Howey, D. S. (1992). Effects of self-generated rules on the development of schedule-controlled behavior. *Journal of the Experimental Analysis of Behavior, 58,* 107–121.

Rosenfeld, H. M., & Baer, D. M. (1969). Unnoticed verbal conditioning of an aware experimenter by a more aware subject: The double-agent effect. *Psychological Review, 76,* 425–432.

Rosenthal, D. M. (1986). Two concepts of consciousness. *Philosophical Studies, 49,* 329–359.

Rosenthal, R. (1966). *Experimenter effects in behavioral research.* New York: Appleton–Century–Crofts.

Rush, C. R., Critchfield, T. S., Troisi, J. R., II, & Griffiths, R. R. (1995). Discriminative stimulus effects of diazepam and buspirone in normal volunteers. *Journal of the Experimental Analysis of Behavior, 63,* 277–294.

Samo, J. A., Tucker, J. A., & Vuchinich, R. E. (1989). Agreement between self-monitoring, recall, and collateral observation measures of alcohol consumption in older adults. *Behavioral Assessment, 11,* 391–401.

Savastano, H. I., & Fantino, E. (1994). Human choice in concurrent ratio-interval schedules of reinforcement. *Journal of the Experimental Analysis of Behavior, 61,* 453–463.

Sherer, K. R., & Ekman, P. (1982). *Handbook of methods in nonverbal behavior research.* London: Cambridge University Press.

Sidman, M. (1960). *Tactics of scientific research.* New York: Basic Books.

Siegel, S., & Castellan, J. (1988). *Nonparametric statistics for the behavioral sciences.* New York: McGraw–Hill.

Skinner, B. F. (1945). The operational analysis of psychological terms. *Psychological Review, 52,* 291–294.

Skinner, B. F. (1957). *Verbal behavior.* New York: Appleton–Century–Crofts.

Skinner, B. F. (1966). What is the experimental analysis of behavior? *Journal of the Experimental Analysis of Behavior, 9,* 213–218.

Sobell, L. C., & Sobell, M. B. (1990a). Self-reports across addictive behaviors: Issues and future directions in clinical and research settings. *Behavioral Assessment, 12,* 1–4.

Sobell, L. C., & Sobell, M. B. (1990b). Self-report issues in alcohol abuse: State of the art and future directions. *Behavioral Assessment, 12,* 77–90.

Speilberger, C. D., & DeNike, L. D. (1966). Descriptive behaviorism versus cognitive theory in verbal operant conditioning. *Psychological Review, 73,* 306–326.

Spetch, M. L., & Wilkie, D. M. (1983). Subjective shortening: A model of pigeons' memory for event duration. *Journal of Experimental Psychology: Animal Behavior Processes, 9,* 14–30.

Stevenson, H. W., Chen, C., & Lee, S. (1993). Mathematics achievement of Chinese, Japanese, and American children: Ten years later. *Science, 259,* 53–58.

Stiles, W. V. (1992). *Analyzing talk: A taxonomy of verbal response modes.* Newbury Park, CA: Sage.

Sudman, S., & Bradburn, N. M. (1974). *Response effects in surveys: A review and synthesis.* Chicado: Aldine.

Sudman, S., & Bradburn, N. M. (1982). *Asking questions.* San Francisco: Jossey–Bass.

Tobin, J., Wu, D., & Davidson, D. (1989). *Preschool in three cultures: Japan, China, and the United States.* New Haven, CT: Yale University Press.

Tomasello, M. (1993). On the interpersonal origins of self-concept. In U. Neisser (Ed.), *The perceived self: Ecological and interpersonal sources of self-knowledge* (pp. 174–184). London: Cambridge University Press.

Troisi, J. R., II, Critchfield, T. S., & Griffiths, R. R. (1993). Buspirone and lorazepam abuse liability in humans: Behavioral effects, subjective effects, and choice. *Behavioural Pharmacology, 4,* 217–230.

Tucker, J. A., Vuchinich, R. E., Harris, C. V., Gavornik, M. G., & Rudd, E. J. (1991). Agreement between subject and collateral verbal reports of alcohol consumption in older adults. *Journal of Studies on Alcohol, 52,* 148–155.

Vuchinich, R. E. (1995). Alcohol abuse as molar choice: An update of a 1982 proposal. *Psychology of Addictive Behaviors, 9,* 223–235.

Vuchinich, R. E., & Tucker, J. A. (1988). Contributions from behavioral theories of choice to an analysis of alcohol abuse. *Journal of Abnormal Psychology, 97,* 181–197.

Vuchinich, R. E., Tucker, J. A., & Harlee, L. M. (1988). Behavioral assessment. In D. M. Donovan & G. A. Marlatt (Eds.), *Assessment of addictive behaviors* (pp. 51–83). New York: Guilford Press.

Walbott, H. G. (1982). Audiovisual recording: Procedures, equipment, and troubleshooting. In K. R. Sherer & P. Ekman (Eds.), *Handbook of methods in nonverbal behavior research* (pp. 542–579). London: Cambridge University Press.

Wanchisen, B. A., & Tatham, T. A. (1991). Behavioral history: A promising challenge in explaining and controlling human operant behavior. *The Behavior Analyst, 14,* 139–144.

Wanchisen, B. A., Tatham, T. A., & Hineline, P. N. (1992). Human choice in "counterintuitive" situations: Fixed-versus progressive-ratio schedules. *Journal of the Experimental Analysis of Behavior, 58,* 67–85.

Wearden, J. H. (1988). Some neglected problems in the analysis of human operant behavior. In G. Davey & C. Cullen (Eds.), *Human operant behavior and behavior modification* (pp. 197–224). New York: Wiley.

Wentland, E. J., & Smith, K. W. (1993). *Survey responses: An evaluation of their validity.* San Diego: Academic Press.

White, P. A. (1988). Knowing more about what we can tell: 'Introspective access' and causal report accuracy 10 years later. *British Journal of Psychology, 79,* 13–45.

Wulfert, E., Dougher, M. J., & Greenway, D. E. (1991). Protocol analysis of the correspondence of verbal behavior and equivalence class formation. *Journal of the Experimental Analysis of Behavior, 56,* 489–504.

Zuriff, G. E. (1985). *Behaviorism: A conceptual reconstruction.* New York: Columbia University Press.

15

Social Behavior

David R. Schmitt

Considered most broadly, a person's behavior is social when its causes or effects include the behavior of others. From the wide range of everyday actions that fit this definition, social scientists have focused on particular, consequential forms of social behavior for experimental study. One of the longest experimental traditions has been the study of cooperation and competition, contrasting social behaviors that are ubiquitous in groups of various types and sizes and the basis of competing economic and organizational philosophies. Although cooperation and competition are often used in a general sense to connote activities that benefit others or gain advantage over them, respectively, definitions in the experimental tradition are more specific. Here cooperation and competition are behaviors that occur in the context of particular contingencies that specify behaviors and the criteria for their reinforcement. With a cooperative contingency, all participants receive a reinforcer if their responses collectively meet a specified performance criterion. With a competitive contingency, reinforcers are distributed unequally based on relative performance.

Although cooperation and competition were treated initially as contrasting alternatives, later analyses have situated them as instances sharing the property of consequence interdependence—each person's consequences depend on the behavior of another. Here others' behaviors typically become discriminative stimuli that affect each person's responding. The basic elements of interdependence have been developed most fully and compellingly by social psychologists Harold Kelley and John Thibaut (Kelley, 1979; Kelley & Thibaut, 1978; Thibaut & Kelley, 1959), who have analyzed interdependence in terms of the outcome matrices used in game theory. Their analysis shows that situations entailing consequence interdependence constitute a definable, socially significant subset of social behaviors. These behaviors, which include cooperation, competition, and exchange, have been studied in a variety of settings by behavior analysts.

David R. Schmitt • Department of Sociology, University of Washington, Seattle, Washington 98195.
Handbook of Research Methods in Human Operant Behavior, edited by Lattal and Perone. Plenum Press, New York, 1998.

PATTERNS OF INTERDEPENDENCE

In situations in which two people are behaving in some manner, each person's consequences can derive from one or more of the following three sources (Kelley & Thibaut, 1978). First, consequences may result from the person's own behavior, for example, reinforcement from watching television, reading a book, or eating a meal (termed *reflexive control* by Kelley & Thibaut). Such consequences have also been termed *nonsocial* or *individual.* Consequences from the other two sources are *socially mediated,* and constitute the two basic types of interdependence. For one the source is solely the other's behavior (termed *fate control* by Kelley & Thibaut). For example, one person may give reinforcers such as approval, assistance, or money to another. Such consequences provided by another person have also been termed *dependent,* and that term will be used here. For the other source, consequences depend in some manner on responses made by *both* people (termed *behavior control* by Kelley & Thibaut). In some instances involving this source, a person's consequences depend completely on combined actions. For example, two people are able to lift a heavy object that neither can lift separately. In other instances, consequences are augmented when responses are combined. For example, a person may enjoy playing the piano, but enjoys playing much more if another person plays guitar as part of a duet. Skinner (1953) noted that the reinforcing effect of an individual act is often increased enormously when a person is part of a group—as when a person cheers in a crowd or jeers in a mob. In all of these examples, the consequences for people making the responses are *correspondent* (or positively correlated). The coordinated responses produce positive consequences for all participants. Consequences, however, can also be *noncorrespondent* (or negatively correlated). In the two-person case, the coordinated responses produce positive consequences for one person and negative (or less positive) ones for the other. In a race, for example, only the winning runner may get a trophy. To distinguish consequences that require that both persons respond in some manner from those that depend on the behavior of only one, the term *joint-dependent* will be used for the former. Whether joint-dependent consequences are correspondent or noncorrespondent is critical because it is the major feature distinguishing cooperation from competition.

Analyses of interdependence in everyday settings are complex because social behaviors are often controlled by both socially mediated and individual consequences. For example, the meal for two that one person prepares can have positive consequences for the preparer (individual) and for the guest (dependent). Two people may enjoy watching a movie singly (individual), but enjoy it much more in the other's presence (joint-dependent). In some instances, then, the social component only partially affects the consequences for each person.

Cooperation and competition share the property of joint-dependent consequences but differ in correspondence of those consequences for the participants. For cooperation, consequences are correspondent—reinforcement is mutual for successful responses. For competition, consequences are noncorrespondent—reinforcement is unequal for winning and losing responses. When interdependence takes the form of dependence, two people can each make a response that provides a reinforcer for the other. If they do so, contingent on the other's reciprocation, another major type of social behavior, exchange, has emerged.

EXPERIMENTAL ANALYSES

Cooperation, competition, and exchange represent three types of social behavior that are considered elementary because of their ubiquity and centrality in social life. The settings and procedures for studying them experimentally in behavior analysis will be described below. There are several distinguishing features of such an analysis. First, the settings have focused on easily measured, readily repeatable responses (e.g., button presses, knob pulls) for which consequences are tangible and significant (e.g., points exchanged later for money). Second, conditions studied are generally maintained long enough for stable, characteristic response patterns to develop. Third, effects of independent variables are assessed, at least in part, using within-subject comparisons, in which each group of interacting subjects (usually a pair) experiences various conditions.

Initial interest in laboratory studies of cooperation, competition, and exchange began during the time when electromechanical programming equipment was used for animal research in behavior analysis. Investigators studying human subjects used similar equipment to control specially designed tasks. Subjects worked at consoles or panels that included counters for registering points earned, stimulus lights, switches for making choices between conditions, and buttons, knobs, or levers for making task responses. Contemporary studies duplicating these functions would typically use computers, where responses are made on keyboards, and monitors are used to display messages, stimulus conditions, and earnings. For this reason, descriptions of these earlier settings will focus on the functions of their various features instead of their physical characteristics. The research reports themselves should be consulted for detailed setting descriptions.

Unlike some other areas of behavior analysis, no single setting has been used and adapted by most investigators who have studied interdependence. Instead, a number of settings have been designed to investigate particular problems. There are thus a variety of starting points for future research. Although some variables have been explored in more than one setting, little is known about the effects of particular setting characteristics on the relations between similar variables. Because most settings have been developed to study two subjects (i.e., a minimal social setting), pairs will be used as illustration in most of the examples that follow.

The experimental analysis of social behavior will be addressed in the next four sections. The first three sections will describe, in turn, laboratory settings for the study of cooperation, exchange, and competition. In each section I will begin by reviewing the array of setting features that need to be considered in investigating the behavior—the setting structure. I will then describe various settings used in the major research. I will emphasize the nature of the setting contingencies, including the types of responses available, number of tasks, and schedules of reinforcement. In the fourth section methodological issues common to all of the settings will be addressed. These include: (1) controlling variables—steps taken to ensure that subjects are responding to each other's behavior and that consequences are effective; (2) initial conditions and instructions—contact allowed between subjects and information used to introduce subjects to experimental conditions; and (3) experimental designs—issues to be considered in designing experiments and recruiting subjects.

COOPERATION

Setting Structure

In studying cooperation, the first requirement is to specify the nature of the cooperative response or task. Although there is general agreement that cooperation requires mutual reinforcement for some response, studies have differed in the features of the responses required. Response requirements are important because the choice of elements determines the effects of other variables on cooperation. As Marwell and Schmitt (1975) noted, cooperative responses have included three major elements. One is *response distribution.* Does the task require that both persons make some response (i.e., a division of labor), or can it be made by only one person? Where the responses need not be made by both people, one person can receive reinforcers noncontingently (i.e., "free-ride"), a feature that can adversely affect group performance for some tasks. Where the cooperative response requires responses by both people, the possibility of *coordination* arises. Must the individual behaviors take place in some specified relation (e.g., in a particular order or in response to a signal)? Finally, if the individual responses are coordinated, must the coordination be *social?* That is, are people responding to stimuli provided by other participants? At the extreme, social coordination implies that participants must be able to see and talk to each other so that the full range of verbal and visual stimuli are available. When people are in separate rooms, other stimuli such as lights, sounds, or messages can be used to convey information. Hake and Olvera (1978) termed such stimuli *quasi-social.* The elements of response distribution, response coordination, and social coordination form a progression with regard to inclusiveness. Thus, social coordination presumes both response distribution and response coordination. Although studies of cooperation have differed with regard to the inclusion of these elements, most have at least used responses requiring some coordination.

A major option in a cooperative setting is the availability of alternative responses to cooperation. The term *forced response* situation is applied when cooperation provides the only reinforcement (Hake & Vukelich, 1972). The term *alternative response* or *choice* situation is applied when one or more alternative responses also provide reinforcement (Hake & Vukelich, 1972). A single alternative to cooperation is typically used. The most common has been a nonsocial, individual response that provides a source of reinforcement that does not depend on the behavior of the other person.

Providing alternative responses can serve various purposes when a specific behavior, such as cooperation, is of interest. First, investigators may be interested in subjects' preference among different kinds of alternatives, such as the choice between cooperation and a particular second response (e.g., working alone, competition). Second, effects of variables that make cooperation more aversive, such as high response requirements or inequitable earnings, are more likely to be observed when an alternative (i.e., concurrent response) can be chosen. For example, subjects who did not readily cease cooperating when it is the only response available were likely to switch to a somewhat less reinforcing alternative response (Marwell & Schmitt, 1975). The strength of a variable's effect on cooperation can be assessed by varying the attractiveness of the alternative (i.e., through changes in reinforcer size or reinforcement frequency), and then observing the point at which the alternative is chosen. Providing alternative reinforcement is particularly important when potentially aversive conditions are studied over a number of sessions using adult subjects. In such cases it is likely that the investigator will be using money as the reinforcer. If the aversive condition is the only source of money, however, subjects forced to remain in that condition may quit the experiment because they earn so little or find the experiment so unpleasant. But, if an adequately paying alternative is available, subjects can avoid the aversive condition after having experienced it. Finally, investigators who are interested in how disrupted cooperation is reestablished may use a reinforcing alternative to temporarily disrupt cooperation (cf. Molm, 1984). For example, making an individual alternative more attractive than cooperation for a period of time will cause cooperation to cease.

When two people are given a choice between two alternatives, the investigator must also specify the consequences when each makes a different choice. In studies where cooperation and individual responding have been the alternatives, cooperative contingencies are typically in effect only when they are chosen by both subjects. If either subject chooses the individual alternative, it is in effect for both subjects. This situation is congruent with most everyday cooperation which requires the agreement of both parties to cooperate. Other choice contingencies are possible, however. The cooperative condition could be in effect unless the individual condition is chosen by both subjects, or one subject's choice could determine the conditions for both subjects.

The structure of cooperative settings is thus defined by three elements: the nature of the cooperative response; the alternatives to cooperation; and, given alternatives, choice contingencies (i.e., how individual choices are combined). Described next are cooperative settings developed by Azrin and Lindsley, Mithaug and Burgess, Lindsley, Schmitt and Marwell, Shimoff and Matthews, and Schmitt which incorporate various of these elements. Also described in brief are matrix games, which have some of these features and have been widely used in the social sciences.

Cooperative Settings

Azrin and Lindsley's Setting

A considerable part of the experimental analysis of cooperation stems from the refinement and elaboration of a setting developed by Azrin and Lindsley (1956). Most previous research on cooperation in social psychology had used discrete, complex tasks in which group members discussed an issue or solved a prob-

FIGURE 15.1.   Azrin and Lindsley's apparatus used for the reinforcement of cooperation between two children.

lem. Based on the success of studies of response rates in animals, Azrin and Lindsley developed a simple, easily repeated response whose frequency was controlled by the subjects (i.e., a free-operant response). The setting was used to demonstrate differential reinforcement and extinction of cooperative responses in nursery school children using a reinforcer that was available to both subjects. As shown in Figure 15.1, two children were seated on opposite sides of a table with a wire screen down the center that permitted them to see each other and communicate. In front of each child were three holes and a stylus. A cooperative response consisted of the children putting their styluses in opposite holes within 0.04 s of each other, a correspondence unlikely to occur by chance. The effective pair of holes was randomized so that subjects had to explore the holes to discover the correct one. When a cooperative response occurred, a red light flashed and a single jelly bean fell into a cup that was accessible to both children. Pairs could divide the candy in any manner. Leader–follower relations typically developed in which one child explored the holes and the other child followed. Figure 15.2 shows cooperative rates for three pairs. High rates typically emerged within 20 min when cooperative responses were reinforced. Rates declined gradually when reinforcement was discontinued (i.e., extinction), and returned quickly to the earlier level when reinforcement was again introduced.

Mithaug and Burgess's Setting

Mithaug and Burgess (1967, 1968) attempted to replicate Azrin and Lindsley's findings in a more complex setting. Subjects were groups of three children instead of two, and 14 alternative responses were provided instead of 3. Three 14-key piano keyboard instruments were aligned against a wall, permitting subjects to see each other (but not all of their responses) and communicate. Each keyboard also contained lights and a counter that could be used to provide individual informa-

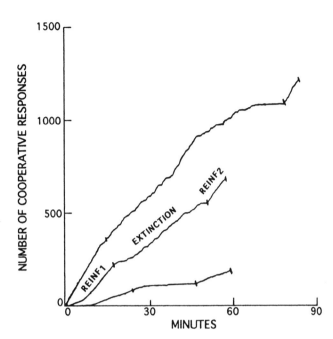

FIGURE 15.2. Cumulative response records for the pairs with the highest, median, and lowest rates of cooperation.

tion to each subject about the accuracy of his or her response. Mounted on the wall was a light board that contained 14 lights corresponding to the piano keys and an additional center light and counter to register cooperative responses. One of the 14 lights was illuminated for a given period (e.g., for 2 min). A cooperative response consisted of each child pressing, within 0.5 s of one another, the key corresponding to the one light illuminated. Following a cooperative response, the center light illuminated on the light board and a count registered. Counts were redeemable later for money or prizes.

When cooperative reinforcement alone was provided in this more complex setting, subjects failed to cooperate (Mithaug & Burgess, 1967). High rates of cooperation did occur, however, when each subject received feedback from a keyboard light for pressing the key signaled on the light board (Mithaug & Burgess, 1968). Mithaug (1969) studied conditions in which subjects could also earn points individually for pressing the correct key. At any time subjects could either coordinate their responses and earn points cooperatively or simply press the correct key and earn them individually. Mithaug varied the number of responses required to earn one point on each of the two alternatives. He found that children made cooperative instead of individual responses only when cooperation required at least 80% fewer responses.

Lindsley's Setting

In order to further explore the leader–follower relations found by Azrin and Lindsley (and to be able to study competition as well), Lindsley developed a more elaborate and flexible two-person setting (Cohen & Lindsley, 1964; Lindsley, 1966). Subjects were seated in laboratory rooms that were separated by a sliding partition that could be opened to reveal a window. A white masking noise prevented conversation between subjects. Each subject faced a panel containing a brass knob (Lindsley knob) that could be pulled, lights, and a dispenser for pennies and candy. When the partition was closed, a subject's knob pull was indicated to the partner by the illumination of a light on the partner's panel (response light) for 0.04 s. A cooperative response consisted of one subject pulling the knob within 0.5 s of the other. Each cooperative response was followed by a 5-s timeout during which the room lights dimmed, a light appeared in the reinforcement bin, and the pennies and candy were dispensed. A light on the subject's panel illuminated when the partner received a reinforcer (reinforcement light). If a subject made a second response before the partner responded (termed a *nonsocial response*), a mild punishment occurred—a 2.5-s timeout accompanied by darkened room lights and a loud tone. The contingencies in Lindsley's setting could also be changed to study competition instead of cooperation. This competitive response will be described in the section on competition.

Lindsley and Cohen (Cohen, 1962; Cohen & Lindsley, 1964; Lindsley, 1966) explored the effects of several variables on the emergence and maintenance of cooperation. One was whether the stimuli in the setting were given a social connotation. In one variation, subjects were brought to the setting alone, with no knowledge of the presence of the other subject. The response and reinforcement lights were operative, but subjects were not told that they were related to the behavior of another person. Under this condition cooperation was acquired very slowly or not at all. However, allowing subjects to see each other through the window or bringing them to the session together brought about rapid acquisition of cooperative responding. Another variable investigated was leadership. It was measured by observing which subject made the first response in each cooperative response pair. The effect of controlled leadership on cooperation was assessed as well. A particular subject needed to make the first response in each pair for reinforcement to occur. A third variable explored was the opportunity for subjects to see each other during the session, in addition to having panel lights that showed the partner's knob pull and reinforcement. Lindsley and Cohen studied variations in leadership requirement and visibility with several pairs and found that they often had a marked effect on the acquisition and maintenance of cooperation. These effects depended, in part, on relationships between subjects that existed prior to the experiment. In Cohen's (1962) study, for example, a 13-year-old boy was paired with his brother, sister, close friend, mother, and a stranger. The various relationships produced markedly different patterns of cooperation and competition.

Schmitt and Marwell's Setting

In Lindsley's setting, subjects responding within 0.5 s of each other were assumed to be attending to each other's behavior to achieve such close coordination—the behavior was assumed to be social (or quasi-social). However, Schmitt and Marwell (1968) found that there were ways that subjects could achieve cooperation without attention to their partner's responding. First, high individual response rates by both subjects (e.g., greater than 120 per min) will necessarily bring

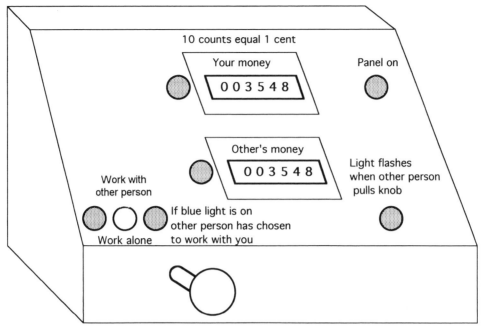

FIGURE 15.3.   Diagram of Schmitt and Marwell's subject panel.

some response pairs within the 0.5-s interval. Second, if both subjects respond immediately after the timeout following reinforcement, a cooperative response results. If either of these patterns occurs often, the subjects' behavior cannot be confidently interpreted as being social. Schmitt and Marwell replicated major features of Lindsley's cooperative setting and procedure using the panel shown in Figure 15.3, but with the switch and lights in the lower left corner removed. (These are part of a procedure described later.) The setting differed from Lindsley's in several respects. The reinforcer was money, but earnings were not dispensed directly to subjects. Accumulated total earnings of the subjects and partner were indicated on separate counters (labeled "Your money" and "Other's money") on each subject's panel. Lights placed next to these counters flashed for every reinforcement count registered. Pulling the knob (Lindsley knob) on the front of the panel illuminated a response light on the partner's panel for 0.1 s. The length of a timeout after a cooperative response was signaled by turning off a light (timeout light) labeled "Panel on" on each subject's panel instead of by dimming the room lights. Subjects worked in separate rooms.

Schmitt and Marwell (1968) studied six pairs of subjects to determine whether the presence of the response lights or the timeout lights was necessary for subjects to cooperate at high rates (where both subjects knew of the other's presence). Results indicated that cooperative response rates were moderate to high when either or both lights were absent. Substantial coordination was obtained either by responding rhythmically or at high individual rates. Although the findings show that high rates of cooperation can occur when either the response or timeout lights are absent, they do not indicate which stimulus tends to be used when both are present. Additional data bear on this point.

Previous research with the apparatus indicated that a reaction time of at least 0.2 s was required for a subject to respond using the partner's pull (response light) as a stimulus. Thus, if the subject pulling second was responding to the partner's behavior, few of the pulls should occur within 0.2 s of the partner's pull. However, if both subjects were responding to the timeout lights, most of the pulls should occur within the 0.2-s interval. Results indicated that response intervals of less than 0.2 s occurred in more than 80% of the cooperative responses for three of the pairs and in less than 20% of the responses for the remaining three. Thus, the controlling stimulus for at least some cooperating pairs was the end of the timeout following reinforcement, a jointly produced event, instead of the partner's behavior.

To try to ensure that all cooperating pairs were responding to the same stimuli, Schmitt and Marwell modified Lindsley's contingencies. The key element was the addition of a delay between the two subjects' responses. Either subject could respond first. That response illuminated the partner's response light for 3 s. If the second subject responded within 0.5 s after the light went out, reinforcement occurred. If the second subject responded before the 3-s response light went out, the response light went out immediately, and the next pull by either subject reinitiated the partner's response light for 3 s. To make the maximum response rate on the modified task comparable to that on Lindsley's, the timeout following reinforcement was reduced from 5 to 2 s. With the 3 s between responses and the 2-s timeout, a minimum of 5 s was required between cooperative responses.

With this modification, Schmitt and Marwell found that the response light initiated by the subject responding first was essential for the follower in making a cooperative response. The six pairs who worked on Lindsley's task described above also worked on the modified task with the response lights and timeout lights present or absent. Results indicated that high cooperative response rates required the lights signaling subjects' responses. Without those lights, few cooperative responses occurred. When both response lights and timeout lights were present, the follower's responses rarely occurred less than 0.2 s after the leader (in no more than 2% of the cooperative responses for any pair). Thus, the only way to cooperate at a high rate was for the follower to respond when the response light turned on by the leader went off.

Before using the modified cooperative contingency, Schmitt and Marwell altered the contingencies in two other respects. Most important was the addition of a nonsocial, individual alternative to cooperation. As shown in the lower left corner of the panel in Figure 15.3, each subject could choose to work under the individual or cooperative tasks by operating a toggle switch up or down. The cooperative task was in effect only if both chose to work together. If either or both chose to work alone, the individual task was available for both subjects. When a subject switched to "Work with other person," two lights illuminated: the light to the left of the subject's own switch, and the light to the right of the partner's switch. When the individual task was made available (by either subject choosing it), a knob pull advanced the subject's counter and illuminated the response light on the partner's panel for 0.1 s. In order to equate the maximum frequency of reinforcement on the individual and cooperative tasks, each individual response was followed by a 5-s timeout during which the panel light was turned off. Neither cooperative nor individual responses could be initiated during timeout periods.

Providing the choice of working individually in a cooperative setting also provides additional assurance that the coordinated responses are cooperative. Subjects who do not want to cooperate can work individually instead of making uncoordinated (noncooperative) responses. Schmitt and Marwell found few uncoordinated responses when the individual response was available and, therefore, eliminated any consequences if a subject made a second response before the partner responded when both had chosen to cooperate. In Lindsley's setting this nonsocial response was followed by a 2.5-s timeout.

Marwell, Schmitt, and their associates used this setting to conduct a number of studies that focused on the effects of two variables that are common in cooperative settings. The first was reinforcer inequity—giving reinforcers of unequal size to the two subjects making a cooperative response. Inequitable consequences led the underpaid subject in previously cooperative pairs to switch from a more profitable cooperative task to a less profitable individual one (Marwell & Schmitt, 1975; Schmitt & Marwell, 1972). For some pairs, a button was added to the upper left-hand corner of the panel permitting subjects to transfer points from one subject to the other. The opportunity to rectify inequities frequently led to transfers and greater cooperation. The second variable studied was the risk of the loss of earnings when subjects cooperated. Choosing to cooperate in everyday life often entails joint access to and control of resources and the risk that one's resources can be taken by another. Thus, cooperation may entail not only a task requirement but also trust. For cooperation to be successful, partners need to refrain from taking each other's resources. Risk was created by providing a button in the upper left-hand corner of the panel that permitted each subject to take points from the other. These buttons were operative whenever both subjects chose to cooperate. When subjects could take a large numbers of points with a single button press, cooperation ceased for most pairs (Marwell & Schmitt, 1972, 1975; Marwell, Schmitt & Shotola, 1971; Schmitt & Marwell, 1971a). Figure 15.4 shows the cumulative cooperative response rates of a typical pair in the presence (take-continuous) and absence (baseline) of the opportunity to take. Subjects were working individually during periods in which no cooperative responses occurred. The abrupt decreases in cooperative response rates following a change in condition are typical when a reinforcing alternative to cooperation is available. This pattern contrasts with the gradual decline in responding found by Azrin and Lindsley (1956) when cooperation was extinguished (shown in Figure 15.2). Marwell, Schmitt, and their associates investigated the effects of risk on cooperation under a number of conditions including variations in risk size, time at risk, and size of the reinforcers for cooperation. They also studied a variety of conditions that might mitigate the disruptive effects of risk, including the ability of subjects to communicate, see each other, and avoid take attempts (Marwell & Schmitt, 1975; Marwell, Schmitt, & Boyesen, 1973; Schmitt & Marwell, 1971b, 1977).

Schmitt (1976) later modified Schmitt and Marwell's setting in order to study cooperation among three people. Each subject's panel contained a switch for work-

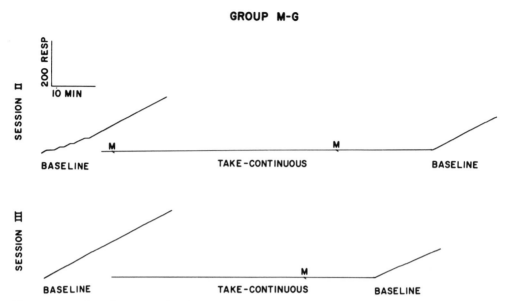

FIGURE 15.4. Cumulative record of the cooperative responses for one pair (Group M–G) during base-line and take-continuous conditions. In take-continuous conditions either subject could take money from the other if both chose to cooperate. "M" shows occasions where Subject M took from Subject G (the only taking).

ing together or alone, a response button (instead of a knob), lights indicating whether each of the other subjects had chosen to work together, and lights show-ing when each of the other subjects responded. Cooperation required that all three subjects choose to work together. With cooperation chosen, the button press by the subject responding first illuminated for 3 s the response lights on the other sub-jects' panels. If both of these subjects pushed their buttons in the 0.5-s period af-ter the response lights went out, points were added to counters adjacent to the pan-els. Other aspects were identical to those of the two-person setting. Schmitt compared the likelihood of cooperation in two- and three-person groups where the alternative was competition. Although less cooperation was found in three-person groups, the cause was the increased attractiveness of competition, not problems in making the cooperative response.

Shimoff and Matthews's Setting

Shimoff and Matthews (1975) studied reinforcer inequities in a choice setting in which two subjects could either cooperate or work independently. Subjects were seated at panels in separate cubicles. A switch was used to choose one of the tasks, and two counters registered own and partner's earnings. Points were ex-changed later for money. Subjects chose one of the tasks at the beginning of each of a series of trials. If both subjects chose cooperation, a sequence of responses us-ing a cooperative response button produced points for both subjects. First, a light on one subject's panel illuminated to indicate that the cooperative response button was to be pressed. Pressing the button extinguished the light and illuminated a second light indicating that the partner's cooperative response button was to be pressed. A completed cooperative response required four such alternations. If either or both subjects chose the independent response, a sequence of responses using two independent response buttons produced points for the subject making the response. Lights signaled when to make four pairs of responses on the two buttons. Following the delivery of points for either a cooperative or independent response, all response buttons were turned off for 9.5 s.

Shimoff and Matthews used this setting to study whether choice was affected by inequities between subjects in the points given for the two responses. Sessions were divided into 20-trial "runs" where the amount paid for cooperation was increased by 1 point on each trial, beginning at 1 point and ending at 20 points. A panel counter showed the prevailing point value. In their first experiment, the independent response always paid 10 points (shown on a panel label). Thus, for the first 9 trials the independent response was more profitable than cooperation; for the last 9 trials it was increasingly less profitable. Inequities in cooperation were created by giving one subject (who was a confederate of the experimenter) an additional number of points on each trial. The effects of inequitable cooperative earnings on the behavior of the underpaid subject were measured in two ways. The first was the point in the run where the underpaid subject began to choose the independent response. To create the second measure, a response was added that allowed either subject to terminate the inequity. Each subject was given a button that could be used once any time during the run to create an equal number of cooperative points on all remaining trials in the run. In addition, some pairs could operate switches on their panels that allowed them to give the extra cooperative points on each trial to the previously underpaid subject. In a second experiment, inequity was created only in the independent response. It provided higher earnings for the subject than the confederate. In general, subjects responded in ways that escaped or avoided reinforcer inequities.

Schmitt's Setting

Schmitt (1987) developed a cooperative setting that enabled the investigator to manipulate the number of responses (i.e., effort) required for cooperation. Two subjects, working at panels in separate rooms, could either cooperate or work alone. As in Schmitt and Marwell's setting, each subject used a switch to select one of the tasks and a knob to make task responses. Two counters registered own and partner's earnings, and a light signaled the partner's response. Points were exchanged later for money. The cooperative task differed from that used by Schmitt and Marwell in not requiring a precise coordination of responses. Reinforcers for cooperation were available at intervals that averaged 30 s and ranged from 1 to 108 s (a constant probability VI 30-s schedule). Points were added to the counters if both subjects pulled their knobs at least once within a specified period of time after the interval ended (a limited hold). Neither the end of the intervals nor the length of the limited holds was signaled for the subjects. Thus, the behavior reinforced in this situation was pulling the knobs at a high rate. How high a rate was determined by the length of the limited hold. For example, with a limited hold of 1 s at the end of each unsignaled interval, at least 60 responses per minute were required to receive all of the scheduled reinforcers. With a reduction of the limited hold from 1 s to 0.4 s, at least 90 additional response were needed to receive all reinforcers. Thus, by reducing the length of the limited hold, the investigator could increase the response rates needed by each subject in order for both to receive most of the reinforcers. Subjects were told the length of the limited hold at the beginning of each condition (e.g., "If both of you pull the knobs within 2/5 second of the right time, each of you will get 6 cents").

The alternative task was in effect if chosen by either subject. Reinforcers were available on the same VI 30-s schedule used for cooperation, but a limited hold period of 1 s was signaled by a panel light. Subjects could thus make a single response each time the panel light went on and receive all of the scheduled reinforcers.

Schmitt was interested in the highest response rate that could be obtained on the cooperative task when earnings favored cooperation by a given amount (e.g., cooperation paid 6 cents and the alternative paid 4 cents). The limited hold for cooperation was set at 10 s initially and was lowered progressively until subjects no longer chose cooperation and spent most of their time on the alternative. Cooperative response rates were compared with rates achieved under individual and competitive contingencies (described in the section on competition).

Matrix Games

In the study of cooperation within social psychology, the most popular format has been the matrix game. This setting is noted here because it focuses on the element of choice where one of the two alternatives is described as cooperative. The most widely used example has been the Prisoner's Dilemma. In a typical Prisoner's Dilemma matrix, shown in Figure 15.5, mutual choice of alternative C, which gives moderate payoffs to both subjects, is termed *cooperation.* Choice of alternative D by either or both subjects is termed *defection* or *exploitation.* The subject choosing D receives the highest payoff and the partner the lowest payoff when the partner chooses C. If both subjects choose D, each receives the next-to-lowest payoff. Studies using matrix games typically require that each subject choose one of the alternatives simultaneously and in isolation from each other. The outcome and points awarded are announced after each trial. Choices are typically made over a number of trials. In essence, a matrix game is a choice setting, but without cooperative or alternative tasks. Points are based only on the combined choices. Matrices such as the Prisoner's Dilemma were developed as mixed-motive games where the motivation to cooperate is only one of several that could affect subjects' choices. Hence, the alternative to cooperation is not a simple individual alternative, but one that exploits the other if chosen unilaterally or punishes both if chosen mutually. Because all of the subjects' outcomes are interdependent, complex response patterns often develop. The choices in matrix games need not have complex outcomes, however. The simpler choices between reinforcer amounts used in the settings above could be studied using the matrix format. (See Matthews's, 1979, investigation of competition.)

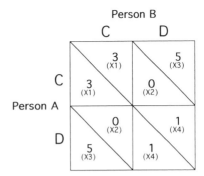

FIGURE 15.5. A 2 × 2 Prisoner's Dilemma game. The Prisoner's Dilemma game is typically defined by the following payoff relations: $X2 < X4 < X1 < X3$; $2X1 > X2 + X3$ (Rapoport & Chammah, 1965).

EXCHANGE

Setting Structure

In cooperative settings reinforcement is mutual when partners' responses meet the response criteria. In exchange settings partners can make responses that provide reinforcers for another, termed *giving,* but these responses need not be reciprocated. Hence, large differences can emerge in reinforcers received. Exchange has been termed *minimal* when there is a mere increase in giving responses by both persons. It is *maximal* when the consequence of giving is a correspondence (typically equality) between partners in the reinforcers given and responses made (Hake & Olvera, 1978). Most research has focused on exchange in the simplest settings where the reinforcer is points or money given to another by means of a simple response. Ability of either or both subjects to give is often manipulated, either through differences in amount given or the number of responses required to give a certain amount. The ability to reciprocate giving has been manipulated as well. In the simplest case either person can give at any time. In more restricted cases giving responses are limited to a single person for a given trial or period of time. Reversing the direction of giving can also require additional responses or some cost. In most studies of exchange, subjects are prevented from communicating with each other.

Because either person can give at different times with varying degrees of frequency, the range of behavior patterns in exchange settings is greater than that for cooperation. The emergence of exchange is often problematic because the initial giving responses are not immediately reciprocated. For the recipient, in fact, the reinforcers could strengthen other behaviors ongoing at the time. Over time, exchange will typically occur only when partners begin to make giving contingent to some degree on receiving. This added subject-initiated element, termed a *dependent contingency* by Weingarten and Mechner (1966), distinguishes exchange from cooperation or competition.

Various patterns of giving can lead to an equitable distribution of reinforcers, that is, maximal exchange. The simplest is where each giving response is reciprocated immediately. For exchanges to be most useful in everyday life, however, periods of giving without reciprocation need to be longer. For example, where friends do favors for each other, it would be cumbersome if every favor had to be reciprocated before another favor was offered. Friends are typically willing to provide a number of favors without reciprocation on the presumption that reciprocation will occur later. The term *expanded exchange* has been given to this pattern (Matthews, 1977). Thus, in expanded exchanges substantial short-term inequities can accompany a high long-term correspondence in giving. Expanded exchange, however, entails the risk that the advantaged partner will leave the relation before the inequity is rectified. Engaging in expanded exchange despite such risks has been termed *trusting behavior* (Hake & Schmid, 1981; Matthews, 1977). In exchange settings, trust can be measured by the number of unreciprocated giving responses that occur in the short term where long-term consequences are correspondent: the larger the number, the greater the trust. Whether expanded exchange is likely should also depend on whether costs are imposed when subjects want to reverse who gives and who receives. Making changes in direction more costly should increase the likelihood that expanded exchange will replace frequent alternation.

Due to the number of interaction possibilities, exchange is less likely to emerge and be maintained than is cooperation. For this reason, an alternative response is particularly significant in exchange settings. An alternative should make attempts at exchange less likely and reduce tolerance of inequitable exchanges. It is also of interest to create individual alternatives that pay the two subjects different amounts in order to study the effects of unequal dependence on the exchange relation.

The structure of exchange settings is thus defined by the nature of the giving responses, the ability to change the direction of giving and receiving, the alternatives to exchange, and the choice contingencies. Described next are exchange settings developed by Burgess and Nielsen, Michaels and Wiggins, Hake, Matthews, and Molm which incorporate various of these elements.

Exchange Settings

Burgess and Nielsen's Setting

Burgess and Nielsen (1974) developed a setting to study variations in the reinforcer amounts subjects received through exchange or working for themselves. Two subjects, seated in separate booths, each worked on a panel (shown in Figure 15.6) with separate buttons that could be pressed to earn points for oneself or give them to the partner. Points were redeemed later for money. Three counters showed own earnings, earnings from other to self, and earnings from self to other. A fourth counter (far left in Figure 15.6) showed the exchange ratio for self and other. The left-hand number on that counter (labeled "Self") indicated the number of presses needed by oneself to give $0.001 to the partner using the "Pay Other" button. The right-hand number (labeled "Other") indicated the number of presses needed by the partner to give $0.001 to oneself (both numbers are 3 in Figure 15.6). The partner's button presses illuminated a light beneath the "Other to Self" counter. The number of presses on the "Pay Self" button needed to add $0.001 to the "Self" counter was shown on a label below the button. Subjects were not shown the num-

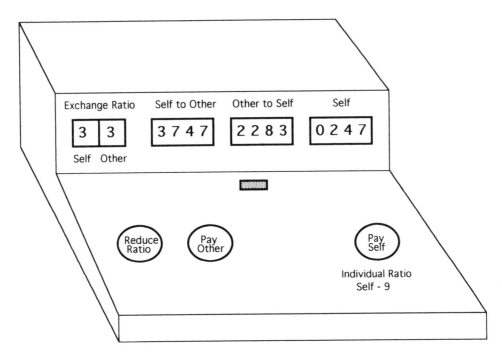

FIGURE 15.6.   Diagram of Burgess and Nielsen's subject panel.

ber of "Pay Self" button presses needed by one's partner to add $0.001. To eliminate differences in maximum response rates, the apparatus did not record responses at a rate grater than two per second. In addition, a subject could not make "Pay Self" and "Pay Other" button presses simultaneously. In some conditions the button labeled "Reduce Ratio" was also activated. Pressing the button reduced for 30 s the number of presses required to give $0.001 to the partner, thereby making exchange more attractive.

The use of ratios allowed earnings on the buttons to be varied for both the exchange and individual responses. Burgess and Nielsen (1974) conducted a series of studies that focused on the effects of changes in the relative number of responses for giving and individual responding. They also created inequities between the two subjects in those response requirements (termed *imbalanced relations*). Both variables affected the probability of exchange.

A setting resembling Burgess and Nielsen's was used by Michaels and Wiggins (1976) to study similar variables. Two buttons were available for adding points to one's own total or to the partner's total. Subjects alternated in either pressing one of the buttons or making no response. Reinforcer differences were created by paying different amounts for a single button press, in contrast to Burgess and Nielsen's procedure of varying the number of responses needed for a given amount. Results were similar, however. The frequency and pattern of exchange depended on relative reinforcer amounts for giving and individual responding and also on inequities between subjects in those amounts.

Hake's Setting

In a series of studies, Hake and his associates developed an exchange setting in which money could be earned by solving matching-to-sample problems. Although they termed behavior in this setting *cooperative,* it involved exchange in the terminology used here. In a study by Hake and Vukelich (1973), two subjects in the same room were seated in front of panels used to solve matching-to-sample problems. Each subject had a sample panel for producing sample stimuli and a matching response panel for matching the sample stimuli. Pressing the sample-producing button on the sample panel produced a red, green, or yellow sample stimulus for 0.5 s. Pressing the corresponding button on the matching response panel was reinforced with points added to a counter. Points were redeemed for money. In later studies Hake and his associates used a more complex matching-to-sample procedure (e.g., Hake, Olvera, & Bell, 1975; Hake, Vukelich, & Kaplan, 1973; Hake, Vukelich, & Olvera, 1975).

In this setting subjects' dependence on each other for problem solving could be varied by changing the physical location of each subject's sample panel. With each subject's sample and matching panels adjacent to each other, problems could be worked most easily individually. Dependence was created by placing each subject's sample panel near the partner's matching panel (as shown in Figure 15.7). With subjects seated some distance apart, working a problem required that the subject either get up and walk over near the partner and press the sample-producing button or ask the partner to press the button. Although the subject's sample panel was some distance away, it still faced the subject, and the stimuli needed for matching could be read at that distance if the partner made the button press. The setting thus allowed each subject to make a response that avoided events that were presumed aversive for the partner, for example, getting up, walking some distance, or spending extra time on each trial. How aversive should depend on the distance between the subjects. Note, however, that although the distance adds to the cost of solving problems alone, it does not prevent that alternative. Hake and Vukelich (1973) found that the likelihood of exchange increased as the sample panels were moved in steps from the subject's own matching response panel to the partner's matching response panel 6 m away.

The observation that subjects frequently checked with their partners to learn how much they had earned prompted Hake et al. (1973) to require that subjects make an explicit response in order to gain access to earnings. This act was termed an *audit response.* An audit that gives access to one's own score is called a *self-audit.* One that gives a subject access to the partner's score is called a *coactor audit.* The response panel was modified by removing the counter showing the subject's own score and adding counters labeled "me" (for self-audit) and "other person" (for coactor audit). Each counter was covered with one-way glass and could be viewed only when illuminated by pressing an adjacent button. The counter remained illuminated as long as the subject pressed the button. When a subject made self- and coactor audits within a brief period of time (e.g., 5 s), they were termed *interpersonal audits* because they suggested that a comparison of scores was occurring.

Requiring audit response allows investigation of conditions under which ac-

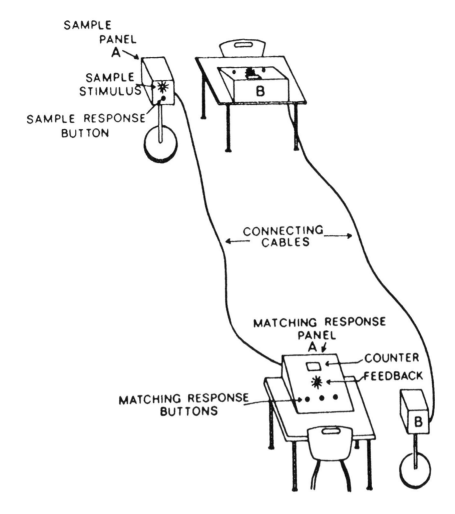

SAMPLE
PANEL
A

SAMPLE
STIMULUS

SAMPLE RESPONSE
BUTTON

B

CONNECTING
CABLES

MATCHING RESPONSE
PANEL
A

COUNTER

FEEDBACK

MATCHING RESPONSE
BUTTONS

B

FIGURE 15.7. Diagram of Hake's matching-to-sample apparatus. Apparatus labeled "A" belongs to one subject and apparatus labeled "B" belongs to the other subject.

cess to scores is reinforcing. Hake et al. (1973) found that when subjects solved problems in each other's presence rather than alone, coactor audits occurred and self-audits increased. Vukelich and Hake (1974) found that subjects made interpersonal audits more frequently when their scores were even with their partner's, as opposed to ahead or behind. Hake and Olvera (1978) suggested that permitting subjects to audit should increase the likelihood of exchange because subjects are better able to adjust their responding to achieve an equitable exchange. It would also be possible to assess the value of audit information to subjects by introducing a procedure that varied its cost, for example, by requiring a number of responses to gain access or by subtracting points for each audit response.

In studies by Hake, Olvera, and Bell (1975) and Hake, Vukelich, and Olvera (1975), the apparatus was modified to allow each subject to choose who would work a single problem on each trial. Problems could no longer be worked alone. Two different procedures were used. In the former study a lever located on the left side on the panel was pushed up to take the problem for oneself (i.e., taking) or down to give the problem to the partner (i.e., giving). The subject who pushed the lever first at the beginning of a trial determined the allocation. In the latter study two knobs were used instead of the lever. Pulling the upper knob a specified number of times (e.g., 75 pulls) took the problem for oneself. Pulling the lower knob a specified number of times gave it to the partner. The use of a response requirement on each knob allowed effort in making a choice to be varied.

The effect of either of these procedures was to provide several alternatives to exchange. First, subjects could *compete* for the single problem available on each trial by responding as quickly as possible to take the problem for oneself. The subject responding first thus received the problem's earnings and left the partner with nothing. Second, the take option could also be used noncompetitively. Subjects could alternate taking and thereby distribute problems equally. This mode of distribution was termed *sharing* as distinct from exchange where the distribution occurred through giving. Finally, equitable distributions could also occur if one of the subjects did all of the distributing. That result was termed *altruism*.

When subjects exchanged, they typically alternated trial by trial in giving problems to each other. Thus, large inequities in earnings typically did not arise. In studies by Hake and Schmid (1981) and Schmid and Hake (1983), the choice procedure was modified so that a choice response was required only if either subject wanted to change the distribution of problems from the previous trial. If no choice response was made the problem was automatically distributed to the subject who had worked the last problem. When this feature was added and the choice response required a number of knob pulls, subjects could minimize effort (i.e., number of choice responses) by allowing one subject to work several problems before giving the problem to the partner. This change led to expanded exchange (i.e., trust), with less frequent alternations and greater short-term inequities in earnings.

Matthews's Setting

Matthews (1977) developed a setting designed specifically to investigate the expansion of exchange—the development of trust. Two subjects worked at panels in separate cubicles. Each panel contained two counters that displayed own and partner's earnings, two response buttons, a switch for choosing between independent work and exchange, and a counter that showed minutes remaining in the session. Subjects could earn points, redeemed later for money, through exchange or independent work on each of a series of trials. One of the two response buttons (earnings button) was used either to earn points for oneself or to give points to the partner. Exchange was possible only if chosen by both subjects. When exchange was chosen, a light labeled "Give" was illuminated on one subject's panel and a light labeled "Get" was illuminated on the partner's panel. For the subject with the illuminated "Give" light, pressing the earnings button gave points to the subject with the illuminated "Get" light. The other of the two response buttons was used to reverse the direction of giving (exchange control button). This button could be used only by the subject with the illuminated "Give" button. If that subject pressed the exchange control button, the "Give" or "Get" light illuminated on each panel was reversed, and giving could occur in the other direction. Only a single "Give" response by one of the subjects was possible on each trial. If either subject chose the "Self" task on a trial, subjects could press the earnings button and earn points for themselves.

Matthews also investigated the effects of a cost in using the exchange control button to reverse the direction of giving. Each time the button was pressed, a fixed number of points was subtracted from both subjects' totals. When giving could be reversed at no cost, subjects typically alternated giving trial by trial. With a cost for reversing giving, exchange expanded—alternation was less frequent and larger reinforcer inequities developed.

In further studies of variables affecting the expansion of exchange, Matthews and Shimoff (1979) provided a monetary bonus to a subject who finished a series of trials a specified number of points ahead of the partner and penalized the subject who was behind. Thus, if an expanded exchange temporarily favored one subject by the specified number of points, that subject could protect the gain by switching permanently to the independent alternative. This condition greatly reduced the expansion of exchange. Matthews, Kordonski, and Shimoff (1983) gave both subjects the ability to punish by making a response that subtracted a given number of points from the partner's counter. Thus, a subject who had received more from a partner in an expanded exchange could not profit by switching permanently to the independent alternative. The partner could take those points. This option facilitated the expansion of exchange.

Molm's Settings

Molm developed several settings to study the effects of variations in reinforcer size on subject's choice of exchange or individual responding. In Molm's (1980, 1984) initial setting, two subjects, seated in separate rooms, worked at panels that contained two response buttons, lights, and a counter. On each of a series of trials, lights signaled the two times (Times 1 and 2) that subjects were to respond on the two response buttons (Buttons 1 and 2). The Time 1 and Time 2 lights were illuminated in sequence on each trial. When one of the lights went on, each subject had to press either Button 1 or 2. Either subject could give to the other by pressing Button 1 at Times 1 and 2. An individual response consisted of Button 2 presses at both time periods, and added points to one's own counter. Lights on each panel showed the partner's button presses and when the partner earned points. A counter and light showed the subject's own points. Points were redeemed later for money. Molm also used this setting to compare exchange with cooperation. A cooperative response consisted of Button 1 presses at both times by the two subjects, and added points to both subjects' counters.

Molm (1981a,b, 1985) later used a simpler response for exchange or individual responding. On each trial subjects made a single response on Button 1 or 2 (no Time 1 and Time 2 responses). A Button 1 press produced money for one's self, and a Button 2 press produced money for one's partner. Both subjects could thus give on the same trial. Molm conducted a series of studies of variables affecting the disruption and recovery of exchange (summarized in Molm, 1984). These included introduction of an individual alternative, reduction in the earnings for exchange, and creation of inequities in earnings. In some of these studies disruption of exchange and cooperation was compared. In other studies the opportunity to work individually and the size of individual earnings differed for the two subjects (termed *power imbalance*).

Molm (1988, 1990) also studied exchange in a context where both giving and taking were possible. Two subjects each had separate buttons for adding or subtracting money from the partner's counter. In place of an individual alternative, a second exchange partner was described as available to each subject. In fact, the second partner was a simulated subject whose responses approximately matched those initiated by the actual subject. On each trial subjects made two choices: which partner to interact with, and whether to add or subtract a fixed number of points from the selected partner's total. Molm studied conditions that differed in the number of points each subject could add or subtract (termed *structural power*), and found that changes in the size of possible additions more strongly affected the patterns of exchange than did changes in size of subtractions.

COMPETITION

Setting Structure

In investigating competition, the initial step is to specify the criteria to be used in first ranking and then differentially reinforcing competitors' responses. A ranking can have two bases. The first is to rank the quantity or quality of responses within a given time period or at a particular time, for example, number of products produced, artistic quality of a painting, height of a pole vault. The second is to rank the time or number of attempts competitors need to reach some response criterion, for example, minutes required to run 10,000 m, days needed to make a given number of sales, strokes to complete a round of golf. With criteria of the second type, the duration of each contest can vary considerably depending on the time it takes competitors to meet them. Although it is customary for a third party to specify in advance the criteria defining a contest, this need not be the case. For example, the ongoing task behaviors of two or more people could be compared at unpredictable intervals and differentially reinforced.

After determining the contest elements, the reinforcer distribution at the contest end must be specified (conventionally termed *payoff distribution*). Distributions can be created in either of two ways. The first is to base the distribution on the relative performances of the competitors, that is, a *proportional distribution.* Each person's proportion of the total payoff equals that person's contribution to the total group performance (assuming that it can be quantified). For example, in a two-person contest where number of responses in a period of time is counted, a person who made twice as many presses as the partner would get two-thirds and the partner one-third of the total payoff. The second way is to fix the proportions of the payoff in advance, that is, a *fixed distribution.* In setting fixed distributions two properties must be considered. One is the proportion of competitors receiving payoffs in each contest. At one extreme, only one competitor receives a payoff; at the other extreme, all competitors receive payoffs, but in varying amounts. The latter is tantamount to giving a payoff to each competitor that is noncontingent on performance—specifically, that amount received by the lowest performer. Maximizing the proportion of competitors earning something should encourage poorer performers to remain in the contests. When payoffs are received by more than one competitor, variation can occur in a second property, payoff differential or spread (i.e., the difference between the highest and lowest payoff amounts in each contest). Maximizing payoff differential should more effectively motivate those who have a chance of winning. The proportion of competitors receiving at least some payoff affects the size of the differential possible, given that the total remains constant. The larger the proportion of competitors receiving at least some payoff, the smaller the maximum differential can be.

Another element arises when a given contest consists of cumulative performances over time or when contests are repeated with the same competitors. Here competitors can be provided with information with regard to their own and others' performances and payoffs, or they can be denied such information. If information is provided, it can be given continuously or intermittently. It can be made available at the experimenter's discretion or it can depend on an audit response made by the subject. Performance information signals the likelihood of reinforcement, and thus it should function as a discriminative stimulus to increase or decrease a competitor's responding (for an extended discussion see Schmitt, 1986). Even if no performance information is given during a contest, some information is available if the same people compete over more than one contest. Competitors necessarily learn at least something about their relative standing (but not the size of performance differences) from the size of their payoffs.

The structure of competitive settings is thus defined by the basis for ranking performances, reinforcer (payoff) distribution, performance information, alternatives to competition, and the choice contingencies. Behavioral analyses of competition have yet to explore the range of contest and information conditions. Most settings focus on competition between pairs of subjects where the winner takes all and subjects have full information about each other's performance and earnings. Described next are competitive settings developed by Lindsley, Schmitt, Buskist, Dougherty and Cherek, and Hake.

Competitive Settings

Lindsley's Setting

As noted in the description of Lindsley's cooperation setting, the apparatus used by Lindsley and Cohen permitted competitive contingencies to be arranged as well (Cohen, 1962; Cohen & Lindsley, 1964; Lindsley, 1966). As with cooperation, competition required a knob pull by each subject, but only one of the responses was reinforced. Reinforcement occurred in either of two response sequences, both of which involved a response first by one subject and then the other. In one, a leader's response was reinforced if the follower's response was delayed more than 0.5 s ("The leader was able to slip in a response when the follower was not alert"). In the other, a follower's response was reinforced if it occurred within

0.5 s of the leader's response ("The follower was alert in responding quickly after the leader"). Each reinforced response was followed by a 5-s timeout during which the room lights dimmed, a light appeared in the reinforcement bin, and reinforcers were dispensed. Lindsley and Cohen found that subjects commonly converted these competitive contingencies to a form of exchange. Subjects alternated leadership in responding and allowed the follower to respond within 0.5 s and receive the reinforcer. Reinforcers were thus equitably distributed. The likely reason for this pattern is that a reinforced competitive response included an atypical requirement. It required responses by *both* subjects—the winner and the loser. A subject who lost continually could prevent the partner from winning by simply ceasing to respond (which prevented any reinforcement). Losers could thus make their continued responding contingent on the winners' permitting winning to be shared over time. The requirement that both competitors must respond for either one to win is neither a necessary nor common feature of everyday competitive settings. If one competitor drops out of a contest or fails to respond, the other competitor usually wins by default.

Schmitt's Settings

Both Lindsley's and Schmitt and Marwell's settings lend themselves to a simpler competitive response in which one competitor cannot block another by failing to respond. Schmitt (1976) took Schmitt and Marwell's earlier task setting (Figure 15.3) and used the panel light as a signal for competitive responding. The first knob pull by one subject after the panel light went on was reinforced by points added to that subject's counter. Points were exchanged later for money. Each reinforcement was followed by a 5-s timeout period during which the panel light was turned off on both panels and neither subject's responses were reinforced. The lights on both panels came on simultaneously after 5 s. Then, the first response by one subject was again reinforced. Success on the competitive task thus depended on responding quickly to the panel light. Pulling continuously at a high rate was also a successful strategy. Schmitt studied competition in a choice situation where Schmitt and Marwell's cooperative task described earlier was the alternative. Effects of differences in reinforcer amounts for cooperation and competition were investigated. This setting was also used to study variations in the choice contingency. In one condition competition was in effect unless both subjects chose cooperation. In another condition cooperation was in effect unless both chose competition. The latter condition produced much more cooperation. Schmitt (1976) also developed a similar three-person competitive setting in which the first response after the panel light went on was reinforced. As noted in the discussion of cooperation, Schmitt compared choice between cooperation and competition in two- and three-person groups, where competition was in effect unless all subjects chose to cooperate.

Finally, Schmitt (1987) also developed a competitive setting designed to produce high response rates. Competitive rates were compared with those from Schmitt's cooperative setting in which response rates needed for reinforcement were varied by changing the length of the limited hold. The procedure was based on one used by Church (1962, 1968) in studies of competition with animals. As with the cooperative task, reinforcers for competition were available at intervals that averaged 30 s and ranged from 1 to 108 s (a constant probability VI 30-s schedule). The availability of reinforcement at the end of an interval was not signaled. Only the subject responding first at that time received a reinforcer (counter points). Thus, a response rate higher than that of one's partner was effective for frequent reinforcement. In effect, the subject's partner was setting the length of the limited hold for a reinforced response. This competitive contingency was studied in a choice setting where the alternative was an individual task that used the same reinforcement schedule but with a signaled limited hold (described earlier with the cooperative task). Schmitt also used another variation of this competitive procedure to study competition without an individual alternative. The counter points received after each subject's winning responses were cumulated, and only the subject with the highest total after a fixed time period (e.g., 20 or 60 min) received a sum of money. As expected, this variation produced higher response rates than the one with the individual alternative.

Buskist's Setting

Buskist and his associates (Buskist, Barry, Morgan, & Rossi, 1984; Buskist & Morgan, 1987) developed a two-person competitive setting based on a fixed-interval reinforcement schedule. Points were delivered only to the pair member who responded first after the interval had elapsed. The end of the interval was not signaled (but was predictable as compared with Schmitt's variable-interval procedure). The response was a lever press, and panel lights indicated which subject earned points after each interval, that is, which subject won. To help prevent subjects from timing the fixed interval, watches were removed. In Buskist and colleagues' study the fixed interval was 30 s in length. In Buskist and Morgan's study fixed intervals of 30, 60, and 90 s were compared. All subjects developed break-and-run response patterns in which a pause after reinforcement was followed by accelerated responding until one of the subject's responses was reinforced. Response rates were higher than those where subjects worked individually on the same fixed-interval schedules.

Dougherty and Cherek (1994) modified Buskist's setting to include a second response option, a noncompetitive fixed-interval schedule. In addition, only one subject actually competed; the behavior of the second subject was simulated. A session began with the subject choosing to earn reinforcers by either competing (pressing a button) or not competing. If the subject chose to compete, four fixed intervals of 30 s followed. After each interval the subject won (earned points) or lost based on a predetermined probability. If the subject chose not to compete, two fixed intervals of 60 s followed where the first response after each interval ended was reinforced with points. Dougherty and Cherek studied the effects of various competitive reinforcer magnitudes and probabilities on the choice to compete. Strong preferences to compete were observed at high and moderate reinforcement probabilities, and also occasionally at very low probabilities.

Hake's Setting

As noted in the description of Hake's exchange setting, the apparatus used by Hake, Olvera, and Bell (1975) allowed each subject to choose who would work a single problem on each trial. Two knobs were available on each subject's panel, one for giving a problem to the partner and the other for taking it for oneself. Thus, subjects could use the giving knob in order to exchange or use the taking knob to either compete or share (alternate taking the problems). In a study by Olvera and Hake (1976), only the taking option was available. The subject who was first to pull the knob a specified number of times worked the problem and received its earnings. Olvera and Hake studied various fixed response ratios ranging from 30 to 100 pulls for each subject. The ratios for both subjects were identical. They found that increasing the ratios increased the likelihood that subjects would cease competition and begin sharing. By alternately taking the problems, subjects reduced the effort in solving problems. Olvera and Hake also used a ratio adjusting procedure that made it less likely that one of the subjects could get a disproportionately large part of the earnings by competing. When inequitable earnings from competition occurred using a given ratio (e.g., FR 30), the losing subject's ratio was reduced by a given number on each trial until that subject won. When the subject won on two consecutive trials, the ratio was increased. This procedure also increased the likelihood that subjects would cease competition and begin sharing.

METHODOLOGICAL ISSUES

Controlling Variables

The various experimental settings for studying cooperation, exchange, and competition all employ arbitrary stimuli that give subjects information about their partner's behavior and provide consequences for various responses. Results from these settings are meaningful, however, only if those stimuli are discriminative for behavior and the consequences for responses are actually reinforcers or punishers (i.e., increase or decrease behavior). The steps taken to ensure that subjects are responding to each other's behavior depend on the behavior being studied. As discussed earlier, cooperative responses have been developed that ensure that subjects attend to each other's behavior. With exchange and competition, however, no single social response is present. Evidence of mutual responsiveness must derive from the behavior patterns that develop. For exchange, the evidence is the correspondence between partners in the number of giving responses and the cumulative reinforcers from those responses (Hake & Olvera, 1978). Additional evidence can come from the emergence of regular, predictable patterns of exchange. The pattern may be simple, as when subjects alternate giving or give simultaneously, or more complex, as with the variety of patterns possible in expanded exchange. For competition, evidence of responsiveness comes from the relation between each person's competitive response rates and wins and losses over a series of contests. Reinforced (winning) responses should be maintained or increase in frequency whereas unreinforced (losing) ones should decrease. When subjects have a choice between competition and a reinforcing alternative, preference for competition should normally be related to the frequency of winning and competitive earnings.

When apparent social responses are made following a choice between social and individual alternatives, the choice itself adds to the evidence that the response is socially controlled. That control, too, can be checked by removing the partner from the setting in a manner obvious to the subject. Hake and Vukelich (1973) made such a change in their match-to-sample exchange setting and found that subjects typically switched immediately to the individual solution.

Various steps can be taken to ensure that the consequences are effective reinforcers. As in single-subject experiments, the reinforcer for a given response can be reduced or discontinued. The demonstration of effect is likely to take longest where reinforcement is discontinued and no alternative source of reinforcement is available—an extinction condition (shown in Figure 15.2). Where two reinforced alternatives are available, discontinuing reinforcement on one typically leads to an almost immediate shift to the other. The demonstration of this effect can be incorporated into a study's training procedure (as described later in Table 15.1).

When money is used as the consequence, it is important to recruit subjects who will find the amounts to be paid reinforcing. Including a reference to the range of earnings in recruiting announcements and consent forms makes their recruitment more likely. When subjects are college students, some may also participate because of a primary interest in learning about experiments, not in earning money. Such subjects may quit experiments they do not find interesting and be less affected by changes in earnings. This problem can be minimized by stressing that the experiment is of interest to those who want to earn money and has little educational benefit (assuming that to be the case).

Initial Conditions and Instructions

After the structure of a setting has been established, the conditions under which subjects learn about the contingencies must be set. These conditions depend in part on the opportunities the setting provides for subjects to communicate or see each other. The ability to communicate directly, either by talking or through written messages, is consequential in various ways. Subjects can clarify the contingencies for each other, make promises or threats, reach agreements, deceive each other, and exchange background information. These activities also provide convincing evidence of the presence of another subject. The presence or absence of communication has been investigated in a variety of settings in social psychology, and the effect is usually substantial (e.g., Sally, 1995). Thus, the initial or baseline conditions in most studies of cooperation, exchange, or competition in behavior analysis do not provide the opportunity to communicate, although communication may be introduced later as a variable. The ability of subjects only to see each other, but not to communicate verbally, confirms the presence of another subject, but can also be used to communicate through signals and facial expressions. Thus, most baseline conditions also prevent subjects from seeing each other during the experimental sessions. When experiments consist of sessions over a number of days, other opportunities might arise outside of the experiment for subjects to communicate or see each other. Thus, if the aim is to prevent communication and observability, experimenters must take additional steps so that subjects do not come into contact. These include having subjects come to widely separated waiting areas before the experiment, escorting them separately to the experimental rooms, and dismissing them separately at the end of each session.

TABLE 15.1
Conditions Defining Training Session

| Period | Counts[a] | | Length of period |
	Cooperation	Individual	
1. Cooperation only	6	none	335 cooperative resp
2. Cooperation or individual responding	1	6	135 individual resp
3. Cooperation or individual responding	6	1	135 cooperative resp
4. Cooperation or individual responding	3	2	15 min

[a]Counts were exchanged for money at end of session.

Subjects may also be asked after the experiment if they saw or communicated with their partner.

As the various settings illustrate, subjects typically learn of the other subject's presence, responses, and reinforcement via stimuli presented on monitors or panels. If the investigator is interested in the minimal conditions necessary for the emergence of a social response such as cooperation or exchange, then these aspects become independent variables of interest (e.g., Lindsley, 1966; Rosenberg, 1960; Sidowski, Wyckoff, & Tabory, 1956). In most research, however, primary interest has not been in the emergence of the response itself, but in the effects of various independent variables on the frequency of that response as an ongoing behavior. The concern is thus with establishing a given social response for which controlling variables can then be experimentally manipulated.

Because of the complexity of many interdependent settings with regard to responses and choice contingencies, investigators have typically used instructions and demonstrations during a training period in order to establish the various responses. The most common procedure has been to provide a few minutes of guided practice in order to show the effects of the various response possibilities. If the response is complex, an additional practice period may follow. As illustration, Table 15.1 shows the 90- to 120-min procedure used by Marwell and Schmitt (1975) in their study of cooperation and individual responding.

Subjects working in separate rooms were addressed by the experimenter via an intercom. In the introduction to Period 1, the experimenter led the subjects through the coordinated responses necessary to cooperate by instructing them on when to pull (using the panel shown in Figure 15.3).

> Notice the brass knob on the front of your panel. The way you make money is by pulling the knob. The amount of money you earn is shown on the counter marked "Your money". The counter below it shows how much money the other person is earning. Now I will demonstrate how you can make money by working with the other person. This requires that you both pull the knobs. To make money, one person pulls the knob first and the other person pulls several seconds later. I will show you how this works.

Subjects made several cooperative responses and were shown that either could pull the knob first. After 335 cooperative responses, the experimenter described the switch for choosing to cooperate or work individually.

> Notice the switch in the corner of the panel. You use this switch to choose to work with the other person or work alone. To work with the other person you both must have your switches up. Now both of you switch to "Work With Other Person." Notice that the blue light is on when the other person has chosen to work with you.

Subjects were instructed to put their switches up or down to show that cooperation required both subjects to choose it. Completion of Periods 2 and 3 provided experience with the switch and the two alternatives, and showed that subjects were responsive to changes in earnings. Period 4 was the baseline condition, which was also repeated in later sessions. How extensive training procedures need to be depends on the difficulty in making the responses. The length of Marwell and Schmitt's procedures was based on the time some subjects required to consistently coordinate their responses. In general subjects making even the simplest social responses usually require practice beyond the instructional period (e.g., 30–60 min) for the responses to be made proficiently.

When verbal or written statements are used to help establish laboratory responses, a concern is that their effects may not be limited to the instructional period. For example, studies have found that subjects who are instructed about effective response patterns on various individual reinforcement schedules are less able to detect schedule changes than those whose initial responses are shaped (for reviews see Cerutti, 1989; Vaughn, 1989). The extensive literature on rule-governed behavior suggests that instruction-following can be a strong, generalized response in a novel situation even though consequences for explicitly complying with the rule are absent (see Shimoff & Catania, Chapter 12). In general, if instructions are used to introduce a repertoire of responses, they should include descriptions or demonstrations of all response alternatives, and should make no reference to performance rates or patterns. Evidence suggests that such procedures, in conjunction with sufficient exposure to the consequences themselves, should not produce long-term instructional effects (Baron & Galizio, 1983; Michael & Bernstein, 1991). Conditions should be maintained through repeated contact with the consequences and until stable behavior patterns are observed.

Instructional procedures with features similar to those used by Marwell and Schmitt have been used in most of the settings described above. Social behaviors in these settings have been shown to be highly responsive to a variety of independent variables, thus providing indirect evidence that instructional effects are probably small. In one instance an explicit attempt was made to exert control by using instructions that ran counter to the immediate reinforcing consequences. One of Marwell and Schmitt's (1975) major findings was that when subjects could take money from cooperating partners, most did so. The original instructions that accompanied the introduction of that option simply described the opportunity to take money from the other and give it to yourself. In two later variations, instructions were elaborated to emphasize the socially undesirable effects of taking. Taking was described as "stealing" or "exploiting," and the instructions referred to the

problems this behavior creates in the university community. These more suggestive instructions failed to prevent a majority of subjects from taking.

Experimental Designs

A distinguishing feature of experimental analyses is the use of within-subject
designs in which each subject's (or pair's) responses in two or more conditions are
compared (see Baron & Perone, Chapter 3). Such designs usually include sessions
that extend over a number of days. When subjects are pairs (or larger groups), obtaining the needed data in the least amount of time becomes particularly important for the investigator. Compared with studies of single subjects, such experiments are not only more expensive to run if subjects are being paid, but they also
run a greater risk of data loss if one subject cancels sessions or quits the experiment. Cancellations can also cause undesirably long periods between sessions.
When college students serve as subjects, illness, conflicting course demands, and
getting a job are commonly cited as reasons for canceling sessions or quitting. Investigators can try to minimize these problems by specifying the maximum number of sessions in advance, ensuring that earnings are substantial, and offering a
bonus for completing the scheduled sessions (see Pilgrim, Chapter 2). When the
responses are very simple and sessions extend over a number of days, boredom
might also reduce sensitivity to condition changes. In a study by Savastano and
Fantino (1994), subjects who reacted in this way said they "did not care about getting points" and "just wanted to finish" the scheduled sessions.

Studies of social behavior have occasionally included between-group comparisons as part of the experimental designs. A major reason is the possibility that
experience under one treatment condition will affect performance under another (presuming that such an effect is not a focus of the experiment). For example,
Schmitt (1987) compared the maximum response rates that could be achieved
working individually, cooperatively, or competitively. All subjects first worked
individually. Instead of subjects then working under cooperative followed by
competitive conditions (or vice versa), half of the subjects worked cooperatively
and half competitively. If the same pair first cooperated and then competed, it is
possible that subjects would be less likely to compete vigorously after a history
of cooperation. If the same pair first competed and then cooperated, it is possible that a subject losing badly in competition would be less likely to cooperate.
Another reason to use between-group comparisons is the presence of an upward
or downward trend in behavior over time. Hake, Vukelich, and Olvera (1975)
found that competition tended to decrease over time without experimental manipulation. This trend was greater when subjects were tested in several sessions
spaced over days then when an equal number of sessions were massed into one
day. In this instance treatment and time-related effects would be difficult to separate if several treatment conditions were studied in sequence. Thus, Hake and
his associates used a between-group comparison to study variables affecting competition.

Most experimental analyses of social behavior have used homogeneous subject populations, namely, adolescents or young adults. They have not studied the

effects of demographic characteristics such as age, education, or cultural background that could merit between-group comparisons. There is one background difference that has been shown to be consequential, however—a prior social relationship, where subjects know who their partners are. Cohen's (1962) study of an adolescent boy and his family and friends showed that prior relation can affect a variety of social responses in Lindsley's setting. Marwell and Schmitt (1975) studied cooperation with couples who were married or close friends and found that cooperation was much less likely to be disrupted by the opportunity to take than when subjects were strangers.

A procedure common in studies using payoff matrices is to simulate the behavior of one of the partners. Subjects are led to believe that they are playing against a real partner, but in fact the partner is either a confederate of the experimenter playing a specified strategy or simply a programmed computer. Simulated partners have been used most frequently when there are particular strategies of interest in a social relation. For example, in the Prisoner's Dilemma matrix a strategy where one subject matches the partner's choice on the previous trial (i.e., tit for tat) has been found to be most effective in producing cooperation (e.g., Axelrod, 1984). In experimental analyses of social behavior, simulated partners have also been used, but infrequently. In the settings described, Marwell and Schmitt (1975) investigated programmed pacifist strategies where subjects could take money from each other if both cooperated, Shimoff and Matthews (1975) used a confederate to study the effects of inequity on cooperation, Dougherty and Cherek (1994) used a simulated competitor, and Molm (1988, 1990) used a simulated partner as an exchange alternative. In addition, Spiga, Cherek, Grabowski, and Bennett (1992) used a fictitious partner in a procedure designed to study drug effects on cooperative behavior. Subjects could press a button that gave money both to themselves and to the fictitious partner when the partner made a response that illuminated a light on the subject's panel. The use of simulated partners raises the issue of the credibility of the information provided to subjects to convince them that a partner exists. Investigators typically rely on postexperiment questions to evoke this information. If subjects voice suspicions, their data are typically discarded, a costly step if a number of sessions have been completed. There are not established criteria for judging the validity of the answers to such questions, however.

Attempts to convince subjects that a simulated partner is a real one are based on the assumption that subjects respond differently to machines than to humans. Increasingly, however, people interact with computers in a humanlike manner—in writing and speech in a variety of job, service, and entertainment contexts. Kiesler, Sproull, and Waters (1996) investigated subjects' responses in a Prisoner's Dilemma game when the "partner" was known by the subject to be either a person or computer-based. In both conditions, the subject and partner discussed options on each trial, and the partner asked the subject for commitments. For both types of partners, agreements and discussion facilitated cooperation, although the effect was stronger with the human partner. Thus, there are occasions where it is the humanlike use of social stimuli and responses by a "partner," not a partner believed to be human, that engenders "social" responses in others. This issue clearly merits further attention.

CONCLUSION

Experimental analyses of behaviors such as cooperation, exchange, and competition have erased initial skepticism that social behaviors could be brought under control in laboratory settings. Stable baseline behavior patterns and reversible treatment effects have been obtained in the manner found for individual behavior. Almost all of these analyses, however, have focused on the minimum number of subjects necessary for social behavior—two. Although this focus has facilitated the development of experimental settings, it has also limited the generality of findings. For all three forms of social behavior, groups larger than two can introduce significant new elements that often characterize those behaviors in everyday situations. For cooperation, the problem of response coordination is greatly magnified if all participants are required to make some response. If failure of a single person can prevent the response required for reinforcement, cooperation in large groups becomes highly tenuous, and less demanding criteria may be needed to maintain responding, for example, an allowance for error. If not all of the participants need to make some response, the problem of free-riding emerges. For exchange, including more than two participants allows the creation of various networks where participants can exchange only with certain others. A variety of exchange networks have been the subject of short-term studies in sociology using monetary exchange games. Exchanges consist of a series of negotiated point splits between pairs of subjects in the larger network. Results indicate that an individual's behavior and payoffs are strongly affected by network type and location in that network (for a review see Molm & Cook, 1995). Several formal models have been developed to predict power and exchange within such networks (for an overview see Willer, 1992). For competition, increasing the number of competitors greatly expands the options in payoff distributions. Both number of competitors receiving some payoff and the differential between the highest and lowest payoff can assume more extreme values in large groups. Evidence also suggests that increasing the number of competitors can lead to an increasing preference for competition under conditions where the *average* earnings from each contest remain constant. Schmitt (1976) investigated preference for competition using contests where the average reinforcer amounts for each person remained constant for two- and three-person groups, and only a single competitor received a reinforcer. The effect of increasing group size is to decrease the likelihood of reinforcement for each competitor but to increase the size of the amount won. Schmitt found that more competition occurred in three-person groups. This result is consistent with the popularity of state lotteries that increase jackpot size at the expense of the probability of winning. Finally, studies that increase group size for any of the social behaviors will typically need to examine or redefine the nature of the tasks, choice contingencies, the stimuli provided, and subjects' attention to those stimuli.

Analyses of cooperation, exchange, and competition have generally used a single type of reinforcer throughout any given series of experiments, typically points redeemed later for money. For cooperation and competition, reinforcers of a single type are characteristic in numerous everyday cases. For example, people often cooperate in solving particular problems where the benefits are the same for all, or compete to win specified prizes. For social exchange, however, reinforcers of a single type are atypical. In everyday exchange relations, a variety of reinforcing consequences (as well as punishing ones) are usually involved, for example, attention, assistance, gifts, information, and so on. How different reinforcers combine in various quantities and schedules to affect the behavior of recipients has not been investigated. Multiple reinforcers have been studied with various single organisms, and research suggests a complex picture (not well understood) regarding the manner in which various reinforcers are substitutable (Green & Freed, 1993). A better understanding of social exchange will require that multiple consequences be investigated, and a dyadic exchange setting would be a reasonable starting point.

In conclusion, investigators during the last several decades have been successful in creating experimental procedures for studying important forms of social behavior in minimal social settings. Development beyond these limits will require further pioneering work.

ACKNOWLEDGMENTS. I thank Joe Parsons and Fran Schmitt for comments on an earlier draft.

REFERENCES

Axelrod, R. (1984). *The evolution of cooperation*. New York: Basic Books.

Azrin, N. H., & Lindsley, O. R. (1956). The reinforcement of cooperation between children. *Journal of Abnormal and Social Psychology, 52*, 100–102.

Baron, A., & Galizio, M. (1983). Instructional control of human operant behavior. *Psychological Record, 33*, 495–520.

Burgess, R. L., & Nielsen, J. M. (1974). An experimental analysis of some structural determinants of equitable and inequitable exchange relations. *American Sociological Review, 39*, 427–443.

Buskist, W. F., Barry, A., Morgan, D., & Rossi, M. (1984). Competitive fixed interval performance in humans: Role of "orienting" instructions. *Psychological Record, 34*, 241–257.

Buskist, W. F., & Morgan, D. (1987). Competitive fixed-interval performance in humans. *Journal of the Experimental Analysis of Behavior, 47*, 145–158.

Cerutti, D. T. (1989). Discrimination theory of rule-governed behavior. *Journal of the Experimental Analysis of Behavior, 51*, 259–276.

Church, R. M. (1962). Effect of relative skill on the amount of competitive facilitation. *Psychological Reports, 11*, 603–614.

Church, R. M. (1968). Applications of behavior theory in social psychology: Imitation and competition. In E. C. Simmel, R. A. Hoppe, & G. A. Milton (Eds.), *Social facilitation and imitative behavior* (pp. 135–167). Boston: Allyn & Bacon.

Cohen, D. J. (1962). Justin and his peers: An experimental analysis of a child's social world. *Child Development, 33*, 697–717.

Cohen, D. J., & Lindsley, O. R. (1964). Catalysis of controlled leadership in cooperation by human stimulation. *Journal of Child Psychological Psychiatry, 5*, 119–137.

Dougherty, D. M., & Cherek, D. R. (1994). Effects of social context, reinforcer probability, and reinforcer magnitude on humans' choices to compete or not to compete. *Journal of the Experimental Analysis of Behavior, 62*, 133–148.

Green, L., & Freed, D. E. (1993). The substitutability of reinforcers. *Journal of the Experimental Analysis of Behavior, 60*, 141–158.

Hake, D. F., & Olvera, D. (1978). Cooperation, competition, and related social phenomena. In A. C. Catania (Ed.), *Handbook of applied behavior analysis* (pp. 208–245). New York: Irvington.

Hake, D. F., Olvera, D., & Bell, J. C. (1975). Switching from competition or cooperation at large response requirements: Competition requires more responding. *Journal of the Experimental Analysis of Behavior, 24,* 343–354.

Hake, D. F., & Schmid, T. L. (1981). Acquisition and maintenance of trusting behavior. *Journal of the Experimental Analysis of Behavior, 35,* 109–124.

Hake, D. F., & Vukelich, R. (1972). A classification and review of cooperation procedures. *Journal of the Experimental Analysis of Behavior, 18,* 333–343.

Hake, D. F., & Vukelich, R. (1973). Analysis of the control exerted by a complex cooperation procedure. *Journal of the Experimental Analysis of Behavior, 19,* 3–16.

Hake, D. F., Vukelich, R., & Kaplan, S. J. (1973). Audit responses: Responses maintained by access to existing self or coactor scores during non-social parallel work, and cooperation procedures. *Journal of the Experimental Analysis of Behavior, 19,* 409–423.

Hake, D. F., Vukelich, R., & Olvera, D. (1975). The measurement of sharing and cooperation as equity effects and some relationships between them. *Journal of the Experimental Analysis of Behavior, 23,* 63–79.

Kelley, H. H. (1979). *Personal relationships: Their structures and processes.* Hillsdale, NJ: Erlbaum.

Kelley, H. H., & Thibaut, J. W. (1978). *Interpersonal relations: A theory of interdependence.* New York: Wiley.

Kiesler, S., Sproull, L., & Waters, K. (1996). A prisoner's dilemma experiment on cooperation with people and human-like computers. *Journal of Personality and Social Psychology, 70,* 47–65.

Lindsley, O. R. (1966). Experimental analysis of cooperation and competition. In T. Verhave (Ed.), *The experimental analysis of behavior* (pp. 470–501). New York: Appleton.

Marwell, G., & Schmitt, D. R. (1972). Cooperation and interpersonal risk: Cross-cultural and cross-procedural generalizations. *Journal of Experimental Social Psychology, 8,* 594–599.

Marwell, G., & Schmitt, D. R. (1975). *Cooperation: An experimental analysis.* New York: Academic Press.

Marwell, G., Schmitt, D. R., & Boyesen, B. (1973). Pacifist strategy and cooperation under interpersonal risk. *Journal of Personality and Social Psychology, 28,* 12–20.

Marwell, G., Schmitt, D. R., & Shotola, R. (1971). Cooperation and interpersonal risk. *Journal of Personality and Social Psychology, 18,* 9–32.

Matthews, B. A. (1977). Magnitudes of score differences produced within sessions in a cooperative exchange procedure. *Journal of the Experimental Analysis of Behavior, 27,* 331–340.

Matthews, B. A. (1979). Effects of fixed and alternated payoff inequity on dyadic competition. *The Psychological Record, 29,* 329–339.

Matthews, B. A., Kordonski, W. M., & Shimoff, E. (1983). Temptation and the maintenance of trust: Effects of bilateral punishment capability. *Journal of Conflict Resolution, 27,* 255–277.

Matthews, B. A., & Shimoff, E. (1979). Monitoring trust levels in ongoing exchange relations. *Journal of Conflict Resolution, 23,* 538–560.

Michael, R., & Bernstein, D. J. (1991). Transient effects of acquisition history on generalization in a matching-to-sample task. *Journal of the Experimental Analysis of Behavior, 56,* 155–166.

Michaels, J. W., & Wiggins, J. A. (1976). Effects of mutual dependency and dependency asymmetry on social exchange. *Sociometry, 39,* 368–376.

Mithaug, D. E. (1969). The development of cooperation in alternative task situations. *Journal of Experimental Child Psychology, 8,* 443–460.

Mithaug, D. E., & Burgess, R. L. (1967). The effects of different reinforcement procedures in the establishment of a group response. *Journal of Experimental Child Psychology, 5,* 441–454.

Mithaug, D. E., & Burgess, R. L. (1968). The effects of different reinforcement contingencies in the development of cooperation. *Journal of Experimental Child Psychology, 6,* 402–426.

Molm, L. D. (1980). The effects of structural variations in social reinforcement contingencies on exchange and cooperation. *Social Psychology Quarterly, 43,* 269–282.

Molm, L. D. (1981a). Power use in the dyad: The effects of structure, knowledge, and interaction history. *Social Psychology Quarterly, 44,* 42–48.

Molm, L. D. (1981b). The conversion of power imbalance to power use. *Social Psychology Quarterly, 44,* 151–163.

Molm, L. D. (1984). The disruption and recovery of dyadic social interaction. In E. J. Lawler (Ed.), *Advances in group process* (Vol. 1, pp. 183–227). Greenwich, CT: JAI Press.

Molm, L. D. (1985). Relative effects of individual dependencies: Further tests of the relation between power imbalance and power use. *Social Forces, 63,* 810–837.

Molm, L. D. (1988). The structure and use of power: A comparison of reward and punishment power. *Social Psychology Quarterly, 51,* 108–122.

Molm, L. D. (1990). Structure, action, and outcomes: The dynamics of power in social exchange. *American Sociological Review, 55,* 427–447.

Molm, L. D., & Cook, K. S. (1995). Social exchange and exchange networks. In K. S. Cook, G. A. Fine, & J. S. House (Eds.), *Sociological perspectives on social psychology* (pp. 209–235). Boston: Allyn & Bacon.

Olvera, D. R., & Hake, D. F. (1976). Producing a change from competition to sharing: Effects of large and adjusting response requirements. *Journal of the Experimental Analysis of Behavior, 26,* 321–333.

Rapoport, A., & Chammah, A. (1965). *Prisoner's dilemma.* Ann Arbor: University of Michigan Press.

Rosenberg, S. (1960). Cooperative behavior in dyads as a function of reinforcement parameters. *Journal of Abnormal and Social Psychology, 60,* 318–333.

Sally, D. (1995). Conversation and cooperation in social dilemmas: A meta-analysis of experiments from 1958 to 1992. *Rationality and Society, 7,* 58–92.

Savastano, H. I., & Fantino, E. (1994). Human choice in concurrent ratio-interval schedules of reinforcement. *Journal of the Experimental Analysis of Behavior, 61,* 453–463.

Schmid, T. L., & Hake, D. F. (1982). Fast acquisition of cooperation and trust: A two-stage view of trusting behavior. *Journal of the Experimental Analysis of Behavior, 40,* 179–192.

Schmitt, D. R. (1976). Some conditions affecting the choice to cooperate or compete. *Journal of the Experimental Analysis of Behavior, 25,* 165–178.

Schmitt, D. R. (1986). Competition: Some behavioral issues. *The Behavior Analyst, 9,* 27–34.

Schmitt, D. R. (1987). Interpersonal contingencies: Performance differences and cost-effectiveness. *Journal of the Experimental Analysis of Behavior, 48,* 221–234.

Schmitt, D. R., & Marwell, G. (1968). Stimulus control in the experimental study of cooperation. *Journal of the Experimental Analysis of Behavior, 11,* 571–574.

Schmitt, D. R., & Marwell, G. (1971a). Taking and the disruption of cooperation. *Journal of the Experimental Analysis of Behavior, 15,* 405–412.

Schmitt, D. R., & Marwell, G. (1971b). Avoidance of risk as a determinant of cooperation. *Journal of the Experimental Analysis of Behavior, 16,* 367–374.

Schmitt, D. R., & Marwell, G. (1972). Withdrawal and reward re-allocation as responses to inequity. *Journal of Experimental Social Psychology, 8,* 207–221.

Schmitt, D. R., & Marwell, G. (1977). Cooperation and the human group. In R. L. Hamblin & J. H. Kunkel (Eds.), *Behavioral theory in sociology* (pp. 171–191). New Brunswick, NJ: Transaction Books.

Shimoff, E., & Matthews, B. A. (1975). Unequal reinforcer magnitudes and relative preference for cooperation in the dyad. *Journal of the Experimental Analysis of Behavior, 24,* 1–16.

Sidowski, J. B., Wyckoff, L. B., & Tabory, L. (1956). The influence of reinforcement and punishment in a minimal social situation. *Journal of Abnormal and Social Psychology, 52,* 115–119.

Skinner, B. F. (1953). *Science and human behavior.* New York: Macmillan Co.

Spiga, R., Cherek, D. R., Grabowski, R., & Bennett, R. H. (1992). Effects of inequity on human free-operant cooperative responding: A validation study. *The Psychological Record, 42,* 29–40.

Thibaut, J. W., & Kelley, H. H. (1959). *The social psychology of groups.* New York: Wiley.

Vaughn, M. (1989). Rule-governed behavior in behavior analysis: A theoretical and experimental history. In S. Hayes (Ed.), *Rule-governed behavior: Cognition, contingencies, and instructional control* (pp. 97–118). New York: Plenum Press.

Vukelich, R., & Hake, D. F. (1974). Effects of the difference between self and coactor scores upon the audit responses that allow access to these scores. *Journal of the Experimental Analysis of Behavior, 22,* 61–71.

Weingarten, R., & Mechner, F. (1966). The contingency as an independent variable of social interaction. In T. Verhave (Ed.), *The experimental analysis of behavior* (pp. 447–459). New York: Appleton–Century–Crofts.

Willer, D. (1992). Predicting power in exchange networks: A brief history and introduction to the issues. *Social Networks, 14,* 187–211.

V

New Directions

16

Establishment of a Laboratory for Continuous Observation of Human Behavior

Daniel J. Bernstein

Since the earliest experimental analyses of behavior, it has been asserted that the conceptual tools derived from operant research would be useful in the understanding, prediction, and influence of human behavior. Although much of the extrapolation of operant principles to human behavior has been verbal speculation only, the last 20 years have seen an explosion of studies of human behavior employing experimental analysis of behavior. No general characterization can be completely accurate, but there appear to have been two main branches of this endeavor. One is applied behavior analysis in which human behavior that occurs in everyday life and in nonlaboratory settings is analyzed and often changed through the systematic application of contingencies. In this area the behavior studied is usually immediately relevant to the human context that generated the interest, and the intervention is carried out over whatever length of time is needed to produce a result that is satisfactory for the client, institution, or researcher. The other branch is the experimental analysis of human behavior in which laboratory researchers engage human participants in studies of the same variables that are investigated with nonhuman animals. In this area the behavior studied is usually moving an arbitrarily selected operandum brought under the control of laboratory-derived stimuli and consequences, and the research is carried out over relatively brief periods (e.g., several 1-hour sessions) as allowed by the availability of student research pools. Recently there has been some growth in the experimental analysis of human verbal behavior, though it is often studied in conjunction with a simple nonverbal task that is a laboratory analogue of more complex human action.

Daniel J. Bernstein • Department of Psychology, University of Nebraska–Lincoln, Lincoln, Nebraska 68588-0308.

Handbook of Research Methods in Human Operant Behavior, edited by Lattal and Perone. Plenum Press, New York, 1998.

In between these two branches there is a twig of research that combines elements of the two major bodies of human operant research. This research is conducted with human participants who live continuously for many weeks in a laboratory apartment; the participants engage in ordinary activities (such as reading, sewing, and artwork) or in arbitrary laboratory activities that are brought into contact with research variables derived from basic experimental analysis. In the line of research on ordinary activities, the primary measure of performance is the percent time devoted to each of the many activities available, and this measure is used to predict the outcomes of reinforcement contingencies in which time devoted to one activity produced access to another activity. In the line of research on arbitrary laboratory activities, the primary measure of performance is the rate of occurrence of the activities as a function of reinforcement schedules or of drug administration. The procedures represent a compromise reached by researchers who want the research repertoire to have the richness of human behavior outside the laboratory while at the same time requiring the experimental control that is typical of research with nonhuman participants. Like all compromises, it is not perfect. For example, it is not often possible to have humans remain in an experiment for the many months needed to reach formal stability criteria, nor is it ethically feasible to reduce humans to 80% of their free-feeding weight so they will work for food with the same intensity as do laboratory animals. Similarly, the kind of activities that humans engage in while living in a laboratory are only a small sample of the potential behavior that occurs in free-ranging humans, and only in rare cases would humans outside the laboratory encounter the kind or amount of control that is routinely found in experimental research. Despite these limits, the compromise has been struck as a large stride toward the generalization of basic operant research to human behavior. When compared with a pigeon pecking a disk for grain, humans engaging in long bouts of reading and sewing in a studio apartment seems a more likely behavioral base for generalization of research to human behavior.

The present account of this program of research is focused on the details of how the research is conducted. Previous accounts (Bernstein & Brady, 1986; Findley, 1966) have given the history of the development of the two main laboratories (Joseph Brady's at Johns Hopkins and mine at Nebraska) and a description of the kinds of research programs undertaken. A reader unfamiliar with this research area may also wish to read reports of research by Bernstein and Ebbesen (1978), Bernstein and Michael (1990), or Foltin et al. (1990).

This chapter will present the details of setting up a laboratory to study human behavior in a naturalistic state, with an emphasis on what practical steps need to be taken to get under way and what assumptions and compromises are made in the process. As part of this account, there will be description of some of the data that have been generated as examples of the benefits of undertaking this long-term detailed analysis. The first section deals with issues that are general to any long-term human laboratory project; it describes the physical space, discusses the selection of the response repertoire to be studied, describes the duration of experiments that can be conducted, and considers the issue of staff and participant resources. The second section examines how similar questions were handled in the particular research projects related to time-based models of reinforcement; it describes how reinforcement operations interact with the selection of behavioral categories, the measurement of response strength, and the stability of behavior. It is hoped that this chapter as a whole will convince more people that research on this scale is worth conducting, despite the difficulties and costs. By the end, someone interested in this kind of work should have a good idea of how to start a research program using continuous observation of naturalistic human behavior.

GENERAL ISSUES IN MANAGING A LONG-TERM HUMAN LABORATORY

The Physical Space

The main element in designing or identifying an appropriate space is that the entire living area should be readily visible from a private observation station behind a one-way mirror. Ideally there is direct access to a private bath/shower room, and that room is the only place in which complete privacy is available. If at all possible, the space should have no windows to the outside, or the windows should be covered to prevent outside viewing. The entire space should be in a relatively private and quiet area, and there should be good sound insulation from the surrounding building activities; participants will likely be distracted and ultimately annoyed by repeated reminders that they are alone in an area surrounded by other people engaging in regular daily activities. Although there should be an excellent two-way sound system between the living space and the observation area, sound insulation is very important between those two areas. Participants often report finding sounds from the observation station particularly disturbing, and their occurrence increases the level of reactivity of the observation system.

The living area can be as small as 50 or 60 square meters, and it should be laid out like a studio apartment with separate locations for different activities and materials. Essential elements include a food preparation area, a bed/sleeping area, a writing desk, a second dedicated work/task desk, a comfortable reading chair in a well-lighted area, and a central table not dedicated to a single activity. If more than one person will participate in the research simultaneously, separate bed/sleeping areas and work spaces should be available. Wherever possible, chairs should be aligned so that participants' hands and the table or desk surface are clearly visible from the observation system. If the participant is sitting with his or her back toward the observation mirror, there will be problems in obtaining reliable data. The bath/shower room should have sufficient space that the sink can be used for cleaning dishes and spreading them out for drying. Some participant time is lost from experimental tasks while they prepare and clean up their own meals, but there are compensating advantages to this approach. In general, participants will like their meals better if they prepare them, and it is significantly less work for the experimenter to shop for groceries once a week than to prepare and deliver food three times a day.

It is not necessary that the laboratory be located in a space that is specifically designed for this research or permanently dedicated to it. Although the conditions described can be achieved most easily with a permanently remodeled facility, successful experimental sessions have been conducted in borrowed space that is located in relatively quiet areas of regular university buildings. Many psychology facilities have rooms set up for observation through one-way mirrors; they are used for supervising clinical sessions, observing children and families, or monitoring participants in group experiments. Residential studies can be conducted during times when other users can plan to function without access to the shared space. If no built-in bathroom is available, the participant could request three or four times each day to visit a bathroom in an adjoining hallway; the experimenter needs only to arrange with other occupants of the area to respect signs designating the space as temporarily off limits. If no facilities for food preparation are allowed in an area, arrangements could be made to have prepared food delivered from campus food services or local franchise sources at specific times. Some flexibility and creativity can go a long way toward adapting available space to a degree that is acceptable. One should not let the research be blocked by the absence of a perfect facility. The most important elements are the behavioral repertoire, the observation methods, and the maintenance of privacy and isolation; these can be accomplished in a variety of physical arrangements.

The Role of Isolation

One fundamental feature of continuous observation research has been that the participants do not interact with people or issues outside the laboratory during the course of the experiment. This means that there are no radios or televisions, no mail, and no telephone connection for the participants. In addition, almost all communication from the experimenter to the participants is delivered by a set of prearranged signal lights that answer questions. Attempts also are made to keep participants from using clocks as a time reference, and the laboratory is located in an area without a lot of walk-through traffic or other auditory distractions. The rationale for these procedures is similar to the reason for putting a pigeon's standard experimental space inside an insulated chamber; for experimental variables to play a relatively large role in influencing behavior, stimuli associated with other variables should not be present in the participant's environment. For example, in my initial long-term study (Bernstein & Ebbesen, 1978) one of the research goals was to identify and measure patterns of responding; how often, when, and for how long the participants distributed time to each activity were primary dependent variables. Having a clock present or having windows to the outside would certainly contribute to those distributions in an orderly and interesting way, but the goal was to find out how the person distributed time without the presence of external cues for temporal spacing.

Similarly, it was anticipated that participants' choice of activities would certainly be influenced by the availability of occasional or ad hoc activities such as phone calls, letters, or broadcast sports events; because those were not the variables being studied, their influence was eliminated by not making them available. Presumably the systematic variability related to experimental factors would be easier to detect in a steady-state stream of behavior observed in an environment free of unpredictable and intermittent distracters. This was carried to an extreme by not allowing even summaries of outside events at prearranged times (such as a prebed news briefing or mail call). Should important events occur outside the laboratory (e.g., sports outcomes, vacillation in partner commitment, or the outbreak of hostilities), the emotional reaction of the participant would possibly add variability to the choice of activities on succeeding days. Although this is potentially an interesting topic to study, it was not part of the present research program, and an attempt was made to keep that source of variance from disrupting steady-state performance.

Initially the laboratory was run without any reference to clock time, and the participant's sleep/wake cycle was allowed to vary without external cues. This procedure created many conflicts with the schedules and sleep patterns of the experimental staff, however, as their behavior remained under the influence of the diurnal cycle outside the laboratory. For reasons of personnel scheduling and the convenience of standard-length data sessions, the laboratory quickly went to a fixed daily schedule of 15 hr light and 9 hr dark. Despite many participants' claims that they never sleep more than 6 or 7 hr and could not possibly adapt to the laboratory schedule, all participants have adjusted within a day or two and sleep the full 9 hr each night without difficulty. In the absence of any outside light or any natural sound cues to indicate the arrival of morning, all participants continued to sleep through the 9-hr dark cycle until the lights were gradually brought up between 9:00 and 9:15 each morning.

It is worth noting that despite appearances, isolation per se has never been the subject of study in this research program. Although there is no doubt some effect on behavior that results from being out of touch with the world at large, all experimental comparisons are made among several conditions all of which are conducted in the same isolated state; no comparisons of isolated versus embedded behavior would even be possible. At least two pairs of participants have shared the space in my own laboratory, and the line of research done at Johns Hopkins (see Bernstein & Brady, 1986) always includes multiple participants. Some of the research done in the Hopkins laboratory was funded by the National Aeronautics and Space Administration (NASA), and the relatively isolated conditions were intended to model space flight. In that research program also, there were no comparisons of behavior under varying conditions of isolation; the contact with people and issues outside the laboratory was kept constant across various experimental conditions.

At many different points attempts have been made to minimize the extent or severity of the isolation, either to save money in payment to participants or to make it easier for participants to complete lengthy experimental commitments. A half-hour walk at bedtime led one participant to quit after only 4 days, noting that contact with a person and the outside world made the laboratory environment harder to accept by comparison. Evenings off and sleeping at home provided other participants with opportunities to engage in home activities that were good substitutes for activities intentionally deprived during the laboratory time; this non-malicious (and often unintentional) reaction to deprivation weakened the effect of the experimental variable being studied. On balance, the best strategy is to recruit people who have the time to stay in the laboratory 24 hr per day, and most participants report becoming quite accustomed to the laboratory after several days. It is probably best not to disrupt that pattern by having the person come and go at various times; maintaining constant environmental conditions appears to yield more stable performance.

The Behavioral Repertoire

The choice of what behavior to study is one of the key focal points of the difference between the experimental and applied branches of behavior analysis. Findley's (1966) original long-term human operant study was clearly modeled after the animal laboratory; the single human participant used arbitrary operanda to obtain consequences available on formal schedules of reinforcement. This laboratory was called a programmed environment because everything in it was part of the scheduled experimental program, and the work at Johns Hopkins (e.g., Bernstein & Brady, 1986; Foltin et al., 1990) has continued the tradition of studying arbitrary laboratory responses. In that approach all activities of interest involve interacting with equipment that automatically records the occurrence of discrete actions; the environment is engineered so that no decisions need to be made about whether or not an activity has occurred; the closure of a microswitch built into the laboratory equipment defines the occurrence of the category. There is no need for considering observer reliability, and typically the equipment provides a rate or frequency measure of discrete instances of behavior. This procedure follows the standard operant research convention in its reliance on sophisticated instrumentation of the environment for detecting instances of the behavior of interest, and it is also congruent with procedures used by NASA during space flight.

The research in my laboratory has gone in the other direction, having participants bring into the laboratory activities they engage in when in their natural circumstances. Participants have devoted time in the laboratory to activities as widely diverse as reading, sewing, candle making, playing the clarinet, studying Russian, lifting weights, doing jigsaw puzzles, playing cards, building models, doing yoga exercises, and producing various forms of artwork. This kind of repertoire has the advantage of being more like the behavior to which we hope to generalize our results, and as such it is part of the big step from the animal laboratory to the experimental analysis of human behavior. In addition, the behavior is extended in time and is maintained by its own naturally occurring consequences; the value of the activities to the participants is not dependent on the delivery of hedonically relevant consequences by the experimenter. One of my goals from the beginning was to bring a behavioral analysis to that kind of human action, beginning the analysis of the kind of behavior that humans engage in during most of their waking time.

There are also a number of disadvantages to the selection of a repertoire of ordinary activities from the participants' natural repertoires. First, the choice appears to go against the fundamental strategy of behavior analysis, namely, the breaking down of complex behavior into the most simple possible units for detailed experimentation. Second, the variety of response forms might make comparisons among results difficult, as there would be topographic differences confounded with experimental differences; identical repertoires would make comparisons of data from different conditions and from different participants more readily interpretable. Third, because the activities come from very different people with unique backgrounds, the natural responses have unknown reinforcement histories that could interact with the present experimental variables and yield apparently anomalous outcomes. Finally, it is much more difficult to measure these activities than it is to measure discrete operations of an operandum. Data from such a repertoire may be contaminated by observer error that could obscure the presence of subtle effects of experimental variables.

On the other hand, the argument for reductionism in experimental analysis has some limits, as seen by the widespread disinterest among behavior analysts in physiological accounts of operant learning. One might argue that breaking complex behavior into units is not a simple process, and ultimately we should welcome any set of molar units that can be shown to yield orderly relations with environmental variables. The decision to use naturalistic categories is then a risky one, for there may not be orderly data to confirm the wisdom of the selection, but such molar categories need not be ruled out on a priori grounds. Similarly, a good case can be made for the inclusion of topographically dissimilar activities in behavior analytic research. The utility of the operant account of human behavior based on laboratory responses by animals rests on the assumption that there is a fundamental conceptual commonality among operant response classes. It would be unduly concrete to claim that reading and sewing are too different from each other to be meaningfully considered equivalent samples of human operant behavior; one needs to view them abstractly as exemplars from a class of responses unified by their relation with the consequences that accrue to the person engaging in the activity. Premack (1959, 1965) made this case initially with regard to time as a measure of responding, and it has been amplified conceptually by others (e.g., Baum & Rachlin, 1969; Timberlake, 1980).

In practice the advantages of the naturalistic repertoire have also outweighed the disadvantages. The measurement procedures (described below) have consistently generated very high reliability assessments (typically above .90), perhaps because they were closely modeled after successful methods used in applied behavior analysis. Also the effects of the experimental variables tend to be very large and consistent so neither the small measurement error nor the previous histories of the response categories have obscured the systematic relations between the independent variables and behavior. When experimental variables are administered over long periods in a controlled environment, variables outside the research program do not compete effectively with the impact of the planned variables. Finally, although it is possible to pay participants enough money to stay in the laboratory while engaging in activities that have no inherent consequences, it is better for long-term maintenance of participants that the repertoire includes activities that they will engage in with only the naturally occurring consequences.

The System of Observation

When a lab is built with fully instrumented operanda that define the rate of occurrence of each activity (see Findley, 1966), observation of participants is useful mostly to ensure that the system is functioning and that participants are not in distress. Data are collected automatically and without need for human interven tion or decision making. When the patterns of naturally occurring categories of behavior are the focus of research, however, observation is essential to the collection of data, and a reliable human system must be established. Operational definitions of the categories selected have rarely been a difficult problem. Most activities can be readily and reliably identified by using a conjunction of manual contact with relevant materials and orientation of the face toward the materials. If a participant looks away from the materials frequently, it is possible to require a minimum off-task gaze time before disrupting the identification of the category. When behavior is observed 15 hr per day, with many hours per category each day, there is no need to struggle with microtopography; the data are orderly at a molar level, and my research issues have never depended on a second-by-second analysis. Both modern digital and traditional electromechanical recording systems can automate the process of ignoring disruptions of a few seconds; larger disruptions could also be treated after the fact during the analysis of the record. When observers make note of every change they see, decisions about glossing over brief interruptions are made in the analysis software; this strategy is clearly the best as the maximum information is in principle available in the data base.

One could in principle use different levels of precision in analyzing the same data and find that level at which reliability of judgment is highest. When observations were calculated in terms of seconds of responding, reliabilities have not been acceptable. When observations have been calculated at the level of minutes, reliabilities are very high (over .90). For example, reading typically takes place in bursts of uninterrupted activity that may be as short as 20 min or as long as 150 min; given the usual topographical criteria, the measurement error in starting and stopping the recording of reading is tiny. The error may be in seconds, so rounding to minutes provides a highly consistent record. Talking, on the other hand, has proven to be a very difficult category to record, even with a molar criterion for judgment. At one point the operational definition of talking included having two people within 2 m of each other (or farther away with observed mutual eye contact) and there having been an utterance from either of them within the last 15 s. When the bouts of talking were calculated in seconds, the reliabilities were in the range of .30 to .50. Rounding each bout of talking to minutes got the reliability of observation into the .70 to .80 range, making the data possibly useful in an experiment.

Although my data have come over the years from paper-and-pencil logs, Esterline-Angus event recorders, relay rack counters and timers, and microcomputers, it is clear that only the last type of recording is presently viable. During the first long-term project undertaken in my laboratory, the recording of the behavior was separate from the analysis. A record of gross total amount of time devoted to each activity was available from pulses directed by hand switches to accumulating counters, and these totals were used to calculate and implement experimental interventions. Analysis of the actual details of responding was done with a separate computer program, and the paper event record for each 15-hr session required 3 hr of hand scoring, 2 hr of data entry, and over 20 hr of computation by a PDP-12 microcomputer. Eventually the computing was switched over to a mainframe that would turn each batch around in only a few hours. Currently, all management of experimental operations and data analysis are handled by a desktop microcomputer; keyboard entries from a menu-driven set of observation screens record each occurrence, calculate and operate experimental operations, and analyze and print the data from a 15-hr session in less than 2 min.

The program itself (see Bernstein & Livingston, 1982) has gone through many iterations, and the most recent version can operate the laboratory with up to three participants simultaneously occupying the same laboratory space. This format will keep independent records of the beginning and ending of each bout of each activity for each participant, as well as operate three independent contingencies on the behavior of each participant. The main features of such a program should include providing sequential options that lead the observer to enter all the necessary information, a routine that checks each entry to make certain that it is at least at logically plausible, and a routine that requires the observer to confirm that an entry is correct after it is first decoded by the machine. This system is different from many laptop observation devices that are commercially available in that it is not intended to handle rapidly occurring brief instances of action; it is structured for the repertoire that can be rounded to minutes without doing damage to the data. The system is like the better commercial programs, however, in that it recognizes that some categories of action can occur simultaneously, and the analysis program can calculate the amount of time that such activities overlap each other. In addition, the program records the participant's location and the status of any experimental variables that vary during the session.

The present program operates on any Apple II series computer or compatible machine, requiring only a clock card and 64K of RAM. Unfortunately, this classic and reliable little computer has become obsolete, and most modern systems cannot operate the programs that worked so well on the old machines. There certainly are good reasons to update these programs onto contemporary machines (mass storage of data on hard drives being the most important), but it has not been accomplished at the time of this writing. The old software is available as free-ware, should anyone want to undertake research of this kind and have access to appropriate hardware. It could also serve as a model for a newer version.

Reactivity of Measurement

People often comment that this research procedure is quite intrusive, and that the entire procedure must be very reactive, that is, the participants' behavior is radically changed by their being in the experimental laboratory and being observed through a large one-way mirror. Just as was true with the isolation inherent in the present procedures, it is almost certain that the participants do not behave exactly as they would in their home environment. The saving element, however, is that the reactivity is present in all of the conditions of the experiment, and all comparisons are made among various experimental conditions with presumably equivalent contamination by this artifact. Unless one can come up with a clearly articulated and reasonable a priori account of how reactivity would specifically interact with the conditions studied, it is unlikely that the experimental results reported are a product of reactivity per se.

It also is worth noting that the effects of being in an experiment, like many other variables, are not constant over time. Most research on experimental demand is done in brief, 1-hr experiments, without any attempt to see how participants would react after 2 hr of research or 5 hr or 5 days. After about 2 days of being in the laboratory and staring at the mirror, the participants typically start doing the kinds of things one would anticipate from someone not worried about who is watching. By the end of 3 days we routinely see participants scratch their privates, belch, and pick their noses while going about their business. They also begin to dress more casually and allow their personal appearance to be more in the style of Sunday at home than Monday at work. Because of this gradual desensitization to the reactivity of the laboratory, in general the first 4 days of data are not used in any experimental analysis. The initial baseline period for each participant is 8 days long, and only the last 4 days are used to calculate the initial baseline percentages of time devoted to activities.

There was also an opportunity to test directly the notion that participants are simply complying with implicit instructions to perform under contingency conditions. On several occasions there have been experimental conditions that included all of the instructions and formal restriction of responding included in a contingency, but there was no deprivation of the activity that functioned as the reinforcer (see Bernstein & Michael, 1990). In most of those cases, there was no increase in the instrumental activity, which is consistent with an interpretation that the experimental variables and not reactivity to the situation were responsible for the behavior observed.

Duration of Conditions

The continuous observation laboratory makes it possible to use the same kind of within-subject experimental designs that have been the hallmark of behavior analysis. As first articulated by Sidman (1960), the preference is for demonstration of replicability of a phenomenon in every participant, and comparisons are made between experimental conditions instituted at different times for the same participant. Although a good case can be made that experimental (or life) history is neither trivial in practice nor an unimportant variable conceptually (e.g., Wanchisen & Tatham, 1991), it has been widely assumed that the variability related to the participant's history will be overcome by the systematic effects of reinforcement operations applied over an extended period of time (e.g., Freeman & Lattal, 1992). Often the experimental analysis of human operant behavior has been based on participation from students enrolled in psychology classes, and many studies are conducted in one or two sessions with a total experimental time of an hour or two. This strategy has some advantages, but as a result the study of human operant behavior has come to resemble social psychology more than behavior analysis (see also Bernstein, 1988). In particular, there are some phenomena reported as fundamental to human behavior that have turned out to be transitory when humans are exposed to sufficient duration of the independent variables (e.g., Michael & Bernstein, 1991). The advantage of a continuous residential laboratory for humans is that researchers can bring the same experimental power to human behavior that has made the experimental analysis of animal behavior such a formidable research tool.

Research in a continuous residential laboratory, however, is expensive in both human time and financial resources, so it is important to have a good estimate of what can be accomplished within a certain period. Given the stability typical of a repertoire of ordinary activities, it is possible to estimate how long each experimental condition will need to be under average conditions. Almost never will it be the case that research with a repertoire of the kind discussed here will afford sufficient data to use formal stability criteria in deciding when to initiate a new experimental condition (see Baron & Perone, Chapter 3). Even after an initial 8-day baseline period to allow for adaptation to the laboratory, a typical research plan can only budget 4 days for each experimental condition and for each baseline.

Despite the fundamental limit on the number of observation days, there are reasonable strategies for demonstrating replicable relations between independent variables and behavior. It is relatively uncommon to find two consecutive days on which the percentage of time devoted to an activity is close to identical (within 3–4%); more typically there will be movement on the order of 8 to 10% in one direction or another. At a minimum then, the design needs a third day in each condition to determine if the level of responding moves back toward the initial value or continues to diverge from the first day. Most often the third point does move back toward the initial estimate, suggesting that there is no large trend in the data; a final fourth day that is within the full range of the first 3 days gives a researcher some confidence that the average amount of time devoted to the activity over those 4 days is a reasonable measure of the participant's relative preference for engaging in the action. Even if one of the points is somewhat different from the other three, there often will be a tolerable range of variability around the condition mean. In the ideal case, the range of daily points for a given experimental condition will have no overlap with the range of points in conditions from which it is thought to be different.

There are several possible exceptions to following this budgeted time plan for conditions. The most important has to do with 4 days of data that show a continuous trend up or down; the data do not represent a stable estimate of the steady-state value of the activity being measured, for that activity continues to change. If the condition is a baseline being used to estimate the values of the activities for purposes of a quantitative prediction or comparison, then baseline should be continued until the last 4 days include the kind of stability just described. On the other hand, there will be times when the main point is simply to demonstrate that an intervention has made a difference in the distribution of time, not to calculate the size of the difference. In such a case one might discontinue an experimental condition that is still changing if the trend is moving away from the comparison baseline and all of the points are outside the range of the comparison period. The qualitative claim can be made that the intervention was effective if the data during the return to baseline condition recover levels comparable to the last previous baseline. Ultimately, the claim will only be accepted if the reversal pattern is replicated both within and across participants, so this strategy will not likely lead to false alarms about the effectiveness of an intervention.

There have been times when early conditions required extra days above the time budgeted, and at least two participants have agreed to extend their stay beyond the initially contracted time. When that has not been possible, it was necessary to delete a few days from later conditions that were planned for the full 4 days.

Only by doing this can the full experimental plan be fitted into the fixed time contracted by the participant. I have used a 3-day condition if all of the daily points are outside the range of the comparison conditions and the trend of the last 2 days is away from the likely value of the succeeding condition of the experiment. Similarly, I have accepted a 2-day baseline between replications of a contingency condition if the two points are within a few percentage points of each other, similar to the last baseline condition, and well outside the range of the daily points in the experimental period. On several occasions these days saved from relatively stable conditions have made up for days given earlier to be certain of obtaining a stable measure of response preference.

In one study the amount of time per condition was fixed by constraints not amenable to change, and it was not possible to consider stability in moving through the planned conditions. Participants devoted time to simulated work activities during a portion of each day of their residence in a continuous environment, and contingencies were arranged among the assigned tasks just as they had been done previously with the participants' own activities. The variability of the daily points was large enough that visual inspection of the ranges of points within and across conditions was not sufficient to make strong claims for the data. Only when the data were aggregated into a mean percentage for each activity for each condition did the order in the data emerge; there were 32 transitions between conditions, and in 29 of them the targeted work activity changed preference in the predicted direction. This example raises the question of the relative value of preserving briefer samples that show variability or aggregating samples into stable estimates. In this research area the major dependent variable is response probability, measured as the percentage of time devoted to each activity. In the purest sense of momentary assessment, an activity can only have a probability of either 1 or 0; at any given moment it is either occurring or it is not. To make this kind of probability description requires aggregating a large number of 1s or 0s over a time period and calculating an expected value. As with the discussion of reductionism and the selection of units of behavior, we should be ready to accept a level of aggregation that shows orderly relations with environmental variables. It is not obvious that the study of ordinary repertoires of activity should be rejected because the stability of the data is not found in data points aggregated from a single hour or even a single day.

The use of ordinary activities results in aggregation of data into much longer periods to produce stable data. In most cases the data from a 15-hr daily session will be stable enough to be used as a data point, and typically four such points will evidence enough stability that the replicated effects of reinforcement operations can be unambiguously interpreted. A clear example of a readily interpretable reinforcement effect with 4-day conditions is presented below in Figure 16.8. The stability of the data can be influenced by the selection of category boundaries for the activity observation system; as described later, smaller activities that readily substitute for each other can be combined into large abstract categories to produce data that will be more consistent from day to day. In general, this approach assumes that the extended exposure to experimental variables will produce effects large enough to be clearly detectable within the variability characteristic of ordinary human activities in a naturalistic environment.

The use of only four data points per condition, and occasionally fewer, is not an ideal strategy for behavior analysis. Even though these conditions typically present data from 60 hr of observation, it would be better to have enough points to use conventional criteria for stability. In this case, we make a trade in which some increased ecological validity is gained in return for some loss in quantitative estimates of responding. Given that the use of the continuous environment is still relatively infrequent, the behavioral audience has accepted the large-scale replications of intervention effectiveness without stable estimates of terminal values in each condition. At the present time, the cost of conducting the research is sufficiently great that it is not advisable to do research in which many parametric variations on a schedule would be called for; it takes too much time to estimate the variables needed, and there are simpler questions as yet unanswered. It is worth noting that a similar argument could be mounted for conducting shorter-term research with human participants engaging in arbitrary laboratory activities; the increment in the quality of the data resulting from improvements in the research may not at the present time justify the costs.

Participant Selection and Maintenance

The single most important issue in conducting this research is the recruitment of a person who will thrive in the relatively impoverished environment of the laboratory. The main criteria that have successfully identified such people are the richness of the proposed repertoire of activities and the current frequency of their occurrence in the person's everyday life. Someone who has several different indoor activities that are engaged in many times each week will find the time in the laboratory enjoyable, whereas someone with one or two possible activities will find the laboratory intolerable. I once spent four difficult days watching someone try to learn to play the guitar by himself before he finally put us both out of our misery by withdrawing.

Participants are recruited with ads in the Help Wanted section of the local newspapers; initial attempts with ads in the Personals and Announcements sections did not produce satisfactory results. The ad describes a live-in psychology experiment and gives the number of days planned and the total stipend ($40, in 1996 dollars, times the number of days) is in large bold characters at the top; it states that applicants must be in good health. Callers leave a name and phone number with a receptionist, and the research staff call each person back for a phone interview. It is not difficult to find interested volunteers; each ad results in at least 100 phone inquiries. Limiting the recruiting to people who can be reached at a phone number increases the general reliability and social stability of the participant pool. The phone interview begins with a brief description of the basics of the research experience, and as many as 50% of the callers sign off after realizing that live-in means 24 hr per day and no TV or phone. If they are still interested, then we collect basic demographic information and ask about health status and any regular medications taken. Finally the candidate is asked to describe the activities that would be brought to the laboratory during the study. The majority of candidates struggle to think of one or two things they might want to do, and only a handful of people generate a reasonable list of likely activities. Candidates also are asked how many times in the last week they have engaged in each of the listed activities; higher reports have been a good predictor of success in the laboratory.

The top three or four candidates are invited to come for an interview at the laboratory. One main function the interview serves is to see if people actually show up; about 30% do not. At the interview the candidates see the laboratory, ask any questions they have thought about since the phone conversation, and answer more detailed questions about their activities. The more a person can describe what is done in an activity, the more likely it is that the activity is done frequently. Based on the breadth of the repertoire and the frequency of occurrence of the individual activities, a final candidate is selected. If there are comparable candidates, a preference is given for activities that generate material consequences (e.g., sewing, artwork, or model building) over activities that do not; these activities have been more stable over extended time in the laboratory.

The finalist is asked to return to the laboratory for an other interview; again, a main consideration is whether or not the person shows up. A lot of work goes into preparing the laboratory for each extended session, and it is essential that the person selected will actually appear at the arranged time. Having successfully met two appointments is a very good predictor of meeting the third appointment—the actual study. The other activity in the second interview is an evaluation conducted by a licensed clinical psychologist; the evaluation includes a basic intelligence test, a broad screen for psychopathology, and an interview. The psychologist is asked only to certify that the person was capable of giving informed consent and that the person is at no obvious risk from being in the experiment. These procedures were instituted at the request of the Institutional Review Board that oversees research with human participants. In addition, the psychologist observes the participant through the observation window roughly every 5 days for any obvious signs of stress or disintegration. The clinician often also offers unsolicited comments about how likely it is the candidate will respond to the contingencies, but these are ignored. In 20 years of research including approximately 30 participants, only one finalist was eliminated based on the screening; he reported having frequent hallucinations, and the psychologist felt he would be at risk in an isolated environment. In that time, only two people have failed to complete the full experimental period, both of these in the first year of the research program. Once the selection criteria and payment options were developed, there were no more problems with participant attrition.

The selected candidate agrees to return about 8 PM the evening before we start to move in and have a final discussion. Using the evening before avoids the loss of a valuable day of data. There is a detailed informed consent document that the participant reads; it describes all of the details that previously have been discussed orally. Key points include the following: The laboratory door is never locked and the participant is free to leave at any time, night or day; there is no deception in the experiment, and all procedures will operate as explained; the participant's privacy in the bathroom and during the dark hours is guaranteed; half of each day's pay is guaranteed, regardless of how long the experiment lasts; the second half of each day's pay accumulates as a bonus for completing the experiment, and is payable only at the end of the contracted time or if the experimenter terminates the study; if the participant leaves before the contracted time, the daily pay will be earned, but not the bonus; the main variable will involve restriction of access to activities, signaled by a red light; violation of the restrictions indicated by the red light will result in termination of the experiment without bonus.

The payment system was negotiated with the Institutional Review Board; the system was designed to make the latter stages of the experimental period as valuable to the participant as they are to the researcher. At first the committee felt that the partial payment was too coercive, but they were responsive to an argument that a partial experiment that was missing essential conditions would be of little value to an experimenter. Just as a publisher would not prorate payment for a book based on the proportion of chapters completed, the researcher should not be expected to pay the full daily rate for only a portion of the complete experiment. The contract provision on the red restriction light is necessary to conduct research on reinforcement. In a reinforcement procedure the participant would have access to certain activities only when time for them had been earned; for example, a drinking tube with saccharin for a rat could be inserted into a cage and withdrawn as the rat engages in the targeted operant behavior. It is not practically possible to remove all reading materials from a room quickly and return them promptly on completion of an instrumental requirement, so a red signal light is used to designate when they are not to be used. No participant has ever violated the conditions of the light, thanks to the simple contract on payment. The contract also specifies that the participant is not to sleep more than an hour during the light period nor spend more than 2 hr total per day in the bathroom, but these conditions have been invoked only rarely. On one occasion a participant left the laboratory for a day to attend a family funeral; the procedure was interrupted and a new baseline was instituted on the following day.

The procedures provide stability in the conditions for the participants without being unduly harsh or inflexible. As a result of a University public relations request, a reporter interviewed several former participants after their permission was obtained without violating their confidentiality. The text of the interviews by this independent source provides evidence to oversight committees that the procedure is benign; participants described their experience using glowing terms such as "self-discovery" and "personal growth." No one reported stress or difficulties with the procedure.

Given the overhead in staff and time, it might be considered advantageous to observe more than one person simultaneously. The laboratory at Johns Hopkins routinely includes three participants at the same time, but the facility is designed so that each person can live in a totally isolated area. In essence, they are conducting three single-participant studies at the same time. In my experience, the addition of a second participant would make interpretation of the data more difficult, and it might be necessary to consider the second participant to be part of the apparatus, like the magazines or art materials. Social interaction would become one of the categories and it could be used as either a reinforcing activity or targeted for change as an instrumental activity. Although such a strategy would open up many new research questions, it doubles the participant costs, and there is no substitute for actual money. So far, there have been more questions that can be answered with a single participant than we have had the energy to address.

Staffing the Laboratory

This research can be done with a minimum of research staff if needed, but most of the time there will be about 10 people working on the project. It is best if observers work around 2 hr at a time; longer times can lead to fatigue and lapses in attention to the task. Using slightly longer shifts in the evening, I managed to cover each day with seven observations periods; each week had around 50 shifts to be covered. In addition, fire safety and ethical concerns require that someone familiar with the building sleep in the laboratory each night, so there are seven overnight shifts to be filled as well. Finally, someone needs to buy groceries about twice a week and do laundry once a week.

It almost always has been possible to find undergraduate students who have done well in a course in learning and who would like to undertake some form of independent study in psychology. They enroll in a research practicum course for variable amounts of credit, depending on how many shifts per semester they will cover. The exact amounts vary in different academic cultures, and the local standards can be employed. The academic content of their experience is based on readings done prior to the session, discussions of the experimental rationale, and performance data on their observation reliability assessments. Expectations for this kind of instruction vary widely across departments, but the experience students get from this participation is widely regarded as valuable academic work. The overnight shifts are usually connected to the observation work, in that the person who has the last shift leading up to midnight usually is the person who stays overnight. As the academic content of being asleep is less substantive, however, a nominal financial stipend accompanies this activity.

It is also possible to use fully paid observation staff if sufficient resources are available. There is less time and energy devoted to teaching and keeping volunteer helpers happy, and multiple-year grant support also means there is more certainty about experimental designs that include a number of participants. In practice a combination of paid and volunteer staff works well; tasks such as supervisory responsibility, doing laundry and shopping, and spending nights in the laboratory can be paid on an hourly basis for those who wish greater commitment and involvement, whereas the actual observation in short shifts can be done by students who are interested in learning about the research area.

All told, the operating costs (excluding institutional costs of maintaining the facility) to conduct the research in the most economical fashion are currently about $60 per day (in 1996 dollars), including participant stipend, food, laundry, and overnight staff. Although this is not the kind of expense a researcher would typically pay from personal money, it is in the range of money that is available from local grants. It is not necessary to compete for and obtain scarce federal research support to conduct research of this type, as it can be accomplished within the context of a typical psychology department. The resources needed are mostly human, and the offer of educational experience and the opportunity to interact with researchers working at their craft is normally sufficient to create a working research group. At the extreme, a graduate student who is beyond the stage of taking classes could conduct research like this with a minimum of assistance; the data presented in Bernstein and Ebbesen (1978) were collected by one person, who was relieved from duty for an hour or two every couple of days.

The only resource that cannot be obtained through educational barter is the time of the participants. Most institutional settings that encourage or require research activity by graduate students and faculty also have some limited financial resources available on a competitive basis; more than 75% of the research I have done in a continuous environment has obtained the necessary cash support from local resources. If one is convinced this form of research is worthwhile, there is no need to be dissuaded because external support is unavailable.

ISSUES SPECIFIC TO RESEARCH ON TIME-BASED REINFORCEMENT

Some of the general issues mentioned above also have specific implications for research that is done on reinforcement in human behavior. There are some interesting ways that decisions made in establishing the laboratory interact with the procedures used in reinforcement research. The second major section describes such interactions in the areas of the identification of appropriate categories of behavior, the use of time as a measure of the strength of behavior, and the temporal stability of measures of behavior.

Selection Observation Categories

Time-based conceptions of reinforcement make predictions from observed distributions of the percentage of time devoted to each of the activities available, and a suitable multiple-response research preparation should have several activities that could be used either as a reinforcer or as a target for change by reinforcement. The results of the contingency operation can then be observed within the context of the distribution of time to all activities (see Bernstein & Ebbesen, 1978). Each participant will present a list of activities to engage in during the experiment. It is usually good to begin the measurement system by having the participant describe the activities and what materials (if any) are used when engaging in it; this will provide a first draft of the final category list that is used in the experiment. One practical rule of thumb is to allow only activities that occur regularly outside the laboratory and only those activities that the participant has engaged in over an extended period of time. The ideal behavioral preparation is one with four or five stable activities that each occur several times every day; a participant who brings in 10 or 15 activities will not likely yield stable day-to-day distributions of time devoted to those activities, especially if they are new to the repertoire.

Careful consideration should be given to the final development of a list of categories to be recorded. The continuous stream of action a person engages in can be broken into any number of pieces, and the category boundaries may influence the data collected. For example, if there are several small categories of handwork, they could be combined into a single abstract category. On any given day, 10% of the time might be devoted to some form of handwork, but each day it would be a different one of the activities. Measuring individual categories would yield an unstable repertoire with individual subactivities alternately filling the handwork time each day, whereas the abstract category would yield an apparently stable class of responses.

Figures 16.1 through 16.4 present examples of combining subcategories to pro-

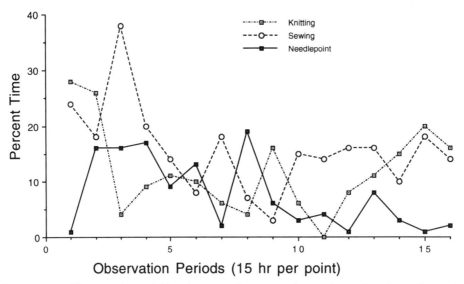

FIGURE 16.1.   Three sewing activities show complementary changes in the time devoted to each.

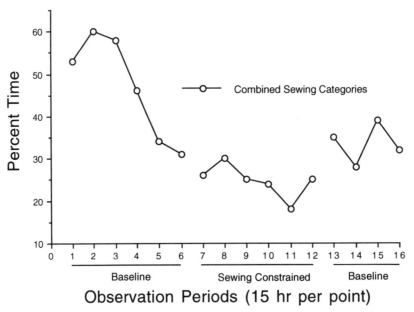

FIGURE 16.2.   Aggregation across sewing categories yielded more stable data, revealing the gradual change of baseline preference. The combined category was also used effectively as a reinforcer (see Figure 16.8).

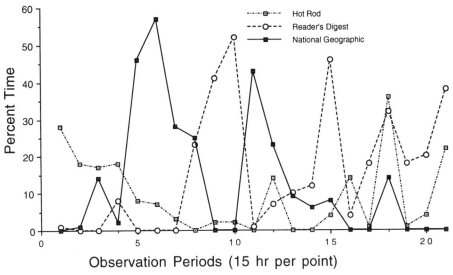

FIGURE 16.3.   Three reading activities show complementary changes in the time devoted to each.

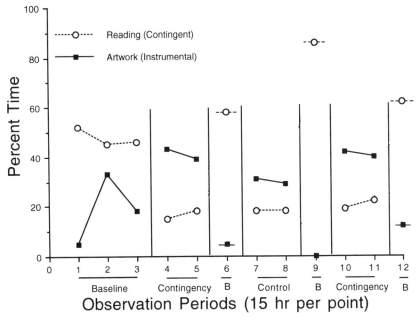

FIGURE 16.4.   Aggregation across reading categories yielded more stable data and allowed for predictions of the outcome of contingencies. Time devoted to artwork was greater during the contingency periods than during the surrounding baselines.

vide useful data on the amount of time devoted to sewing and reading by two different participants (Bernstein, 1974, pp. 212–217). In Figure 16.1 the participant engaged in three handwork activities (sewing, knitting, and embroidery), and the amounts of time devoted to each one varied across individual days. In this case, sewing and embroidery were combined into a single category and knitting remained a second category. The aggregation of sewing and embroidery was based on a modest negative correlation between the time devoted to sewing and the time devoted to embroidery; because the two activities appeared to be good substitutes for each other, they were treated as one category. Figure 16.2 shows the two activities plotted together over the same 16 observation periods. Unlike the individual category data, the combined sewing category shows a more orderly pattern, with far less day-to-day variability than was present in data from the individual categories. These were the first 2 weeks of a 5-week experiment, and there was some adaptation to the setting as sewing generally decreased to a steady level that continued throughout the remaining 3 weeks of the observation. The importance of tracking the changing baseline level will be addressed in a later section.

In Figure 16.3 another participant selected three different magazines to read (*Reader's Digest, Hot Rod,* and *National Geographic*) and they varied widely from day to day in how much time was devoted to each of them. It would have been difficult to interpret changes in the amount of reading from any one of those reading categories, and any attempt to deprive the participant of one reading category would likely result in a compensating increase in one of the other reading categories. When the contingency was implemented, a combined category of all three kinds of reading was used as a reinforcer (contingent activity); time for reading was produced by first devoting time to artwork (instrumental activity). As shown in Figure 16.4, the data for the combined reading category were stable and orderly, and reading was an effective reinforcer for artwork. During the four baseline periods there were six 15-hr periods of observation and during five of them the aggregated reading category was near its overall average; one period showed a somewhat higher value for the combined category. During the four periods in which the full contingency was in place, artwork was increased well above the surrounding baseline periods and clearly above a control condition that included only a portion of the procedure.

There is no single correct strategy for deciding whether to have a few large or many smaller categories. When dealing with any multiple-response repertoire, there will be variations in which activities predominate, and at times there will appear to be orderly and regular substitution of one response for another. This pattern has been documented in both applied (Wahler & Fox, 1983) and basic (Bernstein & Ebbesen, 1978) behavior analysis. If the categories of behavior have some a priori importance for the research, then those boundaries should be used. It would be wise to investigate the substitution properties of those existing categories, however, to avoid misinterpretation of the changes in distribution of time under experimental variables. If one wishes to have a relatively stable repertoire of ordinary activities and there is no reason to favor a particular set of category boundaries, then variable individual categories can be aggregated into larger abstract categories that will provide a more stable experimental preparation. This strategy is especially useful if access to any activities will be deprived as part of the experiment; the availability of readily substitutable alternatives would weaken the impact of the deprivation variable. Whichever decision is made, it should include recognition of the interaction between response substitution and category boundary selection.

As a practical matter, one can begin with a larger number of small categories to see how participants distribute their time among them. If aggregation is desirable, it can be done post hoc during the experiment; breaking down a combined category after the data have been collected is not as easily accomplished. Given the kind of molar activities used in my experiments, a good target range is about six to eight major activities. Most participants engage in three or four main activities that consume the bulk of their open time; it would be unusual for a participant to have more than five activities that consume at least 10% of the 15 hr of light time each day. There is typically a category called "maintenance" that includes all time in personal hygiene, preparing, eating and cleaning up meals, and general picking up; at least 15% of each day is normally devoted to this category. There is also a residual category called "other" that includes any activity not specified, as well as just doing nothing. If this category gets up around 15–20%, there is likely a need to identify the particular activities being included; if that much time is devoted to doing nothing, there may be some issues in participant management.

Measurement of Response Strength

Traditionally in behavior analysis the strength of behavior has been primarily measured by the frequency or rate of responding. In contrast, the models of reinforcement derived from Premack's (1965) account have been based on the duration of activities, measured mostly as the total time on each activity (e.g., Timberlake, 1980). In addition, ethologists interested in human behavior (e.g., Barker, 1963; see also Hackenberg, Chapter 17) and animal behavior (e.g., Kavanau, 1969) had provided some long-term records of how time was distributed among a range of activities, and other researchers have looked at the durations of individual bursts of activities (e.g., Dunham, 1977). Applied behavior analysts recording behavior outside the laboratory had also noted that rate of responding (or frequency) was not the only way to describe the occurrence of nondiscrete responses (e.g., Bijou, Peterson, & Ault, 1968). The observation system used in my continuous laboratory allows for the independent analysis of rate and duration, making it possible to compare various measures of the strength of a category of behavior. This kind of analysis represents an important step in making the principles of behavior analysis useful outside the laboratory with activities that do not lend themselves to automatically instrumented recording of the frequency of discrete and brief occurrences of behavior.

Using time as a measure of behavior strength added an important dimension to the potential utility of behavior analysis. Premack's (1965) approach to reinforcement was new in at least two important ways. First, the model makes a priori predictions about reinforcement operations, avoiding the claims of circularity that haunt purely post-hoc definitions of a reinforcing event. Second, the predictions about the outcome of reinforcement contingencies are based on the relative amount of time devoted to activities during a free-access baseline period, and the predicted result is measured by a redistribution of time devoted to the activities involved. Accordingly, the two major studies from my laboratory (Bernstein & Ebbesen, 1978; Bernstein & Michael, 1990) both used total duration exclusively in creating and implementing reinforcement contingencies among ordinary activities such as studying, knitting, and painting, and the effectiveness of those contingencies was also assessed by examining the overall distribution of time among activities. The rich behavioral record obtained in my continuous laboratory, however, also makes it possible to see whether measures of duration and frequency provide equivalent or differing pictures of the strength of various behavior categories.

The data record consists of several parallel time lines, each of which represents a set of activities or status codes that are mutually exclusive of each other. For example, the main activity set might include reading, sewing, artwork, exercise, maintenance, and other (the residual category). If the participant is doing any one of those activities, it is not possible to meet the definition of engaging in any other activity in the same set. The activity time line consists of alternating activity codes and time markers (in minutes), beginning with 0 min and ending with 900 min (15 hr); each activity listed occurred from the time before it in the list until the time after it, at which time the next listed activity began. At the same time, however, the location set might include the bed, the center table, left desk, right desk, food area, on the floor, standing, and the bathroom; the participant could be simultaneously seated at the left desk and doing artwork, though either could change without the other necessarily being affected. The experimental condition set might indicate whether or not a restricted activity was currently available, and this record would indicate any changes in the status of that variable. Using all three series of events and times of transition, one could know that during a given interval a participant was reading on the bed while sewing was restricted or that a participant was doing artwork at the right desk even though sewing was available. With this complete record of the onset and completion of each bout of each measured activity or location, it is possible after the fact to calculate many alternate descriptions of the stream of human action.

Following in the Premack tradition, the main measure of contingency effectiveness was an increase in the total time devoted to the instrumental activity (that activity that was required to gain access to another activity). Participants could accomplish the required increase by entering into the activity more frequently, engaging in the activity for longer during each bout, or both of those together. One might expect that the time of each occurrence would increase, especially because the contingency specified time (and not rate) as the required characteristic. On the other hand, if rate of responding is a fundamental feature of behavior, an increase in time might be accomplished simply by increasing the frequency of the behavior. Premack (1965) actually used a variant on that analysis in his initial justification of the use of time as a measure of response strength or value; he argued that various activities have characteristic topographies that occur at different rates, and using total time instead of rate allows for comparison of topographically dissimilar activities within a single measure of response strength.

The detailed records of a number of contingencies were examined to see which characteristic of the behavior was changed by contingency procedures that

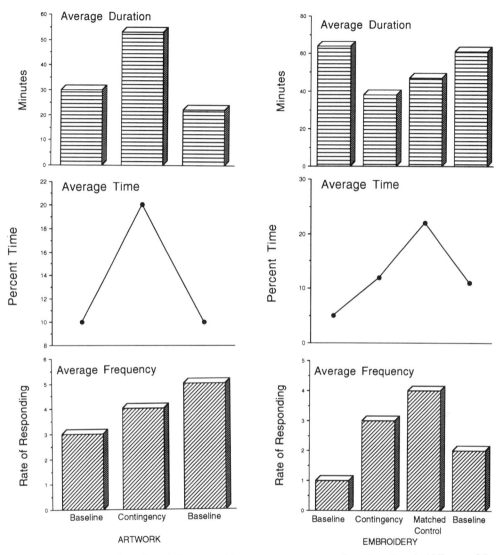

FIGURE 16.5.   Average bout length (top panels), average percentage of session time (middle panels), and average frequency (bottom panels) of two response categories. In the case of artwork (left panels) the percentage of time was driven by changes in the average duration of individual occurrences (top left panel); in the case of embroidery (right panels) the percentage of time was driven by changes in the frequency of individual occurrences (bottom right panel). No one measure gives a complete picture of responding.

were effective in producing an increase in the total amount of time devoted to the behavior. Figure 16.5 shows data from two participants (Bernstein, 1974, pp. 191 and 198) that give two typical but opposite views of this relation. The middle sections of the graph show the primary measure in the experiment. In the left panels, artwork increased from a baseline level of 10% of the total time to 20% and returned to its baseline level; in the right panels, embroidery showed a steady increase from 5% to 25% across the first three conditions and then returned to a moderate level of 10% in the last condition. The top panels show the average duration of a burst of each activity; it is total duration divided by frequency of occurrence. For artwork it can be seen that the pattern of change in percent time is very similar to the pattern of change in the average length of an occurrence. The doubling of time on artwork was accomplished primarily by staying in artwork for longer at each instance, not by doubling the number of occurrences of artwork. The bottom panels show the average number of occurrences of the activity per 15-hr observation period; this is the total frequency of the category divided by the number of observation periods. The decrease back to baseline level was in fact accompanied by a slight increase in the frequency of engaging in artwork, but the average length of each occurrence decreased to a level lower than baseline.

For embroidery the pattern of change in percent time is closely parallel to the changes in frequency over the four conditions. The changes in the total time were accomplished primarily by changing the number of times embroidery occurred, not by changing the duration of each instance of embroidery. In fact, the increase in the second condition and the decrease in the fourth condition were accomplished by strong changes in frequency, despite slight but opposite changes in the average length of each occurrence of embroidery. These data are typical from patterns with three participants (Bernstein, 1974); neither time nor frequency was a more fundamental characteristic of performance, and changes in total time could be primarily a product of either characteristic. Several instances showed a complex interaction in which neither rate nor burst length was comparable to the total duration, and the final result on total time was a product of contrasting changes in average duration and frequency. Analysis of a complex and rich description of performance yielded the conclusion that any description of the effects of contingencies should include both frequency and burst length so it does not miss a potentially interesting relation between behavior and the environment.

Stability of Behavior

This research program did not start out as a long-term project, nor was it intended to demonstrate the superiority of extended exposure to experimental variables. The first study was simply an attempt to demonstrate the Premack principle with human behavior in a laboratory. Volunteer students were recruited to spend 12 hr in a large room, engaging in ordinary activities that they were to bring with them. The first 4 hr was to be a baseline for assessment of the time devoted to the repertoire of activities, the middle 4 hr would be a contingency period, and the last 4 hr would return to baseline conditions to see if the effect of a contingency was reversible and replicable. The first thing learned was that people do not move around among ordinary activities at the same rate that a gerbil alternates among grooming, chewing, running, and digging. The first two participants devoted most of the first baseline period to a single activity, yielding no real estimate of the relative proportion of time devoted to the members of the repertoire. It was not possible to base a contingency on the information collected, so each person was simply observed for 12 hr of continuous baseline. By examining the data in separate blocks of 2, 3, 4, and 6 hr, none of those divisions yielded a hierarchy of response values (measured in percentage of time) that was even remotely stable. The activities were spread out across the day without any regular repetition, and the minimum data point for calculating a measure of relative response strength appeared to be a full day of observation.

At this point two courses of action were possible. One would be to limit the repertoire to activities with brief typical durations, possibly by creating an arbitrary set of operanda like those used by Premack (1965) or Eisenberger, Karpman, and Trattner (1967) to study the same topic in brief sessions. We also considered using puzzles or toys that would be initially engaging but not consuming; this was in the distant past, before VCR or Nintendo were meaningful utterances. For someone who cannot invest weeks or months on time-based reinforcement research, this strategy remains a viable option. Instead, we chose to stick with the leap up to ordinary human activities drawn from the participant's natural daily repertoire, and this meant that the duration of the experiment needed to be extended greatly.

If the basic data point was 1 day, then a minimum of 3 days would be needed for a baseline estimate, 3 days for the contingency, and 3 more for a final baseline. Given the possibility that the data might be sufficiently stable to have a 2-day baseline in there somewhere, a replication of the contingency and a final baseline would be possible in a 2-week experiment. Only when the plan included over 10 days was the notion of 24-hr residence considered. There are many logistical difficulties solved by having the participant simply remain in the laboratory, not the least of which is having the person show up. The isolation and continuous living idea was considered plausible because of Findley's (1966) study of a single person for over 150 days; a mere 14 days seemed very modest relative to that effort.

Construction of the experimental repertoire was also more carefully considered with the second version of the experiment, resulting in some compromises with complete ecological validity. It would be disadvantageous to have several activities that would typically occur for many hours at a sitting; in the first version the participants often read uninterrupted for more than 2 hr. Accordingly, participants were not allowed to bring any books or other lengthy reading material. The laboratory provided an enormous supply of magazines of varying kinds, and participants were allowed to select three magazines for their stay. Several years of each magazine were then provided in the laboratory, with additional issues available if needed. One of the reading options was short stories, but these were not presented in their original bound format. The short story books were systematically torn apart and each story was individually stapled; participants would not just continue reading at the conclusion of each story, for they would have to get up and seek another story from the pile. Although some activities such as exercise or playing music seemed self-limiting, there was no way of knowing in advance how activities such as sewing or artwork would be patterned.

At this early point in the research program, access to television was also ruled out. Later experience indicated that information on television might add random variability, but the decision at this point was based on the likely pattern of television watching. The nature of TV programming is so different on weekends and weekdays that it would not be possible to use weekday baselines to predict contingency performance on the weekend. One solution would be to aggregate TV watching across both programming patterns, but the prospect of having a week of observation count as a single data point made this solution impractical. The same logic was used to eliminate whole books; a baseline of reading based on one book may not be a good predictor of the actual time devoted to reading a different book. At one point 10 years into the research program one participant was allowed to have book-length reading just to see if the research plan was unnecessarily rigid. As luck would have it, the participant finished reading a book just at the end of a baseline period, and the contingency that began on the succeeding days was ineffective. Following a second baseline assessment using the new book, a recalculated contingency was instituted that yielded the expected reinforcement effect. Since that time, reading materials have again been restricted to short items.

At some level it is impossible to guarantee stability of data, regardless of how the repertoire of activities is selected or fashioned. The best one can do is recognize ahead of time how the pattern of behavior will be reflected in stability, so that sufficient observation time is allowed. There inevitably will be some long-term, gradual changes in the amount of time participants devote to activities, especially when the laboratory stay lasts for weeks. Figure 16.6 shows data on two activities from successive baseline periods occurring during a 21-day laboratory stay (Bernstein, 1974, p. 214). The change in baseline values was gradual, and the data from experimental conditions in between any two baselines were interpretable even in the context of the long-term changes. Figure 16.2 from an earlier section shows the experimental procedures interpolated in between these changing baselines; despite the overall drift in artwork and reading, there are clear changes that resulted from the experimental conditions.

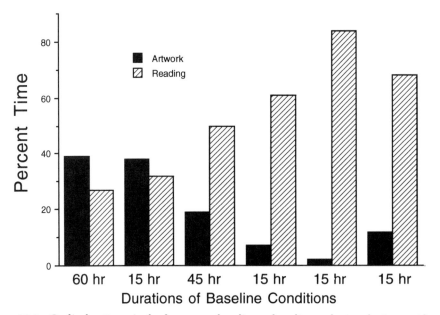

FIGURE 16.6. Cyclical patterns in the free-access baselines of reading and artwork. A recent baseline is needed to make predictions when there are cyclical (and in this case complementary) changes in the percentage of time devoted to activities. Using recent baselines generated effective contingencies (see Figure 16.2).

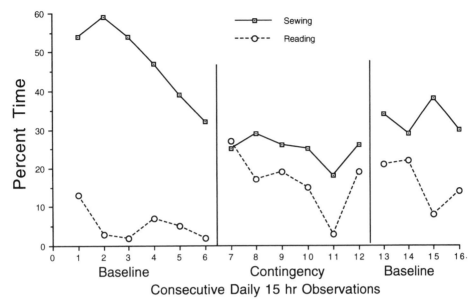

FIGURE 16.7. Changes over time in the baseline values of two responses (sewing and reading) during the initial 16 days of an experiment. Baseline values to be used in contingencies must exclude the data from the initial period of adaptation to the laboratory to give an accurate assessment of the value of the responses at the time of the contingency. The contingency during days 7 to 12 was based on values from the initial baseline and it was not effective when compared with the subsequent baseline.

Some of this variability can be managed by giving participants a sufficient warmup period before using the time estimates in planning experimental interventions. As noted earlier, the initial baseline period in my experiments is currently 8 days. Although this minimizes the reactivity of the experiment, it was implemented originally because the observed distribution of time during the first 4 days is often not typical of a stable pattern of preference that develops after participants have more experience with life in the laboratory apartment. Figure 16.7 shows a 6-day baseline that was used to calculate a contingency between reading and sewing; it appeared that the contingency yielded a modest increase in reading, but the second baseline indicated that the two activities had in fact changed their relative value (Bernstein, 1974, p. 81). Figure 16.8 shows data from a subsequent contingency based on the values in the second baseline. The second baseline data are plotted again as days 13 to 16, and on days 17 to 20 there is a substantial increase in reading (the targeted instrumental activity) above all surrounding baseline levels of reading. The next two baseline days are also plotted, and they show that the new baseline values prevailed throughout the remainder of the stay in the laboratory.

Circadian Distribution of Activities

Another aspect of behavior is its distribution across the day; some activities may be evenly distributed independent of time of day, whereas others may be more

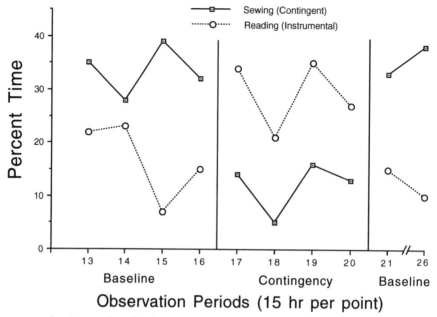

FIGURE 16.8. Contingency based on baseline values collected after 12 days of adaptation was effective in producing an instrumental increase. The time devoted to reading increased above the surrounding baseline periods.

common at certain times than at others. Dunham (1977) suggested that animals may have very strong preferences for these distributions, even to the point of working to preserve them if challenged. Participants in my laboratory have generally shown selective distributions of activities; that is, the time devoted to an activity is not evenly distributed across the day, but typically located in one or several time periods. In one study, participants were prevented from engaging in an activity during its normal time periods of the day, and they were allowed to engage in the behavior only during nontypical periods. Both times when that procedure was implemented, the amount of time devoted to the activity decreased. Dunham also claimed that the average bout length would also be defended by animals, and human participants in my laboratory showed this pattern as well. Using the full record of behavior, it was possible to measure the average bout length of a frequent activity. During a restriction condition, the bout length of this activity was limited to the mean duration (cutting off half of the distribution), and three participants greatly decreased the amount of time they devoted to the activity. The same was true in a fourth instance when the bout length was limited to a value that was half of the average bout length during unrestricted baseline. Overall it was clear that having a continuous record of naturalistic activities of varying lengths made it possible to look at human behavior with very different measures than are possible with only the rate of a brief operant response.

THE EFFORT IS WORTHWHILE

Although it is convenient to assess human behavior by recording the rate at which humans move an arbitrary operandum, there certainly is reason to consider undertaking research with ordinary human behavior. The increased likelihood of generalization can be obtained without losing experimental control if the naturalistic repertoire is studied over extended periods of time and in an environment lacking the distractions of everyday life. Given a repertoire of ordinary activities, it is possible to measure behavior in a more complex way, allowing for more dependent variables than just rate of responding. These records can reveal interesting patterns of performance that can be related to environmental variables just as rate has been in less complex research preparations.

In the end, each researcher decides how much investment of time and intellect can be invested in a project, given the likely return in knowledge and understanding. There is no simple algorithm that gives an answer, and different people pursue research with very different inputs and outputs. The kind of research described here is very long on input, and it is reasonable to ask whether all of that effort is justified. In addition to the inherently interesting nature of the research, I have concluded that the continuous environment research has been productive in at least one very important way. I believe this line of work has greatly enhanced the perception of many readers that a theory of human behavior built around reinforcement can in fact be useful. For me, Premack's (1965) empirical formulation of the reinforcement relation represented a giant step toward using reward outside the laboratory. My early research tried simply to demonstrate that the new model would work when humans and ordinary activities were substituted for laboratory animals and arbitrary operanda. Behavior analysts will likely find it easier to sell our account of human behavior to people outside psychology generalizing from these human research examples.

There was also one modest test of this assumption of generality. After asserting for years that my research would be readily applicable to the workplace, I presented my data to a group of faculty at the College of Business Administration on my campus. Although they were sympathetic to the behavioral model and impressed with the orderliness of the data, they asserted that the research had no implications for the workplace. The research participants engaged in activities they enjoyed (sewing, reading, artwork, and the like), whereas employees generally devote time to assigned activities that they would never engage in without contingent compensation. Here was an audience that not only would not accept animal data, but they would not even grant generalization across apparently similar aspects of a human repertoire.

My first reaction was to conduct another laboratory study using activities that simulated work; each one was boring, repetitive, and of no intrinsic value to the participants. These data perfectly replicated the data from desirable activities, so I went back and gave another presentation to the management crowd. This time they were more impressed, and there followed a collaboration with one of them and his graduate student. We applied the basic formulation to reinforcement of job tasks in a fast-food restaurant; employees engaged in a less preferred task in order to gain assignment to a more preferred work station. Although many researchers worry about taking a phenomenon out of the friendly confines of a laboratory, I was confident that this direct application would be successful. Despite many adaptations to suit the realities and peculiarities of a workplace, the overall procedure produced consistent improvements in the worker's performance as a result of the imposition of the contingencies (Welsh, Bernstein, & Luthans, 1992).

It is that straightforward application of the conceptualization and results of my research with ordinary human activities that gives me the most satisfaction. The laboratory work will also continue, in part because it is easier to work in a research environment than it is to work around the constraints of a functioning business or organization. It has been useful to demonstrate that complex human behavior can have orderly relations with experimental variables when a laboratory environment allows the variables to be strong and to be applied for an extended period. Many other variables in psychology are interesting, and it is clear that under certain conditions they may operate for short periods of time. When time-based contingencies are applied to human behavior under continuous observation and control, however, the results suggest that reinforcement procedures play an enormous role in the distribution of time on everyday activities. Having such a clear view of the effect of behavior analytic variables on human action makes it worthwhile to spend the effort required in establishing and maintaining the experimental conditions of a continuous residential laboratory for the study of human behavior.

REFERENCES

Barker, R. G. (1963). *The stream of behavior.* New York: Appleton–Century.

Baum, W. M., & Rachlin, H. C. (1969). Choice as time allocation. *Journal of the Experimental Analysis of Behavior, 12,* 861–874.

Bernstein, D. (1974). Structure and function in response repertoires of humans (Doctoral dissertation, University of California, San Diego, 1973). *Dissertation Abstracts International, 34,* Series B, p. 4070 (DCJ74-02376, 261 pp.).

Bernstein, D. (1986). Correspondence between verbal and observed estimates of reinforcement value. In L. Parrot & P. Chase (Eds.), *Psychological aspects of language: The West Virginia lectures* (pp. 187–205). Springfield, IL: Thomas.

Bernstein, D. (1988). Laboratory lore and research practices in the experimental analysis of human behavior: Session logistics—How long, how often, how many? *The Behavior Analyst, 11,* 51–58.

Bernstein, D., & Brady, J. V. (1986). The utility of continuous programmed environments in the experimental analysis of human behavior. In H. Reese & L. Parrott (Eds.), *Behavior science: Philosophical, methodological, and empirical advances* (pp. 229–245). Hillsdale, NJ: Erlbaum.

Bernstein, D., & Ebbesen, E. (1978). Reinforcement and substitution in humans: A multiple-response analysis. *Journal of the Experimental Analysis of Behavior, 30,* 243–253.

Bernstein, D., & Livingston, C. (1982). An interactive program for observation and analysis of human behavior in a long-term continuous laboratory. *Behavior Research Methodology and Instrumentation, 14,* 231–235.

Bernstein, D. J., & Michael, R. L. (1990). The utility of verbal and behavioral assessments of value. *Journal of the Experimental Analysis of Behavior, 54,* 173–184.

Bijou, S., Peterson, R., & Ault, M. (1968). A method to integrate descriptive and experimental field studies at the level of data and empirical concepts. *Journal of Applied Behavior Analysis, 1,* 175–191.

Dunham, P. (1977). The nature of reinforcing stimuli. In W. K. Honig & J. E. R. Staddon (Eds.), *Handbook of operant behavior* (pp. 98–124). New York: Appleton–Century–Crofts.

Eisenberger, R., Karpman, M., & Trattner, J. (1967). What is the necessary and sufficient condition for reinforcement in the contingency situation? *Journal of Experimental Psychology, 74*, 342–350.

Findley, J. D. (1966). Programmed environments for the experimental analysis of human behavior. In W. Honig (Ed.), *Operant behavior: Areas of research and application* (pp. 827–848). New York: Appleton–Century.

Foltin, R. W., Fischman, M. W., Brady, J. V., Bernstein, D. J., Capriotti, R. M., Nellis, M. N., & Kelly, T. H. (1990). Motivational effects of smoked marijuana: Behavioral contingencies and low-probability activities. *Journal of the Experimental Analysis of Behavior, 53*, 5–19.

Freeman, T. J., & Lattal, K. A. (1992). Stimulus control of behavioral history. *Journal of the Experimental Analysis of Behavior, 57*, 5–15.

Kavanau, J. L. (1969). Behavior of captive white-footed mice. In E. Willems & H. Raush (Eds.), *Naturalistic viewpoints in psychological research* (pp. 221–270). New York: Holt, Rinehart, & Winston.

Michael, R. L., & Bernstein, D. J. (1991). The transient effect of acquisition history on generalization in a matching-to-sample task. *Journal of the Experimental Analysis of Behavior, 56*, 155–166.

Premack, D. (1959). Toward empirical behavioral laws: I. Positive reinforcement. *Psychological Review, 66*, 219–233.

Premack, D. (1965). Reinforcement theory. In D. Levine (Ed.), *Nebraska symposium on motivation* (pp. 123–180). Lincoln: University of Nebraska Press.

Sidman, M. (1960). *Tactics of scientific research.* New York: Basic Books.

Timberlake, W. (1980). A molar equilibrium theory of learned performance. In G. H. Bower (Ed.), *The psychology of learning and motivation* (Vol. 14, pp. 1–58). New York: Academic Press.

Wahler, R. G., & Fox, J. J. (1983). Response structure in deviant child–parent relationships: Implications for family therapy. In D. Bernstein & H. Howe (Eds.), *Nebraska symposium on motivation* (pp. 1–46). Lincoln: University of Nebraska Press.

Wanchisen, B. A., & Tatham, T. A. (1991). Behavioral history: A promising challenge in explaining and controlling human operant behavior. *The Behavior Analyst, 14*, 139–144.

Welsh, D. H. B., Bernstein, D. J., & Luthans, F. (1992). Application of the Premack principle of reinforcement: Analysis of the impact on quality performance of service employees. *Journal of Organizational Behavioral Management, 13*, 9–32.

17

Laboratory Methods in Human Behavioral Ecology

Timothy D. Hackenberg

Human behavioral ecology is an empirically based set of methods, concepts, and interpretations aimed at understanding human behavior in a biological and social context. As a tradition of research and theory, human behavioral ecology is in its infancy. It is the intellectual offspring of two major approaches to the study of behavior from a biological perspective: behavioral ecology, which focuses primarily on behavior in natural settings, and the experimental analysis of behavior, which focuses primarily on behavior in laboratory settings. The past decade has seen promising attempts at integrating these two complementary approaches to gain a fuller appreciation of behavior in relation to general principles of adaptation and selection (see Fantino & Abarca, 1985; Kamil, Krebs, & Pulliam, 1987).

Although differing somewhat in emphasis, both behavioral ecology and the experimental analysis of behavior share a commitment to environmental determinants of behavior, and to quantitative descriptions of functional relations that extend across species. Whereas cross-species generality has long provided a working assumption in both fields, only recently has human behavior become an explicit focus of investigation in its own right. The experimental analysis of human behavior has grown rapidly over the past decade (Dougherty, Nedelmann, & Alfred, 1993), well represented by the topics covered in the present volume. Over approximately the same time period, terms and concepts from behavioral ecology have been increasingly applied to human behavior, primarily to foraging patterns of hunter-gatherer groups (Smith & Winterhalder, 1992). Human behavioral ecology stands at the interface between the laboratory arrangements of the experimental analysis of behavior and the more naturalistic arrangements of behavioral ecology. Recent findings from the laboratory nicely complement those from the field, but these dual approaches have yet to be combined within a cohesive analytic framework for understanding human behavior. The present chapter is an initial

Timothy D. Hackenberg • Department of Psychology, University of Florida, Gainesville, Florida 32611-2250.

Handbook of Research Methods in Human Operant Behavior, edited by Lattal and Perone. Plenum Press, New York, 1998.

step in that direction. If the fruitful contacts between experimental and ecological approaches to animal behavior are any indication, the future of human behavioral ecology appears very bright indeed.

The goal of this chapter is to sketch a framework for relating laboratory research with that from the field, using some preliminary investigations to illustrate some of the paths human behavioral ecology might follow. The chapter is intended for experimental psychologists interested in learning more about some of the key concepts in behavioral ecology, and for biologists and anthropologists interested in learning more about how analytic tools developed in the behavioral laboratory can be brought to bear on such concepts. In keeping with the methodological focus of the present volume, laboratory methods will be emphasized, although in a field as young as this few data from laboratory preparations exist. Unlike other contributions to this volume with well-defined empirical foundations, the empirical base here is just beginning to develop. The few systematic investigations that do exist are themselves just preliminary stages of work in progress. This chapter will therefore be less a comprehensive review of the literature than a selective overview aimed at highlighting some promising developments. This would appear to be an excellent time to focus on methodological matters. What are the empirical standards that will come to represent this field? How will evidence be evaluated? What are the standard units of measurement? Are there special methodological considerations to take into account when extending to human behavior principles developed primarily with other animals? These are but a few of the questions facing human behavioral ecology. The goal of the present chapter is not so much to answer these questions as to raise them.

The chapter is organized into four main sections. The first section centers on the relationship between laboratory and naturalistic observations, and the circumstances under which laboratory methods might best be utilized in behavioral ecology. The second section will focus on the role of optimization principles in behavioral ecology, including the logic and rationale underlying optimization models. The third section is organized around empirical phenomena from the field and the laboratory, mostly growing out of recent developments in optimal foraging theory. The final section will discuss limitations in current approaches to the subject matter, as well as point to some promising future directions in human behavioral ecology.

LABORATORY METHODS IN BEHAVIORAL ECOLOGY

A major objective of this chapter is to make a case for the laboratory investigation of human behavioral ecology. In doing so, however, it is important to point out that laboratory methods play a somewhat different role in behavioral ecology than they do in many other areas covered in this volume. In a majority of human operant research, core principles and concepts have been developed inside the laboratory, then, in some cases, extended to conditions outside the laboratory. By contrast, the core principles and concepts in human behavioral ecology have been developed outside the laboratory—primarily within the context of field studies; laboratory procedures have come later.

Laboratory methods supply the behavioral ecologist with a powerful set of analytic tools. Such methods can provide a valuable supplement to field studies but only if the rationale underlying their use is clearly specified. The main rationale behind the use of laboratory procedures in behavioral ecology is practical. Faced with the enormous complexity of human behavior in naturally occurring situations, one must make some simplifying assumptions about behavior and how it is related to the environment. As Winterhalder (1981) noted: "The problem is to simplify complex adaptive systems so that they retain essential and interesting (i.e., nontrivial) features, but at the same time become analytically tractable" (p. 18).

An important part of analytic tractability lies in the identification of analytic units. In the laboratory it is possible to break the ongoing behavior stream into some of its constituent functional units. If one is right about the units and the way they fit together, then it should be possible to recombine them in ways that yield complex behavior, a strategy Catania (1992, p. 180) termed a *behavior synthesis.* As MacCorquodale (1970) put it: "In the laboratory, variables are made to act 'one at a time,' for all practical purposes. The real world simply puts the environment back together again" (p. 98). The goal of a laboratory synthesis of behavior is to better understand the functional units of behavior as they might occur in naturally occurring conditions outside the laboratory.

Although recognizing that field studies are and will always be an indispensible part of behavioral ecology, it is appropriate to focus on laboratory methods. As applied to the present issues, laboratory methods hold several practical advantages over field studies. First, they permit isolation of and control over key variables, which is often very difficult under the naturalistic conditions that typify fieldwork in behavioral ecology. Second, laboratory procedures permit continuous monitoring and direct recording of behavior in real time, a decided advantage over the behavior sampling procedures utilized in field studies. Most field studies rely on self-reports and other indirect methods highly susceptible to bias and distortion (see Critchfield, Tucker, & Vuchinich, Chapter 14). Third, examining behavior under well-controlled conditions in the laboratory makes it possible to simulate crucial features of the environment, and to quantify better the relations between those features and behavior. Together, these three features of laboratory methods (enhanced experimental control, more precise measurement, and better quantification of environment–behavior relations) have allowed for more rigorous testing of key predictions of various models and interpretations from behavioral ecology. Reciprocally, the models and interpretations of behavioral ecology have begun to inspire new laboratory procedures that extend and validate models and interpretations from the experimental analysis of behavior.

OPTIMIZATION PRINCIPLES IN BEHAVIORAL ECOLOGY

Most explanatory statements in behavioral ecology are based on a type of cost–benefit analysis in relation to some problem of survival. The formalization of a cost–benefit analysis in behavioral ecology is called an *optimization model.* Because optimization concepts are used in different and often confusing ways, it seems appropriate to briefly discuss the way optimization principles are used in behavioral ecology, as well as the logic and rationale underlying optimization modeling.

The objectives of this section are twofold. The first is to identify some of the conditions under which optimization concepts are appropriate and may be useful to those interested in studying behavior. I will begin by describing some general features of an optimization approach, pointing out some of the conceptual problems that arise from applying optimization principles inappropriately, beyond the specific contexts for which they have been formulated. The second objective is to describe how optimization models are tested, including the core elements most optimization models share. The theoretical flavor of this section may appear to divert attention from the present methodological themes, but is essential in understanding the close interplay between method and theory in behavioral ecology, and the explanatory assumptions that are inherent in ecological methods. In the present context, the term *method* applies not only to specific laboratory techniques for controlling behavior and for isolating functional relations but also to conceptual and quantitative techniques for explicit testing of an optimization model.

General Features of an Optimization Approach

A common misconception about optimization analyses is that they treat optimization as a process, or mechanism, by which adaptation is accomplished. As characterized by behavioral ecologists, however, optimization is not a *process;* rather, it is an inevitable *outcome* of selection, given certain assumptions about adaptation and survival (cf. Staddon & Hinson, 1983). As Smith (1983) put it: "In order to generate explanations of any sort, one must make some assumptions about how the world is put together. Our current understanding of natural selection makes certain types of optimization assumptions plausible guides to theory building" (p. 626).

These assumptions are rooted in principles of variation and selection, and may be summarized as follows: (1) Organisms within a population vary with respect to characteristics important to their survival. These characteristics can be both morphological (relating to anatomical structure and form) and behavioral. The former are concerns of sciences such as comparative physiology and anatomy; the latter are concerns of behavioral ecology. (2) Resources (e.g., food, mates) are finite, so competition among individual members of a species arises. (3) Organisms whose behavior enhances access to these limited resources, relative to other organisms in the population, will, other things being equal, leave a greater number of offspring.

From these three assumptions it follows that the relative frequency of organisms whose behavior enhances access to resources—whose behavior could be said to be *optimal* with respect to those resources—will increase. In this context, *optimal* is simply the name given to that cluster of characteristics, both morphological and behavioral, that collectively contribute to the survival of the organism. Optimization, then, is a natural outgrowth of selection operating on a variable population of organisms. Optimization (or some such concept) is true, by definition, given the basic tenets of natural selection (Foley, 1985).

An important implication of this view is that the concept of optimization is only appropriate at the level of differential survival of the whole organism, not at the level of the individual characteristics that comprise it. As Foley (1985) put it: "Whole organisms tend toward optimality, their component parts do not" (p. 223). In other words, it makes little sense to speak of optimizing a morphological or behavioral characteristic in isolation because that characteristic is only part of the larger evolutionary framework in which optimization concepts are meaningful.

How Optimization Concepts Apply to Behavior

Although morphology and behavior are sometimes discussed as if they were separate domains, in practice, they are frequently interconnected. The bodily structures whereby vision occurs, for example, are selected in part because they make possible certain patterns of behavior that enhance survival. They might do so for various behavioral reasons—because improved visual acuity increases the efficiency of foraging patterns or because it decreases the risk of predation, to name just two. Characterizing and explaining such patterns of behavior as they relate to differential survival of the organism is a central objective of behavioral ecology. According to Krebs and Davies (1993), behavioral ecology

> is about the survival value of behaviour. We call this subject 'behavioural ecology' because the way in which behaviour contributes to survival and reproduction depends on ecology . . . the kind of food [an animal] eats, its enemies, its nesting requirements and so on. (p. 1)

Behavioral ecologists distinguish questions about behavior that contributes to survival from questions about the psychological processes (or mechanisms) by which it does so. As Krebs and McCleery (1984) put it, "there is . . . an important distinction between what the animal is designed to achieve (a question about survival value) and how it does it (a question about mechanisms)" (p. 118). The former are concerned with what are sometimes called *functional* or *ultimate* questions: Why did this particular behavioral adaptation come about? What are the ecological circumstances that gave rise to it and how is it related to differential reproductive success? The latter are concerned with what are sometimes called *causal* or *proximate* questions: What are the ontogenic variables of which the behavior is a function? What are the psychological processes that govern it? These two kinds of questions are complementary, as Shettleworth (1989) pointed out:

> It cannot be emphasized too often that questions about optimality and questions about psychological process are fundamentally different. [Optimality] theory asks the question, 'What should animals do?' Psychological research generally tries to answer the question, 'How do animals do it?' Attempts to answer these questions therefore lead to complementary accounts of behavior, accounts which should ultimately converge. (p. 82)

It will be suggested in the sections that follow that an optimization model provides a structured way of combining these two kinds of questions. It is concerned both with the ecological circumstances that give rise to a particular behavior pattern (its survival value) and with the psychological processes responsible for it (its current behavioral function). I will first describe some basic elements common to optimization models, then outline the steps involved in testing such models. The focus here will be on general features of optimization models; subsequent sections will illustrate how these general features are applied to specific models designed to address specific foraging patterns.

What Is an Optimization Model?

An optimization model is a quantitative description of the costs and benefits of particular behavior patterns in relation to some problem of survival. There is an emphasis on testability, on hypotheses that can be either confirmed or disconfirmed. Optimization models are normally expressed in graphic or algebraic form, and specify how dependent variables (behavior patterns) are related to independent variables (environmental patterns). The functions relating dependent and independent variables "are assumed to be linear, increasing or decreasing over some range—convex, concave, or the like—rather than having exact specifications" (Winterhalder, 1981, p. 18). Like mathematical descriptions in other areas of behavior analysis, an optimization model that specifies a quantitative relationship between independent and dependent variables is useful in the prediction and control of behavior (Shull, 1991).

What distinguishes optimization models from other types of models is an attempt to define independent and dependent variables in ecologically relevant terms (i.e., in terms of an animal's natural habitat). Such an emphasis on ecological relevance improves the external validity of a model, but most optimization models are willing to sacrifice realism for generality. Instead of modeling behavior–environment relations in intricate detail, which may improve understanding of a particular species in a particular habitat, the focus of optimization modeling is on describing general functional relationships that cut across species and the vicissitudes of particular situations and habitats. The primary objective of an optimization model, then, is not to mimic the natural environment in all of its particulars. Rather, it is an attempt to capture what appear to be some important general features of an organism's interaction with its natural environment that may also apply to other organisms, other species, and other environments. As Winterhalder (1981) put it, "The conflicts generated by the necessity to simplify and generalize are irreconcilable, but it is important that they are about methods, not reality, and that models are meant to assist understanding, not to duplicate nature" (p. 20). If one is more interested in the particular details of a species and its habitat, more qualitative, descriptive analyses may be preferred over optimality approaches.

Testing an Optimization Model

Contrary to much popular usage, optimization is not a single unified theory, but rather a family of models and interpretations based on certain shared assumptions. Each model is aimed at a somewhat different problem and is only appropriate with respect to that particular problem. Therefore, as behavioral ecologists maintain, when an optimization model is put to the test, what is tested is not optimization per se (a question about an underlying process), but rather a specific hypothesis about behavior in a particular situation. Outside of that situation, the predictions of a given optimization model are irrelevant and the concept of optimization is meaningless.

To test an optimization model, one must first identify a specific problem area. Traditional problems in behavioral ecology include such things as selecting a mate, defending a territory, or switching from one patch of resources to another, to name just a few. Behavioral ecologists recognize that behavior is multiply controlled by many different, and often overlapping, ecological demands operating at the same time. This is especially true of human behavior. For practical reasons, however, optimization models generally focus on just one problem at a time. Integrating separate optimization models into a comprehensive theoretical account remains an important task for the future of behavioral ecology.

Once a problem has been identified, there is an attempt to define it within the context of a cost–benefit analysis, usually consisting of the following elements: (1) a *decision set*—the range of behavioral possibilities; (2) a *currency*—the scale according to which the elements in the decision set are assessed; and (3) *constraints*—fixed properties of the organism or the environment that limit the range of options included in the decision set. These elements will be discussed in turn, with special emphasis placed on methodological issues.

Decision Set. The term *decision set* (or sometimes *strategy set* or *phenotypic set*) is defined by the range of behavioral alternatives in a given situation. This component of an optimization model arises from the assumption that any behavior for which optimization concepts are appropriate involves two or more courses of action. If this were not the case, an optimization model would offer no insights—at least none that are unique to an optimization account. Optimal behavior is not about what is "best" in some ideal sense; it is about what is "better" than other behavioral alternatives currently available. Only with concurrent alternatives is there a basis for ranking one better than another according to their relative costs and benefits. It is only under these circumstances that an optimization model is potentially useful.

Although the set of actual behavioral alternatives can be quite large, for the sake of convenience and analytic rigor optimization models tend to limit the decision set to a few alternatives. For example, in the optimal foraging models discussed in the following section, the decision set usually consists of a binary choice: accept versus reject a given resource, or stay within versus leave a patch of resources. The focus of most optimization models is on how such binary choices are related to environmental conditions (e.g., the density and distribution of reinforcers like food). In the laboratory, such choices are typically studied in the context of concurrent schedules of reinforcement—two or more schedules simultaneously operative. The experimental study of concurrent schedules has yielded an impressive array of systematic data, including an expanding body of data with human subjects (see Mazur, Chapter 5). Because concurrent-schedule performances often depend on the exact procedures used to generate them, behavioral ecologists interested in using such schedule arrangements as tools for assessing optimization models would be wise to pay careful attention to methodological matters. All of the special methodological considerations described in Chapter 5 apply equally to the choices contained within specific optimization models, including, but not limited to, direct and repeated measurement of performance, assessment of performance under steady-state conditions, experimental isolation of controlling variables, and within- or between-subject replicability of results.

Currency. Once the decision set has been specified, a currency must be selected. In an optimization model, the currency refers to the quantity or commodity subject to optimization—the metric according to which costs and benefits associated with each of the elements in the decision set are calibrated. As Kaplan and Hill (1992) observed, "the currency defines the measurement scale for evaluating the effects of alternative decisions" (p. 169).

Because optimization models are rooted in natural selection, there has traditionally been an attempt to specify currencies in a form that can ultimately be linked to some measure of reproductive success (e.g., inclusive fitness). Initial extensions of optimization models to human behavior have been based on currencies (e.g., net rate of food intake) that are plausibly related to reproductive success. There is growing recognition, however, that successful application of optimization models to human behavior will need to include a broad range of currencies, including those not directly linked to reproductive success (Smith, 1991; Winterhalder, 1987). By this view, a good currency is one that is useful in ordering various behavioral activities according to their costs and benefits, whether or not those costs and benefits can be ultimately tied to reproductive output. This is not to suggest that behavior patterns do not have fitness consequences—many undoubtedly do. Rather, it is to suggest that cost–benefit analyses of human behavior need to define their measurement units more broadly, including, but not limited to, fitness-related criteria.

In the human operant laboratory, currencies vary widely. They sometimes consist of unconditioned reinforcers, such as access to edible items (Forzano & Logue, 1992; Ragotzy, Blakely, & Poling, 1988) or escape from aversive noise (Navarick, 1982; Solnick, Kannenberg, Eckerman, & Waller, 1980; Stockhorst, 1994). More often, currencies are conditioned reinforcers, such as points later exchangeable for access to other reinforcers like money, prizes, or course credit (see Pilgrim, Chapter 2). Sometimes points are not exchanged for other reinforcers at all; subjects are simply told that their task is to produce as many points as possible. In such cases, points seem to serve a purely social function. The social functions of human behavior create the need for more creative and flexible models, but this does not necessarily put human behavior outside the realm of optimization. These issues are explored more fully in a subsequent section.

As a first approximation, then, the currency refers to the type of reinforcer (e.g., points, money, escape from noise). To be analytically useful, however, a currency must be defined more specifically, in a way that permits behavior patterns to be ordered on a common scale. For example, assume a subject is given a choice between two alternatives, one that produces $1 and another that produces $5. The currency in this case is not just money (which both alternatives produce) but *amount* of money—amount being the dimension along which the two alternatives are ordered in cost–benefit terms. Similarly, if Alternative A produced $1 at a rate of two per minute and Alternative B produced $1 at a rate of four per minute, then *rate* of money (rather than just money) would provide the most appropriate currency.

Outside the laboratory, the resources (reinforcers) that follow from different activities usually vary along more than one dimension (e.g., amount and rate), and often differ qualitatively (e.g., food and money). Behavioral ecologists have found the term *profitability* useful in such cases. In its most generic form, profitability refers to net energy gain, but the more usual operational definition is in terms of the overall amount of some resource divided by the time required to obtain it—the rough equivalent to reinforcer amount per unit time. For the present purposes, the term *profitability* will be used in this strictly operational sense.

It should be evident, even from simple hypothetical examples offered here, that the most appropriate currency in a given situation depends on a variety of factors—not only the nature of the reinforcer but also the dimension or dimensions along which it is ordered (e.g., amount, rate, immediacy, probability) and the motivational conditions (e.g., deprivation, instructions) that establish and maintain its effectiveness. An advantage of laboratory procedures is that all of these variables can be experimentally isolated and varied independently; this is often extremely difficult in conditions outside the laboratory. Moreover, once a currency has been specified, laboratory procedures permit direct and detailed measurement of behavior patterns in relation to it, which puts tests of optimization models on especially solid ground.

Constraints. It is important to note that optimization does not predict or imply perfect adaptation, for selection must act on variability that is present. The structure of an organism and its environment limit the behavioral possibilities (or decision set) by narrowing the variability on which selection can operate. In an optimization model, the factors that limit the alternatives in the decision set are called *constraints.* Constraints sometimes describe features of the organism (e.g., the biomechanical makeup of the auditory system places limits on discriminative capacity), sometimes features of the environment (e.g., the density and distribution of resources place limits on food intake). Although it is important to consider both kinds of constraints, behavioral ecologists tend to focus on environmental constraints because they are more amenable to prediction and control.

Constraints are considered fixed properties of the environment. A good example of an environmental constraint is a reinforcement schedule. Such a schedule specifies the contingent relations between behavior and environmental events—relations that place limits on what behavior can accomplish in a given situation. Consider a variable-interval (VI) schedule, in which a reinforcer is made available on an intermittent basis varying around some average value, say, once per minute. This schedule arrangement *constrains* (places a limit on) the overall rate of reinforcement, which reaches an asymptotic rate of one per minute. This asymptotic rate is the theoretical optimum in relation to which performance can be assessed. It would make little sense, then, to speak of a behavior pattern that produces more than one reinforcer per minute because that is the maximum allowable under this schedule.

Of particular interest to behavioral ecologists are schedule arrangements that mimic constraints imposed by an animal's natural habitat. For example, a foraging episode can be conceptualized in very general terms as an extended sequence of behavior in relation to environmental (schedule) constraints, and including at least the following two components: search (locating a resource) and handling (pursuing and capturing/harvesting it once located) (see below). Both of these component responses occur in relation to specific constraints. For example, locating food depends on the rate at which it is encountered, and procuring it depends on how far away the food is and whether it takes evasive action. Ignoring for the moment the different response patterns engendered by these activities, instead focusing on their effects on overall reinforcement rate, it is possible to approach the total foraging episode as a chained reinforcement schedule (a sequence of successive reinforcement schedules). For example, resources are encountered, say, once per minute on average (VI 1-min schedule), and require 2 min to handle once encountered (VI 2-min).

It could be said that overall reinforcement rate is *constrained* by the underlying reinforcement schedules. This is what is meant by constrained optimization—the notion that what is optimal in a given situation depends on what the various constraints make available. When one considers that each of the component schedule requirements (constraints) in the above example can be varied independently under carefully controlled conditions, the advantages of the laboratory are again evident.

Summary

An optimization model consists of a decision set, a currency, and constraints. The decision set is an important component of an optimization model because it specifies the range of behavioral possibilities in relation to which optimization is assessed. Currency provides a metric according to which the behavioral alternatives comprising the decision set can be rank-ordered in cost–benefit terms. And constraints describe conditions that limit the behavioral elements in the decision set, important in delineating the boundary conditions over which an optimization analysis applies.

If a model provides a poor characterization of behavior, it is usually because the currency is inaccurate or the constraints are improperly specified. If, on the other hand, a model provides a good characterization of behavior, it does not *prove* that behavior is optimal, only that the guesses about currency and the constraints were reasonably accurate to at least a first approximation. But a model is never the same as the world it seeks to explain; an optimization model can always be made more realistic by including additional constraints and sharper specifications of currency.

An optimization model is useful not because it predicts optimal behavior, or because it captures all of the crucial elements of an organism's natural environment, but because it is based on problems that can be explicitly stated and directly tested. The term *optimal behavior,* then, is really a bit of a misnomer. Strictly speaking, optimization models do not predict optimal behavior, at least not optimal in the sense of perfect adaptation in some ideal world. Rather, optimization models provide a structured way of asking questions about behavior and a common scale against which to measure it.

The laboratory can be very useful in this context. Although laboratory methods are sometimes criticized for their artificiality, it is their very artificiality that makes them so attractive with respect to evaluating optimization models. Data from laboratory procedures reveal important facts about the internal consistency of a model—whether the predictions work out when all of its simplifying assumptions are met. If an optimization model provides a poor characterization of behavior under the simplified conditions of the laboratory, it will almost certainly fail in the more complex environments it was designed to capture.

EMPIRICAL DEVELOPMENTS IN HUMAN BEHAVIORAL ECOLOGY

Optimization approaches have been applied to various aspects of human behavioral ecology, ranging from territoriality and settlement patterns (Cashdan, 1992; Dyson-Hudson & Smith, 1978; Horn, 1968) to birth spacing and mating systems (Blurton Jones, 1987; Borgerhoff Mulder, 1992), but greatest attention has focused on foraging patterns. This emphasis on foraging is unsurprising given its predominant place in nonhuman behavioral ecology. The collection of models and interpretations designed to address different aspects of foraging within an optimization framework is known collectively as *optimal foraging theory*.

There are probably many reasons foraging has continued to provide a source of inspiration for optimization models in behavioral ecology. Food is a relatively conspicuous resource around which relatively conspicuous patterns of behavior are organized. Costs and benefits can therefore be defined in relatively straightforward ways subject to empirical test. Moreover, food and food-related behavior participate in a wide array of adaptive behavior patterns, and it is reasonable to assume a positive relationship between efficient foraging patterns and reproductive success. The extension of optimal foraging models to human behavior is rich with possibilities, but it should be done with careful attention to the particulars of human activity, including social-cultural patterns not tied directly to reproductive success. Foraging is defined here in the broad sense of choices between different patterns of consequences including, but not limited to, nutritionally based ones.

In this section some recent empirical work from the field and the laboratory will be summarized, with a focus on the two areas in which optimization models have proven most fruitful: (1) diet breadth and resource choice and (2) time allocation and patch choice.

Diet Breadth and Resource Choice

A major concern of optimal foraging theory lies with characterizing patterns of resource choice. Of the many potential resources in a forging environment, which ones should be pursued? Which ones rejected? How many different types of resources should be included in a forager's current "diet"? These are the kinds of questions of concern to the optimal diet model (MacArthur & Pianka, 1966; see also Charnov, 1976a), an optimization approach most widely applied to such problems. In this section I will attempt to lay out some of the assumptions of this model, how it has been tested in the field and in the laboratory, and how it relates to contemporary issues in the experimental analysis of human behavior.

Assumptions and Predictions

The optimal diet model (also known as the *diet breadth model*) is based on a number of simplifying assumptions about the structure of the foraging environment. It includes the following constraints: (1) Resources (reinforcers) are encountered randomly, or at least unpredictably. (2) Resources are uniformly distributed, that is, they are not aggregated into "clumps" or "patches;" other models (see below) have been formulated to address patchy environments. (3) Foraging episodes can be partitioned into two distinct and mutually exhaustive activities: search and handling. Search is the mode during which resources are located and is assumed to occur simultaneously across all resource types. Handling is the mode during which a particular resource is pursued or harvested. Thus, one can search for two or more resources simultaneously, but can handle only one resource at a time. (4) Like other optimization models, the optimal diet model assumes complete "knowledge" of the environment, that is, a relatively stable environment with which the organism has a good deal of experience.

Within this rather broad set of assumptions, the optimal diet model makes some very specific predictions about which items an organism should handle (i.e., choose to pursue when available) and which items it should reject (i.e., pass over in favor of continued search). The decision set thus consists of a binary choice: accept or reject a given resource when it becomes available. Because search and handling are the only two components comprising the foraging episode, rejecting a given item implies continuing to search for other items. Accepting an item implies a commitment to handle that item until it is captured/consumed, at which time the search component is reinstated.

The predictions of the model can be derived from a consideration of the relative costs and benefits of handling a given resource and how they are shifted by ecological conditions. It is first necessary to rank all resources on a common scale according to their costs and benefits; this is the currency component of the model. The currency is defined here in terms of profitability (in a strictly operational sense, as described above), as return rate per unit of handling time, roughly equivalent to reinforcer amount per unit time.

Although the optimal diet model can include a large number of different resource types, for the sake of illustration, consider a situation with just two types, Alternatives A and B. Assume that both require 1 min of handling time once located, but that Alternative A is a $5 bill whereas Alternative B is a $1 bill. The alternatives thus differ in their overall profitability—$5 per min for Alternative A and $1 per min for Alternative B.

Should a person select A—the more profitable alternative—exclusively, or should B sometimes also be selected? According to the optimal diet model, the answer depends on whether B contributes to the overall return rate averaged across resources of both types. If it does, it should be accepted; if not, it should be rejected. Whether the person in this example should specialize (i.e., select A exclusively) or generalize (i.e., select both A and B) depends on how frequently A is encountered (i.e., on the duration of the search phase). If A is encountered sufficiently often, the person should specialize, that is, reject B whenever it is encountered. To see why this is the case, assume that the search phase preceding an encounter with either alternative is 1 min. If A is selected exclusively, the overall return rate would be: $5 (A)/1 min (search) + 1 min (handling), or $2.50 per min.

On the other hand, if B is also selected, the encounter rate increases to two per minute (one of each type) but the overall return rate drops from $2.50 per min when A is selected exclusively to $2.00 per min when both A and B are selected: $5 (A) + $1 (B)/1 min (search) + 1 min (handling A) + 1 min (handling B). Thus, despite the increased encounter rate, the overall return rate decreases because the time devoted to handling the less profitable outcome (B) reduces time that could be devoted to searching for the more profitable outcome (A). Under these circumstances, specializing on Alternative A makes intuitive sense: If a highly profitable outcome is encountered at a sufficiently high rate, it is counterproductive to spend time pursuing a less profitable one. Better to reject it and continue searching for the more profitable item.

The predictions change, however, as the encounter rate with the more profitable item decreases. Assume that the search phase, instead of 1 min, is now 10 min. Selecting A exclusively now yields: $5/10 min (search) + 1 min (handling), or $0.45 per min. Under these circumstances, selecting both A and B now yields a higher return rate than does exclusive preference for A: $5 (A) + $1 (B)/10 min (search) + 1 min (handling A) + 1 min (handling B), or $0.50 per min. Thus, as the overall rate of encounter with highly ranked resource items decreases (as good items become more scarce), the optimal diet model predicts greater acceptance of lower-ranked items (a more general "diet").

Another implication of the model is that such changes in preference should depend only on the availability of the higher-ranked item (in this case, Alternative A), not on the availability of the lower-ranked item (Alternative B). That is, no matter how frequently B is encountered, relative preference for A should not change. To illustrate this counterintuitive prediction, let us return to the example from the preceding paragraph in which the model predicted exclusive preference for A when both alternatives were encountered at a rate of one per minute. Assume A is still encountered at the same rate but B is now encountered twice as often. Thus, for every minute of search, B is encountered (and handled) twice. The overall return rate would now drop to: $5 (A) + $2 (B)/1 min (search) + 1 min (handling A) + 2 min (handling B), or $1.75 per min—still lower than the $2.50 per min that would result from exclusive preference for A. This, too, makes intuitive sense: If a highly profitable item is encountered sufficiently often to result in exclusive preference, it should not matter how abundant less profitable items become; the person should continue to prefer A exclusively no matter how frequently B occurs.

The Laboratory and the Field

The most general prediction of the optimal diet model is that only items that contribute to a forager's overall return rate will be accepted. This prediction has received at least qualitative confirmation in two field studies of human foraging patterns: the Aché Indians of Paraguay (Hawkes, Hill, & O'Connell, 1982) and the Inujjuamiut Eskimos of Eastern Canada (Smith, 1991). Hawkes et al. (1982), for instance, measured return rates for all 16 resource types in the Aché diet at the time of the study, from which they ranked the resources from high profitability (collared peccaries and deer) to low profitability (palm fruit). It was not possible to measure the return rates of all possible resource types the Aché did not pursue, but all 16 of those that were pursued contributed to overall return rates per unit of handling time, consistent with the general prediction of the optimal diet model.

Results such as these suggest that the optimal diet model is a promising approach to understanding human foraging patterns, but more critical tests of the model come from experiments in which encounter rates actually are varied (as in the hypothetical examples described above). Such manipulations, however, are difficult to accomplish in the context of field studies, and, to date, have only been studied systematically in the laboratory (as described in more detail below). Moreover, as researchers in this field acknowledge, it is often difficult to say with certainty that important assumptions of the model have been met. For example, the assumption of random, or unpredictable, encounter rate with resources, though sometimes justifiable, is often difficult to make in practice, especially with seasonal variation in resource distribution (Smith, 1991). This, too, is an area in which laboratory procedures can be very useful. Some procedures used routinely in the experimental analysis of behavior include this feature, and therefore may provide a good model of this aspect of the foraging environment. For example, random-interval (RI) and constant-probability VI schedules of reinforcement arrange reinforcement on a probabilistic basis, unpredictable from moment to moment. The basic structure of these schedules also meets the requirement of uniform (as opposed to "patchy") distribution of resources. Finally, the assumption, common to many optimization models, of a stable environment, can be approached in the laboratory by long-term exposure of subjects to experimental conditions, a distinctive practice in the experimental analysis of behavior (see Baron & Perone, Chapter 3). To further simplify matters, added stimuli can be used to delineate more clearly changes of situation relevant to the model, helping sharpen the distinction between different resource (schedule) types, and between different components in a foraging episode (e.g., search versus handling), both of which are required by the optimal diet model.

These features all come together in two laboratory procedures inspired by optimal foraging theory: successive-choice procedures and simultaneous-choice procedures. In the following section I will outline some of the key features of these procedures, and briefly review some of the experiments with humans and other animals as they relate to the optimal diet model and to current methods in the experimental analysis of behavior.

Successive-Choice Procedures

The separation of search and handling activities, crucial for the predictions of the optimal diet model, is readily accomplished with laboratory procedures. In the successive choice procedure (Collier, 1987; Lea, 1979), the search component is separated from the handling component by means of different schedules of reinforcement, each correlated with different exteroceptive stimuli. For example, in a recent experiment by Stockhorst (1994), each choice cycle began with a search phase, in the presence of a white stimulus light. Figure 17.1 shows a diagram of the basic procedure. Completing the requirements of a short FI schedule during this search phase

FIGURE 17.1.   Flow chart of a successive-choice procedure used with human subjects. The rectangles correspond to different states of the procedure: search, choice, handling, and reinforcement. A cycle begins with a search phase, in the presence of an aversive tone ("noise") and a white light (W). The side keys are dark during this phase. Completing the requirements of a short FI schedule on the button adjacent to the white light produces transition to a choice phase. A red light is illuminated with probability p and a green light with probability $1-p$. (The value of p is generally .5.) The white light and the noise remain on during this phase. If no response is made within 8 s, that cycle terminates without reinforcement, and the search phase is reinstated. This is termed a *rejection*. A single response on the button adjacent to the red (R) or green (G) light in the choice phase produces a transition to the handling phase of the cycle. This is termed an *acceptance*. During the handling phase, a VI 3-s schedule (high-profitability alternative) or a VI 18-s schedule (low-profitability alternative) is in effect in the presence of a red or a green light, respectively. (These schedule-correlated stimuli are counterbalanced across

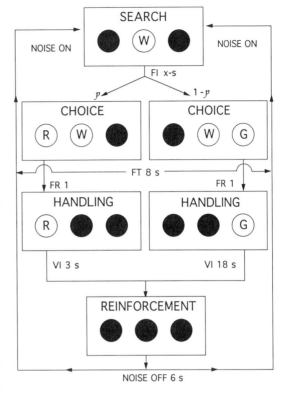

groups of subjects.) The white light is turned off during this phase, but the tone remains on. Satisfying the VI requirements produces reinforcement, in this case, a 6-s termination of the tone, followed by an immediate return to the search phase. Adapted from Stockhorst (1994).

produced a choice phase, during which one of two terminal-link schedules became available, as indicated by distinct exteroceptive stimuli. Each schedule was equally likely to occur. Unlike the more standard concurrent-chains procedure (see Mazur, Chapter 5), the terminal-link alternatives here are arranged successively rather than concurrently. The choice is thus one of *accepting* the schedule available on that cycle or *rejecting* it. To reject the available schedule, a subject must either complete a short ratio requirement or, in some cases, simply wait. In Stockhorst's procedure, a schedule was considered "rejected" if a subject failed to accept it within 8 s (FT 8 s). Rejecting a schedule ended that cycle, and produced an immediate transition to the initial link (search) phase of the next cycle.

To accept the available schedule, a subject must complete a small ratio requirement (a single response, in this case). This produces a transition to a terminal-link situation in which the selected schedule is in effect until its requirements have been met. This terminal-link situation constitutes the handling phase of the trial, in this case consisting of a VI 3-s schedule (more profitable schedule) or VI 18-s schedule (less profitable schedule), each correlated with distinct exteroceptive stimuli. Although positively reinforcing consequences are the more common, Stockhorst's procedure involved negatively reinforcing consequences—termination of a "moderately loud" tone (85 dBA, 3000 Hz) presented to the subjects over headphones. Accepting a schedule also makes all other search and handling responses ineffective. Thus, consistent with the requirements of the optimal diet model, searching results in different resources encountered randomly (the terminal-link schedules are made available on a probabilistic basis), whereas handling is restricted to the resource currently under pursuit (transition to the terminal-link schedule removes all other types from consideration).

Testing the Optimal Diet Model. The successive-choice procedure makes it possible not only to distinguish search from handling phases, but also to vary them independently in ways relevant to the optimal diet model. A key prediction concerns the effects of increased encounter rate with the less profitable outcome on preference for that outcome. To test this prediction, Stockhorst (1994) exposed adult human subjects to a successive-choice procedure like that described above. A diagram of the apparatus is shown in Figure 17.2. Three response boxes (corresponding to the three operanda in Figure 17.1) were arranged on a response console in front of a computer monitor. The computer monitor was used to display messages to the subjects. Each of the response boxes included a translucent button on which presses exceeding 1 N illuminated the button and counted as an effective response. Square translucent disks (stimulus lights) adjacent to each button indicated the current state of the choice cycle. The search phase was in effect when box 1 was illuminated (white). Completing the requirements of the FI schedule made available one of the two terminal-link VI schedules, signaled by the illumination of one of the two response panels to the rear of the panel (boxes 2 and 3), each correlated with a distinctly colored light (either red or green, counterbalanced across subjects). A single response on the illuminated box during this choice phase initiated the terminal-link VI schedule associated with that panel (i.e., "accepted" that schedule), and disabled the other schedule and its associated stimulus. Satisfying the terminal-link VI requirements terminated the noise for 6 s, followed by an immediate return to the search component. If 8 s elapsed during the choice phase without a response, the illuminated panel went dark, and the search component was reinstated (i.e., the schedule was "rejected").

The key manipulation, modeled after an experiment by Fantino and Preston (1988) with pigeons as experimental subjects, involved varying the duration of the FI schedule in the search component preceding the less profitable (VI 18-s) schedule while leaving unchanged the FI preceding the more profitable (VI 3-s) schedule. This made it possible to test the following counterintuitive prediction of the optimal diet model: Increasing the rate at which a less profitable outcome is encountered does not make it any more likely that it will be accepted.

Forty-eight college students were divided into three groups of 16 each. All subjects participated for a single session consisting of 120 trials. The first 10 trials consisted of forced exposure to the terminal-link VI schedules (five of each type), followed by 110 trials of the successive-choice procedure described above. For all subjects, the initial-link (search) phase on the first 50 of these 110 trials consisted of a 7.5-s FI schedule; the terminal-link (handling) phase consisted of the VI 3-s on a randomly determined half of the trials and the VI 18-s schedule on the other half. For the remaining 60 trials, the duration of the search phase preceding the VI

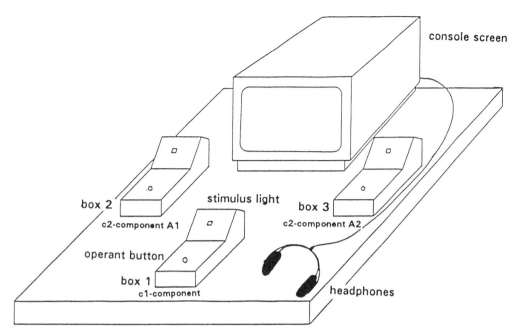

FIGURE 17.2.   Illustration of the apparatus employed in an experiment with adult human subjects using the procedure described in Figure 17.1. Three response buttons and adjacent stimulus lights were arranged on a response console in front of a computer monitor. The response buttons and stimulus lights, which could be illuminated independently from the rear, signaled which phase of the choice cycle was currently in effect. The stimulus light accompanying box 1 (cl-component) was on during the search and choice phases of the cycle and off during the handling phase. On a given cycle, the light accompanying either box 2 (c2-component A1) or box 3 (c2-component A2) was on during the choice and handling phases of the cycle. The console screen was used to display messages to the subject. The headphones were used to present a tone (85 dBA, 3000 Hz), which was on continuously except during 6-s reinforcement periods. See text for other details. Reproduced from Stockhorst (1994).

18-s terminal-link schedule was manipulated across groups of subjects, while the search phase preceding the VI 3-s schedule remained at 7.5 s. For one group of subjects, the search duration preceding the VI 18-s schedule increased (to 22.5 s); for a second group, it decreased (to 2.5 s); for a third group, it remained the same (at 7.5 s).

The data of principal interest concern acceptance of the less profitable outcome (VI 18-s) as a function of the search time preceding it. Figure 17.3 shows mean acceptance of the VI 18-s schedule as a function of the duration of the FI preceding it. Consistent with the predictions of the optimal diet model, increasing the encounter rate with the less profitable schedule did not make it any more likely that it would be accepted. In fact, just the opposite occurred. Acceptability of the less profitable schedule was inversely related to its rate of encounter. This follows directly from a consideration of relative temporal proximities to reinforcement correlated with the onset of the terminal-link schedules relative to the overall average waiting time (timed from the onset of the trial). The availability of the VI 18-s schedule was correlated with a reduction in average waiting time to reinforcement

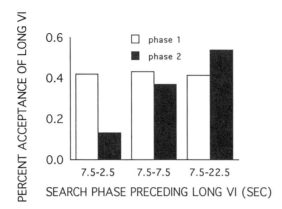

FIGURE 17.3. Percent mean acceptance of 18-s VI schedule of noise termination as function of search duration preceding that schedule for three groups of human subjects exposed to Stockhorst's successive-choice procedure. The VI 18-s schedule was opposed by a more profitable VI 3-s schedule of noise termination. Both outcomes were equally likely. During Phase 1 (50 choice cycles), the search phase preceding both schedules consisted of a 7.5-s FI schedule for subjects in all three groups. During Phase 2 (60 choice cycles), search duration preceding the VI 3-s schedule was held constant, while the search duration preceding the VI 18-s schedule either increased to 22.5 s (right bars), decreased to 2.5 s (left bars), or remained the same (middle bars), correlating with a reduction, an increase, or no change, respectively, in waiting time to noise termination. Adapted from Stockhorst (1994).

for subjects in the group in which search duration increased (rightmost pair of bars in the figure), an increase for subjects in the group in which search duration decreased (leftmost bars), and no significant change for subjects in the group in which search duration stayed the same (middle bars).

This outcome is also predicted by the delay-reduction hypothesis (Fantino, 1969, 1991), a quantitative behavioral model emphasizing relative delays to reinforcement in the context of overall reinforcement rate. According to this model, a schedule should be accepted if it is correlated with a reduction in average time to reinforcement, and rejected if it is correlated with an increase in average time to reinforcement. This is analogous to the prediction of the optimal diet model that only resource types that contribute to increases in return rate (averaged across all resources) are accepted. In fact, Fantino and Abarca (1985) have shown that delay reduction and the optimal diet model make similar predictions on successive-choice procedures across a wide range of manipulations. The convergence of these two models—one with origins in the field and the other with origins in the laboratory—illustrates nicely the complementarity of ecological and experimental approaches to the study of behavior. As such, delay-reduction and other similar models in the experimental analysis of behavior may lend psychological support to optimization models, whose "rules of thumb" are often specified without regard to known behavioral processes.

The results of several other experiments with pigeons as experimental subjects have yielded results broadly consistent with the optimal diet and delay-reduction models. For example, pigeons' choices become more selective (i.e., they are more likely to reject the less profitable schedule) as initial-link (search) duration decreases (Abarca & Fantino, 1982; Lea, 1979). Thus, increased availability of the more profitable alternative leads to increased specialization, as required by the optimal diet and delay-reduction models. This general effect holds whether the profitability of the terminal-link schedules is defined in terms of reinforcement amount (Ito & Fantino, 1986), as in the hypothetical example above, or reinforcement frequency (Abarca & Fantino, 1982; Hanson & Green, 1989; Lea, 1979). Changing the conditions of the handling phase can also alter overall reinforcement rate in ways relevant to the models. For example, Ito and Fantino (1986) found that pigeons were more likely to accept the less profitable of two resource types (3 s of food versus 6 s of food) as the duration of the equal VI schedules in the handling phase increased from 5 s to 20 s. Thus, decreased handling times result in increased specialization, consistent with the predictions of both models. Abarca, Fantino, and Ito (1985) found analogous results when terminal-link reinforcement was made available on a percentage basis (see also Zeiler, 1987). Although no experiments with human subjects involving any of these manipulations have yet been published, these experiments with nonhumans provide solid groundwork for extensions to human behavior.

Some Additional Methodological Considerations. That Stockhorst's humans behaved in ways generally consistent with the behavior of other animals on similar procedures may be related in part to an interesting methodological feature utilized by Stockhorst, namely, the use of a currency of immediate consummatory value. The motivational conditions that establish and maintain the effectiveness of escape from noise as an effective reinforcer are more like those typically used with nonhuman subjects than those typically used with human subjects. The majority of experiments with human subjects have used conditioned reinforcers, such as points or tokens exchangeable for money (see Pilgrim, Chapter 2). Unlike consumable reinforcers, the reinforcing effectiveness of money is not tied to a specific motivational operation. Money thus holds its value across a much wider range of circumstances and states of deprivation inside and outside the laboratory. This procedural difference may limit comparisons across species. Needless to say, if one is interested in cross-species comparisons, every effort should be made to minimize procedural differences, including the nature of the reinforcer, and the motivational conditions that establish and maintain the effectiveness of those reinforcers. At the same time, it should prove interesting in future work in this area to examine a wider range of currencies, including conditioned reinforcers, across a wider range of schedule parameters, to assess the generality of the effects with humans.

Stockhorst's (1994) experiment raises some additional methodological issues that deserve comment. First, the experiment utilized a between-group design, in which the independent variable was manipulated across subjects. This differs from the more typical within-subject manipulations that characterize empirical work in the experimental analysis of behavior (including the experiments with pigeons that inspired Stockhorst's experiment). Although the results revealed clear differences across the three groups of subjects, the individual-subject data did not always correspond well to the group averages. The individual-subject data from one of the two experimental groups (the one for whom encounter rate with the less profitable schedule increased) did correspond well to the group mean (data for 14 of 16 subjects in the expected direction) but the correspondence between the group and individual case was much weaker for the other two groups.

A second, and more serious limitation of Stockhorst's (1994) study concerns the relatively brief exposure of subjects to experimental conditions. Choice proportions often were not stable by the end of the 120 trials. This would appear to violate a key assumption of the optimal diet model relating to the relative stability of the environment (the organism's "knowledge" of it)—an assumption that can be approximated by long-term exposure of subjects to experimental conditions. On the whole, then, Stockhorst's experiment is important in providing an empirical framework with which to examine human behavior in situations relevant to both optimal foraging theory and the experimental analysis of behavior. A greater emphasis on within-subject manipulations and replications that include steady-state assessment of performance would be beneficial in further isolating the controlling variables. It would also permit more detailed and informative comparisons across species.

Simultaneous-Choice Procedures

Optimal foraging theory has also been applied to situations in which resources are encountered simultaneously rather than successively (Engen & Stenseth, 1984). For example, consider a choice between two resources that differ in profitability, say $4 available after 10 min of handling versus $6 available after 20 min. The first alternative is the more profitable because the amount of money per unit time is higher ($0.40 per min versus $0.30 per min) and should be selected consistently. But as search duration increases, the return rates of the two alternatives shift. Search durations less than 10 min still favor the smaller more immediate resource item, but at a search duration of 10 min the overall return rates are equal ($4 every 20 min versus $6 every 30 min both equal $0.20 per min). At search durations exceeding 10 min, the return rates reverse in favor of the more delayed resource type. For example, at a search duration of 20 min, the more immediate resource yields $4 per 30 min ($0.13 per min), whereas the more delayed outcome yields $6 per 40 min ($0.15 per min). Under these circumstances, the formerly more profitable resource lowers the overall return rate, and thus should be rejected.

Fantino and Preston (1989) described a procedure and the results of preliminary research on this topic with pigeon and human subjects. Each choice cycle began with a search phase lasting for x s, followed by the simultaneous presentation of two terminal-link schedules arranged on side keys, as indicated by distinct exteroceptive stimuli. A single response on either side key put that schedule into effect and made other responses unavailable. Each terminal-link schedule involved some combination of reinforcer amount and delay, as described above, differing in profitability. Mean preference for the longer terminal link increased with increases in search duration in both human and pigeon subjects, consistent with the predictions of the successive-encounter version of optimality theory (Engen & Stenseth, 1984). These data, based as they are on a preliminary investigation, should be viewed cautiously. Nevertheless, they suggest that the successive-encounter procedure may be a useful laboratory procedure for more closely examining some important implications of optimal foraging theory as they relate to human behavior.

These data and procedures are also relevant to current issues in the experimental analysis of behavior, such as the time frame over which reinforcement variables (e.g., amount and delay) are balanced. The procedures share many important features with laboratory self-control arrangements (see Mazur, Chapter 5), and may therefore extend models of choice and self-control to new domains. At the same time, it should be recognized that the optimal diet model is explicitly concerned with choices arrayed over multiple resources, yet the laboratory procedures described in this section are limited to pairwise choices. Thus, it could be said that laboratory procedures, by virtue of their ability to carefully test specific predictions, are high in internal validity, but are still somewhat low in external validity. Future laboratory work in this domain should seek to include a wider array of reinforcing consequences, including those that differ qualitatively, to better approximate the ecological circumstances of concern to behavioral ecologists.

Time Allocation and Patch Choice

Another area to which optimal foraging theory has been applied involves patch choice and utilization—which patches to visit and how long to stay in each. The most successful model of patch choice is Charnov's (1976b) marginal value theorem. I will first briefly discuss this model and some of its implications, then turn to some laboratory procedures and results relevant to it.

Assumptions and Predictions

Like the optimal diet model, the marginal value theorem begins with some simplifying assumptions about features of the foraging environment and patterns of movement within it. It includes the following constraints: (1) Resources (reinforcers) are distributed in spatiotemporal clusters, or patches. This is what distinguishes patch choice models like the marginal value theorem from prey choice and other optimal foraging models. (2) Within-patch gains are a negatively accelerating function of time spent foraging in that patch, either because the patch is steadily depleted or because prey disperse or flee to other locations. (3) A foraging episode is divided into two mutually exclusive and exhaustive activities: foraging within a patch and traveling between patches. One cannot search for food and travel between food sources at the same time. (4) Travel time between patches incurs a period of no gain.

Together, these assumptions provide the constraints within which the marginal value theorem applies. Note that all of these constraints relate directly to measurable properties of the environment.

The constraints assumed by the marginal value theorem can be portrayed graphically, as in Figure 17.4. The top panel shows cumulative gain plotted as a function of time in patch. "Gain" is simply a measure of cost–benefit trade-offs, and in this context is equivalent to reinforcers per unit time. The negatively accelerating function defines the situation as one involving diminishing returns; the rate of gain drops off with time spent in the patch. The flat part of the gain curve to the left of (prior to entering) the patch represents the costs (defined in terms of the effort and/or time) of switching to that patch.

Given these constraints, the marginal value model predicts that a patch of the sort portrayed in Figure 17.4 should be vacated before it is completely depleted. More specifically, the patch should be left at the point that maximizes the overall

SITUATION OF DIMINISHING RETURNS
(DEPLETING PATCH)

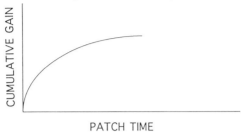

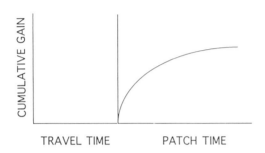

FIGURE 17.4. Hypothetical functions portraying cumulative gain as a function of time within and between depleting patches of resources. Note the negatively accelerating function characteristic of situations of diminishing returns. The bottom panel includes the period of travel between patches, represented by the flat portion of the gain curve. See text for other details.

rate of reinforcement. The top panel of Figure 17.5 shows how one arrives at this optimal point of leaving a depleting patch. The format is similar to that introduced in Figure 17.4. A straight line from the origin to any point on the within-patch gain curve identifies the overall rate of reinforcement that results from switching at that point on the curve, that is, from leaving the patch at that point. The optimal switch point (sometimes called *optimal residence time*) is the line of highest slope from the origin that touches the within-patch curve at its highest point. Of the various switching patterns comprising the decision set, this is the one that maximizes overall rate of reinforcement. One implication of this is that the optimal response unit is an extended sequence of behavior that includes both within-patch behavior and the behavior involved in switching between patches.

A second prediction of the marginal value theorem concerns the effects of between-patch travel time. The bottom panel of Figure 17.5 depicts the relationship between optimal switch point and between-patch travel time. This graph is similar to the one shown in the top panel except that it also includes a shorter between-patch travel time (S) to compare against the original travel time (now, L). The longer the travel time between patches, the farther along the within-patch gain curve the tangent point occurs. This translates into a directly testable (and intuitively sensible) prediction of the marginal value theorem: The longer it takes to move between patches, the longer one should remain within (tolerate a greater depletion within) the current patch.

Less intuitive is the prediction concerning the precise point at which one should leave—the optimal switch point. Because travel time between patches is assumed to incur a period of no gain, leaving a patch often results in short-term

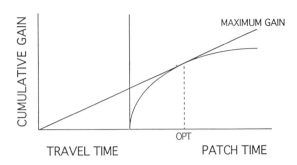

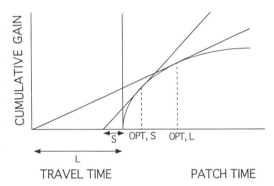

FIGURE 17.5. Optimal point of switching between patches as a function of travel time. (Top) For a given travel time, a straight line from the origin to any point on the within-patch portion of the curve identifies the return rate that results from leaving the patch at that point. The maximum return rate occurs at a point defined by the line of steepest slope from the origin (labeled "OPT" in the figure). (Bottom) The optimal switch points (OPT, S; OPT, L) for short and long travel times, respectively.

losses in gain relative to remaining longer in the patch. Thus, maximizing gain in the long run, as required by the marginal value theorem, often comes at the expense of more proximal outcomes. These contrasting short-term and longer-term outcomes provide an especially strong test of the model, as discussed in more detail below.

Progressive-Schedule Choice Procedures

As with the optimal diet model, rigorous confirmation of the marginal value theorem with data from naturalistic studies has met with serious obstacles. As Smith (1991) pointed out, it is often difficult to verify that the preconditions of the model have been met (e.g., that resources can be regarded as "patchy," or that the gain curve is negatively accelerated), not to mention the practical problems inherent in precise measures of within-patch and between-patch returns rates required for rigorous evaluation of the model. Thus, although some aspects of human forging patterns are consistent in broad outline with the marginal value theorem (Hames & Vickers, 1982; Smith, 1991; Winterhalder, 1981), the available anthropological data cannot be said to offer strong support of the model. Here, again, laboratory procedures that capture some of the crucial features of the foraging environment can be very useful.

A laboratory procedure well-equipped to address human behavior in situations of diminishing returns is based on choices between fixed and progressive schedules of reinforcement (Hackenberg & Axtell, 1993; Jacobs & Hackenberg, 1996; Wanchisen, Tatham, & Hineline, 1992). Although the procedure has been used with a variety of animal species, including pigeons (Hackenberg & Hineline, 1992; Wanchisen, Tatham, & Hineline, 1988) and nonhuman primates (Hineline & Sodetz, 1987; Hodos & Trumbule, 1967), the focus here will be on its use with human subjects.

The basic procedure involves recurrent choices between two work requirements—one constant and the other steadily escalating. The escalating requirements can be arranged by means of either a progressive ratio (PR) or a progressive interval (PI) schedule of reinforcement, depending on whether one is primarily concerned with response-based or time-based requirements. In either case, the requirements for reinforcement increase, typically in fixed increments, with each reinforcer delivered by that schedule. The progressive schedule is opposed by a fixed schedule whose requirements remain constant within a given condition but typically vary across conditions. As with the progressive schedule, this fixed schedule can be either response-based (fixed ratio, or FR) or time-based (fixed interval, or FI). Although the same general relationships hold with ratio and interval schedules, because optimal foraging models of patch choice have been primarily concerned with time allocation, time-based schedules will be emphasized here.

The procedure involves discrete choice points, in which the fixed and progressive schedules are simultaneously available, as indicated by distinct correlated stimuli. In Jacobs and Hackenberg's (1996) experiment, for example, each choice cycle began with the simultaneous illumination of a red (FI) and blue (PI) box, arranged side by side on a standard computer monitor. A choice was made by pressing an arrow key on a standard keyboard: "←" to choose the schedule whose box was on the left or "→" for the schedule whose box was on the right. A single press committed behavior to that option and removed the nonchosen schedule box from the screen for the remainder of that trial. In the terminal-link (outcome) phase, presses on the space bar were required to produce points (later exchangeable for money) according to the requirements of the chosen schedule. Point delivery was signaled by a brief computer-generated tone and by the incrementing of a point counter in the lower corner of the computer screen, and was followed by an immediate return to the choice phase of the next cycle.

Each point produced by the PI schedule increased subsequent PI requirements by a fixed increment. For example, with a PI increment size of 4 s, the first PI selection of a session would make a point available immediately (the first space bar response would produce a point), the second PI selection would make a point available after 4 s, the third PI selection after 8 s, and so on. Under some conditions ("No Reset"), FI selections had no effect on the PI schedule requirements. Under other conditions ("Reset"), each FI selection, in addition to delivering a point when its requirements had been satisfied, reset the PI schedule to its minimum value (usually 0 s). These relationships are diagrammed in Figure 17.6. The top panel shows the No-Reset procedure, in which points earned on the FI schedule have no effect on the PI. The bottom panel shows the Reset procedure, in which points produced by the FI schedule reset the PI to its minimum value of 0 s.

As noted by several authors, these procedures capture some important fea-

FIGURE 17.6. Flow chart of a progressive-schedule choice procedure used with human subjects. In the initial-link (choice) phase, a PI and FI schedule are simultaneously available, as indicated by blue (B) and red (R) squares, respectively, on a computer screen. Selection of the blue square turns off the red square and initiates the requirements of the PI schedule. Similarly, selection of the red square disables the blue square and initiates the FI schedule. The first space-bar press after the programmed interval has elapsed is reinforced by the incrementing of a counter displaying cumulative points (later exchangeable for money), and signaled by a computer-generated beep. The choice phase is reinstated immediately following reinforcement. The PI requirements begin each session at 0 s, but increase in fixed increments (in this case, 8-s increments) following each point delivered by that schedule. The FI requirements remain constant within a session (in this case, 64 s). The only difference between the No Reset procedure (top panel) and the Reset procedure (bottom panel) is that in the latter, points earned on the FI schedule reset the PI schedule to its minimum value of 0 s. Adapted from Jacobs and Hackenberg (1996).

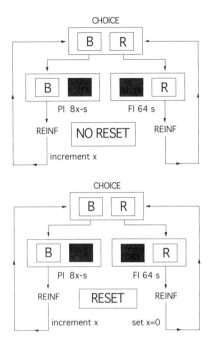

tures of foraging environments relevant to the marginal value theorem. First, the PI schedule provides a diminishing rate of return, representing the steadily increasing costs of foraging in a depleting patch. Second, changing patches (switching from the PI to the FI) produces a period of little or no gain. These travel costs are represented by the FI requirements, which must be met before another patch can be entered. Third, the PI schedule, reset to its minimum, is analogous to entering a new patch abundant with resources.

Computing Optimal Switch Points. The main point of interest on these procedures lies in patterns of switching from the progressive to the fixed schedule. The position in the progressive-schedule sequence at which the fixed schedule is consistently selected is called the *switch point,* and provides a convenient measure of such switching patterns. Evaluating switch points in relation to their net rate of reinforcement makes it possible to identify an optimal switch point.

Under No Reset conditions, computing the optimal switch point is a relatively straightforward matter. It corresponds to switching from the progressive to the fixed schedule when the requirements of the two schedules are equivalent (the so-called *equality point*). For example, assume the FI schedule is 64 s and the PI step size is 8 s. The optimal point of switching occurs when the PI schedule has been driven up to a value of 64 s. Technically, there are two optimal switch points under No Reset conditions: one at the nominal FI value (64 s) and a second at one PI step exceeding that value (72 s); the only difference is whether one of the 64-s intervals is arranged via the PI or the FI. In either case, switching at or one step beyond the equality point is a pattern that both minimizes the delay to the upcoming point delivery and maximizes the overall rate of point delivery.

In contrast to the No Reset procedure, the Reset procedure places delays to up-coming points in conflict with the overall rate of point delivery; what is optimal in the long run entails costs (increases in local delays to points) in the short run. Because of such trade-offs between short-term and longer-term consequences, per-formance under Reset conditions provides an especially strong test of reinforce-ment maximization implicit in the marginal value theorem.

A useful method of computing optimal switch points on the Reset procedure is to calculate and rank order all possible switching patterns according to their net reinforcement rate. Table 17.1 shows for various switching patterns the cumula-tive time invested, the number of reinforcers (PI+FI), the time per reinforcer, and the overall rate of reinforcement (using the schedule parameters from above). By convention, switch points are specified as the PI value confronting the subject when the choice is made rather than the PI on the previous choice. For example, selecting the FI exclusively (when the PI=0) yields 1 reinforcer (on the FI) per 64 s, or 0.94 reinforcer per min; a pattern of strict alternation between FI and PI yields 2 reinforcers (1 on the FI and 1 on the PI) per 64 s, or 1.88 reinforcers per min; choosing the PI twice before switching to the FI yields 3 reinforcers every 72 s, or 2.5 reinforcers per min, and so on. Optimal performance (which occurs at 2.73 re-inforcers per min) entails switching from the PI to the FI after only 3 PI comple-tions—when the PI schedule has only reached 24 s. Although choosing a local de-lay of 64 s per reinforcer (the FI) over a delay of 24 s (the upcoming PI) is costly in the short run, this pattern yields the highest long-term gains—a cumulative time investment of 88 s for 4 reinforcers (3 PI + 1 FI), or 2.73 reinforcers per minute. The net reinforcement rate associated with this pattern compares favorably with that associated with switching at the equality point (1.88 points per min)—the pat-tern that minimizes delays to the upcoming reinforcer.

One of the advantages of this method of computing switch points is that it not only identifies the optimal switch point, it also describes deviations from optimal in clear quantitative terms. Such relationships can be easily seen in Figure 17.7, the top panel of which shows overall reinforcement rates (the rightmost column

TABLE 17.1

Cumulative Time Invested, Number of Reinforcers (on Both Schedules), Seconds per Reinforcer, and Reinforcers per Minute for Each Sequence of Choices Culminating in an FI Choice (in Boldface)

Consecutive PI choices	PI value at switch point	Series of choices	Σ seconds	reinf	seconds per reinf	reinf per min
0	0	**64**	64	1	64	0.94
1	8	0+**64**	64	2	32	1.88
2	16	0+8+**64**	72	3	24	2.50
3	24	0+8+16+**64**	88	4	22	2.73[a]
4	32	0+8+16+24+**64**	112	5	22.4	2.68
5	40	0+8+16+24+32+**64**	144	6	24	2.50
6	48	0+8+16+24+32+40+**64**	184	7	26.3	2.28
7	56	0+8+16+24+32+40+48+**64**	232	8	29	2.07
8	64	0+8+16+24+32+40+48+56+**64**	288	9	32	1.88

[a]Optimal switch point.

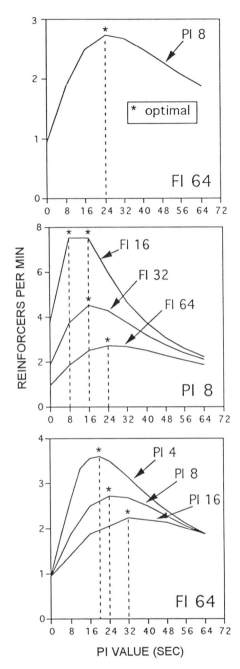

FIGURE 17.7. Hypothetical efficiency functions relating reinforcers per minute to different patterns of switching from the PI to the FI under the Reset version of the progressive-schedule choice procedures. The top panel shows the efficiency function under FI 64 s with a PI step size of 8 s (corresponding to the rightmost column of Table 17.1). The dashed vertical line from the peak of each function to the abscissa identifies the optimal point of switching from the PI to the FI (in this case, corresponding to a PI value of 24 s). The middle and bottom panels show how the efficiency functions (and optimal switch points) change as a function of FI duration and PI step size, respectively.

in Table 17.1) across PI switch points. Note that the peak of the function corresponds to the optimal switch point of 24 s. An interesting feature of many such functions (sometimes called *efficiency functions*) is the asymmetrical decrease in reinforcement rate that results from suboptimal switching. Switching prior to optimal is more costly (results in sharper reductions in reinforcement rate) than switching the same number of PI steps beyond it. For example, a PI switch point of 16 s (one step prior to optimal) produces 13.8 reinforcers per hour less than optimal switching, whereas a PI switch point of 32 s (one step beyond optimal) produces only 3 reinforcers per hour less than optimal switching. With such small differences in overall reinforcement rate, it may be unrealistic to expect switching to be in perfect accord with optimal. Yet with efficiency functions it is still possible to view deviations from optimal in cost–benefit terms. The form of the function allows one to predict the direction of deviations from optimal.

The middle panel of Figure 17.7 shows how the efficiency function varies as a function of FI duration (travel time between patches). This is like the top panel, with a PI step size of 8 s, except that it also includes efficiency functions for shorter FI durations (16 and 32 s) to compare against FI 64 s. In general, as the FI grows larger, the efficiency function peaks later. Thus, consistent with predictions of the marginal value theorem (see bottom panel of Figure 17.5), persistence within a depleting patch should vary directly with the costs of changing patches. Note that at FI 16 s, the peak of the efficiency function is bivalued; switching when the PI equals 8 s produces the same overall return rate (2 reinforcers per 16 s) as switching when the PI equals 16 s (3 reinforcers per 24 s). That some combination of schedule parameters yields more than one optimal switch point should be given careful consideration when selecting schedule parameters.

The bottom panel of Figure 17.7 shows how the peak of the efficiency function (hence, predicted optimal switch point) can change as a function of PI increment size (analogous to different rates of patch depletion). As with FI duration, optimal switch points in this case vary as a direct function of PI step size. The particular schedule values one uses depend on the kind of question one is asking. If one is asking questions about how switch points vary with changes in FI size (travel time) or PI step size (within-patch depletion rate), then it is clearly desirable to sample a range of schedule values across which predicted switch points change (as in most of the conditions shown in the middle and bottom panels). If, on the other hand, one is more interested in using performance under these procedures as a baseline against which to assess the effects of other variables, then it may be less important to select a range of schedule values than to select a particular combination of schedule values for which stable choice patterns can be achieved. In either case, it should be clear that what is optimal in any given situation depends critically on the PI and FI values that are used.

Testing the Marginal Value Theorem. To illustrate how the predictions of the marginal value theorem are brought to bear on actual data, consider the results of a recent experiment by Jacobs and Hackenberg (1996). Four adult humans were given repeated choices between two schedules of point delivery later exchangeable for money—an FI schedule and a PI schedule that increased by a fixed increment with each point delivered by that schedule, as described above. The FI value and the PI step size remained the same within each condition, but were varied independently across conditions in a $3 \times 3 \times 2$ factorial design: Each subject was exposed to all possible combinations of PI step size (4, 8, and 16 s) and FI duration (16, 32, and 64 s) under Reset and No Reset conditions.

A session consisted of five 15-min blocks of choice trials, the final three of

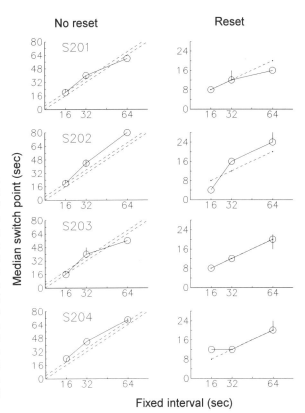

FIGURE 17.8. Points of switching from a PI schedule to an FI schedule as a function of FI duration for each of four adult human subjects. Data from the No Reset procedure are shown in the left panels and from the Reset procedure in the right panels. Data are expressed as means of median switch points over the final three blocks of choice trials in each condition. Increment size of the PI schedule was 4 s. Error bars show the interquartile range of the switch points. The dashed lines and small dots denote the optimal switch points for a given condition. Note that the axes are scaled differently for the two procedures. Adapted from Jacobs and Hackenberg (1996).

which were used to assess stability. Conditions were changed when switch points were deemed stable according to several quantitative criteria. The most common measure of switching patterns on these procedures is the median switch point—the PI value above and below which half of the FI choices occur.

The results will be discussed in relation to the questions raised above. First, do switch points vary with FI duration (travel time between patches)? Figure 17.8 shows median switch points as a function of programmed FI duration under Reset and No Reset conditions for all four subjects. For illustration, only data from the 4-s PI step size are shown, although the functions relating switch points to FI size for the other step sizes are similar. The dashed lines in each plot indicate optimal switch points. The error bars present the interquartile range of the switch points, a common measure of variability in switching patterns. Consistent with the marginal value theorem, switch points varied directly with FI size, indicating sensitivity to the costs of travel between patches, and, in most cases, were very close to predicted optimal switch points. Variability in switching patterns was generally very small; the interquartile range in most cases was close to zero.

Second, do switch points vary with PI step size (rate of patch depletion)? Figure 17.9 shows median switch points as a function of PI step size on the Reset procedure with an FI value of 64 s. (Only performance on the Reset procedure is shown because only on that procedure do predicted switch points vary with PI step size.) As in Figure 17.8, the error bars show interquartile ranges of switch

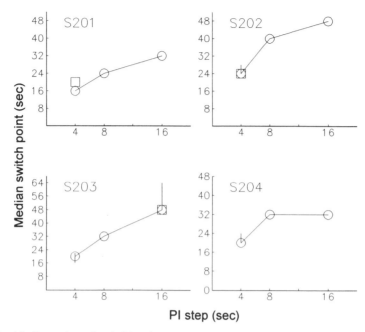

FIGURE 17.9. Median points of switching from a PI schedule to a resetting FI schedule as a function of PI step size for each of four human subjects. The duration of the FI schedule was 64 s. Error bars are interquartile ranges of the switch points. The square, unconnected symbols are from replicated conditions. Note the individually scaled axis for S203. Adapted from Jacobs and Hackenberg (1996).

points, which in most cases were small. Median switch points increased with PI step size, again, broadly consistent with the marginal value model. One additional feature of this figure deserving comment concerns data from conditions that were repeated (represented by the square symbols). Data from these conditions were in close agreement with those from initial exposures, which speaks to the within-subject reliability of the effects.

Finally, does switching occur at the optimal times predicted by the model? Across subjects and conditions, median switch points under steady-state conditions were in perfect quantitative accord with that predicted by the model in 51 of 78 conditions, and within one PI step in all but 2 of the remaining 27 conditions. When switch points did deviate from the predicted optimal points, they did so systematically. Consistent with the asymmetrical form of the efficiency functions shown in Figure 17.7, 25 of 27 deviations from optimal involved switching beyond rather than prior to the predicted optimal point.

The results of these laboratory experiments are in generally close agreement with optimization principles. It must be recognized, however, that the situations of diminishing returns modeled thus far in the laboratory represent a relatively narrow range of naturally occurring circumstances—where the gain curve diminishes at a constant incremental rate and the travel costs are fixed. Although this is an important first step in evaluating some of the simplifying assumptions of an optimization model, future laboratory research should be directed toward examining variations on these simple functions—gain curves defined by hyperbolic or exponential functions, and travel costs that vary around some average value, to name just a few. This would both extend the generality of the marginal value theorem and, at the same time, suggest some new directions in the experimental analysis of choice behavior.

LIMITATIONS AND FUTURE DIRECTIONS

Taken together, the empirical developments from the field and the laboratory described in the preceding sections provide the beginnings of a systematic approach to human behavioral ecology. Despite this promise, many difficult challenges lie ahead. The objectives of this section are to discuss briefly some of the limitations of current approaches, explore potential strategies for overcoming them, and point to some promising areas for future development.

Risky Choice

Classical optimization models have been criticized for their exclusive focus on mean rates of return, neglecting stochastic variation in rate of return. As Caraco (1981) and others have suggested, it is sometimes adaptive for behavior to be sensitive to distributional characteristics of a resource, not just to its average rate of occurrence. Under some circumstances an animal may increase its chances of survival by opting for a risky over a more certain outcome with a similar mean rate of return. Such behavior is termed *risk-prone,* as contrasted with *risk-averse,* the tendency to prefer more certain outcomes. Together, these two patterns define end points on a continuum of *risk sensitivity,* which refers broadly to behavior patterns adjusted to some dimension of variability in return rates.

A key prediction of risk-sensitive models of foraging concerns the effects of deprivation levels. When deprivation is high (thereby creating a negative energy budget), behavior should be more risk-prone than when deprivation is low (positive energy budget). These predictions have received at least qualitative confirmation in experiments with nonhuman animals as subjects (Caraco, Martindale, & Wittam, 1980), but have yet to be applied to human behavior under laboratory conditions.

Research with animals has also revealed important differences in risky choices between fixed versus variable *amounts* of food and fixed versus variable *delays* to food of the same mean value. Animals more strongly prefer variably distributed delays to food (Herrnstein, 1964; Killeen, 1968) than variably distributed amounts of food (Hamm & Shettleworth, 1987; Staddon & Reid, 1987). These effects are also in need of more intensive study with human subjects.

Before embarking on either of these lines of research with human subjects, however, a few methodological considerations seem warranted. First, with respect to the preference for variable over fixed outcomes, a broader definition of *variable outcome* is clearly needed. In the vast majority of work in this area, the variable outcome has been defined solely in terms of a bimodal distribution—only one of many ways outcomes may be distributed in nature or arranged in the laboratory.

Despite the limited ways in which variable distributions have been characterized, theoretical models in this area have proliferated in recent years. Such modeling efforts will be limited without a more thorough understanding of the basic phenomenon, including the range of variable distributions that produce it. Various methods for arranging interreinforcement intervals that have emerged from laboratory work in the experimental analysis of behavior should prove invaluable in this regard (see Ahearn & Hineline, 1992, for a promising approach).

Second, with respect to manipulating energy budgets, one of the main obstacles to research with humans is ethical. The most common method of manipulating energy budget in animals—to vary deprivation levels by restricting an animal's diet between experimental sessions—is not possible with human subjects. How, then, does one arrange conditions with human subjects analogous to varying background deprivation levels with animals? An innovative approach to this problem is suggested by an experiment of Rodriguez and Logue (1988). Human subjects were given a fixed number of noncontingent points (later exchangeable for money) at the beginning of a session. The points were then subtracted (via decrements on a counter to which the subjects had visual access) at a constant rate throughout the session. This manipulation was designed to resemble the discounting of food reinforcers in comparable experiments with animals. One can easily envision a variant of this procedure for studying risky choices in humans, arranging different energy budgets by giving different amounts of money prior to sessions (analogous to varying background deprivation levels).

Procedures used to study risky choice open lines of investigation with human subjects in several directions; toward a more thorough characterization of time discounting functions and of sensitivity to different types of variability in temporally distributed outcomes; toward identifying averaging principles other than arithmetic means (e.g., harmonic, geometric, weighted moving averages) as ways of defining reinforcing effectiveness; and toward the one-shot decisions between probabilistic outcomes studied under the rubric of rational choice theory (Kahneman & Tversky, 1984; see Rachlin, 1989, Chapter 4).

Verbal Behavior

As a result of longstanding participation in verbal communities, humans can acquire behavior appropriate to a given situation in two ways: (1) through direct contact with contingencies and (2) through verbal descriptions of such contingencies, normally in the form of instructions, advice, or warnings from others (Skinner, 1966). Although human verbal functioning has not been an explicit area of focus in classical optimization models, it stands as a key area (perhaps *the* key area) of future development. Among the questions it raises are the following (see Shimoff & Catania, Chapter 12): What role do verbal descriptions of contingencies play in sensitivity to those contingencies? Are verbal descriptions necessary for behavior to come under the control of such contingencies? That is, does sensitivity to environmental contingencies imply verbal "awareness" or "knowledge" of the contingencies? How accurate are verbal reports of contingencies and of behavior? How is behavior affected by verbal descriptions of the contingencies (i.e., instructions)? Is behavior under the control of such instructions identical to behavior under the control of the contingencies specified by those instructions? How is instructional control affected by such factors as instruction accuracy (i.e., by its correspondence with the contingencies it specifies), or by the credibility of its source?

Answers to such questions have important methodological implications for the future of behavioral ecology. Although field researchers favor direct measurement of events whenever possible, they often must rely on "informant recall," that is, on verbal self-reports, sometimes of activities spanning long intervals of time (Hames, 1992). The extent to which reported measures reflect verbal reports of participants versus direct observation by researchers is often not clear. What *is* clear is that verbal reports are often taken as standing in veridical relation with the events on which they are based, that is, they are taken at face value. Research in the experimental analysis of behavior concerned with relations between saying and doing (see Critchfield, Tucker, & Vuchinich, Chapter 14), however, shows that the reliability of verbal reports is a complex function of many factors. Methods *do* exist for improving and verifying verbal report accuracy, thereby enhancing their usefulness as a methodological tool, but the reliability of verbal reports is not something one can take for granted. At minimum, data collection methods should be described in ways that distinguish direct measurement of behavior and environment from verbal reports of such measures.

When human verbal capacity is acknowledged within an optimization account, it is normally construed in a positive light, for example, as enhancing sensitivity to the foraging environment. As Kaplan and Hill (1992) stated:

> Communication systems allow humans rapidly to track changes in their environment, and they actually may be more likely to adhere to the predictions of optimization models than are most other animals, which may instead develop foraging 'rules of thumb.' Human behavior, in general, is more likely to be adaptive in changing environments than can be expected for other organisms. (p. 197)

Research in the experimental analysis of instructional control, however, suggests that this may be an overly optimistic characterization of human abilities. Work in this area reveals that verbal descriptions of contingencies do not always enhance sensitivity to the environment. Rather, by narrowing the range of behavior available to make contact with the environment, instruction following has been shown to disrupt or interfere with control by nonverbal contingencies, resulting in marked insensitivity of behavior to environmental changes (see reviews by Baron & Galizio, 1983, and Hayes, 1989).

For example, in an experiment designed to assess the effects of instructions on optimal performance in humans, Hackenberg and Joker (1994) found that verbal descriptions of the contingencies frequently overrode direct control by those contingencies, even when it came at the expense of monetary earnings. Subjects were given choices between fixed and progressive schedules of points later exchangeable for money, similar to those described earlier. In addition, subjects received written instructions that specified a particular pattern of switching. The degree to which this instruction was "accurate" (i.e., correspond to the programmed contingencies) depended on the step size of the progressive schedule, which was varied systematically across conditions. In the first experimental condition, the instruction was accurate in that it specified the optimal switch point—the pattern of switching that would yield the highest net rate of point delivery. As the progressive-schedule contingencies were altered across conditions, the correspondence between the optimal switch point and the switch point implied by the instructions also changed.

Instructional control was quickly established in all four subjects and was maintained for several conditions thereafter, as the programmed contingencies were manipulated. Although instructional control did eventually give way to more schedule-appropriate patterns, all subjects continued to follow instructions despite their growing inaccuracy with respect to the programmed contingencies, and the loss in potential earnings that was incurred. One subject drove the progressive-schedule requirements to a value more than twice that of the fixed schedule before switching. Such performance reveals the powerful effects of instructions on behavior, and may shed light on aspects of human behavior that appear to be "irrational" or "suboptimal" when considered apart from a verbal context.

In contrast to some of the findings summarized above, which showed that when verbal influences are minimized, choices are in close agreement with molar optimizing, these data reveal circumstances under which such long-term sensitivity to reinforcement variables is overridden by verbal instructions. Such insensitivity of behavior to the environment can be adaptive, as when exposure to natural contingencies would be harmful or inefficient (e.g., when learning to use a power tool or when troubleshooting a computer). On the other hand, by precluding contact with naturally occurring consequences, instruction-following repertoires may actually reduce sensitivity to naturally occurring consequences necessary in the development of adaptive skills. In sum, whether productive or counterproductive, it is clear that verbal descriptions of contingencies are far from simple substitutes for direct contact with those contingencies. Future developments in the experimental analysis of verbal behavior, particularly in instructional control and relations between saying and doing, should advance hand in hand with the next generation of optimization models in human behavioral ecology.

SUMMARY AND CONCLUSIONS

As human behavioral ecology takes shape in the coming years, it will draw on empirical and theoretical developments from both the field and the laboratory. Despite sharing a number of explanatory assumptions, field and laboratory approaches to understanding human behavior from an ecological perspective have to date developed almost entirely in parallel, with little or no recognition of each other's accomplishments. The goal of this chapter has been to identify points of convergence between field and laboratory approaches, and to show how both are necessary elements in casting human behavior in an evolutionary framework. Initial applications of optimization models to human behavior have met with limited but promising success, particularly in those areas in which classical models formulated for use with nonhuman animals are already well developed. The initial successes in these areas provide useful starting points for a systematic approach to human behavioral ecology, but the greatest challenges for the future lie in areas that depart from classical models, particularly those involving human verbal functioning. Integrating functional-analytic approaches to verbal behavior within an ecological framework will promote the development of a truly interdisciplinary approach to understanding human behavior in relation to general principles of adaptation and selection.

ACKNOWLEDGMENTS. Preparation of this chapter was supported in part by Grant R29 MH50249 from the National Institute of Mental Health. The manuscript profited from many helpful comments by Edmund Fantino, Sigrid Glenn, Eric Jacobs, Cynthia Pietras, and Manish Vaidya.

REFERENCES

Abarca, N., & Fantino, E. (1982). Choice and foraging. *Journal of the Experimental Analysis of Behavior, 38*, 117–123.

Abarca, N., Fantino, E., & Ito, M. (1985). Percentage reward in an operant analogue to foraging. *Animal Behaviour, 33*, 1096–1101.

Ahearn, W., & Hineline, P. N. (1992). Relative preferences for various bivalued ratio schedules. *Animal Learning and Behavior, 20*, 407–415.

Baron, A., & Galizio, M. (1983). Instructional control of human operant behavior. *Psychological Record, 33*, 495–520.

Blurton Jones, N. G. (1987). Bushman birth spacing: A test for optimal birth intervals. *Ethology and Sociobiology, 8*, 135–142.

Borgerhoff Mulder, M. (1992). Reproductive decisions. In E. A. Smith & B. Winterhalder (Eds.), *Evolutionary ecology and human behavior* (pp. 339–374). New York: Aldine de Gruyter.

Caraco, T. (1981). Risk sensitivity and foraging groups. *Ecology, 62*, 527–531.

Caraco, T., Martindale, S., & Wittam, T. S. (1980). An empirical demonstration of risk-sensitive foraging preferences. *Animal Behaviour, 28*, 820–830.

Cashdan, E. (1992). Spatial organization and habitat use. In E. A. Smith & B. Winterhalder (Eds.), *Evolutionary ecology and human behavior* (pp. 237–266). New York: Aldine de Gruyter.

Catania, A. C. (1992). *Learning* (3rd ed.). Englewood Cliffs, NJ: Prentice–Hall.

Charnov, E. L. (1976a). Optimal foraging: Attack strategy of a mantid. *American Naturalist, 109*, 343–352.

Charnov, E. L. (1976b). Optimal foraging: The marginal value theorem. *Theoretical Population Biology, 9*, 129–136.

Collier, G. (1987). Operant methodologies for studying feeding and drinking. In F. M. Toates & N. E. Rowland (Eds.), *Feeding and drinking* (pp. 37–76). Amsterdam: Elsevier.

Dougherty, D. M., Nedelmann, M., & Alfred, M. (1993). An analysis and topical bibliography of the last ten years of human operant behavior: From minority to near majority (1982–1992). *The Psychological Record, 43*, 501–530.

Dyson-Hudson, R., & Smith, E. A. (1978). Human territoriality: An ecological reassessment. *American Anthropologist, 80*, 21–41.

Engen, S., & Stenseth, N. C. (1984). A general version of optimal foraging theory: The effect of simultaneous encounters. *Theoretical Population Biology, 26*, 192–204.

Fantino, E. (1969). Choice and rate of reinforcement. *Journal of the Experimental Analysis of Behavior, 12*, 723–730.

Fantino, E. (1991). Behavioral ecology. In I. H. Iversen & K. A. Lattal (Eds.), *Techniques in the behavioral and neural sciences: Vol. 6. Experimental analysis of behavior* (pp. 117–153). Amsterdam: Elsevier/North-Holland.

Fantino, E., & Abarca, N. (1985). Choice, optimal foraging, and the delay-reduction hypothesis. *Behavioral and Brain Sciences, 8*, 315–362 (includes commentary).

Fantino, E., & Preston, R. (1988). The effects of accessibility on acceptability. *Journal of the Experimental Analysis of Behavior, 50,* 395–403.

Fantino, E., & Preston, R. (1989). The delay-reduction hypothesis: Some new tests. In N. W. Bond & D.A.T. Siddle (Eds.), *Psychobiology: Issues and applications* (pp. 457–467). Amsterdam: Elsevier.

Foley, R. (1985). Optimality theory in anthropology. *Man, 20,* 222–242.

Forzano, L. B., & Logue, A. W. (1992). Predictors of adult humans' self-control and impulsiveness for food reinforcers. *Appetite, 19,* 33–47.

Hackenberg, T. D., & Axtell, S.A.M. (1993). Humans' choices in situations of time-based diminishing returns. *Journal of the Experimental Analysis of Behavior, 59,* 445–470.

Hackenberg, T. D., & Hineline, P. N. (1992). Choice in situations of time-based diminishing returns: Immediate versus delayed consequences of action. *Journal of the Experimental Analysis of Behavior, 57,* 67–80.

Hackenberg, T. D., & Joker, V. R. (1994). Instructional versus schedule control of humans' choices in situations of diminishing returns. *Journal of the Experimental Analysis of Behavior, 62,* 367–383.

Hames, R. B. (1992). Time allocation. In E. A. Smith & B. Winterhalder (Eds.), *Evolutionary ecology and human behavior* (pp. 203–235). New York: Aldine de Gruyter.

Hames, R. B., & Vickers, W. T. (1982). Optimal diet breadth theory as a model to explain variability in Amazonian hunting. *American Ethnologist, 9,* 258–278.

Hamm, S. L., & Shettleworth, S. J. (1987). Risk aversion in pigeons. *Journal of Experimental Psychology: Animal Behavior Processes, 13,* 376–383.

Hanson, J., & Green, L. (1989). Foraging decisions: Prey choice by pigeons. *Animal Behaviour, 37,* 429–443.

Hawkes, K., Hill, K., & O'Connell, J. F. (1982). Why hunters gather: Optimal foraging and the Aché of eastern Paraguay. *American Ethnologist, 9,* 379–398.

Hayes, S. C. (Ed.). (1989). *Rule-governed behavior: Cognition, contingencies, and instructional control.* New York: Plenum Press.

Herrnstein, R. J. (1964). Aperiodicity as a factor in choice. *Journal of the Experimental Analysis of Behavior, 7,* 179–182.

Hineline, P. N., & Sodetz, F. J. (1987). Appetitive and aversive schedule preferences: Schedule transitions as intervening events. In M. L. Commons, H. Rachlin, & J. Mazur (Eds.), *Quantitative analysis of behavior: Vol. 5. The effect of delay and of intervening events on reinforcement value* (pp. 141–157). Hillsdale, NJ: Erlbaum.

Hodos, W., & Trumbule, G. H. (1967). Strategies of schedule preference in chimpanzees. *Journal of the Experimental Analysis of Behavior, 10,* 503–514.

Horn, H. (1968). The adaptive significance of colonial nesting in the brewer's blackbird (*Euphagus cyanocephalus*). *Ecology, 49,* 682–694.

Ito, M., & Fantino, E. (1986). Choice, foraging, and reinforcer duration. *Journal of the Experimental Analysis of Behavior, 46,* 93–103.

Jacobs, E. A., & Hackenberg, T. D. (1996). Humans' choices in situations of time-based diminishing returns: Effects of fixed-interval duration and progressive-interval step size. *Journal of the Experimental Analysis of Behavior, 65,* 5–19.

Kahneman, D., & Tversky, A. (1984). Choices, values, and frames. *American Psychologist, 39,* 341–350.

Kamil, A. C., Krebs, J. R., & Pulliam, H. R. (1987). *Foraging behavior.* New York: Plenum Press.

Kaplan, H., & Hill, K. (1992). The evolutionary ecology of food acquisition. In E. A. Smith & B. Winterhalder (Eds.), *Evolutionary ecology and human behavior* (pp. 167–201). New York: Aldine de Gruyter.

Killeen, P. R. (1968). On the measurement of reinforcement frequency in the study of preference. *Journal of the Experimental Analysis of Behavior, 11,* 263–269.

Krebs, J. R., & Davies, N. B. (1993). *An introduction to behavioural ecology* (3rd ed.). Oxford: Blackwell.

Krebs, J. R., & McCleery, R. H. (1984). Optimization in behavioural ecology. In J. R. Krebs & N. B. Davies (Eds.), *Behavioural ecology: An evolutionary approach* (pp. 91–121). Oxford: Blackwell.

Lea, S.E.G. (1979). Foraging and reinforcement schedules in the pigeon: Optimal and non-optimal aspects of choice. *Animal Behaviour, 27,* 875–886.

MacArthur, R. H., & Pianka, E. R. (1966). On optimal use of a patchy environment. *American Naturalist, 100,* 603–609.

MacCorquodale, K. (1970). On Chomsky's review of Skinner's *Verbal Behavior. Journal of the Experimental Analysis of Behavior, 13,* 83–99.

Navarick, D. J. (1982). Negative reinforcement and choice in humans. *Learning and Motivation, 13,* 361–377.

Rachlin, H. (1989). *Judgment, decision, and choice: A cognitive/behavioral synthesis.* San Francisco: Freeman.

Ragotzy, S. P., Blakely, E., & Poling, A. (1988). Self-control in mentally retarded adolescents: Choice as a function of amount and delay of reinforcement. *Journal of the Experimental Analysis of Behavior, 49,* 191–199.

Rodriguez, M. L., & Logue, A. W. (1988). Adjusting delay to reinforcement: Comparing choice in pigeons and humans. *Journal of Experimental Psychology: Animal Behavior Processes, 14,* 105–117.

Shettleworth, S. J. (1989). Animals foraging in the lab: Problems and promises. *Journal of Experimental Psychology: Animal Behavior Processes, 15,* 81–87.

Shull, R. L. (1991). Mathematical description of operant behavior: An introduction. In I. H. Iversen & K. A. Lattal (Eds.), *Techniques in the behavioral and neural sciences: Vol. 6. Experimental analysis of behavior* (pp. 243–282). Amsterdam: Elsevier/North-Holland.

Skinner, B. F. (1966). An operant analysis of problem solving. In B. Kleinmuntz (Ed.), *Problem solving: Research, method, and theory* (pp. 225–257). New York: Wiley.

Smith, E. A. (1983). Anthropological applications of optimal foraging theory: A critical review. *Current Anthropology, 24,* 625–651.

Smith, E. A. (1991). *Inujjuamiut foraging strategies: Evolutionary ecology of an arctic hunting economy.* New York: Aldine de Gruyter.

Smith, E. A., & Winterhalder, B. (Eds.). (1992). *Evolutionary ecology and human behavior.* New York: Aldine de Gruyter.

Solnick, J. V., Kannenberg, C. H., & Eckerman, D. A., & Waller, M. B. (1980). An experimental analysis of impulsivity and impulse control in humans. *Learning and Motivation, 11,* 61–77.

Staddon, J. E. R., & Hinson, J. M. (1983). Optimization: A result or a mechanism? *Science, 221,* 976–977.

Staddon, J. E. R., & Reid, A. K. (1987). Adaptation to reward. In A. C. Kamil, J. R. Krebs, & H. R. Pulliam (Eds.), *Foraging behavior* (pp. 497–523). New York: Plenum Press.

Stockhorst, U. (1994). Effects of different accessibility of reinforcement schedules on choice in humans. *Journal of the Experimental Analysis of Behavior, 62,* 269–292.

Wanchisen, B. A., Tatham, T. A., & Hineline, P. N. (1988). Pigeons' choices in situations of diminishing returns: Fixed- versus progressive-ratio schedules. *Journal of the Experimental Analysis of Behavior, 50,* 375–394.

Wanchisen, B. A., Tatham, T. A., & Hineline, P. N. (1992). Human choice in "counterintuitive" situations: Fixed- versus progressive-ratio schedules. *Journal of the Experimental Analysis of Behavior, 58,* 67–85.

Winterhalder, B. (1981). Optimal foraging strategies and hunter-gatherer research in anthropology: Theory and models. In B. Winterhalder & E. A. Smith (Eds.), *Hunter-gatherer foraging strategies* (pp. 13–35). Chicago: University of Chicago Press.

Winterhalder, B. (1987). The analysis of hunter-gatherer diets: Stalking an optimal foraging model. In M. Harris & E. Ross (Eds.), *Food and evolution: Toward a theory of human food habits* (pp. 311–339). Philadelphia, PA: Temple University Press.

Zeiler, M. D. (1987). On optimal choice strategies. *Journal of Experimental Psychology: Animal Behavior Processes, 13,* 31–39.

18

Human Behavioral Pharmacology
An Overview of Laboratory Methods

Stephen T. Higgins and John R. Hughes

Behavioral pharmacology is a scientific discipline that integrates the principles of behavior analysis and general pharmacology. The origins of this discipline can be traced directly to studies conducted by B. F. Skinner and colleagues during the 1930s using schedules of reinforcement to examine the behavioral effects of drugs (Skinner & Heron, 1937). However, application of Skinner's operant methods to the study of the behavioral effects of drugs did not get under way in any systematic manner until the mid-1950s (see Dews & Morse, 1961). The use of operant methods was well established in numerous laboratories in the United States by that time. The discovery of chlorpromazine and other agents for the treatment of psychiatric disorders during this same period spurred a genuine interest on the part of the pharmaceutical industry in the utilization of operant methods in drug-discovery programs. Operant methods proved quite effective in meeting the challenges presented by the pharmaceutical industry and this new area of scientific inquiry and the discipline of behavioral pharmacology was launched.

Another important event in the development of behavioral pharmacology was the increase in recreational drug use and abuse in the United States during the 1960s (cf. Pickens, 1977). There was a great deal of concern among federal officials, for example, regarding drug abuse among the military in Vietnam, and what the social impact would be when those individuals returned home. Of course, concern extended beyond the military as increased drug use was evident among youth throughout the country. The resulting demand for scientific methods to investigate the etiology and treatment of drug abuse persists today. Again, the methods of be-

Stephen T. Higgins • Human Behavioral Pharmacology Laboratory and Departments of Psychiatry and Psychology, University of Vermont, Burlington, Vermont 05401. **John R. Hughes** • Human Behavioral Pharmacology Laboratory and Departments of Psychiatry, Psychology, and Family Practice, University of Vermont, Burlington, Vermont 05401.

Handbook of Research Methods in Human Operant Behavior, edited by Lattal and Perone. Plenum Press, New York, 1998.

havioral pharmacology were able to contribute effectively to this research endeavor.

Much research in behavioral pharmacology is conducted with laboratory animals. However, interest in research with humans has been evident throughout the history of the discipline. Studies examining the effects of drugs in humans using the methods of behavioral pharmacology were published soon after the advent of the discipline (e.g., Dews & Morse, 1958) and had become an integral part of behavioral pharmacology by the late 1960s and early 1970s (Bigelow & Liebson, 1972; Bigelow, Liebson, & Griffiths, 1974; Mello & Mendelson, 1970). Drug abuse is the area in which human behavioral pharmacology has especially flourished (e.g., T. Thompson & Johanson, 1981). Human behavioral pharmacology also contributes to various other content areas (e.g., developmental disabilities, eating disorders, gerontology), but not nearly to the same extent as to drug abuse. Behavioral pharmacology with humans has not played a role in drug-discovery programs that is comparable to research with laboratory animals. The role that human behavioral pharmacology has played with the pharmaceutical industry is mostly that of testing new drugs for their abuse liability (Fischman & Mello, 1989).

This chapter is intended to introduce readers to laboratory research methods used in human behavioral pharmacology. Human behavioral pharmacology has contributed important methods to treatment research as well, but a review of those contributions falls outside the purview of this chapter and volume. Interested readers might consult Bigelow, Stitzer, Griffiths, and Liebson (1981), Higgins, Budney, and Bickel (1994), and Stitzer and Higgins (1995) for overviews of drug abuse treatment research in human behavioral pharmacology.

A final comment in the way of background has to do with the distinction between the disciplines of behavioral pharmacology and psychopharmacology, both of which are devoted to researching the behavioral effects of drugs. Often there are no meaningful differences between these two disciplines, but the former term typically denotes application of the methods of the experimental analysis of behavior, whereas the latter does not. Also, the term *psychopharmacology* is increasingly being used specifically to describe studies of the effects of drugs on psychiatric symptoms or to refer to a discipline that integrates psychiatry and clinical pharmacology (cf. McKim, 1986). The term *behavioral pharmacology* implies nothing about psychiatric symptoms or psychiatry per se.

SUBJECTS AND SETTINGS

Volunteers for human behavioral pharmacology studies can be recruited via newspapers ads, postings on community bulletin boards, and word of mouth. Clinical populations (e.g., drug abusers, developmentally delayed individuals) are typically recruited from appropriate treatment facilities (e.g., drug abuse treatment clinics). As in any research with humans, protocols must be approved via appropriate institutional review boards and informed consent obtained. There is no general set of guidelines that must be followed regarding the many ethical issues to be considered when conducting drug studies with humans, but a recent position paper regarding human-subject issues in drug abuse research is worth consulting, especially for investigators new to this area (College on Problems of Drug Dependence, 1995). Ultimately, human-subject issues need to be assessed and risk–benefit decisions reached by individual investigators and pertinent review boards on a study-by-study basis (see Brady, 1989).

Subjects should be medically cleared prior to drug testing. The intensity of medical screening needed will vary depending on the drug, dose, and subject population being studied. For example, healthy adults receiving low doses of alcohol may be cleared on the basis of a brief medical history, whereas a careful medical workup and psychiatric screening is necessary prior to administering cocaine to human subjects. Subject screening and safety is an area where new investigators can benefit immensely by consulting with more experienced investigators, many of whom have developed effective subject-screening protocols. To our knowledge, none of those subject-screening protocols have been published. Interested readers can contact us regarding our screening protocols.

Residential and nonresidential laboratory settings are used. Residential settings are those where study participants remain at the laboratory overnight, often located within a hospital setting, sometimes for several weeks or months depending on the purpose and scope of the study. Nonresidential settings are those where study participants visit the laboratory for some portion of the day and otherwise reside in their natural environment. Each setting has advantages and disadvantages. For example, residential settings are more convenient for monitoring a wide variety of drug effects (e.g., effects on sleep, eating patterns, and social interaction), safer for studying higher drug doses and longer-acting compounds, have fewer problems with unauthorized use of other drugs, and provide more uniformity in subjects' daily schedules. Some disadvantages of residential studies are they are more costly, produce difficulties in recruiting subjects other than socially disadvantaged individuals, and typically have fewer individuals participating at the same time, thereby increasing the duration of the study. Nonresidential settings permit the recruitment of less disadvantaged subjects, generally are less costly, and in many other ways are more convenient to subjects and investigators. However, nonresidential studies compromise on the degree of scientific control that can be exerted over subjects' activities outside of the experimental protocol. Concerns about unauthorized drug use are of particular importance in nonresidential studies and necessitate regular objective monitoring (e.g., urine toxicology screening).

PHARMACOLOGICAL PRINCIPLES AND METHODS

We anticipate that many readers of this volume will be relatively unfamiliar with the basic principles and methods of general pharmacology. Hence, we have provided an introduction to these topics below. We cannot discuss these principles and methods in the detail that they merit within the space constraints of this chapter, and so interested readers might consult *Goodman and Gilman's The Pharmacological Basis of Therapeutics* (Hardman, Limbird, Molinoff, Ruddon, & Gilman, 1996), and *The Biochemical Basis of Neuropharmacology* (Cooper, Bloom, & Roth, 1991) for additional information on these and other topics in general pharmacology and neuropharmacology. Readers might also consult an excellent review by Branch (1991) on the principles and methods of pharmacology related to behavioral pharmacology research with laboratory animals and an edited text by Grabowski and VandenBos (1992) on basic mechanisms and applied interventions in psychopharmacology that was prepared specifically for psychologists.

Behaviorally Active Drugs

Defining the term *drug* is a good place to begin this section. A drug is defined broadly as any chemical agent that affects processes involved in living (Benet, 1996). Behavioral pharmacologists, of course, are interested in drugs that affect behavior, which are often referred to as *psychoactive drugs.* We use the more descriptive term *behaviorally active drugs* in this chapter to underscore the explicit subject matter of behavioral pharmacology. Table 18.1 lists the major classes of behaviorally active drugs, representative agents, their therapeutic indications, and some typical effects produced by each (from Johanson, 1992). Each of the drug classes listed in Table 18.1 has been investigated safely in human behavioral pharmacology studies.

Conduct of studies in human behavioral pharmacology requires some familiarity with the basics of pharmacokinetics (drug absorption, distribution, and elimination) and pharmacodynamics (relationships between drug concentration, effect, and mechanisms of drug action), which are discussed next.

Pharmacokinetics

Drug Administration. In human behavioral pharmacology studies, drug is typically administered by a trained research nurse or research assistant who has been authorized to do so by a physician. For most of the drugs studied, physicians need not be present at the time of drug administration, but with certain drugs and routes of administration (e.g., intravenously administered cocaine) this may be necessary. Drugs are usually obtained through and prepared by a hospital pharmacy familiar with research protocols. Depending on the drugs involved and research protocol, a Notice of Claimed Investigational Exemption for a New Drug (IND) from the Food and Drug Administration (FDA) or a license from the Drug Enforcement Agency (DEA) may be necessary. Whether an IND or DEA license is needed is best determined by contacting those agencies directly and consulting with experienced investigators in this research area.

The next challenge in studying the behavioral effects of a drug is identifying a method for getting the drug into the subject, referred to as the route of drug administration. Common routes of drug administration used in human behavioral pharmacology studies are oral, parenteral (intravenous, intramuscular, or subcutaneous injections), inhalation into the lungs, and absorption across mucous membranes (nose, mouth) or skin. As detailed in Table 18.2 (from Benet, Kroetz, & Sheiner, 1996, and Johanson, 1992), each route is associated with advantages and disadvantages. Each of the routes has been used safely in human behavioral pharmacology studies. Use of one route over another is determined exclusively based on the particulars of the study being conducted.

TABLE 18.1
Major Behaviorally Active Drug Classes[a]

Drug class	Representative drugs	Therapeutic indications[b]	Typical effects
Alcohol	Beer Wine Spirits	None	Intoxication Disinhibition Ataxia Impaired judgment and memory Sedation
Antidepressants	Amitryptyline (Elavil) Fluoxetine (Prozac) Lithium	Depression	Dry mouth Dizziness Drowsiness
Antipsychotics-neuroleptics	Haloperidol (Haldol) Chlorpromazine (Thorazine) Clozapine (Clozanil)	Schizophrenia	Sedation Motor depression Dysphoria Extrapyramidal reactions
Barbiturates	Pentobarbital Phenobarbital Secobarbital	Insomnia Seizure disorders	Sedation Ataxia Anesthesia
Benzodiazepines-anxiolytics	Diazepam (Valium) Alprazolam (Xanax) Triazolam (Halcion) Buspirone (Buspar)	Anxiety Insomnia	Muscle relaxation Reduced anxiety Sedation
Cannabis	Marijuana Hashish	Nausea Glaucoma	Sedation Distorted perceptions, memory, and thinking
Hallucinogens	LSD MDMA	None	Distorted perceptions and thinking
Opiates/opioids	Morphine Heroin Codeine Meperidine	Analgesia Cough Diarrhea	Euphoria Nausea Drowsiness
Psychomotor stimulants	Cocaine Amphetamine Methylphenidate (Ritalin)	Obesity Attention deficit disorder Narcolepsy	Increases alertness–motor stimulation Loss of appetite Euphoria

[a]Adapted from Johanson (1992), with permission of the publisher.
[b]Not all representative drugs listed are used for each of the therapeutic indications. For instance, cocaine is a psycho-motor stimulant but is only used as a local anesthetic. Heroin is an opiate, but it is not used therapeutically for any indication. These distinctions are not always related to the pharmacology of the drug but can also be related to legal constraints.

TABLE 18.2
Some Characteristics of Common Routes of Drug Administration[a]

Route	Absorption pattern	Advantages	Disadvantages
Oral (p.o.)	Delayed, variable dependent on many factors	Convenient, safe, economical	Delayed onset, gastric irritation, nausea, erratic absorption, metabolism by stomach or liver
Smoked	Rapid	Rapid onset, no first-pass metabolism in liver	Cumbersome for experimenter to deliver, damage to lungs, not all drugs can be volatilized
Mucosal absorption	Prompt, variable	Convenient to administer	Mucosal irritation, variable absorption
Transdermal	Prompt, effective for sustained absorption across time	Short onset, convenient to administer, sustained release	Not possible with many drugs
Intravenous	Absorption circumvented	Rapid onset, dose titration possible, can be used with substances irritating to other tissue, precise dose manipulation	High risk for overdosing, asepsis required, skill required for injection, cannot be used with oily or insoluble drugs
Intramuscular	Prompt for aqueous solutions slow and sustained for repository preparations	Short onset, can be used with oily drugs and some irritating substances, precise dose manipulation, can be used for some insoluble suspensions	Absorption dependent on vascularity of injection site, asepsis required, possible pain and necrosis at injection site
Subcutaneous	Prompt for aqueous solutions, slow and sustained for repository preparations	Short onset, can be used with some insoluble substances and for implantation of solid pellets	Not suitable for large volumes, asepsis required, possible pain and necrosis at injection site

[a]Adapted from Benet, Kroetz, and Sheiner (1996); and Johanson (1992), with permission of the publishers.

Drug Absorption and Distribution. Once a drug is administered, it must reach its site(s) of action in order to produce an effect. Behaviorally active drugs are distributed systemically (i.e., via the circulatory system) to sites of action in the central nervous system (brain and spinal cord). With an intravenous route of administration, drug is injected directly into the circulatory system, thereby circumventing absorption. With each of the other routes, the drug must be absorbed, that is, transported from its site of administration through cell membranes into the circulatory system. The rate and efficiency with which a drug is absorbed into the circulatory system via the different routes of administration are basic factors that must be considered in designing a behavioral pharmacology experiment. For example, with an inhalation route of administration absorption is directly into the arterial system so that drug will reach the brain in a few seconds. With the oral route of administration, absorption can take 30 min or more depending on factors such as how recently the person ate. Such information will be essential, for example, in deciding how soon after drug administration to begin experimental sessions, the duration of sessions, and so forth. For most drugs studied in human behavioral pharmacology, a search of MEDLINE (computerized Index Medicus), available through any university library, is sufficient to locate relevant pharmacokinetic studies, and the *Physicians' Desk Reference* (1997) is a convenient source for obtaining that information on prescribed drugs.

Drug Elimination. How rapidly a drug is cleared or eliminated from the system is another pharmacokinetic factor that must be considered in designing experiments in this area. Most drugs are metabolized (i.e., changed to another molecule) before being eliminated from the body. Generally, this involves transforming the drug from a fat-soluble to a water-soluble compound, which usually occurs in the liver via enzymatic reactions. Certain drugs need to be administered intravenously, buccally (via mucosal lining of mouth), or inhaled in order to bypass initial metabolism in the liver (i.e., first-pass metabolism) before reaching their sites of action. Following metabolism, the transformed molecule is typically removed from the circulatory system by the kidney and excreted in urine.

Pharmacologists estimate the time needed to metabolize and excrete a drug in terms of an elimination half-life, which is the time required to eliminate 50% of the total amount of drug in the body. Consider as an example a 100-mg dose of a hypothetical drug with an elimination half-life of 12 hr. After 12 hr, approximately 50 mg will remain in the body; after 24 hr, 25 mg will remain; after 36 hr, 12.5 mg will remain; and so on, until all drug has been eliminated. As a rule of thumb, a drug is considered to be eliminated after five half-lives. Knowing a drug's elimination half-life is necessary for making decisions about the frequency of drug administration. For example, with an acute drug-dosing regimen, administrations are typically spaced so that all drug from the prior administration has been eliminated before the next administration. With a chronic dosing regimen, doses are typically spaced so as to achieve and maintain a stable level of drug in the system. In both instances, one needs to know the elimination half-life of the drug under investigation in order to implement the desired dosing regimen.

Many factors can influence drug metabolism and elimination, including genetics, age, gender, disease, body size and composition (% body fat), and current and past history of drug and toxin exposure. Older age and smoking status are two of the more common factors that affect metabolism and elimination. These many factors need to be considered in determining subject inclusion and exclusion criteria for drug studies. Certain of them may be especially important in studying a particular drug, and that is usually learned by reviewing the scientific literature as was noted above. With new drugs, this information may have to be provided by the pharmaceutical company. Concerns about possible between-subject differences related to body size are typically addressed by adjusting drug dose according to body weight. Depending on the potency of the drug, such adjustments typically are made on a gram or milligram of drug per kilogram of body weight basis. Finally, careful monitoring and recording of unexpected or adverse drug effects during and between experimental sessions is essential for detecting problems related to drug metabolism and elimination.

Pharamcodynamics

Receptor Action. Most behaviorally active drugs produce effects by binding to receptors. Drug receptors are large molecules located on the surface of cells that typically, but not always, serve as receptors for the body's normal regulatory ligands (e.g., hormones, neurotransmitters) (Benet et al., 1996). Consistent with the specificity inherent in endogenous regulatory systems, there is great specificity in drug–receptor binding. Pharmacologists use the term *affinity* to refer to the propensity of a drug to bind to a particular receptor type. Once bound, drugs differ in the magnitude of effect they produce, which is referred to as *intrinsic activity* or *efficacy*. Drugs that have affinity and intrinsic activity are termed *agonists;* those that have affinity and no intrinsic activity are termed *antagonists;* those that have affinity and intermediate activity relative to a known agonist are termed *partial agonists*. Affinity and intrinsic activity are based on the chemical structure of the drug, and even minor modifications in a drug's structure can produce profound changes in its profile of effects.

In addition to intrinsic efficacy, another determinant of the magnitude of drug effect observed is the concentration of drug available at the receptor site. Effects generally increase as an orderly function of increasing drug concentration. The most common method of varying drug concentration is varying the dose of drug administered.

Dose-Response Curves. The dose–response relationship is perhaps the most fundamental of all relationships in pharmacology research (cf. Branch, 1991). A dose–response curve graphically expresses the relationship between the magnitude of effect observed on some dependent variable (shown on the vertical or Y axis) as a function of the dose of drug administered (shown on the horizontal or X axis) (see upper panel of Figure 18.1). The scale type used on the Y axis varies within and across studies, but the X axis (drug dose) is usually displayed on a log scale. Displaying drug dose on a log scale permits easy display of a wide range of drug doses and facilitates qualitative and quantitative comparisons of the potency and efficacy of different drugs in producing a particular effect (Ross, 1996).

Several basic characteristics of dose–response curves common in human behavioral pharmacology are illustrated in the upper panel of Figure 18.1. That pan-

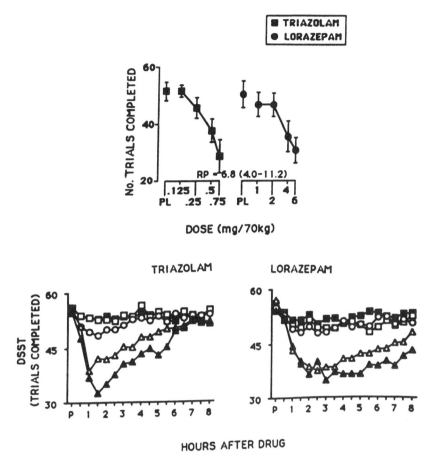

FIGURE 18.1.   (Upper) Dose–response functions during peak effects of triazolam and lorazepam on the number of DSST trials completed. Data points are means from eight subjects during peak drug effects; brackets represent ± 1 SEM. Data points above PL represent placebo values. X axis: dose expressed in milligrams. Y axis: mean number of trials completed. Relative potencies (RP) are expressed as milligrams of lorazepam equivalent to 1 mg of triazolam; confidence intervals (95%) are shown in parentheses. (Lower) Separate time–response functions for the effects of triazolam and lorazepam. X axis: time after drug in hours with values above P indicating predrug observations. Y axis: number of trials completed. Data are means from eight subjects. ■, placebo; □, 0.125 mg/70 kg triazolam or 1 mg/70 kg lorazepam; ○, 0.25 mg/70 kg triazolam or 2 mg/70 kg lorazepam; △, 0.5 mg/70 kg triazolam or 4 mg/70 kg lorazepam; ▲, 0.75 mg/70 kg triazolam or 6 mg/70 kg lorazepam. From Rush et al. (1993), with permission of the publisher.

el depicts dose–response relationships for the acute effects of two benzodi-azepines, triazolam and lorazepam, in normal, adult volunteers performing the Digit Symbol Substitution Test (DSST; described below in the section Procedures Involving Arbitrary Operants) (Rush, Higgins, Bickel, & Hughes, 1993). Both drugs decreased the mean number of DSST trials completed as a graded, monotonic function of dose. We refer to these curves as graded because the magnitude of effects increased in a stepped fashion as dose increased, and monotonic because effects moved in only one direction (i.e., downward). Bitonic curves, in which effects move in two directions, are also common in human behavioral pharmacology research, especially curves that have an inverted U shape (i.e., effects increase at low to moderate doses and decrease at higher doses).

The curves in Figure 18.1 differ in two additional characteristics that merit comment. Note that the effects of triazolam occur at lower doses than those of lorazepam. On that basis, triazolam is said to have greater potency than lorazepam in producing these effects. Note also that the two drugs produced comparable maximal effects. On that basis, triazolam and lorazepam are said to be equally efficacious in producing this effect. These comparisons can be expressed quantitatively as relative potency estimates (Finney, 1964). For the effects on DSST performance in Figure 18.1, for example, approximately 6.8 mg of lorazepam was needed to produce the equivalent effect of 1 mg of triazolam. With bitonic curves, potency and efficacy need to be estimated separately for the increasing and decreasing segments of the curve.

The potency and efficacy differences observed in the study depicted in Figure 18.1 can be related back to the receptor actions discussed above. Triazolam and lorazepam operate through the same receptor system. Hence, the observed potency differences indicate that triazolam has greater receptor affinity than lorazepam, that is, triazolam more readily binds to the receptor than lorazepam. The comparable maximal effects observed indicate that once bound, triazolam and lorazepam have comparable intrinsic activity at the receptor(s) involved in producing the effect, that is, the two drugs produce comparable effects per bound molecule at the receptor site.

This example explored a wide range of drug doses of each compound, including at least one dose at the lower end that produced no or minimal effects and several intermediate and higher doses. Ideally, additional higher doses might have been included to ensure that maximal effects were observed. However, when working with humans, safety concerns often preclude testing doses that produce maximal effects. The goal in determining a dose–effect function in humans is to test as wide a dose range as is ethically and practically feasible. It is important to remember that drug effects can differ quantitatively and qualitatively depending on dose. Thus, a drug's action can only be fully characterized by testing a wide range of doses.

Drug Interactions. Drug use in a common feature of everyday living. For example, 80% of the U.S. adult population are daily users of caffeinated beverages and 30% are regular cigarette smokers. Any drug administered to these individuals, whether it be administered for recreational (e.g., alcohol) or therapeutic (e.g., anxiolytic) purposes, will be acting in concert with caffeine and nicotine. Even if the regularly used drug is not present in the body when the second drug is administered, certain behavioral and physiological adaptations associated with chronic drug exposure can still produce an altered drug response (e.g., tolerance). Such alterations in drug response related to prior drug exposure are most effectively characterized in terms of changes in dose–response functions.

An example of how exposure to an agonist drug can alter subsequent response to another agonist from the same drug class is shown in Figure 18.2. The mean respiration rates are plotted for two groups of human subjects following acute, intravenous injections of hydromorphone, an opioid agonist that acts on mu-opioid re-

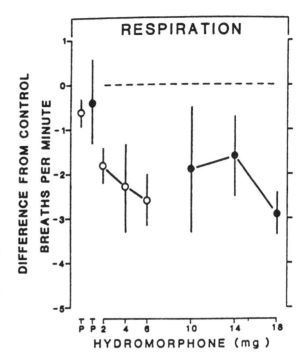

FIGURE 18.2. Effects of intravenous hydromorphone on respiration rate in opiate-free (○) and methadone-maintained (●) subjects. Unconnected symbols show results of placebo administration. Error bars represent ± 1 SEM. From McCaul et al. (1983), with permission of the publisher.

ceptors (McCaul, Stitzer, Bigelow, & Liebson, 1983). All subjects had prior experience with opioid drugs, but one group was currently undergoing a chronic, daily regimen of orally administered methadone, another mu-opioid-receptor agonist, whereas the other group was receiving no other drug exposure. Note that the dose–response curve for the group that was receiving methadone was shifted in a rightward, parallel manner relative to the curve obtained with the group without recent drug exposure. In pharmacological terms, such a rightward shift is referred to as *tolerance*. Because in this example the drug to which subjects were chronically exposed was from the same class but was not the actual test compound, this is more precisely referred to as an example of *cross-tolerance*. Had the chronic exposure to methadone shifted the dose–response curve of morphine to the left, this would have been referred to as an example of *sensitization* or, more precisely, *cross-sensitization*. The mechanisms of action responsible for such rightward and leftward shifts can be quite complex. That complexity notwithstanding, in pharmacology the terms *tolerance* and *sensitization* refer to leftward and rightward shifts in the dose–response curve resulting from prior drug exposure.

Figure 18.3 illustrates changes in a dose–response function resulting from combining antagonist and agonist drugs. In this example, the effects of subcutaneously administered morphine (also a mu-opioid-receptor agonist) on subject-rated drug effects were assessed in opioid abusers in the presence and absence of twice-daily treatment with an orally administered 15-mg dose of naltrexone (a mu-opioid-receptor antagonist) (Martin, Jasinski, & Mansky, 1973). When administered during naltrexone treatment, morphine competes with naltrexone for recep-

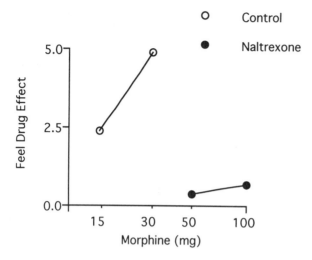

FIGURE 18.3. Effects of subcutaneously administered morphine (X axis) on subjects' ratings of feel effect of drug (Y axis). Each value represents the mean, for six subjects, of the sum of responses for the first 5 hr following drug administration. Open symbols show effects of morphine alone and closed symbols show effects of morphine injections in the presence of twice-daily, oral administration of 15 mg naltrexone. From Martin et al. (1973), with permission of the publisher.

tor sites. Thus, higher doses of morphine are required to produce the same effect that was produced with lower doses when morphine was tested without naltrexone. In terms of the dose–effect curve, this interaction results in the morphine dose–effect curve being shifted rightward and downward from the curve obtained with morphine administered in the absence of naltrexone. In pharmacological terms, this shift is referred to as *antagonism*. Perhaps because of concern for subject safety, the morphine dose was not increased further in the naltrexone condition in this study. Had it been increased further, the eventual outcome likely would have been maximal effects in the naltrexone condition equal to those observed with morphine alone. This is referred to as a *surmountable antagonism* (antagonism that can be surmounted by increasing dose). Antagonism that cannot be surmounted via dose increases is referred to as *insurmountable antagonism*. Because morphine and naltrexone each act at mu-opioid receptors, this interaction is referred to as *competitive antagonism* (i.e., agonist and antagonist compete for receptor occupancy). When antagonism is observed with drugs that do not share a common mechanism of action, it is referred to as *functional antagonism*.

Had the effects of the drug combination been a leftward shift in the dose–response function, it would have been referred to as *synergism*. No qualifiers are used with *synergism* that are directly comparable to the *surmountable, insurmountable, competitive,* and *functional* terms used with *antagonism*. However, leftward shifts are sometimes further characterized as being additive, less-than-additive, or supraadditive if the respective shift in the curve is equal to, less than, or exceeds the algebraic sum of combining the agonist effects observed when the two drugs involved were administered alone.

Note that, while informative, the above examples illustrated shifts in the hydromorphone and morphine dose–effect functions following exposure to only single doses of methadone and naltrexone. A thorough analysis of the combined effects of these compounds would require determining the effects of these two agonists in the presence of a full range of doses of methadone and naltrexone (cf. Branch, 1991). Because of such possible drug–drug interactions, detailed histories of subjects' drug use are necessary in human behavioral pharmacology studies as are restrictions on other drug use during studies.

Time–Effect Functions. In addition to dose–response relationships, characterizing time–effect functions is also important in characterizing the behavioral effects of drugs. Shown in the lower panel of Figure 18.1 are two time–response functions for the effects of triazolam and lorazepam on DSST performance, which correspond to the dose–response functions shown in the upper panel of that figure. Five characteristics of time–response functions are often noted: time to onset of drug effects, time to maximal or peak effects, time to offset of effects, duration of peak effects, and overall duration of effects. Each of these aspects of the time–response function can differ as a function of drug or dose. With regard to drug differences in the example shown in Figure 18.1, effects of triazolam were discernible, peaked, and dissipated earlier, and had briefer peak and overall durations than those of lorazepam. With regard to dose differences, effects of higher doses of both compounds were discernible earlier and had a longer overall duration of action than lower doses. These drug and dose differences can be understood in terms of differences in the pharmacokinetic factors (drug absorption, distribution, and elimination times) discussed above.

Placebo-Controlled, Double-Blind, Randomized Testing

Certain control conditions are necessary in experimental drug studies in order to permit causal inferences to be made regarding relationships between drug and effect. One common control is a placebo, which is an inert substance that is administered in the same manner as the drug under investigation. A placebo control permits experimenters to estimate the influence, if any, of the drug administration and monitoring procedures on the dependent variables under investigation. Instructions that one is receiving a drug or the act of ingesting capsules or receiving an injection might in and of themselves change the dependent variable. By including a placebo condition, such effects can be measured and compared with the effects observed when drug was administered. Because the same administration procedures are used, any differences between the effects observed in the placebo and drug conditions can be attributed to the drug.

Parenterally administered drugs need to be dissolved in a saline or other solution before being injected, which is referred to as a *vehicle*. Injection of vehicle alone is a common placebo as is the administration of capsules filled with lactose in studies in which drug is being administered orally in capsules.

In addition to keeping the administration procedures uniform across drug and placebo conditions, it is also important that all other aspects of the experimental setting be kept as uniform as possible. For that reason, it is preferable that placebo and drug be administered under double-blind conditions, meaning that neither staff nor subjects are informed whether drug or placebo is being tested in a particular session. In a between-group design, assignment of subjects to a placebo or drug condition is determined randomly and staff and subjects are blinded to (i.e., uninformed about) that assignment. In a within-subjects design, the order of testing placebo and drug within and across subjects is determined randomly and staff and subjects are blinded to that determination. These double-blind, randomized testing practices help to establish a uniform set of conditions across placebo and drug sessions.

BEHAVIORAL AND PHYSIOLOGICAL METHODS

This section assumes that readers are familiar with principles of behavior. A discussion of principles related to the physiological methods discussed in this section was omitted for space concerns and because such information is available elsewhere (e.g., Guyton, 1997). This section is devoted to reviewing *methods.*

The behavioral methods used in laboratory studies in human behavioral pharmacology can be divided into two general types: (1) methods used to examine how drugs alter the rate, accuracy, or other aspects of responding, often referred to as measures of the direct effects of drugs, and (2) methods used to investigate how drugs serve as antecedents and consequences for responding, often referred to as measures of the stimulus functions of drugs. The former are used throughout the various content areas in human behavioral pharmacology, whereas the latter are more common in studies related to drug abuse.

Direct Behavioral Effects of Drugs

Characterizing how drugs directly alter behavior is of interest to human behavioral pharmacologists for several reasons. First, drugs can produce a myriad of behavioral effects, some of which can be harmful or toxic to the user and those around them. The methods of human behavioral pharmacology are useful in characterizing the nature of such effects, and in assessing similarities and differences across various drugs, doses, and dosing regimens in producing them. In other instances, questions might address more theoretical or basic issues regarding, for example, the mechanisms by which environmental factors may modulate the behavioral effects of drugs (e.g., understanding the relationship between the degree of stimulus control and sensitivity to drug-produced behavioral effects). In still other instances, questions might pertain to behavioral effects thought to influence the initiation or maintenance of drug abuse. For example, abused drugs from diverse pharmacological classes often facilitate social interaction, which may contribute to their abuse liability (Higgins, Hughes, & Bickel, 1989; Stitzer, Griffiths, Bigelow, & Liebson, 1981).

Procedures used to assess the direct behavioral effects of abused drugs comprise four categories: (1) procedures utilizing trained, arbitrary operant responses; (2) laboratory-analogue procedures to study human social behavior; (3) use of residential settings to study various aspects of naturalistic human behavior; and (4) observer and subject ratings of drug effects.

Procedures Involving Arbitrary Operants

As in studies conducted with laboratory animals (Branch, 1991), procedures in which subjects emit stable levels of an arbitrary operant response have proven useful in characterizing the acute and chronic effects of drugs on human behavior.

These procedures are chosen largely because they produce stable behavioral base-lines that are sensitive to the effects of drugs, and not because they have any di-rect topographical similarities to naturalistic human activities. They are useful both for pragmatic questions concerning the degree of behavioral disruption asso-ciated with a particular drug, and also for more basic questions concerning envi-ronmental factors that modulate the behavioral effects of drugs.

Digit Symbol Substitution Test and Circular Lights Procedure. A computerized version of the DSST (McLeod, Griffiths, Bigelow, & Yingling, 1982) and the Circu-lar Lights procedure (Griffiths, Bigelow, & Liebson, 1983) are two arbitrary-oper-ant procedures that have been used rather extensively in human behavioral phar-macology studies. In the DSST procedure, a list of 10 symbol codes are presented across the top of a video screen. The codes are numbered in sequence from 1 through 10 and aligned in ascending numerical order from left to right. Each of the 10 symbol codes is comprised of an identical 3 $\times$ 3 matrix of symbols (i.e., a 3 $\times$ 3 matrix of asterisks). That 3 $\times$ 3 matrix of symbols corresponds to a 3 $\times$ 3 matrix of response keys that subjects use to record their responses. In addition to their nu-merical order, the 10 symbol codes are also differentiated through highlighting. Three of the nine symbols in each code are highlighted and the pattern of high-lighting is varied across the 10 codes. Located in the center of the video screen is a single digit that can vary from 1 through 10. That digit indicates which of the 10 codes listed at the top of the screen is signaling the availability of reinforcement (e.g., points exchangeable for money). If the response sequence is completed cor-rectly, a point is added to a running tally, and a new digit is displayed in the cen-ter of the screen. In operant terms, the task is a signaled, three-response chained schedule of reinforcement across nine operanda. Test sessions typically last 90 s and are repeated at different temporal intervals following drug administration. Subjects are instructed to obtain as many points as possible during each 90-s ses-sion.

Drug testing with the DSST does not begin until responding on the procedure is deemed to be stable based on visual inspection of the data or a predetermined stability criterion. A sufficient level of stability for initiating drug testing general-ly is achieved following approximately thirty 90-s trials. The procedure is sensi-tive to both performance-enhancing (e.g., Higgins, Bickel, Hughes, Lynn, Capeless, & Fenwick, 1990) and disrupting (e.g., Rush et al., 1993) effects of drugs.

In the Circular Lights procedure, subjects cumulate points, often exchange-able for money, by pressing a circular series of buttons as rapidly as possible in re-sponse to the randomly sequenced illumination of an associated display of lights. This represents a fixed-ratio 1 schedule of reinforcement across multiple operan-da. Sessions typically are limited to 60 s in duration and are repeated at different temporal intervals following drug administration. Rates of overall and correct re-sponding generally are affected as an orderly function of dose and time by a vari-ety of different drugs including alcohol, benzodiazepines, and barbiturates (e.g., Griffiths et al., 1983; Roache, Cherek, Bennett, Schenkler, & Cowan, 1993).

The orderly dose– and time–response relationships that can be obtained with the DSST were discussed above and shown in Figure 18.1. To illustrate further the utility of the DSST and to illustrate effects observed with the Circular Lights pro-cedure, dose–response functions displaying peak effects of acutely administered triazolam and ethanol (alcohol) on these measures are shown in Figure 18.4. Mean total number of correct three-response sequences made during 90-s sessions are shown for the DSST and mean total number of correct single responses made during 60-s sessions are shown for the Circular Lights procedure. Results are from a double-blind comparison of the effects of these two drugs in eight healthy volunteers (Roache et al., 1993). The two drugs produced equal maximal effects across both procedures. The dose–response functions for triazolam tended to be more graded than those for alcohol. That is, the intermediate doses of triazolam tended to produce greater effects than the intermediate doses of alcohol across both procedures, but those differences only achieved statistical significance with the DSST.

The DSST and Circular Lights procedure offer the advantage of generating stable behavioral baselines that are sensitive to the effects of a wide variety of abused drugs. In addition, they are sufficiently simple such that with most subjects, responding stabilizes quickly. These attributes notwithstanding, these procedures are intended only as examples, and not an exhaustive list, of the kind of arbitrary-operant procedures that are used to assess the direct behavioral effects of drugs in human behavioral pharmacology research.

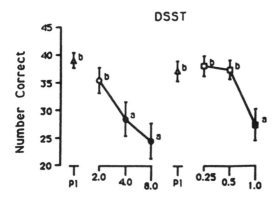

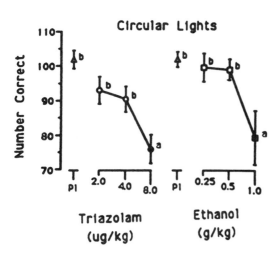

FIGURE 18.4. Effects of triazolam (circles), ethanol (squares), and placebo (unconnected triangles) on DSST (upper panels) and Circular Lights (lower panels) performance. X axis: drug in micrograms (triazolam) or grams (ethanol) per kilogram body weight; Pl designates placebo. Y axis: number of correct response sequences (DSST) and responses (Circular Lights). Data points are means from eight subjects; vertical bars represent ± 1 SEM. Closed symbols indicate a significant difference from placebo observations and letter codes indicate results of multiple comparisons between data points; any two means having the same letter do not differ significantly. From Roache et al. (1993), with permission of the publisher.

Repeated Acquisition of Behavioral Chains. Another important aspect of human behavior known to be sensitive to drug effects is the ability to acquire new behavior (i.e., learning). A common way to study drug effects on learning with laboratory animals and humans involves a procedure known as Repeated Acquisition of Behavioral Chains (Thompson & Moerschbaecher, 1979). The procedure typically is arranged so that in each session reinforcement delivery is contingent on subjects acquiring a new and predetermined response sequence across three or four operanda. In nonhumans, the length of the sequence is typically restricted to 3 or 4 steps, whereas with humans it may be as high as 15 steps. After sufficient training, the number of errors made in learning a new sequence and rates of responding stabilize, thereby providing a stable baseline to study drug effects on learning within a single subject.

In an adaptation of this procedure for use with humans, reinforcement delivery is contingent on depressing three response keys (A, B, C) in a predetermined order in the presence of the numbers 0 to 9, which appear sequentially in the center of a video screen (Desjardins, Moerschbaecher, & Thompson, 1982; Higgins, Bickel, O'Leary, & Yingling, 1987). For example, reinforcement delivery may be contingent on depressing the keys in the sequence C, A, B, C, B, A, C, B, A, C in the presence of the screen numbers 0 to 9, respectively. Each correct response advances the screen number by one step, whereas each incorrect response initiates a brief timeout. Each completed sequence adds a point, typically exchangeable for money, to a counter and returns the number in the center of the video screen to zero for the start of the next trial. Subjects typically complete sets of 20 trials at various temporal intervals following drug administration. Accuracy and rates of responding typically stabilize after approximately 30 training sessions, conducted at a rate of 5–10 per day.

Figure 18.5 displays dose–response functions from a study of the acute effects of varying doses of orally administered alcohol and intranasally administered cocaine tested alone and in combination on Repeated Acquisition (Higgins et al., 1992). Subjects were seven healthy, adult volunteers. Results are shown for the percentage of responses that were errors expressed as area-under-the-time-action-curve (AUC) values. AUC is a statistical method commonly used in pharmacology studies for representing as a single data point the overall duration and magnitude of effects observed with different drugs and doses (Dixon, 1988). Cocaine administered alone did not reliably increase errors above placebo levels. Alcohol administered alone increased errors above placebo levels as a graded function of dose. Combining either dose of cocaine with either dose of alcohol antagonized the error-increasing effects observed with alcohol alone. Because alcohol and cocaine do not share a common mechanism of action, such an effect represents functional antagonism.

Analogues of Naturalistic Human Behavior

Drugs of abuse can significantly alter human social interaction in numerous ways (e.g., Stitzer et al., 1981). Moreover, much drug use and abuse occurs in a social context. Thus, the study of drug effects on social interaction is necessary for a thorough understanding of not only the consequences of drug abuse but also the

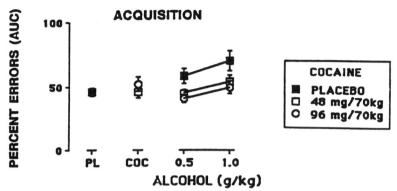

FIGURE 18.5.   Area-under-the-time-action-curve values (Y axis) averaged across seven subjects who received all dose conditions are shown as a function of alcohol dose (X axis). Data point above PL represents effects of placebo alcohol and placebo cocaine; those above COC represent effects of cocaine administered alone. Connected data points represent effects of the two alcohol doses alone (■), and in combination with the 48 mg/70 kg (□) and 96 mg/70 kg (○) doses of cocaine. Brackets represent ± 1 SEM. From Higgins et al. (1992), with permission of the publisher.

factors that influence drug use. Two examples are provided of procedures developed by behavioral pharmacologists to study aspects of such interactions in non-residential, laboratory settings.

One of these examples involved the use of a concurrent schedule to study the increases in social interaction commonly observed with abused drugs (Higgins, Hughes, & Bickel, 1989). Two mutually exclusive options were concurrently available to eight volunteers during 60-min experimental sessions. Every 3 min, subjects chose between conversing with another same-sex volunteer or providing speech monologues for monetary reinforcement. In each of the available options, the topography of the response was the same (i.e., talking). The important distinction was that in one option talking was maintained via social reinforcement from another volunteer whereas in the other option talking was maintained by monetary reinforcement. Acute administration of *d*-amphetamine significantly increased choice of social over monetary reinforcement, suggesting that drug may enhance the relative reinforcing effects of social interaction (Figure 18.6). The lower panel of Figure 18.6 illustrates the reliability of this effect at the level of the individual subject. Similar effects have been observed with other abused drugs from different pharmacological classes suggesting that this shared behavioral effect may contribute to the abuse liability of particular drugs (e.g., Griffiths, Bigelow, & Liebson, 1975; Heishman & Stitzer 1989).

A second example involves the use of a concurrent schedule to study human aggression (Cherek, Bennett, & Grabowski, 1991). Eight healthy male tobacco smokers were provided deceptive instructions indicating that during experimental sessions they were paired with another individual who was located elsewhere in the building. The instructions indicated how to earn points and that any points subtracted from their earnings were added to the earnings of this other individual. Five 25-min experimental sessions were conducted each test day. Two response options were concurrently available. One was maintained under a fixed-ratio 100

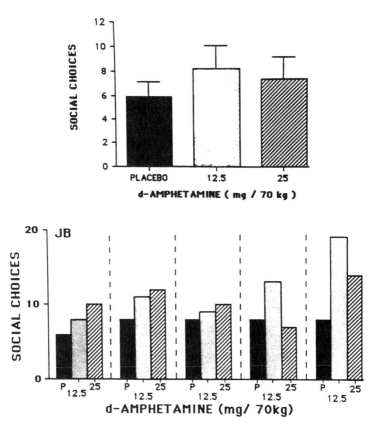

FIGURE 18.6. (Upper) Average number of choices of the social option as a function of placebo, 12.5, and 25 mg/70 kg d-amphetamine. Each bar is the mean for eight subjects and brackets represent 1 SEM. (Lower) Number of choices for the social option as a function of d-amphetamine dose for an individual subject (JB) across five sequential (left to right) dose–effect determinations. From Higgins et al. (1989), with permission of the publisher.

schedule of point presentation, with points being exchangeable for money (nonaggressive option). The second option was a fixed-ratio 10 schedule of ostensible subtraction of points from the other person paired with the subject (aggressive option). Responding on the second option was considered aggressive because it ostensibly resulted in infliction of harm to another person. Aggressive responding was provoked by intermittent experimenter-programmed point losses that were attributed to the other individual. Across successive test days, subjects were tobacco deprived and tested under four conditions: (1) ad-lib smoking, (2) placebo gum, (3) nicotine gum, and (4) no gum or smoking. On days when subjects received no gum or smoking, provocation increased aggressive responding significantly above levels observed under ad-lib smoking conditions. On days when subjects smoked or received active or placebo gum, aggression levels were intermediate between these two extremes. The significant differences observed between the conditions of ad-lib smoking and no smoking or gum provided objective evidence to substantiate prior reports of increased irritability during acute tobacco abstinence.

More recently, laboratory-analogue procedures have been developed to study drug effects on human cooperation and competition (e.g., Dougherty & Cherek, 1994; Spiga, Bennett, Cherek, & Grabowski, 1994; Spiga, Bennett, Schmitz, & Cherek, 1994). This approach of developing analogues of human social interaction for careful study of drug effects under controlled laboratory conditions has a great deal of unrealized potential. For additional information about methods to analyze social behavior, see Schmitt (Chapter 15).

Naturalistic Behavior in Residential Settings

As was noted above, residential settings offer opportunities to systematically study drug effects on naturalistic aspects of human social interaction. The following examples illustrate methods used for that purpose.

In one study, 12 men with histories of sedative abuse resided on an eight-bed research ward and were randomized to receive either placebo and two active doses of diazepam (placebo, 50, and 100 mg), a benzodiazepine, or placebo and two active doses of pentobarbital (placebo, 200, and 400 mg), a barbiturate (Griffiths et al., 1983). Subjects were exposed to each of the three dose conditions for 5 consecutive days. Ten to fourteen-day "washout" periods were interspersed between dose conditions to allow sufficient time for drug to be eliminated before beginning testing in the next condition. Dose order was randomized across subjects. Staff completed a global mood and behavior questionnaire rating mood, complaints, general behavior, and social interaction twice daily. Assessment in each of the areas involved four- or five-point rating scales, yes–no questions, and space for written comments.

Mean rating-scale scores during diazepam and pentobarbital treatment and placebo-washout periods are shown in Figure 18.7. Diazepam, but not pentobarbital, decreased staff ratings of subjects' mood and social interactions, and increased ratings of hostility, complaining, and unusual behavior. Those effects of diazepam dissipated during the placebo-washout periods. By routinely and systematically observing subjects' naturalistic behavior, a diazepam-specific deterioration in their social behavior was detected. Such observations can be of obvious clinical importance as sedative and other behaviorally active medications are often taken under chronic-dosing regimens.

In a second example, groups of three subjects resided in a residential ward designed for continuous 24-hr observation (Foltin et al., 1990). No staff came onto the ward during the experiment. The ward consisted of three identical efficiency apartments and a common social/recreation area and bathroom. Subjects were observed continuously by staff via audio and visual monitoring equipment except when in private dressing and toilet facilities. The purpose of this particular experiment was to assess the "amotivational" effects (i.e., decreased likelihood of initiating or sustaining responding) of smoked marijuana on responding maintained under behavioral contingencies. Following a baseline period in which subjects' preferred and nonpreferred activities were determined, contingencies were implemented requiring subjects to spend time in a nonpreferred activity (instrumental response) in order to earn time for engaging in a preferred activity (contingent activity). Subjects smoked 1-g marijuana cigarettes containing 0 (placebo)

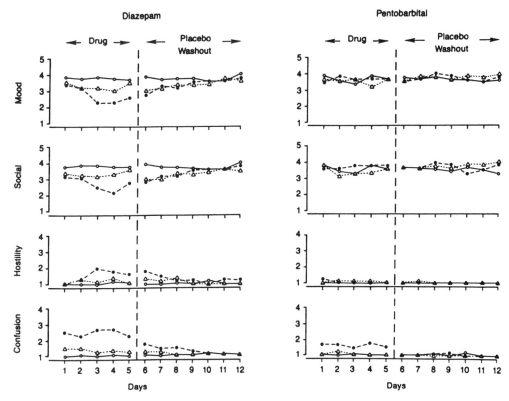

FIGURE 18.7. Effects of diazepam at left with placebo (○), 50 mg/day dose (△), and 100 mg/day dose (●) and pentobarbital at right with placebo (○), 200 mg/day dose (△), and 400 mg/day dose (●) on staff ratings of mood, social interactions, hostility, and confusion during 5-day drug periods, followed by 7-day placebo-washout periods. X axis: days: Y axis: staff ratings. From Griffiths et al. (1983), with permission of the publisher.

or 1.3–2.7% delta-9 THC twice daily. Implementation of the contingency reliably increased the amount of time subjects engaged in instrumental activities. However, in contrast to extant theories about the amotivational effects of marijuana, smoking the active marijuana cigarettes actually resulted in still further increases in the amount of time allocated to instrumental activities. Thus, these arrangements can be useful for rigorously examining the validity of commonly held beliefs about the behavioral effects of certain drugs, which often are based on anecdotal observation and may be incorrect. However, such issues must be treated cautiously because, as this chapter is illustrating, the behavioral effects of drugs are modulated by many factors. Whether laboratory-analogue arrangements or residential settings include the determinants necessary to observe certain drug effects that are reported to occur under more naturalistic conditions is a difficult challenge to which researchers in this area must and generally do remain sensitive. For a detailed discussion of some of the general problems and prospects in research conducted in residential environments, see Bernstein (Chapter 16).

Observer and Subject Rating Scales

Observer Ratings. A detailed example of the effective use of observer ratings was described in the immediately preceding section and shown in Figure 18.7. Observer ratings are also commonly used in studies examining the effects of abrupt cessation of chronic drug use (i.e., withdrawal scales). Hughes and Hatsukami (1986), for example, used an observer-rating scale in their study characterizing signs and symptoms of tobacco withdrawal. In that study, 31 smokers who had abruptly discontinued smoking were rated (0–3 scales) daily by their significant others (spouse, relative, or friend) on seven signs of withdrawal. Ratings were completed during 2 days of ad-lib smoking and the initial 4 days of tobacco abstinence. Observer ratings increased significantly on five of the seven items (Table 18.3, from Hughes & Hatsukami, 1986), providing further objective support for the validity of a tobacco withdrawal syndrome. Similar observer-rating scales are commonly used in characterizing opioid agonist and withdrawal effects in human behavioral pharmacology studies (e.g., Bickel, Stitzer, Liebson, & Bigelow, 1988; Preston, Bigelow, & Liebson, 1988).

Subject Ratings. Subject ratings of drug effects are commonly included in human behavioral pharmacology studies related to drug abuse. Commonly used methods are visual-analogue scales, the short form of the Addiction Research Center Inventory (ARCI) (Haertzen, 1966), and the Profile of Mood States (POMS) (McNair, Lorr, & Droppleman, 1971). Visual-analogue scales are typically 100-point scales marked at opposite ends with phrases such as "not at all" and "extremely." Questions often address specific aspects of drug effects (e.g., How high are you?), mood (e.g., Are you elated?), and other items of interest (e.g., How sleepy are you?). The ARCI is a 49-item true–false questionnaire that has been empirically separated into the following five subscales associated with different drug classes: amphetamine (A) and benzedrine (BG) scales designed to measure stimulant effects, the morphine–benzedrine group scale (MBG), which putatively measures euphoric effects, the pentobarbital–chlorpromazine–alcohol group scale (PCAG) designed to measure sedative effects, and the lysergic acid scale (LSD) designed to measure psychotomimetic effects. The POMS consists of 72 adjectives describing mood

TABLE 18.3
Mean (SE) for Observer Ratings[a]

	Baseline	Abstinence	t
Observer ratings ($n = 31$)			
Irritability	0.4 (0.1)	0.9 (0.1)	5.0*
Anxiety	0.6 (0.1)	1.1 (0.1)	4.0*
Restlessness	0.4 (0.1)	0.9 (0.1)	5.0*
Drowsiness	0.3 (0.1)	0.3 (0.1)	NS
Fatigue	0.3 (0.1)	0.4 (0.1)	NS
Impatience	0.5 (0.1)	1.0 (0.1)	4.3[b]
Somatic complaints	0.2 (0.1)	0.4 (0.1)	2.8[c]

[a]Adapted from Hughes and Hatsukami (1986), with permission of the publisher.
[b]$p < .001$.
[c]$p < .05$.

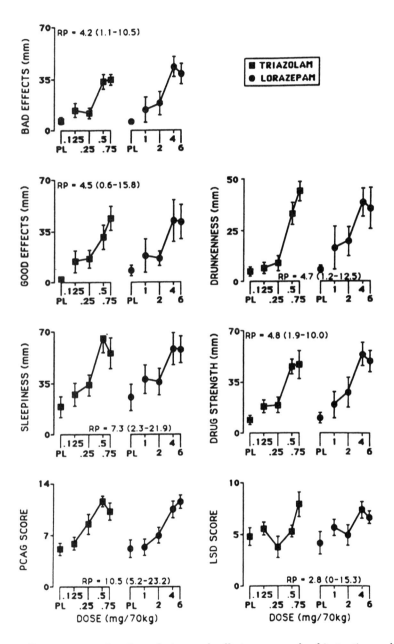

FIGURE 18.8. Dose–response functions during peak effects on several subject-rating scales. X axis: dose expressed in milligrams per 70 kg body weight. Y axis: mean ratings. All else as in upper panel of Figure 18.1. From Rush et al. (1993), with permission of the publisher.

states and separated into the following empirically derived clusters: anxiety, depression, vigor, fatigue, confusion, friendliness.

Subjects typically receive no or minimal training with these scales prior to drug testing. Nevertheless, the scales often prove to be sensitive to drug effects, to differentiate between drugs, and to yield orderly dose–response relationships. Figure 18.8 shows results from the study by Rush et al. (1993) described above comparing the acute effects of triazolam and lorazepam, and illustrates the orderly and useful information that can be obtained using these methods. For a general discussion of self-report methods in behavior analysis, see Critchfield, Tucker, and Vuchinich (Chapter 14).

Stimulus Functions of Drugs

Drugs as Antecedents

Drug-Discrimination Procedures. Abused drugs produce a variety of interoceptive (arising within the body) stimulus effects, and those effects can acquire discriminative control over operant behavior. In the same manner that lights and various other types of exteroceptive (arising outside the body) stimuli can serve discriminative functions, so can the interoceptive stimulus effects of drugs.

Drug-discrimination procedures have been widely studied with nonhuman subjects (see Stolerman, 1993). The basic method is to reinforce a particular operant response (e.g., pressing the left lever) following administration of the training drug but not a control substance, and conversely, to reinforce a different operant response (e.g., pressing the right lever) following administration of the control substance but not the training drug. The discriminations trained in such studies are typically characterized by a high degree of pharmacological specificity. For example, after a morphine versus saline discrimination is established, administration of pharmacologically unrelated drugs (e.g., *d*-amphetamine) do not occasion morphinelike responding, whereas administration of other mu-opioid-receptor agonists (e.g., hydromorphone) do so consistently. Because of the high degree of pharmacological specificity observed with drug-discrimination procedures, they have been used extensively in assessing similarities among drugs from the same and different pharmacological classes. There is also a high degree of concordance between the results of drug-discrimination and neuropharmacological receptor-binding studies. For example, the relative potencies of various benzodiazepines for occasioning diazepam-appropriate responding in organisms trained to discriminate diazepam from placebo are highly correlated with their potencies in displacing tritiated diazepam from brain receptors (Glennon & Young, 1987). Hence, these procedures have become standard assays in both behavioral and neuropharmacology research (cf. Branch, 1984; Colpaert, 1986).

Drug-discrimination procedures have been adapted for use with humans only recently. Thus far, opioids (e.g., Bickel, Bigelow, Preston, & Liebson, 1989; Preston et al., 1987), sedatives (e.g., Oliveto, Bickel, Hughes, Higgins, & Fenwick, 1992), and stimulants (e.g., Chait, Uhlenhuth, & Johanson, 1984; Oliveto, Rosen, Woods, & Kosten, 1995) have been successfully established as discriminative stimuli in humans. The most basic procedure used with humans is the two-key discrimination described above in which two operants are differentially reinforced depending on whether the training drug or a control substance was administered. A study with caffeine illustrates the procedure (Oliveto, Bickel, Hughes, Shea, et al., 1992). Healthy male and female volunteers learned a discrimination between a 320 mg/70 kg oral dose of caffeine and placebo administered under double-blind conditions. Drugs were assigned arbitrary letter codes of A and B. During four training sessions (Sessions 1–4), subjects were (a) exposed twice to each substance on separate days, (b) informed of the drug's letter code at the time of administration, (c) instructed to learn to distinguish between the two compounds, and (d) instructed that money could be earned by correctly identifying the administered drug by letter code. Next (Sessions 5–11), subjects entered a test-of-acquisition phase, during which they received Drugs A and B on different days under double-blind conditions. During the experimental session, subjects were provided two 3-min periods in which they could earn points exchangeable for money under a fixed-interval (FI) 1-s schedule of reinforcement by distributing responses across two options corresponding to the letter-coded drugs. Subjects did not receive feedback regarding the accuracy of their responses on any of these procedures until the end of the session when the correct letter code was revealed and subjects were paid money according to the accuracy of their responses during the session (e.g., if Drug A was administered, only responses on the option corresponding to that drug earned money). When subjects achieved a predetermined accuracy criterion (≥ 85% accuracy on four consecutive sessions) during the test-of-acquisition phase, they entered a test phase during which different doses of caffeine (four subjects) and a novel drug, triazolam (three subjects), were tested across separate sessions.

Results from the four subjects who completed testing with caffeine and three subjects who were tested with triazolam are shown in Figure 18.9. Accuracy of responding approximated 100% at the 320 mg/70 kg training dose and then decreased as a graded function of decreasing caffeine dose, thereby producing an orderly generalization gradient (upper left panel). None of the caffeine doses affected rates of responding (lower left panel). Testing with varying doses of triazolam did not occasion responding on the caffeine lever above placebo levels, demonstrating the pharmacological specificity of the caffeine discrimination (upper right panel). The two higher doses of triazolam were behaviorally active as indicated by the decreases in rates of responding observed with them (lower right panel).

Overall, this study demonstrated that the interoceptive stimulus effects of caffeine can acquire a discriminative function in humans that generalizes to novel doses of the same drug but not to doses of a novel drug from a different pharmacological class.

Drug-discrimination studies in humans also can be conducted using a three-drug discrimination (Drug A versus Drug B versus placebo). An advantage of the three-drug discrimination is greater specificity because subjects are required to discriminate between two active drugs. For example, subjects with histories of drug abuse resided on a residential ward and were trained to discriminate between hydromorphone (a mu-opioid-receptor agonist), pentazocine (a mixed opioid agonist-antagonist that has affinity for multiple opioid receptor subtypes), and placebo (Bickel et al., 1989). Procedures generally were the same as described above except for additional training sessions to accommodate the additional drug. The

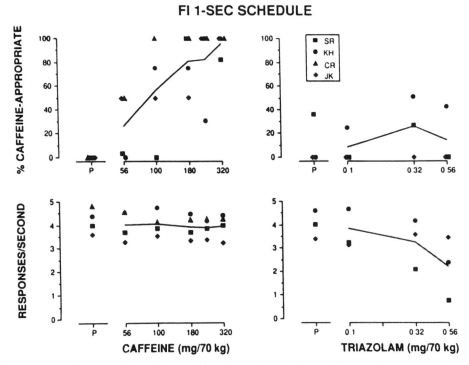

FIGURE 18.9.   Effects of caffeine (left panels) and triazolam (right panels) on performance under an FI
1-s schedule of point presentation. Y axis: discrimination performance expressed as percentage of total responding that occurred on the response key paired with caffeine (top panels) and rate of responding expressed as responses per second. X axis: dose of caffeine (left panels) and triazolam (right
panels) expressed as mg/70 kg body weight. Data points above P represent performance when placebo
was administered. Each line represents the mean of four subjects for caffeine and three subjects for triazolam. One subject terminated participation in the study before testing with triazolam was conducted. From Oliveto, Bickel, Hughes, Shea, Higgins, and Fenwick, (1992), with permission of the publisher.

results from this study demonstrated that a three-drug discrimination could be established in humans, and testing with a wide range of doses of the training drugs
resulted in dose-related increases in discriminative performance consistent with
the effects of caffeine described above. Also consistent with the results with caffeine, the discriminative stimulus effects of hydromorphone did not generalize to
the effects of novel drugs such as *d*-amphetamine, lorazepam, and secobarbital.
Some partial generalization between the effects of hydromorphone and those of
pentazocine and saline was observed.

   An interesting methodological advance in this research area that to date has
been used only with human subjects is a novel-response procedure (Bickel, Oliveto, Kamien, Higgins, & Hughes, 1993). This procedure is designed to add still
greater specificity to the discrimination procedures. In the conventional drug-discrimination procedures, novel drugs that are pharmacologically dissimilar to the
drugs subjects have been trained to discriminate typically occasion responding on
the placebo lever, that is, subjects emit responses on the key on which responses

were reinforced following placebo administration. Interpretation of such responding is difficult because it may be occasioned by the absence of any drug effect or the absence of a specific drug effect.

To begin to address this issue, a procedure was developed in which subjects were trained to respond on a "novel" key when drug effects occurred that were unlike those produced by the training drug. Instructions indicated that only responses on the novel key would be reinforced in the presence of unfamiliar drug effects. Four healthy male volunteers were trained to discriminate 0.32 mg/70 kg of orally administered triazolam from placebo. Following training to criterion levels of performance, a range of doses of triazolam, the training drug, and d-amphetamine, a novel drug, were tested using a standard two-key procedure (drug key versus placebo key) and this new novel-key procedure (drug key versus placebo key versus novel-drug key). Triazolam produced dose-related increases in responding on the drug key in both procedures. d-Amphetamine produced predominately placebo-key responding with the two-key procedure and predominately novel-key responding in the novel-key procedure. That is, the novel-key procedure generated greater selectivity than the two-key procedure in terms of the conditions that would occasion responding on the placebo key, and provided a more detailed characterization of the profile of interoceptive stimulus effects produced by the compounds tested. Additional studies have been completed with this new procedure illustrating its utility for increasing specificity in human drug-discrimination testing (Kamien et al., 1994; Oliveto, Bickel, Kamien, Hughes, & Higgins, 1994).

Human drug-discrimination procedures offer a unique method to investigate similarities and differences between various drugs. The high degree of specificity that can be obtained permits subtle distinctions between seemingly similar drugs. These procedures are sufficiently similar to those used with laboratory animals to facilitate fruitful cross-species comparisons and an impressive degree of generality has been observed (Kamien, Bickel, Hughes, Higgins, & Smith, 1993).

Along with many important and positive features, drug-discrimination procedures are associated with several disadvantages. One is that training and testing can require many sessions (e.g., > 50 sessions), with attendant problems with subject recruitment and retention. Extended training also involves numerous drug exposures that can increase risks to subjects and involve greater costs in payment to subjects and staff. Although nonresidential settings reduce costs, they have some limitations, including restriction to lower drug doses and attendant loss of specificity of the discrimination. An effective compromise is to conduct studies in nonresidential settings, but have subjects remain on site while under the influence of drug.

Use of cumulative dosing also could prove very helpful. With moderate and longer-acting drugs, it is possible to administer an initial dose, measure its effects, administer a second dose, which because the first dose is still acting approximates the sum of the first and second doses, measure its effects, administer a third dose, which approximates the sum of the first, second, and third doses, and so on, until you have tested a full range of doses within a single session. This procedure is used with some regularity in behavioral pharmacology studies with nonhumans (cf. Branch, 1991), and is currently being investigated and appears to be effective in human drug-discrimination research (Smith, Bickel, Higgins, Hughes, & Kamien, 1995).

Drug-Discrimination and Stimulus-Equivalence Procedures. A potentially important but little-researched topic in this area of research involves an integration of drug-discrimination and stimulus-equivalence procedures (see Green & Saunders, Chapter 8). In stimulus-equivalence research, relations are trained between different environmental stimuli via matching-to-sample procedures (Sidman & Tailby, 1982). First, a relationship is trained between stimuli A and B and stimuli B and C. For example, when stimulus A is the sample stimulus and stimuli B and X are comparison stimuli, choosing stimulus B is reinforced. Similarly, when stimulus B is the sample stimulus and stimuli C and X are comparison stimuli, choosing stimulus C is reinforced. With such training, an untrained relation emerges between A and C; that is, if stimulus A is presented as the sample stimulus and stimuli C and X as comparison stimuli, subjects choose stimulus C even though this relation was never trained. Adding another relationship, this time between stimulus C and a new stimulus D would produce the novel untrained relationships between A and D and between B and D. This process is generative in that each new relationship that is added produces a still greater yield of untrained relations. All of these stimulus relations, trained and untrained, are considered to share membership in a stimulus class.

In what, to our knowledge, is the only study combining drug-discrimination and stimulus-equivalence procedures, DeGrandpre and colleagues (DeGrandpre, Bickel, & Higgins, 1992) examined whether the interoceptive stimulus effects of an orally administered dose of triazolam (0.375 mg/70 kg) could enter into stimulus-equivalence relations with exteroceptive stimuli. Through the same generative development described above, the drug stimulus and numerous other trained and untrained exteroceptive stimuli came to control the same response, that is, they became members of the same stimulus class. This research is important in that it illustrates a mechanism whereby formerly neutral environmental stimuli can come to control druglike responses even though they were never directly paired with the drug itself. Although this line of research is in its very early stages, it has important implications for understanding the pervasive control that abused drugs often exert over the behavior of dependent individuals (see DeGrandpre & Bickel, 1993).

Drugs as Consequences

Drug Self-Administration. Of fundamental importance in drug abuse is the act of drug taking or, more technically, drug self-administration. Without drug self-administration, there can be no problem of drug abuse. An extensive body of research with laboratory animals and humans demonstrates that drug self-administration is a form of operant behavior that is maintained by the reinforcing effects of drugs (Brady, 1981; Griffiths, Bigelow, & Henningfield, 1980). This empirical observation represents an important advance because it permits investigators to apply to the study of drug abuse the methodological and conceptual advances previously established with other forms of operant behavior.

In self-administration research, drug reinforcement is inferred when the rate of drug intake, or choice of drug, exceeds levels observed with a placebo. The levels of self administration maintained by drug and placebo can be compared sequentially or concurrently.

Sequential Self-Administration Testing. In sequential comparisons, subjects are provided access to active drug and placebo across sequential conditions of the experiment and drug reinforcement is inferred when the drug is self-administered at a rate that reliably exceeds levels observed with placebo.

This procedure is illustrated in a study on sedative self-administration (Griffiths, Bigelow, & Liebson, 1979). Nineteen sedative abusers residing on a research ward were provided an opportunity to self-administer different drugs and doses during sequential 5- to 15-day periods. A maximum of 10 ingestions per day were available under a contingency wherein subjects had to ride an exercycle for 15 min per ingestion. Daily rates of pentobarbital self-administration are shown in Figure 18.10. Rates of self-administration varied as an orderly function of dose, with 90

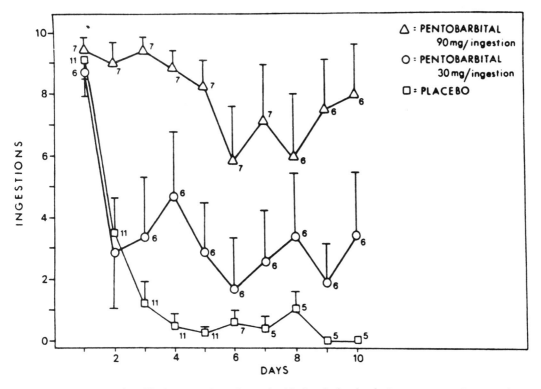

FIGURE 18.10.   Daily self-administration of pentobarbital and placebo during 10 consecutive experimental days. Y axis: ingestions. X axis: consecutive experimental days. Points show mean number of ingestions consumed daily for pentobarbital 90 mg/ingestion (△), pentobarbital 30 mg/ingestion (○), and placebo (□). Brackets indicate 1 SEM. Numerals indicate number of subjects. From Griffiths et al. (1979), with permission of the publisher.

mg/ingestion maintaining the highest rate, 30 mg/ingestion an intermediate rate, and the placebo dose the lowest rate. The increased rates of self-administration of the active drug doses compared with placebo indicated that pentobarbital functioned as a reinforcer.

Concurrent Self-Administration Testing. When using concurrent procedures, reinforcement is inferred when drug is chosen over placebo during either discrete-trials (e.g., Griffiths, Bigelow, & Liebson, 1989) or free-operant (e.g., Hughes et al., 1991) access to the two substances.

A study on caffeine self-administration using a discrete-trials procedure illustrates the use of concurrent testing (Griffiths et al., 1989). Six heavy coffee drinkers residing on a research ward were provided hourly opportunities during 12-hr periods to ingest color-coded capsules containing 100 mg of caffeine or placebo, or to take no capsules. Permitting subjects the option of forgoing either capsule was an important feature for inferring reinforcement. Otherwise, it would have been a forced-choice arrangement wherein, for example, subjects may have simply chosen between the least of two undesirable alternatives. Testing was double-blind. Capsules were available contingent on a simple verbal request. Caffeine was reliably chosen over placebo capsules in all six subjects tested, and was ingested at daily rates exceeding twelve 100-mg capsules in some subjects. Under these conditions, the experimenter could infer that caffeine functioned as a reinforcer in maintaining choice behavior.

Multiple-Choice Procedure. Griffiths and colleagues (Griffiths, Troisi, Silverman, & Mumford, 1993) recently made an interesting methodological contribution to the use of choice procedures to study drug self-administration in humans. With this procedure, referred to as the Multiple Choice Procedure, subjects are first exposed to various drugs or drug doses. In subsequent sessions, they are provided a questionnaire that lists two-item choices between the various drugs or doses to which subjects have been exposed. Choices between the drugs and varying amounts of money are also listed. Subjects indicate on the questionnaire their preferences between the listed items. On completion of the questionnaire, one of the preferences listed on the questionnaire is delivered by the experimenter. Which of the many choices that subjects have listed is consequated is determined randomly.

In the seminal study using this procedure, the information obtained regarding preference for pentobarbital was consistent with results obtained with more conventional drug self-administration procedures (Griffiths et al., 1993). The procedure has since been used effectively in additional studies of human drug self-administration (e.g., Griffiths, Rush, & Puhala, 1996; Silverman, Mumford, & Griffiths, 1994). This method has great potential for assessing preference between numerous reinforcers in humans in a single, brief experimental test session. Of course, drug exposure sessions are needed as well, but even with exposure sessions included, this new method has the potential to substantially shorten the duration of self-administration studies while also increasing the amount and diversity of information obtained. To our knowledge, the procedure only has been used to study drug reinforcement, but would appear to have applicability to the study of a wide variety of reinforcers in humans.

Environmental Factors Influencing Drug Self-Administration. Many environmental factors influence human drug self-administration, including drug dose (Griffiths et al., 1979), response requirement (Bickel, DeGrandpre, Hughes, & Higgins, 1991), environmental context (Silverman, Kirby, & Griffiths, 1994), experimenter instructions (Hughes, Pickens, Spring, & Keenan, 1985), and history of drug use (Hughes et al., 1990). Studies of the modulation of drug reinforcement by environmental factors under controlled laboratory conditions can have important potential clinical implications.

A study examining the influence of an alternative, monetary reinforcer on preference for intranasal doses of cocaine serves as a good example (Higgins, Bickel, & Hughes, 1994). Subjects were current users of cocaine who reported no evidence of current or past cocaine or other drug dependence, with the exception of nicotine dependence. In a discrete-trial arrangement, subjects were permitted to make a maximum of 10 exclusive choices between 10 mg of cocaine, varying amounts of money, or neither. Drug and money were available under fixed-ratio 10 schedules of reinforcement. The drug option exerted exclusive control when the value in the monetary option was zero, demonstrating the high degree of behavioral control cocaine can exert under some conditions (Figure 18.11). How-

□ **First Exposure**
■ **Second Exposure**

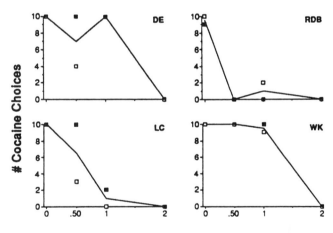

FIGURE 18.11. Number of choices (Y axis) are plotted as a function of the value of money available per choice in the monetary option (X axis). Subjects made a maximum of 10 choices between cocaine versus money each session. Data are presented for each of four individual subjects and as a group average. Results from the first and second exposures to the different monetary values are shown separately. From Higgins, Bickel, and Hughes (1994), with permission of the publisher.

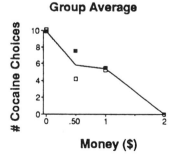

ever, as the monetary value increased, choice of the drug option decreased, with the monetary option exerting exclusive control at the $2 per choice value. The shift in control from the drug to the monetary option in this study illustrates that the degree of behavioral control exerted by cocaine's reinforcing effects is dependent on the availability and magnitude of alternative reinforcers. These results provide important additional empirical support for the positive results obtained in treatment studies with cocaine-dependent samples in which the contingent provision of prosocial, alternative reinforcers increased cocaine abstinence (Higgins, Budney, Bickel, Foerg, et al., 1994; Silverman et al., 1996). Similar results also have been obtained in laboratory studies with nonhumans self-administering cocaine (e.g., Nader & Woolverton, 1991), further strengthening the evidence for the fundamental role of reinforcement and behavioral context in cocaine use and abuse.

Schedules of Drug Reinforcement. Most of the simple schedules of reinforcement have been used in drug self-administration studies with humans, but their relative merits have not been systematically examined. Choice of one over another at this time appears to be determined by the larger experimental question under investigation. Second-order schedules and progressive-ratio schedules, which are commonly used in self-administration research with nonhumans, have each been successfully adapted for use with humans (Lamb et al., 1991; McLeod & Griffiths, 1983; Mello & Mendelson, 1987; Mello, Mendelson, & Kuehnle, 1982). A great deal remains to be learned about the influence of the schedule of reinforcement on the genesis and maintenance of human drug self-administration.

Behavioral Economics. An important advance in drug self-administration research was the application of the concepts and methods of behavioral economics to this subject matter (see Bickel, DeGrandpre, & Higgins, 1993, for a review). A study of human cigarette smoking under controlled laboratory conditions provides a good illustration of this approach (Bickel et al., 1991). The study examined the interaction of various fixed-ratio values and reinforcer magnitudes (number of puffs on a cigarette) on responding maintained by cigarette smoking in three male and two female deprived smokers. The central question was whether unit price (response requirement/reinforcer magnitude) was the important determinant of the level of drug consumption (i.e., the number of puffs taken). As shown in Figure 18.12, drug consumption was comparable at the same unit price independent of which combination of response requirement and reinforcer magnitude made up that unit price. Increasing unit price generally decreased consumption.

The scientific importance of this observation was that schedule of availability and reinforcer magnitude, which were previously treated as two separate variables, were shown to operate as a single variable, unit price. The ability of unit price to more parsimoniously summarize the influence of the schedule of drug availability and dose or reinforcer magnitude does not appear to be unique to human cigarette smoking. A review of selected self-administration studies conducted with laboratory animals supported the generality of this unit-price analysis to other species, drugs, and routes of drug administration (Bickel, DeGrandpre, Higgins, & Hughes, 1990). Behavioral economics also has been effective in elucidating how drug pretreatment and the availability of nondrug reinforcers influence

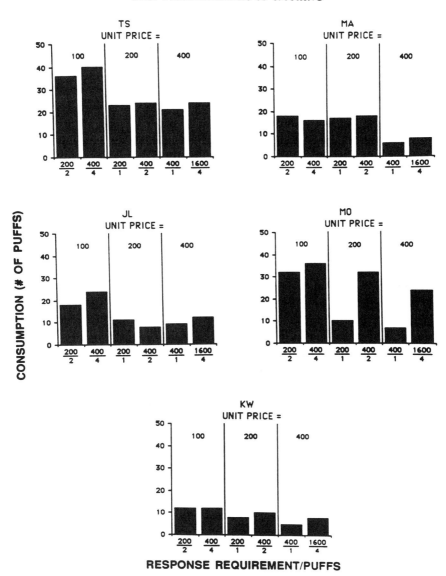

UNIT-PRICE ANALYSIS OF SMOKING

FIGURE 18.12.   Consumption (number of puffs on a cigarette) is shown on the Y axis for five individual subjects at three replicated unit prices (100, 200, and 400) for each subject. Response requirements
and reinforcer magnitudes making up each unit price (unit price = response requirement/number of
puffs) are shown on the X axis. From Bickel et al. (1991), with permission of the publisher.

drug self-administration in humans and laboratory animals (Bickel, DeGrandpre &
Higgins, 1993; Carroll, Carmona, & May, 1991).

Selecting a Self-Administration Method. No general rules have been established concerning which methods or procedures are more effective for studying
drug self-administration in humans. The most important determinant continues to

be the experimental question. For example, second-order schedules with brief stimulus presentations would be a good procedure to study the influence of conditioned reinforcers on human drug self-administration, but may be unnecessarily cumbersome in assessing new drugs for reinforcing effects (i.e., abuse liability testing). Investigators must choose a method based on the experimental question being addressed and other particulars of the study.

Aversive Effects of Drugs. In addition to reinforcing effects, drugs also can produce aversive effects. Aversive effects of drugs have been demonstrated in numerous studies conducted with laboratory animals (e.g., Downs & Woods, 1976; Goldberg & Spealman, 1982) but, to our knowledge, in only one study conducted with humans (Henningfield & Goldberg, 1983). In the study with humans, response-independent intravenous injections of nicotine or vehicle were delivered at designated intervals. Injections could be avoided by pressing a lever under a fixed-ratio 10 schedule. Avoidance responding was well maintained during nicotine but not vehicle conditions, demonstrating that responding was maintained by the aversive effects of the drug. Obviously, under other conditions nicotine can function as a reinforcer in humans. An important point to be made about these multiple functions of nicotine is that whether drugs function as aversive or reinforcing stimuli is not an inherent characteristic of their physical properties alone, but, rather, is dependent on a myriad of environmental factors (Hughes, 1989).

Monitoring Physiological Responses to Drugs

Physiological effects of drugs are commonly recorded in human behavioral pharmacology studies. The physiological responses recorded vary widely across studies, depending on the type of drug being investigated and purpose of the study. Some common physiological responses that are studied include cardiac functioning (heart rate, blood pressure, electrocardiogram), respiration rate, skin temperature, pupil diameter, and drug levels in body fluids (blood, urine, expired air, saliva). The methods and equipment used to record these responses vary across studies. New investigators can benefit from consulting the published literature on studies related to their interests, consulting established investigators, and contacting suppliers of medical equipment.

The kind of physiological results routinely reported in human behavioral pharmacology studies is displayed in Figure 18.13. Time–response functions are shown for the effects of varying doses of intranasally administered cocaine on several measures of cardiac functioning and skin temperature in eight healthy, adult volunteers (Higgins et al., 1990). Cocaine produced orderly dose- and time-dependent effects across each of the physiological measures. Those physiological measures provided an important complement to the measures of learning, performance, and subject-rated drug effects that were also included in this report.

CONCLUSIONS

Human behavioral pharmacology has made substantive methodological advances during the approximately 25 years it has been thriving. Effective laborato-

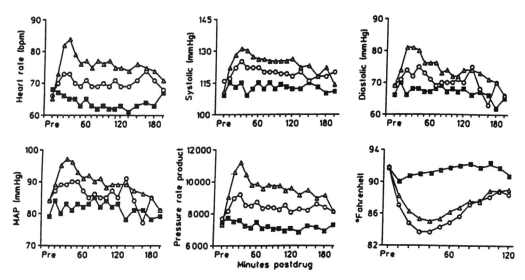

FIGURE 18.13.   Time–response functions for the effects of cocaine dose on cardiac measures and skin temperature. Data points represent means for eight subjects across two observations per dose. ■, placebo; ○, 48 mg/70 kg; △, 96 mg/70 kg. From Higgins et al. (1990), with permission of the publisher.

ry methods have been developed to research drug effects on a wide spectrum of arbitrary and naturalistic forms of human behavior and physiological functioning. The comprehensive nature of the available methods is impressive. Methods are in place for making contributions ranging from basic-science issues regarding relationships between behavioral and neuropharmacological effects of drugs to the development of laboratory analogues of human social interaction. These contributions have been recognized by others and research in this area generally is well supported via research grants and contracts from federal agencies and pharmaceutical companies. As such, human behavioral pharmacology should be considered a viable career option for students and an important area in which funding can be obtained to conduct and expand basic human-operant research.

ACKNOWLEDGMENTS. Preparation of this chapter was supported by Grants DA08076, DA04843, and K0200109 from the National Institute on Drug Abuse. Thanks to Jennifer Tidy, Ph.D., for comments on the manuscript, and Dale Desranleau and Mindee Peterson for their assistance.

REFERENCES

Benet, L. Z. (1996). Introduction. In J. G. Hardman, L. E. Limbird, P. B. Molinoff, R. W. Ruddon, & A. G. Gilman (Eds.), *Goodman and Gilman's the pharmacological basis of therapeutics* (9th ed., pp. 1–2). New York: McGraw–Hill.

Benet, L. Z., Kroetz, D. L., & Sheiner, L. B. (1996). Pharmacokinetics: The dynamics of drug absorption, distribution, and elimination. In J. G. Hardman, L. E. Limbird, P. B. Molinoff, R. W. Ruddon, & A. G. Gilman (Eds.), *Goodman and Gilman's the pharmacological basis of therapeutics* (9th ed., pp. 3–27). New York: McGraw–Hill.

Bickel, W. K., Bigelow, G. E., Preston, K. L., & Liebson, I. A. (1989). Opioid drug discrimination in humans: Stability, specificity and relation to self-reported drug effect. *Journal of Pharmacology and Experimental Therapeutics, 251,* 1053–1063.

Bickel, W. K., DeGrandpre, R. J., & Higgins, S. T. (1993). Behavioral economics: A novel experimental approach to the study of drug dependence. *Drug and Alcohol Dependence, 33,* 173–192.

Bickel, W. K., DeGrandpre, R. J., Higgins, S. T., & Hughes, J. R. (1990). Behavioral economics of drug self-administration. I. Functional equivalence of response requirement and drug dose. *Life Sciences, 47,* 1501–1510.

Bickel, W. K., DeGrandpre, R. J., Hughes, J. R., & Higgins, S. T. (1991). Behavioral economics of drug self-administration. II. A unit-price analysis of cigarette smoking. *Journal of the Experimental Analysis of Behavior, 55,* 145–154.

Bickel, W. K., Oliveto, A. H., Kamien, J. B., Higgins, S. T., & Hughes, J. R. (1993). A novel-response procedure enhances the selectivity and sensitivity of a triazolam discrimination in humans. *Journal of Pharmacology and Experimental Therapeutics, 264,* 360–367.

Bickel, W. K., Stitzer, M. L., Liebson, I. A., & Bigelow, G. E. (1988). Acute physical dependence in man: Effects of naloxone after brief morphine exposure. *Journal of Pharmacology and Experimental Therapeutics, 244,* 126–132.

Bigelow, G., & Liebson, I. (1972). Cost factors controlling alcoholic drinking. *Psychological Record, 22,* 305–314.

Bigelow, G., Liebson, I., & Griffiths, R. (1974). Alcoholic drinking: Suppression by a brief time-out procedure. *Behavior Research and Therapy, 12,* 107–115.

Bigelow, G. E., Stitzer, M. L., Griffiths, R. R., & Liebson, I. A. (1981). Contingency management approaches to drug self-administration and drug abuse: Efficacy and limitations. *Addictive Behaviors, 6,* 241–252.

Brady, J. V. (1981). Common mechanisms in substance abuse. In T. Thompson & C. E. Johanson (Eds.), *Behavioral pharmacology of human drug dependence, NIDA Research Monograph 37* (DHHS Publication No. ADM 81-1137, pp. 11–20). Washington, DC: U.S. Government Printing Office.

Brady, J. V. (1989). Issues in human drug abuse liability testing: Overview and prospects for the future. In M. W. Fischman & N. K. Mello (Eds.), *Testing for abuse liability of drugs in humans, NIDA Research Monograph 92* (DHHS Publication No. ADM 89-1613, pp. 357–370). Washington, DC: U.S. Government Printing Office.

Branch, M. N. (1984). Rate dependency, behavioral mechanisms, and behavioral pharmacology. *Journal of the Experimental Analysis of Behavior, 42,* 512–522.

Branch, M. N. (1991). Behavioral pharmacology. In I. H. Iversen & K. A. Lattal (Eds.), *Experimental analysis of behavior: Part 2* (pp. 21–77). Amsterdam: Elsevier.

Carroll, M. E., Carmona, G. G., & May, S. A. (1991). Modifying drug reinforced behavior by altering the economic conditions of the drug and nondrug reinforcer. *Journal of the Experimental Analysis of Behavior, 56,* 361–376.

Chait, L. D., Uhlenhuth, E. H., & Johanson, C. E. (1984). An experimental paradigm for studying the discriminative stimulus properties of drugs in humans. *Psychopharmacology, 82,* 272–274.

Cherek, D. R., Bennett, R. H., & Grabowski, J. (1991). Human aggressive responding during acute tobacco abstinence: Effects of nicotine and placebo gum. *Psychopharmacology, 104,* 317–322.

College on Problems of Drug Dependence. (1995). Human subject issues in drug abuse research. *Drug and Alcohol Dependence, 37,* 167–173.

Colpaert, F. C. (1986). Drug discrimination: Behavioral, pharmacological, and molecular mechanisms of discriminative drug effects. In S. R. Goldberg & I. P. Stolerman (Eds.), *Behavioral analysis of drug dependence* (pp. 161–193). New York: Academic Press.

Cooper, J. R., Bloom, F. E., & Roth, R. H. (1991). *The biochemical basis of neuropharamcology* (6th ed.). London: Oxford University Press.

DeGrandpre, R. J., & Bickel, W. K. (1993). Stimulus control and drug dependence. *The Psychological Record, 43,* 651–666.

DeGrandpre, R. J., Bickel, W. K., & Higgins, S. T. (1992). Emergent equivalence relations between interoceptive (drug) and exteroceptive (visual) stimuli. *Journal of the Experimental Analysis of Behavior, 58,* 9–18.

Desjardins, P. J., Moerschbaecher, J. M., & Thompson, D. M. (1982). Intravenous diazepam in humans: Effects on acquisition and performance of response chains. *Pharmacology Biochemistry and Behavior, 17,* 1055–1059.

Dews, P. B., & Morse, W. H. (1958). Some observations on an operant in human subjects and its modification by dextro amphetamine. *Journal of the Experimental Analysis of Behavior, 1,* 359–364.

Dews, P. B., & Morse, W. H. (1961). Behavioral pharmacology. *Annual Reviews of Pharmacology, 1,* 145–174.

Dixon, W. J. (1988). *BMDP statistical manual* (Vol. 1). Berkeley: University of California Press.

Dougherty, D. M., & Cherek, D. R. (1994). Effects of social context, reinforcer probability, and reinforcer magnitude on humans' choices to compete or not compete. *Journal of the Experimental Analysis of Behavior, 62,* 133–148.

Downs, D. A., & Woods, J. H. (1976). Naloxone as a negative reinforcer in rhesus monkeys: Effects of dose, schedule, and narcotic regimen. *Pharmacological Reviews, 27,* 397–406.

Finney, J. D. (1964). *Statistical methods in biological assay.* New York: Hafner.

Fischman, M. W., & Mello, N. K. (Eds.). (1989). *Testing for abuse liability of drugs in humans, NIDA Research Monograph 92* (DHHS Publication No. ADM 98-1613). Washington, DC: U.S. Government Printing Office.

Foltin, R. W., Fischman, M. W., Brady, J. V., Bernstein, D. J., Capriotti, R. M., Nellis, M. J., & Kelly, T. H. (1990). Motivational effects of smoked marijuana: Behavioral contingencies and low probability activities. *Journal of the Experimental Analysis of Behavior, 53,* 5–19.

Glennon, R. A., & Young, R. (1987). The study of structure–activity relationships using drug discrimination methodology. In M. A. Bozarth (Ed.), *Methods of assessing the reinforcing properties of abused rugs* (pp. 373–390). Berlin: Springer-Verlag.

Goldberg, S. R., & Spealman, R. D. (1982). Maintenance and suppression of responding by intravenous nicotine injections in squirrel monkeys. *Federation Proceedings, 41,* 216–220.

Grabowski, J., & VandenBos, G. R. (Eds.). (1992). *Psychopharmacology: Basic mechanisms and applied interventions.* Washington, DC: American Psychological Association.

Griffiths, R. R., Bigelow, G. E., & Henningfield, J. E. (1980). Similarities in animal and human drug taking behavior. In N. K. Mello (Ed.), *Advances in substance abuse: Behavioral and biological research* (pp. 1–90). Greenwich, CT: JAI Press.

Griffiths, R. R., Bigelow, G. E., & Liebson, I. (1975). Effects of ethanol self-administration on choice behavior: Money vs. socializing. *Pharmacology Biochemistry and Behavior, 34,* 303–311.

Griffiths, R. R., Bigelow, G., & Liebson, I. A. (1979). Human drug self-administration: Double-blind comparison of pentobarbital, diazepam, chlorpromazine and placebo. *Journal of Pharmacology and Experimental Therapeutics, 210,* 301–310.

Griffiths, R. R., Bigelow, G. E., & Liebson, I. A. (1983). Differential effects of diazepam and pentobarbital on mood and behavior. *Archives of General Psychiatry, 40,* 865–873.

Griffiths, R. R., Bigelow, G. E., & Liebson, I. A. (1989). Reinforcing effects of caffeine in coffee and capsules. *Journal of the Experimental Analysis of Behavior, 52,* 127–140.

Griffiths, R. R., Rush, C. R., & Puhala, K. A. (1996). Validation for the multiple-choice procedure for investigating drug reinforcement in humans. *Experimental and Clinical Psychopharmacology, 4,* 97–106.

Griffiths, R. R., Troisi, J. R., Silverman, K., & Mumford, G. K. (1993). Multiple-choice procedure: An efficient approach for investigating drug reinforcement in humans. *Behavioural Pharmacology, 4,* 3–13.

Guyton, A. C. (1997). *Human physiology and mechanisms of disease* (6th ed.). Philadelphia: Saunders.

Haertzen, C. A. (1966). Development of scales based on patterns of drug effects, using the Addiction Research Center Inventory (ARCI). *Psychological Reports, 18,* 163–194.

Hardman, J. G., Limbird, L. E., Molinoff, P. B., Ruddon, R. W., & Gilman, A. G. (Eds.). (1996). *Goodman and Gilman's the pharmacological basis of therapeutics* (9th ed.). New York: McGraw–Hill.

Heishman, S. J., & Stitzer, M. L. (1989). Effects of d-amphetamine secobarbital and marijuana on choice behavior: Social versus nonsocial options. *Psychopharmacology, 99,* 156–162.

Henningfield, J. E., & Goldberg, S. R. (1983). Control of behavior by intravenous nicotine injections in human subjects. *Pharmacology Biochemistry and Behavior, 19,* 1021–1026.

Higgins, S. T., Bickel, W. K., & Hughes, J. R. (1994). Influence of an alternative reinforcer on human cocaine self-administration. *Life Sciences, 55,* 179–187.

Higgins, S. T., Bickel, W. K., Hughes, J. R., Lynn, M., Capeless, M. A., & Fenwick, J. W. (1990). Effects of intranasal cocaine on human learning, performance and physiology. *Psychopharmacology, 102,* 451–458.

Higgins, S. T., Bickel, W. K., O'Leary, D. K., & Yingling, J. (1987). Acute effects of ethanol and diazepam on the acquisition and performance of response sequences in humans. *Journal of Pharmacology and Experimental Therapeutics, 243,* 1–8.

Higgins, S. T., Budney, A. J., & Bickel, W. K. (1994). Applying behavioral concepts and principles to the treatment of cocaine dependence. *Drug and Alcohol Dependence, 34,* 87–97.

Higgins, S. T., Budney, A. J., Bickel, W. K., Foerg, F. E., Donham, R., & Badger, G. J. (1994). Incentives improve outcome in outpatient treatment of cocaine dependence. *Archives of General Psychiatry, 51,* 568–576.

Higgins, S. T., Hughes, J. R., & Bickel, W. K. (1989). Effects of *d*-amphetamine on choice of social versus monetary reinforcement: A discrete-trial test. *Pharmacology Biochemistry and Behavior, 34,* 297–301.

Higgins, S. T., Rush, C. R., Hughes, J. R., Bickel, W. K., Lynn, M., & Capeless, M. A. (1992). Effects of cocaine and alcohol, alone and in combination, on human learning and performance. *Journal of the Experimental Analysis of Behavior, 58,* 87–105.

Hughes, J. R. (1989). Environmental determinants of the reinforcing effects of nicotine. *Journal of Substance Abuse, 1,* 319–329.

Hughes, J. R., & Hatsukami, D. (1986). Signs and symptoms of tobacco withdrawal. *Archives of General Psychiatry, 43,* 289–294.

Hughes, J. R., Higgins, S. T., Bickel, W. K., Hunt, W. K., Fenwick, J. W., Gulliver, S. B., & Mireault, G. C. (1991). Caffeine self-administration, withdrawal, and adverse effects among coffee drinkers. *Archives of General Psychiatry, 48,* 611–617.

Hughes, J. R., Pickens, R. W., Spring, W., & Keenan, R. (1985). Instructions control whether nicotine will serve as a reinforcer. *Journal of Pharmacology and Experimental Therapeutics, 235,* 106–112.

Hughes, J. R., Strickler, G., King, D., Higgins, S. T., Fenwick, J., Gulliver, S. B., & Mireault, G. (1990). Smoking history, instructions, and the effects of nicotine: Two pilot studies. *Pharmacology Biochemistry and Behavior, 34,* 149–155.

Johanson, C. E. (1992). Biochemical mechanisms and pharmacological principles of drug action. In J. Grabowski & G. R. VandenBos (Eds.), *Psychopharmacology: Basic mechanisms and applied interventions* (pp. 11–58). Washington, DC: American Psychological Association.

Kamien, J. B., Bickel, W. K., Hughes, J. R., Higgins, S. T., & Smith, B. J. (1993). Drug discrimination by humans compared to nonhumans: Current status and future directions. *Psychopharmacology, 111,* 259–270.

Kamien, J. B., Bickel, W. K., Oliveto, A. H., Smith, B. J., Higgins, S. T., Hughes, J. R., & Badger, G. J. (1994). Triazolam discrimination by humans under a novel response procedure: Effects of buspirone and lorazepam. *Behavioural Pharmacology, 5,* 315–325.

Lamb, R. J., Preston, K. L., Schindler, C. W., Meisch, R. A., Davis, F., Katz, J. L., Henningfield, J. E., & Goldberg, S. R. (1991). The reinforcing and subjective effects of morphine in post-addicts: A dose–response study. *Journal of Pharmacology and Experimental Therapeutics, 259,* 1165–1173.

Martin, W. R., Jasinski, D. R., & Mansky, P. A. (1973). Naltrexone, an antagonist for the treatment of heroin dependence. *Archives of General Psychiatry, 28,* 784–791.

McCaul, M. E., Stitzer, M. L., Bigelow, G. E., & Liebson, G. E. (1983). Intravenous hydromorphone: Effects in opiate-free and methadone maintenance subjects. In L. S. Harris (Ed.), *Problems of drug dependence 1982: Proceedings of the 44th annual scientific meeting of the Committee on Problems of Drug Dependence, Inc. NIDA Research Monograph 43* (DHHS Publication No. 83-1264, pp. 238–244). Rockville, MD: National Institute on Drug Abuse.

McKim, W. A. (1986). *Drugs and behavior: An introduction to behavioral pharmacology.* Englewood Cliffs, NJ: Prentice–Hall.

McLeod, D. R., & Griffiths, R. R. (1983). Human progressive-ratio performance: Maintenance by pentobarbital. *Psychopharmacology, 79,* 4–9.

McLeod, D. R., Griffiths, R. R., Bigelow, G. E., & Yingling, J. (1982). An automated version of the digit symbol substitution test (DSST). *Behavior Research Methods and Instrumentation, 14,* 463–466.

McNair, D. M., Lorr, M., & Droppleman, L. F. (1971). *Profile of Mood States (manual).* San Diego, CA: Educational and Industrial Testing Services.

Mello, N. K., & Mendelson, J. H. (1970). Experimentally induced intoxication in alcoholics—A comparison between programmed and spontaneous drinking. *Journal of Pharmacology and Experimental Therapeutics, 173,* 101–116.

Mello, N. K., & Mendelson, J. H. (1987). Operant analysis of human drug self-administration: Marijuana, alcohol, heroin, and polydrug use. In M. A. Bozarth (Ed.), *Methods of assessing the reinforcing properties of abused drugs* (pp. 525–558). Berlin: Springer-Verlag.

Mello, N. K., Mendelson, J. H., & Kuehnle, J. C. (1982). Buprenorphine effects on human heroin self-administration: An operant analysis. *Journal of Pharmacology and Experimental Therapeutics, 223,* 30–39.

Nader, M. A., & Woolverton, W. L. (1991). Effects of increasing the magnitude of an alternative reinforcer on drug choice in a discrete-trials choice procedure. *Psychopharmacology, 105,* 169–174.

Oliveto, A. H., Bickel, W. K., Hughes, J. R., Higgins, S. T., & Fenwick, J. W. (1992). Triazolam as a discriminative stimulus in humans. *Drug and Alcohol Dependence, 30,* 133–142.

Oliveto, A. H., Bickel, W. K., Hughes, J. R., Shea, P. J., Higgins, S. T., & Fenwick, J. W. (1992). Caffeine drug discrimination in humans: Acquisition, specificity and correlation with self-reports. *Journal of Pharmacology and Experimental Therapeutics, 261,* 885–894.

Oliveto, A. H., Bickel, W. K., Kamien, J. B., Hughes, J. R., & Higgins, S. T. (1994). Effects of diazepam and hydromorphone in triazolam-trained humans under a novel-response drug discrimination procedure. *Psychopharmacology, 114,* 417–423.

Oliveto, A. H., Rosen, M. I., Woods, S. W., & Kosten, T. R. (1995). Discriminative stimulus, self-reported and cardiovascular effects of orally administered cocaine in humans. *Journal of Pharmacology and Experimental Therapeutics, 272,* 231–241.

Physician's desk reference. (1997). Montvale, NJ: Medical Economics Company.

Pickens, R. (1977). Behavioral pharmacology: A brief history. In T. Thompson & P. B. Dews (Eds.), *Advances in behavioral pharmacology* (Vol. 1, pp. 230–257). New York: Academic Press.

Preston, K. L., Bigelow, G. E., Bickel, W. K., & Liebson, I. A. (1987). Three-choice drug discrimination in opioid-dependent humans: Hydromorphone, naloxone and saline. *Journal of Pharmacology and Experimental Therapeutics, 243,* 1002–1009.

Preston, K. L., Bigelow, G. E., & Liebson, I. A. (1988). Butorphanol-precipitated withdrawal in opioid-dependent volunteers. *Journal of Pharmacology and Experimental Therapeutics, 246,* 441–448.

Roache, J. D., Cherek, D. R., Bennett, R. H., Schenkler, J. C., & Cowan, K. A. (1993). Differential effects of triazolam and ethanol on awareness, memory, and psychomotor performance. *Journal of Clinical Psychopharmacology, 13,* 3–15.

Ross, E. M. (1996). Pharmacodynamics: Mechanisms of drug action and the relationship between drug concentration and effect. In J. G. Hardman, L. E. Limbird, P. B. Molinoff, R. W. Ruddon, & A. G. Gilman (Eds.), *Goodman and Gilman's the pharmacological basis of therapeutics* (9th ed., pp. 29–42). New York: McGraw–Hill.

Rush, C. R., Higgins, S. T., Bickel, W. K., & Hughes, J. R. (1993). Acute effects of triazolam and lorazepam on human learning, performance and subject ratings. *Journal of Pharmacology and Experimental Therapeutics, 264,* 1218–1226.

Sidman, M., & Tailby, W. (1982). Conditional discrimination vs. matching to sample: An expansion of the testing paradigm. *Journal of the Experimental Analysis of Behavior, 37,* 5–22.

Silverman, K., Higgins, S. T., Brooner, R. K., Montoya, I. D., Cone, E. J., Schuster, C. R., & Preston, K. L. (1996). Sustained cocaine abstinence in methadone maintenance patients through voucher-based reinforcement therapy. *Archives of General Psychiatry, 53,* 409–415.

Silverman, K., Kirby, K. C., & Griffiths, R. R. (1994). Modulation of drug reinforcement by behavioral requirements following drug ingestion. *Psychopharmacology, 114,* 243–247.

Silverman, K., Mumford, G. K., & Griffiths, R. R. (1994). Enhancing caffeine reinforcement by behavioral requirements following drug ingestion. *Psychopharmacology, 114,* 424–432.

Skinner, B. F., & Heron, W. T. (1937). Effects of caffeine and benzedrine upon conditioning and extinction. *The Psychological Record, 1,* 340–346.

Smith, B. J., Bickel, W. K., Higgins, S. T., Hughes, J. R., & Kamien, J. B. (1995). Cumulative dosing for human triazolam discrimination using a novel response procedure. In L. S. Harris (Ed.), *Problems of drug dependence 1994: Proceedings of the 56th annual scientific meeting of the College on Problems of Drug Dependence, Inc. (Volume II). NIDA Research Monograph 153* (NIH Publication No. 95-3883, p. 241). Rockville, MD: National Institute on Drug Abuse.

Spiga, R., Bennett, R. H., Cherek, D. R., & Grabowski, J. (1994). Effects of ethanol on human free-operant cooperative responding. *Drug and Alcohol Dependence, 34,* 139–147.

Spiga, R., Bennett, R. H., Schmitz, J., & Cherek, D. R. (1994). Effects of nicotine on cooperative responding among abstinent male smokers. *Behavioural Pharmacology, 5,* 337–343.

Stitzer, M. L., Griffiths, R. R., Bigelow, G. E., & Liebson, I. A. (1981). Social stimulus factors in drug effects in human subjects. In T. Thompson & C. E. Johanson (Eds.), *Behavioral pharmacology of human drug dependence, NIDA Research Monograph 37* (DHHS Publication No. ADM 81-1137, pp. 130–154). Washington, DC: U.S. Government Printing Office.

Stitzer, M. L., & Higgins, S. T. (1995). Behavioral treatment of drug and alcohol abuse. In F. E. Bloom & D. J. Kupfer (Eds.), *Psychopharmacology: The fourth generation of progress* (pp. 1807–1819). New York: Raven Press.

Stolerman, I. P. (1993). Drug discrimination. In F. van Haaren (Ed.), *Methods in behavioral pharmacology* (pp. 217–243). Amsterdam: Elsevier.

Thompson, D. M., & Moerschbaecher, J. M. (1979). Drug effects on repeated acquisition. In T. Thompson & P. B. Dews (Eds.), *Advances in behavioral pharmacology* (Vol. 2, pp. 229–259). New York: Academic Press.

Thompson, T., & Johanson, C. E. (Eds.). (1981). *Behavioral pharmacology of human drug dependence, NIDA Research Monograph 37* (DHHS Publication No. ADM 81-1137). Washington, DC: U.S. Government Printing Office.

19

Self-Experimentation

Seth Roberts and Allen Neuringer

> That you can learn how to do things by doing them has somehow always
> seemed mysterious to me.
> —KERMODE (1995, p. 164)

By *self-experimentation* we mean experiments in which the researcher studies
him- or herself. We contrast it with *conventional* research in which the experimenter studies other people or animals. This chapter tries to show that self-experiments are useful for gaining knowledge and solving problems, and that self-
experimentation and conventional research have complementary strengths.

The earliest recorded self-experiment may be the work of Santorio Santorio, a
seventeenth-century physician. He determined that the weight of his food and
drink was usually more than twice the weight of his excretions, leading him to
posit the existence of *insensible perspiration* (Castiglioni, 1931). Indeed, we sweat
constantly in tiny amounts (Tokura, Shimomoto, Tsurutani, & Ohta, 1978). Since
Santorio, many self-experimenters have been physicians interested in the causes
and treatment of disease (Altman, 1972, 1987; K. Brown, 1995; Franklin & Sutherland, 1984). Early this century, Joseph Goldberger ingested excretions of pellagra
patients to show that pellagra was not contagious. Werner Forssmann threaded a
catheter to his heart through a vein in his arm to show the feasibility of the procedure (which won him the 1956 Nobel Prize in medicine). More recently, in 1984
Barry Marshall, an Australian doctor, drank a flask of water full of *Helicobacter py-
lori* bacteria to show that they cause ulcers. His theory of causation, now accepted as correct, was contrary to what most people believed at the time (Brown, 1995).
Marshall's work began a new area of medical research: the role of bacteria in chronic disease ("Bugged by disease," 1998).

Some medical self-experiments have involved personal problems. In 1969,
Richard Bernstein, an engineer with diabetes, started to measure his blood glu-

---

Seth Roberts • Department of Psychology, University of California, Berkeley, California 94720-1650.
Allen Neuringer • Department of Psychology, Reed College, Portland, Oregon 97202.
Handbook of Research Methods in Human Operant Behavior, edited by Lattal and Perone. Plenum
Press, New York, 1998.

cose several times a day. He discovered that it varied widely over a day, even though he was carefully following his doctor's recommendations. Both high and low glucose have bad effects. To reduce the variation, he began to do simple experiments. He discovered that many small doses of insulin, spread out over the day (similar to what the pancreas does for nondiabetics) maintained more stable glucose levels than one large daily dose of insulin, the usual prescription at the time. Lack of professional standing made it difficult for him to publicize his results, but he persisted and eventually his ideas spread. Glucose self-monitoring is now a $3 billion/year industry (Bernstein, 1984, 1990, 1994, personal communication, September 11, 1996), with products sold in every drug store ("Blood-glucose meters," 1996).

In psychology, the best-known self-experiments are the memory studies of Ebbinghaus (1885/1913). Using lists of nonsense syllables as the material to be remembered, he measured speed of learning as a function of list length, retention as a function of time, and many other things. Conventional researchers have confirmed many of his conclusions (Cofer, 1979). One of Ebbinghaus's discoveries—that memory after sleep was better than expected from shorter retention intervals (Ebbinghaus, 1885/1913, pp. 76–77)—is still an active research topic (Barinaga, 1994). It is now well-accepted that sleep improves retention (Barinaga, 1994; Jenkins & Dallenbach, 1924).

The early history of psychology contains many other examples of self-experimentation (Neuringer, 1981). Thomas Young immobilized one of his eyeballs to test whether its movement was responsible for accommodation. This and other self-experiments led him to conclude correctly that accommodation is related to changes in the shape of the lens (Boring, 1942). Stratton (1897/1966) wore lenses that inverted the world both left-right and up-down and described his ability to adapt. Early behavioral psychologists, such as Thorndike (1900), joined early cognitive psychologists, such as Wundt (Bolles, 1993) and Titchener (1896), in reporting the results of experiments on their own thoughts, emotions, and behavior.

Self-experimentation has also been applied to practical psychological problems. The self-change literature contains many examples of this (e.g., Steinhauer & Bol, 1988; Watson & Tharp, 1993). Mahoney (1974, 1979) suggested that self-experimentation be used as a method of psychological treatment, recommending that "clients" be taught basic scientific methods so as to become "personal scientists."

Despite a long and productive history, self-experimentation is not now a major force in psychology. This is unfortunate, we argue here. Computers and other modern devices have made self-experimentation easier and more powerful than ever before, but quite apart from these advances, self-experiments can do many things more easily than conventional experiments.

In this chapter we try to show the value of self-experimentation, mainly through examples from our own research. The following "case studies" demonstrate the diversity of questions that self-experiments can help answer and some methods we have found worthwhile. Some of our examples were motivated by scientific interest, like Ebbinghaus's research, others by the desire to solve personal problems, like Bernstein's work. In the final sections of this chapter, we draw conclusions about self-experimentation in general.

EXAMPLES

Behavioral Variability (A. N.)

Variation in behavior is often useful. When a moth detects the ultrasound of a bat, the moth's flight path becomes highly unpredictable, helping the moth to elude the bat. Similarly, behavioral variation may be helpful when a person tries to solve a problem, be creative, or avoid an opponent in a game or battle.

Experimental psychologists have studied the limits of behavioral unpredictability by asking whether human subjects can generate random sequences of responses. Randomness implies that knowledge of prior history does not permit better prediction than no knowledge. Hundreds of studies have found that when people are asked to produce random sequences, for example, of heads and tails, the resulting sequences can readily be distinguished by statistical tests from those produced by a random generator. Researchers have often concluded from these results that people are *unable* to behave randomly (Reichenbach, 1957; Tune, 1964; Wagenaar, 1972).

There is a problem with this conclusion, however. Although people may commonly observe random events, they may never have needed to behave randomly. If you asked whether individuals had ever listened to a violin, most would answer "yes," but if you then provided a violin and asked the same individuals to play, few would be able to make music. It would be wrong, of course, to conclude that people are unable to play the violin, because training is necessary. Perhaps training is also necessary for random behavior, a conjecture that led me (A. N.) to try to teach myself to behave randomly.

I entered the digits 0 through 9 on a computer keyboard as randomly as possible. At the end of each trial (consisting of 100 responses), I was shown on the computer screen a *random number generator score* (RNG), a measure of randomness used by conventional researchers (Evans, 1978). RNG assesses equality of dyads—how often "1" was followed by "1," "1" followed by "2," and so on, for all possible pairs. If all dyads occurred with equal frequencies, the RNG score was 0. If responding was highly repetitive, RNG approached 1.0. The main result, shown in Figure 19.1, was that, over the 140 trials, RNG scores decreased. To assess the generality of the effect, a college student, M. S., received the same contingencies and feedback as I had, with similar results (Figure 19.1). These data showed that people can learn to improve one measure of the randomness of a response sequence.

One possible explanation for the lowered RNG scores with training involves memory for past behaviors, namely, that M. S. and I learned to avoid repetitions of response patterns. Consistent with this explanation was the finding that attention-competing tasks increased RNG scores (Evans & Graham, 1980). To test the memory explanation, I systematically varied how quickly I responded. The memory hypothesis predicted that the more slowly I responded, the less likely it was that I would remember my previous responses and the more likely, therefore, that patterns would be repeated. All contingencies were identical to the first experiment except that the time between each response (*interresponse time,* IRT) was

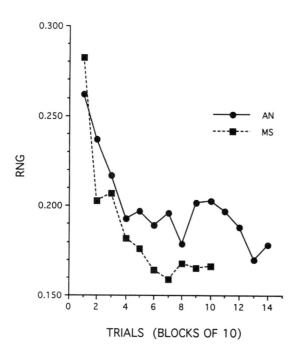

FIGURE 19.1. RNG, a measure of sequence uncertainty, as a function of training trials (averaged across blocks of 10) for the author (AN) and an experimentally naive subject (MS). (High RNG values indicate repetitious sequences, lower values indicate more variable sequences.)

controlled. Figure 19.2 shows that RNG scores *decreased* as a function of IRT between 0.3 and 7.5 s, opposite to the prediction. To test this finding, I compared a 5-s IRT with a 20-s IRT in ABA fashion (three replications of each value). RNG at 5-s IRT was .161 ± .006 (mean ± standard error) and at 20 s was .153 ± .008. Thus, slow responding increased response unpredictability, a result also found in conventional studies with people (Baddeley, 1966), as well as with animals (Neuringer, 1991). An extended discussion of these results would take us far afield from self-experimentation, but it appears that there are at least two strategies for behaving variably, one based on memory for prior events, another that appears to mimic a random generator, responses from which are relatively independent of history (Neuringer, 1986; Neuringer & Voss, 1993; Page & Neuringer, 1985).

One aspect of the above research was bothersome. When a random generator was programmed to generate 100 responses per trial, average RNG score was about .245, a value higher than many of the values in my experiments. Recall that high scores indicate *less* variability. The problem appeared to be that RNG was based on equality of dyads, and my dyads were more equal than expected from a random generator. One possible solution, and the one I followed, was to change the goal from that of minimizing a particular statistic to *matching* the output of a random generator according to many different statistics. A complete discussion is again beyond the scope of this chapter, but there is no single test of randomness (Knuth, 1969); many tests are needed to demonstrate approximations to random performance.

I therefore attempted to match a random generator on six different levels of the RNG metric. In the above experiments, RNG was based on *contiguous* pairs of

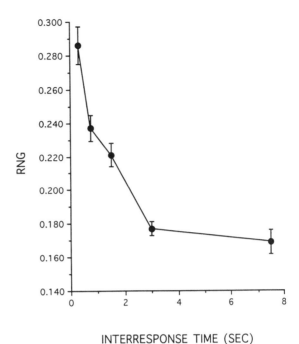

FIGURE 19.2.   RNG as a function of interresponse time. (Each point is an average of 10 trials; the error bars show standard errors.)

INTERRESPONSE TIME (SEC)

responses, what is called "lag 1." Similar measures could come from responses separated by one response (lag 2), separated by two responses (lag 3), and so forth. At the end of each trial, I received feedback from six lags, my goal being to match the random generator at each of the lags. Table 19.1 compares my performance over the last 100 trials in a set of more than 300 trials with 100 trials from a random generator. At the end of training, I was generating RNG scores that did not differ significantly, across the six lags, from the scores produced by the random generator.

I later extended this work to as many as 30 different statistical tests, many used to evaluate the adequacy of RNGs (Knuth, 1969; Neuringer, 1986). The random generator was programmed to make 100 responses per trial (digits 0 through 9), and the data from 100 trials were then evaluated according to each of the 30 test statistics, with means and standard deviations calculated for each statistic. Following each trial, I received feedback in terms of how I differed (in standard deviation units) from the random generator on each of these 30 statistics. Figure 19.3 shows an example of this feedback. At the beginning of training, most scores diverged greatly from those of the random generator, but by the end of 6 months of training, scores did not differ statistically from the random model according to these 30 statistical tests. Thus, a person can learn to approximate a random sequence of responses, as assessed by a large number of measures.

These results provide a challenge to the behaviorist's goal of prediction and control of instrumental behavior (Zuriff, 1985). Feedback can generate different levels of predictability, from highly predictable response rates in operant chambers to highly unpredictable performances. The results also suggest how behav-

TABLE 19.1
Comparison of 100 Trials by A. N. with 100 Trials by Berkeley-Pascal
Random Number Generator (RNG)

	Mean		Standard deviation			
Lag	A. N.	RNG	A. N.	RNG	t	p
1	.245	.242	.028	.024	0.85	>.4
2	.239	.243	.037	.023	1.01	>.2
3	.243	.245	.027	.025	0.60	>.5
4	.240	.246	.025	.023	1.71	>.05
5	.243	.243	.028	.026	0.01	>.8
6	.241	.244	.027	.026	0.56	>.5

ioral variability may be engendered when creativity, problem solving, or learning of new skills is required (Holman, Goetz, & Baer, 1977; Siegler, 1994; Stokes, 1995).

Commentary

An objection often raised to self-experimentation is that expectations bias results. However, as shown above, self-experiments often produce results that differ from expected. Another common objection is that the results may be relevant only to the single subject involved. However, when the last experiment was repeated with high-school and college students as subjects, and simpler feedback and procedure, the results were consistent with those from the self-experiments (Neuringer, 1986). Others have extended this line of research to animals, allowing the study of drugs, motivation, and genetic differences, including gender (Cohen, Neuringer, & Rhodes, 1990; Machado, 1989; McElroy & Neuringer, 1990; Mook & Neuringer, 1994; Neuringer & Huntley, 1991). Thus, conventional studies have yielded results consistent with those from the self-experiments.

Thought, Memory, and Physical Movement (A. N.)

I tend to pace whenever I write a paper or prepare a lecture; and during long walks I seem to generate more novel ideas than at other times. These observations led me to ask if physical activity facilitates intellectual activity. I tried to generate new and interesting ideas (on any topic) under two conditions. In the *sit* condition, I sat quietly at my desk. In the *move* condition, I walked, paced, swayed, or danced around a small room. The experiment consisted of 20 trials, 14 of these 15 min in duration each, the remainder 5 min each. Sit and move trials were pre-

---

FIGURE 19.3.   Some of the feedback given the author (A. N.) after each trial. (Each trial consisted of 100 responses. Shown are 8 of the 30 statistics provided at the end of a trial. The dashed lines show the means for the performance of a random number generator; the letters indicate performance by the subject relative to the random generator in standard deviation units, with A = +0.5, B = +1.0, a = −0.5, b = −1.0, and so on.)

RNG Lag1   -8.231628406795298e-01

RNG Lag2   2.925655620615034e+00

RNG Lag3   5.360304904290396e+00

RNG Lag4   6.729524789030080e-01

Chisquare   -7.734553775743719e+00

Serial Corr. Lag1   2.126379364753748e+00

Serial Corr. Lag2   3.748303979912194e+00

Serial Corr. Lag3   1.082412297441927e+01

sented in pairs—one sit and one move—with order counterbalanced and trial durations equal. Whenever a new and interesting idea came to mind, I would stop and record it on a pad. (I stopped the trial-duration timer while writing.) I wrote more ideas during move (1.05/min) than during sit (0.72/min), a significant difference (Wilcoxon matched-pairs signed-ranks test, two-tailed $p < .01$). Days after completing the trials, I subjectively judged the overall novelty and interest (one measure) of each idea. While judging, I was unaware of the condition in which the ideas had been generated (that information was coded on the back of each sheet of paper). Estimated novelty and interest was higher in the move condition than in sit, although the difference was not significant. Other experiments compared reading speed (I read 8% faster when moving than sitting, a significant difference), performance on the Miller Analogies test of intelligence (contrary to expectations, I performed *worse* while moving than sitting), and speed of learning to associate names with faces (see Neuringer, 1981).

To do this last experiment, pictures of people who worked for a large corporation were attached to one side of index cards with the individuals' names on the other. The cards were divided into 20 sets of 20 cards each, with 10 sets arbitrarily allocated to the move condition and the other 10 to sit. The task consisted of learning the names of the individuals until I was able to go through the set of 20 cards without any errors, and do this three times in a row. In the sit condition, I sat at my desk, taking care to have not engaged in strenuous exercise for the preceding few hours. To increase the amount of activity in the move condition, I now exercised (ran or swam) for about 30 min before each move trial, in addition to moving during the trial. Again, move and sit sessions alternated. Figure 19.4 shows that learning was facilitated by exercise and movement. In the move condition, each set of cards took about 7.5 repetitions to learn to perfection; in sit, 9.7 repetitions—again, a statistically significant difference (Wilcoxon matched-pairs signed-ranks test, two-tailed $p < .05$).

Commentary

Self-experimentation speeds up the feedback loop involved in developing methods. In the memory experiment, for example, I first learned names of flowers, than names of trees, and then French–English equivalents, all while developing the procedure. Because the experimenter serves as his or her own subject, many additional unexpected results may emerge. In the course of this research, it became clear to me that exercise enhanced my moods. A conventional study later supported the observation (Gurley, Neuringer, & Massee, 1984).

Weight (S. R.)

The setpoint theory of weight control assumes that amount of body fat is controlled by a feedback system (Hervey, 1969), similar to the thermostatic control of room temperature. The amount of fat that the regulatory system tries to maintain is the *setpoint*. When actual body fat is below the setpoint, the system acts to increase body fat by increasing hunger and reducing metabolic rate. According to this theory, fat people have a higher setpoint than thin people.

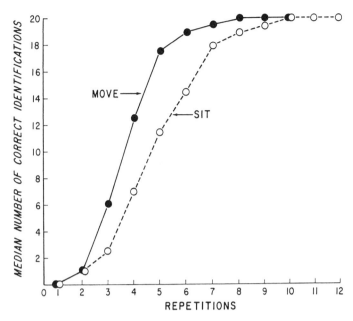

FIGURE 19.4. Learning curves for the Move and Sit conditions showing the average number of faces correctly identified (in a list of 20 faces) as a function of the number of times the list had been studied.

Most weight-control researchers believe it is hard to change one's setpoint in adulthood (e.g., Gibbs, 1996, p. 91). But some studies contradict this conclusion. Sclafani and Springer (1976) found that adult rats allowed to eat unlimited amounts of "supermarket foods" (p. 461), such as cookies, salami, cheese, banana, and marshmallows, gained considerable weigh relative to rats given unlimited lab chow. The supermarket rats gained weight two to three times faster than one would expect from a high-fat diet (A. Sclafani, personal communication, July 2, 1996). Similarly, Cabanac and Rabe (1976) found that adult humans who consumed Renutril (a bland liquid food, like Metrecal) in place of their regular diet lost substantial weight, even though they could consume as much as they wanted. The two studies were done independently, yet both suggested the same conclusion: The tastiness of one's food controls one's setpoint. Tasty food (supermarket food, a normal human diet) produces a higher setpoint than bland food (lab chow, Renutril). If correct, this conclusion implies there is a way to lose weight without going hungry: eat less-tasty food.

In 1993, I (S. R.) wanted to lose weight and decided to test this conclusion. I am 5′ 11″ (1.80 m) and at the time weighed 197 pounds (89.4 kg). I reasoned that what makes food tasty is *processing* (including home processing). Fruit juice tastes better than whole fruit. Cooked food tastes better than raw. So I reduced the amount of processing in my food. I stopped eating deli foods, bread, sweets (e.g., scones), fruit juice, and fancy frozen food (e.g., Stouffer's Lean Cuisine), ate less meat and chicken (because meat and chicken are higher on the food chain than fish), and more fruits and vegetables. I ate mostly soups, salads, fish, steamed vegetables, rice, potatoes, and fruit.

FIGURE 19.5. Body weight as a function of day. (Weights were normalized by subtracting the prediet weight for each subject. Prediet weights were, in pounds, 197 for SR, 167 for JH, and 146 for AL.)

Over 3 weeks, never going hungry, I lost 11 pounds (5.0 kg), which I have kept off without effort. At first the food seemed boring, but after a few days I came to enjoy my new diet and dislike my old one. The time course of my weight change is shown in Figure 19.5. (These measurements ended when the scale broke.) Later, two students (J. H. and A. L.) tried the same diet. They too lost weight; and when they returned to their original diets, they gained weight (Figure 19.5), providing more evidence that eating less-processed food produces substantial weight loss. Experiments in which subjects changed from a "modern" diet to an "indigenous" one support the same conclusion (O'Dea, 1984; Shintani, Hughes, Beckham, & O'Connor, 1991).

I eventually resumed measuring my weight, now using three scales. In 1996, an acquaintance told me that, starting at 190 pounds (86 kg), he had lost 45 pounds (20 kg) when he switched from an ordinary American diet to a diet of fruits, vegetables, rice, lots of water, and small amounts of fish and chicken (Tray Critelli, personal communication, June 5, 1996). The weight change was remarkably large, and his diet contained an unusual element: lots of water. To learn if water intake affects weight, I started to drink 5 liters of water a day, much more than my usual intake (about 1 liter daily).

I lost weight quickly, 7 pounds (3.2 kg) in 10 days, even though I always ate as much as I wanted (Figure 19.6). The results were consistent with the idea that drinking more water lowered my setpoint. Because I drank almost all of the water between meals, it was unlikely that the weight loss occurred because the water was "filling," i.e., influenced satiety mechanisms that control meal length. It was not easy to drink that much water every day, so eventually I reduced my water intake from 5 to 3 liters/day. Figure 19.6 shows that soon after the change I gained about 3 pounds (1.4 kg).

These two observations—the effect of processing and the effect of water—were not easy to explain in conventional terms (amount of calories, amount of fat). Neither involved caloric restriction (eating less than desired). Drinking water did not change the amount of fat in my diet. Eating less-processed food probably reduced my fat intake, but the resulting weight loss was much more than the weight loss

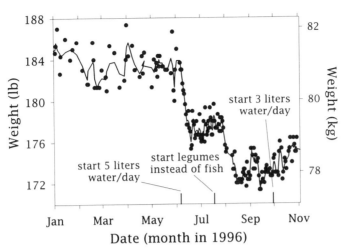

FIGURE 19.6.   S. R.'s body weight as a function of day. (Each weight is the average of three scales. Each scale could be read to the nearest pound. The wiggly line is a moving average [mean] of 3 days.)

produced by a low-fat diet (Kendall, Levitsky, Strupp, & Lissner, 1991; Raben, Jensen, Marckmann, Sandström, & Astrup, 1995; Sheppard, Kristal, & Kushi, 1991).

Around this time, I developed a theory of weight control (see below) that predicted that eating what I call *slow calories*—food with calories that are detected relatively slowly—would lower one's setpoint. In the United States, the main sources of slow calories are legumes (beans, peas, lentils). Hearing this prediction, a friend said her boyfriend had been much thinner in high school, when he ate a lot of beans and rice (Joyce Friedlander, personal communication, August 17, 1996). At the time of this conversation, my main sources of calories were fish and rice. The next day, I started eating legumes instead of fish. Again, I lost weight quickly for a short time (Figure 19.6). I lost about 6 pounds (2.7 kg) in 20 days, not counting 7 days out of town when I went off the diet.

The theory of weight control that I developed, which explains these results, was inspired by the results of Ramirez (1990) with rats. Its main assumption is that one's setpoint is controlled by the strength of the taste–calorie associations in one's diet. Tastes become associated with calories when the two co-occur—when a taste signal (generated in the mouth) happens shortly before a calorie signal (probably generated in the stomach). Many rat experiments have shown that the taste of a food becomes associated with its caloric content (e.g., Bolles, Hayward, & Crandall, 1981). The theory assumes that the brain keeps a running average of the calories associated with the tastes of one's food. The greater the value—the more strongly the tastes in the diet signal calories—the higher the setpoint (more body fat). This makes evolutionary sense: When calories are relatively abundant, we should try to stockpile more of them (via body fat) than when they are scarce.

To explain the effect of processing (Figure 19.5) this theory makes an additional assumption: The more strongly a food's taste is associated with calories, the better the food tastes—in behavioral terms, the more likely you will choose that food if given a choice. This assumption is supported by rat experiments that used preference tests to show the existence of taste–calorie associations (e.g., Bolles et al., 1981). Pairing a taste with calories increased choice of the taste.

Processed food is generally preferred to the same food unprocessed (as revealed, for instance, by willingness to pay more for the processed food). For example, most people prefer roasted nuts to raw nuts, orange juice to oranges, food with spices to food without spices. Probably the main reason processing makes food taste better is that it strengthens taste-calorie associations. The details of common processing methods support this argument. The strength of taste–caloric associations, like other examples of Pavlovian conditions, depends on (1) conditioned-stimulus (CS) intensity, that is, taste intensity, and (2) unconditioned-stimulus (US) intensity, that is, calorie intensity. Many processing methods plausibly increase CS intensity or complexity: adding spices, sauces, flavorings, or small amounts of fat (many flavoring agents are fat-soluble). Many other processing methods plausibly increase US intensity, the amount of calories detected soon after the taste: cooking, mashing, adding large amounts of sugar or fat. Adding fat or sugar adds calories, but cooking and adding spices do not. Thus, the effects of processing cannot be explained just in terms of calories. Processed food, in other words, produces stronger taste-calorie associations than the same food unprocessed, even when the calorie content is unchanged.

Water reduces weight (Figure 19.6) because its taste is associated with zero calories. So it lowers the running average the brain uses to judge the abundance of calories. Legumes reduce weight (Figure 19.6) because they produce a relatively slow calorie signal, an assumption based on the relatively slow rate at which they raise blood glucose (Foster-Powell & Brand-Miller, 1995; the technical term for this measurement is *glycemic index*). Thus, the taste signal and the calorie signal produced by legumes are relatively far apart in time, reducing their association.

In summary, this work suggests three ways to lose weight without going hungry: eat less-processed food; consume more water or any other source of taste and few calories (tea, pickles, low-calorie soup); and eat more legumes.

Commentary

Self-experimentation was helpful in several ways. *It connected laboratory and real life.* Self-experiments are often more realistic than conventional experiments. The Sclafani and Springer experiments (rat subjects, supermarket food; 1976) and the Cabanac and Rabe experiment (human subjects, liquid food; 1976) suggested that eating less-tasty food lowers the setpoint, but did so in situations remote from everyday life. My self-experiment about processing (Figure 19.5) showed the practical use of these discoveries. The Ramirez experiments (rat subjects, liquid food, effect of saccharine; 1990) pointed to a new mechanism of weight control, but gave no indication of the importance of that mechanism in the real-life control of human weight. My results suggest it plays a large role because it explained and predicted large effects (Figures 19.5 and 19.6). *It was a good precursor to clinical trials* because I tested treatments (diets) on myself before I tested them on others. Medical self-experiments have often served this purpose (Altman, 1987). Finally, *it helped me lose weight.* I lost about 17 pounds (8 kg). I never went hungry, took no drugs, and ended up eating a healthier diet (more fruit, vegetables, fiber). Unlike many people who lose weight, I know the crucial features of what worked; maybe that helps avoid backsliding based on wishful thinking.

Sleep (S. R.)

I used to suffer from what is called *early awakening.* I awoke at 3 or 4 AM, still tired but unable to sleep. Not until a few hours later would I be able to fall back asleep. About 15% of United States adults have this problem (Gallup Organization, 1991).

In the 1980s, I began to try to solve the problem with self-experimentation. The Psychology Department electronics shop made a small device that helped record when I slept. I pushed one button when I turned off the lights to try to fall asleep, another button when I got out of bed. I defined an instance of early awakening to be a morning when I fell back asleep between 10 min and 6 hr after getting up. The lower limit (10 min) was meant to eliminate trivial awakenings (e.g., getting up to urinate), the upper limit (6 hr) to eliminate afternoon naps. My life was well suited for sleep experiments. Because the hours I worked were flexible, I never used an alarm clock and almost always could fall back asleep if I wanted to. It also helped that I lived alone.

Despite such favorable conditions, for years I made little progress. I tried many treatments, most involving morning light. Some helped, but none eliminated early awakening. At best, I awoke too early on a third of all days. All my ideas about the cause(s) of early awakening were apparently wrong, but it was not clear how to find better ideas. I was stuck.

In January 1993, during routine data analysis, I looked at a graph of my daily sleep duration (how long I slept each day, including naps) as a function of day. Figure 19.7 is an updated version of what I saw. The graph showed a sharp drop in sleep duration during 1992. The drop (about 40 min) occurred at the same time I lost weight by eating less-processed food (Figure 19.5; smoothing makes the sleep decrease appear to start before the weight loss).

The coincidence of these events (diet change, weight loss, less sleep) suggests that either weight or diet controls how much sleep we want. Other data suggest that it is weight, not diet, that is crucial because diverse ways of changing weight have similar effects. Loss (or gain) of weight has been associated with less (or more) total sleep time (Crisp, Stonehill, & Fenton, 1971; Crisp, Stonehill, Fenton, & Fenwick, 1973; Lacey, Crisp, Kalucy, Hartmann, & Chen, 1975; Neuringer, 1981). In surveys, less weight has been associated with less total sleep time (Paxton et al., 1984; Shephard, Jones, Ishii, Kaneko, & Olbrecht, 1969; Walsh, Goetz, Roose, Fingeroth, & Glassman, 1985). A connection between body fat and sleep makes functional sense. Sleep is a luxury, a kind of vacation: While you sleep, you use more calories than you take in. The greater your wealth (in terms of body fat), the more sleep you can afford.

I showed my students a graph similar to Figure 19.7. It inspired one of them to tell me, a few weeks later, that eating a diet high in water content (e.g., fruit) had reduced how much sleep he needed (Michael Lee, personal communication, March 1993). This was fascinating. I tried the diet he suggested, at first eating four

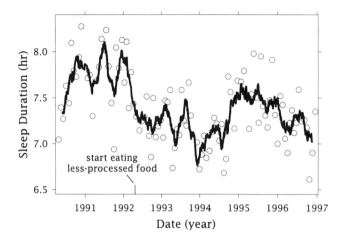

FIGURE 19.7. Long-term record of S. R.'s sleep duration. (Each data point is the 10% trimmed mean of 21 days. The wiggly line gives the moving averages [means] of 93 days. The tick marks for each year indicate the first day of that year.)

pieces of fruit a day. My sleep duration did not change. When I told him my results, he said, "I eat *six* pieces of fruit per day." So I started eating six pieces of fruit daily. To do this, I had to change my breakfast—there was nowhere else to put the extra fruit. Instead of eating oatmeal for breakfast, I started eating two pieces of fruit (often a banana and an apple).

My sleep duration remained about the same. However, after about a week of fruit breakfasts I noticed that my early awakening had gotten *worse*—I woke up too early every morning instead of a third of all mornings. Was this a coincidence? I alternated between fruit and oatmeal breakfasts and established that it was cause and effect. A fruit breakfast made early awakening the next morning much more likely than an oatmeal breakfast.

The connection was a total surprise; when I awoke at 3 or 4 AM, I did not feel hungry. Yet I had known for years about laboratory observations of food-anticipatory activity, a well-established effect in animals (Bolles & Stokes, 1965; Boulos & Terman, 1980). Mammals, birds, and fish become more active shortly before the time of day that they are fed (Boulos & Terman, 1980). Despite its cross-species generality, to my knowledge, the effect had never been related to human behavior. The animal results made a cause-and-effect relation between breakfast and early awakening much more credible. However, they did not make clear how to reduce early awakening.

I had been eating oatmeal for breakfast for reasons unrelated to sleep. Because a randomly chosen breakfast was unlikely to be optimal, some other breakfast would probably produce less early awakening. Oatmeal produced less sleep disturbance than fruit, and the obvious nutritional difference between them is that oatmeal has more protein. This led me to try a variety of high-protein breakfasts, but always with the same result: I continued to wake up too early quite often.

Mistlberger, Houpt, and Moore-Ede (1990), studying rats, found that carbohydrate, protein, and fat can each produce anticipatory activity. I learned of these results during my study of different breakfasts, and they made me realize that I needed to consider more than just protein in my search for a better breakfast. That was not easy. Food can be described on many dimensions (e.g., calories, fat, cholesterol, sugar) and I had no idea which were important.

FIGURE 19.8. Probability of having fallen back asleep as a function of breakfast and time since first getting up. (Probability of having fallen back asleep after 2 hr = number of days on which S. R. fell back asleep within 2 hr after getting up/number of days included in the condition. The functions are based on days both with and without early awakening, i.e., both the days on which S. R. fell back asleep after getting up and the days on which he did not fall back asleep after getting up. The results are from the mornings *after* eating the indicated breakfasts. For instance, if fruit was the breakfast Monday through Friday, the fruit results would be based on Tuesday through Saturday morning. The "oatmeal" function is based on the 300 days before the breakfast variations began, during which oatmeal was almost always the breakfast. The "none–1st" function is based on the first 102 days when no breakfast was eaten, omitting the first 8 days. The "fruit" function is based on the following 47 days, when breakfast was one piece of fruit. The "none–2nd" function comes from the 62 days after that, omitting the first 2, when again no breakfast was eaten.)

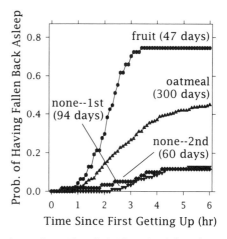

My experimental comparisons had contrasted one breakfast (e.g., oatmeal) with another (e.g., fruit). To make interpretation easier, I decided to compare something (one breakfast) with nothing (no breakfast). I began with a baseline of no breakfast (nothing to eat or drink before 11 AM). The result: My early awakening disappeared! It went away gradually, during the first week of no breakfast. To check that the absence of early awakening was related to the absence of breakfast, I started eating breakfast again (one piece of fruit between 7 and 8 AM). Early awakening returned. When I stopped eating breakfast again, early awakening disappeared. These changes also affected how I felt: When I ate no breakfast, I woke up feeling more rested.

Figure 19.8 shows the results of this ABA experiment in detail. It plots the probability that I had fallen back asleep as a function of time since getting up. The *oatmeal* function is from the 300 days before I started varying my breakfast. The *none–1st* function is from the first period when I ate no breakfast, omitting the first 8 days (when the treatment was gradually taking effect). The *fruit* function is from the days when I ate one piece of fruit for breakfast. The *none–2nd* function is from the beginning of the second block of days when I ate no breakfast, omitting the first 2 days. As Figure 19.8 shows, skipping breakfast greatly reduced early awakening.

Details of my results resembled food anticipation in rats. In rats, anticipatory activity begins a few hours before food when large amounts of food are given (e.g., Bolles & Stokes, 1965). During the fruit phase of my experiment, I ate between 7 and 8 AM, and I awoke on average at 5:35 ± 0:11 AM (10% trimmed mean ± standard error). Rat experiments have found that when food stops, the anticipatory activity gradually disappears over the next 5–10 days (Boulos, Rosenwasser, & Terman, 1980). When I stopped eating breakfast, waking up too early took about 8 days to nearly disappear. Calling the first morning with no breakfast Morning 1, I woke up too early on Mornings 2, 4, 5, 6, 9, and much less often after that. These similarities between rat and human results make the human results more credible.

Although skipping breakfast reduced early awakening, it did not eliminate it.

During the two no-breakfast periods of Figure 19.8, I awoke early on 12% of the mornings. This suggested that early awakening had more than one cause. More evidence for a second cause was that the absence of breakfast changed the "latency" of falling back asleep (the time between when I got up and when I fell back asleep). It was less during the fruit phase (2.1 ± 0.1 hr) than during the two no-breakfast phases (3.3 ± 0.2 hr). When one cause (breakfast) was removed, the existence of another cause—which produced falling back asleep with a different latency—became apparent.

The data of Figure 19.8 are from September 1992 to May 1994. During the following months, early awakening became much more frequent, eventually happening on about 60% of mornings, even though I never ate before 10 AM. I had no idea what caused this increase, but it was more evidence that early awakening had more than one environmental cause, if my conclusions about breakfast were correct.

In February 1995, searching for other causes, I started watching TV every morning. Although this had a large effect on my mood (see below), it had little effect on the probability of early awakening, despite great expectations and considerable trial and error. The lack of change was an especially clear indication that expectations and hopes did not substantially influence the results.

A second solution to the problem turned up by accident, like the first solution (no breakfast). Asking friends about weight control, I had heard two anecdotes in which a person who walked much more than usual (many hours a day) lost significant weight. Perhaps it was cause and effect: Walking a lot caused weight loss. Walking combines movement with standing (placing all of your weight on your feet). Either might have caused the weight loss.

I could not walk many hours a day but could stand many hours a day if I stood while working at my desk. This lifestyle change interested me partly because I assumed that our hunter-gatherer ancestors usually stood much more than I did (about 3–4 hr/day), and my breakfast and mood results had suggested that solutions to psychological problems can often be found in aspects of Stone Age life. On August 27, 1996, I began to stand much more. I raised my computer screen and keyboard so that I wrote standing up, stood during phone calls, walked more, bicycled less. At first this was exhausting but after a few days I got used to it. I used the stopwatch on my wristwatch and a small notecard to keep track of how long I stood each day. I included any time all my weight was on my feet: standing still, walking, playing racquetball. My weight did not change. Within a few days, however, it became obvious that I was waking too early much less often. During the 3 months before August 27, I had woken up too early on about 60% of days; during the first few months after August 27, on about 20% of days.

How long I stood each day varied, mostly because of variation in events during which I had to sit (e.g., meals, meetings). After I noticed the effect of standing, I initially assumed that any substantial amount of standing (e.g., 6 hr) would be enough to reduce early awakening. However, in October 1996 I analyzed my data in preparation for a talk. The analysis suggested that the amount of standing necessary to get the maximum benefit was much more than I had thought (Table 19.2). Standing from 5 to 8 hr had little effect on early awakening, judging from the pretreatment baseline (before August 27); standing from 8.0 to 8.8 hr reduced early

TABLE 19.2
Correlation between Standing and Early Awakening

When	Standing (hr)	Days	Median standing (hr)	Days with early awakening the next morning	Proportion (%)
May 18– August 26, 1996	Not measured	100	Not measured	57	57
August 27–	5.0–8.0	20	7.0	12	60
October 24, 1996	8.0–8.8	34	8.5	5	15
	8.8–11.0	5	9.3	0	0
October 25, 1996–	5.0–8.0	10	6.8	6	60
February 28, 1997	8.0–8.8	8	8.5	2	25
	8.8–11.0	90	9.3	1	1

Note. Early awakening = fell back asleep between 10 min and 6 hr after getting up. Because of travel and illness, some days were not included. Median standing gives the median duration of standing for the days in that category; e.g., 7.0 is the median of 20 days.

awakening, but did not eliminate it; and standing 8.8 hr or more eliminated early awakening. After noticing this, I tried to stand at least 9 hr every day. This completely solved the problem (Table 19.2). After a day during which I stood at least 8.8 hr, I almost never awoke too early. Although the data of Table 19.2 are correlational, the correlation implies causation because the correlation is strong, long-lasting, unexpected, and seems to have no other plausible explanation.

That standing affects sleep makes functional sense. The muscles we use to stand no doubt did more work in an average Stone Age day than any other muscles. Because we sleep lying down, sleep time can be used to do routine maintenance on these muscles. And if these muscles were shaped by evolution to *take advantage* of sleep for maintenance, then they will *need* sleep for maintenance. The more use during the day, the more maintenance is needed at night. So we will need a system that makes us sleep more than usual after we have stood more than usual. At the time our sleep-controlling system evolved into the form it now has, people probably stood many hours every day. Without the pressure to sleep provided by considerable standing, sleep is not deep enough.

Figure 19.9 summarizes 7 years of research. The wiggly line in the upper panel is a smooth of the data, a moving average based on 31 points (the 15 days before the target day, the target day, the 15 days after the target day). The wiggly line in the lower panel indicates the probability of early awakening (i.e., the density of points in the upper panel); each point on the wiggly line is based on the 31 neighboring days. Smoothing should be part of the analysis of any longtime series (Tukey, 1977), which self-experimentation sometimes generates. It often reveals previously unnoticed structure. Figure 19.9 provides three examples. (1) In the upper panel, the smoothed latency rises from about 1.5 to 3 hr starting when morning TV began. It is only a correlation, but it raises the possibility that morning TV affected the mechanism(s) that cause early awakening, even though morning TV had no clear effect on the probability of early awakening (lower panel). (2) The function in the lower panel suggests there was a yearly rhythm in early awakening—it was more frequent during the summer. (3) The lower panel also shows that

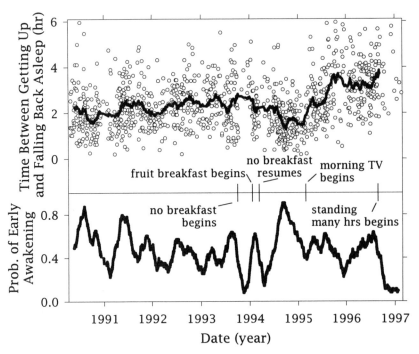

FIGURE 19.9. S. R.'s early awakening 1990–1997. (Each point is a different day that early awakening occurred. The height of the points indicates the time between getting up and falling back asleep; the density of the points indicates the probability of early awakening. In the upper panel, the wiggly line shows the moving average [mean] of 31 points. In the lower panel—based on exactly the same data as the upper panel—the wiggly line gives the probability of early awakening based on the 31 days in the neighborhood of the day at which the point is plotted—the 15 days before, the day itself, and the 15 days after. The tick mark for each year indicates the first day of that year. The data are from April 10, 1990, through February 28, 1997.)

standing many hours was associated with a more sustained reduction in early awakening than ever before—more evidence for the power of standing. Early awakening remained very rare from the end of the period covered by Figure 19.9 until the time of this writing (March 1998).

In summary, my early awakening was apparently caused by eating breakfast and not standing enough. To reduce early awakening, try (1) eating your first meal of the day no sooner than 3 hr after you get up and (2) standing at least 9 hr a day.

Commentary

These self-experimental results challenge some widely held beliefs. That skipping breakfast was helpful contradicts the popular idea that breakfast is "the most important meal of the day" (Bender, 1993, p. 488). (Bender [1993] found no clear support for the popular view.) Most sleep researchers believe that light and time awake are the main environmental events that control when we sleep (e.g., Borbély, 1982; Moore-Ede, Sulzman, & Fuller, 1982). This work found that breakfast and standing can also have powerful effects. The effect of breakfast is just an ex-tension of animal research on food-anticipatory activity (e.g., Boulos & Terman, 1980) but the effect of standing seems to be without precedent.

A common criticism of self-experimentation, mentioned earlier, is that the ex-perimenter's expectations and desires may shape the results. When I first began self-experiments to reduce early awakening, I worried about this possibility. I *could* consciously control whether or not I fell back asleep after getting up, main-ly by deciding whether or not to lie down. But the longer the research continued, the less I worried. Because I failed for years to find a solution (despite wanting to), because a solution I strongly expected to work (morning TV) did not, and because the solutions I eventually found (no breakfast and standing a lot) were unexpect-ed, it became clear that desires and expectations had little effect.

Serendipity, often important in conventional research (Siegel & Zeigler, 1976; Skinner, 1956), played a large role. I noticed the connection between breakfast and early awakening while trying to sleep less; I noticed the connection between stand-ing and early awakening while trying to lose weight. Yet these discoveries were not accidental, because the lifestyle change that made the difference was no acci-dent (e.g., I stood more on purpose). Self-experiments lend themselves to this sort of discovery because they implicitly measure many things at once. Even when fo-cused on one measure (e.g., weight), you can easily notice if other measures change. The next section describes another example of serendipity.

Mood (S. R.)

Because early awakening persisted after I stopped eating breakfast, breakfast was not its only cause. Trying to think of other possible causes, I realized there might be a general lesson to be learned from the effect of breakfast. Our brains were shaped by evolution to work well during long-ago living conditions. Our Pleis-tocene ancestors, I believed, could not regularly eat a rich breakfast soon after wak-ing up, but I could—and a rich breakfast caused early awakening. Maybe other "un-natural" aspects of my life also caused early awakening.

Based on studies of people living with no time-of-day information (e.g., in caves), Wever (1979) concluded that human contact affects the phase of an inter-nal clock that controls when we sleep. Wever's evidence for this conclusion could be interpreted in other ways, and later commentators have been skeptical (e.g., Moore-Ede et al., 1982). However, Wever's conclusion makes evolutionary sense. An internal clock "set" by human contact would tend to make us awake when oth-er people are awake, just as the internal clock that causes food anticipation tends to make us awake when food is available. Our Stone Age ancestors lived in groups, of course, and field studies of technologically primitive cultures (e.g., Chagnon, 1983) suggest that our ancestors had a great deal of contact with other people every morning. In contrast, I lived alone and often worked more or less alone all morn-ing. Maybe lack of morning human contact caused early awakening.

In 1964–66, an international survey of time use found that adults in the Unit-ed States stayed awake an hour later than adults in each of 11 other countries (Sza-lai, 1973). In every country except the United States, adults fell asleep about 11 PM; in the United States, they fell asleep about midnight. Only one other activity measured in the survey differed so dramatically in its timing between the United States and other countries—television watching. Americans watched TV an hour later than everyone else. Watching TV resembles human contact in many ways. The survey results raised the possibility that the aspects of human contact that control when we sleep could be supplied by TV.

In February 1995 this reasoning led me one morning to watch about 20 min of TV soon after I awoke—specifically, a tape of the Leno and Letterman monologues (resembling what Americans were watching at 11 PM). There was no obvious effect, and I fell back asleep about an hour later. The next morning, however, soon after I awoke I felt exceptionally good—cheerful, refreshed, relaxed, energetic. I could not remember ever feeling so good early in the morning. We do not usually attribute how we feel in the morning to whether we watched TV the previous morning. Yet the prior days had been ordinary in every way, except for the morning TV. Over the next few weeks, I watched morning TV some days and not others and became convinced that the morning TV/next-day mood correlation I had observed reflected causation. Whether I watched TV one morning (e.g., Monday) clearly affected how I felt the next morning (Tuesday), despite having no noticeable effect on my mood while watching or soon afterwards and being drastically different from what we usually think controls happiness.

As mentioned above, my first detailed study of TV effects tried to find an arrangement that eliminated early awakening. Although I was not carefully measuring my mood, I noticed that several shows I wanted to watch did not improve my mood the next day—in particular, The Simpsons, The Real World, documentaries, and the O.J. Simpson criminal trial. In contrast, stand-up comedy seemed to work fine. These observations suggested that the crucial stimulus was a reasonably large face looking more or less straight at the camera (i.e., both eyes visible). The Simpsons had no real faces. Documentaries and The Real World rarely showed a face looking at the camera. The Simpson trial had plenty of faces but almost always in profile. Stand-up comedy is usually a person looking at the camera. I also found that playing racquetball (i.e., one form of actual human contact) was not effective. During racquetball, you rarely see your opponent's face. Apparently the visual aspect of human contact (seeing a face) was far more important than the auditory aspect (hearing a voice), the cognitive aspect (decoding language, thinking about people), or the emotional aspect (feeling happy, sad, etc.), all of which the ineffective stimuli (The Simpsons, and so on) provided.

The conclusion that the effective stimulus was a front view of a face led me to measure face time, defined as the duration of faces at least 2 inches (5 cm) wide with two eyes visible. (I watched TV with my eyes about 40 inches [1 m] from a 20-inch [51 cm] TV.) I used 2 inches as the minimum width because it was slightly less than a stimulus that I knew was effective—the average width of Jay Leno's face during his monologue. I kept track of face time using a stopwatch. After I realized the importance of faces, I usually watched a mix of shows with a high ratio of face time to total time (Charlie Rose, Charles Grodin, Rivera Live, much of The News Hour with Jim Lehrer), and shows that I liked more but which showed fewer large faces (Friends, 60 Minutes). I watched everything on tape, of course.

Eventually I stopped trying to reduce early awakening with morning TV and instead studied the mood effect more carefully. To quantify it, I measured my mood

TABLE 19.3
Mood Scales

	Dimension		
Rating	Unhappy → happy	Irritable → serene	Reluctant → eager
9.5	extremely happy	extremely serene	extremely eager
9	very happy	very serene	very eager
8	quite happy	quite serene	quite eager
7.5	happy	serene	eager
7	somewhat happy	somewhat serene	somewhat eager
6	slightly happy	slightly serene	slightly eager
5	neither happy nor unhappy	neither serene nor irritable	neither eager nor reluctant
4	slightly unhappy	slightly irritable	slightly reluctant
3	somewhat unhappy	somewhat irritable	somewhat reluctant
2.5	unhappy	irritable	reluctant
2	quite unhappy	quite irritable	quite reluctant
1	very unhappy	very irritable	very reluctant
0.5	extremely unhappy	extremely irritable	extremely reluctant

at about 11 AM each day on three 0.5–9.5 scales (Table 19.3). The three scales—happiness, serenity, and eagerness—reflected the three most obvious ways that watching TV in the morning seemed to make a difference: I felt happier, more serene (less irritable, less easily upset), and more eager to do things. The three measures were almost always close (happiness and eagerness about equal, serenity about 1 point higher) so I give only their average. (Later work found that each measure could change independently from the other two, so it was a good idea to measure all three.)

Figure 19.10 presents the results of an experiment done to show the basic effect. During the first phase, a baseline, I watched TV every morning (40 min of face time, starting at 7 AM). When I was sick for a few days, I did not record my mood. During the second phase, I did not watch TV. My mood got worse, but the change happened a day after the change in treatment. The final phase was a return to baseline: I watched TV every morning, just as in the first phase. My mood improved but again it took at least a day for the change to take place.

How much TV was needed to get the maximum effect? Figure 19.11 shows the results of conditions done to answer this question. (It includes the data shown in more detail in Figure 19.10.) I tested 0, 20, 30, and 40 min of face time in the order shown in Figure 19.11 (30, 40, 0, 40, 20, 30), each for several days. Twenty minutes of face time produced a better mood the next day than 0 min ($t[8] = 3.8$, one-tailed $p < .005$). (I did statistical tests by averaging the three mood ratings for each day to get a single number, then treated that number as an independent random sample.) Thirty minutes was more effective than 20 min ($t[13] = 2.8$, $p < .01$); 30 and 40 min produced similar effects.

Figure 19.12 shows the results of conditions run to learn more about what controls the effect. I interspersed blocks of baseline days with blocks of days during which I changed the baseline treatment in various ways. The baseline treatment was watching enough TV to get 30 min of face time, starting at 7 AM, with

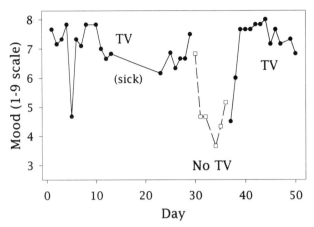

FIGURE 19.10. Mood as a function of morning TV and day. (Each mood rating is a mean of the ratings on the three scales of Table 19.3. No ratings were made during a block of days during the first phase because of sickness.)

my eyes about 40 inches [1 m] from the TV screen. The four baseline conditions of Figure 19.12 did not differ reliably, $F(3, 21) = 1.7$. Watching TV 1 hr later lowered mood, $t(29) = 6.4$, $p < .001$, comparing the "1 hr later" results to the combined baseline results. To my surprise, watching TV 1 hr *earlier* also lowered mood, $t(28) = 3.7$, $p < .001$. Watching TV twice as far from the screen (80 inches [2 m] rather than 40 inches [1 m]) lowered mood, $t(29) = 8.3$, $p < .001$.

In order to obtain the desired amount of face time (e.g., 30 min), the *total* time I watched TV each morning varied with what I watched. Watching 10 min of *Charlie Rose* yielded about 8 min of face time; watching 10 min of *Friends* yielded about 2 min of face time. Was the difference between *Charlie Rose* and *Friends* important? Soon after the results of Figure 19.12, I looked at a scatterplot of some of the data. I computed *face density,* defined as

$$\text{face density} = \text{face duration/total duration}$$

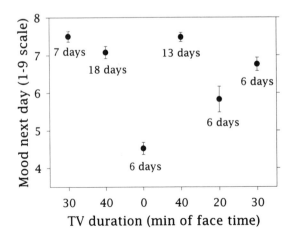

FIGURE 19.11. Mood next day as a function of face time. (The number of days indicated by each data point is the number of days that contributed to that datum. The mood for each day was an average over the three scales of Table 19.3. The results for each duration were taken from the days *after* the treatment was used. For instance, if a treatment was used Monday through Thursday, the results for that treatment came from the mood ratings on Tuesday through Friday. Averages over days were 10% trimmed means, with standard errors computed using the jackknife [Mosteller & Tukey, 1977, Chapter 8].)

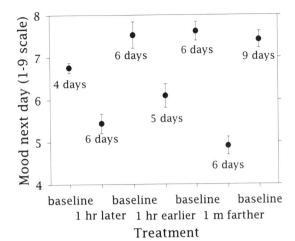

FIGURE 19.12. Mood next day as a function of TV starting time and distance. (See the caption of Figure 19.11 for more information.)

for each TV session. For instance, if it had taken 50 min of TV to accumulate 30 min of face time, face density = 0.6. I plotted mood the next day versus face density (Figure 19.13). I used all of the "baseline" data I had collected at that time—all days with 30 or 40 min of face time, 7 AM starting time, and 1 m viewing distance. Figure 19.13 suggests that density or something correlated with density made a difference. Except for two outliers, greater face densities were associated with higher next-day mood.

Did the correlation shown in Figure 19.13 reflect causation? Table 19.4 gives the results of an ABA experiment done to find out. During Phases 1 and 3, face density was relatively high; during Phase 2, it was lower. I manipulated density by varying what I watched (always on tape); to increase density, I watched more *Charlie Rose, Charles Grodin,* and the like. I kept face time constant across conditions. The results showed that density (or some correlate) made a difference. My mood ratings were higher during Phases 1 and 3 than during Phase 2, $t(15) = 6.7$, $p < .001$.

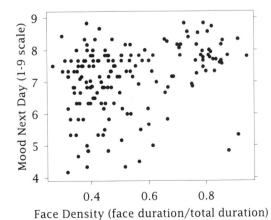

FIGURE 19.13. Mood next day as a function of face density. (Each point is a different day. The data come only from days where face time was 30 or 40 min, the viewing distance was 1 m, and the starting time was 7 AM.)

TABLE 19.4
Face Density and Duration Effects on Mood

Phase	Days	Face duration (min)	Total duration (min)	Face density	Mood
Before experiment	33	30	67	46%	7.4 ± 0.1
1	7	30	36	83%	7.9 ± 0.1
2	4	30	76	40%	6.7 ± 0.1
3	6	30	39	78%	7.8 ± 0.1
After experiment	10	50	64	79%	8.5 ± 0.1

Note. Values in the columns Face duration, Total duration, Face density, and Mood are 10% trimmed means of the values for individual days. Standard errors were computed with the jackknife (Mosteller & Tukey, 1977, Chapter 8).

A possible explanation of the density effect of Table 19.4 is that the potency of faces declines with time, i.e., that faces soon after 7 AM have more effect than later faces. As this explanation predicts, watching 1 hr later lowers mood (Figure 19.12). If this explanation is correct, then the results of Figure 19.11 could be misleading. Because 30 and 40 min of face time had the same effect, the results of Figure 19.11 seem to imply that 30 min of face "saturates" the system. However, the difference between 30 and 40 min—the additional 10 min—may have had no effect because it happened too late. Maybe it would have made a difference if it happened earlier. The last row of Table 19.4 shows the results of a test of this idea. Indeed, 50 min of dense face produced higher mood ratings than 30 min of dense face, $t(18) = 4.7$, $p < .001$, in contrast to the results of Figure 19.11. (Later work found that 70 min of dense face produced higher ratings than 50 min.) The density-by-duration interaction supports the idea that faces more than a few hours after 7 AM have little effect. Another possible explanation of the density effect of Table 19.4, not yet tested, is that density was confounded with face size (e.g., faces on *Charlie Rose* are larger than faces on *Friends*) and that face size makes a difference.

The parametric results (Figures 19.11–19.13, Table 19.4) helped show how to get a large effect and pointed toward an explanation of the basic effect (Figure 19.10). Faces (or part of them) were surely the crucial feature. This conclusion is supported not only by my informal observations (e.g., that *The Simpsons* was ineffective) but also by other results. That distance from the screen mattered (Figure 19.12) implies that the crucial stimulus is visual, a conclusion supported by two additional findings: (1) Size of TV mattered. A 27-inch TV produced a higher mood than a 20-inch TV or a 32-inch TV. Full-screen faces on a 27-inch TV are closer to life-size than on the smaller and bigger TVs. (2) Angle of view mattered. Looking down at the TV (at a 35° angle) produced a lower mood than looking straight ahead. Any theory that assumes faces are *not* the crucial stimulus will have difficulty explaining the finding that under some conditions *decreasing* the total duration of TV increased the effect (Table 19.4). The best stimulus seems to be close to what you see during an ordinary conversation.

Also impressive is the importance of time of day. One hour is a small fraction of a day, yet a 1-hr change in time of exposure to TV, in either direction, made a clear and consistent difference (Figure 19.12). This suggests that the TV acts on an internal mechanism that changes considerably and consistently from one hour of the day to the next (e.g., from 7 AM to 8 AM). The obvious candidate for such a mechanism is an internal circadian clock.

Thus, the results point to the existence of an internal circadian oscillator that is (1) sensitive to faces and (2) controls mood. This theory predicts there will be large-amplitude circadian rhythms in happiness, serenity, and eagerness. (There will be a circadian rhythm of some size in almost any biological measure—what is interesting is finding a *large* circadian rhythm.) Many conventional studies have observed circadian variation in mood (Boivin et al., 1997), albeit relatively small. Hundreds of times I measured my mood throughout the day and found what the theory predicts. My average mood was low in the early morning (roughly 4 soon after waking up, at 4–6 AM), rose to a maximum (about 8.5 under optimal conditions) from about noon to 4 PM, and declined sharply after that to below 5 around 9 PM (I fell asleep 10–11 PM).

The existence and properties of this clock make evolutionary sense. As mentioned earlier, people who live together should be active at the same time. This clock tends to produce such synchronization. It obviously controls the timing of sleep, and its sensitivity to conversational faces makes us tend to be awake at the same times of day we have conversations. I did not study the effect of TV on when I slept because the effect was so clear. When I stopped watching the 11 PM news, for example, I started falling asleep an hour earlier.

That this clock controls several dimensions of mood also makes evolutionary sense. Eagerness—a desire to do things—is helpful during the day but harmful at night, because activity at night will prevent you from falling asleep and may keep your neighbors awake. A daily rhythm in serenity helps protect sleep. If you are irritable when awakened, others will try to avoid awakening you (good). But if you are irritable during the day, others will avoid you during the day (bad). The function of a daily rhythm in happiness is less obvious. Perhaps a clock-controlled lowering of happiness makes problems more urgent. Suppose that problems (e.g., hunger) reduce happiness but only when your level of happiness goes below neutral—you become unhappy—do you take strenuous action to solve the problems (e.g., get food)? (In agreement with this idea, the term *happy* is sometimes used to mean *satisfied:* "Are you happy?") A clock may reduce happiness as bedtime approaches because existing problems become more urgent at that time: if not solved, they will interfere with sleep.

My results raise the possibility that we have an internal clock (or clocks) that, to work properly, needs (1) daily exposure to faces (30 min or more) in the morning and (2) nonexposure to faces at night. If so, many people have malfunctioning clocks, because many people get too little exposure to faces in the morning and/or too much exposure to faces at night. If this clock controls both sleep and mood, we should see many cases where the two are disrupted simultaneously. In fact, simultaneous disruption of sleep, happiness, serenity, and eagerness is a good description of the mental disorder depression. An oscillator can malfunction with either the wrong phase or low amplitude. Wrong phase will cause trouble falling asleep; low amplitude will cause difficulty staying asleep. Both problems are common features of depression (American Psychiatric Association, 1994, *Diagnostic and Statistical Manual of Mental Disorders,* 4th ed.; Brown & Harris, 1978), and insomnia is correlated with depression (Soldatos, 1994). Wrong phase and low-ered amplitude of the happiness, serenity, and eagerness rhythms would cause someone to be less happy, more irritable, and less eager to do things than usual (at least, while awake). Lack of eagerness to do things is the core symptom of depres-sion (DSM-IV), and lack of happiness and irritability are common concomitants (DSM-IV; Brown & Harris, 1978). (They are not *inevitable* concomitants, however, suggesting that depression has other causes, too. For example, this theory does not easily explain Seasonal Affective Disorder.) Many other facts about depression also link it to circadian rhythms (Van den Hoofdakker, 1994; Wehr & Goodwin, 1983). Several theories have assumed that a circadian-rhythm disturbance is the source of depression (e.g., Ehlers, Frank, & Kupfer, 1988; Kripke, 1984; Van Cauter & Turek, 1986; reviewed by Van den Hoofdakker, 1994), but this is the first to sug-gest the crucial role of exposure to faces.

Commentary

This is a good illustration of how self-experimentation and conventional re-search can work together. My self-experiments were stimulated by the conven-tional research of Wever (1969) and Szalai (1973). In the area of circadian-rhythm research, the study of social zeitgebers (a *zeitgeber* is an environmental event, such as light, that entrains an internal oscillator) is moribund; *The Journal of Bio-logical Rhythms,* which began publication in 1986, has, as of early 1998, never car-ried an article on the topic. Several years ago, psychiatrists who were not circadi-an-rhythm researchers proposed that depression was due to disruption of "social rhythms" (Ehlers, Frank, & Kupfer, 1988, p. 948). They had a good idea, but could not effectively follow it up; working with a clinical population (depressives), it would have been extraordinarily difficult to do experiments to isolate the crucial ingredient of social rhythms—experiments that presumably would have found that the sight of life-size faces in the morning, at a conversational distance, for 30 min or more, is the potent ingredient. That the effect of faces is apparent only a day later would have made the research even more difficult; most depressed pa-tients are not hospitalized, so they are almost never tested two days in a row. Self-experiments not only made it much easier to discover the effect of morning faces on next-day mood, they also made it much easier to explore the "parameter space" of the effect, the many procedural dimensions that might influence its size.

On the other hand, self-experimentation can only raise the question of whether lack of morning faces (and/or exposure to faces at night) is an important cause of depression; it can do little to answer it. For that, conventional research with depressed subjects is needed.

Summary

The examples show that self-experimentation can take many forms. The goal may be mainly scientific (A. N.'s randomness work) or highly practical (S. R.'s sleep research). The setting can be a laboratory (A. N.'s randomness work) or the real world (S. R.'s sleep research). It may start with an apparent solution to a prob-lem (S. R.'s weight research) or may find solutions only after much trial and error

(S. R.'s sleep research). A series of experiments may emphasize the various effects of an interesting treatment (A. N.'s movement work), study in detail one effect of one treatment (S. R.'s mood research), or test a wide range of treatments (S. R.'s weight and sleep work). Treatments may be familiar (feedback) or novel (standing 9 hr/day), may involve small changes in lifestyle (one of our students found that her acne disappeared when she stopped using soap to clean her face [Neuringer, 1981]) or large ones (standing 9 hr/day). The measures may be objective (A. N.'s randomness work) or subjective (S. R.'s mood work). Data collection may last weeks (many of our students do short-term self-experiments) or many years (S. R.'s sleep research). Self-experiments can explore a completely new area or test pre-existing beliefs about a familiar one. Some of the examples (behavioral variability, cognitive effects of movement) helped confirm the experimenter's hypotheses. In other cases (sleep, mood), the main results were a complete surprise.

Within psychology, Ebbinghaus is the best-known example of self-experimentation. However, our examples show that some of the less attractive features of Ebbinghaus's work—the tedious nature of the measurements (learning and relearning lists), the artificial nature of the memorized items (nonsense syllables)—do not describe all self-experimentation. Most experiments contain artificial aspects, usually to reduce variation (i.e., noise). Yet many of our examples involved no artificial elements—the experiments studied exactly the measure of interest under natural conditions (e.g., S. R.'s studies of sleep and mood). Self-experimentation can be sufficiently powerful to handle the variability of everyday life.

Above all, the examples show that self-experimentation can generate valuable data and theory that would be hard to get in other ways. Most of the topics we studied had been the subject of a great deal of conventional research, yet the self-experiments uncovered new, strong, and useful effects.

METHODOLOGICAL LESSONS LEARNED

We began self-experimentation with the belief that it was done the same way as conventional experimentation. Our experiences mostly supported that belief. However, we also learned some lessons, not necessarily specific to self-experimentation:

1. *Measure something you care about.* Self-experimentation is often exploratory, and exploratory research is often difficult because of its uncertainty and unfamiliarity. The more you care about a topic, the more likely you will persist despite difficulties. S. R.'s extensive self-experiments began with bothersome personal problems—first, acne, later, early awakening. The acne research made progress within months, but the sleep research lasted 8 years before substantial progress was made. A. N. was intrigued by the many implications of the questions "can behavioral variability be trained?" and "if so, what are the limits of such training?" He has done self-experiments on these questions for years.

2. *Make data collection and analysis as easy as possible.* Progress on serious problems will probably be slow. If you want to do something every day for many days, ease and convenience are important (Skinner, 1956). S. R.'s collection and analysis of sleep data improved considerably when he obtained a cus-

tom-made recording device and a home computer, making data analysis much easier.

3. *Taking more than one measure is usually worth the trouble* (in slight contradiction to Lesson 2). A few measures of behavior are almost always better than one, if adding the extra measures is not hard. This obviously makes sense if the additional measures reflect different dimensions. A. N. evaluated a number of different effects of activity and used multiple measures of response variability. What may be less obvious is that use of multiple measures also makes sense if the additional measures reflect the *same* dimension as the first. S. R. began measuring his weight using only one scale. When that scale was damaged, it became hard to compare new weights with old weights. When he resumed, he weighed himself each day on three different scales. Use of three scales made it possible to be much surer that any weight change was not the result of a scale change, and made it possible to measure weight more precisely. However, some measurement procedures are too time-consuming. Early in his TV research, S. R. measured mood with a well-known questionnaire, the Profile of Mood States (the short form, Curran, Andrykowski, & Studts, 1995), in which the subject rates how much he feels each of 30 emotions (e.g., tense, angry, lively) on a 5-point scale (from 0 = not at all to 5 = extremely). This took several minutes—too hard to do each day for many days.

4. *Make graphs.* Graphs help find surprises (Tukey, 1977). S. R. did not notice his decrease in sleep duration coincident with weight loss (Figure 19.7) until he plotted sleep duration over time. A. N. and his students have found that graph-keeping helps maintain research activities, what the self-control literature calls a "reactive" effect, similar to the usefulness of monitoring in self-control projects (e.g., Nelson, Boykin, & Hayes, 1982; Taylor, 1985).

5. *Communicate.* To have new ideas, it is said, tell others the ideas you have now. A newsletter, *Self-Experimentation/Self-Control Communication,* distributed by Irene Grote, of the Department of Human Development, University of Kansas, has facilitated communication among self-experimenters.

6. *A flawed experiment is better than none.* In our experience, obvious flaws and weaknesses are inevitable, but rarely fatal. S. R.'s acne research involved counting the number of new pimples each day, a measurement with so much room for error that S. R. wondered if it could be worthwhile. It was. Measurements of mood (Table 19.3) are inevitably subjective and vague, yet produced useful results. Moreover, doing research on a question today may increase the likelihood that you will do research on that question in the future (Neuringer, 1988). Paul Halmos, a renowned math teacher, taught his students that "the best way to learn is to do" (Halmos, 1975, p. 466). The best way to learn how to do a better experiment is often to do an imperfect one.

7. *Value simplicity.* The smallest step forward—the simplest, easiest way to increase what you know—is often the best. Complex or difficult experiments usually make more assumptions than simpler or easier ones—for example, assumptions about how quickly a treatment will act if it has any effect. Unless you know that those assumptions are true—because you have done simpler experiments that test the assumption rather than require it—some of them are likely to be wrong, making the results of complex experiments hard to interpret. The overconfidence that causes us to overvalue complex experiments also causes us to undervalue sim-

ple ones. As several of our examples show (e.g., S. R.'s discovery of the mood-altering effect of morning TV), simple manipulations often turn out to be more revealing or helpful than expected.

STATISTICAL ISSUES

Some writers have claimed that experiments with a single subject require different statistics than other experiments (e.g., Edgington, 1987, Chapter 10). This is wrong. *Every* experiment is $n = 1$ in many ways—one school, one stimulus set, one place, one time of day, and so forth (Tukey, 1969). If an experiment uses only one school, it cannot generalize across schools; if it uses only one subject, it cannot generalize across subjects. If an experiment has 10 subjects, a *t*-test with $n = 10$ will indicate what to expect if the experiment is done again with a similar group of subjects (different subjects chosen in a similar way). If an experiment has one subject, and data are collected from 10 days, a *t*-test with $n = 10$ will indicate what to expect if the experiment is done again with the same subject and a similar group of days (different days chosen in a similar way). R. A. Fisher, who originated the statistical concept of significant difference, used a single-subject experiment (a woman tasting tea) to explain the concept (Fisher, 1951). The number of subjects in an experiment affects *what* can be concluded but not *how* those conclusions are reached.

Repetition of self-experiments is often relatively easy. The purpose of inferential statistics (e.g., *t* tests) is to predict what would happen if the experiment were done again. *The more you use actual repetition to answer this question, the less you need to rely on statistics* (e.g., Comstock, Bush, & Helzlsouer, 1992; Tukey, 1969). That is, the less you need to assume that the requirements of your statistical test (e.g., independent samples) are close enough to the truth. If you are worried about the validity of a statistical inference (a test says that A and B are different—is this correct?), the best check is to repeat the experiment.

STRENGTHS OF SELF-EXPERIMENTATION

In a situation where self-experimentation and conventional research are both possible, self-experiments have several attractive features:

1. *Easy to measure treatment effects.* "Does X influence Y?" is the most basic question of experimental science. All of our self-experiments answered this question more easily than a conventional experiment would have. The difference in required effort can be large. S. R. has done similar sleep experiments on himself and others. It required about 50–100 times more of the experimenter's time to do similar experiments with others than with himself. The conventional experiments required more time for recruitment, instructions, travel, and data collection. The self-experiments, unlike the conventional experiments, could be done without help, did not have subjects stop in the middle, did not require subject payments, and had fewer concerns about treatment and measurement accuracy. Likewise, A. N. found it easier to develop methods to train behavioral variability when he used himself as subject than when he studied others.

Not only are self-experiments usually less time-consuming and expensive than conventional research, they often have more resolving power, that is, they better distinguish signal from noise. They can use more potent treatments, increasing signal. S. R. would not ask anyone else to drink 5 liters of water a day for many days but did not mind doing it himself. Other features decrease noise. The subject is usually experienced and always well-motivated, and the experiment can last a long time. A. N. could not have easily convinced others to spend hundreds of hours entering "random digits" (as he did) to develop methods to study operant variability.

The ease and power of self-experiments allow a researcher to answer many questions using self-experiments with the same effort it would take to answer one question using conventional methods. Self-experiments are well-suited for exploring a parameter space and finding optimal values. A. N.'s randomness work (Figure 19.2) and S. R.'s mood experiments (Figures 19.11 and 19.12) illustrate this point. When it comes time to do a conventional experiment to assess generality, these parametric results will help the researcher choose procedural details. The high power/effort ratio of self-experimentation also allows a researcher to do studies that seem to have a low or uncertain probability of success, as shown by many of our examples.

2. *Can detect many changes and correlations without formal measurement.* A self-experimenter's deep involvement helps him or her to notice when uncontrolled factors make a difference. Early in his work on variability, A. N. noticed that his behavior was less variable in the evening (when he was tired) than early in the day (when he was rested). After that, he did the research before noon. A later self-experiment showed that, indeed, time of day affected the randomness of his sequences. Likewise, a self-experimenter can easily notice when the experimental treatment changes something that is not being measured. After serving as his own subject in an experiment on thermoregulation, which involved prolonged immersion in hot water, Cabanac accidentally noticed that very cold water felt pleasant. This observation led to a great deal of research (Cabanac, 1995). S. R.'s mood and sleep research also illustrate the value of incidental observations. A self-experimenter knows in detail what a subject thinks and feels.

3. *Encourage action.* Because self-experiments are often easy, they encourage the researcher to do *something.* Our examples show how actions based on wrong ideas can be helpful.

4. *Personally helpful.* S. R. became enthusiastic about self-experimentation after it reduced his acne by 80% in 1 year. To S. R., the mood boost produced by morning TV is well worth 1–2 hours a day, quite apart from its research value. A. N.'s exercise research caused him to swim each day at about 4 o'clock, thereby improving his ability to work on academic and scientific tasks during the late afternoon and early evening.

5. *Long-term records allow instructive correlations to be noticed.* Self-experimentation often leads to months or years of measurements. Such records allow uncontrolled environmental changes ("experiments of nature") to yield useful information. When the data base is long, changes that take months can be noticed and interpreted (e.g., Figure 19.7). Day-to-day variation can also help show the "dosage" of a treatment needed to get the full effect (Table 19.2).

These strengths can be summed up by saying that self-experimentation often facilitates three basic activities of science:

First, *hypothesis elimination.* Self-experiments often make it relatively easy to test an idea and hard to dismiss the results when they contradict a favored theory. Because you know so clearly what happened (Strength 2), there may be little room for post-hoc explanations ("well, that was because . . .").

Second, *hypothesis generation.* Because self-experiments produce many results (Strength 1), they tend to produce many surprises, and surprises often lead to new ideas. The surprise may be an unexpected change (Strength 2) or correlation (Strengths 2 and 5). Or it may be the convincing elimination of a favorite hypothesis. Because the surprises of psychological self-experiments involve the experimenter's own behavior, they are especially thought-provoking.

Finally, *trial and error.* Edison's description of genius ("99% perspiration") could have been "99% making mistakes." Because mistakes in a self-experiment have a relatively low cost (Strength 1), more can be made.

WEAKNESSES OF SELF-EXPERIMENTATION

Self-experiments have important limitations, of course. In rough order of importance (most important first):

1. *Expectations may influence results.* In most cases, self-experiments cannot be run "blind," which allows expectations to vary with treatment and cause differences between treatments (Rosenthal, 1966). However, the results of our and our students' self-experiments have often been surprising, implying that expectations often have small or short-lived effects. Examples come from studies of random sequence generation, acne, study efficiency, sleep, mood, and weight, among others. A simple test of the power of expectations is to ask if the results have always turned out as expected; if so, expectations may be powerful in that situation.

A researcher may notice that two rare events happened at about the same time and do an experiment to ask if one caused the other. For instance, S. R.'s TV/mood research began when he noticed that he woke up feeling refreshed and cheerful (rare) the day after he watched TV early in the morning (rare). These correlations are interesting *because* they are unexpected, and thus could not be the result of expectations. If an experiment confirms the correlation—if intended variation of X produces the effect that the correlation suggested—this implies that the experimental effect was not the result of expectations.

A few self-experiments *can* be done completely blind. One of our students studied the effect of caffeine by having a friend place caffeinated instant coffee in a jar marked "A" and identical-looking decaffeinated instant coffee in a jar marked "B." Following an ABA design, she alternated between jars. Contrary to what she expected, she found her behavior and mood to be strongly affected by caffeine (Neuringer, 1981).

2. *Generality across subjects unclear.* As discussed earlier, every experiment is $n = 1$ in many ways. Yet because people plainly differ in important ways the fact that a self-experiment involves only one person is an obvious concern. The best way to assess generality across subjects is of course to do the same experiment

with other subjects. However, other sources of data also help answer questions about generality.

One is history. In dozens of cases, the conclusions from self-experiments have turned out to be widely true (e.g., Altman, 1987); we know of no case where the result of a self-experiment was misleading because the subject was unusual. Psychologists care about individual differences partly because any sensitive experiment will reveal them—different subjects are affected differently by the same treatment. However, experimental reports with data for individual subjects show that between-subject differences are generally differences in the *size* of the effect, not its *direction*.

And few self-experiments stand alone. In our experience, other evidence usually sheds light on the generality of the results. S. R.'s breakfast results, for instance, closely resembled food-anticipatory activity in animals. S. R.'s discovery that morning TV improved his mood suggested a theory about depression supported by data from other subjects (e.g., data linking depression and circadian rhythms).

3. *Limited subject matter.* Self-experiments can study only a few of the topics that experimental psychologists investigate. Many experiments compare different groups of people, e.g., studies of sex differences. The experimenter may not belong to the group of interest, e.g., persons with an illness or disability.

4. *Easy to lie.* Self-interest should minimize this problem. It is hardly in the experimenter's interest to do a long series of self-experiments based on false or misleading results, to do conventional experiments based on false or misleading results (based on earlier self-experiments), or to publish false or misleading results. Moreover, attempts by other experimenters to replicate important findings provide protection, just as with conventional research.

5. *Interferes with daily life.* Self-experimentation is sometimes a burden, but not always. Self-experimentation led S. R. to stop eating breakfast, maybe *saving* a half-hour each day. Weight loss due to self-experimentation caused him to sleep about one half-hour less each night; more time saved. Standing rather than sitting took no additional time. S. R.'s TV/mood research was time-consuming (1–2 hours a day) and intrusive, but as mentioned earlier, the benefits made the cost seem a bargain.

6. *Real life noisier than lab.* A common objection to self-experimentation is "my life varies too much." In some cases, this is probably true. A student who works the graveyard shift (11 PM to 7 AM) two nights a week should probably not try to do an experiment on circadian rhythms. On the other hand, our examples show that a lot can be learned from real-life experiments and that real-life noise is not always a problem. Some self-experiments, like Ebbinghaus's memory studies and A. N.'s randomness work, can be done in labs or lablike isolation. In some cases, treatment effects are much larger than real-life noise, e.g., S. R.'s body-weight results (Figures 19.5 and 19.6). Often, enough data can be collected to greatly reduce noise by averaging (e.g., Figure 19.7).

CONCLUSIONS

Biological diversity (in terms of number of species) is especially high along boundaries between two different habitats (e.g., forest and meadow), a phenomenon that ecologists call the *edge effect* (Harris, 1988, p. 330). Much the same principle holds for economies: Cities prosper and diversify their economic activity where a number of economic conditions coexist (Jacobs, 1984). Something similar should be true for psychology: the combination of self-experimentation and conventional research will be more fruitful than either alone.

Self-experimentation and conventional research have complementary strengths. The essential strength of self-experiments is how easy they are (compared with conventional research on the same topic). They can try many treatments, measure many things at once, generate and test many ideas, allow considerable trial and error. However, some topics cannot be studied, the subject pool is limited, and generality across subjects is unclear. Conventional experiments are usually more difficult, but are also more versatile—they can study a wider range of topics and subjects, including animals—and more convincing. The use of complementary methods is central to public health research, where epidemiology, laboratory research, and clinical trials work well together. Epidemiology (i.e., survey research) is better than laboratory work and clinical trials for generating ideas about cause and effect, but worse for testing them.

Self-experiments and conventional research can help each other in several ways. Self-experiments can suggest conventional ones. For instance, self-experiments can filter anecdotal evidence. Despite plenty of anecdotes about water and weight loss, no conventional experiments have measured the effect of water intake on weight. S. R.'s self-experiment that showed a clear effect of water on weight provides a better basis for conventional experimentation than an anecdote would. In addition, self-experiments can help decide the details of conventional experiments (e.g., how long treatments should last). Help can flow the other way, too. Self-experiments can take a scientific question raised by conventional research and try to answer it, as in A. N.'s randomness work. Conventional research may suggest solutions to practical problems; self-experiments can ask if the solutions work. S. R.'s weight experiments, for instance, were partly inspired by animal studies. Conventional research may also help show that a surprising observation in a self-experiment is correct, e.g., S. R.'s sleep and mood research.

When self-experimentation and conventional experiments are both possible (when a researcher has a choice), the difference between them often resembles the difference between learning and showing: *Self-experiments are better for discovery* (solving an everyday problem, answering a scientific question) *but worse for convincing others* that the solution is helpful or the answer is correct. Of course, most scientists want to do both—discover something *and* convince others of their discovery. Thus, psychologists should consider doing both self-experiments and conventional ones, if self-experiments would help answer the question they are asking. The best use of resources may often be self-experiments followed by conventional ones. The researcher begins with self-experiments that, if all goes well, find large effects and/or generate and eliminate many hypotheses. This exploratory and theory-building phase lasts until a convenient solution or large effect is found. Then the researcher uses self-experiments to find the procedural parameters (e.g., duration, time of day, intensity) that optimize the solution or maximize the effect. Only then would the researcher begin conventional experiments, using the optimized parameters.

Science involves both hypothesis creation and hypothesis testing; the tools that are best for one are unlikely to be best for the other. Unfortunately, education in scientific methods emphasizes testing far more than creation. Statistics textbooks, for example, are full of ideas about how to test hypotheses but often ignore methods of hypothesis creation. Our examples show that self-experimentation is especially good for hypothesis creation.

New techniques and equipment often lead to bursts of scientific progress shortly after they become available. Self-experimentation is an old technique but also, our examples suggest, an unwisely neglected one. Unlike most new tools—unlike, say, a magnetic resonance imaging machine—self-experimentation is available to everyone at a price everyone can afford. It will never be the last word, but it may often be a good place to start.

ACKNOWLEDGMENT. Writing of this chapter was supported by a grant to Allen Neuringer from the National Science Foundation.

REFERENCES

Altman, L. K. (1972). Auto-experimentation: An unappreciated tradition in medical science. *New England Journal of Medicine, 286,* 346–352.

Altman, L. K. (1987). *Who goes first? The story of self-experimentation in medicine.* New York: Random House.

American Psychiatric Association. (1994). *Diagnostic and statistical manual of mental disorders* (4th ed.). Washington, DC: Author.

Baddeley, A. D. (1966). The capacity for generating information by randomization. *Quarterly Journal of Experimental Psychology, 18,* 119–129.

Barinaga, M. (1994). To sleep, perchance to . . . learn? New studies say yes. *Science, 265,* 603–604.

Bender, A. E. (1993). Breakfast—role in the diet. In R. Macrae, R. K. Robinson, & M. J. Sadler (Eds.), *Encyclopaedia of food science, food technology, and nutrition* (Vol. 1, pp. 488–490). London: Academic Press.

Bernstein, R. K. (1984). *Diabetes: The glucograF method for normalizing blood sugar.* Los Angeles: J. P. Tarcher.

Bernstein, R. K. (1990). *Diabetes type II: Living a long, healthy life through blood sugar normalization.* New York: Prentice Hall Press.

Bernstein, R. K. (1994, March 12). To control diabetes, cut down carbohydrates. *New York Times, 143,* 14 (National Edition).

Blood-glucose meters: They're small, fast, and reliable. (1996). *Consumer Reports, 61,* 53–55.

Boivin, D. B., Czeisler, C. A., Dijk, D.-J., Duffy, J. F., Folkard, S., Minors, D. S., Totterdell, P., & Waterhouse, J. M. (1997). Complex interaction of the sleep–wake cycle and circadian phase modulates mood in healthy subjects. *Archives of General Psychiatry, 54,* 145–152.

Bolles, R. C. (1993). *The story of psychology: A thematic history.* Pacific Grove, CA: Brooks/Cole.

Bolles, R. C., Hayward, L., & Crandall, C. (1981). Conditioned taste preferences based on caloric density. *Journal of Experimental Psychology: Animal Behavior Processes, 7,* 59–69.

Bolles, R. C., & Stokes, L. W. (1965). Rat's anticipation of diurnal and adiurnal feeding. *Journal of Comparative and Physiological Psychology, 60,* 290–294.

Borbély, A. A. (1982). A two process model of sleep regulation. *Human Neurobiology, 1,* 195–204.

Boring, E. G. (1942). *Sensation and perception in the history of experimental psychology.* New York Appleton–Century–Crofts.

Boulos, Z., Rosenwasser, A. M., & Terman, M. (1980). Feeding schedules and the circadian organization of behavior in the rat. *Behavioral Brain Research, 1,* 39–65.

Boulos, Z., & Terman, M. (1980). Food availability and daily biological rhythms. *Neuroscience and Biobehavioral Reviews, 4,* 119–131.

Brown, G. W., & Harris, T. (1978). *Social origins of depression.* New York: Free Press.

Brown, K. S. (1995, December 11). Testing the most curious subject—oneself. *The Scientist, 9* (No. 24), pp. 1, 10.

Bugged by disease. (1998). *The Economist, 346,* 93–94.

Cabanac, M. (1995). *La quête du plaisir.* Montreal: Liber.

Cabanac, M., & Rabe, E. F. (1976). Influence of a monotonous food on body weight regulation in humans. *Physiology and Behavior, 17,* 675–678.

Castiglioni, A. (1931). Life and work of Sanctorius. *Medical Life, 38,* 729–785.

Chagnon, N. A. (1983). *Yanomamo: The fierce people.* New York: Holt, Rinehart & Winston.

Cofer, C. N. (1979). Human learning and memory. In E. Hearst (Ed.), *The first century of experimental psychology* (pp. 323–370). Hillsdale, NJ: Erlbaum.

Cohen, L., Neuringer, A., & Rhodes, D. (1990). Effects of ethanol on reinforced variations and repetitions by rats under a multiple schedule. *Journal of the Experimental Analysis of Behavior, 54,* 1–12.

Comstock, G. W., Bush, T. L., & Helzlsouer, K. (1992). Serum retinol, beta-carotene, vitamin E, and selenium as related to subsequent cancer of specific sites. *American Journal of Epidemiology, 135,* 115–121.

Crisp, A. H., Stonehill, E., & Fenton, G. W. (1971). The relationship between sleep, nutrition, and mood: A study of patients with anorexia nervosa. *Postgraduate Medical Journal, 47,* 207–213.

Crisp, A. H., Stonehill, E., Fenton, G. W., & Fenwick, P. B. C. (1973). Sleep patterns in obese patients during weight reduction. *Psychotherapy and Psychosomatics, 22,* 159–165.

Curran, S. L., Andrykowski, M. A., & Studts, J. L. (1995). Short Form of the Profile of Mood States (POMS-SF): Psychometric information. *Psychological Assessment, 7,* 80–83.

Ebbinghaus, H. (1913). *Memory: A contribution to experimental psychology.* New York: Columbia University Press. (Original work published 1885).

Edgington, E. S. (1987). *Randomization tests* (2nd ed.). New York: Dekker.

Ehlers, C. L., Frank, E., & Kupfer, D. J. (1988). Social zeitgebers and biological rhythms. A unified approach to understanding the etiology of depression. *Archives of General Psychiatry, 45,* 948–952.

Evans, F. J. (1978). Monitoring attention deployment by random number generation: An index to measure subjective randomness. *Bulletin of the Psychonomic Society, 12,* 35–38.

Evans, F. J., & Graham, C. (1980). Subjective random number generation and attention deployment during acquisition and overlearning of a motor skill. *Bulletin of the Psychonomic Society, 15,* 391–394.

Fisher, R. A. (1951). *The design of experiments* (6th ed.). London: Hafner.

Foster-Powell, K., & Brand-Miller, J. (1995). International tables of glycemic index. *American Journal of Clinical Nutrition, 62,* 871S–893S.

Franklin, J., & Sutherland, J. (1984). *Guinea pig doctors: The drama of medical research through self-experimentation.* New York: Morrow.

Gallup Organization. (1991). *Sleep in America.* Princeton, NJ: The Gallup Organization.

Gibbs, W. W. (1996, August). Gaining on fat. *Scientific American, 275,* 88–94.

Gurley, V., Neuringer, A., & Massee, J. (1984). Dance and sports compared: Effects on psychological well-being. *The Journal of Sports Medicine and Physical Fitness, 24,* 58–68.

Halmos, P. R. (1975). The problem of learning to teach: I. The teaching of problem solving. *American Mathematical Monthly, 82,* 466–470.

Harris, L. D. (1988). Edge effects and conservation of biotic diversity. *Conservation Biology, 2,* 330–332.

Hecht, S., Schlaer, S., & Pirenne, M. H. (1942). Energy, quanta, and vision. *Journal of General Physiology, 25,* 819–840.

Hervey, G. R. (1969). Regulation of energy balance. *Nature, 222,* 629–631.

Holman, J., Goetz, E. M., & Baer, D. M. (1977). The training of creativity as an operant and an examination of its generalization characteristics. In B. Etzel, J. Le Bland, & D. Baer (Eds.), *New developments in behavioral research: Theory, method and application* (pp. 441–471). Hillsdale, NJ: Erlbaum.

Jacobs, J. (1984). *Cities and the wealth of nations.* New York: Random House.

Jenkins, J. G., & Dallenbach, K. M. (1924). Oblivescence during sleep and waking. *American Journal of Psychology, 35,* 605–612.

Kendall, A., Levitsky, D. A., Strupp, B. J., & Lissner, L. (1991). Weight loss on a low-fat diet: Consequence of the imprecision of the control of food intake in humans. *American Journal of Clinical Nutrition, 53,* 1124–1129.

Kermode, F. (1995). *Not entitled.* New York: Farrar, Straus & Giroux.

Knuth, D. E. (1969). *The art of computer programming: Vol. 2. Semi-numerical algorithms.* Reading, MA: Addison–Wesley.

Kripke, D. F. (1984). Critical interval hypotheses for depression. *Chronobiology International, 1,* 73–80.

Kristofferson, A. B. (1976). Low-variance stimulus–response latencies: Deterministic internal delays? *Perception and Psychophysics, 20,* 89–100.

Kristofferson, A. B. (1977). A real-time criterion theory of duration discrimination. *Perception and Psychophysics, 21,* 105–117.

Kristofferson, A. B. (1980). A quantal step function in duration discrimination. *Perception and Psychophysics, 27,* 300–306.

Lacey, J. H., Crisp, A. H., Kalucy, K. S., Hartmann, M. K., & Chen, C. N. (1975). Weight gain and sleeping electroencephalogram: Study of 10 patients with anorexia nervosa. *British Medical Journal, 4,* 556–558.

Machado, A. (1989). Operant conditioning of behavioral variability using a percentile reinforcement schedule. *Journal of the Experimental Analysis of Behavior, 52,* 155–166.

Mahoney, M. J. (1974). *Cognition and behavior modification.* Cambridge, MA: Ballinger.

Mahoney, M. J. (1979). *Self-change: Strategies for solving personal problems.* New York: Norton.

McElroy, E., & Neuringer, A. (1990). Effects of alcohol on reinforced repetitions and reinforced variations in rats. *Psychopharmacology, 102,* 49–55.

Mistlberger, R. E., Houpt, T. A., & Moore-Ede, M. C. (1990). Food-anticipatory rhythms under 24-hour schedules of limited access to single macronutrients. *Journal of Biological Rhythms, 5,* 35–46.

Mook, D. M., & Neuringer, A. (1994). Different effects of amphetamine on reinforced variations versus repetitions in spontaneously hypertensive rats (SHR). *Physiology and Behavior, 56,* 939–944.

Moore-Ede, M. C., Sulzman, F. M., & Fuller, C. A. (1982). *The clocks that time us: Physiology of the circadian timing system.* Cambridge, MA: Harvard University Press.

Mosteller, F., & Tukey, J. W. (1977). *Data analysis and regression: A second course in statistics.* Reading, MA: Addison–Wesley.

Nelson, R. O., Boykin, R. A., & Hayes, S. C. (1982). Long-term effects of self-monitoring on reactivity and on accuracy. *Behaviour Research and Therapy, 20,* 357–363.

Neuringer, A. (1981). Self-experimentation: A call for change. *Behaviorism, 9,* 79–94.

Neuringer, A. (1986). Can people behave "randomly"? The role of feedback. *Journal of Experimental Psychology: General, 115,* 62–75.

Neuringer, A. (1988). Personal paths to peace. *Behavior Analysis and Social Action, 6,* 51–56.

Neuringer, A. (1991). Operant variability and repetition as functions of interresponse time. *Journal of Experimental Psychology: Animal Behavior Processes, 17,* 3–12.

Neuringer, A., & Huntley, R. W. (1991). Reinforced variability in rats: Effects of gender, age and contingency. *Physiology and Behavior, 51,* 145–149.

Neuringer, A., & Voss, C. (1993). Approximately chaotic behavior. *Psychological Science, 4,* 113–119.

O'Dea, K. (1984). Marked improvement in carbohydrate and lipid metabolism in diabetic Australian aborigines after temporary reversion to traditional lifestyle. *Diabetes, 33,* 596–603.

Page, S., & Neuringer, A. (1985). Variability is an operant. *Journal of Experimental Psychology: Animal Behavior Processes, 11,* 429–452.

Paxton, S. J., Trinder, J., Montgomery, I., Oswald, I., Adam, K., & Shapiro, C. (1984). Body composition and human sleep. *Australian Journal of Psychology, 36,* 181–189.

Raben, A., Due Jensen, N., Marckmann, P., Sandström, B., & Astrup, A. (1995). Spontaneous weight loss during 11 weeks' *ad libitum* intake of a low fat/high fiber diet in young normal subjects. *International Journal of Obesity, 19,* 916–923.

Ramirez, I. (1990). Stimulation of energy intake and growth by saccharin in rats. *Journal of Nutrition, 120,* 123–133.

Reichenbach, H. (1957). *The rise of scientific philosophy.* Berkeley: University of California Press.

Rosenthal, R. (1966). *Experimenter effects in behavioral research.* New York: Appleton–Century–Crofts.

Sclafani, A., & Springer, D. (1976). Dietary obesity in adult rats: Similarities to hypothalamic and human obesity syndromes. *Physiology & Behavior, 17,* 461–471.

Shepard, R. J., Jones, G., Ishii, K., Kaneko, M., & Olbrecht, A. J. (1969). Factors affecting body density and thickness of subcutaneous fat. Data on 518 Canadian city dwellers. *American Journal of Clinical Nutrition, 22,* 1175–1189.

Sheppard, L., Kristal, A. R., & Kushi, L. H. (1991). Weight loss in women participating in a randomized trial of low-fat diets. *American Journal of Clinical Nutrition, 54,* 821–828.

Shintani, T. T., Hughes, C. K., Beckham, S., & O'Connor, H. K. (1991). Obesity and cardiovascular risk intervention through the *ab libitum* feeding of traditional Hawaiian diet. *American Journal of Clinical Nutrition, 53,* 1647S–1651S.

Siegel, M. H., & Zeigler, H. P. (1976). *Psychological research: The inside story.* New York: Harper & Row.

Siegler, R. S. (1994). Cognitive variability: A key to understanding cognitive development. *Current Directions in Psychological Science, 3,* 1–5.

Skinner, B. F. (1956). A case history in scientific method. *American Psychologist, 11,* 221–233.

Soldatos, C. R. (1994). Insomnia in relation to depression and anxiety: Epidemiological considerations. *Journal of Psychosomatic Research, 38, Suppl. 1,* 3–8.

Steinhauer, G. D., & Bol, L. (1988). *Computer assisted self observation.* Berkeley, CA: Artificial Behavior, Inc.

Stokes, P. (1995). Learned variability. *Animal Learning and Behavior, 23,* 164–176.

Stratton, G. M. (1966). Vision without inversion of the retinal image. In R. J. Herrnstein & E. G. Boring (Eds.), *A source book in the history of psychology* (pp. 103–112). Cambridge, MA: Harvard University Press. (Original work published 1897).

Szalai, A. (1973). *The use of time.* The Hague: Mouton.

Taylor, I. L. (1985). The reactive effect of self-monitoring of target activities in agoraphobics: A pilot study. *Scandinavian Journal of Behavioral Therapy, 14,* 17–22.

Thorndike, E. (1900). Mental fatigue. *Psychological Review, 7,* 466–482.

Titchener, E. B. (1896). *An outline of psychology.* New York: Macmillan Co.

Tokura, H., Shimomoto, M., Tsurutani, T., & Ohta, T. (1978). Circadian variation of insensible perspiration in man. *International Journal of Biometeorology, 22,* 271–278.

Tukey, J. W. (1969). Analyzing data: Sanctification or detective work. *American Psychologist, 24,* 83–91.

Tukey, J. W. (1977). *Exploratory data analysis.* Reading, MA: Addison–Wesley.

Tune, G. S. (1964). A brief survey of variables that influence random generation. *Perceptual and Motor Skills, 18,* 705–710.

Van Cauter, E., & Turek, F. W. (1986). Depression: A disorder of timekeeping? *Perspectives in Biology and Medicine, 29,* 510–519.

Van den Hoofdakker, R. H. (1994). Chronobiological theories of nonseasonal affective disorders and their implications for treatment. *Journal of Biological Rhythms, 9,* 157–183.

Wagenaar, W. A. (1972). Generation of random sequences by human subjects: A critical survey of literature. *Psychological Bulletin, 77,* 65–72.

Walsh, B. T., Goetz, R., Roose, S. P., Fingeroth, S., & Glassman, A. H. (1985). EEG-monitored sleep in anorexia nervosa and bulimia. *Biological Psychiatry, 20,* 947–956.

Watson, D. L., & Tharp, R. G. (1993). *Self-directed behavior: Self-modification for personal adjustment* (6th ed.). Pacific Grove, CA: Brooks/Cole.

Wever, R. A. (1979). *The circadian system of man: Results of experiments under temporal isolation.* Berlin: Springer-Verlag.

Zuriff, G. E. (1985). *Behaviorism: A conceptual reconstruction.* New York: Columbia University Press.

Appendix
Ethical Guidelines in Research with Humans

The "Ethical Principles of Psychologists and Code of Conduct" (American Psychological Association, 1992) includes several provisions that guide ethical research with human subjects. The material below is excerpted from Section 6, "Teaching, Training Supervision, Research, and Publishing." Included are the standards that address specific issues in research with humans, as well as general issues in planning research and storing, sharing, and publishing the results of research.

6.06 Planning Research

(a) Psychologists design, conduct, and report research in accordance with recognized standards of scientific competence and ethical research.

(b) Psychologists plan their research so as to minimize the possibility that results will be misleading.

(c) In planning research, psychologists consider its ethical acceptability under the Ethics Code. If an ethical issue is unclear, psychologists seek to resolve the issue through consultation with institutional review boards, animal care and use committees, peer consultations, or other proper mechanisms.

(d) Psychologists take reasonable steps to implement appropriate protections for the rights and welfare of human participants, other persons affected by the research, and the welfare of animal subjects.

6.07 Responsibility

(a) Psychologists conduct research competently and with due concern for the dignity and welfare of the participants.

(b) Psychologists are responsible for the ethical conduct of research conducted by them or by others under their supervision or control.

(c) Researchers and assistants are permitted to perform only those tasks for which they are appropriately trained and prepared.

(d) As part of the process of development and implementation of research projects, psychologists consult those with expertise concerning any special population under investigation or most likely to be affected.

6.08 Compliance with Law and Standards

Psychologists plan and conduct research in a manner consistent with federal and state law and regulations, as well as professional standards governing the conduct of research, and particularly those standards governing research with human participants and animal subjects.

6.09 Institutional Approval

Psychologists obtain from host institutions or organizations appropriate approval prior to conducting research, and they provide accurate information about their research proposals. They conduct the research in accordance with the approved research protocol.

6.10 Research Responsibilities

Prior to conducting research (except research involving only anonymous surveys, naturalistic observations, or similar research), psychologists enter into an agreement with participants that clarifies the nature of the research and the responsibilities of each party.

6.11 Informed Consent to Research

(a) Psychologists use language that is reasonably understandable to research participants in obtaining their appropriate informed consent (except as provided in Standard 6.12, Dispensing with Informed Consent). Such informed consent is appropriately documented.

(b) Using language that is reasonably understandable to participants, psychologists inform participants of the nature of the research; they inform participants that they are free to participate or to decline to participate or to withdraw from the research; they explain the foreseeable consequences of declining or withdrawing; they inform participants of significant factors that may be expected to influence their willingness to participate (such as risks, discomfort, adverse effects, or limitations on confidentiality, except as provided in Standard 6.15, Deception in Research); and they explain other aspects about which the prospective participants inquire.

(c) When psychologists conduct research with individuals such as students or subordinates, psychologists take special care to protect the prospective participants from adverse consequences of declining or withdrawing from participation.

(d) When research participation is a course requirement or opportunity for extra credit, the prospective participant is given the choice of equitable alternative activities.

(e) For persons who are legally incapable of giving informed consent, psychologists nevertheless (1) provide an appropriate explanation, (2) obtain the participant's assent, and (3) obtain appropriate permission from a legally authorized person, if such substitute consent is permitted by law.

6.12 Dispensing with Informed Consent

Before determining that planned research (such as research involving only anonymous questionnaires, naturalistic observations, or certain kinds of archival research) does not require the informed consent of research participants, psychologists consider applicable regulations and institutional review board requirements, and they consult with colleagues as appropriate.

6.13 Informed Consent in Research Filming or Recording

Psychologists obtain informed consent from research participants prior to filming or recording them in any form, unless the research involves simply naturalistic observations in public places and it is not anticipated that the recording will be used in a manner that could cause personal identification or harm.

6.14 Offering Inducements for Research Participants

(a) In offering professional services as an inducement to obtain research participants, psychologists make clear the nature of the services, as well as the risks, obligations, and limitations.

(b) Psychologists do not offer excessive or inappropriate financial or other inducements to obtain research participants, particularly when it might tend to coerce participation.

6.15 Deception in Research

(a) Psychologists do not conduct a study involving deception unless they have determined that the use of deceptive techniques is justified by the study's prospective scientific, educational, or applied value and that equally effective alternative procedures that do not use deception are not feasible.

(b) Psychologists never deceive research participants about significant aspects that would affect their willingness to participate, such as physical risks, discomfort, or unpleasant emotional experiences.

(c) Any other deception that is an integral feature of the design and conduct of an experiment must be explained to participants as early as is feasible, preferably at the conclusion of their participation, but no later than at the conclusion of the research. (See also Standard 6.18, Providing Participants With Information About the Study.)

6.16 Sharing and Utilizing Data

Psychologists inform research participants of their anticipated sharing or further use of personally identifiable research data and of the possibility of unanticipated future uses.

6.17 Minimizing Invasiveness

In conducting research, psychologists interfere with the participants or milieu from which data are collected only in a manner that is warranted by an appropriate research design and that is consistent with psychologists' roles as scientific investigators.

6.18 Providing Participants with Information About the Study

(a) Psychologists provide a prompt opportunity for participants to obtain appropriate information about the nature, results, and conclusions of the research, and psychologists attempt to correct any misconceptions that participants may have.

(b) If scientific or humane values justify delaying or withholding this information, psychologists take reasonable measures to reduce the risk of harm.

6.19 Honoring Commitments

Psychologists take reasonable measures to honor all commitments they have made to research participants.

6.21 Reporting of Results

(a) Psychologists do not fabricate data or falsify results in their publications.

(b) If psychologists discover significant errors in their published data, they take reasonable steps to correct such errors in a correction, retraction, erratum, or other appropriate publication means.

6.22 Plagiarism

Psychologists do not present substantial portions or elements of another's work or data as their own, even if the other work or data source is cited occasionally.

6.23 Publication Credit

(a) Psychologists take responsibility and credit, including authorship credit, only for work they have actually performed or to which they have contributed.

(b) Principal authorship and other publication credits accurately reflect the relative scientific or professional contributions of the individuals involved, regardless of their relative status. Mere possession of an institutional position, such as Department Chair, does not justify authorship credit. Minor contributions to the research or to the writing for publications are appropriately acknowledged, such as in footnotes or in an introductory statement.

(c) A student is usually listed as principal author on any multiple-authored article that is substantially based on the student's dissertation or thesis.

6.24 Duplicate Publication of Data

Psychologists do not publish, as original data, data that have been previously published. This does not preclude republishing data when they are accompanied by proper acknowledgment.

6.25 Sharing Data

After research results are published, psychologists do not withhold the data on which their conclusions are based from other competent professionals who seek to verify the substantive claims through reanalysis and who intend to use such data only for that purpose, provided that the confidentiality of the participants can be protected and unless legal rights concerning proprietary data preclude their release.

6.26 Professional Reviewers

Psychologists who review material submitted for publication, grant, or other research proposal review respect the confidentiality of and the proprietary rights in such information of those who submitted it.

REFERENCE

American Psychological Association. (1992). *Ethical principles of psychologists and code of conduct.* Washington, DC: Author.

Index

ISBN 0-306-45668-0

90000